Illustrations By

HELEN B. DAVIDSON, KATHRYN LUND,
GENEVIEVE VAUGHT and CLAUDIA BAILEY

CAMP COUNSELING

Fifth Edition

A. VIOLA MITCHELL, A.B., M.A.
Former Assistant Professor, Hanover College,
Winthrop College and University of Maryland

JULIA D. ROBBERSON, B.A., M.Ed.
Associate Professor, Missouri Valley College

JUNE W. OBLEY, B.S., M.S.
Counselor, Wichita, Kansas Public Schools
Consultant, Outdoor Dynamics, Inc.

1977

W. B. SAUNDERS COMPANY Philadelphia • London • Toronto

W. B. Saunders Company: West Washington Square
Philadelphia, PA 19105

1 St. Anne's Road
Eastbourne, East Sussex BN21 3UN, England

1 Goldthorne Avenue
Toronto, Ontario M8Z 5T9, Canada

Front cover photograph courtesy of Peter Gabel, Cheley Colorado Camps, Estes Park, Colorado

Back cover photograph courtesy of National Music Camp, Interlochen Center for the Arts, Interlochen, Michigan

Front endpaper courtesy of Camp Fire Girls, Inc., Ventura, California (Walt Dibblee)

Back endpaper courtesy of Camp Kooch-I-Ching, International Falls, Minnesota

Listed here is the latest translated edition of this book together with the language of the translation and the publisher.

Japanese (*3rd Edition*)—Baseball Magazine Sha, Tokyo, Japan

Camp Counseling ISBN 0-7216-6407-5

Last digit is the print number: 9 8 7 6 5 4 3 2 1

To

THE CAMPING MOVEMENT

May It Continue To Enrich and
Broaden the Lives of Campers
Everywhere

TO AN OLD CAMPER

You may think, my dear, when you grow quite old,
You have left camp days behind,
But I know the scent of wood smoke
Will always call to mind
Little fires at twilight
And trails, you used to find.

You may think some day you have quite grown up,
And feel so worldly wise,
But suddenly from out of the past
A vision will arise,
Of merry folk with brown, bare knees
And laughter in their eyes.

You may live in a house built to your taste
In the nicest part of town,
But some day for your old camp togs
You'd change your latest gown,
And trade it all for a balsam bed
Where the stars all night look down.

You may find yourself grown wealthy,—
Have all that gold can buy,
But you'd toss aside a fortune
For days 'neath an open sky,
With sunlight on blue water
And white clouds sailing high.

For once you have been a camper
Then something has come to stay
Deep in your heart forever
Which nothing can take away,
And heaven can only be heaven
With a camp in which to play.

—*Mary S. Edgar*

From *Wood-Fire and Candle-Light*
Published by The Macmillan Co.

Preface

In this revision of CAMP COUNSELING, we have kept the old where applicable while adding new materials to conform with current camp practices and philosophy. To reflect changes in organized camping, certain parts of the text have been expanded while others have been reduced. The book is intended to prove helpful to at least five groups of people: (1) colleges offering courses in camp counseling; (2) agencies and other organizations sponsoring camps, for use in between-camp session training courses or for recommended reading for their prospective counselors; (3) camp directors conducting pre-camp or in-camp training courses; (4) experienced and neophyte counselors who want to work independently to prepare themselves to do their jobs more adequately; and (5) individuals who want to enjoy and benefit more from their own camping experiences.

Working with youngsters in an organized camp offers an unparalleled opportunity to make a positive contribution to society. Opportunity is knocking, but only those with adequate training and skills can open the door to take maximum advantage of it.

A person must, first of all, know what organized camping is all about, including its background and present status. He must know what its objectives are and how to accomplish them. To these ends, Part I was written.

But a counselor is not working with sticks and stones; he is working with real, live youngsters, and his ability to understand them and to devise ways to lead them successfully is even more important than the skills he teaches them. Part II was designed to give help in this area. Working intimately with youngsters in a rustic camp situation is, of course, not everyone's cup of tea. Therefore, Part II also attempts to paint a rather detailed picture of the type of person most likely to be a successful counselor and the duties he will be expected to perform, along with hints for doing them.

However, children would get too bored and restless for words if all their leader did was sit around and understand them. Children want action and excitement and plenty of it in a variety of forms. Part III describes and tells how to conduct many activities especially suited for use in the informal, rustic atmosphere of a modern camp.

Part IV treats in some detail the campcraft and woodcraft skills that are necessary for living comfortably in the out-of-doors. After all, this out-of-door environment and the skills essential to it play an important part in distinguishing the camping experience from the child's other activities and materially helps us to obtain our objectives.

The reader will find countless ideas for "Program" scattered throughout the book in addition to those in the specific sections devoted to that topic. For those wanting to specialize in or learn more about any particular phase, such as waterfront, dramatics, or music, the suggested readings at the end of each chapter will point the way. These bibliographies have been thoroughly revised and updated for this edition.

To save space and to avoid undue repetition, only skeletal information is given when a specific reference work is cited in several chapters; complete information about each can be found in the Selected General Bibliography in Appendix A. Directories of magazines, organizations, publishers, and commercial films concerned with camping and related activities can be found in Appendices B, C, D, and E, respectively. The index is complete and includes extensive cross-references to help the reader to quickly locate the information he wants on any specific subject.

Many new photographs and drawings are included, some to add flavor, others, we hope, to amuse, and still others to clarify techniques discussed in the text.

Rapidly changing attitudes in several areas that directly affect camping have made it difficult to know just what to include in this edition. An example is our belated realization of the urgent need to take immediate action to clean our air and water and to conserve our dwindling natural resources. Our shortsightedness and wasteful practices of the past, together with a rapidly expanding population and attendant demands for replacing the natural environment with farmland, buildings, roads, parking areas, and commercial paraphernalia, have made this problem acute. Those now traveling on some of the more popular hiking trails report that, whereas an encounter with anyone else along the way during a full day's hike was a rarity in the past, other parties now abound and the trails are crowded and filled with an assortment of old camp and fire sites left by parties that felt it necessary to carve out new places for themselves in the wilderness. In an effort to minimize this depredation, some parks and recreational areas are now placing Adirondack shelters and permanent fire sites at strategic points along the trail so that users will be encouraged to leave the rest of the trail unspoiled.

As a result of our dwindling wood supply, many recreational areas frown upon the use of wood for fires or camp construction. A growing number have now made such activities illegal, and this trend will no doubt increase in the future. In these locations, certain skills once considered essential to good camping have been rendered largely useless. However, there are doubtless other areas that have relatively few users and a wood supply that is plentiful and that is being adequately replaced by new growth; in these places, campers can, with good conscience, still build wood fires if they use discretion and care. For them, a section on the building of wood fires is still included, together with a discussion of the use of such wood substitutes as charcoal, propane, and butane for heat and cooking.

We hope that you will find this edition of interest and of practical use. Your comments and suggestions will, as always, be deeply appreciated.

Viola Mitchell

June Obley

Helpful References for Those Training and Dealing with Counselors

(For an explanation of abbreviations and abbreviated forms used, see page 25.)

Blair, Glenn M., and R. Stewart Jones: *Psychology of Adolescence for Teachers.* Macmillan, 1964, 118 pp., $2.50, paper.

Camp Administration Course Outline. ACA, 1961, 29 pp., 75¢, paper.

Campcraft Instructor's Manual (Including Tripcraft).

Campcraft Training Program and Personal Record. (A description of the ACA campcraft program.) ACA, 1973, 16 pp., 25¢, paper.

Crow, Lester and Alice: *Readings in Child and Adolescent Psychology.* McKay, 1961, $3.95, paper.

Galloway, Howard: *Sources of Summer Staff.* Galloway, 149 pp., $3.95, paper.

A Guide for College Credit for Camp Field Experience. ACA, 1970, 6 pp., 25¢, paper.

A Guide for the Director of Campcraft Instructors. ACA, 1970, 16 pp., 75¢, paper.

Hammett, Catherine T.: *A Camp Director Trains His Own Staff.* ACA, 32 pp., 50¢, paper.

Hartwig, Mary, and Bette Myers: *Camping Leadership: Counseling and Programing.* Mosby, 1976, 224 pp., $6.00. (A workbook.)

Interpretive Guide. (Includes state camping regulations; boating regulations; fire protection; waterfront; riflery; archery; food service.) ACA, 1966, 39 pp., 30¢, paper.

Kinnamon, Ron, and Armin Luehrs: *Camp Leadership Focus.* Campac, 12138 Landlock Drive, Dallas, Tex. 75218, 1974, $17.50.

Rodney and Ford: *Camp Administration.*

Shivers: *Camping,* ch. 5.

Trecker, Harleigh, B.: *Social Group Work—Principles and Practices.* Ass'n Press, rev., $12.95.

van der Smissen, Elizabeth: *Bibliography of Studies and Research in Camping and Outdoor Education.* ACA, 1962, 57 pp., $1, paper.

Weitz, Henry: *Behavior Change Through Guidance.* Wiley, 1964, 225 pp., $9.25.

Magazine Articles

Camping Magazine:

"An Old Problem—Integrating New Staff with Old." (YMCA Camp Cherrio, N.C.) Apr., 1972, p. 10.

Berk, Harvey D.: "Audio-Visual Aids Can Help You Pep Up Staff Meetings (And Get More Ideas Across)." Apr., 1971, p. 12.

Boxer, Dr. Arthur D.: "Camps and 'The New Morality.'" Sept./Oct., 1969, p. 15.

Brower, Robert: "Sensitivity Training Aids Our Staff Development Program." Nov./Dec., 1970, p. 14.

Brown, Stewart A.: "Camp Objectives Must Be *Specific* If They Are To Be *Meaningful.*" Nov./Dec., 1970, p. 15.

Dimock, Hedley G.: "How to Choose Only Successful Camp Counselors." Apr., 1970, p. 8.

Fried, Anne, Ph.D.: "Today's Counselors Are Different." Feb., 1969, p. 8.

Gillespie, Virginia: "Training Volunteer Camp Staff." Apr., 1971, p. 16.

Hamilton, Fanchon: "Camp Staff Members, Just as Campers, Need Individual Guidance." Apr., 1971, p. 8.

"How Two Camps and Colleges Cooperate in Camp Staff Training." Apr., 1972, p. 8.

"How You Can Conduct Better Staff Interviews." Jan., 1970, p. 22.

Jones, Dr. Orville E.: "What Are Today's College-Age Counselors Really Like?" Jan., 1971, p. 11.

Klein, Edith: "How to Plan Your Pre-Camp and In-Camp Staff Training." June, 1970, p. 15.
Moon, Dr. Peter: "Better Interviewing Can Mean Better Staff." Jan., 1969, p. 17.
Riggins, Ron: "When Classroom Theory Is Put Into Outdoor Practice, Students Learn Campcraft Skills." Feb., 1973, p. 14.
Rotman, Charles B.: "The Camp Director's Role in Staff Orientation." Apr., 1970, p. 11.
Rotman, Charles B., and Charles S. Clayman: "Human Relations Training for Camp Staff Members." Apr., 1971, p. 10.
Sacerdote, John R.: "College Credit for Counselors? Here are 44 Ways To Get It." Jan., 1972, p. 14.
Sharenow, Arthur: "A Camp Should Be a Benevolent Dictatorship." Apr., 1970, p. 16.
Shellenberger, Don: "The Big Question—What Kind of Staff Training Helps Both Staff and Campers Attain Best Personal Growth." Mar., 1969, p. 12.
Silverman, Martin: "Professionalizing Your Staff Development." Mar., 1971, p. 13.
"Staff Problems in a Co-Ed Camp." Mar., 1972, p. 15.
Steinman, Richard, Ph.D.: "From Campus to Camp—The Counter-Culture Is Imported." Feb., 1972, p. 12.
Talley, Eidola Jean: "To What Extent Should Staff Be Involved in Camp Operations?" Apr., 1973, p. 22.
Tener, Morton: "Training Your Staff To Handle Ecological Programs." Feb., 1971, p. 11.
Trueheart, Vell: "A Staff Training Program for Integrated Camps." Apr., 1973, p. 13.
Van Matre, Steve: "Counselor Hair Styles—A Staff Person's View on a Nagging Problem for Boys' Camp Director." May, 1970, p. 15.
Webb, Dr. Dwight: "What Will Your Counselors Communicate to Campers?" Apr., 1971, p. 14.
Witkovsky, Jerry: "Understanding College-Age Youth Will Help a Director in Selecting Staff." Mar., 1973, p. 11.

Counselor-in-Training (C.I.T.)

Guide to a CIT Program. ACA National Leadership Committee, ACA, 1964, 30 pp., $1, paper.

Magazine Articles

Camping Magazine:

Guerard, Edmund R.: "Revamped CIT Program Trains for All Camp Staff Positions." Apr., 1972, pp. 13–14.
Hennessey, Pamela: "Be Specific when You Plan Your C-I-T Program." Jan., 1972, p. 26.
Rupp, Nancy C.: "Let's Challenge Our CIT's in Outdoor Living." Apr., 1973, p. 11.
Sim, Andrew L., Jr.: "CIT Program Combines Pre-Camp Home Study with In-Camp Training." May, 1972, p. 20.
Sterk, Sam: "How To Give Real Meaning to C-I-T Programs." Mar., 1971, p. 15.
Webb, Susan H.: "Convention Study Group Offers Guidelines for Better CIT Training." May, 1969, p. 26.

Suggestions for Conducting Courses in Camp Counseling

This book has been designed particularly to be used by those in college courses in camp counseling, but it will be equally useful for participants in C.I.T. (counselor-in-training), pre-camp, and in-training courses as well as for those already employed in a camp situation. The purposes of the four sections of this book and the persons for whom it is intended have been discussed in the Preface. Since a successful camp counselor must be a well-rounded, knowledgeable person who understands people, harbors proper attitudes, and possesses specialized skills, it seems obvious that if he is to do an adequate job, a number of methods of training and preparing him will be necessary. Like the children with whom he expects to work, he will profit most from a course that is lively and varied and that seems meaningful to him. The theoretical aspects of the course can be covered with the usual lectures, discussions, testing, and such, but something more is needed. There must also be some provision for laboratory periods to give practice in skills such as telling stories, using tools, and working effectively with groups. There should also be at least a few excursions to practice outdoor cooking and overnight camping and, ideally, these will culminate in a 6 to 10 day camping trip to note how things actually work out on a long-term basis and to catch the flavor of living in the out-of-doors. If some actual work with children can also be included, so much the better.

Since we know that some learn best by *seeing,* others by *hearing,* and still others by *doing,* it seems logical to use all of these methods of instruction, just as our prospective counselor will be doing later on a modified basis with his own campers. Use variety to spark interest and develop a sense of what being a counselor means. Here are some suggestions that may prove helpful:

1. Study the text, supporting it with lectures, class discussions, demonstrations, testing, and the like.
2. Assign supplementary reading. No student can be prepared adequately who has not been exposed to different opinions and methods, as well as to some, at least, of the excellent publications now available in the field. Require certain readings from everyone; in addition, permit choices from diverse fields such as ecology, aquatics, and dramatics to allow for per-

sonal interests and to help counselors to prepare for the specific jobs they may hold.

3. Hold buzz sessions and discussions—round table or panel fashion or led by a group member—about topics of general interest, perhaps chosen by the class.
4. Have class members make oral presentations. These, unfortunately, can be so colorless and dry that they provide a good nap period for everyone. Point out that a person who uses a group's time should try to be so well prepared and dynamic that all will feel that their time has been well spent. Emphasize that singsong, drab presentations will never hold the attention of either their classmates or the children with whom they will be working. Encourage them to be innovative and to seek ways to present material in an exciting manner that will challenge them and appeal to several of the senses. Let the class evaluate the methods used.
5. Let individuals take turns at instructing their classmates on chosen topics, such as how to lead a discussion, plan a campfire program, lay a fire, pitch a tent, use and care for a knife, waterproof matches, and so on. Discuss methods of presenting such material to campers.
6. Assign special projects—collecting and making a booklet containing poetry or songs suitable for camp use; making articles for camp or personal use later; making spatter prints or plaster casts.
7. Bring in outside speakers or visiting consultants—a Boy Scout, Girl Scout or Camp Fire leader, camp director, first aid worker, conservation agent, forest ranger, and the like. Also invite persons from such related teaching fields as sociology, elementary education, and home economics.
8. Keep bulletin boards that are attractive and instructive, and have students participate by changing them frequently. Use such attention getters as colored mounting paper and thumbtacks, posters, actual specimens, prominent topical headings, current newspaper and magazine clippings, pictures, and diagrams.
9. Use some of the many good slides and movies now available on camping and related topics.
10. Make a large chart to use for checking off each student's course requirements as he completes them—demonstrating how to care for and use a knife properly, taking satisfactory notes on required readings, packing a pack properly, helping to plan and prepare for a cookout or overnight trip, writing a playlet, and so forth.
11. Collect and display such things as camp bulletins, pamphlets published by the American Camping Association and other organizations, selected books about camping, a miniature model of an outdoor campsite, arts and crafts using native materials, small models of various fires and their uses, a model council ring, nature lore, and the like.
12. Schedule laboratory periods for practicing campcraft and woodcraft skills, perhaps inviting in a group of neighborhood children to receive instruction.

13. Have students prepare an annotated bibliography or card file of literature on camping. Students will find such a compilation invaluable later, as it enables them to quickly put their finger on what will give them the information they need or guide them in making future purchases.
14. Have each student write a special report or term paper concerning some phase of camping he wants to learn more about, perhaps in preparation for a job he has accepted.
15. Have class members plan and participate in cookouts, overnights, and longer camping trips. This gives experience in using a committee system, delegating responsibility, and working democratically with others to put into practice some of the things studied about only in theory.
16. Collect useful materials to put into a loose-leaf notebook or scrapbook.
17. Plan and make sets of flip charts or lesson cards (at least 18 by 24 inches) to use when explaining techniques to others.
18. Tape record a student's presentation as he tells a story, teaches a song, leads a discussion, or conducts an evening vespers service. Let him evaluate the play-back.
19. Take photographs or slides or make motion pictures to use for arousing interest or to present a special topic.
20. Use various group methods, such as role playing, circular discussion, and others described in the text.
21. Study various types of camping equipment available, using the catalogues of various outfitters (see Appendix E). Visit outfitting stores or arrange to borrow items of equipment for careful study and comparison.
22. Attend meetings and workshops sponsored by ACA and related organizations. Encourage student membership in ACA.

Although courses in counselor training continue to grow in both number and quality, the supply of those completing them still lags far behind the demand. Anyone who contemplates offering such training is urged to contact the American Camping Association about the courses in campcraft they have set up. Provision is made for giving ratings on four levels (see page 36); when the courses are conducted by instructors approved by the association, appropriate certificates are available for those satisfactorily completing them. Become qualified to conduct such courses yourself.

Obviously, no practical course in camping can be carried on without a minimum of equipment, such as knives, hatchets, saws, stoves, cooking utensils, files, tents, and the like. Students may buy their own or rent or borrow them from the sponsoring organization.

Users of this book will probably find the lists of additional readings given at the ends of the chapters too extensive for the limited time they have available. Even though lack of space has necessitated omitting many valuable references, the lists have purposely been left quite long to permit the user to eliminate those not available to him and to select from the rest those he finds most appropriate to his needs and personal taste.

Viola Mitchell

Suggestions for Conducting Camp CIT (Counselor-in-Training) Courses

By Nancy C. Rupp

Assistant Professor,
University of New Hampshire,
Durham, New Hampshire

INTRODUCTION

Today, more than ever before, young and old are taking to the out-of-doors where they can get away from it all and enjoy the beauty of the natural environment. Anyone in the field of camping, recreation, and outdoor living should keep himself up-to-date and knowledgeable concerning the protection of our environment and should practice, as well as teach, ways to live in the out-of-doors without destroying it. Although outdoor and wilderness ethics can be learned partially from books, practice in "doing it" is also necessary.

Today, there is much discussion about the proper use of the wilderness by groups and individuals. Many states have compiled their own regulations, guidelines, and tips concerning this, although individual states sometimes fail to agree on specifics. For example, in order to protect the forest ground cover, some states suggest that campers sleep in hammocks instead of tents, and many prefer that campers cook with small portable stoves in order to conserve wood.

An experienced or inexperienced individual engaged in camp counseling or leadership in the out-of-doors can gain much knowledge and skill from using this book. It will acquaint him with skills, teaching methods, and techniques for taking care of himself in the out-of-doors in a camp setting. It will serve as an excellent text for courses in leadership conducted in a day, year-round, or summer camp program. College students who spend much time in the out-of-doors and are interested in camping, outdoor education, and/or recreation leadership will also find this text quite valuable as an effective guide and reference book containing much supplementary information relating to the fields of recreation and camping.

Individuals involved in teaching college camp leadership courses or CIT courses during the camp season will find *Camp Counseling* an excellent text. The CIT course, and the implementation of it, will, of course, depend upon such factors as the nature and philosophy of the camp, the type of CIT program (one or two years), the number of CIT personnel involved, and the facilities available. The following course outline is intended to serve merely as a guide for the person who has chosen this text for the course.

SUGGESTED CIT COURSE OUTLINE FOR A TWO-YEAR COURSE

I. First summer.
   A. Objectives. What are the objectives of your camp? Guided by them, develop your own objectives, including knowledge and understanding to be gained, skills and habits to be developed, feelings, attitudes, and interests to be encouraged.
   B. A survey of camping today. Examine issues and problems, campers' needs, your camp's philosophy, background of the camping field, types of camps, organizations and agencies, camp program.
   C. Developing your own skills and knowledge in camp and sports activities. Leadership roles in activities should be stressed. Emphasis depends upon your camp's philosophy and program.
      1. Land sports—tennis, archery, riding, etc.
      2. Music—songs and song-leading.
      3. Creative activities—arts and crafts, dramatics, story telling, dance, etc.
      4. Special activities—special programs, campfires, evening programs, rainy day activities.
      5. Campcraft, trip camping, outdoor living (these areas should be given a great deal of emphasis).
         (a) Health, safety, and first aid.
         (b) Conservation, naturelore, woodlore, ecology.
         (c) Basic skills—hiking, backpacking, canoeing, kayaking, toolcraft, ropecraft, gear and shelter, firecraft, map and compass, food and menu planning, outdoor cooking.
         (d) Waterfront activities—swimming (Water Safety Aide, Senior Life Saving), sailing, waterskiing, canoeing, kayaking.
   D. Developing leadership and teaching skills. Experience in analyzing skills. Transition from senior camper to CIT by functioning as a teacher aide assistant to counselors and director.
      1. Role of the CIT.
         (a) With each other—peer teaching and interaction.
         (b) With campers—act as teacher aide under counselor while teaching and working with children of all ages and in a variety of activities.
         (c) Organize specific camp activities and events—Sunday services, camp sports' day, visits to other camps, etc.

(d) Develop an understanding of camper behavior and age group characteristics.
(1) Observe campers during activities, in cabin, and on trips.
(2) Teach campers as *individuals.*

2. CIT evaluation—attitudes, background, experience, strengths and weaknesses, leadership potential (see Chapter 4). (Evaluate at the beginning, during the summer, and at the end, as desired).
(a) Self evaluation.
(b) Counselor evaluation.
(c) Unit and activity heads and director evaluations.
(d) Recommendations concerning the advisability of having the CIT return to continue the course next summer. Does he really want to come back to continue living in the out-of-doors and working with children?

II. Second summer.
A. Continuation of development of skills and knowledge of camping and sports techniques.
B. Further experience as assistant "student teacher" or aide.
1. Live in different age group units for several weeks, acquiring a variety of experiences and assuming various camp roles.
2. Practice teach in camp activities under the direction of various counselors.
3. Assist on trips and in various camp activities.
C. Group interaction and discussion concerning camper backgrounds and needs, means of assessing their abilities and problems, and discussions of specific situations.
D. Visit other camps and discuss their philosophies.
E. Evaluation of the CIT or aide.
1. Self evaluation.
2. Counselor evaluations.
3. Unit and activity heads and director evaluations.

CONDUCTING THE PROGRAM

Learning about leadership in the outdoors should and can be fun, adventurous, and challenging in a camp setting. It is important that this material be presented in an interesting and individualized way, with "being involved" and "doing" stressed in order to motivate both experienced and inexperienced CITs. When teaching such a course, one should be familiar with the teaching-learning process. It is also important that the CIT be familiar with and know how to analyze various camp and sport skills so that when teaching individual campers he will be able to preplan his techniques to include various kinds of progressive and meaningful learning experiences. In order to assist a camper in acquiring skills and knowledge, the CIT must know and understand the individual and be aware of any experience he has had with the skill to be learned.

It is also important to review and discuss various teaching methods and techniques. Ordinarily, emphasis should be placed on a creative, individualized, and informal approach rather than one that is structured and formal, and it should be geared to the ability of the group. However, when teaching some camp and sport skills where safety or time are important, a more structured, formal approach may be best.

CITs should practice as teacher aides as soon as possible, working with all types of individuals in order to experience success and gain confidence.

The group should also be involved as early as possible in group tasks, projects, and problems requiring initiative in order to develop mutual support and respect within the group. Individuals should learn to react to each other as well as to situations, realizing that the success or failure of the group depends on the efforts of all its members. Individuals, as well as groups, can be assigned various topics to discuss. They can also be assigned outside readings on which to report and lead discussions. Leadership skills are most important, and as much experience as possible should be given in this area in order to practice and develop them. Hopefully, at the conclusion of each chapter or topic, the CITs will be encouraged to acquaint themselves with the most recent developments and philosophies and to keep their knowledge up-to-date by reading current literature. It may also be helpful to encourage persons to engage in independent study and contract teaching. Assigned progressive study work sheets for those keenly interested in specific areas will help them to communicate information to each other and to you effectively as well as to help them to evaluate what they have learned.

Acknowledgments

It would be almost impossible, from the point of view of both time and space, to cite each of the many individuals and organizations that have contributed in helpful ways toward making this revised edition possible. Be assured, however, that warm thoughts and deep appreciation go out to all of you.

Grateful acknowledgment is made to the individuals and publishers who gave kind permission to use quoted material. Credit has been given when the source was known, but unfortunately, despite diligent efforts and much correspondence, it has sometimes been impossible to ascertain the exact source of some of the quotations and ideas used. Whoever and wherever you are, please accept our apologies for not being able to give credit where it is so richly deserved.

Many of the ideas included in this book have derived from several years of association with various individuals in camping and the reading of the rich quantity of camping literature now available.

Appreciation is expressed to Helen B. Davidson, Kay Lund, and Genevieve Vaught for illustrations used from previous editions of this book and to Genevieve Vaught and Claudia Bailey for new illustrations.

Particular thanks are due to Elsie Fisher, Camping Administration Specialist, Camp Fire Girls, for her generous sharing of time and ideas, which has been of great help in preparing this revision. Gratitude is also expressed to Peter Gabel of the Cheley Colorado Camps and to Jeanne Bassett of Miami University (Ohio) for helpful suggestions and to Nancy Rupp of the University of New Hampshire for the section on the conducting of Counselor-in-Training (C.I.T.) courses.

Sincere thanks to Karla Allison Hannaford for her skillful and painstaking help with the preparation of the first part of the manuscript.

Appreciation is also expressed to the following people who so kindly submitted new photographs for use in this edition: Armand Ball and Dwight Jewson of Camp Widjiwagan, Ely, Minnesota; Theodore Cavins of Camp Mishawaka, Grand Rapids, Minnesota; Elsie Fisher of Camp Fire Girls, Inc., New York, New York; Peter Gabel of Cheley Colorado Camps, Estes Park, Colorado; Agnes Guinn of the Wichita Area Girl Scout Council, Wichita, Kansas; Mabel Hammersmith and Elspeth B. Anderson of the Girl Scouts of the United States of America, New York, New York; Marie Hartwig and Melba Bram of the National Music Camp, Interlochen, Michigan; Mrs. Brigadier James G. Henderson of Star Lake Camp, Bloomingdale, New Jersey; John Holden of Camp Kooch-I-Ching, International Falls, Minnesota; John J. Kirk of Camp Wapalanne, Branchville, New Jersey; Frederick Lorenz of Gnaw Bone Camp, Nashville, Indiana; John C. Page of Boy Scouts of America, North Brunswick, New Jersey; Chuck Shom of Alpine Trails

Outings, Denver, Colorado; Robert Telleen of Camp Manito-Wish, Boulder Junction, Wisconsin; Dorothy Walker and Dan Hemphill of Camp Summer Life, Taos, New Mexico; Mr. and Mrs. John H. Walker of Camp Teela-Wooket, Inc., Roxbury, Vermont; and Mrs. R. C. Woodcock of Camp Mary White, Mayhill, New Mexico.

Last, but not least, I would like to express appreciation to the members of the editorial and production staffs of the W. B. Saunders Company and especially to Ellen Murray, whose skillful assistance has been deeply appreciated.

Viola Mitchell

Table of Contents

Part One

Growth and Objectives of Camping

COULD YOU AFFORD IT?

Suppose God charged us for the rain,
Or put a price on a song-bird's strain
Of music—the dawn—mist on the plain.
How much would autumn landscapes
cost,
Or a window etched with winter's frost,
And the rainbow's glory so quickly
lost?
Suppose that people had to pay
To see the sunset's crimson play
And the magic stars of the Milky Way.
Suppose it was fifty cents a night
To watch the pale moon's silvery light,
Or watch a gull in graceful flight.
How much, I wonder, would it be worth
To smell the good, brown, fragrant
earth
In spring? The miracle of birth—
How much do you think people would
pay
For a baby's laugh at the close of day?
Suppose God charged us for them, I
say!
Suppose we paid to look at the hills,
For the rippling mountain rills,
Or the mating song of the whippoorwills,
Or curving breakers of the sea,
For grace, and beauty, and majesty?
And all these things He gives us free!

—AUTHOR UNKNOWN

Chapter 1

Camping

Figure 1-1 For Purple Mountain Majesties.

I know not where the white road runs,
nor what the blue hills are,
But man can have the sun for a friend,
and for his guide a star;
And there's no end of voyaging when once
the voice is heard,
For the river calls and the road calls,
and oh, the call of a bird!

—AUTHOR UNKNOWN. (Reprinted from Webb: *Light from a Thousand Campfires.*)

The organized summer camp is the most important step in education that America has given the world.

—CHARLES W. ELIOT,
President, Harvard University

FAMILY CAMPING

Don and Betty Perkins were just entering Blank National Forest. It was about four o'clock in the afternoon and they had driven a pleasant 100 miles from their home on Sunset Boulevard in Oswego, Ohio. They had planned their arrival for early in the afternoon to allow them some choice of campsites and time to leisurely settle in and do some exploring of nearby areas before supper time. Their children, Barry, 12, and Judy, 10, were in the back seat, agog with interest, as they neared the area they had chosen for their first night's stay.

All winter, the four members of the Perkins family had spent long evenings poring over road maps and piles of literature picturesquely describing the joys and adventures to be found in the several different areas they considered visiting. Step by step, the four of them had evolved a plan involving travel through various types of terrain, some rugged, some smooth, but each interesting and beautiful in its own unique way. There would be travel through historic areas with stops at appropriate places to make sections of the children's history books literally come alive and bring to all a deeper knowledge and appreciation of our wonderful American heritage.

Their usual plan called for making one- or two-night stops in some National Park or National Forest. Don had been a Boy Scout for many years and had also spent two summers at a private camp, and Betty had gone to Girl Scout camp for several summers and then served as a counselor for two seasons in a Camp Fire Girls camp. These experiences had given them some of the knowledge and skills necessary for living comfortably in the out-of-doors, as well as a love of informal rustic living which inevitably drew them to spend their summer vacation and as many weekends as possible in secluded areas far from the busyness of city life. Each had a two-week summer vacation, planned to coincide and scheduled so that the children would be back to attend regular sessions in organized camps. As much as Don and Betty believed in and enjoyed camping together as a family, they realized how much they would be shortchanging their children if they deprived them of the opportunity to participate with their peers in the planned and well-coordinated program of a good organized camp.

Since their early married life, Don and Betty had taken to the wilds on every possible occasion, so the children grew up accepting this as a way of life. In addition to learning with and from their parents, they had also profited from their experiences in youth organizations and at organized camps. Don and Betty looked forward to these opportunities to get away from the discordant jangle of telephones, automobile horns, alarm clocks, television sets and noisy home appliances. Like most children, Barry and Judy found the experience one continuous lark from beginning to end. They found it hard to wait until it was time to take off again.

Their trip was not regimented and formally planned, for they wanted most of all to get away from schedules and having to rush frantically about to be somewhere on time or do what someone else wanted or thought they *should* do. They preferred a leisurely expedition with freedom to linger or move on as the mood dictated. They shuddered at the thought of engaging in a speed derby like some of their friends who tried to cover as many miles as possible in order to outboast their friends on their return home. Instead, they preferred a fuller experience, returning happy and rested, with hearts, minds and souls jammed full of memories of companionship, fun-filled activities, beautiful scenery and the scamperings of such enchanting creatures as chipmunks, squirrels, a noisy jay, a strange bug or a doe and her fawn pausing to drink at a distant water hole. The children wouldn't have traded places with their city-bound playmates for anything, no matter how much money their doting parents might have spent on canned pleasure and entertainment.

Although none of the Perkins family ever consciously thought of it or tried to put it into words, each sensed unconsciously how much these shared experiences helped to weld them into an affectionate, closely knit family. Through all their planning and the trip itself, everything was done democratically and, as with any group of individuals, although opinions sometimes differed, each was flexible and willing to give as well as take, so that amicable compromises were usually possible. The children came to see their parents, as well as each other, in an entirely different light as the daily chores and pleasures of communal living brought out the virtues and lovable traits of each in contrast to his relatively few shortcomings. How different this way of life was from that of some city dwellers where each family member is so busy pursuing his or her own particular interests with his or her own particular associates that home becomes little more than a place to eat, sleep, take a bath and change clothes. Likewise, Don and Betty came to a new understanding of each other as well as of each child and found many opportunities to counsel and guide the children along desired paths. These close and warm relationships carried over into their city life to bear out the saying, "A family that plays together, stays together."

Don and Betty had learned how difficult it is during peak season to find

(Courtesy of the U.S. Forest Service.)

a choice campsite along main roads in popular camping areas. Even if they were lucky enough to find one it would offer little privacy and they could probably stay for only a limited time because of other demands for the site. From the relatively small band of about a million people, mostly hunters and fishermen, who camped in 1924, it is estimated that today over 34 million camp (approximately one of every seven people), many of them several times during a season. The number is increasing so rapidly that, despite valiant efforts by all concerned, the supply of new campsites produced annually lags farther and farther behind the demand.

Although one might logically assume that these mainly urban-dwelling campers would seek solitude and relief from crowds, this is not always the case. As the average newcomer arrives, he almost invariably stops at an already crowded location as close to the main road as possible. The Perkins family, however, are not bothered by this for they know that even the best known forests and parks are extensive and contain quantities of little used acreage providing choice campsites for those willing to wander off the beaten path and settle for simple facilities instead of the elaborate luxury of the more populated sites. Others, however, prefer to live among crowds, for much of their pleasure comes from rubbing elbows with those with varied backgrounds, occupations, experiences and views about life.

Most people in public camping areas are friendly, courteous and considerate. Unfortunately, however, sooner or later campers will encounter a few who are quite ignorant or unmindful of the meaning of good outdoor manners and will engage in vandalism, mutilating or destroying wildlife, cutting down trees, carving initials in public places or on living trees, keeping or leaving a messy campsite or being overly inquisitive and intruding where they are not wanted. There may also be an occasional group who pull in late at night, shining headlights and flashlights about indiscriminately, slamming car doors and conversing in loud tones as they unload and stash away an interminable amount of gear instead of quietly unpacking only the bare necessities for bedding down, leaving the rest until morning. Most knowledgeable campers retire early, ready to arise and take full advantage of daylight for their next day's activities, but eventually these campers will probably encounter a collection of characters who apparently equate enjoyment with noisiness. They may consume quantities of alcohol to release inhibitions and sing loudly, if not melodiously, until long after fellow campers are in bed, and consequently, both the party of midnight revelers and the other campers are unhappy when morning comes and it is time to stir about groggily.

HOW THEY CAMP

When Don and Betty first started camping they pooled their individual equipment from their earlier camping experiences, supplementing it with a few items rented from a nearby supply house. This saved money and gave them a chance to try out and compare different pieces of equipment before deciding which to buy. They took advantage of opportunities to learn from the experiences of others and pored over each new supply catalogue carefully. They also acquired a few good books about family camping. They wanted to avoid learning by trial and error methods in the school of experience whose theme song is "ouch." They chose each new purchase thoughtfully, weighing both its sturdiness and cost, for while they wanted what was necessary for comfort and safety, they avoided frills and gadgets which would add expense and weight, take up space and have to be moved about each time they wanted to get to some specific article.

A variety of recreational vehicles (RV's) are available. For those who want to duplicate home life as nearly as possible, there are the extra-large, gas-guzzling *motor homes,* featuring such amenities as wall-to-wall carpeting, separate rooms, air conditioning, a hot shower, an indoor toilet, a wall furnace, hot water, electric lights and a compact and cleverly built-in kitchen with all sorts of equipment ready to be plugged in at the electrical outlets available at many campgrounds. Some of these campgrounds rival plush resorts, with showers, flush toilets, laundromats, indoor dining rooms, swimming pools, recreation rooms and planned recreation programs, televisions, museums, conducted tours and trips, and nearby tennis courts and golf courses.

A popular form of mobile shelter is the *tent trailer* or *camping trailer,* which consists of a metal box on wheels with a collapsible pop-up tent folded inside, leaving about three-fourths of the space for stowing equipment. The outfit is about as high as the trunk of the car so that it does not interfere with the driver's rear view. When ready to use, one slides out the sides or folds them down level with the bottom to form a floor for the tent, which is brought up and erected above. The *truck camper* consists of a coach which slides onto the bed of a pickup truck. Some campers travel in the family car, stowing a tent and accessories in the back seat and trunk or in a cartopper or small trailer. A *station wagon,* sometimes equipped with a removable kitchen cabinet and a cartopper which erects into a tent, is also a favorite. There are several types of small *buses* or *land cruisers* fitted out for camping, and some campers use converted school or commercial buses.

Figure 1-2 I Wonder What We Forgot!

Modern tents are a far cry from the old type of heavy, bulky drill or canvas in drab gray or tan. They were difficult to pitch and strike and their heavy materials and wooden or metal poles challenged the skill and patience of almost everyone. Modern tents come in all shapes and sizes and in colorful, lightweight materials with screened windows and doors and zippered storm flaps. Some have awnings, screened-in porches and separate or sewed-in waterproof floors to keep out dampness and unwanted "critters." Poles, when necessary, are of lightweight fiber glass or aluminum. Some tents are so easy to pitch and strike that a child can do it in almost no time at all. Foldaway beds, with air mattresses and pillows inflated by a foot or electric pump, and convenient sleeping bags make sleeping as restful as at home.

Lightweight, nested cooking and eating kits and the wide assortment of dehydrated and pre-prepared foods now available from supermarkets or camp suppliers, take the drudgery out of preparing meals and make it possible to serve almost anything you would at home. Plastic or paper dishes and plastic eating utensils, with paper tablecloths and napkins, let you dine in style, yet forget dishwashing as you chuck the refuse into a conveniently located trash can. Compact gasoline, butane gas or liquid fuel stoves have clip-on ovens and work almost as efficiently as your own kitchen stove. You can also get a stove to heat your living quarters if it gets chilly.

Other conveniences are folding tables and chairs, air mattresses which snap together to make chaise lounges, lanterns which provide good light, effective insect repellents, and transistor radios to keep you abreast of what is going on back in the hubbub. It is impossible to even imagine what new devices will come from the creative minds of the manufacturers who look upon this tremendous mushrooming of interest in camping as big business.

If you are a novice, beware lest a clever advertisement or glib salesman tempt you to spend unnecessarily large sums of money and burden yourself with a multitude of gadgets you neither need nor want. If you truly love camping for its own sake, you will welcome worthwhile innovations but will confine yourself to what you actually need to live comfortably.

If you enjoy being innovative and resourceful, improvise some of your own equipment from materials you have around home or can purchase

Figure 1–3 And Would You Care for One of Our Finest Five-Mile Extension Cords?

cheaply, or invest in some of the kits now available from reputable manufacturers. Don and Betty often do this and it cuts down on expenses and gives them the same satisfaction they first felt when they improvised with tin cans and other cast-offs during their childhood camping trips. However, they realize that not everyone wants to rough it, and they willingly grant each person the right to do *his* camping as *he* sees fit.

WHY THEY CAMP

It is difficult to explain the rapidly growing interest in outdoor life and a way of living somewhat akin to that of our forefathers. It is probable that each person has his own strictly personal reasons for finding satisfaction in outdoor living.

One explanation lies in the nomadic urge, present in each of us to some extent, which bids us cast off the tried and routine and be up and away. Travel and camping sound red-blooded and glamorous and seem to offer welcome relief from an everyday humdrum existence. We long to walk away from our daily grind and association with equally bored people, and the almost inevitable pressures, frictions and misunderstandings which develop. On the other hand, some people may be frustrated and lonely from too few personal contacts and welcome camping as a chance to get into the maelstrom of life where they can mingle socially with their peers.

Many find in camping a rewarding way to spend the increased amount of leisure time now available through shorter working hours, longer paid vacations and increasingly numerous labor-saving devices which minimize the time necessary for home chores. Powerful automobiles and excellent roads crisscrossing the country tempt even those with only a limited amount of time to head for one of the camping areas within easy driving distance of practically everyone.

Our affluent society and the fact that often both husband and wife work, make such extras as camping equipment and vacation trips financially possible. Owning two cars is a matter of convenience or sometimes necessity for many families, making a station wagon or other vehicle adaptable to camping a logical choice for the second car.

On the other side of the economic picture, the inflated prices charged by modern motels and resorts strain the pocketbooks of those of moderate means or with large families. One can easily spend hundreds of dollars for even a short resort vacation, and this same amount is enough to buy basic camping equipment. Once outfitted, except for transportation expenses and the nominal fees charged in most camping areas, you can camp almost as cheaply as you can stay at home, for you carry your shelter with you and prepare your own food just as you normally would.

For some, camping satisfies nostalgic memories of a rural childhood or participation in organized camping. Memories keep intruding, with the tantalizing smell of an open fire, bread toasting over the coals, bacon and eggs frying in the pan and coffee boiling in the pot, all perfect for satisfying appetites made ravenous by hours of activity in the out-of-doors. We long to sit once again around the embers of a dying campfire, dreaming and chatting until it's time to ease our pleasantly fatigued muscles into a cozy bedroll and drift off to sleep 'neath a canopy of stars, lulled by the croaking of bullfrogs in the distance and the sound of the waters of a nearby creek bubbling over its rocky bottom. We might not even look askance at the ominous warnings of an approaching thunderstorm as we recall the blissful feeling of cuddling safe and secure in our bedrolls, listening as the first raindrops come tattooing down on our sturdy tent roof.

Many of us who would shy away from the hardships and deprivations of camping in a rough and rugged style, open our eyes for another look when apprised of the completely modernized, lightweight and convenient equipment and well-designed campsites now available. Many places offer so many program possibilities that it would be hard not to find at least one interesting activity to pursue. Among the choices are exploring, studying nature, hiking, swimming, boating, fishing, hunting, playing golf or shuffleboard, folk or square dancing, joining with other enthusiasts in a game of bridge or just lolling around on the beach or in a deck chair under a shady tree while attempting to concentrate on that good book you've been intending to read all winter. Some camping and recreation areas even provide babysitters and recreation directors to entertain your children while you and your spouse take off for a brief trip by yourselves.

On the other hand, some of us long to break away from the softness and ease so much a part of today's living. Camping appeals because it provides an opportunity to rough it, to improvise and make do, and to test our wits against the forces of nature. Many people leading sedentary lives feel vaguely uncomfortable about their loss of physical fitness and want to do something about it. Vigorous camp life seems to offer a way to take positive steps toward getting back into shape again. Those who have been trying to shed excess weight see in the strenuous life a possible way to fortify the exercise and diet programs of the city which have proved all too ineffective.

Many parents, like Don and Betty Perkins, look upon camping as a prime means of promoting close family ties as well as providing many other advantages and benefits for their children. Here they can acquire many valuable skills, attitudes and bits of lore not ordinarily gained in school or from their usual city activities. There are opportunities to learn more about ecology, geography, history, geology, botany, zoology and astronomy. Even practical sociology and psychology come into use as they mingle with a hodgepodge of people under diverse circumstances. They are usually safer when camping than they would be at home in a city with its traffic hazards and potentially harmful influences. When children are carefully supervised by adults and instructed about such possible hazards as poison ivy, being too venturesome with strange animals, snakes, bugs, berries and such, and cautioned never to wander off alone, there is little to fear.

Figure 1–4 All Nature's Creatures Are Fascinating for Those With Eyes to See.

Appetites are keen and no nagging or bribing is necessary to get the children to consume quantities of plain, nourishing food.

No doubt many who join in the camping parade do so because it is currently the "in" thing to do. We read about camping, see it in the movies and on television and hear about it from friends, relatives and acquaintances. In many ways, America is a nation of conformists, and whatever others are doing, we want to do too. Luckily, many of us who are first motivated to try camping for this reason, and approach it as gingerly as when gradually working up the courage to stick our toes in cold water, are quickly "hooked" and transformed into as enthusiastic campers as anyone else.

WHERE THEY CAMP

The day is long past when a traveler could simply pull off the road and make himself at home wherever he wished and for as long as he wished. Such freedom is now denied, largely because of the population explosion, as well as the thoughtlessness and selfishness displayed by an occasional camper who settled in without a "by-your-leave" and proceeded to chop down the straightest, most valuable young trees and limbs from seasoned timber for firewood and camp "fixin's," broke down fences and trampled over flowers and growing crops with careless abandon. He was occasionally so trigger-happy and unversed in farm lore as to mistake some valuable barnyard animal for wild game and kill or maim it. He built huge bonfires which sometimes got out of control or were left smoldering to later burst into flame and destroy acres of crops, wildlife, timber, farm buildings and even human beings. He was sometimes foul talking and boisterous. When he finally decided to move on, he was not soon forgotten because of the messy array of bottles, cans, partly eaten food, ashes, charred wood and other debris left behind. Need we go further to explain why so many present day landowners grimace as they see some new group approach to "squat" on their property, which represents so much of their time and money?

Fortunately, toward the end of the nineteenth century, a few farsighted individuals realized how rapidly private ownership and commercial usage were removing vast quantities of public land from the public domain and depleting it of its natural resources by indiscriminate logging, mining, and grazing, and by converting it into farms, cities, highways, parking areas, oil wells, factories, dams, and reservoirs. These early conservationists pleaded with all who would listen to take immediate and decisive steps to stop this wholesale rape of the land and retain quantities of it in public ownership and in its native state, unspoiled by man's greed and selfishness. They feared that future generations would have nowhere to go to find the beauty, solitude and peace so much needed. Too few listened and still fewer acted, so that today only about 10 per cent of the unspoiled forests and plains which greeted our first settlers remain in our 50 states. A large part of this is located in the National Forests, National Parks,

State Parks and Wildlife Refuges and Ranges. The Wilderness Act of 1964 defines wilderness as "an area where earth and its community of life are untrammeled by man, where man himself is a visitor who does not remain."

National Parks. At the present time, Congress has provided for the establishment of 38 National Parks covering almost 15 million acres. To qualify as a National Park, an area must contain something of unusual scenic beauty, or historic or recreational interest. The Parks are administered by the National Park Service, a bureau of the Department of the Interior, and embrace such famous phenomena as the Grand Tetons, Mammoth Cave, the subtropical Everglades, Mount Rainier, the Carlsbad Caverns and the Petrified Forest. The Park Service, in its administration of the Parks, follows the general policy of "the greatest good for the greatest number while keeping them as primitive and unspoiled for future generations as possible." Thus, no hunting is allowed and the number of roads, lodges and other man-made refinements is kept at a minimum. If a tree falls, it will probably be left where it fell as long as it is not blocking a road; some administrators have even gone so far as to advocate letting lightning-caused fires run their courses as long as they create no special hazards. Dams for hydroelectric power, artificial lakes, logging, mining and cattle grazing are frowned upon. This creates of the parks great outdoor museums where one can see the true balance of nature in action. The Park System operates 6,591 miles of well-marked trails, some accessible only on foot or horseback. Camping is encouraged and over 300,000 campsites are available, ranging from the most primitive to the more refined, sometimes with resort hotels, motels, boat liveries, stores, restaurants and other services operated by concessionaires under the direction of the Park Service.

Figure 1-5 Busy, Aren't They?

The Service also administers areas of historical significance, trying to maintain them or, if necessary, restore them as nearly as possible to their original condition. Such areas range from Lincoln's birthplace to the Statue of Liberty and Gettysburg National Military Park. Aware of the problem of a decreasing amount of open space for a rapidly expanding population, the Service has added a third area of interest in the form of National Recreation Areas. These are mostly on withdrawn public lands and are administered by the Bureau of Reclamation for dam or reservoir projects. The areas usually center on or about water, often a manmade lake. For further information, write to Public Inquiries Department, National Park Service, Washington, D. C. 20240.

National Forests. The 155 National Forests and 19 National Grasslands are scattered over 44 states and Puerto Rico and contain some 187 million acres. They are under the administration of the foresters of the Forest Service, under the Department of Agriculture. Instead of leaving their welfare largely up to the forces of nature as the Park Service does, the policy is to manage their resources under a system of coordinated multiple use which yields water, timber, livestock, wildlife, minerals and recreation. This permits "harvesting" an amount of the renewable resources each year equal to what will be restored by the year's growth. For instance, as many mature trees are marked and cut down each year as will be replaced by new tree growth. This furnishes about one-fifth of the nation's annual timber crop. This harvesting actually improves the forest by providing room for young trees to grow as well as improving the cover and food supply for livestock and forest wildlife. Livestock grazing is permitted, but only to the extent that the forage and browse consumed will be replaced. Watersheds are managed and protected to safeguard water supplies, prevent erosion and reduce floods; forests and watercourses are maintained in suitable condition for game and fish. One-third of the country's big game animals live in these forests. Controlled hunting and fishing are permitted, except in certain designated wildlife refuges, and this is again on a sustaining basis.

The Forest Service constantly tries to increase its recreation areas insofar as possible without interfering with the welfare and attractiveness of the forests. "The aim is the harmonious and coordinated management of the several resources without impairment of the productivity of the land." *

Some 150,000 miles of roads are located in the forests; many of them are used primarily for carrying fire-fighting and maintenance equipment, but are usually open to visitors as well. There are 88 wilderness areas and 112,000 miles of trails to provide a veritable wonderland of adventure for the backpacker or horseback rider. Their 81,000 miles of streams and lakes delight lovers of water sports and of travel by canoe or boat, and Forest Service acreage furnishes the locale for 80 per cent of the snow skiing in the West. Of the total acreage, 94 per cent is forest covered, with some 6,400 camping areas and 53,000 individual campsites, some accessible only by quiet forest roads or wilderness trails. Most camping areas are equipped with tables, benches and firegrates, with toilets and water supplies centrally located. Firewood is usually available at nominal cost. For further information, write to Forest Service, U.S. Department of Agriculture, Washington, D. C. 20250.

State Parks. Although usually smaller than the National Parks, the State Parks have been rapidly increasing in number and importance. Varying

---

**National Parks and National Forests*, U. S. Government Printing Office, 1962.

greatly in size, some are historic, some scenic, some primitive, and others highly developed. Some have rangers and, sometimes, naturalists, and many provide facilities for camping.

Private Campgrounds. Commercial firms, such as those dealing in timber, pulpwood for paper and power and utility companies, have opened some 50 million acres of their privately owned virgin wilderness and streams and lakes for the use of hunters, fishermen and other vacationers. Several Indian Reservations are now developing campground facilities with a definite Indian flavor to attract vacationers. One of the most rapidly growing trends is the ownership and development of private camping and recreational areas. Here, for a modest sum, families or individuals can stay to fish in well-stocked lakes and streams or hunt in woodlands stocked with game. Many offer other sorts of recreation, such as trail rides or tours with experienced guides, food, equipment and transportation; sometimes they help groups to plan their own excursions. Guests stay in lodges, tents, light housekeeping cabins or bring their own trailers or tents. Home-cooked meals are available in a central dining room, or those who wish to may cook their own. There may be programs and supervision for children, leaving the parents free to do what they want. Grocery staples and other supplies are available on the site or nearby, and boats, canoes, horses, fishing tackle and other equipment may be rented.

American Youth Hostels

Although American Youth Hostels (AYH) does not sponsor camping as such, it fosters a way of life quite in accord with the spirit of camping. The name implies that it is primarily devoted to serving the needs of young people, but membership is open to people of all ages, as well as family groups.

The word *hostel* comes from the Old English and means resting place. The movement was started in Germany in 1909 by a young schoolteacher and rapidly spread throughout Europe. In 1934 two American teachers who had been hosteling in Europe brought the idea back with them to the United States, and within a year or two a chain of hostels had sprung up throughout the Green and White Mountains of New Hampshire and Vermont.

Hostelers travel under their own steam by hiking, bicycling, canoeing, sailing, horseback riding or skiing, and bunk down for the night at some simple building such as a house, converted barn, school, church, camp or mountain lodge known as a *hostel*. There are separate dormitories for boys and girls (and sometimes family groups), and the hostel provides beds, mattresses, blankets, stoves, refrigerators and pots and pans. Hostelers bring their own sheets or sleeping sacks, eating utensils, clothing and food.

Service is strictly on a do-it-yourself basis, with each group doing its own cooking, and assisting with the general clean-up of the quarters. Certain rules are observed; drinking and the use of illegal drugs are forbidden, smoking is restricted to specified areas, and going to bed and rising must be at reasonable hours. When distances to or between hostels are great, hostelers sometimes camp out.

Each hostel is supervised by houseparents who ordinarily volunteer their services because of their liking for

Figure 1–6 He's Hard to Keep Up With.

people and their belief in the values of the program. Advance reservations are usually required and cost from $1 to $3 a night in this country, and 50¢ to $1.25 in foreign countries. There are now 128 hostels in the United States, scattered across the various states, including Hawaii and Alaska.

There are 29 local councils which sponsor hostels and a year-round program of local trips and other outdoor activities. The National Travel Department of AYH sponsors over 50 hosteling trips each summer, lasting from three to four weeks, to various areas of the United States as well as to Canada, Mexico, Europe, Hawaii and Israel. Trips are under the supervision of carefully selected and trained leaders and the groups are kept small, usually having from seven to ten people. AYH travel is one of the most pleasant and least expensive ways to meet others and see the world.

Individual memberships cost $5 a year for those under 18, and $10 for those older. Family memberships cost $12 and cover all children under 18. All members receive an AYH pass and a copy of the *Hostel Guide and Handbook,* which contains pertinent information about each hostel in this country, as well as much valuable general information about camping and hosteling.

There are now over 75,000 American Youth Hostel passholders. The organization is international and has a total membership of some 2,079,000, with a total of 4,245 Federation Hostels located in 48 countries. By mutual agreement, the pass of any person will be honored in any of the participating countries.

The AYH National Campus has recently been moved to a new 62-acre location. There, among other things, they hope to enlarge their curriculum of leadership courses and ecology studies, some offering the possibility of college credit. For further information about membership, trips and other services offered, contact American Youth Hostels, Inc., National Campus, Delaplane, Virginia 22025.

ORGANIZED CAMPING

WHAT IS ORGANIZED CAMPING?

Our past discussion has centered around the types of informal camping people do as and when they will. However, this book is primarily concerned with organized camping. An *organized camp* is one conducted primarily for young people, usually from 7 to 16 years old, where they can dwell more or less in a world of their own, working, playing, worshiping and carrying on the daily business of living together under the watchful eye of a staff of counselors and other camp personnel. Organized camps are of many types and are conducted in various ways and for various purposes.

TYPES OF CAMPS

Camps may be classified into five types: (1) resident or established camps, (2) trip or travel camps, (3) day camps, (4) school camps, and (5) special camps.

Resident or Established Camps. A *resident* or *established camp* is one in which campers live for a period of time, usually ranging from a few days to eight or more weeks. There are usually several permanent buildings surrounded by a broad expanse of woods and meadows, left pretty much in their natural state and located away from the main roads to provide privacy and freedom from intrusions by those without legitimate camp connections.

Resident camps are of many types, usually with many points of similarity, yet differing in certain aspects, so that each has a distinct personality of its own. Some are purposely kept quite primitive and rustic, featuring a somewhat rugged and simple way of life quite different from the average camper's home environment. Others go to the opposite extreme, providing most of the refinements and conveniences of modern urban life. These camps might better be termed summer resorts, for they often contribute little of what is generally considered a good camping experience. All good camps, no matter how rustic, maintain the qualities essential for good, safe and healthful living.

A typical large camp contains quantities of woodland and meadows, often with brooklets meandering through and crisscrossed by several trails traced by the feet of scores of adventuresome counselors and campers. Here, all types of plant and animal life abound, for the attitude of camp people toward wildlife is one of friendliness and appreciation rather than indifference or destructiveness. These unspoiled natural surroundings provide the background for a real organized camp experience.

Campers and staff may live in somewhat rustic cabins, teepees or tents on wooden platforms, usually grouped into separate units of from 12 to 24 campers with their counselors, and somewhat segregated from the other units to promote a feeling of solidarity and privacy. In some camps each living unit is entirely self-sufficient. However, most camps feature centrally located buildings to provide a common dining room and kitchen, a large lodge or recreation room, an arts and crafts shop, washrooms, showers, toilets, laundry facilities, a camp office, tool houses and sheds for camp storage and the caretaker's equipment, a health center, trading post, counselors' retreat, nature museum, camp library and a center to house equipment and supplies for cook-outs or trips away from camp.

Some camps have fields and courts for such sports as tennis, archery, softball, badminton, horseshoes, riflery and golf, an amphitheater, an outdoor chapel and a council ring. Located at the ends of certain trails and at some distance from the main camp will probably be outposts or campsites where those with sufficient campcraft skills can go to break the monotony of camp life and experience the thrill of living comfortably and simply under more primitive conditions. There may be a stable, tack room, riding ring and riding trails. A popular spot is the waterfront on a lake, river or seashore with an array of rowboats, canoes, sailboats and possibly even power boats. Most camps also have a swimming pool, for few are fortunate enough to possess natural bodies of water still free enough from contamination to be safe for swimming and lifesaving activities. Some camps specialize in certain activities, such as tennis, horseback riding or water sports; others offer a wide variety, running the gamut from woodworking, ballet dancing and tutoring through electronics and nuclear physics. Most lie somewhere in between.

Figure 1-7 So Fleet His Hoofs.

This word picture of a more or less typical camp depicts a busy, thriving community, and that is exactly what it is. A large camp represents a big investment and may be populated by as many as a hundred or even several hundred lively youngsters and a fairly large staff of counselors and other personnel.

Trip or Travel Camps. Those participating in *trip* or *travel camping* start from a common base, traveling by foot, canoe, bicycle, horseback, sailboat, a horse-drawn "covered wagon" or almost any other conceivable means of transportation. They make camp each night at a new location and may use a map and compass to find their way over a predetermined route. Some travel groups consist of older campers from a resident camp who have won this privilege by demonstrating their knowledge and skills in camping techniques; others are made up of individuals who come together for the express purpose of making the trip, which is often commercially sponsored and led by an experienced guide or guides. *Wilderness, pioneer* or *survival camping* is a specialized form of primitive camping undertaken by older campers specially trained for it. Participants are usually transported to a takeoff spot where they set out with only rudimentary equipment and supplies, getting most of their food and other necessities from what nature provides along the way. One or more skilled counselors or guides are in charge, and the trip may last from a week to an entire summer.

Day Camps. A *day camp* is one set up to accommodate campers who commute from home each day. They ordinarily run from one to five days a week, with the children arriving by bus or private car soon after breakfast and returning home in the late afternoon, although some camps lengthen the hours to accommodate the children of employed mothers. The children spend the day participating in various camping activities and may cook part or all of their lunch, using ingredients brought from home.

Day camping is most common in or near metropolitan areas, and often the camp utilizes parks or other public recreational facilities. Sponsorship is often by the city or town itself or some service organization such as the Boy Scouts, Girl Scouts, Camp Fire Girls, Boys' or Girls' Clubs, YMCA or YWCA. Privately owned day camps, operated for profit from fees paid by those attending, are now on the increase. Nearly all the activities of a resident camp are possible in a day camp, except for those of early morning or nighttime and, of course, sleeping on the campgrounds. Some camps even work in a measure of these by sponsoring overnight sleep-outs and occasional trips for those able to participate, using borrowed tents or a park shelterhouse in case of inclement weather. Programming in a day camp is especially challenging since the campers choose to return or stay away each day, depending upon how appealing the previous day's activities were. Day camps make an important contribution to camping by extending its benefits to those who are too young or who are financially unable to attend resident camps. They also prepare beginning campers for later participation in a resident or travel camp.

Special Camps. Most organized camps offer a well-rounded program, including such activities as woodcraft, campcraft, aquatics, nature study and arts and crafts; however, some concentrate on only one or a few activities in order to serve those with special interests or needs. For example, there are salt water camps, ranch camps, farm camps, mountain climbing camps and trip and pioneering camps, which build their programs around their particular environments. Others stress specific activities such as field hockey, tennis, aquatics, basketball, horseback riding, nature or science study, dramatics, music, dance, religious education, tutoring or language study. Still others serve those with special problems such as diabetics, the deaf, the mentally retarded, cardiacs, epileptics, the physically handicapped or the socially maladjusted. Some camps are coed, and others accommodate special groups such as families, adults or golden age persons (those over age 60).

Outdoor Education and School Camping. Although people sometimes use these terms interchangeably, they are not the same. *Outdoor education* includes all types of experiences which improve one's knowledge, attitudes or skills in the out-of-doors and render him more appreciative of it and better able to enjoy himself in it. Outdoor education may involve anyone, of any age, at any time and in various situations. In school the first experience may come as a teacher takes his class out on the playground to observe cloud formations, soil erosion or the activities of the surprisingly large number of plants and animals living there. It may consist of a trip to a farm, zoo, museum, dam, wildlife refuge, fish hatchery or municipal or state park. It may include viewing films and slides about nature and ecology or growing plants or caring for pet animals in the classroom. It may involve instruction in fishing, hunting, hiking or camping techniques.

School camping, on the other hand, consists of a camping trip taken by one or more school classes to a regular campsite, accompanied by their teachers and other personnel and lasting from a few days to several weeks. Neither school camping nor outdoor education is new, for progressive teachers have always tried to acquaint their students with the world around them. However, recent years have brought an awakening interest in this field, and more and more school districts and states are now incorporating school camping into their programs, and as their experience grows, school camping practices will improve.

(Courtesy of Crystal Lake Camps, Hughesville, Pennsylvania.)

Objectives of School Camping. Although the objectives of school camping are somewhat similar to those of general organized camping, a definite effort is made to closely correlate the camping experience with what is occurring in the classroom. Thus, when properly carried out, it supplements and makes more meaningful certain phases of the regular school curriculum. Throughout recent years it has become evident that society is making progressively greater demands on the school to accept increasing responsibility for rounding out and totally educating the child, not only in the new subject matter necessitated by our increasingly complex society, but also in other areas of learning formerly taught by the neighborhood, church and family. When this country was largely agricultural, each child had chores to perform and did them under the close supervision of his family and neighbors. Families and friends conversed for long hours, uninterrupted by radio, television, movies or other modern forms of entertainment. Now children have few, if any, chores to do, and family members often make little effort to instruct the child in even rudimentary tasks. Consequently, the school has been asked to provide more and more of the training needed to help the child to become a healthy, happy citizen with the knowledge and skills to earn a living and the attitudes and abilities to use wisely his rapidly increasing leisure time.

Since most educators now recognize the important contributions a good camping experience can make, they would like to provide every child with this experience, not just the relatively small percentage presently enjoying it. Some parents do not send their child to summer camp because they fail to recognize its values and so do not encourage attendance. Others feel they cannot afford even the modest fees charged by organization camps, while some fear interference with family vacations. Therefore, the logical solution seems to be for the school to take on this added responsibility.

The school's approach to camping should be educational rather than merely recreational, for usurping school time can scarcely be justified unless the results make a definite contribution to general school objectives. However, even though school camping is not specifically designed to entertain children, they usually enjoy it thoroughly because,when the program is well administrated, every waking hour is filled with novel, exciting things to do, seemingly expressly designed to stimulate and enchant youngsters. They often become so completely absorbed in what they are doing that previous discipline problems, psychosomatic allergies and antagonistic attitudes evaporate into thin air, since they are no longer needed to fulfill personal needs or to gain attention. Since most normal children possess a big bump of curiosity and are naturally observant and eager to know, learning takes place unconsciously, and children previously lackadaisical in the classroom may discover for the first time just how much fun it is to learn.

A school camping trip is not a spree or a vacation trip. Instead, it has been carefully planned to correlate with what has been taking place in the classroom and, like the laboratory experience it really is, can develop more meaningful attitudes and knowledge in such fields as health, housekeeping, woodworking, arts and crafts, ecology and nature study, history, language arts, arithmetic, dramatics, music, social studies and moral and spiritual values. The aim is to retain for the classroom those activities and studies best handled there while transferring to the camping situation those that are especially suitable for that environment. This necessitates careful planning before the trip, as well as a

Figure 1–8 Just Some of the Natives Coming Out to Look Us Over.

thoughtful analysis and evaluation upon returning, so that the next trip will be even more successful.

The child's learning begins as he pores over maps to trace the school bus route to the campsite, and continues as he plans nutritional menus, consults with his classmates on such matters as what individual and group equipment will be needed and decides what types of information can be gained and what questions can be answered by observation and experimentation while at camp.

Camping offers an unparalleled opportunity to develop social skills. A child who has seldom if ever been away from home before learns to depend on himself and to make his own decisions with the help of accompanying adults. Here he must assume responsibility for washing and dressing himself and caring for his own clothing. He must keep his own quarters neat and also do his share in caring for group facilities. He learns to be punctual in performing assigned chores. He realizes that there are several ways of doing a given task and that some may even be superior to the way he is used to at home. If he comes from a disadvantaged or poorly supervised home, he may absorb much from the teaching and example of others in such areas as personal grooming, cleanliness, proper setting of tables, dishwashing, table manners, proper eating habits, the saying of grace before meals and appropriate conduct at such ceremonies as flag raising and lowering. Teachable moments occur frequently for leaders skilled enough to see them. Camp living is democratic and a child learns how group decisions are made, why a certain number of rules and guidelines are necessary to safeguard the welfare and rights of all, and that privileges are always accompanied by responsibilities. He learns the roles of a leader and followers in a group. By close association with others, he recognizes that no two individuals are precisely alike and that, in order to be happy in a group, he must learn to appreciate the good qualities of each, while accepting his shortcomings. Thus, he sees how slow learner John excels at the waterfront, whereas ordinarily scatterbrained Kathy efficiently plans and carries out the details of a campfire program. He has a golden opportunity to acquire the social graces and amenities necessary to live happily and cooperatively with others.

A youngster experiences the satisfaction of serving others and helping those less skilled than he. He acts as a good citizen while helping with a camp or community project such as planting trees or controlling erosion to benefit future campers. Ecology and nature study, carried on in natural surroundings, assume new importance and elicit his enthusiastic support for all wise conservation methods. He may also acquire valuable skills and a lifelong interest in such forms of recreation as camping, hiking, water sports, hunting, fishing, geology and nature study. Without these interests and appreciations, he is likely to become just one more person to join the crowd in its trek to our parks, forests and other outdoor recreation areas where he will probably become extremely bored away from the gadgets and diversions he is used to in the city. Can you imagine our forests cluttered up with beer parlors, golf courses, slot machines, motion picture theaters and such, all put there to entertain unimaginative and unresourceful citizens?

Educators have long realized that greater progress is made when students and teachers work in an informal but controlled situation where they learn to know and appreciate each other as individuals. The school camp, where they eat, work, study and play together 24 hours a day, presents an ideal opportunity for this to occur.

ORGANIZATION AND ADMINISTRATION. Most schools enter school camping on a modest basis. starting with a weekend spent camping by one or two classes in the fall. As momentum grows and parents, school and community become more enthusiastic and supportive, the program expands, with the same classes camping for a week or two, while additional grades are brought into the program as rapidly as possible. Camping may eventually extend into the winter months, necessitating the use of winterized facilities, and some school systems even extend school camping into the summer months.

The fourth, fifth and sixth grades are the ones most commonly included, although some schools extend the program up to those of high school age. It seems best not to have more than two classes or a total of 30 youngsters present at one time, since larger numbers tend to destroy the feelings of intimacy and solidarity which are so desirable. If there are more, they should be separated into smaller groups and each conducted as independently as possible.

Figure 1-9 Wish My Umbrella was Portable.

Each class is accompanied by its own teacher to allow for better integration of camp life and classroom work and also to provide for the informal associations between the two which have been previously mentioned. This sometimes presents a problem, because many classroom teachers have had little, if any, training or experience in camping and outdoor living and are reluctant to try it, since they may lose confidence when away from the familiar classroom environment.

To overcome this difficulty, many schools of education now offer courses and hold workshops and institutes in outdoor education for teachers. These usually take place on a campsite and include instruction in camping techniques as well as in planning programs tailored for the teacher's particular class. They are designed to show him how to integrate the camp experience with what is done in the classroom in order to improve both. For instance, children will realize how practical such a subject as arithmetic can be when they use it to measure the ingredients for recipes or the height of a tree or the width and depth of a river.

A school camp usually has a professional camp director, cooks and persons trained in campcraft techniques, and schools with an extended program may hire a permanent camp staff to serve on an annual basis. In addition, resource personnel, such as astronomers, conservationists, foresters, geologists, agriculturalists and nature study experts may be invited.

FINANCING THE PROGRAM. The

school district usually pays for instruction, equipment and supplies just as it does for other school activities and also assumes the cost of capital improvements and maintenance for the campsite. Grounds and buildings may be available in a state or local park, a summer resident camp may be rented, or the school district may build its own campsite.

Local service clubs or the PTA may aid financially and, as the Federal Government has become more and more interested in camping programs, it has provided substantial help in several areas. Children can pay for their own food and lodging by starting a Camp Fund Bank early in the year in which each deposits small amounts in his own account. This provides a valuable lesson in economics and banking procedures as the children note how rapidly their nickels and dimes, earned by doing odd jobs or set aside from their allowances, add up. The aid of clubs or other service organizations can be enlisted to provide for indigent children. The class may also raise money by such projects as paper drives, class carnivals, cookie sales or chili suppers. Insurance is often provided in the comprehensive insurance policies of the school or sometimes through the family policies carried by the parents.

PLANNING. Whether a school camping trip is a complete waste of time or one of the most valuable experiences of the school year depends largely on how carefully it is planned for cooperatively by teachers, parents and children. In introducing school camping to a community, a first step may well be to call a meeting of all interested parties for a general discussion and the appointment of committees to handle various phases of the project. The purpose and procedures must be interpreted to the entire community as well as to parents so that all come to regard it as a valuable educational experience, rather than just another frill on which to spend school time and taxpayers' money. As enthusiasm rises, individuals will begin to help by giving suggestions and such tangible services as aid with finances, facilities, supplies, work needed at the campsite, transportation and proper physical and psychological preparation of the youngsters.

Figure 1-10 Bucky Beaver.

SPONSORSHIP OF CAMPS

Organization or Agency Camps. Many youth organizations or organizations with branches to serve youth find camping an excellent way to further their own objectives and consequently conduct their own camps, tailored to meet their specific purposes. These organizations are supported largely by the public through the United Fund, government funds, public taxation, fund-raising projects and private subscription. Campers, therefore, need pay only nominal fees, bringing camping well within the reach even of those from low income groups; there are often camperships* available for those unable to pay even this small sum. Since the facilities are limited and they must accommodate large numbers, a child's stay is often limited to a week or two. Fortunately, this is not necessarily as great a handicap as it may seem, for the camping experience is

---

*A "campership" is a grant or scholarship given to a deserving child to enable him to attend camp.

(Courtesy of Camp Teela-Wooket, Inc., Roxbury, Vermont.)

often merely an extension of what the child has been doing in the organization's regular city program, conducted by the same leaders. An organization camp is usually located near the campers it serves and this cuts down on transportation costs. These camps often have high standards and follow excellent camping practices and have been instrumental in introducing many worthwhile practices into camping. Since they handle so many children from so many social strata, they play an important role in the attempt to bring camping to all.

So many organizations now promote camping as a part of their programs that it is next to impossible to list all of them. The following, however, are noteworthy:

American Red Cross
Associations for handicapped children and adults
Big Brother Association
Boy Scouts
Boys' Clubs of America
Camp Fire Girls
Church groups
Four-H Clubs
Girl Scouts
Girls' Clubs of America
Municipalities
Pioneer Girls
Salvation Army
Settlement houses
Volunteers of America
Woodcraft Rangers
YMCA
YMHA
YWCA
YWHA

Independent or Private Camps. *Independent* or *private camps* are owned by an individual or individuals and are usually run for profit. They are often incorporated, and some sell stock. Since they receive no public moneys, they must usually charge a supportive fee of from $500 to $1000 or more a season. This tends to limit their patronage to children of the upper-middle or high income groups, although many have camperships which are available to selected children from lower income families. Private camps often draw their clientele from widespread areas, a practice which gives many campers the benefit of seeing a new part of the country and mingling with children whose customs and ways of life may be different.

The greater financial resources of private camps sometimes enable them to provide somewhat more in the way of equipment and facilities; this, of course, does not necessarily mean that they offer a better program, since those in charge may lack the wisdom and will to make good use of these material things. This, fortunately, is seldom the case, for most private camp directors are public spirited and sincerely dedicated to conducting their camps for the best interests of children.

A camper in a private camp ordinarily remains four to eight weeks, which allows enough time to thoroughly acclimate him and make real progress toward achieving camp objectives.

Throughout their history, private camps have generally been quite progressive and have made many valuable contributions to the camping field. Unfortunately, there have been a few which put monetary gains above the welfare of the children or which cater too much to the whims of parents and children, giving them what they want rather than what would be most beneficial. Thus, they sponsor city-type activities or those offering glamor and prestige instead of those which would make maximum use of their wonderful outdoor environment, unavailable to most of the children elsewhere.

LENGTH OF THE CAMP SEASON

Summer camps ordinarily operate during the months of July and August, called the *camp season.* In some camps, the season may be divided into several shorter periods known as *camp sessions.* In *long-term camps,* campers may stay for a half or the entire camp season of 4 to 8 weeks. In others, their stay may be limited to one session, lasting a week, ten days or two weeks. These are known as *short-term camps.* Because they must serve a large number of campers, most camps sponsored by agencies or organizations are short-term camps.

SOME FIGURES REVEALED BY AN ACA NATIONAL SURVEY

As a result of a 1969 national survey of ACA member camps,* it was found that 48 per cent were agency, 35 per cent private independent, 13 per cent church, 1 per cent school and 3 per cent in the miscellaneous category. Although there were several combinations of resident and day camps and travel camps, 79 per cent were resident, 20 per cent day and 1 per cent travel camps. Of every 31 ACA camps, 12 were for girls, 9 for boys and 10 were coed.

A 1973 study revealed that the average ACA camp encompassed 286.4 acres and represented an average investment of $403,081. Of course, these are only averages, and many camps vary markedly from them.

ADDITIONAL READINGS

(For an explanation of abbreviations and abbreviated forms used, see page 25.)

Church Camping

Bogardus, LaDonna: *Outdoor Living.* Abingdon, 1971, Leader's Guide, $1.50; Packet 1 (Guidelines for Discussion, Songs, Games), $1.25; Packet 2 (Outdoor Living Skills, Recipes, Crafts), $1.25; Packet 3 (Discovery Guides, Ecology Activities), $1.25.

---

*Schmidt, Ernest F.: An Accounting to ACA Members, *Camping Magazine,* May, 1969, p. 5.

Cues for Church Camping. (For counselors of junior and senior highs) Geneva, 1962, 80 pp., $1, paper.
Davis, Robert Pickens: *Church Camping.* Knox, 1969, 140 pp., $3.25, paper.
Ensign, John and Ruth: *Camping Together as Christians.* Knox, 1958, 148 pp.
Giese, Geneva: *Camping in Covenant Community.* Knox, 1967.
How to Be a Camp Counselor. Scripture, rev. 1967, 48 pp., 75¢, paper.
MacKay, Joy: *Creative Counseling for Christian Camps.* Scripture, 1966, 128 pp., $1.95, paper.
Purchase, Richard and Betty: *Let's Go Outdoors With Children.* Westminster, 1972, 32 pp., $1.50.
Seeking Meaning With Junior Highs in Camp. Geneva Press, 1956, 192 pp., $1.85, paper.
Springer, James C.: *Boys, Girls and God.* Vantage, 1971, 82 pp., $3.75.
Todd: *Camping for Christian Youth.*

Day Camping

So You Want to Start a Day Camp. ACA, 1964, 24 pp., $1.25.

MAGAZINE ARTICLES

Camping Magazine:
Hall, Mrs. William, and Grant Southwell: "Keep 'Camp' in Day Camping." June, 1967, p. 12.
Melamed, Monte: "Day Camp Busing." May, 1970, p. 17.
Papich, Robert: "Real Camp Program in a City Park Day Camp? Of Course You Can!" Feb., 1971, p. 20.
Recreation:
Musselman, Virginia: "Factors Affecting the Day Camp Program." Mar., 1963, p. 131.

Family Camping

Ade, Ginny: *A Guide to the Wonderful World of Camping.* Order from ACA, 1970, 50¢, paper.
Bernstein, Edwin G.: *Recreation Program in a Private Family Campground.* Order from ACA, 1969, 14 pp., 50¢, paper.
Better Homes and Gardens Family Camping Book.
Bridge: *America's Backpacking Book,* ch. 23.
Bugg, Ralph: *When Your Family Goes Camping.* Order from ACA, 1967, 72 pp., 75¢, paper.
Coffey, Cecil: *Camper's Digest.* Follett, 1970, 320 pp., $4.95, paper.
Gould: *The Complete Book of Camping,* ch. 7.
Langer: *The Joy of Camping,* pp. 125–132.
Manning: *Backpacking One Step at a Time,* ch. 18.
Outdoor Tips, pp. 54–65.
Riviere: *The Camper's Bible.*
Riviere: *The Family Camper's Cookbook.*
Sunset Camping Handbook. Lane, 1970, 96 pp., $1.95, paper.
Wells, George S.: *Guide to Family Camping.* Stackpole, 1973, 188 pp., $2.95, paper.
Wood: *Pleasure Packing,* ch. 12.
Note: Camping Journal includes a wealth of information about family camping in various issues.

Miscellaneous

Broome, Harvey: *Faces of the Wilderness.* Mountain Press, 1972, 271 pp., $7.95.
Camp, The Child's World. ACA, 1962, 32 pp., 85¢, paper.
Everhart, William C.: *The National Park Service.* Praeger, 1972, 275 pp., $9.
Frome, Michael: *The Forest Service.* Praeger, 1971, 241 pp., $8.75.
Kimball, James W.: *The Spirit of the Wilderness.* Denison, 1970, 302 pp., $6.95.
Leopold, Aldo: *A Sand County Almanac (and Sketches Here and There).* Order from ACA, 1966, 226 pp., $6.60; $1.95, paper.
Preparing Your Child for Camp. ACA, 1966, 25¢, paper.
Price, Carl E.: *Trails and Turnpikes.* Abingdon, 1969, 128 pp., $2.75.
Rodney and Ford: *Camp Administration,* ch. 1, pp. 1–12 and 21–24; ch. 16.
Rowlands, John J.: *Cache Lake Country.* Norton, 1959, 272 pp., $5.95.
Rutstrum, Calvin: *Challenge of the Wilderness.* Denison, 1970, 196 pp., $6.95.
Shivers: *Camping,* chs. 1 and 16.
Singer, Miriam and Murray: *Summer Camping—A Parent's Guide.* ACA, 1965, 17 pp., 15¢, paper.
Webb, Kenneth (Ed.): *Camping for American Youth—A Declaration for Action.* ACA, 1962, 26 pp., 75¢, paper.
Webb: *Light From a Thousand Campfires.*

MAGAZINE ARTICLES

Camping Magazine:
Webb, Kenneth B.: "So You Want to Start a Camp." May, 1964, p. 23.

School Camping and Outdoor Education

Education In and For the Outdoors. Nat'l Ed. Ass'n, 1963, 96 pp., $2.
Donaldson, George W. (Ed.): *Perspectives on Outdoor Education—Readings.* Brown, 1972, 233 pp., $3.95, paper.
Garrison, Cecil: *Outdoor Education: Principles and Practice.*
Hammerman and Hammerman (Eds.): *Outdoor Education: A Book of Readings.*
Hammerman and Hammerman: *Teaching in the Outdoors.*
Jensen, Clayne R., and Clark T. Thorstenson: *New Issues in Outdoor Recreation (A Collection of Contemporary Readings).* Burgess, 1972, 425 pp., $4.95.
Mand: *Outdoor Education.*

Outdoor Education. A.A.H.P.E.R., rev., 1970, 32 pp., $1.25, paper.
Outdoor Recreation Research: A Reference Catalog. Supt. of Documents, 1970, $1.25.
Sanford, Jean: *Bibliography of School Camping and Outdoor Education*. ACA, 1962, 29 pp., 75¢, paper.
Schramm, Wilbur: *Classroom Out-of-Doors—Education Through Camping*. Sequoia, 1969, 192 pp., $3.25.
Smith et al.: *Outdoor Education*.
Swan, Malcolm D. (Ed.): *Tips and Tricks in Outdoor Education*. (Compiled by members of the Department of Outdoor Education at Northern Illinois University's Lorado Taft Field Campus) Interstate, 1970, 184 pp., $3.95, paper.
van der Smissen, Dr. Betty (Chairman): *Use of Resident Camps for School Programs*. ACA, 1972, 22 pp., $1, paper.

EXPLANATION OF ABBREVIATED FORMS USED IN BIBLIOGRAPHIES

The reader will note that the bibliographies sometimes contain only skeleton information about a book and author. This practice has been followed for those books deemed of especial interest to the reader or for those cited in several chapters. You will find complete data about these books in the *Selected General Bibliography* in Appendices A and B. Likewise, abbreviated forms are sometimes given for publishers; their complete names and addresses will be found in the *Directory of Publishers and Organizations*, also located in Appendix D. Prices given are, of course, only approximate.

Order books through your local bookstore, directly from the publisher or from the National Recreation and Park Association (NRPA) or the American Camping Association (ACA). The latter two carry a rather extensive list of publications in the fields of camping and recreation and offer the convenience of ordering books from a single source. They sell these books at list price and the American Camping Association even offers a discount to members. Catalogues of their selections are free upon request. Their addresses are:

American Camping Association
Bradford Woods
Martinsville, Indiana 46151

National Recreation and Park Association
1601 North Kent St.
Arlington, Virginia 22209

Chapter 2

History of Camping

Figure 2-1 An Early American Expert in Camping.

THE TAPESTRY OF LIFE*

I wonder what the other side will be when I am finished weaving all my thread. I do not know the pattern or the end of this great piece of work which is for me. I only know that I must weave with care the colors that are given me, day by day, and make them a fabric firm and true which will be of service for my fellow men.

The work is held in place by the Master's Hand. The Master's mind made the design for me, if I but weave the shuttle to and fro and blend the colors as best I know. Perhaps when it is finished, He will say, "'Tis good," and lay it on the footstool at my feet.

—CLARISSA L. G. ZONS

EARLY CAMPERS

Camping is, no doubt, as old as man, for early people were often nomadic, moving with the changing seasons in search of food, better climate or in pursuit of or flight from their enemies. Some lived in caves while others constructed temporary, and sometimes portable, shelters.

The American Indians were among this country's early campers, and experts they were, for we still marvel at the vast amount of wood lore and camping know-how they acquired and passed on from one generation to the next. From the first moment the Pilgrims landed, they also became campers, for their long ocean voyage had depleted their supplies and they needed to supplement them with whatever game and vegetation they could find while hurrying to construct shelters against the worsening weather. Regardless of how history and movies have pictured them, many of the Indians were friendly and gave invaluable help; without them, our problem-ridden ancestors probably could not have survived.

Almost every growing thing was of interest to these early settlers. Many plants were valuable as sources of food, tools, medicine, clothing or shelter, while others were a hindrance to be gotten rid of to make room for growing crops, erecting buildings or grazing cattle. These people *had* to know nature intimately, for there was no time for mistakes when selecting proper

*Reprinted by permission from *Modern Maturity*, Dec.-Jan., 1966.

wood for a box or axe handle or finding things to eat or some herb to relieve illness and pain. Hunting and trapping animals for fur, food, leather and clothing required cunning and an intimate knowledge of animal life.

Tales of the ingenuity and courage of our early settlers fascinate us and we appreciate their proficiency at wresting a livelihood from the vast wilderness surrounding them. We are spellbound at the derring-do and high adventure of such early American campers as Lewis and Clark, Daniel Boone, and Kit Carson, and later outdoorsmen such as Theodore Roosevelt, Daniel Beard and Ernest Thompson Seton. But it is human nature to recall the pleasant and forget the painful and distasteful; thus we bask in the glamor and excitement of the exploits of the early settlers and explorers while glossing over the privations, dangers and hardships which formed the very core of their daily lives.

EARLY RURAL LIFE

At the time of the signing of the Constitution, 98 per cent of the population lived in rural areas. With the coming of the machine age, industries developed in the larger towns and cities, and as more lucrative employment opportunities appeared in the more populated areas, people left the farms and turned the settlements into towns and the towns into cities. This movement still continues, so that now, less than 200 years later, only about 27 per cent of our population remain in rural areas while less than 16 per cent actually live on "farms" as defined by the 1970 census. This exodus from the farm to the city, with its mechanization and gadgetry, has greatly affected our way of life, especially that of young people.

In the farm environment of several generations ago, boys and girls grew up with an intimate knowledge of nature, for nearly every plant, tree and animal was of interest since if it was not useful, it needed to be controlled or eliminated if possible. Children grew up as jacks-of-all-trades, for most things were grown or made at home and repaired by the user. Thus, shop or manual training, arts and crafts and homemaking were learned and practiced from the cradle on, under the close supervision of parents and often grandparents. Formal school training in "readin', writin' and 'rithmetic" was confined to a few winter months when the children could be spared from their farm duties.

Chores about the farm furnished vigorous exercise and the whole countryside provided room for running, jumping and shouting. There was no lack of social contacts, for families were large and closely knit and children enjoyed the companionship of brothers and sisters as they worked and played together. Guests provided welcome diversion and were urged to make an extended stay, for distances were too great and traveling too hazardous and uncomfortable to warrant brief overnight or casual evening visits. For those living nearby, there were numerous social affairs such as corn huskings, bellings, house and barn warmings, taffy pulls, spelling bees and singing schools. Attendance at church services was regular, and camp meetings drew people from great distances.

All this changed as people moved to cities and began to specialize in one trade or occupation, earning wages which they used to buy services or commodities from other specialists. Gone were the intimate contacts with nature experienced while tilling the soil or rambling over woods and fields.

MODERN URBAN LIFE

Today's child spends a long nine or ten months in an often overcrowded school, perhaps followed by summer

(Courtesy of Alpine Trails Outings, Denver, Colorado.)

school to catch up on work missed or to forge ahead in the struggle for college acceptance. Although there have been improvements, school is still too often geared mainly to meet college entrance requirements, and classes are sometimes so large that little attention can be given to the individual and his particular difficulties and needs. A child's life is regulated by schedules and bells and he is subjected to the somewhat formal teaching methods made necessary when large numbers of students must meet course and credit requirements.

Many children get very little exercise; except for a few perfunctory physical education periods each week, little more than lip service is paid to this extremely important aspect of their development. A parent or a school bus takes them to and from school, and their out-of-school hours are crammed with band practice, dramatics, trips to the movies or long periods spent in front of the television set.

The present economy does not encourage the large families of a former day and the child often lives entirely with adults in a small house or apartment where there is no room to run, jump, or climb. When he indulges his perfectly normal craving for action, his antics are likely to end unhappily as his ball crashes through the Kwality Grocery's plate glass window, or he tramples in Mrs. Jones' prize petunia bed or his noise drives old Grandma Smith to bellicose retribution. For engaging in what should be the birthright of every child, he is likely to receive a good "bawling out," physical punishment or may even be treated as a juvenile delinquent. Can we wonder that he is puzzled and sometimes rebellious? Our modern knowledge of children shows us how irritating and warping it can be to live amidst the constant "do's" and "don'ts" of people crowded in on all sides like sardines.

Both parents are often employed outside the home and spend their free time in pursuits which continue to segregate them from their offspring. There is too little time for recreation or even being together. Instead of giving of themselves through companionship, understanding and sympathy, parents try to substitute with liberal allowances for movies and comic books, baby sitters, television shows and other makeshifts which are supposed to supply happiness.

With few chores to do, children now have a great deal of leisure time, but unfortunately, they quickly fall into the pattern set by their parents and become afflicted with "spectatoritis," depending on commercial organizations to supply them with ready-made entertainment and recreation, which are all too often merely time-consuming busywork. It is easy to understand the elation that a child from such a background usually derives from struggling and sweating to dig a beanhole or construct a nature trail, for this activity fulfills the universal desire to do something constructive and useful, to display something *he* has made with *his* own hands. Children work like little beavers on camp projects and do not consider it work at all, for, as Sir James Barrie said, "Work is only work when you would rather be doing something else."

THE BEGINNINGS OF ORGANIZED CAMPING

As early as the latter half of the nineteenth century, some of those who had rushed to the city for its purported advantages found that the life there was not as idyllic as anticipated. Problems immediately arose, as they do when many live in close proximity to one another, and some were plagued with nostalgic memories of the peace and quiet of the old days and the buoyant good health resulting from their vigorous lives in the open. Perhaps of even greater concern was the manner in which their children were growing up. Although children from poorer families were kept busy with household chores and apprenticeships at trades or other outside jobs, those from well-to-do families had servants to satisfy their every need, which left them with time on their hands to loaf about and perhaps get into mischief or evil pursuits. A camping experience seemed to offer an acceptable solution; in this way, organized camping began in the United States, as devoted men and women organized groups of young people for outings in the woods.

THE FIRST SCHOOL CAMP (1861)

Frederick William Gunn, who is generally regarded as the *Father of Organized Camping,* was the founder and head of the Gunnery School for Boys in Washington, Connecticut. With the coming of the Civil War, his students, like typical boys, wanted to live like soldiers and were sometimes permitted to march, roll up in their blankets and sleep outdoors. The school ran through part of the summer and in 1861, yielding to the wishes of the boys, Mr. and Mrs. Gunn packed all of them up for a gypsy trip to Milford on the Sound, 4 miles away. There they spent two weeks boating, sailing, hiking and fishing. The experiment proved so successful that it was repeated in 1863 and 1865, with some of the former students returning to join in the excursion.

Later, a new site was selected at Point Beautiful on Lake Waramauge, 7 miles from the school, and the name was changed from Camp Comfort to Gunnery Camp; it continued to exist until 1879. Although Mr. Gunn's camp might be considered the beginning of school camping (he simply moved his already organized school outdoors for a brief session), the objectives and procedures of today's school camping are quite different from those of Mr. Gunn's camp. However, his camp was

(Courtesy of the U.S. Forest Service.)

actually the first organized camp in the world and so established the United States as the birthplace of organized camping.

THE FIRST PRIVATE CAMP (1876)

Dr. Joseph Trimble Rothrock was a practicing physician in Wilkes-Barre, Pennsylvania, who combined his hobbies of forestry and conservation with his desire to do something for frail boys by establishing the North Mountain School of Physical Culture. Here he felt that the children's health would improve since they could live out-of-doors in tents while continuing their education. The school was located on North Mountain in Luzerne County, Pennsylvania, and lasted from June 15 to October 15; there were 20 pupils and five teachers. Each student paid $200 tuition, but income failed to meet expenses, and Dr. Rothrock abandoned the idea in favor of spending the next year on an Alaskan expedition. Various attempts to revive the school under different leadership likewise proved unprofitable and it was permanently closed within a few years.

THE FIRST CHURCH CAMP (1880)

The Reverend George W. Hinckley of West Hartford, Connecticut, was the next to try an established camp, for he saw in its informal atmosphere an opportunity to get to know the boys of his congregation more intimately and so perhaps to influence them more permanently. Consequently, in 1880 he took seven members of his church on a camping trip to Gardner's Island, Wakefield, Rhode Island. The results must have been gratifying, for he later founded The Good Will Farm for Boys at Hinckley, Maine. His schedule called for a "sane and sensible" religious and educational morning program, with afternoons spent in such activities as swimming, baseball and tennis, and evenings devoted to singing, talks and various other forms of entertainment.

THE FIRST PRIVATE CAMP ORGANIZED TO MEET SPECIFIC EDUCATIONAL NEEDS (1881)

That same year, in 1880, while Ernest Berkely Balch was traveling on Asquam Lake near Holderness, New Hampshire, he chanced upon Burnt Island, which seemed to be unowned and appeared to be an ideal spot to bring to a reality his aspiration to give boys from well-to-do families a summer of adventure instead of letting them idle away their time in resort hotels. Consequently, in 1881 he returned with five boys and erected a small frame shanty which they christened "Old '81." The group was somewhat surprised, no doubt, by the unexpected appearance of a man claiming to own the island, but they were certainly not outdone for they tendered the magnificent sum of $40 in complete payment for the entire island. They called their retreat Camp Chocorua because of its superb view of Chocorua Mountain, 30 miles away, and the camp continued to exist for eight years until 1889.

The boys wore camp uniforms of gray flannel shorts and shirts with scarlet belts, caps and shirt lacings. All work was done by the boys, who were divided into four crews, each with a leader called the "stroke." One crew was off duty each day while the other three spent about five hours as kitchen, dish or police crews. Spiritual life was carefully planned and the services must have been quite impressive as the boys came singing through the woods, dressed in cotta and cassock (a short surplice over a long garment reaching to the feet), to the altar of their chapel, which was set deep in a grove of silver maples.

Figure 2-2 Wonder at God's Creations.

The camp had an average of five staff members and 25 boys who competed in tennis, sailing, swimming, diving and baseball. Winners were awarded ribbons bearing their names, the event and the date. Mr. Balch was the first to set down definite objectives for his camp, which were the development in the boy of (1) a sense of responsibility, both for himself and others and (2) an appreciation of the worthwhileness of work. The Camp Chocorua silver pin was given annually to the two or three campers best incorporating qualities of "manliness, justice, truth and conscientiousness." It was intended as a symbol of recognition for innate qualities and not as a reward to be worked for; in fact, those who consciously set out to win it were said to stand little chance of doing so and no award at all was made in the years when none were judged worthy.

THE FIRST INSTITUTIONAL CAMP (1885)

Sumner F. Dudley, a young resident of Brooklyn, was associated with his father and brother in the manufacture of surgical instruments. His first venture in camping was to take seven members of the Newburgh, New York, YMCA on an eight-day fishing, swimming and boating trip to Pine Point on Orange Lake, six miles away. Since the boys had had their heads shaved close in what they deemed proper preparation for the trip, their camp was appropriately dubbed Camp Bald Head.

Figure 2-3 So That's Why They Called It Camp Bald Head!

Dudley spent the next several years conducting other camping trips for boys and entered the YMCA as a full-time worker in 1887. He died in 1897 at the age of 43. His last camp on Lake Champlain near Westport, New York, was renamed Camp Dudley in his honor and is the oldest organized camp still in existence.

CAMPING FOR GIRLS (1890, 1892 AND 1902)

In 1890 Luther Halsey Gulick opened a private camp for his daughter and her friends. He later founded the Camp Fire Girls.

In 1891 Professor Arey of Rochester, New York, established Camp Arey as a natural science camp and a year later he lent it for a month's use by girls. Mr. and Mrs. Andre C. Fontaine took over the camp in 1912 and from that time on conducted it as a camp exclusively for girls.

Laura Mattoon founded what is generally regarded as the first camp exclusively for girls in 1902 at Wolfeboro, New Hampshire, calling it Camp Kehonka for Girls.

THE DEVELOPMENTAL PERIODS OF CAMPING

Early organized camping was classified by Dimock* into three stages of development, according to its main emphasis at the time. These were (1) the recreational stage, (2) the educational stage and (3) the stage of social orientation and responsibility. As with any movement, no sharp line of demarcation can be drawn between these periods, for the changes were gradual and overlapping and at no time was there perfect unanimity among leaders or uniformity as to the programs and practices of the various camps.

THE RECREATIONAL STAGE (1861–1920)

Early camps were sponsored mainly by conscientious, public-spirited men who saw in them a chance

---

*Dimock, Hedley S.: *Administration of the Modern Camp.* Association Press, 1948, p. 24.

to get boys out into the open and away from potentially harmful pursuits in the city. They believed that the rugged, outdoor life would strengthen the boys physically and keep them engaged in wholesome, enjoyable activities. Bible study often played a prominent part in the program; high moral and spiritual values were held in high esteem, and it was believed that they could be "caught" like mumps or measles from mere association with fine, upright leaders. There was no thought of financial gain from the project, and the lack of adequate monetary backing caused the early demise of many camps.

It was common for one or two adults to start out on a trip with as many as 40 or 50 boys and a meager supply of equipment. The expeditions were, almost without exception, built around the strong personality of a man who kept the respect and admiration of the boys by his unselfish motives, sympathetic understanding, tactful leadership and sound principles concerning the intermixture of work and play. Ralph Waldo Emerson's statement that "Every institution is but the lengthened shadow of a man" certainly applies to these early camps.

The movement was slow to "catch on," for there were probably no more than 25 to 60 camps in existence in 1900.

THE EDUCATIONAL STAGE (1920–1930)

Great changes and exciting developments often follow wars, and the years after World War I were no exception. Organized camps increased rapidly in number and there were marked changes in their methods and programs. "Progressive education," with its foundations of psychology and mental hygiene, was coming to the fore, fostering increased emphasis on satisfying the needs of each child instead of trying to fit all of them into a preconceived mold. Camps fell in line, adding various activities, such as dramatics, arts and crafts, dancing and music, designed to supplement the enlarged school curriculum. Almost all 24 hours a day of a camper's time were strictly regimented and they were enrolled in scheduled classes much as at school with stress on competition, often with an elaborate system of awards. One cause of this change in philosophy was the development of new testing methods which had demonstrated that personality, character and spiritual growth were *not* inevitably "caught" but must be taught and planned for to obtain optimum results.

THE STAGE OF SOCIAL ORIENTATION AND RESPONSIBILITY (1930–   )

Continued research in testing methods and evaluation showed that camps were not always measuring up to the high aspirations held for them, but, as always, ever-resourceful camp directors proved equal to the occasion and continued to forge ahead.

Camping enthusiasts had assumed that the active outdoor life was invariably invigorating and healthful and were quite shocked when a 1930 study of over 100 camps showed that, instead, camping was actually sometimes detrimental to health and that the longer a child stayed in camp the more likely his health was to suffer. In an attempt to remedy the situation, camp directors added physicians, nurses and trained dietitians to their staffs and instituted more healthful practices in their programs, allowing campers more freedom of choice in activities and generally reducing the hectic tempo of camp life.

Society has long been aware that its strength can be only as great as that of its individual citizens and we in the United States are well aware that the best way to strengthen and preserve our form of government is to give each citizen a solid foundation in the principles of democracy. Camping leaders early realized that they had not only an opportunity but also a very real responsibility in this respect since they were dealing with young people during their most formative years. Consequently, progressive camps have tried to offer young people a chance to experience democratic living in a democratic atmosphere. Ideally, camping is an experience in group living at its best, with each individual camper encouraged to develop independence, self-control and self-reliance as he helps to plan and accept responsibility for his own way of life under the friendly guidance and example of wholesome adults. Camp personnel are becoming ever more aware of the necessity for adapting programs to the needs of the individual rather than trying to fit him into the "system."

The 1970's have brought a reevaluation of where we have been and where we are going in camping. There is more awareness of what is happening between groups of people with corresponding changes in the conduct and organization of the modern camp. (These changes will be discussed in more detail in Chapter 3.)

THE ORGANIZATION OF THE CAMPING PROFESSION

Each early camp was a highly individualized project, carried on largely according to the beliefs, past experiences and particular ideals and aspirations of the person or organization sponsoring it. Before long, however, some of the more progressive camp directors and other interested individuals began to recognize the values of meeting informally with others for fellowship and an exchange of experiences about common successes, problems and failures. These gatherings proved so helpful and inspirational that a formal meeting was held in Boston in 1903 with about 100 people in attendance.

Additional meetings followed and, in 1910, a decision was made to form a definite organization to be known as the *Camp Directors' Association of America* with Charles R. Scott as its first president and 11 charter members. The *National Association of Directors of Girls Camps* was formed in 1916 with Mrs. Luther Halsey (Charlotte V.) Gulick as president, and the *Mid-West Camp Directors' Association* followed in 1921. These three organizations joined forces as the *Camp Directors' Association of America* in 1924 with George L. Meylan as president. In 1926 the Association began to issue a magazine called *The Camp Directors' Bulletin* which was later changed to *Camping*.

THE AMERICAN CAMPING ASSOCIATION (ACA)

The Camp Directors' Association was renamed the *American Camping Association* in 1935 and, since that time the organization has continued to grow steadily in both membership and influence. It is a nationwide, nonprofit professional organization dedicated to the promotion and improvement of organized camping for children and adults, with members in 50 states and 10 foreign countries. Among its members are camps, camp owners, camp directors and staff, educators, clergymen, commercial firms supplying camps, family camping leaders and others with diverse training and experience who are interested in camping. It has six categories of membership which provide for an equitable system of dues for camp and individual members; students enjoy a special reduced rate.

Objectives. The stated objectives of the American Camping Association are:

1. Through camping, to further the welfare of children and adults.

Figure 2-4 Members of ACA May Use this Official Insignia.

2. To extend the recreational and educational benefits of out-of-door living.

3. To give emphasis in camping to citizenship training in keeping with the principles and traditions of American democracy.

4. To provide opportunities for developing awareness and appreciation of the interdependence of all living and nonliving resources and a sense of responsibility for them.

5. To give emphasis to spiritual opportunities through camping.

6. To provide opportunities for fellowship among camp leaders.

7. To stimulate high professional standards of camp leadership.

8. To provide for the exchange of experiences and successful practices and for developing materials, standards and other aids for the progress of camping.

9. To interpret camping to related groups and to the public.

Organization. The American Camping Association is composed of five Regions which are subdivided into 36 Sections. National Conventions are held in March of the even-numbered years, with Regional Conventions in the intervening years; the Sections also hold meetings. Working directly with the elected National President of ACA are a full-time Executive Vice President and three professional staff members who operate from the national headquarters at Bradford Woods, near Martinsville, Indiana. Much of the work of the organization is carried on by volunteers. Serving with the president are five elected vice presidents: (1) V.P. for Development of Finances, (2) V.P. for Field Service, (3) V.P. for Private/Independent Camping, (4) V.P. for Program, and (5) V.P. for Related Groups, an office not yet activated. The responsibility for policy and operations of the Association is vested in four governing bodies: (1) Section Leadership, (2) Regional Advisory Boards, (3) The National Board of Directors, which includes the national officers, regional representatives and standing committee chairmen of the Association, and (4) the Council of Delegates, which consists of the National Board of Directors and over 100 delegates elected by the Sections.*

Publications. Since 1926, ACA's official publication has been *Camping Magazine*, which appears eight times a year; monthly from January through June, and bi-monthly from September through December. It also publishes a quarterly newsletter called the *American Camper* which all members receive. All private independent camps belonging to ACA receive a PIC Council Information Bulletin, *Smoke Signals*, as well as the monthly *PIC Newsletter*.

ACA's annual *National Directory of Accredited Camps for Boys and Girls* lists all the camps that are accredited by ACA, together with pertinent information about each. This serves as a valuable reference for those seeking camp employment, as well as for parents seeking a good camping experience for their children. The Family

*From "Together We Serve," ACA.

Camping Federation, an affiliate of ACA, publishes the *Family Camping Leader* for members of that organization.

ACA members may subscribe to the *Camping Law Abstract,* which is published 10 times a year and is designed to keep readers abreast of new state and federal laws and pending bills which are likely to affect camping.

ACA encourages studies and research pertaining to camping and fosters the writing and publication of needed literature in the field. Its National Publications Services carries several hundred publications in the fields of camping and recreation which are available to members at a 10 per cent discount from list price. This service provides the convenience of ordering from one source instead of having to contact numerous publishers and bookstores. A catalogue of publications carried is available free upon request.

Leadership Training. ACA provides leadership training course outlines in camp counseling and administration to serve as guides for colleges, camp directors and others giving such courses. It also sponsors campcraft courses leading to certification on four levels: Campcrafter, Advanced Campcrafter, Tripcrafter and Trip Leader. These courses are given on a Sectional basis under the direction of a Leadership Chairman and Campcraft Instructors. Areas covered are firecraft, food, toolcraft, ropecraft, gear and shelter, campsite, maps and compass, health and safety, nature and conservation, trips, and leadership. Interested parties can obtain details from their local Sections of ACA.

Camp Director Institute training programs are held on a Regional basis in cooperation with certain colleges and universities. Participants in these programs can earn certification as Certified Camp Directors. ACA has also developed curricula to train staff in such specialized areas as camp ecology and naturalist training, and training for camp health directors; these courses are given periodically at various places around the country.

Accreditation and Other Services. One of the outstanding accomplishments of ACA has been its contribution to the general upgrading of camp operation and performance. Since 1948 it has carried on a program of camp accreditation which it constantly re-evaluates and revises. To be accredited by ACA, a camp must be visited by one or more official ACA Camp Visitors, who rate it in eight areas of overall operation: administration, program, personnel, campsite and facilities, health, safety, sanitation, and transportation. Accredited camps are permitted to display and otherwise use the insignia shown in Figure 2-5. An accredited camp is subject to revisitation every five years. The accreditation program is of great value to camp directors and other personnel because it provides a means of evaluating the quality of their camp. It is also useful as a guide to prospective camp staff members and parents seeking a quality camp for their children.

Among its other services, ACA sponsors meetings, conventions and workshops where interested parties can meet to exchange ideas, learn of new developments, and receive instruction

Figure 2-5 Only Camps Accredited by ACA May Display this Insignia.

and inspiration from experts in the field while enjoying good fellowship. It keeps abreast of proposed legislation which would affect camping and provides guidance and counseling to lawmakers at local, state and federal levels. Through consultation, ACA helps camp personnel in solving professional, legal or other problems they may encounter. It also conducts an ongoing public relations program, with news releases, newspaper articles and radio and television spots. ACA also conducts a counselor placement service, usually on a Sectional basis, to bring together camp directors and staff and counselors seeking jobs.

THE FUND FOR ADVANCEMENT OF CAMPING (FAC)

The Fund for Advancement of Camping (FAC) is part of the Development Division of the American Camping Association and plans cooperatively with it. Its purpose is to raise funds to support needed and worthwhile projects in camping which cannot be included in the regular ACA budget. It arose as an outgrowth of a private camp "cracker-barrel" session in 1962 and was first known as the American Camping Association Foundation. In 1966 its headquarters were moved to Chicago and its name was changed to the Fund for Advancement of Camping. Its general management is the responsibility of an elected Board of Trustees, and it depends entirely upon voluntary contributions from individuals, Sections of ACA, foundations and other sources.

FAC has contributed to the publication of certain books and pamphlets, and has funded many new and innovative projects in such areas as camp standards and evaluation, research, leadership training, the use of government funds for the purchase of camping services, a survey of the values of camping, a study of the history of camping and a study on acclimatization. A recent project, Camping Unlimited, has as its objective the promotion of integrated camping for those of different religious, racial and cultural backgrounds. This program is being carried out in many existing camps under the auspices of various ACA Sections.

ADDITIONAL READINGS

(For an explanation of abbreviations and abbreviated forms used, see page 25.)

Hammerman and Hammerman (Eds.): *Outdoor Education: A Book of Readings:* Gibson, H. W.: "The History of Organized Camping," pp. 62–76.
Mand: *Outdoor Education,* ch. 2.
Rodney and Ford: *Camp Administration,* pp. 21–24.
Shivers: *Camping,* pp. 11–20.
Todd: *Camping for Christian Youth,* chs. 1 and 2.
Webb: *Light From a Thousand Campfires:*
Sinn, Mrs. B. A., and Kenneth Webb: "A Brief History of the American Camping Association," p. 371.

The American Camping Association (ACA)

A Guide for the Director of Campcraft Instructors. ACA, 1970, 16 pp., 75¢, paper.
A Listing of American Camping Association Standards for Organized Camps. ACA, 1973, 22 pp., 25¢, paper.
Campcraft Instructor's Manual.
Campcraft Training Program and Personal Record of ______________. ACA, 1973, 16 pp., 25¢, paper.
Camp Standards With Interpretations for the Accreditation of Organized Camps. ACA, 1972, 64 pp., $3, paper.
National Directory of Accredited Camps for Boys and Girls. ACA, $3, paper. (Issued annually.)
Rodney and Ford: *Camp Administration,* pp. 21–24.

MAGAZINE ARTICLES

Camping Magazine:
"ACA Interracial-Interfaith Policy." Jan., 1972, p. 19.
Burns, Gerald A.: "A Short History of Camping." Feb., Mar. and Apr., 1949.
Eels, Eleanor P.: "Fund for Advancement of Camping." Nov./Dec., 1973, p. 16.
Morash, Tal: "Revised Standards Accreditation Program To Be Voted on by Council of Delegates." Jan., 1972, p. 19.
"Proposed Bylaws for ACA." Nov./Dec., 1973, p. 25.

Chapter 3

Objectives of and Trends in Organized Camping

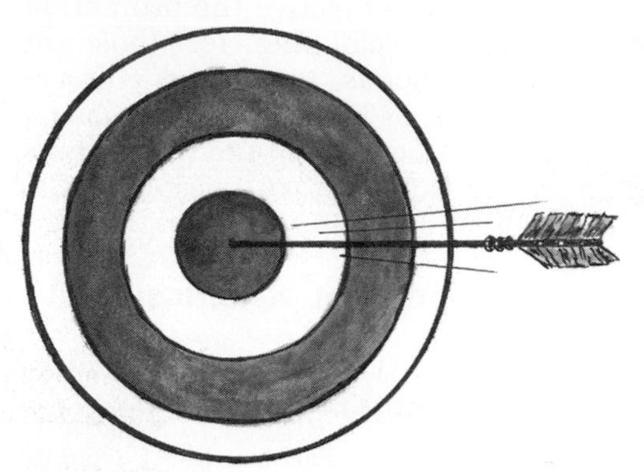

Figure 3–1 Are You On Target With Your Objectives?

I WONDER

I wonder, when you pack away this week
The things you've used at camp and need no
more,
Whether in fancy you will put away
Some other treasures gained, among your store.

I wonder, if within the garment folds,
The scent of new-learned flowers may be laid,
Or hidden in the corner of your trunk
A bird wing or a bit of pine tree shade.

I wonder if perhaps when you unpack,
Attempting to shake out a stubborn fold,
There may come tumbling out before your eyes
A sunset sky or tiny star of gold.

I wonder if, when you can do no more,
And all the tray is packed quite firm and tight,
You'll softly step and o'er it gently lay
A moonlight mist you saw, some lovely night.

I wonder if the very last of all,
Because your trunk is locked to go away,
You might just slip within your heart's small
wall,
Some of the peace and love you learned at
Onaway.

—FRANCES M. FROST,
Director, Camp Onaway.

CAMPING IS EDUCATION

What are the objectives of organized camping and why do we believe that the camping environment is particularly well-suited for accomplishing them? What is there about camping that has caused it to grow so rapidly and be deemed worthy of all the time and money that camping personnel and parents have been willing to devote to it? The ultimate aim of all education is, of course, to help youngsters to develop into happy, healthy, well-adjusted, contributing members of society. Unfortunately, to many people, education is only what takes place within the classroom. However, a little reflection reveals that every single experience a child has during his waking and even sleeping hours plays a part in making him what he is and what he will become. Every person he comes in contact with, be it parent, teacher, playmate, or even a policeman on the beat or a clerk in a store, leaves some impression. He is also influenced by the organizations he belongs to, the books he reads, the television programs he watches, and the movies he attends. While some influences are quite positive, others he might better be without.

Obviously, a stay in a well-conducted camp can be quite educational and beneficial. A good camp will take advantage of its unique environment to strengthen the values instilled in campers by others and to teach new values which are particularly meaningful in the camp setting.

UNIQUE CHARACTERISTICS OF THE CAMPING ENVIRONMENT AND THEIR POTENTIAL BENEFITS

> It is not the primary function of the summer camp to entertain children, but to provide a setting, an environment, a program and a leadership out of which children will find their own entertainment. With the proper motivation in an outdoors environment, children entertain themselves and acquire much of the kind of education they need most.*
>
> —C. Walton Johnson, *The Unique Mission of the Summer Camp.*

*Used by permission of the author.

CAMP POSSESSES A CAMPER WHOLLY

Camp possesses a camper completely, for he eats, sleeps, works, talks, and plays there 24 hours a day, seven days a week, with almost no outside influences to distract him. The camper lives in a child's world, associating closely with his counselors and the campers in his cabin group, and often doing things with his entire unit or the camp as a whole. Not even his family spends as much time with him each day as do his counselors and fellow campers. In terms of hours, two months spent in camp are the equivalent of a whole year in school. Camp is at once home, school, gang, church, and playground to him, in contrast to his city "assembly line" existence where he is passed along like a product on a conveyor belt to have spiritual development screwed on at one spot, a few nuts and bolts in his mind adjusted at another, then home for refueling and repairs and off with the gang for some rounding out as to the "facts of life."

THE OUT-OF-DOOR SETTING

Most camps pride themselves on their large grounds of varied terrain, most of it left in a relatively primitive and unspoiled state. Here, the camper spends most of his waking, as well as an appreciable amount of his sleeping, hours outdoors with only a tent or the sky for his roof. His frequent hikes and rambles as well as his participation in the many camp activities geared or adapted especially to outdoor living attune him to a life in the open. All of his senses undergo constant stimulation by the smells, sights, sounds, textures and possibly even tastes of nature.

Some potential benefits of this out-of-door setting are:

1. An intimate knowledge of nature and a lasting love of the outdoors which can form the basis for a lifelong

Figure 3–2 One of Nature's Miracles.

interest in outdoor activities and related hobbies.

2. A keen insight into nature's blueprint for keeping all things in balance and an appreciation of the interdependence of all living things and of man's proper place in the natural world.

3. A meaningful spiritual awakening as a camper realizes that all of this could have been created only by the hand of the Master. He is overwhelmed by a sense of awe and inspiration as he gazes at the majesty of a high mountain, the peace of a quiet valley, the glory of a colorful sunset, the glint of sunlight on the lake, or dewdrops glistening on an intricate spider web.

4. An understanding of the urgency of conserving our natural resources lest there be none left for future generations to enjoy after so many years of abuse and destruction. A good camp's practices of recycling, conservation, and ecology will likely be noted and continued at home by every observant camper.

5. The development of esthetic tastes as he lives with nature's panorama of unsurpassed beauty, largely unmarred by man and his creations. He will gain an appreciation of her peace and serenity, unbroken except for the occasional sound of some wild creature or the laughter and happy banter of his peers as they carry on their activities.

LIVING 24 HOURS A DAY WITH OTHERS OF VARIED BACKGROUNDS

Many youngsters spend much of their non-school time with adults, and the children whom they do associate with often have very similar social backgrounds. In camp children live continuously with a variety of individuals representing almost every conceivable personality and background.

Some potential benefits of this social diversity are:

1. Learning to accept those different from himself, appreciating their good qualities and minimizing their idiosyncrasies, just as he hopes they will do for him.

2. Learning that flexibility, sharing, and consideration for others are essential for happy group living. If a camper has not learned this and does not quickly shape up, he will probably be subjected to that most powerful force, the lack of acceptance by his peers. If he fails to grasp the situation and remedy it on his own, some observant staff member will most likely come to his rescue and help set him on the right road.

3. Reinforcing good home training, or supplying it when lacking, in such areas as proper table decorum, good grooming, general good manners, and satisfactory eating and health habits.

4. Deep and lasting friendships develop with both peers and older persons with whom he has laughed and exchanged confidences while sharing the varied experiences of trail and camp living.

5. Helping him to mature by gradually weaning him away from what may have been overdependence on his family. He must eventually make this break if he is ever to stand on his own two feet and play his rightful role as an adult in society. Life in his small, friendly, closely knit cabin and unit groups helps to ease the pangs of this first separation.

LIVING IN A DEMOCRATIC COMMUNITY

The usual camp method of handling problems and topics of general in-

(Courtesy of the Children's Aid Society, New York, N. Y.)

terest in a group is through group discussion with a counselor, or sometimes a camper, serving as leader. Matters concerning the whole camp are similarly handled through the Camp Council, composed of representatives and staff from each of the smaller groups. This gives campers an opportunity to share in formulating procedures and rules which are within their province.

Some potential benefits of democratic group living are:

1. Learning how the democratic process works, how to serve effectively as a leader or follower, and how to express himself clearly and without being obnoxious or usurping an undue amount of time and attention.

2. Understanding camp rules or "how we do things at Camp Wahoo" as general discussion brings out the necessity for having at least a few rules in order to protect the rights of each individual and to make things run smoothly with a minimum of friction. Such experiences help a camper to be-

Figure 3–3 Guess I'll Try This On for Size.

come a cooperative, law-abiding citizen; people rarely flout laws when they understand the reasons for them, especially if they have shared in making them.

3. Gaining the courage to take an active part in a meeting and to express honest opinions, even though they may not coincide with what is popular. Recognizing the right of others to differ and learning to listen and actually think about what they are saying.

4. Learning to abide by the will of the majority while still having concern for the rights and wishes of the minority. Being willing to compromise instead of always insisting on having his own way.

5. Learning to get the facts before making a decision, consulting knowledgeable people or reference sources if necessary, and then analyzing and evaluating all the pros and cons before making up his mind.

6. Learning to bring problems and disputes out into the open instead of sulking, grumbling, becoming bitter, or discussing them only with those who are no better informed than he or in no better position to do anything about the situation.

7. Gaining experience in problem-solving, for in camp living questions frequently arise about what to do and how to do it.

A BROAD PROGRAM OF ACTIVITIES

Most camps offer a wide variety of activities with special emphasis on those concerned with camping and outdoor living. Many of these activities are unlikely to be available elsewhere, at least not in the same form, since they depend upon an outdoor environment and the general atmosphere of a typical camp. A camper can select many of his own activities and, with so many possibilities, he can sample and choose almost as though he were selecting goodies in a candy store.

Some potential benefits of a varied program are:

1. Developing lifetime hobbies, perhaps even a vocation. Participation in a wide variety of activities often discloses unsuspected interests and aptitudes, broadens perspectives, and enables a camper to appreciate the interests and accomplishments of others. The average camp aims to develop general, all-around abilities rather than specialized ones, as is so often done in school sports and other activities where only a few are chosen to participate and the large majority are left to cheer on the sidelines.

2. Encouraging a camper to try his best as he attempts to improve his own performance (in effect, competes against himself). Although there is enough competition to challenge those with superior ability, the emphasis is on self-improvement. This is preferable to a highly competitive program in which a few consistently do well and often become smug and conceited, while others are usually well down on the scale and so become dejected and unwilling to try.

3. Being a good loser; giving his all to provide his opponent with the satisfaction of having defeated him at his best, but learning to lose graciously and without rancor or excuses.

4. Having just plain *fun* and enjoying the excitement and new experi-

(Courtesy of Camp Teela-Wooket, Inc., Roxbury, Vermont.)

ences every child craves, but doing so in a wholly safe and sane way. A youngster who has learned to satisfy his desire for adventure and fun in wholesome ways will never need to resort to stealing, fighting or killing just for "kicks"!

> Every little boy has inside of him an aching void which demands interesting and exciting play. And if you don't fill it with something that is interesting and exciting and good for him, he is going to fill it with something that is interesting and exciting and isn't good for him.
>
> —THEODORE ROOSEVELT, JR.

5. Satisfying his curiosity and desire to investigate and learn. The whole camp approach is "let's go together and find out."

6. Learning how to properly balance work, play, and rest; alternating vigorous activities with quieter ones, while observing regular hours for rest and sleep.

7. Education in the wise use of leisure time; choosing activities which give true enjoyment and satisfaction rather than merely kill time. This fulfills an increasingly pressing need as lessened working hours provide more leisure time. Many camp activities such as canoeing, swimming, hiking, backpacking, boating, fishing, camping out, nature study and ecology, photography, tennis, and horseback riding provide the interests and skills required to make full use of our rapidly expanding parks and other recreational facilities. Although football and basketball may be fine school sports, few will continue to play them after school days are over, and this may be just as well since they are too strenuous for those who are out of condition or past the prime of life.

8. Enjoying simple pastimes which cost little or nothing, and learning to entertain himself instead of depending on others or on canned entertainment.

9. Patriotism and appreciation of

our American heritage through participation in such activities as flag-raising ceremonies, the Fourth of July celebration, studying local history, and living somewhat like our pioneers and early heroes.

10. Learning to appreciate seriousness and thoughtfulness as he participates in vespers and Sunday and campfire programs built on thought-provoking themes and rituals.

SUFFICIENT FREE TIME FOR MEDITATING AND DREAMING AND REGULAR HOURS FOR REST AND SLEEP

Modern society seems intent upon converting a child into an adult just as rapidly as possible. His clothing, games, and social activities are closely patterned after those of adults, and his after-school hours are crammed with such things as music and dancing lessons, training for competitive athletics, hours of homework and watching television. This greatly complicates the problem of setting aside regular hours for rest and sleep and leaving free time for just sitting, meditating, and dreaming dreams. "Hurry! Hurry! Hurry!" seems to be the order of the day and even summer vacations no longer provide lazy, carefree days to spend in fishing, wading in a brook, browsing in a book, or just whiling away the hours in the hundreds of ways young people find enjoyable.

As previously mentioned, camps long ago recognized the folly of cramming each day so full of a frenzy of activities that the camper ended up with nervous exhaustion from his constant struggle to catch up with what he was supposed to be doing an hour ago. Today's camp leaves time for a camper to just wonder as he wanders.

Some potential benefits of sufficient free time are:

1. Having time to think and examine so that a youngster can come to

(Courtesy of Camp Manito-Wish, Y.M.C.A., Boulder Junction, Wisconsin.)

better understand who and what he is as well as the world he lives in.

2. A sense of calmness and well-being. A child who has learned to solve his problems and live sanely, exercising enough to produce healthful physical fatigue then relaxing completely at something he enjoys, is unlikely to become one of the millions of adults who feel they must rely upon such crutches as aspirin, sleeping pills, and tranquilizers in order to keep going.

A HIGH RATIO OF TRAINED AND ESPECIALLY SELECTED STAFF TO CAMPERS

The American Camping Association recommends the following ratio of counselors to campers, according to age group:*

Age Served	*Number of Campers*
6 and under	5
7–8	6
9–14	8
15–18	10
19 and over	20

A staff is usually made up of a nucleus of older experienced persons, supplemented by college students, younger counselors, teachers, and others especially trained and interested in youth work. This provides distinct advantages, since any child who needs or wants advice or craves a sympathetic adult ear for his hopes, frustrations, accomplishments, and problems can almost always find it.

Some potential benefits of a high ratio of staff to campers are:

1. Learning to regard adults in a new light. A cabin counselor acts as a sort of big brother to his little group and establishes a warm, friendly atmosphere, planning, working, sharing, laughing and having fun with them.

**Camp Standards with Interpretations for the Accreditation of Organized Camps.* ACA, 1973, p. 23.

Figure 3–4 We're Good Friends.

Other staff members play a similar role on occasion and present to the child, perhaps for the first time, a picture of adults as interesting, helpful people whom he can trust and enjoy.

2. Learning desirable traits and characteristics by example as well as by precept. It is a well-known fact that both desirable and undesirable traits are at least as likely to be "caught" as taught. Informal camp living creates an atmosphere of closeness and camer-aderie which is quite favorable for learning. Most campers are still in the stage of "hero worship" and a coun-selor or other staff member may well be chosen as the beloved model. Mira-cles can happen if the chosen one puts his best foot forward on all occasions and uses skill in handling situations.

SIMPLE LIVING IN RUSTIC SURROUNDINGS

Although camp buildings are often quite simple and rustic, they are fully equipped to serve their purposes, but without the ornateness and unneces-sary gadgetry so common in city build-ings. Such facilities as the health service and camp kitchen are strictly modern and kept spotlessly clean and sanitary, but the attractiveness of the whole camp depends upon simplicity and ruggedness. "Do it yourself" is the usual motto as each camper cares for his own quarters and possessions and shares in the upkeep of buildings and camp grounds used in common. He also shares in such chores as washing dishes, setting tables, sweeping the lodge, and preparing and cooking out-door meals. He learns to dress for the weather and pack his own trip duffel, uncomplainingly carrying it, as well as his share of the group equipment, even when the trail is long, the sun hot, the hill steep or a summer rain is beating down on his well-protected head and shoulders.

Some potential benefits of simple camp living are:

1. A new self-respect and self-confidence comes as a camper learns to shift for himself and do things others may previously have done for him. Everyone else is too busy with his own job to pamper him and pick up the paper he dropped or put away the clothes he left on the floor where he stepped out of them.

2. A new and more realistic sense of values is gained as he notes how relatively unimportant such things as money, material possessions, IQ and fine clothes are in assessing the true worth of an individual. In camp he finds that the happiest, best liked and most respected counselors and campers have earned their enviable status be-cause of what they are inside rather than because of their outward appear-ances and material possessions.

3. A feeling of community and camp pride and satisfaction comes from serving others, as he shares in maintaining his cabin, unit and entire camp or sometimes aids in projects to improve them for the benefit of present and future campers.

4. A pride in his ability to impro-vise and make do with what he has, for at camp he cannot run to the store to replace something he has damaged or to satisfy his whim of the moment.

Figure 3–5 Happiness Is An Indoor John.

5. A feeling of at-homeness in the out-of-doors as he learns the unique part each element plays in the make-up of the total environment.

6. A respect for the dignity of work and the satisfaction which comes from sweating and struggling to cook in a beanhole or construct a needed lean-to shelter or bridge across a meandering stream.

7. Pride in the good health and physical fitness that vigorous outdoor life brings as it stimulates his lungs and heart, exercises his large muscles, and produces a ravenous appetite for the simple, nutritious meals cooked outdoors or planned and served indoors by the dietitian and kitchen staff.

8. Skill in doing such household tasks as making beds, sweeping, washing dishes, planning and cooking well-balanced meals, setting tables, and constructing, repairing, and maintaining equipment and clothing.

9. A deeper appreciation of our American heritage as his own simple life somewhat resembles that of our early pioneers and other historical figures. This appreciation may be enhanced through appropriate dramatics, storytelling, reading, trips to nearby points of historical interest and exhibitions of early Americana.

PARENTS CREED*

"If a child lives with criticism, he learns to condemn . . .
If a child lives with hostility, he learns to fight . . .
If a child lives with fear, he learns to be apprehensive . . .
If a child lives with jealousy, he learns to feel guilty . . .
If a child lives with tolerance, he learns to be patient . . .
If a child lives with encouragement, he learns to be confident . . .
If a child lives with praise, he learns to be appreciative . . .
If a child lives with acceptance, he learns to love . . .
If a child lives with approval, he learns to like himself . . .
If a child lives with recognition, he learns it is good to have a goal . . .
If a child lives with honesty, he learns what truth is . . .
If a child lives with fairness, he learns justice . . .
If a child lives with security, he learns to have faith in himself and in those about him . . .
If a child lives with friendliness, he learns the world is a nice place in which to live."

—DOROTHY LAW NOLTE

*Reprinted by permission of the John Philip Company, 1070 Florence Way, Campbell, California 95008. Parents Creed available in a 14 × 26-inch hand-screened felt scroll, in red/blue or blue/green for $3 postpaid.

ACCOMPLISHING OBJECTIVES

Camps can indeed accomplish these objectives, but not by being a camp in name only, coasting along on the good name of camping and doing nothing more dynamic than waving a magic wand and saying "abracadabra." Worthy achievements come only when those in charge have made careful, intelligent plans, based upon the sincere belief that a camp's highest accomplishment is to help youngsters develop to their highest potential. It is the task of the administration to lay the groundwork and unite the whole staff into a team which pulls together toward a common goal. Each staff member must then strive to convert the objectives into action, being quick to recognize and take advantage of each opportunity that arises and sometimes even creating them.

Your camp will probably have already set down its own objectives (a requirement for any camp accredited by ACA), which you will learn about during precamp training. These will, of course, provide the framework within which you will set up the specific ob-

Figure 3-6 Jeffie Is Timid and Shy.

jectives for your particular group. Take into consideration your own ideas and abilities as well as what your campers want for themselves and what their parents wish. Assess their present status and build upon it. Set down your objectives in writing; be specific and express them in simple terms and avoid high-flown generalities. Be sure they are realistic and attainable, then write out exact procedures for accomplishing them. Your objectives may well vary for each individual camper, depending on his needs and personality.

Don't try to be Superman and don't expect to accomplish miracles in the brief time you have available. Be prepared for disappointments and setbacks, for habits are hard to break and personality changes come slowly. Review your objectives frequently to refresh your memory and assess your progress, and don't hesitate to alter your goals as experience and a better understanding of your group dictate. Try hard to help each person to achieve at least a few constructive things as the season progresses; this encourages him to try harder.

It is sometimes better not to make your specific objectives too obvious since youngsters tend to rebel at too much "preachment" or nagging. Although a camper may dutifully say that he wants to become "neater" or "more punctual," he is probably only mouthing what he thinks you want to hear instead of what he really wants, which may be just to have fun or to learn to swim or to pass his canoeing test so he can go on the next trip. Obviously you will need a great deal of tact and understanding to discern what he really wants and then help him to achieve it.

One of the best ways to change attitudes and plant new ideas is to set an example yourself. Another is to recognize and take advantage of the "teachable moments" that arise during the activities of the day. These "moments" occur when a camper is truly interested and recognizes his need for guidance or information and is therefore alert and ready to look, listen, and learn. At these times, a brief anecdote (even if you have to make it up) is often an effective way to make your point.

Now and then, sit down and evaluate what has been accomplished with each individual and with the group. Informal chats with individuals and the group as a whole are helpful both in setting up your initial objectives and in keeping tabs on just how each camper feels about the progress he is making.

Make a complete assessment for each camper at the end of the season; this presents a realistic picture of the value of your work during the summer. (There are several ways to do this which will be discussed in later chapters.) Camps often request such an evaluation and may also ask each camper to fill out a questionnaire about his accomplishments. Sometimes questionnaires are also sent to parents to learn what changes they have observed in their child and which seem likely to be lasting.

MODERN TRENDS IN CAMPING

As in every other phase of American life, rapid changes are occurring in the field of camping. Many are necessary and desirable, but in our haste to accept each new proposal just because it is new, we must take care to preserve and improve on what is good of the old and combine it with promising new innovations. The following seem prominent among today's trends.

NUMBER AND TYPES OF CAMPS

Although some decrease in the number of regular resident camps is apparent, especially among the smaller camps, some of the larger ones have become still larger so that perhaps as many or even more campers can be accommodated. As some camps close others are opening, many of which are purposely kept small in order to accomplish some specific purpose or goal. There are now more special camps such as day, trip, school, 4-H, and religious camps, as well as camps for particular groups, such as the retarded, the handicapped, older citizens, and the emotionally disturbed, and for particular activities, such as music, dramatics, weight gain or loss, conversational languages, sports, dance, and almost everything else under the sun. Some of the latter would hardly qualify as camps as we interpret the name, but the term "camp" has apparently caught the American fancy, and like an umbrella, it is used to cover everything, leaving anyone free to capitalize upon its good name and apply it to situations not even remotely resembling true camping.

SIZE OF CAMPS AND DECENTRALIZATION

The increase in the size of some of the larger camps is probably a response to growing demand to accommodate more people or an attempt to use the economies of bigness to meet constantly spiraling expenses. However, as we have noted, a large group tends to lose the individual touch and close intimacy so essential to achieving optimal objectives.

Early camps were laid out in the manner of army camps with living quarters arranged in straight lines on either side of a central street or in the form of a hollow circle or square with buildings of common use such as the mess hall and camp lodge centrally located, Multiple-occupant sleeping units, like army barracks, contained cots arranged in long rows. The stress was on all-camp activities or on various activities from which the camper could choose, so that he was usually associated with either the entire camp group or with a constantly shifting collection of individuals who had chosen the same activities as he. This type of organization might be called *centralized camping.*

As camps grew larger, some enrolling as many as a hundred or even several hundred campers, the individual was often lost in the shuffle and found himself in an impersonal atmosphere that lacked the warmth, close intimacy, and personal attention that are so essential to a constructive camp experience. Some camps have responded to this problem by establishing several smaller independent camps, and nearly all camps, even those of modest size, have now adopted what is known as a *decentralization* plan, pioneered by the Girl Scouts. Here the entire camp is divided into groups of 12 to 24 campers, each living and operating somewhat like an independent camp. Each group, which may be called a unit, section, division, or village, is somewhat homogeneous, its members having been selected on some common basis, such as age, camping experience, general development, or interests. Each unit has its own buildings, situated close enough to the main dining room and lodge for convenience, yet sufficiently secluded to provide privacy and to allow the unit to function independently. Unit buildings usually consist of a unit house for group meetings, a latrine and bath house, and an outdoor kitchen. Unit members take most of their meals in the main dining room and occasionally participate in all-camp activities in order to provide a happy blending of living in a small group while sharing in the life of the whole camp community.

COMPETITION FOR CAMPERS

Camps are now encountering more competition in their quest for camper patronage. One reason is the decreasing birth rate of the past few years, which is causing a constantly dwindling number of children of camp age. In addition, there are now more counterattractions to camp, such as Little League, extensive park and recreation programs, experimentation with the 12-month school year, tutoring in special subjects or summer school, driver education programs, band or baton instruction, summer travel, youth hosteling, social work, or summer jobs. Family camping is now becoming the "in" thing to do as longer weekends and vacations and increased income furnish the time and money for travel and for camping equipment and such accessories as station wagons and recreational vehicles, boats, summer cottages, and horses.

Because today's youth are more sophisticated and often have substantial amounts of money at their disposal, they are disenchanted with those camps which still offer the dull, lackluster programs that sufficed in former days. In response to this, many camps today are successfully promoting red-blooded, exciting, challenging programs which have real appeal for youngsters. In addition, many camps, particularly private independent camps, that once offered one six- or eight-week program during the summer now offer several short sessions of two or three weeks so that youngsters can attend camp and still have time for other summer activities.

WAYS OF WORKING WITH CAMPERS

Today's youth are generally more aggressive and inclined to question authority, tradition, and old ways of doing things. They demand a greater role in planning their own programs and formulating their own rules of conduct, and they are likely to resist such requirements as observing a stated time for "lights out," attendance at vespers and other religious or general programs, honoring the flag, and the like. They bring with them potential problems such as the abuse of alcohol and drugs. Successful leaders are using democratic methods to locate and bring out into the open possible sources of conflict so that they can work jointly with campers to find acceptable solutions.

CAMP BUILDINGS

Old buildings are being modernized and new ones are sometimes more elaborate, largely because of camper or parent demands and more specific health, safety, and building regulations at all levels of government. Buildings are frequently being winterized and pipe and sewer lines laid underground to permit camps to be used during cold weather.

CAMP PERSONNEL

The majority of camps now make a conscious effort to bring together both campers and staff from various social, religious, and economic backgrounds. Many counselors from foreign countries are being hired. Instead of remaining largely a middle class institution, camps are truly becoming melting pots as those from minority and innercity groups receive camperships and other financial aid from many sources, such as foundations, government agencies, and the Camping Unlimited movement of ACA's Fund for the Advancement of Camping.

AGES OF CAMPERS

There was a period when campers became progressively younger as those who had previously attended stayed away in droves, preferring to stay at home rather than spend a boring summer repeating what they did last year. Wide-awake camps are successfully meeting this challenge by offering new activities each succeeding summer that are built upon techniques and skills acquired the previous summer. Teenagers are now returning in relatively large numbers, attracted by such challenging and exciting possibilities as wilderness camping (sometimes modeled after the Outward Bound program), mountain climbing, spelunking, travel and trip camping, and Counselor-In-Training programs.

CAMP STAFF ARE BETTER QUALIFIED AND MORE PROFESSIONAL

The first counselors were often college athletes who were selected because of their ability in sports, with their primary appeal derived from their prowess on field or court. They often knew little and cared less about the needs, desires, and natures of children.

With the changes in camp philosophy and program has come a demand for counselors who not only love children but also know how to work with them in an atmosphere of mutual confidence and friendly rapport. Although program specialists are still needed in such areas as campcraft and trip camping, aquatics, health, crafts, and dramatics, the modern tendency to do most things together as a cabin or unit group has produced a need for more general counselors with broad interests, versatility, and training and skills in group leadership.

Today's staff are much better trained for several reasons. Better and more diversified camping literature is available, and colleges and other organizations are offering more and better courses for training camp leaders. The precamp training period conducted by camps is now considerably longer and better-planned and is used to *train* counselors, in contrast to the earlier custom of using the period to get free help from incoming counselors in doing the physical work of getting the camp ready to open. Many camps are now "growing" their own counselors by conducting excellent CIT courses for older campers. ACA has established standards and guidelines and is fostering courses leading to certification as Campcrafter, Advanced Campcrafter, Trip Crafter, and Trip Leader. Staff members are taking courses in such specialized fields as ecology and working on the waterfront. Increasing numbers of camp directors approach their jobs in a more professional manner as they study and acquire special training through such programs as the ACA-sponsored courses leading to a Camp Director Certificate. More help is coming from such allied fields as health, psychology, sociology, and education. All of these factors combine to assure us that camping people are indeed becoming more professional and camping a true profession.

CAMP PROGRAM IS CHANGING

The program of an early centralized camp was rigidly scheduled; activities were arranged like school classes and each camper was required to participate in those that were considered "good for him." He was supposed to come "bug-eyed" with curiosity about nature study at 8 o'clock and maintain this state of blissful attention for exactly one hour, then magically change into an equally enthusiastic tennis student, and so on throughout the day. The program was planned by the camp or program director, sometimes with the assistance of a few chosen counselors, and was intended to fill every waking moment of the day. Tutoring in school subjects or special instruction in music, dramatics, or dancing was included at the request of parents.

We no longer take this narrow view of program as being merely the schedule of activities offered each day or week. Rather, we regard it as the sum total of every experience a child has from the time he enters camp until his final "good-bye." There is now much more flexibility and the camper has more freedom to choose where he will go and what he will do, as campers, counselors, and general staff share in planning the program. The modern camp is child-centered with emphasis on what is happening to the camper as a person instead of merely on what physical skills he is developing. The growing sophistication of campers has caused corresponding changes in the program, such as a greater variety of creative arts and more environmental study.

CAMPER MOTIVATION

To motivate campers in the old program, an elaborate system of achievement charts and awards was set up. As a result, there was competition in almost every area, which was sometimes overstressed. Some modern camps have over-reacted to this so violently that they now refuse to use anything resembling a check list or awards of any type. Some of their reasons for this aversion are: (1) Campers become so intent on working for awards that they miss the real values inherent in the activities themselves. (2) Regardless of the care taken in planning any system of awards, for every winner there must be one or several losers. Since some campers or groups seldom win they may acquire a hopeless "what's the use of trying" attitude, while others win too frequently and become insufferably cocky. (3) The extreme competitive spirit engendered results in petty bickerings and jealousies which are in direct conflict with the atmosphere camps are trying to create. The desire to win sometimes becomes so keen that it leads to such regrettable incidents as one cabin sprinkling sand on another cabin's floor to keep it from winning a neatness award. (4) The motivating power of the awards is so great that lazy counselors can lie down on the job and exert themselves no more than if they were watching dogs chase a mechanical rabbit at a dog race.

Although modern camps may give awards, they minimize their importance and give them on the basis of doing one's best rather than attaining a specific goal. High camp morale, tradition, a word of commendation from sincere and enthusiastic counselors, the inner glow of self-satisfaction an individual feels at having done his best, and the impetus of group approval furnish enough reward to promote activities which have natural appeal for youngsters.

UTILIZING GROUP DYNAMICS

The modern camp tries to ascertain the wishes and needs of each camper and set up a wide range of possibilities for meeting them. Units in a decentralized system usually plan their activities around their own living needs. The unit is small enough to permit the close-knit atmosphere of family life; each camper is recognized as a personality whose opinions are respected and whose needs are considered by understanding fellow-campers and counselors.

At one time it was customary to assign campers to their cabins without making any effort to determine how they would fit in. Sometimes, in fact, a deliberate attempt was made to separate friends and break up cliques so that campers would be forced to form new friendships. We now know that a child benefits from camp in direct proportion to his happiness in it, and so most camps prefer to help him keep his old friends while learning to live comfortably and appreciatively with others from a variety of backgrounds. It is hoped that such intergrouping will be an enriching experience which will better prepare him for life in today's society.

Figure 3-7 Camp Should Be Free From Pressures.

HEALTH PRACTICES

Health has always been claimed as an important objective of camping, but early camps deluded themselves into believing that good nourishing food plus an active life in the out-of-doors would add up to good health as inevitably as night follows day. After a 1930 study exploded this theory, great changes came about in camp health practices and programs. A complete health examination for every camper and staff member just prior to camp opening became customary, but now an examination anytime within the preceding year is deemed adequate to reveal any individual weaknesses needing correction, or at least protection, by a modified program. All campers are given a check-up on arrival at camp in order to find those with problems needing immediate attention. Trained nurses and doctors, and sometimes dieticians, are a part of the regular camp staff.

Camp personnel now realize the serious error of scheduling every moment so that campers engage in a feverish round of strenuous activities from reveille to taps. Serenity and calm are at last winning due recognition, and campers, with careful guidance, are more often being left to follow their own interests even though these may occasionally involve nothing more strenuous than sitting under a tree daydreaming or watching a colony of ants as they carry on their particular form of social living. Often there is a rest hour following lunch and campers are encouraged at all times to strike a sane balance between active and inactive pursuits, while enough vigorous exercise is provided to keep them strong and to produce a pleasant, healthful tiredness by nightfall.

CAMP STANDARDS AND GOVERNMENT INVOLVEMENT

There is now a definite trend to set and follow recognized camping standards, which are usually based upon those established by the camping profession itself, under the leadership of ACA, as requirements for accreditation. There has also been more involvement by all levels of government in such areas as financial support, state licensing, and regulations concerning medical examination of food handlers and other personnel, sewage and garbage disposal, fire prevention, milk supply, licensing of the camp store, boating, fishing, and minimum wage laws. More recently, camps have been affected by regulations concerning the use of pesticides, solid waste disposal, air pollution by refuse-burning and other types of fires, child welfare and day care, and legislation such as the Occupational Health and Safety Act. Further government participation seems imminent, as seen in a proposed Camp Safety Act which is under consideration by Congress at the time of this writing.

RESEARCH IN CAMPING

Although there is still a great need for research in the field of camping, encouraging progress has been made. Financial support for research has come from such sources as the Fund for the Advancement of Camping, ACA, various foundations, and the federal government.

YEAR-ROUND AND MULTIPLE USE OF CAMP FACILITIES

In an attempt to meet constantly spiraling costs and still maintain a reasonable return on a considerable investment, many camps are now promoting multiple and year-round use of their facilities. Among the positive results have been innovative programs and greater possibilities for year-round employment of those with camp program and administrative skills. As previously mentioned, buildings are being winterized and water and sewer lines placed underground to permit winter use.

Off-season usage is being promoted for such activities as winter sports and camping, school camping and outdoor education, college camping and administration workshops, college orientation programs, dude ranch experiences, senior citizen camping, family camping and family reunions, long weekends, and vacations. Camps are also being used as retreats for conferences and for football teams, marching bands, and similar groups.

ECOLOGY AND CONSERVATION INFLUENCES

As land for camping has become scarcer and more expensive, those responsible have become more concerned about taking care of what they have. Portable facilities are now being used, and paths and program activities are shifted about to provide rotation of land usage and thus minimize the harmful effects of overuse. Primitive camping programs, instead of depending largely upon the use of natural resources, now rely mainly upon manmade products (stoves for cooking and warmth, lanterns for lighting, etc.). New thinking embraces the concept that you take everything you need to the campsite, then bring it all back again in order to disturb the environment as little as possible. Owners and users of land are now feeling a greater sense of stewardship, or responsibility for its wise use and care. Among other things, this involves planting trees to replace those lost to disease, accident, fire, or old age, controlling plant diseases, and preventing forest fires.

(Courtesy of Girl Scouts, U.S.A.)

The use of wood from federal or state lands for camp program, building wood fires, and the like is increasingly discouraged, and in many areas is now prohibited by law. Such legislation will no doubt be more prevalent in the immediate future. We in camping who are interested in preserving our natural heritage should voluntarily support these conservation practices instead of waiting for legislation to force compliance.

TAXATION OF CAMPS

All levels of government, from local to federal, are re-examining their tax bases as they try to meet increasing demands for tax monies. Some camps which have been largely tax-exempt are now being taxed and this practice seems likely to become much more widespread.

DEMAND FOR MORE URBAN CAMPSITES

The growing desire among all types of people for outdoor experiences of every kind is increasing the demand for facilities in or near population centers to accommodate those with limited time, money, or transportation.

SMALL GROUP CAMPING

Camping expeditions by small groups such as a Boy or Girl Scout Troop and its leader(s), often for short periods ranging from one to several days, are on the increase.

THE CAMPING PROFESSION IS BECOMING MORE SOPHISTICATED

As camping matures and its leaders become better trained and more experienced, we acquire greater ability to look at ourselves objectively and gain a clearer picture of where we, as a profession, have been and in what direction we should be going and how best to get there.

ADDITIONAL READINGS

(For an explanation of abbreviations and abbreviated forms used, see page 25.)

Objectives

Camp Standards With Interpretations, pp. 15, 47, and 55–56.
Camping Is Education.
Convention Highlights:
Clark, Walter: "Fitness for American Youth." p. 85.
Gibbs, Howard G.: "The Search for What Is Important in Camping." p. 65.
Ledlie, John A.: "The Camp Community—A Laboratory in Citizenship Training." p. 96.
Hammerman and Hammerman: *Outdoor Education: A Book of Readings:*
Donaldson, Lou and George: "A Camp Is a Children's Community." p. 33.
Hammerman, Donald R.: "A Case for Outdoor Education." p. 45.
Kilpatrick, W. H.: "The Role of Camping in Education Today." p. 16.
Masters, Hugh B.: "Values of School Camping." p. 21.
Miller, Paul S.: "The Summer Camp Reinforces Education." p. 77.
Mitchell, Elmer D.: "The Interests of Education in Camping." p. 80.
Partridge, E. DeAlton: "Some Psychological Backgrounds of Camping." p. 12.
Sharp, L. P., and E. DeAlton Partridge: "Some Historical Backgrounds of Camping." p. 57.
Vinal, William Gould: "The School Camp Line-Up for Nature Education." p. 28.
Johnson, C. Walton: *The Unique Mission of the Summer Camp.* ACA, 24 pp., $1, paper.
Lowry, Thomas Power (Ed.): *Camping Therapy: Its Uses in Psychiatry and Rehabilitation.* Thomas, 1974, 160 pp., $7.75.
Rodney and Ford: *Camp Administration,* pp. 12–21.
Smith, et al. *Outdoor Education,* chs. 1, 2.
Todd: *Camping for Christian Youth,* ch. 4.
Webb, Kenneth B.: *As Sparks Fly Upward.* Phoenix, 1973, 196 pp., $6.95.
Webb, Kenneth B. (Ed.): *Camping for American Youth—A Declaration for Action.* ACA, 1962, 26 pp., 85¢, paper.
Webb: *Light From a Thousand Campfires:*
Gibson, H. W.: "Is It Worth While?" p. 41.
Hill, Ralph: "Creative Activity in Camping." p. 56.
Johnston, Margaret J.: "The Ministry of Nature." p. 260.
Kuebler, Clark G.: "Education for What?" p. 65.
Lorber, Max: "Give To Your Campers Work to Do." p. 311.
Reiley, Catharine C.: "Our Common Heritage." p. 67.
Roehrig, Gilbert H.: "There's a Reason for This Yearning." p. 51.
Vincent, E. Lee: "What a Piece of Work Is Man!" p. 59.
Webb: *Summer Camps—Security in the Midst of Change.*

MAGAZINE ARTICLES

Camping Magazine:
Adelman, Norman: "How Does Program Planning Help Camper Integration?" Feb., 1965, p. 19.
Brackeen, Margaret: "There's a Big Difference (and an Important One) Between Integration and Acceptance." Feb., 1971, p. 12.
Carpenter, Larry: "Do You Encourage Campers to Think for Themselves?" Feb., 1965, p. 20.
Charpentier, Bruce and Helen: "Eight Values Camps Can Give." Sept./Oct., 1971, p. 14.
Cullen, William J.: "Foreign Counselors Come to Camp." Jan., 1971, p. 26.
Ford, Dr. Phyllis M.: "Two Modern Challenges for Every Camp Director." May, 1969, p. 12.
Goldsmith, Ann, and Robert Hellerson: "Our Commitment Is to . . . Diversification of Campers." Mar., 1969, p. 19.
Kirk, John J.: "Camping Can Be Unique If We Only Let It." June, 1969, p. 8.
Konopka, Gisela: "How to Make Camping Significant in the 1970's." Jan., 1970, p. 8.
Krieger, William D.: "Study on Self-concept Changes in Campers." Apr., 1973, p. 16.
Liener, Martin: "Seven Step Program Helps to Integrate Camp." Sept./Oct., 1970, p. 14.
Penn, Matthew: "Learning in Camp: The Fourth Force in Total Education." June, 1970, p. 13.
Ramey, John H.: "We Need to Try Harder —Innercity Children Need Active Recruitment." Feb., 1969, p. 12.
Schmidt, Ernest F.: "How Parents Select a Camp." Mar., 1974, p. 4.
Tener, Dr. Morton: "Camp Can Be Much More Than Just 'Fun and Games'." Jan., 1970, p. 14.

Wylie, James A.: "How Camping Contributes to Educational Needs of Children." June, 1964, p. 10.

Trends

Gabel, Dr. Peter S.: *Camping Creates Community*. ACA, 1971, 17 pp., 50¢, paper.
Rodney and Ford: *Camp Administration,* pp. 24–26.

MAGAZINE ARTICLES

Camping Magazine:
Ball, Armand: "A Hard Look at Camping —Today and Tomorrow." May, 1973, p. 12.
Buynak, Michael F.: "Facing the Camping Future With Confidence." Feb., 1972, p. 8.
Catlin, Glenn: "Eminent Domain . . . the Common Good and Camps." Apr., 1972, p. 20.
Cowle, Irving: "Some Goals for the Seventies." Jan., 1969, p. 10.
Hibbard, Roger: "What Criteria Must Be Met in Order to Make Camping a Profession?" Feb., 1973, p. 10.
"How to Think About the Extended School Year." ACA National Staff, Sept./Oct., 1971, p. 8.
Makoff, Stephen J.: "Preparing Groups for Weekend Camp Programs." Mar., 1970, p. 46.
Melzer, Asher O.: "Camping—Where Do We Go From Here?" Jan., 1972, p. 8.
Ramey, John H.: "Eminent Domain Is A Coin With Two Sides." Nov., 1972, p. 15.
Sanborn, Roger: "And What Do You Do In the Winter?" Nov./Dec., 1970, p. 8.
Smith, Ellis S., Jr.: "How To Use Your Camp All Year Long," Nov./Dec., 1969, p. 16.

Part Two

HOW DO YOU MEASURE UP?

The Camp Counselor and His Role in Guidance

YOU NEVER KNOW*

"You never know when someone
May catch a dream from you.
You never know when a little word
Or something you may do
May open up the windows
Of a mind that seeks the light—
The way you live may not matter at all
But you never know—it might.

And just in case it could be
That another's life, through you,
Might possibly change for the better,
With a broader and brighter view,
It seems it might be worth a try
At pointing the way to the right—
Of course, it may not matter at all,
But then again—it might."

—HELEN LOWRIE MARSHALL

---

*"You Never Know" from *Hold to Your Dream* by Helen Lowrie Marshall. Copyright © 1965 by Helen Lowrie Marshall. Used by permission of Mrs. Marshall and Doubleday & Company, Inc.

Chapter 4

The Camp Counselor

Ideals are like the stars; you will not succeed in touching them with your hands, but like the seafaring man on the desert of waters, you choose them as your guides, and, following them, you reach your destiny.

—CARL SCHURZ*

Figure 4-1 What Is a Counselor?

Camp counseling provides a fascinating summer occupation for thousands of people who return to it summer after summer but, as with any field of endeavor, not everyone is suited to it. Only when there is mutual admiration between the counselor, who likes almost everything about the camp, and the camp, which likes nearly everything about the counselor, can there be that happy blending which makes the days fly by all too quickly. Therefore, in this chapter, we shall try to consider some ways to predetermine how you would fit into the camping picture.

*Reproduced by permission of Coronet Magazine.

CHARACTERISTICS OF A GOOD COUNSELOR

APPRECIATION OF AND LIKING FOR PEOPLE

To enjoy a happy camp experience, you obviously must be a person who would rather work with people than with things and ideas, though you will be called upon to do plenty of the latter, too. You must have a genuine interest in, liking for, and faith in people of all kinds and ages, since camp life involves associating with such an assortment practically 24 hours a day. These qualities, or the lack of them, will quickly show up in your relationships with both your cabin group and your fellow staff members.

Your first consideration will be fitting in with other staff members; there will probably be a number of fellow counselors of approximately your own age, and older persons as well. All will have different personalities, interests, experiences, and camp duties. You must be versatile and adaptable, for, as you work, you will have frequent contacts with the camp nurse, in regard to your campers' health, the dietitian or head cook, in planning cookouts, and the waterfront director, the handy man, the camp director, and others. Good camp morale and good working relationships do not necessarily follow because a member of the camp administration has painstakingly made out a chart depicting the specific duties and responsibilities of each worker in the total camp undertaking; rather, they result when each staff member shows an enthusiastic willingness to combine with all others into a closely knit, harmonious camp family.

As a staff member, you must know and understand people and be able and willing to find good traits and qualities to appreciate in each, ungrudgingly accepting his quirks and peculiarities, just as you hope he will accept yours. Basically, you must be aware of and able to seek out and acknowledge the intrinsic worth of each, both to himself and to society, while still realizing that he, like you, is unique and different from everyone else.

On the whole, you'll probably find your fellow counselors to be a pretty fine group, for they are the kinds of people who are ordinarily attracted to summer camp work. Among them you'll most likely find several who are very congenial and may become lifelong friends.

Secondly, you must sincerely enjoy children, even when they are noisy, uncooperative, impulsive, or demanding. You must not like just some children but must extend your affection to the whole assortment. In fact, the shy, reticent, socially unattractive child needs and hungers for the bit of affection and appreciation you can give much more than the one with an outgoing personality who, with little conscious effort on his part, almost instinctively attracts others to him. You must be able to perceive the hidden possibilities in each individual, especially the ungifted child who seems to be "all thumbs"; you must be able to see behind the "front" of the misfit and maladjusted who are trying in their immature way to find their place in a society which is too complex for them. Your sincere concern for each as an individual will be evident to them, and will win their trust and good will and ideally set the stage for you to help them toward acceptance of and by the group. You must be able to tolerate children in large and frequent doses with continued patience and good humor, for you will be foster parent, teacher, friend, confidante, taskmaster, and model to them.

Granted, you must indeed like children, but not to the point of being sweetly sentimental about them; you will sometimes have to be stern with them when their actions endanger their welfare or clash with camp objectives and policies. Yet withal, you must maintain their good will and respect as you skillfully weld them into a community, learning to live together peacefully, harmoniously, and happily.

EMPATHY

The ability to put yourself in another's place and actually sense how *he* feels is called *empathy*. It is a rare and valuable quality that you are more likely to acquire if you have had many experiences and felt a variety of emotions yourself, such as joy, sadness, love, hate, anger, fear, depression, and loneliness. Such a broad background provides you with a basis for recognizing and correctly interpreting these emotions when you see them in another, so that you can more nearly step into his shoes and sense his problems and emotional needs as *he* sees them. Only then can you determine how best to help him.

WANTED: BETTER LEADERSHIP!

You, as a leader, must exemplify by your own habits and conduct the ideals and objectives of the camp. An ability to attract youngsters is an almost priceless asset, but it would be much better to stay at home if the example you set is not of the best, for your very attractiveness will then make your influence the more pernicious. Campers may pick up bad habits and become boisterous, slangy, vulgar, complaining, or boastful, if you set such a pattern.

Pretense and sham are soon spotted in the intimacy of camp life. You might as well face it: everything you are and say and do will be carefully observed by your bright-eyed youngsters, who will be quick to detect and equally quick to dislike hypocrisy. They will soon see through your attempt to cover up sloppiness by an "Oh, I just never could keep my room straight"; a weak-kneed excuse, such as "I just didn't have time," is similarly revealing.

Youth is the period of hero worship and a child's heart is full of faith and love. Consequently, there is nothing in the world more painful or demoralizing to him than to discover that his beloved idol has feet of common clay and that his first favorable impression was false. Every prospective counselor must ask himself if he is willing to conduct himself as an inspiring rather than a disillusioning model.

BE THE EXAMPLE!

Try in all ways to be a person worthy of emulation, for you are the leader

(Courtesy of the U.S. Forest Service.)

and set the pattern for tomorrow's adults. Younger campers are particularly impressionable because often they are away from parental authority for the first time. They are quick to recognize one who has a zest for living and are irresistibly drawn to him.

You must be able to seize on or create opportunities through which each youth can develop and grow through his camping experiences. Help each to recognize and develop his own potentialities and encourage him to think through his own problems and, with a minimum of help from you, arrive at his own decisions.

YOUTHFUL IN SPIRIT, YET MATURE IN JUDGMENT

Camp directors demand counselors with mature judgment. This is one of the reasons why the American Camping Association has stated that, as one of its requirements for ACA accreditation, at least 80 per cent of the camp's counselors and program staff must be at least 18 years old, the rest at least 2 years older than their campers, and at least 20 per cent of them must have bachelor's degrees. However, mature judgment is not always a matter of chronological age or experience, for some people attain it early, whereas others live to be 90 without ever having demonstrated a particle of it. Campers are too precious to entrust to those whose actions are determined by caprice and whim. Yet along with good judgment, you must retain a youthfulness of spirit and interest which keeps you forever curious and craving new experiences, so that, regardless of passing birthdays, you can still enjoy wading in a babbling brook, hunting the hiding place of a frog, or digging for pirates' gold with your campers. You're glad to be alive, and your enthusiasm should be contagious to everyone in the camp.

LOVE OF THE OUT-OF-DOORS

Even the most luxurious camp usually has rustic surroundings and facilities, since these provide the basic setting necessary for accomplishing some of the main camping objectives. A good program calls for having both the counselor and his campers spend many hours out in the open, participating in a variety of activities and sharing many experiences. Therefore, you must have the ability to adapt yourself to such an environment and enjoy such things as rambling down a woodland path, beachcombing, just sitting on a hill watching the sun set in a blaze of color, sharing thoughts and ideas with your campers, or joining a group on a cookout around a campfire. You must like all types of weather, even the rain, for you will be working as well as playing in the wide open spaces. Does this discourage you? Don't let it, unless you have already had a well-planned and somewhat extensive experience in outdoor living and know for sure that you don't like it; often a counselor has come to camp as green as the grass and trees only to find himself completely captivated with outdoor living before the season is over. If you've never tried it, why not give it a chance?

CAMPING SKILLS

Having definite skills is of utmost importance to you as a counselor, for a camper likes to feel that his counselor excels at some one thing, be it diving, telling a good story, or being the kindest, most considerate person in camp. What is important is that you be able to do at least one thing well and that it be readily apparent to the camp as a whole. This may seem unimportant, yet it plays an important part in gaining the respect of your campers and establishing rapport with them. What can you do? Is there any area in which you excel? Is your tennis, camp cookery, swimming, or woodcraft of such quality that you can demonstrate and teach it to someone else? Can you step into a group which is unduly alarmed over a snake and, by looking at it, assure them that it is harmless and quite essential to nature's well-balanced plan? Can you start a fire in a steady downpour to dry out sopping campers? Can you oversee packing a canoe so that it rides properly in the water? Can you tell poison ivy from Virginia creeper? Can you tell stories, sing, play an instrument, or perform reasonably well in some phase of arts and crafts?

Even a program specialist needs a general background in wood lore and camping skills, for camping is essentially an outdoor process, and a good modern camp coordinates the many facets of its program into one grand experience in out-of-door living. It isn't enough to just "love" nature; you must know something about it.

As a counselor, you may get along beautifully with children, and the warmth of your personality may be evident to everyone, but unless you can *do* something, your charming smile will soon wear thin. However, you need not despair if you do not already possess such skills; the main requirement is that you be willing to acquire them, for you will certainly not lack for opportunities to learn from others, and you can read the many excellent printed materials now in existence and probably available in your camp library. Many of the best counselors have acquired their knowledge and "know-how" while on the job in camp.

PERSISTENCE

You must be able to find happiness in doing a job well and in serving others without thought of personal gain or self-aggrandizement. You must like hard work and plenty of it, for, except for brief periods of "time off," you will be on duty 24 hours a day. You must have enough persistence and will power to replace your "wishbone" with backbone, and you must realize that genius is but "1 per cent inspiration mixed with 99 per cent perspiration." If you really feel challenged by an opportunity to spend a summer where you can do something and be something worthwhile, then in you and those like you lie the hope and future of camping. Every director knows and admits deep in his heart that, no matter how capable he may be, or how good his planning or elaborate his buildings and equipment, the real success of his camp depends upon the quality of his counselors.

WHAT IS YOUR SELF-CONCEPT?

EVALUATE YOURSELF REALISTICALLY

As a counselor, you will be expected to zealously fulfill all your responsibilities, and hopefully you will volunteer in other areas where there are needs which you can capably fill; therefore, it is essential that you seek out and recognize your own capabilities and limitations. When frankly assessing your own strengths and weaknesses, you must acknowledge each of your limitations as well as any special skills, talents, and competencies you have. This open-minded and frank approach will be noted by others, and there will then be no need for you to go to extremes to either display or conceal what you really are—behavior which is almost universally disliked and would undoubtedly start you off on the wrong foot with your associates. Keep in mind this bit of wisdom:

> Modesty is becoming to the great. What is difficult is to be modest when one is nobody.
>
> —JULES RENARD

In order to better assess your possibilities for success and enjoyment as a counselor, it may help you to rate yourself, using Chart I. Remember that there is nothing to be gained by "cheating," for the real showdown comes when you begin working with fellow staff members and campers on the job.

Rate yourself by placing a dot in the appropriate column opposite each trait; then connect them with a line to achieve your "profile." Try to be honest and objective with each item. Now look at the "profile" and note your strengths and weaknesses as the line moves from left to right.

Chart I

Physical Health	Poor 1	Below Average 2	Average 3	Above Average 4	Superior 5
1. Stamina enough to last through a strenuous day					
2. Well-balanced meals eaten regularly					
3. Day planned well enough to get regular sleep in sufficient quantity					
4. Smoking, not at all or moderately, and in an appropriate place					
5. No intoxicating liquors or drug abuse (can't be tolerated at camp)					
6. Sufficient vigorous exercise each day					

General Qualities	Poor 1	Below Average 2	Average 3	Above Average 4	Superior 5
1. Curiosity (want to know about many things just for the sake of knowing)					
2. Cleanliness of person and clothing					
3. Pleasing appearance					
4. Graciousness and mannerliness					
5. Tact (speak truthfully, but without offending or hurting others)					
6. Cooperativeness (even when carrying out the plans of others)					
7. Cheerfulness (no sulking or moodiness)					

General Qualities (*Continued*)	Poor 1	Below Average 2	Average 3	Above Average 4	Superior 5
8. Sense of humor (even when the joke's on you)					
9. Ability to communicate well					
10. Warmth (a friendly personality that attracts others to you)					
11. Poise (even in emergencies or embarrassing situations)					
12. Appreciation of the beautiful in actions, nature, music, and literature					
13. Sincere liking for children (even unattractive and obnoxious ones)					
14. Ability to work well with a group of children					
15. Willingness to work hard even though it means getting dirty					
16. Skills and knowledge of outdoor living (in rain, as well as sunshine)					
17. Adaptability (can happily change plans to fit in with others or the weather)					
18. Can follow as well as lead					
19. Love of fun (can see possibilities for enjoyment in almost any situation)					
20. Interested in many things					
21. Skill in at least one camp activity that children like to do					
22. Initiative (ability to start without outside prodding or suggestion)					
23. Promptness at all appointments and in performing all tasks					
24. Dependability (do *what* you say you will *when* you say you will)					
25. Persistence (finish what you start with dispatch and thoroughness)					
26. Good organization of your personal possessions					

EMOTIONAL MATURITY

WHAT IS EMOTIONAL MATURITY?

"When I was a child, I spake as a child, . . . but when I became a man, I put away childish things" is not necessarily true of adults, who sometimes unconsciously cling to childish ways of thinking and acting. A person who harbors such childish traits is said to be emotionally immature, and, though frequently at a loss to understand why, he is often unhappy, for his behavior keeps him constantly at odds with himself and his associates; he often feels mistreated and deprived. Camp directors look upon a counselor's degree of emotional maturity as one of the surest indices of his probable success, for he can scarcely expect to fulfill his job of helping his campers to mature unless he can set an example.

Your physical and intellectual maturity tell nothing of your emotional maturity, for the fact that you are as strong as an ox or as fleet as a deer does not indicate that you have learned to face up to life squarely and solve your problems in an adult way. Indeed, you may be a straight "A" student at school and still be unable to apply your intelligence to solve your own problems and to help you to deal more effectively with people.

How often we hear some exasperated person say to another, "Why don't you grow up?" What actions and attitudes determine why one person is considered mature while another is not? First of all, a mature person has awakened to the fact that every person around him has wants and needs similar to his own and he therefore cannot always have his own way. For instance, if he has set his heart on doing something with a particular buddy on his day off, he doesn't sulk, try to get even, or throw a tantrum if he finds that his pal has made other plans or that unforeseen developments have made it necessary for one of them to remain on duty in camp. He tries to persuade others to agree with his way of thinking, but he does it by reasoning with them, not by pouting, wheedling, flattering, or being so disagreeable that others give in rather than suffer the consequences.

When someone with obviously good intentions criticizes something about him, he is smart enough to analyze the remark and profit by any truth there is in it, instead of flaring up at the thought that another would even hint that he is anything less than perfect; a mature person realizes that learning to accept deserved criticism is a necessary part of growing up. He has pride and faith in himself, yet displays a becoming modesty, and doesn't feel it necessary to excuse every shortcoming. He isn't a "doormat" who lets everyone walk over him at will; he may even on occasion rise up in righteous anger or resentment about things important enough to really matter.

Understanding Yourself

Are you a well-integrated person who feels secure about himself and adequate to carry on in his surroundings? Many psychologists believe that feelings of security come to persons who from childhood have enjoyed many successful experiences. Eventually these persons develop an increasing sense of competence and self-confidence sufficient to meet new circumstances.

Do you really know yourself? If you are an emotionally mature person, you will be able to realistically analyze your own behavior patterns and personality makeup so that you can better understand your own actions and reactions and your own motives and drives as you attempt to satisfy them. This will help you to gain keener insights into others as you recognize in them these same desires and needs and note the similar ways in which they attempt to satisfy them.

Other Signs of Maturity

If you are emotionally mature, you take pride in your ability to influence others, using it always to help them and lead them in the right direction, and never misusing it to build up your own ego by making willing slaves of any hero-worshiping campers or younger counselors who might be willing to grovel at your feet. Your greatest satisfaction comes from watching young people become increasingly independent; you don't encourage their dependence in order to feel powerful or superior. Instead of trying to run their lives, you concentrate on improving your own. You respect the rights of others and refrain from quarrels and undue anger or grudges. You readily and easily adapt yourself to the routines of camp living, cheerfully accepting all camp rules, since you realize that without these rules for group living, a few might take advantage and selfishly jeopardize the rights and privileges of everyone else. Most of all, you try your best to be thoughtful of others and considerate of their needs and wishes even though they sometimes conflict with your own.

Perhaps the surest indication of emotional maturity is that the person's actions are governed by his reason, not his emotions.

Chart II can be used to make a rough estimate of your overall emotional maturity. Total all scores and divide by 25 (the number of items rated). If you have proceeded honestly and objectively, an average of 4 or 5 means you are quite acceptable, 3 indicates you are average and 1 or 2 shows that you are below average and should "grow up."

Chart II

EMOTIONAL MATURITY	Poor 1	Below Average 2	Average 3	Above Average 4	Superior 5
1. Can you accept criticism without undue anger or hurt, acting upon it if justified, disregarding it if not?					
2. Are you tolerant of others and willing to overlook their faults?					
3. Do you feel genuinely happy at the success of others and sincerely congratulate them?					
4. Do you refrain from listening to and repeating gossip about others?					
5. Do you converse about other things and persons? Test this by checking your conversation to see how frequently you use "I."					
6. Are you altruistic, often putting the welfare and happiness of others above your own?					
7. Do you refrain from emotional outbursts of anger, tears, etc.?					
8. Do you face disagreeable duties promptly and without trying to escape by feigning sickness or making excuses?					
9. Can you stay away from home a month or more without undue homesickness?					
10. Can you weigh facts and make decisions promptly, then abide by your decisions?					
11. Are you willing to postpone things you want to do now in favor of greater benefits or pleasure later?					
12. Are you usually on good terms with your family and associates?					
13. When things go wrong, can you objectively determine the cause and remedy it without making excuses for yourself or blaming it on other people or things?					

(Chart continues on following page.)

EMOTIONAL MATURITY (*Continued*)	Poor 1	Below Average 2	Average 3	Above Average 4	Superior 5
14. When disagreeing with another, can you discuss it calmly and usually work out a mutually satisfactory agreement without hard feelings?					
15. Can you enter into informal social events of many types wholeheartedly?					
16. Do you really enjoy doing little things for others, even though you know they will likely go unnoticed and unappreciated?					
17. Do you dress appropriately for the occasion?					
18. Can you dismiss past mistakes that can't be remedied now without dwelling on them?					
19. Can you be objective about making decisions regarding others?					
20. Do you work democratically with others, neither dictating to nor forcing your will on others?					
21. Are you loyal to your friends, minimizing or not mentioning their faults to others?					
22. Are you free from "touchiness," so that others do not have to handle you with kid gloves?					
23. Do you act according to your honest convictions regardless of what others may think or say?					
24. Do you have a kindly feeling toward most people, a deep affection for some, and no unhealthy attachments to any?					
25. Do you feel that you usually get what you deserve? Are you free from a feeling that others "have it in for" you?					

Here are some suggestions to help you to attain emotional maturity:

1. Recognize your deficiencies honestly and plan to improve, then evaluate your progress periodically.

2. Set out to acquire definite skills and interests which have social rather than selfish or purely personal value.

3. Make it a point to associate with a number of emotionally mature people. Observe them and try to determine why they seem mature. Hold a discussion with others and try to determine why certain of your acquaintances seem to you to be emotionally mature.

4. If you feel a need for help, seek someone qualified and discuss the problem frankly with him, and then be willing to give his recommendations serious consideration.

5. Avoid dwelling on yourself and your problems by becoming involved in absorbing and worthwhile activities. Volunteer to help with such organizations as the Girl Scouts and Boys' Clubs; in this way, you will gain experience in dealing with a variety of people, and you will gain skills and knowledge that can be of benefit to yourself and others.

The traits enumerated in Charts I and II characterize an ideal counselor and have no doubt convinced you by now that no camp director need waste his time looking for such a paragon of virtue on earth. Certainly no one but an angel with a halo cocked over one ear and strumming on a harp of gold could qualify! Do not be discouraged, however, for anyone can improve himself if he is willing to recognize his problems honestly and to make a sincere effort to solve them.

Figure 4-2 Does the Halo Fit?

THE COUNSELOR'S REWARDS

The satisfactions and rewards of camp counseling, as with any other occupation, will vary with the individual and the situation. The degree of effort you put into your job will largely determine what you will receive from the experience.

If you have had no experience and little special training, your actual salary may be meager, but you must realize that you are also receiving free room and board as well as the privilege of living in an environment for which campers may be paying several hundreds or even thousands of dollars. You should not pass over these benefits lightly. Camps sometimes pay a part or all of your transportation expenses and some provide for doing part or all of your laundry. An increasing number of colleges now offer college credit for work experience as a member of a summer camp staff. There are few needs and little temptation to spend money in camp, making it easier for you to save whatever cash you receive.

Many benefits, however, are of inestimable value but come in nonmonetary and intangible forms. As a counselor, you will have almost unlimited opportunities and stimuli to achieve the objectives of camping for yourself. You will be spending your time in the out-of-doors, under the same sun, and in the same friendly, cooperative atmosphere as the campers.

You will probably form some very close and lasting friendships with those of all ages and occupations, and you will have an unparalleled opportunity to acquire the techniques of successful group living, while furthering your own development as an emotionally mature person. You will also have a chance to improve your own skills in camp activities. In addition, counseling offers one of the best possible opportunities for learning the art of leadership and gaining experience in working with people; these skills can be of inestimable value to you if you choose to enter certain vocations.

As a counselor, you will know the joy of helping youngsters with their own personal growth and maturity; in fact, you will experience the same deep and rewarding satisfaction which comes to all good leaders of youth—the knowledge that you have made a real contribution toward developing good citizens who will not only have more zest for living but will also be better fitted to become the leaders of the future.

Figure 4-3 Happiness Is When a Counselor Gets a Letter From Home With Money in It.

GETTING A JOB OFFER

THE JOB WON'T COME TO YOU

This statement is important to bear in mind once you have decided you might like to become a camp counselor. Some of you may already be experienced campers and may have participated actively in C.I.T. (Counselor-in-Training) programs, whereas others may have had no previous camping experience but feel an interest in working with youth in a camp setting. You are likely to be wondering, "Where and how do I start?" It is important for you to start to look for a counseling position as soon as possible; winter is not too early, for by late spring the position you want may already be filled.

There are a number of possible sources for learning of positions:

1. School placement bureaus or your school counselor.

2. School recreation and physical education departments.

3. Local camping associations.

4. Your city's social and welfare agencies, such as Boy Scouts, Girl Scouts, Camp Fire Girls, YWCA and YMCA headquarters.

5. Private employment agencies and the state and Federal employment services.

6. Advertisements in newspapers and certain magazines which feature camp listings and job opportunities.

7. Personal contacts.

8. Current issue of the American Camping Association *National Directory of Accredited Camps for Boys and Girls.** (The 1973 issue listed almost 3,000 member camps.) Consult ACA

*Order current issue from the American Camping Association, Bradford Woods, Martinsville, Ind. 46151. Price, $3.00.

Figure 4–4 Expect Quality in a Camp Which Displays this Insignia.

about its services for employers and job seekers.

9. Chambers of Commerce in areas which interest you.

Investigate a number of camps, reading their booklets and, if possible, talking with their present or former counselors and campers. Select from three to five that especially appeal to you because of their location, length and dates of the camp season, general policies, programs, objectives, or types and ages of children served. If you select camps which are accredited by the American Camping Association, you can be sure that they have met and continue to maintain high standards of camping practices in order to retain their accreditation.

YOUR RÉSUMÉ OR DATA SHEET

Since all employers are interested in certain data about a prospective employee, you may be able to save both your own and their time by collecting such information in a neat and logical order on one or two sheets, having copies reproduced if you anticipate needing several. This provides a summary that they can scan quickly to determine if or where you might fit into their situation. Chart III provides a sample résumé on which to model your own.

YOUR LETTER OF APPLICATION

Since you are including a personal data sheet with your letter, you can make it brief, concentrating on explaining why you are especially attracted to this particular camp and describing the qualities you possess which will, you believe, enable you to make a real contribution to it.

Before starting to compose the letter, analyze your experience and ability by asking yourself:

1. What have I successfully accomplished and been commended for?

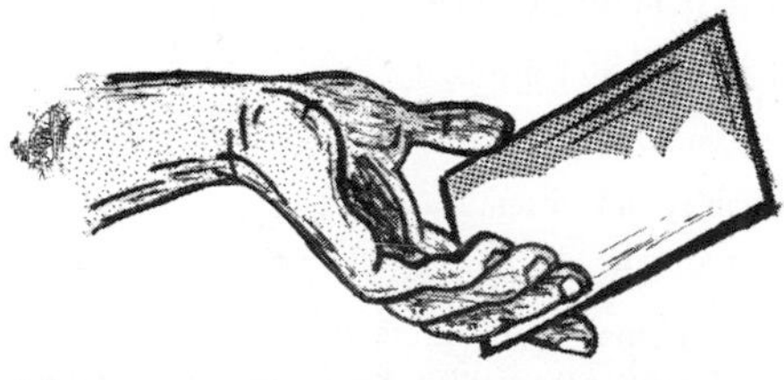

Figure 4–5 Your Data Sheet Is Your Calling Card.

Chart III

PERSONAL DATA SHEET (RÉSUMÉ)

IDENTIFICATION:

Name____________________

Permanent address__________ Permanent phone number__________

Present address__________ Present phone number__________

Position(s) applied for (in order of preference)__________

VOCATIONAL OBJECTIVES:

(Describe your short- and long-range plans.)

PERSONAL DATA:

Date of birth__________ Height__________ Weight__________

Mo. Day Year

Father's name__________ Father's occupation__________

Mother's name__________ Mother's occupation__________

Ages of brothers__________ Ages of sisters__________

Religious preference__________

Physical limitations (if any)__________

EDUCATION:
(List in reverse chronological order.)

Colleges attended	Years attended	Graduated
__________	__________	__________

High schools attended	Years attended	Graduated
__________	__________	__________

Major field of study__________ Minor__________

Scholastic standing__________ School honors and activities__________

Special training (Include special courses you have taken, such as camp counseling, sociology, psychology, human relations, education, music, physical education, mental health, first aid, aquatics, arts and crafts, journalism, creative writing, geology, astronomy, dramatics, or ecology.)

____

WORK EXPERIENCE:

Present occupation__________ Years employed__________

TYPE OF WORK PERFORMED:
(Start with present position and record employment data in reverse chronological order with dates employed and type of work.)

____

OTHER INFORMATION:

Special skills and hobbies__________

Travel, knowledge of foreign languages, etc.__________

Community activities__________ Other__________

REFERENCES:

(Give the names and addresses of three references [teachers, youth leaders, previous employers, and the like] who know you well and can speak authoritatively about you; be sure to secure their permission before listing them.)

____

2. What jobs have I held?

3. What specific skills do I have which are appropriate for camp and which I could help others to develop?

4. What are the things that I really like to do? What are the things I don't like to do?

A well-written application letter is quite important and well worth your time and best efforts, since it may be quite influential in opening the door to future contacts and perhaps eventually may lead to a personal interview. Evaluate yourself honestly, and avoid overstating your abilities or experience, for you, as well as the camp, will be the loser if you step into a job you can't adequately fill. Be specific in all your statements, especially as to the kind of job for which you are applying. Keep it brief, clear, concise, interesting, courteous and convincing. Address it to the proper person, for example, Mr. Harry Williams, Director of Camp High Standards; open with "Dear Mr. Williams," and write specifically to *him,* enclosing a stamped, self-addressed envelope to make it easy for him to reply.

Make a rough draft first, then make revisions until you are sure it represents your best efforts. Then transcribe it neatly onto good stationery, preferably using a typewriter. It is a good idea to keep a copy so that you will know exactly what you have said. A camp director receives many applications each season and doesn't read business letters for pleasure; therefore, sloppy, poorly written letters usually land in the wastebasket where they rightfully belong.

THE INTERVIEW

If you are invited for an interview, remember that your attitudes and personality will be showing and that you are presenting a valuable product: yourself. Employers are as concerned about your personality as they are about the factual information you included in your résumé. When two applicants have approximately equal qualifications, the interview usually determines why the job is offered to one and not the other.

You must remember that you are trying to sell yourself and that merchandise always sells better when attractively packaged. Before appearing for the interview, get a good night's sleep, eat sensibly and come with a neat appearance and a clear and alert mind. Be prepared to talk about yourself in terms of the needs or requirements of the camp director. What do you have to offer that would make you an asset to the camp? Why do you want to be there, and why will he be glad to have you? (Remember, this is what most interests him.) Have you thought of pertinent areas in which you want to obtain further information, such as:

1. The philosophy and program structure of the camp.

2. The camp setting itself and its location.

3. The exact dates on which your job would begin and end.

4. General camp policies.

5. Does the camp specialize in particular activities such as aquatics, riding, or arts and crafts, or does it instead provide a balanced general program?

6. What living quarters and conditions are provided for staff? (Will you share a cabin with other staff members or be expected to live in the cabin with your campers?)

7. What age group will you be working with?

8. What are the regulations regarding time off, smoking in camp, the use of alcohol or drugs in and out of camp, having your own car, etc.?

9. What will be the remuneration, including possible transportation to and from camp, laundry services, use

Figure 4-6 Boy, Isn't that Director Lucky!

of camp equipment and extras such as riding and boating privileges?

10. What will be your definite responsibilities and duties on the job? Most reputable camps will usually be able to furnish you with such information through a definite and detailed written job description. Ask about it. (For a more detailed discussion of the job description, see Chapter 5.)

Throughout the interview the camp director will be evaluating your maturity, cooperativeness, physical and mental alertness, motivation, enthusiasm, and any other qualities that will help him to assess your willingness to work and your ability to get along with others.

ACCEPTING A POSITION

If you receive an offer of a position, do not accept it until you are reasonably sure that the camp's philosophy is sufficiently compatible with your own to enable you to give it your utmost loyalty and devotion. Now is the time for you to clear up all questions and doubts, for after having accepted a job, you have assumed obligations which you must fulfill. If you have applied to several camps, and receive an offer from one before you have heard from others in which you may be interested, it is entirely appropriate for you to call those camps which have not yet replied to determine the status of your application. Don't feel shy about inquiring; your honesty and initiative will usually be appreciated. Answer all correspondence promptly, since the director may lose other desirable applicants while you are trying to make up your mind. A signed contract is your word of honor that you will arrive on schedule, prepared to carry out your agreements to the best of your ability.

After you have returned a signed contract, you will, in all probability, receive various literature and correspondence from the camp. Read each carefully to better orient yourself and

Some Do's and Don't's in Successful Interviewing

Do's	Don't's
1. Be prompt, neat, courteous, and appropriately dressed.	1. DON'T arrive late and breathless for the interview. Be a few minutes early to allow time to compose yourself.
2. Act naturally; be poised and friendly and remember to smile.	2. DON'T be extreme in mannerisms, grooming, or dress (no smoking or gum chewing).
3. Try to overcome nervousness or shortness of breath. (It may help to take a deep breath and sit back comfortably in your chair as you talk.)	3. DON'T display a passive or indifferent attitude.
4. Answer questions honestly and straightforwardly.	4. DON'T be overaggressive or inflexible.
5. An interview is a two-way street, so feel free to ask for information about the camp and its policies.	5. DON'T become impatient or emotional.
6. Recognize your limitations.	6. DON'T make claims if you can't "deliver" on the job.
7. Indicate your flexibility and readiness to learn.	7. DON'T be a "know-it-all" or person who can't take instructions or suggestions.
8. Make yourself clear and be sure he understands what you mean; enunciate clearly and use good grammar and sentence structure.	8. DON'T speak indistinctly or in a muffled voice. Keep your head up and look directly at the employer as you talk.
9. Modestly point out the specific contributions you can make to his camp.	9. DON'T show undue concern about salary.
10. Give the employer an opportunity to express himself and listen closely to what he says.	10. DON'T unnecessarily prolong the interview. Watch for signals that indicate that he is ready to conclude the interview, and leave promptly unless you have a reason for lingering.

fix pertinent details in your mind, for everything sent to you will help you to learn more about the camp. You should now proceed to prepare yourself to assume your duties. If possible, enroll in, or at least audit, helpful school courses and study any general camping books and materials in allied fields that are available in your school or community library. If you want to start your own camping library, you can find many worthwhile books, pamphlets, and articles available free or at modest cost. One of the most helpful things you can do is to start a camping notebook in which to jot down every bit of useful information and helpful ideas that come your way. A loose-leaf cover, holding sheets $3\frac{3}{4}$ by $6\frac{3}{4}$ inches, is suggested, for it is a convenient size for recording and is small enough to carry with you on trips or at camp. Take advantage of opportunities to gain further experience in working with groups of children.

Whispering wind in the tree tops,
Shimmering sun on the lake,

From all of the world's occupations
A life in the open I'd take.*

ADDITIONAL READINGS

(For an explanation of abbreviations and abbreviated forms, see page 25.)

A Guide for College Credit for Camp Field Experience. ACA, 1970, 6 pp., 25¢, paper.
Bannon, Joseph J.: *Problem Solving in Recreation and Parks.* Prentice-Hall, 1972, 347 pp., $5.95, paper.
Camp Counseling Is Channel Number One. ACA, 10¢, paper.
Camp Staff Application. ACA, 2¢.
Careers in Camping. ACA, 1972, 10¢, paper.
Dudley, Geoffrey A.: *Your Personality and How to Use It.* Emerson, 1962, $3.95.
MacKay: *Creative Counseling for Christian Camps,* ch. 2.
National Directory of Accredited Camps for Boys and Girls. ACA, issued annually, $3. (Lists all of the camps accredited by ACA with pertinent information about each)
Perry, Marian L.: *The Relationship of Selected Variables to the Success of Camp Counselors, Research Monograph #2.* ACA, 1964, 20 pp., $1, paper.
Rodney and Ford: *Camp Administration,* chs. 6, 7, Appendices B, C, D, F.
Shivers: *Camping,* ch. 2, ch. 6 to p. 126.
Van Krevelen: *Children In Groups: Psychology and the Summer Camp,* ch. 9 to p. 123.
Webb: *Light From a Thousand Campfires:*
Allen, Hugh: "Let's Take Stock," p. 198.
Graham, Abbie: "On Being a Counselor," p. 150.
Joy, Barbara Ellen: "It's Fair to Expect," p. 157.
Link, Dr. Robert: "What Makes a Good Counselor?" p. 162.
Sharp, Dr. Lloyd B.: "The Campers' Prayer," p. 201.
Woal, S. Theodore: "Yours Is a Tough Assignment," p. 154.
Welch, Emily: *Its Fun to Be a Counselor.* Ass'n Press, 1956, 63 pp., $1.

MAGAZINE ARTICLES

Camping Magazine:
Ballentine, A. Cooper, and Lois Orr: "The Camp Leaders We Seek—And Those We Avoid." Jan., 1965, p. 17.
Brackeen, Margaret E.: "Some Questions Camp Directors Should Ask to Insure Good Staff Selection." Apr., 1973, p. 9.
Perry, Marion L.: "Camp Counselor Selection." Feb., 1964, p. 22.
Roberts, Kenneth: "The Fringe Benefits of Camp Counseling." June, 1964, p. 22.
Steinman, Richard, Ph.D.: "From Campus to Camp—the Counter-Culture Is Imported." Feb., 1972, p. 12.
Stevenson, Jack L.: "Qualities a Director Looks for in a Camp Dietitian." Mar., 1973, p. 15.

*From *Deep-River Jim's Wilderness Trail Book.* Used by permission of The Open-Road Publishing Co.

Chapter 5

The Counselor on the Job (Part I)

A great deal of the joy of life consists in doing perfectly, or at least to the best of one's ability, everything which he attempts to do. There is a sense of satisfaction, a pride in surveying such a work—a work which is rounded, full, exact, complete in all its parts—which the superficial man, who leaves his work in a slovenly, slipshod, half-finished condition, can never know. It is this conscientious completeness which turns work into art. The smallest thing, well done, becomes artistic.

—WILLIAM MATHEWS

Figure 5–1 You're His Big Brother.

In this chapter we shall survey some of the general aspects of a counselor's duties. Please study the chart in Figure 5–2 to gain an overall view of the general staff organization.

Figure 5–2 shows the lines of responsibility in the typical staff organization of a large camp. There may be many variations on it as each camp tailors its own plan, adapted to its own

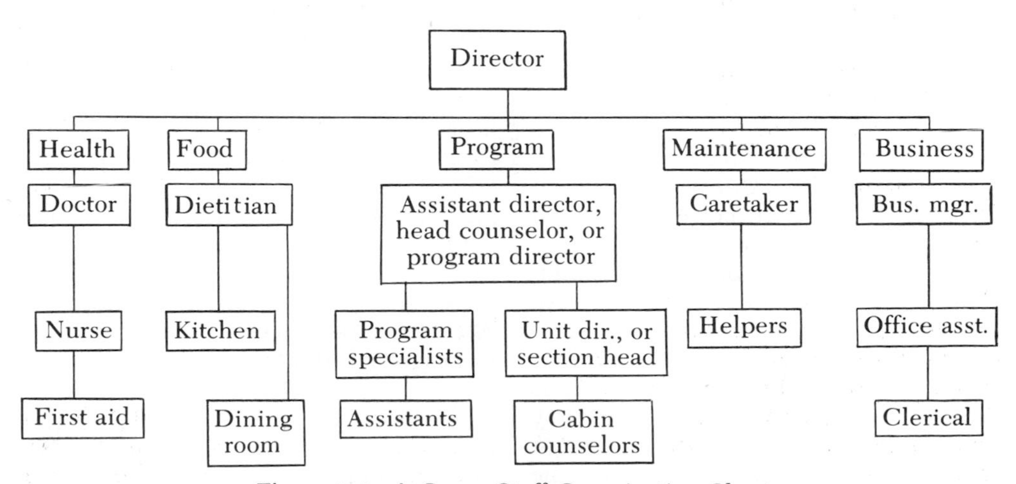

Figure 5–2 A Camp Staff Organization Chart.

size, the capabilities of its staff, its individual program and facilities, and the objectives and personal preferences of the director or sponsoring agency; for instance, a director may prefer to assume some of the duties shown here as delegated to the assistant director.

The chart, however, does give an overall view of staff organization and indicates lines of authority and the particular staff member to whom each person is directly responsible. Note that there is one individual in charge of each of the five main areas of health, food, program, maintenance, and business, and that each is directly accountable to the director for the conduct of his particular area.

THE CAMP STAFF

CAMP DIRECTOR

You will note that the camp director is at the top of the chart. He is the highest authority in camp and is ultimately responsible for everything that occurs there. All staff members are accountable to him, even though they may be under the immediate supervision of someone to whom the director has delegated responsibility. There will be general camp policies and rules to cover routine procedures, and those in charge of a certain area may be authorized to make important decisions in that area; however, every other decision of major importance must be referred to the camp director for his final approval and consent.

The director is basically responsible for the welfare of each camper and staff member and carries out these responsibilities through the abilities and training of his staff, as well as through the camp rules, philosophy and objectives and the methods used to carry them out. Obviously he must be a person of diverse abilities, since he serves simultaneously as an administrator, financial wizard, child welfare expert, educator, recreation director, and advisor to his counselors and other staff members.

Since he realizes that a camp can be only as strong as its staff, he tries to procure the best personnel available. Then, to obtain the optimum in total team performance, he must recognize the inherent potentialities of each team member and help him to develop and use his abilities to best advantage in combination with whatever physical and natural resources the camp offers. At the same time, he must realize that each staff member has needs and desires of his own which must be fulfilled.

The director, then, is the hub of the wheel, about which each staff member revolves as he contributes his efforts toward the summer's achievements.

ASSISTANT CAMP DIRECTOR

The person second in position is called by various titles, such as assistant director, head counselor, or program director, and serves as the liaison man or coordinator of the whole camp program. He is accountable to the camp director and works directly with program specialists, unit directors, and sometimes their assistants. He is the mainspring of the whole camp, and the morale of both campers and staff is largely dependent upon him. His specific duties vary according to the size, philosophy, and general setup of the camp.

PROGRAM SPECIALISTS OR DEPARTMENT HEADS

Program specialists or department heads are usually found in larger numbers in long-term camps or those tending toward a more centralized system, though nearly every camp has a few, such as a riding instructor and a waterfront director. They head such specialized areas as equitation, tennis, campcraft, arts and crafts, ecology, sailing, trip camping, music, and dramatics; each may have assistants to help him to carry on his particular activity.

A program specialist may perform his duties in a variety of ways. In some camps, he keeps his work area open at definite hours for any who wish to come, whereas in others, each group is scheduled to come at a certain time. In camps which follow the recent trend of giving each living group a freer hand in planning and carrying out its own activities, the group asks for the use of the services and facilities of the program specialist when they see fit.

A program specialist may or may not be assigned regular cabin duties, depending on the philosophy of the camp and how demanding his special program is. In addition to instructing and advising, his duties usually involve requisitioning the supplies he needs and seeing that his work quarters and equipment are kept in good condition. He will also be held responsible for taking an inventory and packing away his supplies and equipment at the end of the season. He should also list any supplies needed and make recommendations for improving the program for the following year.

UNIT DIRECTORS AND COUNSELORS (ASSISTANTS)

A unit director, sometimes called a village or section head, presides over a living unit of four to six cabins or tents. Usually under him are assistant unit heads or cabin counselors in direct charge of the cabins in the unit and the four to nine campers who live in each.

Prior to camp opening, the unit director works closely with his assistants in planning a skeleton unit program for the summer, suited to the needs and interests of their particular campers. The details of the plan are then worked out and altered, if necessary, with the help of the campers after they arrive. He also works with his assistants to decide such matters as the division of unit duties and time off, and serves as their liaison with the assistant director. He must see that the unit program coordinates with the overall program of the camp and with its general objectives and philosophy.

THE JOB DESCRIPTION

A job description is a written statement which spells out the exact terms of employment for a particular staff member and includes not only a detailed outline of his responsibilities to the camp, but also the obligations of the camp to him. The job description in a particular camp may develop in various ways and may be revised in succeeding years as experience or changing camp philosophy and customs dictate. At the end of a season, the camp administration usually reviews each employee's job description with him to ascertain his reaction to it and to receive any suggestions he may have for ways to improve it.

When applying for a job, you may be shown the job description during your interview; if not, you should certainly ask for it before making your final decision to accept so that you will have a clear picture of what the job involves, in specific and written form.

WHAT A JOB DESCRIPTION INCLUDES

Job descriptions may be written in many different ways, but all should include the following information:

1. Title of the position.

2. To whom employee is accountable.
3. General responsibilities.
   a. Degree of responsibility and performance expected.
4. Specific duties.
5. Qualifications.
   a. Prior training and experience.
   b. Skills and interests needed.
6. The relationship of the position to other positions in the camp, as well as to the camp's total program.

ADVANTAGES OF A JOB DESCRIPTION

A job description aids the camp by (1) helping to recruit staff specifically suited for a particular position; (2) serving to remind an immediate supervisor of exactly what each of his subordinate's duties are in order to avoid having duties overlap or leaving important areas unassigned; (3) serving as an objective basis for evaluating an employee's performance during and at the end of the season; and (4) producing more satisfied and more confident staff members, since each knows just what he can expect and what is expected of him before he accepts the job. The job description also serves as a guide for the counselor to follow on the job.

The job description is important to the staff member because (1) it prevents the misunderstandings and confusion that often result from verbal discussions; (2) it informs him of what his particular job entails, where to turn for help and guidance, to whom he is responsible, with whom he works, their positions in relation to his and how they interrelate; (3) it lends status to his position and helps him to take pride in his job; (4) it assures him that the camp is efficiently administered and that concern for its personnel is a high priority; (5) it gives him something specific to refer to as questions arise on the job; and (6) it helps him to plan by supplying definite information about what is expected of him and when he is expected to do it (for instance, what reports he is to make out periodically and at the close of camp).

THE STAFF MANUAL

Most camps have a staff manual which will be either sent to you before camp opens or given to you soon after you arrive. It is a comprehensive reference book, with specific information and material, which you should study thoroughly and keep for future reference. It will probably contain information concerning the camp's philosophy and objectives, the history of the camp, the camp staff organization chart, personnel policies and privileges, camp customs, sample record forms, a description of the camp layout with a map of the units and facilities, emergency procedures, policies regarding staff time off and staff use of equipment and facilities, staff meetings, in-camp training procedures, and, *hopefully,* a bibliography of camp library materials available for use when you need help in carrying out various phases of your job.

BEFORE THE CAMPERS ARRIVE

PRE-CAMP TRAINING

Counselors and other staff personnel are often asked to report for duty several days to a week or more ahead of the campers. This pre-camp training session is a very important orientation period for new counselors, as well as a review for returning staff, and gives everyone a chance to get acquainted with one another and to familiarize himself with the camp site, routines, program, and customs and traditions.

(Courtesy of Missouri Valley College, Marshall, Missouri.)

You will have a chance to do some planning for the summer, both individually and with various groups, and you will probably be learning or reviewing all sorts of campcraft skills, from making a beanhole to building a campfire and bedding down for an "overnight," as you go through some of the routines and activities your campers will be doing. You may be asked to do a certain amount of assigned reading and to participate in discussions conducted by various members of the staff. Several unit staff meetings may be held to help you to plan for your own unit program.

If you are an experienced camper or counselor, remember your own feelings of insecurity and uncertainty upon first coming to camp. Extend a hand of fellowship to your inexperienced colleagues to help them through those first trying days; show them the same sensitivity, understanding, and cordiality you expect to extend later to your incoming campers. If you are new to the camp, remember that, despite outward appearances of self-assurance, nearly everyone else is as anxious as you to become adjusted and feel at ease with the group; meet them halfway, or even a little more.

PREVIEWING CAMPERS

You will probably soon learn something of your incoming campers, if only their names and ages. Camp regulations usually require that each camper submit a personal record for the information of the camp office and staff. This record contains a great deal of information about the camper, some of which may be of a highly personal nature, which is one of the reasons why the privilege of examining it is often denied to counselors. If you do receive this privilege, be professional and keep its contents strictly confidential, discussing it with no one except authorized persons; use it solely to help you to gain a better understanding of the camper before you meet him face to face. If you study it objectively and with that purpose in mind, it may help you to anticipate and prevent future behavior problems and reveal the possible interests and abilities of the camper, as well as provide an overall image of your entire group.

Your wise handling of pre-camp evaluations will offer a real challenge to demonstrate your maturity and good judgment. Because these records contain only factual information, it is easy for a person examining them to jump to conclusions and form inaccurate judgments based upon single or isolated bits of information. It is also unwise and unfair to assume that episodes which may have occurred during one period of a camper's life necessarily forecast what he will do or be at a later period.

If he has been in camp before, records of his previous accomplishments and staff evaluations of his personality, social adaptability, adjustment to adult and peer groups, and general behavior may be available. His past health records and the health examination report of his home physician, made prior to camp opening, will be of importance, and it is your responsibility to note any limitations regarding strenuous activities, swimming and diving, and any allergies or food idiosyncrasies and to see that recommendations regarding them are carried out.

YOUR OWN PERSONAL ADJUSTMENT

When you pack your bag to come to camp, remember to include your sense of humor, patience, fondness for children, ability to be fair and impartial, kindness, and, last but not least, love of the out-of-doors. These qualities are necessary for working both with your campers and with the entire camp staff, and they will help you to fit comfortably into the group and adjust quickly and happily to camp ways. You have voluntarily closed the door on the local drive-in, dances, sports car rides, and long telephone conversations, but in exchange, you will find yourself on the threshold of a new, exciting, and rewarding way of life.

Figure 5-3 The Counselor's Dream.

Camp counseling may well be one of the highlights of your entire life, ending with treasured memories of close friendships and fun, and the joy of a job well done helping a group of campers to grow and develop into better persons. The results largely depend on your attitude toward counseling and the wholehearted manner in which you approach it. You'll know you've succeeded when some grubby little paw is placed trustingly in yours at the end of the season and a small voice says, "Hey, you'll be back next summer, won't you? 'Cause I don't wanna come if you don't."

RELATIONSHIPS WITH THE STAFF

It isn't your position that makes you happy or unhappy; it's your disposition.

—AUTHOR UNKNOWN

WITH THE CAMP DIRECTOR

A camp director has usually spent long months preparing for the approaching season and is naturally very concerned about its success. Though he has delegated many duties and responsibilities to others, he still retains the primary responsibility for the administration of the camp, and he will be held accountable for any serious errors in judgment made by his staff. Remember this when he seems to you to be overly cautious or unbending about things you propose. Obviously, he has a more comprehensive view of the whole camp situation, and there are a multitude of details and problems demanding his attention. Regard yourself as someone to help him to bear the load instead of unnecessarily adding to his burdens by making thoughtless, selfish requests or by failing to fully and efficiently carry out all tasks assigned to you.

Keep the aims and objectives of the camp foremost in your mind and direct all your efforts toward their accomplishment, for, after all, you shouldn't have accepted the job if you couldn't enthusiastically accept and support them. Be conscious always that *camp is for the campers* and that their moral, spiritual, and physical welfare must take precedence over the self-centered desires of any individual or group.

Neither ask for nor expect special favors, for no administrator can afford to show partiality; you wouldn't like to have others receive privileges denied to you. Obey the spirit as well as the letter of camp rules and regulations. Turn in all required reports on time and be sure they are complete down to the last detail.

Camp equipment is expensive so it is foolish to waste or abuse it. Since every camp has only a limited budget, the unnecessary destruction of equipment may mean that staff and campers must forego other things they might very much like to have.

Though it will often be difficult, you must be able to distinguish between problems and decisions you can handle yourself and those which you should refer to your superiors for their action or advice. On the one hand, you have been hired because you have a level head and mature judgment; these qualities will enable you to make minor decisions within your jurisdiction instead of "passing the buck." On the other hand, you must be quick to recognize major problems which must be referred to your unit head, the camp nurse or doctor, or the head counselor. If the problem is of great urgency or importance, you may even need to take it directly to the camp director.

WITH FELLOW STAFF MEMBERS

Camping is not only a pleasant and satisfying way to spend the summer months; it is also a way of life and a valuable experience in adapting yourself to living harmoniously in close association with others 24 hours a day. The esprit de corps of the staff largely determines the spirit of the entire camp, for no person can be truly happy and do his best work when laboring under disharmony, tension, and vague feelings of insecurity and frustration. Good staff morale is the vital component almost invariably found in every successful camp, but, unfortunately, it can't be produced by ordering the personnel to acquire it. Therefore, each

Figure 5-4 Happiness Is When a Counselor Gets a Box of Goodies From Home and Shares Them.

person should exert himself to the utmost to promote harmonious and cooperative relationships. This is essential not only for yourself, but also for the well-being of the campers and the attainment of camp objectives, for campers are quick to perceive any lack of staff unity and, like their elders, will discuss it among themselves and may even take sides with one feuding party or the other.

A bit of petty gossip or a careless comment can cause the first break in staff morale. Avoid being critical of those whose ways differ from yours, and regard each person as an individual who will never be duplicated; learn to respect and accept his distinctive characteristics, remembering that you probably sometimes seem odd and cantankerous to others. How can you hope to develop tolerance and broadmindedness in campers if you have not yet acquired them yourself?

Do not look for wrong and evil—
You will find them if you do;
As you measure for your neighbor
He will measure back to you.
Look for goodness, look for gladness—
You will meet them all the while;
If you bring a smiling visage
To the glass, you meet a smile.

—AUTHOR UNKNOWN

Camp consists of a blending of many different activities and experiences, and most of the good that is accomplished results from this blending into a whole, rather than from the parts individually. Many times this is hard for an ambitious, conscientious counselor to remember, for he often becomes so absorbed in trying to conduct his own particular part of the program that he loses sight of the camp picture *in toto*. Immature counselors can often be spotted by their attempts to vie with each other in attracting the greatest camper clientele; this, of course, is very short-sighted and selfish and may seriously jeopardize the welfare of both the camp and the campers. As previously stated, to be a truly topnotch counselor you must maintain an inquiring, adventure-seeking mind and be interested in many things. When you belittle other activities and staff positions or personnel, you are only showing your own smallness and poor sense of values. You will find it is to your benefit to encourage your fellow workers by showing an interest in their activities and trying to learn more about them. We all respond well to others who show an interest in us and what we are doing, and by doing this yourself, you will often find that you have thereby acquired a new friend and a new field of interest whch may well provide you with lasting enjoyment. Be modest about your own accomplishments, for conceit is never an endearing trait and certainly not one to cultivate.

Recognize the importance of each person on the staff. Without the maintenance man, who would fix the plumbing or electricity? The kitchen staff? You like to eat, don't you? When you need help from the dietitian, camp nurse, or other specialist, exercise consideration and patience, remembering that they already have busy schedules which leave little time or flexibility for adding extra chores.

Cooperate and help others whenever you can and be the first to volunteer for special duties, even though they may involve hard work. It is said that when a piano is to be moved, there are usually several volunteers to help but always one or two who hang back and look on or merely offer to carry the stool. Are you a helper or only an onlooker?

It is usually best neither to borrow nor to lend money, clothing, or other personal possessions, for such practices often lead to misunderstandings and hard feelings between those involved.

Make friends with many and avoid cliques or special and inseparable pals,

Figure 5–5 Happiness Is a Counselor Who Sings Stark Naked in the Shower.

for such exclusive friendships can damage camp morale and eventually make the participants themselves suffer as other staff members shun them. Old counselors, who are reuniting after a winter's separation, must be especially careful about this, for in their joy at being together again, they may unconsciously exclude new staff members, making them feel lonely and estranged from the rest of the camp family. "Mix 'em up" in every way that you can, for mingling with many broadens your circle of friends and often exposes you to interesting, congenial personalities.

Like most people, you will, of course, want others to like you and seek out your companionship, but don't sacrifice your individuality or principles to gain acceptance or to be "one of the gang." Such ill-gained popularity is shallow and fleeting, and such "friends" often desert you, leaving you lonely and disillusioned about people in general.

Take your job, but not yourself, seriously and be the first to acknowledge your mistakes and laugh at your blunders. Worthwhile personal relationships do not spring up by themselves like weeds; they are delicate plants which thrive best under careful cultivation. Esprit de corps and good camp morale are the end products when staff members live by these principles.

> Morale is when your hands and feet keep on working after your head says it can't be done.
>
> —Admiral Ben Morcell (Quoted in *Forbes*)

WELCOMING YOUR CABIN GROUP

PLANNING FOR THEIR ARRIVAL

If you are a cabin counselor, you will be living intimately with your small group nearly 24 hours a day and will come to know them and they to know you very, very well. Remember that decentralized camping came into being precisely to provide this experience of living in a small group, where each member plays an important role and enjoys the feeling of being an integral part of his group, sharing in its work, play, joys, and sorrows just as in a closely knit family. Hopefully, this living arrangement will give each camper a feeling of security and belonging.

Many activities will involve only the small group, yet, like any well-adjusted family, the group will frequently engage in "community" activities with other groups and the camp as a whole. It will be your job to teach your campers to function effectively in both their own and larger groups, and the proceedings during the first few camp days will be instrumental in setting the stage for this undertaking.

First contacts are most important and will largely determine the attitude of the campers toward one another and you. It is therefore important for you to plan in some detail what you will do and how you will do it during these first crucial hours and days. Most camps feel that a large share of this time should be spent in the small group, so that the counselor can weld them together and build up a climate of "oneness" and loyalty which will instill in each the courage to go out and take his place with larger groups.

Some camps wait until the campers arrive before assigning them to living quarters, preferring to wait until they have met and surveyed the entire assemblage. Others feel it is better to make assignments ahead of time, hoping to add to a youngster's feeling of security by letting him know in advance that there is a definite bed in a definite room ready and waiting for him.

Some camps ask the counselor to send a brief note to each of his campers, timed to reach him a few days before he leaves for camp. This is often quite helpful, for a person can often face a new experience more confidently if he knows that there is a definite person expecting him and looking forward to his arrival. You will not want to do this unless someone in authority has approved it, and you should adapt the tone and type of your communication to the age of the camper; naturally, a letter suitable for a six-year-old will be inappropriate for a teenager.

Figure 5-6 I'm Here at Last.

WHEN THE CAMPERS ARRIVE

The process of getting the campers settled will differ, depending on whether they arrive simultaneously, or come singly or in small groups. If all the campers arrive at one time, all staff members should be present together, for many hands will be needed to take care of a multitude of details. If campers dribble in a few at a time, one unit staff member may remain in the quarters as a host to greet each camper, show him his bunk, and help him to get settled. Program specialists and other staff may act as guides to receive the newcomers and assign them to quarters, keeping an accurate record of who has checked in. Spare staff or returning campers may act as "runners" to help the new arrival with his baggage and show him to his living unit. Those coming by train, bus, or plane often have a staff member assigned to meet them at some central gathering place and to care for their needs during the trip to camp.

To guide you in your conduct at this time, imagine yourself as a small child, leaving your parents, familiar surroundings, friends, and pets, perhaps for the first time. You would probably be overwhelmed by feelings of excitement and anticipation, tempered by some uncertainty and, perhaps, anxiety, without the support of family or friends. You would probably be asking yourself such questions as: "Will I like the camp, my counselor, the other campers?" "Will they like me?"

Wouldn't it reassure you to have a cordial, friendly counselor greet you with an outstretched hand and a smile?

Wouldn't you like to have him tell you his name and ask you yours, particularly your favorite nickname by which you want to be known in camp? Wouldn't it make you feel warm inside to have him say, "Here's your bed, Sandy, and these are your storage spaces for the summer. Bill, here, will help you to unpack and stow away your gear. You can get into some comfortable clothes and come out to meet the rest of the gang. Then we'll take a tour of the camp to get the hang of it and see where we're going to have a lot of fun together this summer."

If your camper doesn't have a nickname but wants one, help him to select a suitable one which appeals to him, and start calling him by it immediately. No matter what a person's age, it boosts his ego to have a new acquaintance remember him and call him by name; this is one of the secrets known and practiced by those who have the knack of quickly making friends and establishing rapport with people. The first nickname chosen will not necessarily stay with the person and may later be replaced by one spontaneously adopted after some funny happening or camp occurrence which gives it a special significance to those involved. This is fine if the person concerned is happy with this name, but don't let a youngster get "stuck" with something he dislikes or finds uncomplimentary. Almost anyone would be sensitive to and hurt by a name such as "Horse Face," "Fatso" or "Dumbo," and even though a child may seem to take such "kidding" good-naturedly, it can make him truly miserable and can even cause long-lasting damage to his dignity and self-esteem.

Introduce campers to each other and see that each is provided with a name tag which can be read easily from a distance. Getting everyone on a first name basis breaks down barriers and helps to start things off in a spirit of friendliness.

SETTLING IN YOUR CABIN GROUP

Encouraging a camper to unpack, put his belongings in *his* particular storage place, make up *his* bed, and get into his comfortable camp clothes, with one particular person assigned to be his buddy and help him, combine to make him feel at home and settled in for a long stay and help to dispel his first instinct to "turn tail" on the unknown and unfamiliar and run back home to mommy and daddy. As long as he is dressed in his traveling clothes, with his bags still packed, it is all too easy for him to yield to his fears and latch onto any excuse he can think of to get back to the tried and familiar.

The camp will probably have asked him to bring an inventory of the things in his baggage. Ask him to check off each item as he unpacks and, if there is a discrepancy, make sure it is not something merely overlooked and then report the discrepancy to the camp office. If he has no inventory, see that he makes one as he unpacks and file it at the camp office to use when it is time to pack to return home. The camp will probably have requested that everything be clearly marked with his name; if it isn't, mark it, for children often leave things carelessly about where they remain unidentified and unclaimed after all have departed at the end of the season.

Show him how to make up his bed with the square corners he will be using all season. Indicate where the latrine and washrooms are and invite him to take a shower if he wants one. Keep up a friendly informal conversation, designed to involve everyone.

Most camps request that all campers' medicines and first aid equipment be collected and turned over to the nurse or doctor, for it is advisable to have anyone needing medical attention, no matter how minor, referred to the professional person in charge. Unless specifically directed otherwise, you, the counselor, should not give any kind of medical treatment, except first aid in a real emergency. Collect return trip tickets, money, and other valuables to store at the camp office or other designated place.

All campers usually check in with the doctor or nurse soon after their arrival and then meet with the waterfront staff to be classified according to ability and to receive a preliminary briefing about swimming procedures and the use of boats and canoes. Be sure to have your group report at the proper place and time during this unusually busy period for the waterfront staff.

A veteran camper placed in a cabin unit with neophytes can become a problem to them, himself, and his counselor. If aggressive, he may become bossy or dictatorial and try to take over running your cabin for you, or he may try to play practical jokes on the newcomers. This "showing off" is an attempt to get attention and cover up his underlying feelings of insecurity and his failure to gain what he considers rightful recognition. Satisfy his needs through useful channels by asking him to assume certain responsibilities, such as helping newcomers to unpack and get settled, showing them around the camp, preparing and passing out name tags, or running errands. Use discretion here, for delegating too much responsibility can make some individuals insufferably conceited, while others will feel like failures, if the responsibilities given are more than they can handle. Keep yourself tactfully but firmly in the "driver's seat" and in full control of the situation, welcoming and using as much help as the returning camper can capably give.

When a child's parents have not brought him to camp, he should write a card to go out in the first mail, telling of his safe arrival. As a friendly gesture on your part, write them a short, friendly note within a day or two to establish a friendly rapport and to assure them that their precious possession is in the hands of someone who is really interested in him and concerned with his welfare.

As the occasion presents itself during the day, bring out some of the main points of camp life, such as mail call and basic camp rules, and discuss with your campers their importance to the general welfare of the camp family. Campers don't resent reasonable rules if they understand the "why" of them, so approach the subject from that angle. Ask them to figure out the reasons for the rules; you'll be surprised at how well they do. It isn't hard for Tommy to see that if he doesn't wash his share of the dishes, someone else will have to work overtime; that if he doesn't bring his canoe back on time, another who is waiting will be cheated; or that he will be too tired to enjoy the cookout planned for tomorrow if he "raises Cain" all night instead of sleeping. If possible, let youngsters help to formulate some of the rules which will affect them; this will help to give them a sense of responsibility for and participation in the camp community. Since the word "rules" often carries a negative connotation and may arouse antagonism and resentment in some, you may want to give them a more innocuous name, such as "Guidelines," "Camp Robin Hood Customs," or "Ways we do things in Chipmunk Unit." Don't try to tell your campers everything at once, however; present what is most important first and save details for later.

DEVELOPING GROUP UNITY AND FEELINGS OF ACCEPTANCE

As soon as most of your campers are settled in and seem ready, proceed with some activities you have planned to break the ice and get them on easy terms with one another. This may be a good time to play some sure-fire "fun"

Figure 5–7 Play Some "Fun" Games.

games or to take them on a tour of the camp, pointing out such points of interest as the dining room, arts and crafts building, general lodge, and waterfront. You may want to pair them off, using the "buddy" system in which each camper stays close by his buddy for a designated period; this establishes a more than casual relationship with at least one other person.

When it seems appropriate, launch into a brief, informal group discussion, suggesting exciting adventures they may want to plan for the near future or long-term projects to think about now and decide on at a later date. Notice we said *group* discussion, which means encouraging each and every one to contribute. Try to generate enthusiasm and paint word pictures which will leave each starry-eyed and dreaming of the many happy times to come. This will help to keep their minds occupied, crowding out feelings of homesickness and loneliness which are particularly likely to appear as night draws near. Work hard at this, for it will also give you a chance to establish yourself as a forceful, understanding leader who is as anxious as they to fill each day with excitement and fun. Keep your initial long-term plans flexible so that they can be altered as the group gets acquainted and becomes more aware of the possibilities of the camp, but make detailed and definite plans for the immediate future instead of waiting for chance inspiration.

Before the first meal, discuss dining room procedures and give them an idea of what to expect. Later on, as the need arises, you can delve more deeply into dining room conduct and table manners, stressing such points as sitting up straight, keeping elbows off the table, passing food properly, chewing with mouth closed and conversing *quietly;* be observant so you will know which children are most in need of this instruction. Stress the importance of cleanliness and being well groomed at all times, especially when in the dining room. Ask returning campers to volunteer to wait on tables and carry out other duties until newcomers have had a chance to observe operations and become familiar with procedures.

THE FIRST NIGHT

Some camps have an all-camp council ring or other all-camp meeting on the first night to give everyone a chance to see the whole group and have the entire staff introduced to them. At this time, the staff may put on a skit or other entertainment to introduce themselves in a more informal way. Other camps prefer to arrange for unit or cabin programs, believing that a camper should become well acquainted with his own small group before tackling the large one.

The time just before taps is a critical one, and that is when new campers need a little extra attention from you. Arrange for an early bedtime, for most of the group will be more tired than they realize from the day's emotional strain and excitement; it may be desirable to have them brush their teeth, wash their faces, don their pajamas, and perform other bedtime rituals before dark. Personally check to see that each performs these chores adequately, and that he is properly clad for the weather conditions. Leave some time for a short evening program of discussion or a good bedtime story in the coziness of the cabin before you accompany them on a last trip to the latrine. Explain the procedure for morning rising and breakfast, and stress that taps is the signal for complete silence, with everyone in bed ready to go to sleep promptly, so they can arise rested and fresh for a day of fun tomorrow. You may want to tuck younger children in and give them a reassuring goodnight pat. Take a little extra time this first night to show each of your campers that you are interested in him as an individual and to assure him that you will be nearby where he can call you if he needs to go to the latrine or becomes *really* frightened. Remember that urban children may have never heard an owl before, and even the small rustlings of wild things out hunting their suppers, a tree creaking in the wind, or a twig falling on the cabin roof may be quite alarming in the unaccustomed stillness of an outdoor environment. Young children in camp for the first time are often encouraged to bring a precious, familiar toy or possession with them to give them a feeling of security at this crucial time.

Figure 5-9 Her Security Blanket.

Figure 5-8 Misery Is an Outdoor John.

THOSE IMPORTANT FIRST DAYS

Set a shining example from the start, for your charges will model their behavior on yours. Be the first out of bed in the morning to check on the weather, and advise campers how to dress accordingly; greet your sleepyheads with a friendly "hello" and a smile as they arise, and, instead of dwelling on inconsequential irritations, keep yourself in a positive frame of mind by reminding yourself and your group of how fortunate you are to be spending this time in God's wonderful outdoor setting. Maintain an outward optimism, even though it hurts sometimes, and try to see the funny side of things; joking and good-natured banter can help to start the day on a cheerful note. Perform the morning routines of washing, brushing teeth, and combing hair with dispatch. Campers and counselors who have gone to bed on time find it much easier to be cheerful and alert; if you find yourself with the disposition of a bear and a bit on the droopy-eyed side, you need to decide whether those late evening hours are really worth it.

Campers like to have you join them in their morning routines, and this makes it easy for you to see that each practices proper habits of cleanliness and good grooming. Encourage those who awaken early to read or write letters, so that they will not disturb others.

Homesickness is particularly likely to occur during the first few days of camp, and one of the best ways to forestall it is to get individuals deeply involved in things that absorb them. Constantly plan exciting adventures for the future so that there is always something to look forward to. If you spend some extra time with them during the first few days and work hard to achieve the spirit of friendly camaraderie and cooperation you want, it will be easier to maintain this spirit throughout the summer.

Seize every available opportunity for informal chats, for there is no better way to get to know your campers and to find out why they came to camp, what their hobbies and interests are, and what they have looked forward to experiencing in camp. Listen attentively to campers' chatter, for, being wholly unplanned and uninhibited, it provides real insight into their current hopes, plans, interests, capacities, and ambitions. Initiate conversations with your campers, individually and in groups, so that you feel at ease with each other; make a special effort to include "loners" and "misfits." These conversations will also give you an opportunity to spot any camper who shows a tendency to stir up trouble or dissension within the group.

Don't try to tell your campers everything about camp customs at once, but gradually introduce them to such things as camp *kapers* (camper duties). Work out a rotation system for keeping cabins and unit quarters neat and clean, as well as for each to contribute his share to the upkeep of the whole camp. Present information as the need for it arises; ears are much keener and minds more receptive when an individual sees that what is being presented can be put to use right away. As the days pass, appropriate occasions will arise to inform your group about such matters as camp traditions, programs, special events, camp government and how it works, waterfront procedures, fire drills, safety and health practices, and sick call.

Each unit or cabin should have its own bulletin board for posting timely material such as schedules, notices, "A Thought for the Day," and poems written by campers. A committee may supervise it, planning what is to appear, taking down "dead" material, changing it frequently and seeing that it is arranged attractively.

One of the first things campers will want to do is to make their living quarters comfortable and attractive. By all means let them help with planning what is to be done, for the work then becomes more interesting to them and keeps them happily occupied. This is usually such a worthwhile project that

	Mary	**Helen**	**Jean**	**Sarah**	**Peggy**	**Joan**	**Ruth**
Clean-up squad—sweep cabin floor	Su	M	Tu	W	Th	F	S
Woodsmen—clean out ashes in fireplace, bring in wood	M	T	W	Th	F	S	Su
Table setters—set tables and help prepare vegetables	Tu	W	Th	F	S	Su	M
Hoppers—wait on and clear tables	W	Th	F	S	Su	M	Tu
Ground keepers—clean up campsite	Th	F	S	Su	M	Tu	W
Kitchen police—help do dishes	F	S	Su	M	Tu	W	Th
Unit duty—help at the Unit house	S	Su	M	Tu	W	Th	F

Figure 5–10 A Typical Kapers Chart.

some camps strip the cabins quite bare and tear down all the things the departing campers have built in order to give the incoming campers the thrill of planning their own cabin furnishings, decorations, and other camp "fixings," such as crate tables and chairs, lashed wooden clothes pegs and rustic clothes hangers, wall plaques and other objects. The campers can also devote their energies to "sprucing up" the unit grounds. Safety may call for removing such hazards as glass, pieces of metal, and protruding tree roots. Gaily painted stones make a decorative border for paths, and many other "improvements" will suggest themselves once the campers get started.

Before long, your group will probably want to plan a menu and program for a cookout and, if you casually steer them toward a good spot you have previously located, they will soon see its possibilities as a perfect place for a unit outpost camp. These projects, interspersed with their other camp activities, will happily solve your program problems for some time to come.

CAMP HOUSEKEEPING

IN GENERAL

Since many campers have learned virtually nothing of good housekeeping practices at home, you may need to demonstrate and give specific help with techniques. Right after breakfast is a good time for the whole group to straighten up the cabin and adjacent unit area; they may also be expected to help out in cleaning up the entire camp. Make a check list for each job so that the camper will know how to proceed. Your attitude toward camp duties is important, for if you pitch in enthusiastically, your campers will follow suit and will soon learn the satisfaction of work well done and the pleasure of living in clean, orderly surroundings. Try to be especially happy and cheerful as you go about your tasks and see how time flies when everyone joins in singing old favorites or learning a new song. Discourage bickering and grumbling by substituting banter and lighthearted chatter.

(Courtesy of Detroit Area Council, Camp Fire Girls, Inc., Connie Coutellier.)

On rainy mornings, make up beds promptly to keep out the dampness, and on sunny days, hang out sheets and blankets to air, bringing them in before five o'clock to avoid evening dampness. Air and turn mattresses and put on fresh linen each week, making up beds with square corners.

Each person should hang up his clothing or fold it neatly and put it away, tidy his personal effects, and collect his soiled clothing in a bag, ready to send to the laundry. Remind your campers that prompt repair can keep a small tear from becoming a big hole, and that a button sewed on now may prevent later embarrassment or inconvenience.

Most camps have tent or cabin inspection at least once a day, usually unannounced and at varying times, in order to encourage habitual orderliness rather than a periodic tidying up for an inspection. A cabin or unit which has met high standards should be recognized by awarding it some trifle, such as a brightly colored cardboard broom or mop, to display all day. Group pressure will soon bring backsliders into line so that the group can qualify for the award.

Toilet articles and towels should never be borrowed, and other borrowing is discouraged and is permissible only with the express permission of the owner; when done without permission, "borrowing" isn't the correct name for such practices.

In many camps, campers help with various chores, sometimes in an effort to reduce expenses and thus make it easier financially for them to attend camp, and always to create in them an appreciation of the dignity and respectability of good, honest work. Such duties may include keeping unit showers, latrines, cabins, unit houses, and the main lodge in order, collecting and disposing of trash, helping to prepare vegetables and fruit, setting and waiting on tables, and washing dishes. Counselors should pitch in when their group is on duty, to lend a hand and to see that the work is done properly. Cooperate in devising ways to complete the job more quickly and efficiently and discourage tendencies to dawdle.

Paint trash cans in bright colors and place them conveniently about the camp site, so that no one can plead failure to see them as an excuse for cluttering up the grounds. Point out how thoughtless it is to throw trash on the ground today where you or a camper serving as grounds keeper must pick it up tomorrow.

Let campers help you to work out some equitable way to share camp duties. You may work out a rotating kapers (duties) chart such as the one shown in Figure 5-10, or place slips with the names of duties or symbols for them (such as a fork for dishwashing or a broom for cleaning the cabin) in a hat and let each camper draw one out, or conceal them under the campers' plates at the table.

DISHWASHING

After meals, some groups may be assigned certain duties such as washing dishes and cleaning up the dining room. These responsibilities are usually rotated among groups, or each table is held responsible for taking care of its own things. Some camps hire special staff members for these jobs and provide such equipment as electric dishwashers, but even though your camp has these aids, everyone needs to know proper methods of dishwashing by hand, for you certainly can't take an electric dishwasher on a cookout or camp trip, and even in the most luxurious home the dishwasher breaks down, the electricity goes off, or the maid takes her day off. Dishwashing and cleanup shouldn't and needn't be

(Courtesy of Dogwood Trails Girl Scout Council, Springfield, Missouri.)

dreaded chores; instead, they often become scenes of busy, happy groups, enjoying themselves in a common task, with joking, singing, and storytelling to leaven the atmosphere, resulting in a thoroughly enjoyable experience.

You cannot assume that everyone will already know how to wash dishes, for many modern homes are now equipped with dishwashers, poor practices are followed, or children are not allowed to help with such tasks. Therefore, you will need to explain the process favored at your camp and review it several times. Again you will of course be there, cheerfully helping as you check to see that the work is proceeding as it should. You probably will have learned your camp's procedures during pre-camp training; you may have received written instructions or found them posted conveniently near the dishwashing area.

Dishwashing on Cookouts

On a cookout, one counselor, with camper help, should see that water is heating, ready for use as soon as the meal is over. Start washing immediately, for food comes off more easily before it has been allowed to dry. A counselor should always handle hot water when young campers are involved, for they could scald themselves or someone nearby.

Use hot, soapy water and wash in the following order: glassware, silver, dishes, and, finally, pots and pans. Keep enough water heating to replace the dishwater as it gets greasy or cold. Thorough washing and rinsing greatly decrease the number of bacteria on dishes, so, after the wash and rinse, sanitize them by one of the following methods:

1. Place them in a long-handled basket or net bag and immerse them in

enough water at 170° F. or hotter to cover them. Leave them for at least 30 seconds, or longer if possible; merely pouring boiling water over them is definitely not sufficient.

2. Use a good chemical sanitizer, following the directions which come with it. After sanitizing, remove the dishes from the hot solution with sterilized forceps, arrange them on a drying rack, cover them with clean cloths, and leave them to air dry. This is more sanitary than drying them with towels, for each swipe of the towel adds more bacteria to be deposited on all dishes dried subsequently. The less you handle dishes, the more sanitary they remain; however, you should towel dry silverware and pots and pans which might rust.

Dishwashing Kapers

1. *First scraper*—uses rubber scraper to remove food from dishes and places utensils which have held eggs, or starchy or sticky foods in cold water to soak.

2. *Polisher*—supplements efforts of first scraper, using paper napkins. If facilities are available, he rinses the dishes and stacks them into piles.

3. *Dishwasher*—washes dishes in clean water and a detergent.

4. *Rinser*—arranges washed dishes in the long-handled wire dishdrainers or net bags, ready for sterilization.

5. *Sterilizer* (always a counselor)—lowers the containers of dishes into the sanitizing agent and removes them at the prescribed time.

6. *Dish dryer and storer*—removes dishes and arranges them on the drying racks, covering them with clean cloths and leaving them to air dry. (When on a trip, you can place them in net bags to lower into the hot sterilizer and hang the bags on a convenient limb or bush to dry.) Wash out the used dishcloths and towels in hot, soapy water and hang them out to dry, away from dust and other sources of contamination.

7. *Handyman or cleanup man*—cleans the tables and the area around them after the dishes have been covered or put away. Cleans dishpans, sinks and work surfaces.

Keep a close eye on your campers to make sure that the dishes are really clean and sanitary.

ADDITIONAL READINGS

(See bibliography at the end of Chapter 6.)

Chapter 6

Figure 6–1 You Might Even Have To Do This.

The Counselor on the Job (Part II)

Do not stop with doing necessary kindnesses;
The unnecessary ones are of far greater importance.

—AUTHOR UNKNOWN

The liar's punishment is not that he is not believed, but that he cannot believe anyone else.

—GEORGE BERNARD SHAW

OTHER CAMP ROUTINES

CLEANLINESS

Being at camp is no excuse for disregarding personal cleanliness, for various skin disturbances and infections can be traced directly to unhygienic practices. A swim is no substitute for a daily or at least thrice-weekly warm soap bath, which can be taken from a wash pan if no other facilities are available. Hair should be washed at least every week, with counselor help if necessary. See that campers use fresh towels and washcloths as needed and, of course, that they never use anyone else's, and hang towels and washcloths out to air and dry after use. Casually inspect each camper daily for cleanliness, scanning particularly the ears, elbows, and neck, and inconspicuously call any deficiencies to his attention. Never assume that, because you tell a youngster to wash and clean up, he will do so.

Impress upon your campers the importance of washing hands before eating and after going to the toilet and see that they brush their teeth each morning and again before retiring. Urge boys and girls with long fingernails or toenails to clip them, for they are inappropriate for camp life.

See that each camper puts on fresh clothing (including underwear) each day and collects his soiled garments in the proper place. Often a youngster is inclined to stuff his wet clothing or swimsuit in a corner, under his bed, or in his suitcase or laundry bag in his rush to get on to something more exciting, so be sure that he hangs them out to dry, pointing out that storing wet clothing causes mildew which can permanently damage clothing. Make sure, too, that your campers rotate wearing the clothing they have brought, for a

Figure 6–2 A Long, Dry Summer.

DO-IT-YOURSELF LAUNDERING

Although machine washing is preferable, it is economical and not at all difficult to wash clothes by hand, and it usually becomes a necessity on a camping trip. Be sure to turn pockets inside out to see that nothing has been left in them, then soak the clothes for 30 minutes in a bucketful of hot, soapy water, and then douse them up and down several times or, better still, use a rubber plunger on them. Scrub especially soiled parts with a brush and extra soap. Rinse them thoroughly and hang them out to dry on your camp rope suspended between two trees or on bushes or branches. If you are in a hurry for them to dry, wring them out as completely as possible and turn them over every half hour or so. Be sure to check the label inside synthetic garments for washing instructions.

youngster often has a few choice garments he puts on day after day, never even completely unpacking all the things his parents sent.

If campers send their laundry out to be done, see that each places his in an appropriate bag, lists the items, and deposits them at the appointed place on time. Each item must be marked with his name.

Cabins, units, or whole camps often enjoy a special cleanup day when everyone washes his clothes, helps to spruce up the cabin and grounds, and then finishes with a shampoo and hot bath for himself. These cleanup days can help in developing a spirit of fun and camaraderie, as each camper learns to be self-sufficient while lending a helping hand to others. You should be there, helping with and enjoying it too, as you display an appreciation of the importance of personal and camp cleanliness and experience the self-respect which comes from taking care of your own personal needs.

DRESSING THE PART

A wholesome, well-groomed counselor usually sets the example for his campers. If you wear dirty clothes or fail to stow your extras away neatly, what can you expect from them? Like you, they should wear clothing appropriate for the weather and the activity; since mornings and evenings are usually cool, extra clothing will be needed then. Bring to their attention the importance that star athletes place on wearing sweat shirts or jackets in cool weather or after participating in strenuous activity, since they know that it is one of the best ways to prevent colds and stiff muscles and hence to keep themselves in top condition, ready to come through with their best performance.

A camper should wear shoes at all times, and he should be completely "waterproofed" when venturing out on rainy days. Point out that he will be the loser if he neglects this, for he may step

Figure 6–3 Happiness Is Running Through the Grass with Bare Feet? Sorry, That's a No-No!

on some sharp object and get an infection or develop a cold which may keep him in bed and away from all the fun others are having. Older campers, in particular, tend to dress improperly for the weather or the occasion in an attempt to demonstrate how rough and tough they are. This offers you an opportunity to point out the difference between mollycoddling themselves and being foolhardy.

Keep an eye out for a camper whose big toe is peeking out of his undarned sock or whose shorts are threatening to do a strip tease act because of missing buttons; he may not have even an inkling as to which end of a needle the thread goes through, and you will have to show him. One of the greatest benefits of camp may be to show campers how pleasant it is to live among neat, clean people in spick-and-span, though rough and rustic, surroundings. They will realize, too, that utter chaos will result, with so many living in such close quarters, if each just lets things drop where they are when through with them. The subject of an early group discussion might be how to best utilize facilities, with each possession having a "home base" so no time is wasted in looking for it.

Trading or selling personal possessions is taboo, for parents will not be overjoyed when little Babette returns with a perfectly "delightful" pair of ragged cut-off jeans instead of the plush new "wake-to-music" radio they started her off with. Some camps, particularly day camps, solve this problem by sponsoring special trading days when children, *with the permission of their parents,* bring things they have grown tired of, such as old toys, books, or records, to exchange for similar unwanted things offered by others.

HEALTH

CHANGING ATTITUDES

You must work closely with the health staff in protecting and maintaining the health of your charges, for your proximity to them places you in a particularly advantageous position to note many things of vital importance. What camping objective could be more important than keeping campers in the best of health?

Camps and parents once considered a set of scales the best yardstick for measuring the health benefits of camp, for they assumed that a gain in weight clearly indicated a corresponding gain in health. We now know how foolish this belief was, for unless a youngster is underweight, any weight gain beyond what is normal for his age and build may create serious physical or psychological problems. Unless he is one of those extremely rare individuals with a physical defect causing his abnormal weight gain, it indicates merely a super-abundance of sweets and carbohydrates.

Another far too prevalent idea was that, in order to look like a *real* camper, he must appear as weather-beaten, sunburned, and flea-bitten as possible. Furthermore, he must not deign to notice such minor details as scratches, blisters, and mosquito bites. Such scars of battle were considered medals of honor since they showed that he had been "roughing it" and could "take it." Modern camps would consider it a disgrace to turn out such a representative, for they pride themselves on their elaborate provisions to insure optimum health benefits for all.

During precamp training, you will have become familiar with the health facilities of your particular camp. Most camps have one or more nurses on duty and a physician in residence or on call. These health officials have their headquarters in an infirmary with ample space for those indisposed or in need of special food, rest, or individual care. Since children are imaginative, the facility is often called the Health Lodge or Nightingale Cottage, instead of the hospital or infirmary.

DAILY CARE

Each morning, while campers are dressing, eating breakfast, or doing cabin cleanup, scan them for signs of illness or injury and note any symptoms, such as headache, sore throat, indigestion, sneezing, cough, fever (as indicated by hot, flushed skin), pimples, skin rashes, weight loss, paleness, swelling, cuts or other irritations, and any signs of fatigue, such as listlessness, irritability, excitable talking, or undue noisiness. If you suspect a child is injured or ill, take him to the nurse immediately, escorting him there if necessary, for a camper sometimes avoids the Health Lodge, fearing that he will be banned from swimming or another favorite activity. Show him the wisdom of taking a few moments now to prevent the development of an illness which could curtail his activities for days or even weeks. Some camps require counselors to turn in health reports each morning, so that the nurse can note and call in any camper needing further attention.

When signs of fatigue are widespread in a group, it indicates an overstrenuous program, and a light schedule is advisable for a few days, with extra time provided for rest and sleep. Prevent fatigue by alternating quiet and active pursuits, seeing that competition is not carried to the point of overstimulation, and insisting on strict observation of hours for rest and sleep.

Although it is true that a swim can be invigorating for one who is tired, you must use discretion, since it can be the last straw for one who is really exhausted. Campers should not go in the water immediately after eating and should wear shoes and robes of some sort both to and from the swimming area and not loiter about in wet suits.

If you are in tick-infested country, everyone, including yourself, should be inspected twice a day. The U.S. Public

Figure 6-4 Where Are Your Shoes?

Health Service has stated that there is little chance of being infected with Rocky Mountain spotted fever if infected ticks are removed within four to six hours. Don't try to pull them loose or crush them with your fingers, for the head may remain embedded and may cause a serious infection. If you cannot take the victim to the nurse, touch a lighted match to the insect, screw it out counterclockwise with tweezers, or cover it with butter or grease to smother it.

SUNBURN

Sunburn can be a serious as well as painful condition, for researchers now feel that there may be a causal relationship between repeated overexposure to the sun and the later development of skin cancer. If you want to acquire a deep tan, you must do so gradually, for if you try to hurry it too much, you will defeat your own purpose by acquiring a painful sunburn which eventually peels off, leaving you to start all over again. Begin with a maximum of 15 minutes of exposure the first day and increase it by 15 minutes on each succeeding day. Apply a good suntan lotion and replenish it occasionally, since the protective coating wears off after a time. When going out for long periods, as on a canoe trip or hike, wear long shirt sleeves, long trousers and a wide-brimmed hat to prevent overexposure, and provide yourself with sunglasses which adequately protect your eyes. When sunbathing, cover your face, particularly your eyes, with a towel.

THE HEALTH LODGE

When a camper has been injured or shows symptoms of illness, *take,* don't *send,* him to the Health Lodge or get another responsible person to accompany him. If he's feeling bad, he particularly needs the assurance of your personal interest at this time, and

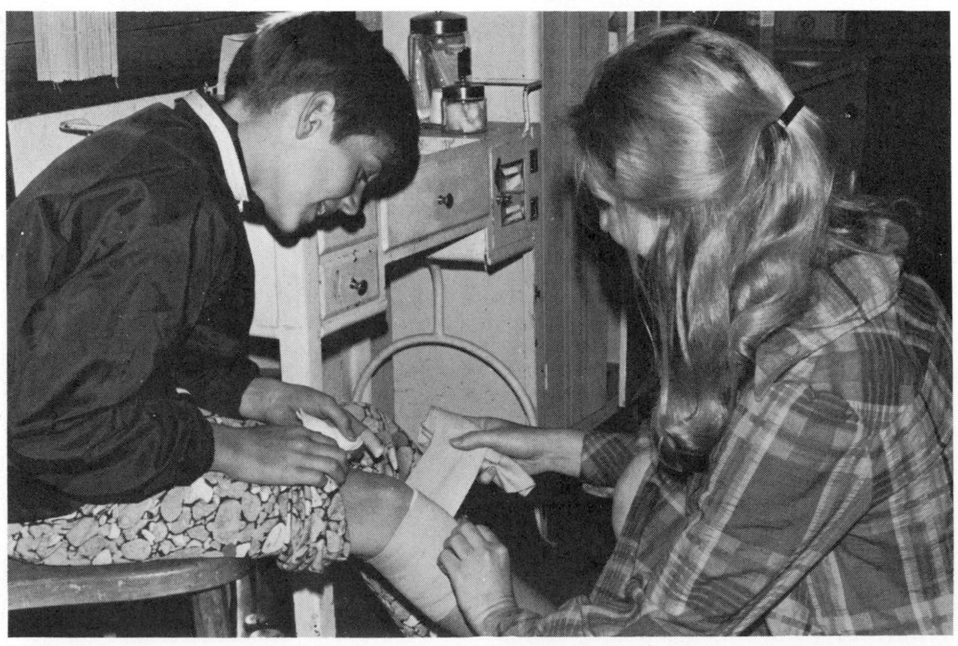

(Courtesy of Cheley Colorado Camps, Estes Park, Colorado.)

by making sure he goes to the Health Lodge, you express this interest while insuring his receiving prompt treatment, which may later prove of great importance. If he is detained overnight, see that he has the proper clothing, toilet articles, and means to entertain himself if he is well enough to want some amusement.

Most camps send a camper home or to the hospital if his illness is likely to last more than a few days or is of a serious nature. However, minor illnesses may detain him at the Health Lodge for what may seem like wearisome hours or even days. If those in charge approve, it makes the time pass faster if his friends send a small token of remembrance, such as a round-robin letter, an informal diary of what they are doing, an original poem, a small arts and crafts gift with his name on it, or give him a personal serenade from outside. A visit is welcome if the nurse permits; if not, just waving to him through the window helps. With the approval of the nurse, keep him supplied with puzzles, a radio, light reading matter, or tell or read him a story; something to occupy his hands and mind, such as a crafts project, his scrapbook, making favors for a group party or labels for the nature trail his group is constructing, also helps. The particular amusements you provide are not important as long as the camper knows that you and his friends miss him and are thinking of him.

When he has been released, make sure that the instructions of the doctor or nurse are followed. He may be likely to "overdo it" in trying to make up for lost time, so you must insist that he maintain a proper balance of rest and exercise for a few days to prevent a possible relapse.

SAFETY

Your camp has probably established rules and guidelines regarding safety, which you will need to interpret to your campers, and, most important of all, you will also need to develop in them a proper attitude toward the whole area of safety and safe procedures. Camp safety standards are based upon long years of experience as reflected in state and federal laws and in the recommendations of such authoritative bodies as the American Camping Association and the American Red Cross. This again gives you an opportunity to demonstrate your ability as a leader, for if you invariably respect and observe good practices yourself, you will elicit a like response from campers.

Safety doesn't end with merely obeying established mandates, however, but also involves developing a proper state of mind, so that you recognize potential hazards, such as bits of broken glass, tin cans with sharp edges, or a board with protruding nails, and are willing to pick them up and dispose of them properly.

Your campers, likewise, might show their awareness of good safety practices by spotting such hazards as a jagged stump near the path to the latrine which, for the protection of sleepy nighttime travelers, needs to be removed or tagged with a bit of phosphorescent paint or tape. Some low overhanging branches may need to be trimmed from a path, or the whole group may set aside an hour to pick up debris around the swimming area. Know where the fire extinguishers are and how to use them and conduct fire drills and fire prevention discussions with your group. Keep a careful eye on youngsters using knives, axes, or other possibly dangerous equipment, and see that each carries and uses his own flashlight at night. When you are about to lead your group in an unfamiliar experience, try to anticipate any possible hazards and brief your campers as to what could happen and necessary precautions to take. Follow up by preventing needless risk-taking and correcting faulty techniques, and, if the welfare or safety of anyone is imperiled, be very firm and insist on immediate response to your directions. Of course, adventure and a certain amount of daring and trying the unknown are desirable adjuncts of the camping experience, and you must not err on the side of caution. As with many other camp problems, a group discussion may enable your campers to work out very creditable standards which they'll more willingly follow since they weren't imposed by someone else.

DINING ROOM PROCEDURES

ASSEMBLING IN THE DINING ROOM

Counselors and campers should arrive on time for meals, with hair combed and hands and faces washed. Those arriving early often enjoy singing while waiting to enter the dining room, and some camps have developed a tradition of assembling early to sing or carry on some other interesting activity to solve the problem of latecomers who straggle into the dining room.

Many different plans exist for seating in the dining area; in some cases, each camper and counselor simply walks in and sits at his previously assigned place, or a counselor will lead his assigned group to their table. The group may be his regular living unit, or a rotating system may be used to enable each individual to widen his circle of acquaintances. A less formal procedure consists of having campers enter the dining room first and fill in camper places at tables as they choose; the counselors then follow and seat themselves at tables, making it a point to choose a different one each meal. All these methods avoid the melee which often occurs when counselors enter first, followed by the campers who often engage in a mad scramble to secure seats with the most popular counselors.

MEAL TIME PROCEDURES

Counselors customarily occupy the places at the foot and head of a table, where they can act as hosts, serving the food, seeing that refills are provided as needed, giving second servings as requested, signaling for the tables to be cleared, and so forth. Campers stand quietly behind their benches or chairs until the counselors are seated, then the meal is opened with a grace, either sung, said in unison or by some individual, or observed silently. With younger campers it is better to serve plates family style, since heavy or hot platters often cause accidents when passed around. When possible, left-handers should be seated on the left where their eating movements will be unhampered.

Camps usually make it a point to serve tasty, well-cooked, and nutritious meals which often have been carefully planned by a trained dietitian. These efforts will be wasted, however, if campers are allowed to pick and choose what they eat. Although you must make allowances for food allergies or stipulated special diets, do not accept a camper's word about these, since he may be using them as an excuse to avoid eating foods he doesn't care for. Consult the health staff about problems in this respect, and report a child who is absent from a meal to the proper person. You can allow an individual to ask for only a small portion if he really dislikes the item, but insist that he eat at least this much of it, for in this way he often learns to like something he has never tasted before or refuses in imitation of an admired older person who has made disparaging remarks about it. Serve small portions, especially to younger campers, encouraging them to clean up their plates before asking for seconds, instead of starting off with large quantities, much of which will go to waste. You can often invent games and otherwise use your ingenuity to encourage finicky or troublesome eaters by such tactics as forming a "Jack Spratt Club," open only to those who clean up their plates. You are doing campers a real favor when you teach them to broaden their tastes and learn to eat a wide variety of foods. Seconds and even thirds are usually available for those who want them, but only after others, particularly slow eaters, have had their fair share. This encourages good table manners, since there is no incentive to gulp down food like uncivilized animals.

A crowd of girls usually includes a few "reducers," for, as Franklin P. Jones has said, "Women are never satisfied. They are trying either to put on weight, take it off, or rearrange it." Encourage overweight campers, either boys or girls, to cut down *sensibly* on their intake of fattening foods; most reducers, however, should be discouraged in their attempts, for camp life is so strenuous that large quantities of energy-yielding foods are needed. Some camps maintain special diet tables for those with idiosyncrasies or those who need to gain or lose weight. In planning cookouts, it is easy to introduce good dietetic practices and to explain the necessity of maintaining a varied and well-balanced diet. When youngsters understand the importance of each item, they usually become quite cooperative about their eating.

DINING ROOM ATMOSPHERE

The dining room atmosphere should be one of leisurely relaxation, with quiet, though sprightly, conversation. As host, you can set the pace for your table by keeping your voice well modulated and by trying to introduce topics of general interest instead of letting a few monopolize the conversation. These conversations can provide good social training, as each learns to respect the right of the person speaking to finish what he is saying before adding his own comments. Keep your voice low as an example, for when a few individuals or a whole table becomes boisterous, others must raise their voices in order to be heard at all, and soon the whole dining room is in a rising crescendo which is most unpleasant to hear. You may want to inconspicuously seat a shy or unpopular child next to you during his first few meals to draw him out and give him self-confidence.

Everyone waits to eat until all are served and the host has taken his first bite. Talking to those at another table is always in poor taste; if you *must* communicate, ask to be excused and go over and speak to him quietly. No one but "hoppers" leaves the table until all are ready to go; in case of emergency, campers should ask the host to be excused.

Camps have different ways of calling for silence when an announcement is to be made. Some have a pleasant chime, which is certainly better than banging loudly on glasses or the table; another method which proves quite successful is for the person wanting attention to merely raise his hand; then each in turn raises his own hand and shuts his mouth as soon as he sees the signal, and in almost no time at all the whole group is ready to listen. Be sure you aren't the counselor who raises his hand for silence while continuing to chatter away at 50 words a second.

GOOD TABLE MANNERS

Observe all the precepts of good table manners, reminding campers not to toy with their utensils while waiting until all are served and ready to eat, not to talk when the mouth is full, to break

Figure 6–5 Good Table Manners Are Always Observed?

bread slices into quarters and butter only one portion at a time, to cut meat a piece at a time as it is eaten, to handle knife and fork properly, to chew food with the mouth closed, and the like. Unfavorable comments about the food and griping or bickering of any sort create an unpleasant atmosphere and are strictly taboo. Do not make a public scene when a camper has violated good etiquette. It is usually better to discuss it with him privately, since such lapses are more likely to be due to his lack of training in the past, being ill at ease, or a desire for attention, rather than willful misbehavior; in addition, consideration must be given to differences in children's cultural backgrounds.

AFTER EATING

Each camp usually has a definite system for clearing tables: serving dishes are usually removed first, then when all have finished eating, campers pass their dishes to the counselor at the head of the table, who scrapes them, stacks them neatly, and signals his "hopper" to clear them from the table. Most camps forbid taking anything edible from the dining hall except on certain occasions when specific permission is given.

Singing songs, especially those requiring movements, distracts slow eaters and interferes with clearing tables, washing dishes, and putting food away. It also detracts from the quality of the singing, since some are still trying to eat and those singing tend to stress loudness instead of harmony and sweetness in an attempt to be heard above the noise of scraping dishes and clearing tables. It is probably better to wait until tables are cleared and then engage in a songfest led by a designated song leader. Obviously, no activity should be scheduled too soon after the meal lest it cause campers to race to get through.

EATING BETWEEN MEALS

Camp meals are planned to include enough sweets to satisfy normal needs, and campers are consequently not encouraged to supplement them with between-meal soft drinks, candy, and other "goodies" which may offset the good effects of the carefully planned diet. When snacks are permitted at all, a limit is usually set on the daily amount and should be rigidly enforced.

Watch for the camper who tries to buy quantities of such contraband to bring back with him from a hiking trip or other expedition, and guard against the promiscuous picking and eating of such things as green apples or berries while on a trip. This is not only a question of health, but also one of ethics when done on non-camp property.

No matter what steps the camp takes, it seems that many parents must demonstrate their love by sending their children "goodies" from home. Some camps warn parents before camp that such food will be returned unless they want to send enough to substitute for a regular dessert for the whole cabin or table group; others simply save the individual packages until there are enough to make a treat for all. It is

Figure 6-6 Misery Is Having a Camper Catch You Eating the Candy You Took Away From Him!

sometimes effective to encourage parents to substitute fruit or small items, such as a piece of camping equipment, when they feel they must send something to show their affection.

Campers readily understand the reasons for not keeping or eating food around living quarters when you point out to them that ants, flies, mice, and other unwelcome "guests" will be attracted by the crumbs.

REST AND SLEEP

REST HOUR

As Sancho Panza said, "God bless the man who first invented sleep," and busy camp life makes campers and counselors thankful for the rest hour, which usually comes right after lunch in order to rejuvenate them for the remainder of the day. It is a siesta in which everyone either sleeps or engages in some quiet activity which is restful for him without interfering with others who may wish to sleep. These activities can include reading, writing letters, telling stories, playing quiet games or working on a craft project. Stay with your campers to see that they observe this period, and set an example by observing it properly yourself, for you need to recharge your own batteries. Your camp may choose an individ-

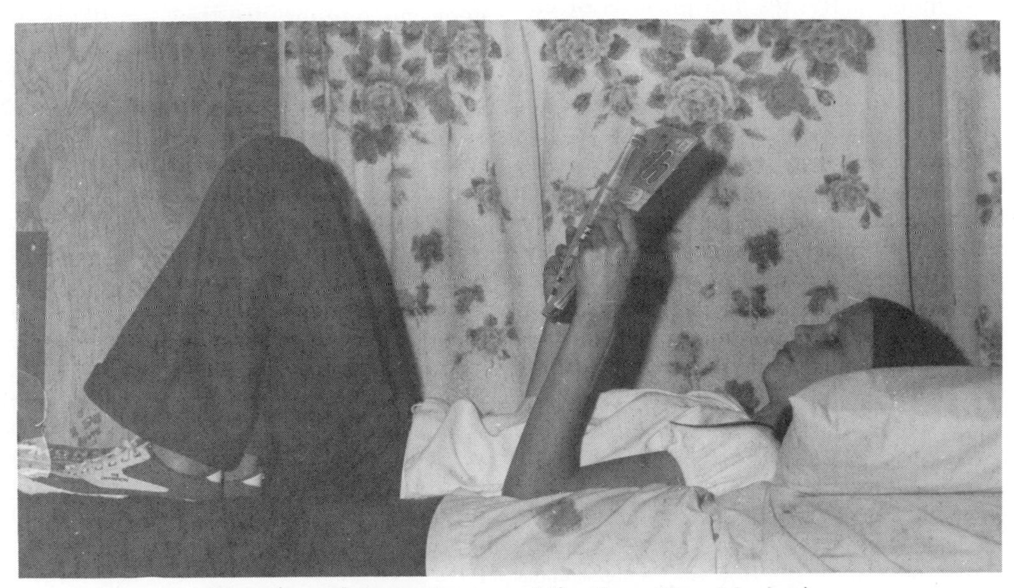

(Courtesy of Camp Summer Life, Taos, New Mexico.)

ual name for the rest hour, such as Siesta or FOB (Feet on Bed and Flat on Back).* The camp which firmly insists upon a proper rest hour is a happier, healthier camp.

SLEEP

Camp life is so strenuous that only those who get plenty of sleep can keep up and enjoy it to the fullest. Administering to this need constitutes one of your main responsibilities. The following amounts of sleep (in addition to the one-hour rest period) are recommended:

Ages	Hours of Sleep
6–8	11
9–11	10½
12–14	10
15–17	9
Staff	8

Children, like adults, differ in their reactions to the excitement and "busyness" of camp life, so some may need rest over and above this amount.

As previously mentioned, a common mistake has been to try to crowd too many activities and periods of excitement into the camp day. This is especially true as the last weeks of camp draw near and each counselor grows intent on squeezing some highlight of his particular activity into a last "roundup" of water carnivals, arts and crafts exhibits, horse shows, and whatnot. The wise camp tries to adopt the saner practice of spreading these special events over the entire summer, so that campers can leave camp rested and healthy instead of completely frazzled.

Children sleep better when healthily fatigued, but moderation is advisable, for too much excitement and tiredness cause fitful and restless sleep. A few individuals seem to run on sheer nerves, so watch for them and help them to organize and distribute their time, saving enough for rest and sleep.

*Smith, Billie F.: "How 40 Camps Handle Rest Hour." *Camping Magazine*, Dec., 1952.

BEDTIME

The period just before bedtime (taps) usually provides one of the best opportunities for building up group rapport. First come the routine procedures of washing, brushing teeth, and making the final trip to the latrine. Plan to have these taken care of in time to leave a few minutes for group activities, such as evening devotions, a discussion period, planning future activities, inactive games, a quiet bedtime story, stargazing, singing, or listening to soft music before "lights out." It is quite important to create the right atmosphere just before your campers go to sleep, for when youngsters engage in roughhousing, horseplay, exciting games, or telling ghost stories, you will have difficulty in getting them to quiet down and go to sleep. It is essential to have some well-planned activities, however, since otherwise they are likely to lie in bed thinking of home, their parents, or their pets until they have built up a real case of homesickness.

Take time to participate with them wholeheartedly instead of seeing how quickly you can hurry them into bed in order to squeeze out more time for yourself. Sit at the foot of a bed and chat with them until they are relaxed and ready for sleep, filled with pleasant thoughts of what they have just done and of what tomorrow holds in store. Before you leave the cabin, wander leisurely about with a special "goodnight" for those still awake and see that each is comfortably tucked in. Use blanket pins for very small tots who have a tendency to squirm about and so expose various odds and ends of their anatomy.

Taps is the signal for lights out and absolute quiet. Enforce it from the first night in camp, for allowing exceptions usually leads to a never-ending bombardment of requests for further favors.

Unit counselors usually take turns on night duty in the unit, so that some may get away for a little free time. When it is your turn to be on duty, stay there, for if you make a practice of leaving as soon as you think the campers are asleep, they'll "play possum" until you are gone and then bedlam will break loose. When on duty in the unit, you will probably be expected to stay in your counselor quarters, which are usually close by. Youngsters need assurance that you are near, ready to help if they become frightened or need you; this is especially important during a thunder and lightning storm. Youngsters should not get up again except for trips to the latrine, which should be quick and quiet, and there must be no disturbance of any kind until reveille. Night raids on other cabins and impromptu moonlight excursions are definitely prohibited.

STARTING THE DAY

The rising signal should sound long enough before breakfast to allow ample time for a last stretch, washroom procedures, and putting bedding outside or turning it down to air. When the rising signal sounds, you should be the first out of bed and should see that all arise promptly. This will probably not be a problem during the first few days of camp, for some campers will be so excited they'll wake at the crack of dawn and will need to be restrained so others can sleep. If your group is going out extra early for a bird walk, don't wake the whole camp as you go by.

You may need to help younger campers to manipulate buttons and hairbrushes, but encourage them to do

Figure 6–7 Be the First To *Spring* Out of Bed!

these things for themselves as soon as they can. A morning dip may be permitted, but it should certainly not be required, for many people react unfavorably to cold water and exercise so soon after rising. For the same reason, a compulsory exercise program before breakfast is frowned upon.

VISITORS' AND PARENTS' DAYS

POLICIES

Each camp has its own policies regarding visitors' and parents' days, based upon its own philosophy, the length of the session, the nature of the camp, camp activities, and the ages of the campers. Visitors are always a disturbance to the smooth-running routines of a camp and, for this reason, some short-term camps discourage or prohibit visitors, or plan to carry on their regular activities, so that interference is minimized and visitors get a better picture of regular camp happenings. Long-term camps of six to eight weeks sometimes set aside specified hours and days for visitation and encourage family and friends to come, in the belief that it boosts camper morale and satisfies natural parental concern about how little Charlotte really is and in what kind of environment she is spending her summer. Many camps plan special events for such occasions, such as horse shows, aquatic activities, campfire programs, and sightseeing tours around the camp grounds. If parents must travel a great distance, the camp sometimes sends them advance information about places nearby where they can stay overnight. Inviting parents to eat in the camp dining room or at an outdoor cookout helps to avoid the problem of parents who want to take their child out of camp to eat, a practice most camps disapprove of.

Some camps have several visiting days, so parents can choose the one they want to attend. This provides more flexibility and also avoids having too many visitors in camp at once. Children with no visitors need your attention, so that they will not feel left out. Keep them busy by using them as guides to escort parents to their child's living unit or to help to prepare for the coming program.

PREPARATIONS FOR VISITORS' DAY

Successful visiting days require careful planning and preparation of everything from the camp grounds down to Joe's elbows, which must be looking their best. Campers must be well-groomed and clean, ready to greet their guests and show off their camp and living quarters. You may need to explain to them some of the duties of a gracious host or hostess, such as introducing their guests to the camp administration, their counselors, and fellow campers and taking time to be pleasant to the guests of others. Encourage them to include friends without visitors in some of their activities, although they should reserve some time to be alone with their parents. Guests are usually requested not to bring extra food, for the reasons previously discussed, and also to avoid having campers consciously or unconsciously compare the "haul" each has made.

Figure 6-8 Scrub Those Elbows, Too!

THE GUESTS ARRIVE

Do not dread visiting day, for you will probably enjoy it thoroughly if you enter into it wholeheartedly. Meeting your campers' families lays the groundwork for better understanding on everyone's part. Since you have been serving as substitute parent, friend, and guide to each of your group, you will have at least one very important thing in common with parents—the welfare of their child. Step confidently into your role as host and be cordial and friendly to all and available for a short visit with each. Stay near your unit where they can find you, and be on your best behavior, courteous and considerate to all. Parents go home

Figure 6-9 Misery Is Meeting a Camper's Parents After She Has Told Them You Snore.

much happier and with a deepened sense of security when favorably impressed by their child's counselors. Be diplomatic in talking with them, remembering that the center of their attention is their pride and joy. Comment positively about any good points, achievements, or signs of improvement you have noticed, but be sincere and avoid "gushing," for most parents are fully aware that their children fall far short of being angels, and so will be quick to recognize insincerity. Never let yourself be drawn into long, involved discussions and never make unfavorable comments; if parents persist, refer them to the camp director or head counselor. Avoid being monopolized by a few, and share your time equally with all visitors. Closely adhere to the camp's policy regarding acceptance of tips and expensive gifts from parents.

As guests leave at the end of the day, you will often be faced with severe emotional reactions by campers, some of whom may even want to return home with their families. Plan exciting activities to follow parental departures in order to regain campers' attention and reestablish the normal tempo and atmosphere of camp life. Some camps minimize the pangs of actual goodbyes by asking the parents to bid their adieux and then silently steal away while the campers are occupied in some activity, such as a vespers service or flag-lowering ceremony. Unless well handled, visitors' day may seriously distract campers' attention from their regular camp activities and can undermine progress made toward the important camp objective of emancipating the camper from his possibly too doting or domineering parents.

WRITING AND RECEIVING LETTERS

Each camp will probably have its own letter writing policy, which may require that a camper write home regularly, either daily, every other day, or weekly, although some leave this up to the discretion of the camper. No matter what guideline your camp sets up, you will find it advantageous to encourage your group to set aside time for this activity, and you can catch up on your own correspondence at the same time. You may be called on for guidance, especially to help your younger campers to spell difficult words and to master the essentials of good letter writing. Suggest such topics as the activities his group has been engaging in, the new skills he has acquired, his new friends, bunkmates, the food, and the weather. Encouraging him to write about the positive side of camp life keeps him from recounting small grievances and unhappy incidents, which are often only moods of the moment that will be entirely forgotten by the time the letter reaches its destination. These complaints may also be attempts to get attention or sympathy, especially during

Figure 6–10 Gosh, I Got One!

the first few days of camp when feelings of homesickness and loneliness are common to nearly everyone. Whatever the camper's motivation for writing such letters, they often prove quite upsetting to parents, who magnify their importance out of all proportion and sometimes make long distance calls or come to camp to investigate and take the camper home.

See that envelopes are correctly and legibly addressed and that the letters are promptly mailed, for campers often misplace them, and soon parents are making frantic calls to see why they have heard nothing. Go as a group, take turns, or elect a runner to post them at the camp post office.

It is heartbreaking to see a child's face drop when he consistently receives nothing in the daily mail call. Bring the problem to the attention of the head counselor or camp director, who may write, or ask you to write, a tactful letter to his family, suggesting how much it would boost the child's morale if they wrote more often. You may want to send him a special card on your day off, but you must, of course, be careful not to arouse jealousy in other campers.

RECORDS AND REPORTS

Doing little things well is a step toward doing big things better.

—Author Unknown

You may be asked to keep various records concerning your campers, including those previously mentioned. Although these often seem like odious chores and a waste of time, they actually take only a few moments if you keep up with them. Try to see the purposes of each report and the ultimate way in which it will be used. Records are important for several reasons: (1) One prime purpose may be to keep a systematic record of each individual's amount, rate, and direction of growth in various areas. (2) They also serve to give the busy camp director and head counselor a composite picture of what is really happening throughout the camp. (3) They provide an accurate and detailed written record of what actually takes place, since they are made at frequent intervals while memories are still fresh. This sometimes proves to be quite important later on. (4) They make you analyze and evaluate your own work, as you note evidences of your failures and successes.

Written reports mean different things to different people and you should never regard them as just busy work or an extra chore with no inherent value. Unfortunately, counselors are sometimes not told the ultimate purpose of these records and the exact information they should include, so ask for more information along these lines if you feel you need it. Here are a few simple, basic rules to follow in writing out reports:

1. Try to be *completely objective* and *impartial* in every statement you make.

2. Record all observations *accurately* and *correctly*. It is better to omit something than to risk being incorrect in important details.

3. If an incident with a camper has

produced a strong emotional reaction in you, delay recounting it until you have had time to calm down and look at it objectively.

4. It often helps to include a brief description of the background or social setting in which certain actions took place.

5. Write down unusual behavior that you note frequently in an individual, together with the situations or circumstances which cause or accompany it. Note what you did about it and what resulted.

6. Make your report personal and reflective of your own individuality. This conveys more meaningful information to those who read it than a dry stereotyped report which reflects no real understanding of the child or situation.

You may want to keep records beyond those required by the camp just for your own benefit. Include such things as accounts of the individual camper's activities, reactions, growths, problems, and health. This helps to create a total picture of him which enables you or others to understand his needs and how to go about meeting and fulfilling them. The reports that the sponsoring agency, camp director, or head counselor send to parents or headquarters during or at the end of the camping season are based partially upon your evaluations; therefore, you can see the importance of making them honestly, objectively, completely, and thoroughly.

Camps commonly ask staff members to make a written report of any accident or injury to a camper, no matter how trivial. You will usually be furnished with a form on which to do this, which you should fill out as soon as possible before you have forgotten exactly what happened. Be accurate, and go into some detail and include what was done about it; this may be of the utmost importance if later complications or questions arise.

You may also be asked to make out certain reports at the end of the season, such as an inventory of the equipment and supplies in your unit or cabin or an activity with which you have worked, together with recommendations for additions or changes for next year. Again, devote time and thought to the procedure, for it will be instrumental in helping you or your successor to do an even better job next season.

TIME OFF

All camps give counselors some time off—usually an hour or two each day, and a longer period each week or two weeks; you probably learned the particulars of this when you signed your contract. This interlude can and should be of great benefit to both you and the camp. Dealing in such intimacy with many personalities can deplete physical and emotional energy and cause patience to grow short, emotions to boil over at trifles, and a sense of humor to completely forsake its owner. Counselors are sometimes unaware of this gradual accumulation of emotional and nervous fatigue and become so attached to their jobs that they are reluctant to leave them, even when given time off. Such zealous overdevotion to duty is a sad mistake, for sooner or later it will produce a dull, cross, bearish person who cannot possibly do his job effectively.

If you hold your nose to the grindstone rough,
And hold it down there long enough,
You'll soon forget there are such things,
As brooks that babble and birds that sing;
These three things will your world compose,
Just you, and a stone and your darned old nose!

—Author Unknown

It is important for you to get your

(Courtesy of Girl Scouts, U.S.A.)

mind off camp, so use your time off to write letters, do your laundry or mending, or go off with a companion or two to bowl, eat out, shop, roller skate, dance, attend the movies, or engage in any other favorite pastime which will temporarily erase camp from your mind.

When out in public, you must remember that you represent your camp, so conduct yourself so that your actions and appearance reflect creditably upon it. Drinking in public, driving recklessly, and any sort of boisterous or socially unacceptable conduct are in very poor taste. Treat the citizens of the town courteously and fairly in the same manner in which you expect them to treat you.

You may be able to arrange to use camp equipment, and a good workout on the tennis courts or a boat trip will relax those kinks in your brain and emotions. Use all the time you have, but do not take time from the job to start getting ready to leave, return late, or spend the day after your return in recuperating and talking about the big time you had. The purpose of time off is to return you rested and with renewed enthusiasm, and it is up to you to plan so that it accomplishes this purpose.

Figure 6–11 I'll Never Make It Tomorrow!

OTHER DETAILS

PERSONAL HABITS

Most camps request that counselors who smoke do so at designated times and in designated places, never in front of campers. Such requests are not based on moral issues, but reflect the example that a sincere counselor would want to set in view of recent medical findings concerning the health dangers of smoking, as well as a recognition of the fire hazard created by indiscriminate smoking in rural areas, which are often equipped with only simple fire-fighting equipment. The use of alcoholic beverages is prohibited on the camp site and often on time off, for even parents who themselves indulge are likely to object to placing their children in charge of leaders who do, and it is likely to bring unfavorable community reaction toward the camp. The non-medical use of drugs in camp is inappropriate as well as illegal, and engaging in any activity during time off which in any way interferes with a staff member's judgment or job performance is unwise.

LOYALTY

You owe loyalty first, last, and always to your camp and camp director. You chose this camp above all others because it seemed to be most compatible with your objectives and ideals, but as in any situation, you will find things which are not just as you would wish them. When this occurs, keep it to yourself and think it over for a few days, for you will probably see the situation in a different perspective as camp life unfolds and you get a better picture of the whole scene. If your problem still seems as important, don't complain about it or talk to others who are as unable as you to interpret things from a different perspective or to do anything about them; instead, go to someone who can give you the right answers, even the director himself if necessary. If you still cannot accept the situation and adjust happily to it, consider asking for a release from fulfilling the rest of your contract, for both you and the camp may be better off if you part company. Never, under any circumstances, criticize the camp to outsiders or other counselors, and, of course, never do so in front of campers. Even when started as good-natured small talk, griping will sooner or later prove ruinous to good morale and also will reflect unfavorably on you.

COLLECTING IDEAS

Carry your camp notebook and pencil as regularly as you wear your shoes, for the worst lead pencil in the world is better than a good memory, and many a conscientious, well-meaning counselor has failed because he "forgot." Add to your collection of ideas and projects constantly, jotting down games, program material, that new recipe for clam chowder, the sure way to keep Jim's shoestrings from coming untied, and refresher notes about the needs, interests, accomplishments, and signs of improvement on the part of your campers. Drop in at the camp library now and then for new ideas or new ways of doing things.

COUNSELOR-IN-TRAINING PROGRAMS

CONDUCT OF THE PROGRAM

Many camps conduct Counselor-In-Training (CIT) programs, designed to prepare older campers for possible future positions as full-fledged counselors. Candidates are usually 17 or 18 years old and have had several seasons of successful camping experience. Although they sometimes admit outsiders, many camps use the training program as a means of "growing" some of their own future staff members by choosing outstanding campers with definite leadership qualities and abilities. A CIT program is a professional undertaking and should never be used as a way to keep older campers on the camp roster, provide "busy work," or get cheap help around the kitchen, campgrounds, or as substitutes for regular counselors. Indeed, it is a distinct honor to be chosen as a CIT, since stringent requirements are usually set up and only those who are deemed worthy of consideration as future staff members are admitted. Each camp has its own standards, rules, regulations, fees, and course content, but most have similar objectives in mind.

The course is carried out on the camp site during the regular camp session and usually lasts over two seasons in order to do justice to all the material to be covered. It is conducted by one or more trained leaders who are familiar with the purposes of the program, their responsibilities as instructors, and proper course content and teaching methods.

OBJECTIVES AND VALUES OF THE PROGRAM

1. A well-conducted CIT program provides an opportunity for the discussion of such topics as camp philosophy, history and development, objectives, program and activities, and the growth and behavior patterns of children at different ages, as well as their varying individual needs and how to understand and meet them.

2. The program is stimulating in itself, since it permits each participant to enjoy satisfying experiences with his own peer group while observing the workings of group dynamics.

3. It gives each participant the opportunity to perfect or learn new skills and to increase his appreciation of and sense of security in the out-of-doors.

4. It helps him to develop his own potential as he evaluates his own particular strengths and weaknesses, improving them when he can and, when necessary, accepting his limitations and learning to live with them. It helps him to mature as he exercises the necessary self-discipline to complete the course and to understand himself and find acceptable ways to discover who he is, to establish a place for himself in society, and to satisfy his own needs.

5. The better CIT programs allow him to work with campers, applying and practicing the techniques and skills he has been studying and assuming increasing responsibility as he assists in planning and carrying out such camp activities as evening programs, cookouts, song leading and teaching new songs, initiating games, planning activities for rainy days, taking the initiative in starting new camp projects, assisting in particular departments, such as aquatics or arts and crafts, and sometimes living with and working closely with counselors and their cabin group, always under close supervision and with the guidance of an older, more experienced person.

Although CIT training involves hard work, the trainee will find it quite enjoyable, for he will gain added self-respect by learning to take responsibility and feeling the thrill of seeing what he has planned succeed. CITs usually receive special privileges, such as living in their own cabin without a counselor, being permitted to stay up longer than younger campers, developing and enforcing their own codes of behavior; and planning their own social programs.

Actually, CITs often set the tone and become the "spark plugs" of the whole camp, attracting others by their youthful enthusiasm and good cheer.

Their special status in younger campers' eyes constantly challenges them to set a good example by adhering closely to all camp rules and regulations, for, because of their proximity in age, their young protégés often adopt them as models and try to emulate their behavior and attitudes.

The CIT program is very important and can be lots of fun and most rewarding to the individuals involved. What better opportunity could anyone ask if he is enthusiastic about camping and is interested in working with people?

ADDITIONAL READINGS

(For Chapters 5 and 6)

(For an explanation of abbreviations and abbreviated forms, see page 25.)

Accident Report Form. ACA, 1 sheet, 2¢.
Bloom et al.: *Camper Guidance—In the Routines of Daily Living.*
Camp Health Record Form. ACA, 2¢.
Camp Job Descriptions.
Camper Guidance—A Basic Handbook for Counselors. ACA, 1961, 24 pp., 85¢, paper.
Ensign: *Camping Together As Christians,* Part I, ch. 3; Part II, ch. 1.
Ledlie and Holbein: *Camp Counselor's Manual.*
Ott: *So You Want to Be a Camp Counselor.*
Rodney and Ford: *Camp Administration,* ch. 10; Appendix E.
Schmidt, Ernest F.: *Camping Safety.* ACA, 1971, 43 pp., 50¢, paper.
Shivers: *Camping,* ch. 2 and pp. 126–139.
Todd: *Camping for Christian Youth,* pp. 140–144; 151–152.
Universal Health Examination Form. ACA, rev., 1968, 2¢.
Van Krevelen: *Children in Groups: Psychology and the Summer Camp,* chs. 6, 7; ch. 9 from p. 123.

MAGAZINE ARTICLES

Camping Magazine:
Borkowski, Richard P.: "A Camp Director Is—" Feb., 1972, p. 11.
Ford, Dr. Phyllis M.: "Hireth Thou Me for I Shall Do Guidance." June, 1965, p. 14.
Hansen, Robert H.: "A Structure for Counseling." May, 1966, p. 16.
Jones, Dr. Orville E.: "Does Staff Accept Campers or Just Tolerate Them?" June, 1965, p. 19.
Kaufman, Abraham M.: "When Campers Write Home." June, 1963, p. 7.
Lomen, L. D.: "A Camp Experience Should Leave Time to Learn By Doing." June, 1973, p. 14.
Marley, Dr. William P.: "Sedentary Camper Syndrome." May, 1971, p. 14.
Northway, Mary L.: "Counselors Must Have Ability to *Camp* and to *Counsel.*" Apr., 1964, p. 16.
"Share These Tested Aids to Better Counseling." May, 1965, p. 22.
Thwing, Dr. Henry W.: "Campers Make More Friends If Your Dining Room Seating Is Scientifically Designed to Aid Them." June, 1970, p. 16.
Woal, S. Theodore: "Be Sure to Welcome Campers on That Important First Day." Apr., 1965, p. 16.
Woal, S. Theodore: "Get a Quieter Dining Room With These Practical Ideas." June, 1965, p. 21.

First Aid, Health and Safety in Camp

Arnold, Robert E., M. D.: *What to Do About Bites and Stings of Venomous Animals.* Collier, 1973, 122 pp., $1.95.
Auld, Margaret E., and Graceann Ehlke: *Guide to Camp Nursing.* ACA, 1974, 44 pp., $2, paper.
Corbin: *Recreation Leadership,* ch. 9.
Emergency Preparedness (No. 3366). Boy Scouts, 1972, 64 pp., 45¢, paper.
First Aid. A.R.C.
First Aid (No. 3276). Boy Scouts, 1972, 64 pp., 45¢, paper.
Hafen, Brent O., et al.: *First Aid—Contemporary Practices and Principles.* Burgess, 1972, 214 pp., $3.50, paper.
Hamessley, Mary Lou, R.N.: *Handbook for Camp Nurses and Other Camp Health Workers.* Tiresias, 1973, 160 pp., $3.95.
Johnson, Loren A., M.D.: *Survivit Manual.* Survivit Company, Lake McQueeney, Texas, 1973, $1.
Kodet, E. Russel, M.D., and Bradford Angier: *Being Your Own Wilderness Doctor.* Stackpole, 1968, 128 pp., $3.95.
Rodney and Ford: *Camp Administration,* Appendix A.
Safety (No. 3347). Boy Scouts, 1971, 64 pp., 45¢, paper.
Schmidt, Ernest F.: *Camping Safety.* ACA, 1971, 44 pp., 50¢, paper.
Suggested Policies and Standing Orders for Camp Nursing Services. ACA, rev., 1968, 25¢, paper.

The Camp Nurse. ACA Health and Safety Committee, ACA, 26 pp., 50¢, paper.
The Camp Physician's Manual. Thomas, 1967, 192 pp., $8.50.

Magazine Articles

Camping Magazine:
Andzel, Walter: "How to Handle Heat Illnesses." June, 1973, p. 25.
Austin, Glenn: "It is Time We Outgrow Camp Physical Exams." Feb., 1970, p. 14.
"14 Camp Accidents Which Could Have Been Avoided." Jan., 1970, p. 16.
Jordan, Lynn: "Turned-On Teaching at Camp." Apr., 1972, p. 16.
Means, Elizabeth, R.N.: "Helpful Hints From a Camp Nurse." Apr., 1970, p. 20.
Putt, Arlene M.: "The Most Important Element in Camping Must Be Our Concern for Camper's Health and Safety." Feb., 1973, p. 20.
Stevenson, Dr. Jack L.: "Safety Is a Never-Ending Job." Apr., 1972, p. 22.

Chapter 7

The Counselor Must Understand People

Figure 7-1 What Is A Boy?

No one really understands humans except a dog and a sophomore psychology major.

—MARY L. NORTHWAY

WHAT IS A BOY?*

A boy is a person who is going to carry on what you have started. He is going to sit right where you are sitting and, when you are gone, attend to those things you think are important. You may adopt all the policies you please, but how they will be carried out depends on him.

He will assume control of your cities, states and nations. He is going to move and take over your churches, schools, universities and corporations.

All your books are going to be judged, praised or condemned by him. The fate of Humanity is in his hands.

So it might be well to pay him some attention!

—AUTHOR UNKNOWN

OBJECTIVES AND HOW TO OBTAIN THEM

In order to be happy in this world, one must live in harmony with one's associates. The person who says he doesn't care what other people think of him is almost always covering up his deep disappointment and frustration by pretending to scorn what he really desires—the respect and affection of others. Getting along well with others is most important to you as a counselor, for you may be sure that you will be neither happy nor successful in influencing campers unless you gain their respect, admiration, and friendly cooperation.

*Reprinted from *The Royal Rangers Leader's Manual,* 1962.

(Courtesy of Gnaw Bone Camp, Nashville, Indiana.)

There are three main components of camp life which will have a major effect on the camper's growth and improvement. These are the camp environment or facilities, the camp program or what is done in camp, and the camp personnel. The last component is by far the most important of the three, for not only do camp staff influence campers by their actions, words, and example, but it is only through their skillful manipulation of the other two components that the potential of the whole camp experience can be realized. In order to function most effectively in this role, you must understand campers and their needs and how to satisfy them, for, without such an awareness, these components may be misused and may have decidedly undesirable effects. For instance, a camp which offers elaborate facilities and services and has someone to perform all disagreeable and tedious tasks for campers may be turning out helpless, dependent snobs instead of independent, self-reliant people. A camp which motivates its campers wholly by elaborate awards, public acclamation, and publicity in the camper's hometown paper may be teaching the participants that winning is the only important thing, no matter what the means or consequences, and that those who try, yet fail, are to be brushed aside as insignificant "also-rans." Thus, you must have a clear idea of what you actually want to accomplish, and these objectives must be definite, concrete and specific. You will not achieve these objectives by presenting them in the form of generalities or platitudes; you must be able to apply them in the context of everyday camp life.

Since you will be trying to promote the best in camper behavior and attitudes, you must consider the possible ways in which you can influence others.

HOW WE INFLUENCE OTHERS

Let us assume that you have a quite definite mental picture of what you want to accomplish and are trying to find a way to induce a camper to act in accordance with your objectives. One way is to order him to do it, perhaps threatening to punish him or withhold something he wants, such as his regular swimming period, if he disobeys. Though this may bring about the desired action, no lasting improvements in the camper's behavior are likely, for as soon as the force is removed, he will probably revert to his former behavior and may resent the experience so much that he may act in a worse manner than before. It may also teach him to dislike and resist authority and anyone symbolizing it. He will probably rebel inwardly, but, through fear, will keep his feelings bottled up inside until his bitterness gradually builds up and eventually bursts forth in full force when he feels old enough or big enough to dare to express it. He may eventually come to hate whatever it was you commanded him to do, despite his true feelings toward it, because of its association with the unpleasantness of the whole experience.

Therefore, let us turn to a better way, which is to persuade him to act in a certain way because *he* wants to. When you stop to think of it, almost everything we do is in response to some want. We go to bed because we want to rest; we eat because we want the taste of food or to satisfy hunger; we work because we want the things we can buy with the money we earn; we practice long hours on the basketball court because we want to be a good player or because we seek the social prestige which comes with playing on the team. It seems obvious, therefore, that it is futile to try to persuade anyone to do something because *we* want him to, if *he* couldn't care less; like everyone else, he is primarily interested in and motivated by his own desires.

Let us face the fact that nearly everyone is selfish to some degree and much more interested in himself than in anyone else. Therefore, we are usually successful in bringing about lasting changes in a camper's conduct only when we show him that the desired improvement will satisfy one of *his* wants. Suppose he very much desires to pass his endurance tests in swimming in order to qualify for a canoe trip. He'll drink his milk willingly and ask for more and be the first one in his bunk and asleep, once he realizes that good eating habits and rest are essential for swimming endurance. How much better both the results and his attitude will be than they would have been had you nagged him and tried to force him to do what you want; now, he'll probably get angry with you if you try to keep him from doing it. Suppose one cabin group "goofs off" and finds excuses for putting off cabin cleanup after breakfast. Can you imagine the whirlwind of activity if a choice activity is offered for the first cabin group to finish (with requirements for thoroughness, of course)?

Both of these examples illustrate the positive rather than negative approach to a problem and the use of the principle of self-motivation in persuading people of any age to do what "is good for them." This approach really works, but, of course, you must carefully disguise your techniques and use them skillfully, for people heartily dislike the feeling that others are manipulating them. Let us repeat this important point: *persuade people to do what you want them to do by making them realize that doing so will satisfy one of their wants.* Now, let us consider what people want.

THE FUNDAMENTAL WISHES

Though it is quite obvious that people are different, nevertheless, they are also alike in many ways, and among the things they have in common are five desires or wishes that are present in every normal person. Though these vary in intensity, they are usually so strong and compelling that we can understand almost anything a person does when we recognize it as an attempt to satisfy one of these desires. As we shall see, a well-adjusted person finds ways to fulfill his wishes in a socially acceptable manner, but when he can't or thinks he can't do this, he may resort to unacceptable ways; compelling inner demands require fulfillment, no matter how this is accomplished. When these attempts to satisfy needs are carried to extremes, the person often becomes stamped as a social misfit, a juvenile delinquent, or even a hardened criminal.

THE WISH FOR AFFECTION

One powerful wish is to be accepted and regarded affectionately by one's friends and associates. The sense of inner contentment a camper feels when his peers select him for a tentmate or greet him with a friendly word and smile when he enters the cabin door and the thrill he gets when his cabinmates choose him to represent them on the Camp Council result from the fulfillment of this basic desire. The longing to be loved, appreciated, needed, and missed is universal. When fulfilled, it produces a feeling of well-being and contentment; when unfulfilled, it brings inconsolable loneliness and unhappiness. Be wary of the camper who says, "I don't wanna go on their old cookout 'cause I don't like them," as he goes off to read a book or stroll through the woods in solitude; the chances are he is really miserable and desperately longing to be accepted as part of the group. You may need to exercise the utmost tact and persistence to penetrate the wall he has built around himself, but the resulting happier, better-adjusted camper will amply reward your efforts.

Figure 7–2 Misery Is Not Being Part of the Group.

From the first day, your efforts to build cabin morale and a feeling of group unity and friendly camaraderie are aimed at helping each newcomer to feel wanted and accepted. You may need to take special pains with those who are shy and retiring or who aren't the type others readily take to, and pairing them off with a "buddy" or getting an old camper to take a newcomer in tow is often helpful. The naturally unattractive camper will especially challenge you to search for his good points and help him to fit in. A wise father, consoling his befreckled little daughter said, "I love every one of your freckles because they are *you.*"

Find out why a camper is disliked or ignored, then set out diligently to help him to remedy the situation.

See that your program is broad and varied enough to provide for every youngster's interests and abilities, be he an athlete, a musician, a social introvert, a bookworm, or any other species of young human being. Be especially aware of the quiet, retiring youngster who tends to be overlooked and may be hiding a deep unhappiness and sense of loneliness.

A thoughtful counselor can find many ways to satisfy a camper's desire for affection. A friendly "hello," a willingness to listen to their achievements, a pat on the back and a "well done," a bedtime story, or a moment spent seeing that each is tucked in for the night will usually do the trick.

When you notice a child who needs help, it is best to spare his pride by using an indirect approach and unobtrusively devising ways to draw him into the group. Occasionally it may be best to approach the problem directly and have a frank talk with him, impressing him with the fact that you really like him and consider him a very worthwhile person. Guide your conversation skillfully so that you lead him to eventually conclude that it is his own selfishness and lack of consideration for others, his boasting, shirking of responsibility, or crude manners that cause others to dislike him and shun his company. On rare occasions, you may deem it best to choose a time when he is absent and discuss the situation with all or a few of his mates, for they can often help most of all by making a special effort to include him in the group and help him to make a new start. Most children are basically sympathetic and warmhearted, and when shown how their thoughtlessness is hurting someone else, are only too glad to help him to turn over a new leaf. Tolerance and forgiveness for the shortcomings of others are certainly desirable traits to cultivate, and any improvement in the fellow camper will be a cause for rejoicing as his comrades realize that their efforts helped him to adjust. Helping others is one of the most satisfying ways to fulfill our fundamental wishes for recognition and power, as we shall see.

A serious case of maladjustment or continued failure to fit in may necessitate referral to the camp director or head counselor, for those with insufficient training and experience to handle the situation often succeed only in compounding the problem. It may sometimes be best to transfer the camper to another cabin, but this should be a last resort, for it will give him much more satisfaction and do him more permanent good if you help him to confront and solve his problems and don't allow him to run away from them.

THE WISH FOR ACHIEVEMENT

The desire to have others feel that we are important and to exercise power over ourselves or others is also universal. A camper knows this satisfaction when he masters the backstroke, catches and cooks his own fish dinner, or propels a canoe down the river. He also demonstrates power over himself when he cures a bad habit such as procrastinating or keeping an untidy room, or when he disciplines himself to do a good job of cleaning up a section of the waterfront or constructing a new footbridge across a stream. He shows power over others when, as chairman of a committee, he steers it to a successful completion of its duties, when he sways others to his way of thinking during a cabin discussion, or talks his pal Joe out of some proposed misdeed. Everyone likes to think that he counts for something in the world, and a feeling of accomplishment at some task

(Courtesy of Camp Kooch-I-Ching, International Falls, Minnesota.)

acts as a powerful spur to further accomplishments.

Consequently, a camper suffers frustration and disappointment when asked to compete with those of superior age, experience, or ability; this is the danger in carrying competition to extremes, for consistent winners may get inflated egos, while consistent losers may develop inferiority complexes. A good substitute is to have an individual compete against himself as he tries to better his former record or strives to pass standard tests set up for swimming or boating classifications or for the skills required for participation in a cookout or a canoe trip. Again we see the advisability of having a program which will include something in which *each* camper can experience a satisfactory degree of success.

A misdirected sense of power may explain the bully who controls others through fear, the leader of the gang who dominates and does the thinking for his weaker followers, the individual who enjoys capturing and torturing helpless animals, or the speedboat or automobile driver who goes roaring on his merry way, without regard for the comfort or safety of others or even of himself and his passengers.

THE WISH FOR SECURITY

Every person wants to feel safe and secure in his surroundings and with his associates. A camper, particularly if away from home for the first time, misses his familiar routines and ways of life. He finds camp ways new and is inexperienced in living with such a large number of other children, especially if he is an only child. He has learned to predict with some certainty how his parents and home playmates will react to what he does, and often has become quite adept at "getting around" or wheedling what he wants out of one or both parents. Now he is associated with strange adults, as well as new youngsters of his own age, and doesn't quite know what to expect. If someone makes a cross remark to him or shows an outburst of temper, it hurts his ego, and he may respond in kind, run to someone else for sympathy, or retreat into his shell and brood. The experience may well set the stage for a bad case of homesickness.

We have previously discussed several things you can do to add to the camper's sense of security. Be friendly and pleasant, but be firm when the need arises, and above all be consistent, for a counselor who is kindly and full of fun one minute and angry or temperamental the next will certainly not impart a sense of security to his young charges.

Encourage your campers to chatter freely with you and feel flattered when one discloses his secrets, but never betray his confidences or let him overhear you discussing his personality or problems with others. Establish yourself as a never-failing friend to whom he can always feel free to bring his fondest hopes and dreams, as well as his worries and problems.

A camper's sense of security must include freedom from fear of harm, both physical and social. Fear of being injured or ridiculed even interferes with physical coordination, and this explains the superior results obtained by a modern swimming counselor who works his swimmers hard but gives praise and encouragement when due, instead of using the old method of throwing a nonswimmer into deep water and letting him sink or swim. Children who are worried and afraid of being made fun of may react by stuttering, bed-wetting, retiring into a shell, fighting back, criticizing others, or engaging in malicious gossip.

THE WISH FOR NEW ADVENTURES

The desire to do something different and to try one's wings in uncon-

(Courtesy of Camp Kooch-I-Ching, International Falls, Minnesota.)

quered fields, though the opposite of the desire for security, is often just as strong, and when denied too long brings boredom, bad temper, and misbehavior just to create a little excitement. Varying camp routines and letting campers help to plan their own programs to include new exciting things which interest them help to satisfy this wish.

Keeping campers busy at things which give them a feeling of accomplishment is one of the secrets of a happy camp. Trips, cookouts, "special days," work projects in camp or on a neighboring farm, a hobby display, a camp play, building a tree house, rustic bridge, or nature trail, folk dancing, a visit from a camp neighbor with interesting experiences to relate, all help to meet this demand for new adventures.

THE WISH FOR RECOGNITION AND APPROVAL

Each camper has a deep-seated wish to stand out as an individual and to do at least one or several things better than others. He will consequently work like a beaver to run faster, swim better, swear more fluently, make more noise, or recognize more birds than his cabinmates. From his early days, this deep urge drives him from one field of endeavor to another in a search for activities in which *he* can excel. Often his reluctance to engage in a suggested activity is based on a deep-seated inner fear that he does not or cannot do it well; John's excuses for not going in the water during his swimming period may stem from his self-consciousness about his lack of ability, heightened by the unthinking but unkind remarks of some fellow camper or counselor. His attitude may well change to one of tolerance or even enthusiasm when a wise counselor searches out some good point to compliment him on or offers help to improve his technique. To work successfully with youngsters, or in fact with persons of any age, you need to remember that praise brings better results than criticism. Praise your campers frequently, but avoid overdoing it or giving it when it is not deserved; others are quick to detect insincerity and will consequently lose faith in and respect for you.

If Sue is overweight, her disinclination to join the group in hiking may be based on her inability to "keep up" and her fear of receiving cruel comments on her weight from other hikers. If her problem goes unsolved, she may learn to snap back and make herself disagreeable, just as a tethered dog does when mischievous children tease it. She may claim to have a headache or give some other excuse to avoid the activity, and will probably compensate for her inner unhappiness by indulging herself by eating more and exercising less. A tactful talk with her may arouse her interest in bringing her weight down to normal. In the meantime, encourage her to capitalize on her strong points, such as her ready wit which keeps her tentmates in stitches.

Bill, who rows poorly and knows it, may be so overwhelmed by the thoughtless taunts and jeers of others that he loses what little coordination he has and flails the water in a truly ludicrous way. You may help him most by unobtrusively suggesting a little private coaching in a remote spot where he can concentrate on his technique without worrying about what others are saying or thinking.

A youngster's desire to be accepted by his peers demands that he receive recognition from them for something he does well. Oftentimes you may find it worthwhile to rearrange the program to make use of some talent not called for by the regular routines. Quiet, socially inept Jane may really shine when her ability to draw well and make attractive posters is needed to advertise the all-camp fair or circus. We are reminded of a story about a camper, Jean, whose lone outstanding trait seemed to be an ability to make more noise than anyone else. Her counselor, realizing that her frequently annoying breaches of good conduct were in reality an unconscious attempt to get the personal attention she could get in no other way, decided to stage a contest to see who could yell the loudest. Of course Jean won as anticipated, and thus achieved her place in the limelight.

A camper would prefer to have *favorable* distinction if he can get it. However, his desire for recognition is so strong that he will go to almost any length to satisfy it, settling for unfavorable attention if necessary. The actions of the constant troublemaker or camp mimic may be explained in this way, for he has at least achieved *some* distinction and would rather be known as bad than be treated as a nonentity. Nevertheless, this camper has a gnawing sense of inadequacy and unhappiness, and you will render him a real service if you show him how to achieve distinction in a more satisfactory way. No quick cure can be expected, however, and there will very likely be occasional discouraging relapses along the way.

Be especially eager to help the shy, retiring camper to achieve success and recognition. "The child who feels inferior can usually be helped to develop abilities which will in time make him truly superior along certain lines. Genuine superiority often grows out of a sense of inferiority which has served as a spur to unusual effort."*

WHEN WISHES ARE THWARTED

Children are a combination of a great deal of good spiced by a bit of bad, and those who long for the perfectly behaved child should remember this little poem:

> Tommy does as he is told!
> No one ever has to scold!
> Quick! Drag him by the wrist
> To see the psychoanalyst!
>
> —AUTHOR UNKNOWN

Let us summarize by recalling that, when a child is "bad," it is usually because he has not found a satisfying and socially acceptable way to fulfill one or more of his basic needs. Therefore, when trouble arises, seek and eliminate the cause. Basic wishes are strong and will be fulfilled by fair means or foul, but children aren't anxious to sacrifice social approval to satisfy their desires, if they can avoid it.

MENTAL HEALTH

The wish for good mental health is universal, for although most of us would fail miserably if asked to tell just what the term means, we all recognize that it involves a general sense of well-being and of living at peace with oneself and the world. A well-adjusted person has stopped "reaching for the moon" by attempting things beyond his capabilities, yet, at the same time, he has recognized his strong points and developed them to a high degree. He has learned to expect and to accept a certain amount of disappointment in life and has kept his sense of humor, so that he can laugh at himself when he stumbles and try once or many times again. He likes people and has learned that it is wiser to emphasize their good traits than to pick out their faults and magnify them out of all proportion. He is friendly and outgoing, yet not a backslapper whose shallowness soon shows through. He is cheerful and optimistic, yet recognizes and meets problems and takes constructive steps to solve them instead of wasting his time

*Henry C. Link: *The Rediscovery of Man*, 1938, published by The Macmillan Company and used with their permission.

in ineffective worry and indecision. What is perhaps most characteristic of a well-adjusted person is that he has gone beyond exclusive, childish self-interest and has developed a concern for others and a desire to use his time and talents to serve them and so make the world a better place in which to live.

CHARACTERISTICS OF CHILDREN

As previously pointed out, individuals are too different to classify and fit into pigeonholes, with instructions for understanding and handling each placed neatly in a nearby file. Each has a unique personality, created from his own genetic background and the totality of experiences and knowledge he has absorbed from his particular environment. We cannot truthfully say that there is such a thing as an average child, but only average characteristics of children. Nevertheless, it is helpful to understand these average characteristics, since they represent basic patterns upon which each child's own individual characteristics are superimposed. As a counselor, it is essential that you understand the various stages of maturation and patterns of growth and development of children in order to counsel with and build a meaningful program for them.

THE CAMPER FROM 6 TO 8

This period might be termed the *individualistic period,* since although he is not so completely self-centered as he was, a child's thoughts are still largely centered upon himself, with only a superficial and transitory interest in others. A friend may be completely spurned or disliked one minute and accepted again as a boon companion a short time later. In fact, a child of this age shows more interest in pleasing adults than in pleasing his contemporaries, and thus you can easily motivate him to desirable conduct by a bit of praise or other sign of approval.

He tends to be incessantly active and cannot be kept physically quiet for long. His interests are keen but fleeting, and you must be prepared for him to suddenly drop a project or game in which he has been absorbed and clamor for something entirely new and different. He is quite impulsive and highly unpredictable. He likes to be first and likes to win.

His imagination knows no bounds and he goes into a frenzy of activity as he clears his cabin dooryard and lines a path with rocks to the door of the "White House" or "pioneer's cabin" where he and his campmates bunk. He loves to try to creep silently through the woods, stalking in the best manner of Daniel Boone or a fierce Cherokee brave, yet only moments later, a few touches of costume have transformed him into an astronaut, piloting his rocket toward the moon.

It is very important at this time to encourage him to try out his skills in many fields so that he can sample everything and find out where his true interests and abilities lie, for he's greatly excited about anything new at this age. However, his coordination is not dependable, and his control over his finer muscles is so poor that he finds concentration on painstaking, exacting techniques wearisome and unsatisfying; simple, large-muscle activities such as running and jumping are best. He needs to be protected against overexcitement and fatigue, which tend to interfere with his getting sufficient rest and sleep.

THE CAMPER FROM 9 TO 11

A camper of this age is beginning to prize the approval of his peers above that of parents and other adults. At the same time, he is entering the age of hero worship and may adopt some adult, perhaps a famous athlete or even you, his counselor, as a model after whom to pattern his behavior. He seeks an intimate relationship with one or two special buddies, perhaps in a club or gang, with whom he can share closely-guarded secrets. He is a bundle of energy engaged in a constant whirlwind of activity, so you will need to watch him closely for signs of fatigue or overexcitement and see that he observes rest hour and gets an adequate amount of sleep.

He has a good sense of humor, although it may be of the slapstick variety, and at times he may be effervescent and talk incessantly, sometimes imagining or exaggerating things. He loves to collect things, be they nature specimens, trading stamps, or model airplanes. His interests are so many and so varied and he is so intent on learning everything he can about this beautiful world that little time and interest are left for keeping himself and his possessions clean and in good order. He wants to know the "why" of everything and what makes things work, even if he has to tear them apart to find out. He likes to read, but at the same time, enjoys being out-of-doors.

Figure 7-3 Daring, But May Be Harmful To Both Boy and Tree.

His improved coordination and muscle control enable him to acquire new skills in many fields, such as tennis, swimming, crafts, or the use of simple tools for camp construction. He enjoys working in a group on such activities as planning a campfire skit or program, an outdoor cookout or "gypsy" trip, or a cleanup project for his unit or cabin. He has a tendency to throw himself wholeheartedly into a chosen task and work furiously, but often after a day or two, he will lose interest and abandon the project even though it is not yet finished.

Avoid using sarcasm or ridicule, even though his boastfulness and braggadocio may irritate you, for these are often signs of an underlying lack of confidence and a desire for your attention. He is striving to grow up and exercise more independence, and consequently will resent it if you use a bossy, dictatorial approach, so try an understanding, friendly one and elicit his cooperation by a "let's" instead of by pressure or direct orders. His imagination is still strong and he finds doing things much more fun when he can picture himself as a "forty-niner," an Indian brave, or a beloved character from his history book or a favorite story.

THE CAMPER FROM 12 TO 15

This age is often referred to as the *gang age* because self-interests are now becoming subservient to a deeper loyalty to the group or gang. (This sense of gang loyalty is not usually quite so strong in girls as in boys.) Desire for the approval of his group is becoming so strong that to be different or to stand out from the rest is a major catastrophe. All want to act and dress as nearly alike as possible, even to the extent of cutting off and fringing their jeans, engaging in minor acts of vandalism and disobedience, or wearing outlandish clothing of some sort. Don't forcibly try to stop this tendency, for adolescents of this age very much resent authoritative methods and their antagonism can be easily aroused; instead, try to employ this peer pressure in constructive ways to further camp objectives. A camper of this age is very anxious for independence, but must be encouraged to recognize that more independence always brings with it increased responsibilities.

This loyalty to and enthusiasm for working as a group plus a growing ability to discuss and see several sides of a question make this an ideal time to give campers more responsibility for planning their own program and working out common problems. Rely on camper leadership whenever you can do so confidently and safely, and encourage individuals and committees to assume responsibilities and to develop a social consciousness, so that each camper realizes his own responsibility for and obligations to others.

This is the age of acute hero worship and "crushes," and the choice of the right models can be a very potent force for good. Campers are thrilled by examples of thoughtfulness, self-sacrifice, valor, and honesty in their models, and they themselves (even though loudly protesting) really want to be held to high standards, with reasonable rules and regulations consistently and fairly, but not over-rigidly, enforced. Above all, avoid the fatal error of striving for personal popularity by overleniency or by trying to be "just one of the gang," for these youngsters will take advantage of this mistake and will lose respect for you in the process.

This age group will vacillate between "clowning around" and showing off and moodiness and introspection, and it is often impossible to predict what any camper will do or say next. It is difficult to tell whether this period, with its rapid change of moods, interests, and general reactions to life, is harder on the individual or on those who associate with him. Rapid physical changes bring profound unrest, making the girls extremely self-conscious about their changing physical appearance and keeping the boys in constant anguish as their voices range without warning from treble to bass. Arms and legs are lengthening and hands and feet are rapidly increasing in size, leaving the owner embarrassed as he tries to maintain control over their changing proportions. Puzzled by these rapid physical, emotional, and social changes, the youngster often covers up his self-consciousness by loud talk and laughter and general boisterousness. He very much needs someone to confide in, and you can help to fulfill this need.

THE CAMPER FROM 15 TO 18

This older adolescent is nearing both physical and mental adulthood and the rapid changes taking place may both embarrass and puzzle him. He is gregarious by nature, and now more than ever, is anxious to achieve a place of status and acceptance with his peers. He will go to almost any length to conform to whatever is currently the "in" thing in matters of dress, language, or behavior, and he sometimes may even be willing to sacrifice his own personal standards if group approval demands it. The combination of peer pressure and the older teenager's desire for new experiences often provides the impetus for experimentation with tobacco, drugs, or alcohol.

His maturing sexual development intensifies his quest for sex information, and he is much more interested in the opposite sex and in seeking social contacts with them. "Going steady" is commonplace because it provides this desired companionship, and also be-

(Courtesy of Camp Kooch-I-Ching, International Falls, Minnesota.)

cause it fulfills an increased need for security by providing someone he can count on, one who prefers *his* company to that of others.

A camper of this age wants to be accepted as a thinking, self-reliant adult by other adults, and bitterly opposes anyone who treats him otherwise; this is why he so often refuses to accept suggestions or advice from his elders or those in positions of authority. He is in a transitional stage where he is no longer a child but not yet an adult. Striving for identification as a person in his own right, he tries to resolve the conflict between what adults expect of him, what he expects of himself, and most of all, what his peers expect. He wants adults, as well as his peers, to take him seriously, so that he can respect himself as a person of consequence, and if he fails to achieve this in a satisfactory way, he may be inclined to find less desirable means to accomplish it.

This is a period of idealism and of wanting to participate in social causes and "save the world." There is interest in a wide variety of topics, including those of national and international scope, as well as various topics of a religious and philosophical nature. Group discussions and informal "rap" sessions are popular, and participation by older persons who have had interesting experiences is welcome. A sense of values and standards is rapidly taking form now, and this presents a distinct challenge to the sincere camp counselor.

A camper of this age craves adventure and activities that challenge his growing skills and ability to plan and think things out. In order to retain his interest, a progressive program is necessary that is free from repetition of activities of previous years, or what he now considers "kid stuff." It is mandatory that you recognize his budding powers of self-direction by letting him play a major role in program planning and camp government. A minimum of wise and tactful guidance is still necessary, however, since this fledgling adult is inclined to fluctuate between his new-found maturity and his former immaturity. Enlist his help in planning longer and more rugged trips, more elaborate unit improvements and outpost activities, occasional co-ed activities, and opportunities to explore and satisfy individual interests and developing skills. Many camps have found that a Counselor-In-Training (CIT) or junior counselor program is very effective with campers of this age.

BASIC EMOTIONS

Love can be of several types and is one of the deep basic needs in normal development. It begins in the very young child with self-love, and later grows to include affection for parents, brothers, sisters, and pets, then affection for persons of the same sex and, finally, love for a member of the opposite sex.

Fear is characterized by dread of impending harm to one's physical or emotional well-being and makes the individual want to either fight or run away from whatever menaces him. Fears are mostly learned reactions, for few of those which later develop are present in a baby. The swimming instructor will be faced with the camper who is afraid of water yet wants to learn to swim, and you may have a camper who is afraid of the dark and loudly protests when lights go out at taps. A certain amount of fear is normal and important, since it causes us to temper our actions with caution, and keeps us from taking foolhardy chances. However, children as well as adults sometimes have unreasonable or unduly magnified fears, which may have developed from past traumatic experiences or from having others pass on their own fears to them. They may also result from exposure to too many ghost or horror stories, or from certain all-too-prevalent types of television programs and movies.

Worry is a form of anxiety about possible future happenings. Though sometimes pinpointed to dread of a specific thing or event, it is often quite vague and is merely a general feeling that something bad may happen. Some children are constant worriers, with such symptoms as insomnia, indigestion, nail-biting, or bed-wetting. Chronic worriers often have deep feelings of insecurity and inferiority, and therefore our efforts to make them feel wanted and approved of may result in rapid cessation of these often seemingly unrelated manifestations.

Inferiority feelings are probably present, at least occasionally, in everyone, for even some of the most outwardly composed, self-confident people confess to having shaky knees or butterflies in their stomachs even when doing something they have done repeatedly in the past, as the athlete about to start an important game or the professional actor or public speaker who is once again before the public. Some, however, experience such feelings almost constantly and in nearly everything they do, because they are convinced that they are inferior to their associates, either physically, mentally, or socially.

Anger usually results when one's plans or wishes are thwarted. A camper may respond to such frustration by going into a temper tantrum or screaming, biting, crying, or throwing things. He may have found these tactics to be effective in getting his own way in the past and may have practiced them so often that they have become almost unconscious reaction patterns with him.

Jealousy results from the actual or feared loss of the affection of someone dear, such as a parent, friend, or pet, or of failing to attain some goal which the individual holds dear, such as winning a tennis match or being elected to some office. Naturally, his jealousy is often directed at the person who did win the thing coveted and may cause

(Courtesy of Camp Fire Girls, Inc., New York.)

him to intensely dislike that person, often belittling him or finding fault with him in an effort to downgrade him while building up his own ego. Feelings of both fear and inferiority usually accompany jealousy, and the child will respond to these feelings in the way which promises the most satisfaction and pleasure. He may show some of the symptoms of the chronic worrier mentioned previously, or he may refuse to eat, suck his thumb, pretend to be ill, or even run away or threaten to kill himself in an effort to gain the sympathy and attention he craves.

CAMPERS ARE INDIVIDUALS

Although we have attempted to summarize the typical characteristics of children according to age, these are obviously mere generalizations, for changes take place gradually, and a youngster doesn't miraculously change from a 10-year-old into an 11-year-old on his eleventh birthday. Development proceeds at different rates in different individuals and even in the same individual, as in a child who suddenly increases in height and weight while remaining relatively immature emotionally and socially. A 12-year-old might well have the physique of a 14-year-old, a 10-year-old's mentality, a social adaptability level of a 9-year-old, and an emotional development of only an 8-year-old.

Campers are usually placed in living groups according to such factors as chronological age, camping experience, and school grade in an attempt to get as homogeneous a grouping as possible, but you will undoubtedly still find quite a bit of diversity among them, owing to these variations in personal development.

We have noted many points of similarity among individuals, and yet we know that there is no one in the whole world exactly like anyone else. Each person's unique personality results from his particular heredity, environment, and associates, for even in his

Figure 7–4 Campers Come in All 57 Varieties Too!

short lifetime, a camper has been in contact with hundreds or even thousands of people, situations, and experiences, each of which has left its stamp of influence on him. The importance of developing what we call a good personality cannot be overestimated, for it opens many doors to an individual and helps him to fit smoothly and happily into our society because he finds it easy to fulfill his needs and wishes in socially acceptable ways. All of us have a general idea as to what we mean by a pleasing personality, but we might find it hard to define in specific terms. In assessing it, we usually refer to the general impression the person makes, based upon such diverse qualities as his posture and general appearance, his facial expression, his voice, the way he handles his body, his choice of vocabulary and manner of speaking, his manners, and, most of all, his way of reacting to and mixing with others. Just as a camper is growing in height and weight, he likewise is developing his personality for better or for worse.

It would be impossible as well as undesirable for us to try to eliminate campers' individual differences, for society needs a wide variety of personalities. You as a counselor must be mature enough to understand and accept each of your campers and encourage him to be *himself* rather than try to change him to fit into a common mold, which would result in a monotonous assortment indeed. It is true that we learn much by imitating others, but an individual attains a feeling of true fulfillment only when he asserts his own individuality while still retaining enough conformity and adaptability to be acceptable to the group.

We tend to notice and perhaps give more attention to the confident, effervescent, outgoing child, for he stands out through his capacity to successfully meet new and untried situations, his sense of security and being loved, and his eagerness to accept responsibility. For these reasons, we especially need to concentrate some of our attention on the quiet, plodding, conscientious introvert, who is often unsure of himself and tends to shrink into the background, keeping his joys and sorrows largely to himself. He is often subservient to others in order to please them and get the reassurance he needs, and he is likely to be a "me-too-er," going along with the crowd and seldom initiating anything himself for fear of failing. This type of child needs your understanding and encouragement to help him to realize that his qualities and contributions are just as valuable as those of the more outgoing, popular child.

Not everyone is geared to the same speed, and constantly admonishing a naturally slow person to hurry may frustrate him until he becomes uncoordinated and extremely nervous. Campers also differ in their vital capacity or stamina, and the large, husky child isn't necessarily "goofing off" when he protests at carrying a heavy pack or hiking over the miles a small, wiry companion can take with ease. Be careful not to confuse physical size with strength and endurance.

The problem, then, becomes one of determining just how much pressure to exert to bring an individual up to what is deemed an acceptable level. On the one hand, you must challenge him to reach his full potential, but at the same time, you must avoid overpressuring him to attempt attainments beyond his capacity. Thus, you must become adept at restraining with one hand while pushing with the other and must use all of your wits to determine the proper proportion of each.

You must keep a cool head and a steady hand at the helm. Your prayer might well be, "Dear God, give me the strength to accept with serenity the things that cannot be changed. Give me courage to change the things that can and should be changed and wisdom to distinguish one from the other."*

LEARNING ABOUT YOUR CAMPERS

SOURCES OF INFORMATION

It becomes evident that in order to treat campers as the individuals they are, you must learn as much as you can about each. Here are some of the possible sources of information:

1. The parental information blank, filled in by parents before camp begins.
2. The camper information blank, filled in by the camper. Keep both eyes open when you study this, for unless questions are skillfully stated, the answers may be what the camper thinks he *should* say rather than what he actually *feels*. For instance, we can be suspicious when a camper states as his objective for coming to camp that he "wants to learn to be more socially acceptable."
3. Organizational records compiled by the sponsoring group, such as the Boy or Girl Scouts.
4. Records from the previous summer if he is a returning camper. These may include health records, activities records, and anecdotal or other "profile" records compiled by former counselors and other staff members.
5. The current health examination report from his home physician.
6. Chats with the camper himself. These should usually be informal and initiated by the counselor in a spontaneous way in order to put the camper at ease and in a mood to talk freely.
7. Observations of the camper as he participates in activities and the routines of group living.
8. Observations of the reactions of other campers to him and comments gleaned by listening to their conversations.
9. Some camps give the counselor the names of his campers before the season starts and suggest that he write an informal, personal letter to each, introducing himself and requesting them to answer with such information as their interests and hobbies. Many times much firsthand information can thus be gained, and it helps to establish camper-counselor rapport before they even meet.

---

*George Sessions Perry and Isabel Leighton: *Where Away*. Whittlesey House. (Used by permission of publishers.)

ADDITIONAL READINGS

(For an explanation of abbreviations and abbreviated forms, see page 25.)

Bloom et al.: *Camper Guidance—A Basic Handbook for Counselors.*

Bossard, James H. S., and E. S. Boll: *The Sociology of Child Development.* Harper & Row, 4th ed., 1966, $10.95.

Coleman, James S.: *The Adolescent Society.* Free Press, 1971, $8.50; $3.95, paper.

Donaldson, Lou and George: *Teaching in the Field.* The Donaldsons, Box 203, Oregon, Ill. 61061, 1971, 31 pp., 75¢.

Fedder, Ruth: *A Girl Grows Up.* McGraw-Hill, 4th ed., 1964, $4.95.

Gardner, Richard A., M. D.: *Understanding Children.* Jason Aronson, Inc., 59 Fourth Avenue, New York, N. Y. 10003, 1973, 258 pp., $10.

Hauck, Paul A.: *The Rational Management of Children.* Libra, 2nd ed., 1972, 190 pp., $5.95.

Hollander, Sandra, and Sox Saville: *Games People Ought to Play: Reality Games.* Macmillan, 1972, pp. 19–348.

James, Muriel, and Dorothy Jangeward: *Born to Win.* Addison-Wesley Publishing Company, Reading, Mass., 1971, pp. 1–433.

Jourard, Sidney M.: *The Transparent Self.* Van Nostrand, 1971, pp. 3–207.

MacKay: *Creative Counseling for Christian Camps,* ch. 3.

Shivers: *Camping,* ch. 7 to p. 148; ch. 8.
Todd: *Camping for Christian Youth,* ch. 14.
Van Krevelen: *Children in Groups: Psychology and the Summer Camp,* chs. 1, 2.

MAGAZINE ARTICLES

Camping Magazine:
"Camping for Older Girls." Mar., 1974, p. 11.
Gabel, Dr. Peter S.: "Teenage—the Best Age for Camping." Nov./Dec., 1973, p. 10.
Krieger, William, Ed. D.: "Study on Self-Concept Change in Campers Receives ACA's 1972 Research Award." Apr., 1973, p. 16.
Loren, Harold: "What Can We Do About the Camp Drop Out." Nov./Dec., 1969, p. 14.
McMaster, Robert: "Camp Rules for Adolescents," May, 1974, p. 11.
Solimine, Alexander, Jr.: "Seven-Year-Olds Meet Challenges of Real Wilderness Tripping." Sept., 1972, p. 19.

Chapter 8

The Counselor as a Leader

Figure 8-1 Stepping in Your Footsteps.

A LITTLE FELLOW FOLLOWS ME

A careful man I ought to be,
  A little fellow follows me.
I dare not go astray,
  For fear he'll go the self-same way.
I cannot once escape his eyes.
  Whate'er he sees me do he tries.
Like me, he says, he's going to be,
  The little chap who follows me.
He thinks that I am good and fine,
  Believes in every word of mine.
The base in me he must not see,
  That little chap who follows me.
I must remember as I go,
  Thru summers' sun and winters' snow,
I am building for the years to be,
  In that little chap who follows me.

—AUTHOR UNKNOWN

LEADERSHIP

DESIRABLE CHANGES DO NOT AUTOMATICALLY OCCUR

Let us review some of the satisfying changes which can take place in a camper through his camp experiences. He can attain a deeper sense of self-respect as he learns, with adult guidance, to weigh the pros and cons of possible actions and to decide for himself which will give him the most lasting satisfaction. He can attain a deeper sense of security as he acquires the ability to understand and accept others, and in turn learns to fit harmoniously into the group. He thus experiences the warm feeling which comes when one is respected and accepted by others.

He enjoys the freedom and pleasures of democratic living in a more or less self-sustaining group that determines many of its own activities and standards of conduct, but he sees that such living also demands respect for the rights of others and carries with it certain responsibilities. He learns to care for his own possessions and person and to perform many tasks which someone else may have previously done for him, for in camp there is no maid or self-sacrificing mother to do things for him. He learns to provide his own entertainment and acquires many new skills, particularly those concerned with living in an out-of-door environment under more or less primitive conditions.

Note that while we have mentioned all these things as being possible, we have not meant to imply that they will magically appear like a rabbit out of a magician's hat just because the child is living in an organized camp, for unfortunately, camps come in all varieties. Some camps can do immense damage to their campers or at best leave them pretty much as they were when they came.

First and foremost, to realize the camp's greatest potentials, its philosophy, organization, and personnel must be designed and utilized with the express purpose of providing a favorable climate for desirable camper participation and growth. You, the counselor, must then follow up by effectively grasping and making use of the opportunities provided, for they will lie dormant and unproductive unless you furnish the spark to set them in motion. This is a big responsibility, to be sure, for even though you are dedicated and well-intentioned, your utmost efforts will come to nothing unless you know what to do and when and how to do it.

As we have repeatedly pointed out, it is most important that you yourself exemplify the qualities and ways of living you wish your campers to develop, for despite its triteness, there is still truth to the saying that "What you do speaks so loudly I can't hear what you say." You must be constantly mindful of the general characteristics of the age group with which you are working and must have the astuteness and sensitivity to note and allow for the variations among individuals which will inevitably exist. In fact, you may find that your whole group varies in important aspects from what is generally considered the norm, owing to such background factors as race, culture, region of the country, economic status, past experiences, and a host of others. You will need the perceptive, analytical, and constructive abilities of an engineer, since in one sense you will be serving as a "human engineer" throughout your summer's undertakings. Your methods of dealing with individuals and groups will largely determine your success, and when puzzled as to how to proceed in given situations, you might well ask yourself, "If I were a camper, what kind of person would I want my leader (counselor) to be?" or "How would I want my counselor to act toward me and my fellow campers?" Why not discuss the situation with them and let them help you to arrive at a decision?

Figure 8-2 A Leader.

WHAT DYNAMIC LEADERSHIP INVOLVES

EVERY GROUP HAS A LEADER

The ability to exert the positive leadership we are talking about will not automatically come to you just because you have secured a position as a leader or have been designated as one by someone in authority. Though a group may feel dutybound to pay deference to an appointed leader, they may actually be influenced to a much greater extent by someone else who has no official status at all. This unofficial leader is often a member of the group who, because of his personality and behavior, is able to crystallize their thinking and sway them toward his point of view.

Every group of individuals acting together has some sort of leader, either appointed, elected by the group, or just spontaneously followed. For instance, a street gang engaged in brawling, vandalism, and general rowdiness often has a very potent leader, for there must be someone to decide upon and direct their various escapades, which often involve painstaking "briefing of the case" and careful planning of details, from how best to utilize the talents of each member to how to dispose of the loot and divide the spoils. Punishment must also be designed for those who "chicken out," "rat on," or fail to execute their assignments in an approved manner. This leader often possesses an uncanny ability to lead and organize and shows great talent for "sizing up" and dealing with individuals, as well as the group as a whole. What a waste of both his and his gang's potentialities, for their abilities and energies are misdirected toward the detriment of society rather than its benefit. It seems obvious that, at least in some cases and in a different environment, a dynamic and constructive leader could steer them into socially approved ways of satisfying their feelings of rebellion and natural youthful craving for thrills, adventure, excitement and their need to be a member of a group.

REQUIREMENTS FOR LEADERSHIP

As a counselor, you have a chance to demonstrate true leadership by guiding your group into constructive endeavors. Although you will be teaching skills and performing many other duties, your most important contribution will be your efforts to help your campers to develop a proper sense of values, together with desirable attitudes and ways of thinking.

Before becoming a good leader, one should learn to be a good follower. Dr. Joel W. Bloom and associates have defined *followership* as "the ability to serve in a democratic group situation under the leadership of a member of that group but still retain the capacity to suggest, criticize and evaluate, as well as serve in the project."* Through constant practice, you should have already acquired the skills of living congenially with a group. Heading the list of your attributes will probably be a spirit of cooperation and teamwork, for a good group member works *with* his fellow members and is often called upon to willingly and unselfishly sacrifice his own wishes for their best interests.

Ideally, you will, as a leader, possess the ability to weld your group into such a well-coordinated team, with each contributing according to his abilities, that it functions like a well-oiled piece of machinery. Although personality clashes and dissension will inevitably occur, since so many personalities and individual desires are involved, a spirit of harmony and goodwill should prevail most of the time. Group spirit should deepen and strengthen as each successive project comes to fruition, but it must never be allowed to reach a point where it creates an unfriendly feeling or undue rivalry with other groups or a willingness to sacrifice the welfare of the whole camp.

As a leader, you will not only be learning to understand and counsel in-

---

*Bloom et al.: *Camper Guidance—A Basic Handbook for Counselors.* ACA, 1960, p. 16.

dividuals, but you will also be mastering the techniques of dealing formally and informally with a group as a whole. We will now consider additional ways to increase your effectiveness in these areas.

LEADERSHIP

The boss drives his men; the leader coaches them.
The boss depends upon authority; the leader on goodwill.
The boss inspires fear; the leader inspires enthusiasm.
The boss says, "I"; the leader says, "We."
The boss assigns the tasks; the leader sets the pace.
The boss says, "Get here on time"; the leader gets there ahead of time.
The boss fixes the blame for the breakdown; the leader fixes the breakdown.
The boss knows how it is done; the leader shows how.
The boss makes work a drudgery; the leader makes it a game.
The boss says, "Go"; the leader says, "Let's go."
The world needs leaders; but nobody wants a boss.*

TYPES OF LEADERS

There are three basic types of leaders: (1) an *autocratic leader* makes all important decisions himself and controls his group mainly by force and fear; (2) a *laissez-faire leader* is almost the exact opposite, for he is overly lenient, allowing his group to decide everything for themselves and to do whatever they wish, with a minimum of adult interference; (3) a *democratic leader* is a combination of the two. He can assume control and use discipline on the few occasions when he finds it necessary, but he ordinarily assumes the role of big brother, influencing his young followers through the respect and confidence engendered in them by what he is and what he stands for and his skill in planning and working cooperatively with them. Most leaders fall somewhere within this last, broad category, between the extremes of the autocratic and the laissez-faire leaders.

*Dodge, Dora E.: *Thirty Years of Girls' Club Experience.*

THE AUTOCRATIC LEADER

The autocratic leader singlehandedly decides upon the activities, goals, and procedures for his group, then draws up step-by-step instructions for them to follow. He is apparently oblivious to the reactions of his campers and seldom considers their opinions or desires; he seems to believe that his own judgments and decisions are so superior that he needs no advice or help from anyone else. He feels that he knows what is best for everyone and is therefore justified in enforcing his mandates on them willy-nilly. His "big stick" methods of control brook no lapse of discipline or questioning of his authority, and he threatens drastic and certain punishment for all dissenters and nonconformists.

His high-handed tactics accomplish little permanent good, for as we have previously noted, exemplary conduct evoked by fear or force lasts only while the leader is present. Some will respond to such a leader with passivity and subservience, often becoming so dependent that they lose the ability to make decisions for themselves. Others react by resisting or rebelling, and often develop an intense hatred for discipline and authority of any kind or from any source.

Under an autocratic leader, groups have a tendency to destroy more property when working, to be more aggressive, and to show much more hostility, often channeling their frustrations toward some scapegoat in the group, since they are afraid to direct them against the true target, the leader. On the whole, the members are more de-

Figure 8-3 The Autocratic Leader From Camp No-It-All.

pendent and submissive and tend to show less individuality than those under other types of leadership. Although autocratic methods may sometimes be efficient or even necessary, as during an emergency, they should be the exception rather than the rule, since when used habitually, they reduce the initiative and creativity of those subjected to them, as well as producing the undesirable results mentioned previously.

Unfortunately, an autocratic leader sometimes assumes these dictatorial qualities unconsciously, in a mistaken belief that such conduct is expected of a leader and indicates that he is forceful, aggressive, and strong. Instead of feeling cocky, self-assured, and confident, as his outward manner suggests, in reality, he is often covering up deep-seated feelings of insecurity and inadequacy for which bossing others seems to compensate. He may be satisfying his desire for power over others in this unhealthy way, and he demonstrates his emotional inmaturity by meeting misdemeanors and resistance with loss of temper, harsh scoldings, and even physical punishment.

THE LAISSEZ-FAIRE LEADER

The laissez-faire leader is almost the exact opposite of the autocratic leader, for he asserts no authority or leadership at all, under the misapprehension that a group can develop independence and self-reliance only by practicing *complete* self-direction. He realizes that campers should be happy, but is laboring under the delusion that happiness comes only when people are left entirely free to do what they want whenever they want, and that his wishy-washy methods are therefore necessary; nothing could be further from the truth.

He tries to be "one of the gang," going along with whatever they suggest, apparently in the hope of gaining popularity with them. Although they may like him in a lukewarm way, they soon lose respect for him when they recognize his weakness and lack of direction. Children subconsciously expect their appointed leader to be stronger and wiser than they and to act in a dynamic and positive fashion. Although they frequently protest against it, studies have shown that children really want a certain amount of discipline.

When campers are left entirely on their own to work out a program, their inexperience and limited awareness of possibilities often result in a pointless and fragmented program with which they soon become bored. They are then likely to sink into indifference and apathy, arguing among themselves over who will act as leader and getting into mischief just to create some excitement and break the monotony. The counselor will then find it almost impossible to reassert his authority and regain control of the group, for by this time, the campers will have little faith in someone who has allowed the situation to deteriorate to this point. Groups under a laissez-faire leader accomplish very little, and even that is usually of poor quality.

THE DEMOCRATIC LEADER

The democratic leader strikes a balance between the autocratic and laissez-faire approaches to leadership. He is a "good sport" and a firm believer in fun and good times, yet he can be firm and can exercise control or administer swift and just discipline when necessary.

He is able to relax and have a good time, for he has mastered the art of working *with, for,* and *in* the group without losing control of them; however, he knows where to draw the line when things start to get out of hand, involve physical hazards, or are against camp policies and objectives. He encourages group members to express their views and to participate in camp government and program planning insofar as their ages and abilities permit. He realizes that if his group has not previously been allowed such freedom, it may at first "kick up its heels" and be as undisciplined and aggressive as a spring colt, and so he continues to patiently and persistently work with them, gradually assigning them more freedom and responsibility as they want it and prove able to handle it. Progress by the democratic process is slow, for explanations, discussions, and group action take time and although the leader may often be tempted to resort to doing it himself or using autocratic methods, he realizes that his campers can grow and mature only

(Courtesy of National Music Camp, Interlochen, Michigan.)

through solving problems for themselves and that what happens inside the campers is more important, in the long run, than the material things they accomplish. A democratic leader is not overly cautious through fear of losing status by making a mistake, and he honestly admits his errors, for his relationship with the group is such that they respect his honesty and realize that, being human, he will not be infallible.

In the best sense of the word, a democratic group is one which has learned to live together in comparative harmony while initiating, conducting and evaluating its own program; it is willing to accept and abide by the results of its own decisions. Citizens in a democracy must learn to be good "choosers" and each must be willing to accept group decisions and do his share to carry them out, even though they are not his own choice. The leader stays somewhat in the background, acting as a friendly adviser and guide, helping when and where he is needed and seeing that responsibilities and privileges are distributed equitably.

Many counselors only give lip service to democratic planning with their group, holding perfunctory discussions with them but giving them little real control over decisions. Test yourself by thinking back over your own recent planning sessions and discussions to see how much talking you did and to determine whether the ideas and plans were truly group decisions or were instead simply your own ideas.

When true democratic procedures exist throughout the camp, every person has a chance to express himself and share in the decision-making processes of the camp, either directly, within his cabin group, or indirectly, through his representatives on the unit council and all-camp council.

One trouble with being a leader is that you can't be sure whether the people are following you or chasing you.

—AUTHOR UNKNOWN

CHARACTERISTICS OF A GOOD LEADER

1. A good leader leads by example. What he *does* agrees with what he *says*.

2. He has a good sense of humor and exercises it to avert crises and to keep minor problems from becoming major ones. He can see the humorous side of things and always has time for a good joke, even when it's on him.

3. His thoughts are not always centered on himself and how each situation and decision will affect him, but are instead extended outward toward the group as a whole.

4. In order to tactfully introduce worthwhile ideas or projects, he often relies upon the power of suggestion. He casually mentions an idea without insisting that it be adopted; he suggests rather than commands. In this way, the group is free to elaborate on his idea and to improve and alter it, as many minds will when working together toward a common goal. Often his suggestions come from some casual comments his campers have made, which give him a clue as to their needs and interests.

5. He tactfully avoids misunderstandings and feuds whenever he can and sincerely attempts to see things from others' viewpoints. He realizes that when he arouses another's antagonism, he diminishes his ability to influence him in the future.

6. When there is work to be done, he is in the midst of it, sleeves rolled up and hands just as dirty as anybody else's.

7. He understands the force of group pressure and group opinion, but also realizes that there is danger in letting campers entirely rule themselves, for their judgment is still immature and they sometimes get carried away by their own enthusiasm.

8. He is ever-mindful of the value of "fun," for happy, self-motivated campers seldom become problems to themselves or others. When teaching a

new skill, he is thorough, but patient and understanding, and proceeds in an informal, friendly manner. He devises ways to make chores fun instead of irksome tasks.

9. He knows that campers, no matter how much they complain, do not really enjoy slovenly, careless standards of conduct or performance, and that they will soon lose respect for him if he tolerates laxness or haphazardness. He recognizes that a suggestion such as "Don't you think the path to the waterfront looks pretty crummy?" or "Who would like to help me put the cabin tools in tip-top shape this rainy afternoon?" gets a better response than an order; he also realizes that there are occasions when orders are necessary, and that once issued, they must be enforced without exception, unless he sees that they were in error in the first place.

10. He gives praise freely and can see some good in nearly everything and everybody, but he realizes that when praise is insincere or overused, it is quickly detected and discounted. He avoids nagging and excessive fussiness about detail, for he knows that they tend to destroy campers' enthusiasm and interest, and he seldom, if ever, resorts to sarcasm or ridicule.

11. He can foresee an impending problem and tries to avert it if he can. If Johnny is chanting how much he dislikes spinach, he does not wait until everyone at the table is wailing about their pet dislikes, but quietly reminds Johnny, "We try to talk about pleasant things at the table."

12. He shuns public scenes whenever possible. A "bawling out" before others hurts a camper's pride and makes him react by giving up or growing resentful and intent on revenge. He knows that emotional hurts are even more serious than physical ones and gives the erring camper a chance to "save face" by ignoring the misdemeanor in public, but discussing it later on in private in a frank and friendly manner. He knows that "badness" often occurs because a camper feels hurt or embarrassed or simply doesn't know what is appropriate behavior in a given situation. He rejects the bad conduct but not the camper, and he never sends a camper away feeling dejected and hopeless, but tries to leave him with the feeling that he still has faith in him and trusts him not to make the same mistake twice.

Figure 8-4 Never Leave a Camper with a Feeling of Rejection.

13. He seldom *tells* a camper what to do, but instead discusses the problem with him, skillfully leading him to analyze the situation himself and eventually arrive at his own solution.

14. He never uses physical punishment, for it seldom brings about the desired result, is usually against camp policies, and might involve him or the camp in legal difficulties.

15. He uses disciplinary measures sparingly and only when convinced that they will benefit the culprit; he never uses them vindictively or in an effort to save his own pride. Punishment is so easy to administer and gets such quick and sure results (outwardly,

at least) that it is often misused or overused. A superior counselor handles his group so skillfully that serious disciplinary problems are reduced to a minimum, but even so, sooner or later the day will come when action can no longer be postponed. He will find that children are usually good sports about accepting punishment they deserve, if no partiality or spite is involved. When discipline is necessary, it should follow the misdemeanor as closely as possible and preferably should bear some relationship to it; for instance, depriving a camper of his dessert would probably be appropriate only for a dining room misdemeanor. Using work as a punitive measure belittles it and drags it down from the place of honor it ought to hold; however, it may sometimes be appropriately meted out to a camper who has caused unnecessary work for others, such as by cluttering up the grounds or throwing food around the dining room.

16. He knows that people tend to live up to what others expect of them, and that one of the best ways to get a camper to improve is to let him feel that you expect nothing but the best from him. Issuing a challenge is a very potent force to bring out the best in anyone.

17. He does not take a camper's bad conduct as a personal affront, realizing that it is more likely to be a reaction to some past experience or an outside worry. When a camper rebels at even a reasonable amount of discipline, it may be because of previous overdoses of it at home or school.

18. He satisfies his own basic needs or wishes in a positive way and so keeps himself mentally healthy. For

Figure 8-5 A Counselor Is Not!!!

instance, he does not secure the affection he needs by taking advantage of campers' tendencies toward hero worship or crushes, or by encouraging special or exclusive friendships with his campers or peers.

19. He seldom yields to sudden bursts of anger, because he uses a "cooling off" period to give himself time to get all the facts and to see the situation from another perspective when his head is cooler and his judgment sounder. There are a few occasions, however, when justified anger, kept well under control, may serve a useful purpose.

20. He is firm but friendly, remaining objective toward all. He tries to stay on amicable terms with those who personally disagree with him.

21. He takes his position seriously, justifiably taking pride in any small successes, but not letting them make him bossy or conceited. As a true leader, he works tirelessly and unceasingly for a cause, realizing that even superhuman efforts may bring him little honor or thanks. His true reward must come from his own inner sense of satisfaction at having contributed his best efforts toward making the world a better place in which to live.

22. Although in being honest it is sometimes necessary to hurt people, he does so only when all other methods fail. He is careful to show the person that he still likes him and is merely trying to show him how to live more harmoniously with others.

ALL IN THE POINT OF VIEW*

"I am firm
You are determined
He is obstinate
We are resolved
You are persistent
They are pig-headed fools."

—*A.D.*, July, 1973.

*Permission of the publishers.

WORKING WITH A GROUP

THE USE OF SOCIODRAMA

WHAT IT IS

Sociodrama is a form of play-acting in which individuals play the roles of certain people, creating the dialogue as they go along or using a previously prepared script; it is especially effective with older campers. It adds spice and variety to the program and can be useful as a teaching method and as a means of pinpointing and solving problems, especially when followed by a discussion of what took place and its implications. Keep it lively and never allow it to drift off into silliness or exaggeration, but expect some touches of humor to creep in as the actors inject their own personalities into the roles they are playing.

WHAT IT CAN DO

Sociodrama can serve many purposes, for example:

1. To instruct or get a point across. It is particularly useful in working with a CIT group or regular counselors during training sessions. A hypothetical situation is presented, with actors assigned to play such roles as camp director or other camp administrators, counselors, campers, or visiting parents. They may then act out proper (or improper) ways to behave on such occasions as visitors' day, the counselors' visit to the neighboring village on their day off, the counselor during rest hour or in the hour just before taps, and so forth. If desired, several others may act out their personal versions of proper procedures at these times, with the group then discussing and evaluating each presentation. In the same way, campers may act out such things as acceptable and unacceptable conservation practices (carving initials,

strewing leftovers from a cookout around or dumping them in the lake, causing or controlling erosion, eliminating fire hazards), washing dishes, conduct in the dining room, and so forth.

2. To solve a problem. The sociodrama may deal with a problem of campers, counselors, or both; possible topics are "Mary, who won't observe quiet after taps or during rest hour"; "John, who has poor habits of personal cleanliness and neatness"; "Susan, who shirks her share of cabin cleanup duties"; or "Henry, who is bossy and always wants to run the show." This may provide a tactful way to allow a person to see himself in a new light, as he notes how disagreeable some of his ways seem to others. (Be careful not to make the characterization so pointed that it hurts feelings.) The problem may be a real or imaginary one, with each acting out his idea of the best solution, followed by a general appraisal and discussion.

3. To develop *empathy* or attempt to put yourself in another's place, so that you understand how he is feeling. Mary, again, is a camper who won't observe quiet after taps; why does Mary act as she does and how do the others feel about having her keep them awake? How does a member of a minority group feel? What about Jimmy, who never gets any mail at mail call, or the counselor who is dead tired after a strenuous day, yet whose campers won't quiet down at taps so that she can go to her cabin for some much-needed rest? How does the busy dietician feel when campers are a half hour late for an appointment to plan the menu for a cookout, or the busy caretaker, when campers don't return his tools promptly or damage them by careless use? Younger campers may even want to take the part of an animal, such as a squirrel, who won't have enough to eat next winter because campers are gathering *all* the nuts.

4. To learn desirable and undesirable ways to do something, such as launch a canoe, build a fire, act as leader of a discussion, serve as camper leader to organize an overnight, carry on cabin cleanup, or wash dishes. How can his cabinmates help a camper who is painfully shy or who feels left out? The usual discussion and evaluation then follow.

5. To develop better communication within the camp and to give insights or awaken emotions the person never realized himself capable of before. After participating in such activities, each person will probably mull over what happened and his own and others' feelings about it and perhaps discuss it further with his fellow campers or counselors.

Obviously there are many possible variations, such as secretly selecting someone each day to play the role of a braggart, practical joker, or daredevil; the group is then asked to pick out the actor for the day and the good and bad qualities he was depicting. Another variation is to ask individuals to perform certain skills such as building a fire, launching or docking a canoe, or packing for a trip, deliberately making certain mistakes to see if the group observes them. You may want to ask the group to suggest topics, or leave it up to a committee or the cabin council to suggest problems they think might lend themselves well to such techniques.

LEADING A DISCUSSION

I dislike him because he only listens when he talks.

—GEORGE BERNARD SHAW

DISCUSSIONS IN CAMP

Everyone enjoys taking part in a discussion, and campers are no exception. Discussion should be regarded as a valuable part of the camp experience, for the interchange of ideas and opinions is important to a camper's development as a person.

In addition to the usual spontaneous, informal discussions, there will probably be some of a more formal nature that are planned by you, either at your own instigation or in response to requests from campers. At other times, you may want to introduce a topic in a casual way, so that the ensuing discussion is more spontaneous. Unless a situation calls for an immediate discussion, it is best to hold them on rainy days, late afternoons, or during the period just before taps. In the camp situation, a relaxed, friendly, informal atmosphere is usually most appropriate.

REASONS FOR DISCUSSIONS

People often engage in discussions merely to exchange opinions or acquire information about almost anything under the sun. One of the most fascinating things about people of camp age is their insatiable curiosity and desire to know the how, where, what, and why of countless things, not only in their own environment, but also in far-away times and places. They often enjoy discussing such diverse topics as college life, vocations, dating, love and marriage, personal grooming, Indian lore, fishing, camping techniques, cheating, religion, current inventions, and world affairs. Through these conversations, campers can acquire information, broaden their interests and insights, and learn to better communicate with and understand others.

Discussion is also one of the best ways to clear up misunderstandings and solve problems, such as how to divide cabin duties and thus avoid shirkers and "workhorses," how to deal with campers who lie, steal, or spread malicious gossip, or to explain the reasons for certain camp rules, such as why all must wear shoes to and from the waterfront. When a wise counselor detects undercurrents of unrest which seem to be building up to a crisis, he gives his campers the opportunity to express their dissatisfaction and "blow off steam." It is better to bring controversial matters out into the open and let everyone discuss what is bothering him before tensions build up and tempers reach the boiling point. A frank and open discussion will often be enough to solve the problem, for increased goodwill and mutual understanding will result once perfectly well-meaning people learn how their thoughtless actions have been irritating others or find that their suspicions and distrust were based largely on imagination, idle rumor, or gossip, or a chance act or statement that was misinterpreted.

Discussion is the best and most democratic way to plan a group project such as an overnight hike, a three-day canoe trip, a cabin name and slogan, a camp safety week, a stunt for stunt night, or ways of beautifying unit grounds.

Current events are, or can be made, much more interesting to youngsters than we often realize. They should be included in discussions, for being in camp should not isolate a person to the extent that he seems like Rip Van Winkle awakening from a long sleep when he returns to "civilization."

A camper often has a problem or interest that he hesitates to discuss privately with anyone or that he feels free to discuss only with a buddy or a few of his peers. Questions of general morality, personal health problems, standards of conduct for self or group, relationships with the opposite sex, camp rules or customs, the use of tobacco, alcohol and drugs, or other campers who disturb or puzzle him often fall into this category. He may feel somewhat ashamed of his interest or unsure of how adults or his peers will react to it, so he will need your assurance that you recognize his concerns as being perfectly normal and common to those of his age. When these topics are brought up before the group, he is often relieved to find that others share his interests and gladly enter into the discussion. The more relevant discussions are to the real problems and interests of campers, the more valuable they become.

THE ROLE OF THE COUNSELOR IN DISCUSSION

If you can gain enough of the group's confidence to be freely admitted into their discussions, you can give them the benefit of the wider knowledge and more mature viewpoint and way of thinking your greater age and experience should provide. It will also draw them closer to you when they find you so human and understanding. There is nothing to be gained from burying your head in the sand and refusing to admit that your campers are curious about sex, drugs, and other moral and ethical questions, for whether or not these subjects are brought out into the open, your campers will discuss them. With this in mind, make sure that your influence is for the good, and instruct, inform, and discuss as seems desirable.

Try to keep your campers from overstressing or going overboard in any one area, for there are too many exciting things to do and talk about in this world to concentrate exclusively on only a few. There is a dangerous trend in our society toward overemphasizing sex and certain other topics; with the aid of people like you, camping can help to offset this by recognizing the importance of these matters, but at the same time, showing campers how much they will miss if they allow their interests to become so limited. Are you ma-

(Courtesy of National Music Camp, Interlochen, Michigan.)

ture enough to maintain for yourself and pass on to others a balanced set of values?

PREPARING FOR A PLANNED OR SEMIFORMAL DISCUSSION

The how, when, where, and what of a planned discussion are important considerations. A group of six to eight individuals (never more than fifteen) works best, for it permits a small, intimate grouping in which each can clearly hear and be heard, (a particularly important consideration in the out-of-door setting so common in camp). It also promotes a friendly climate where each feels free to speak frankly, and even the timid can enter in without fear or embarrassment, and it encourages a tendency to think in terms of "We" instead of "I."

Either a counselor or a capable camper may serve as leader or chairman. When serving in this capacity, it is your task to see that everything is in readiness; this includes setting a suitable time and place, notifying participants, and taking care of such details as lighting and seating. If participants are not already aware of what is on the agenda, you may want to inform them of it ahead of time, so that they can come with well-thought-out ideas, instead of talking off the top of their heads and saying things they don't mean or may later regret. You, as leader, may likewise want to prepare yourself, securing pertinent information and planning in some detail how to conduct the meeting. For instance, you may want to plan your opening remarks and outline the logical steps to follow in progressing to a meaningful conclusion in order to avoid having the discussion lag or become bogged down in digressions.

CONDUCTING THE DISCUSSION

It is usually best for everyone to sit in a circle, so that each can see everyone else; you can join the circle yourself if the group is small and informal. It often creates a good atmosphere and makes people more willing to participate if you invite them to bring along a piece of handiwork, such as whittling or some arts and crafts project. If members are new to each other, have each introduce himself and supply a bit of pertinent data about himself. (A variation might be to pair them off to exchange information, each then introducing the other.)

A good first step is to help them to define or arrive at a clear under-

Figure 8–6 Deep in a Discussion.

standing of the exact topic or problem to be discussed and what they hope to accomplish. This starts everyone off on common ground and curbs any tendency to flounder about or bring in irrelevancies. As things progress, it helps to have someone record in large, legible characters such things as data presented, summarizations of decisions made and lists of duties and personnel. This may be done on a blackboard or with a crayon or broad felt pen on a large artist's pad or sheet of butcher's paper, arranged easel-style. Someone may also be designated as secretary to keep a permanent record of proceedings. If several topics are up for discussion, you may want to ask the group to arrange them in the order of their importance, putting near the end those which could possibly be postponed until a later meeting. However, if discussion of topics cannot be postponed, draw up a schedule and allot the necessary time to each topic and make sure the schedule is followed.

You are now ready to introduce the first topic. Once the discussion has gotten started, you should retire into the background, for the discussion should largely be between group members, not between you and the group. Your main function is to keep the discussion going in an orderly fashion, summarizing main points as they develop, and steering the group members on to the next step as rapidly as is feasible, in order to reach a satisfying conclusion. Though it is occasionally wise to permit some digression from the subject, you must use good judgment as to just how much and how far this should go before you tactfully but forcefully bring them back on course again. Keep a sharp eye out for signs of unrest or disinterest, for young children, in particular, have short interest spans, and, even more than their elders, grow impatient with purposeless monologues or repetitions by the long-winded who seem to crop up in every group.

One of the best ways to launch a subject, bring a wandering group back on course, or move them on to another topic is to ask a question. Express it as briefly as possible, choosing your words carefully to clearly bring out your meaning. Ask questions which will require a thoughtful answer rather than a simple "yes" or "no." For instance, you might begin by asking, "Since our meeting is to decide what to do Wednesday night, who has a suggestion to make?" (List the suggestions on the blackboard and encourage discussion until they finally agree on two or three.) Then, if the choice lies between going on an overnight star-gazing trip or working on their outdoor cooking site, you might say, "Since you seem about equally divided between the star-gazing trip and work on the outdoor site, who would like to speak for or against the star-gazing trip?" After a similar discussion on working on the outdoor site, call for a final vote. If they decide on the trip, ask what preparations will have to be made for it; they will probably mention such things as deciding on when to leave, menu, program, personal and group equipment needed, assembling and packing supplies and work committees and their duties. Record these on the blackboard and then work out the details involved in each.

Before concluding the meeting, summarize what you have accomplished in some way, as by asking each to state the most important things he gained from it or by briefly restating important decisions reached or responsibilities assumed by individuals or the group, and when, where, and how they are to be carried out. Keep notes for yourself, and in order to ascertain what progress is being made, follow up at a later meeting or ask individuals such questions as, "Jack, how are those plans for stunt night coming?" or "How many of you were in your seats and quiet before vespers began last night?"

ADDITIONAL HINTS FOR THE LEADER

If your group lacks experience or has drifted into bad discussion habits, plan an early meeting to consider with them how to prepare and carry on a good discussion. This may call for a review of important rules of order and some of the courtesies and techniques of participation; for instance, each person should respect the rights of the one who has the floor and should listen intently and open-mindedly to what he has to say. Conversely, he should never rudely interrupt or be so involved in his own point of view that he doesn't listen or closes his mind to the good points others make. He should avoid wasting time by restating points already made, using more than his share of time, or not thinking out what he wants to say so that he can be brief and to the point. After the group has reached a decision, each should accept it gracefully and wholeheartedly join in helping to carry it out.

With younger campers, you will need to take quite a bit of the decision-making responsibility yourself, but you can and should let older campers gradually do more, since they are increasingly resentful of being dominated by their elders and are eager to demonstrate their own growing abilities to decide things for themselves and carry them out. Encourage them in this, even though they may make mistakes, and promote a spirit of cooperation rather than of competition.

This is a good time for you to demonstrate your understanding of the true meaning of democratic leadership. Your campers will often surprise you with their good judgment and ingenuity when challenged and will enter into projects they have planned with enthusiasm and determination, for it will have become a matter of individual as well as group pride to them. This "hands off" policy is hard for most of us to maintain, for we have a tendency to be impatient and to want to boost our own egos by stepping in to suggest what should be done and how and by whom. Yet our role should be one of standing by to prevent really serious mistakes, instructing and assisting as needed, and exerting a restraining hand only when necessary, for the most important thing is what is happening inside the campers, not how much gets done.

Of the best leaders, the people only know
that they exist;
The next best, they love and praise;
The next, they fear;
And the next, they revile.
When they do not command the people's
faith,
Some will lose faith in them,
And then they resort to recrimination,
But of the best, when their task is accomplished,
Their work done,
The people all remark: "We have done it
ourselves."

—Author Unknown

(Reprinted from Douglas Monahan, *Let's Look at Leadership.* Character Craft, 1958.)

Introduce older campers to the committee system of work in which committees do certain parts of the job or perform preliminary work, and then report back to the entire group. Ordinarily, the group should choose its own leaders and committee members, for they often know their peers much better than you, and when impressed with the importance of selecting people who will be responsible and capable, will usually choose wisely and will follow those chosen more willingly. Point out that one of the main duties of a good committee leader or chairman is to maintain enthusiasm and a spirit of teamwork in his group, in addition to getting the job done.

If there is some question as to whether it will be possible to carry through on a proposed project because of needed permission, expense, supplies, or the availability of certain personnel, clear up these problems first, before expending your energy and getting too enthusiastic about it.

Strike a happy medium between letting a discussion drag and rushing through it; undue haste and demonstrations of impatience on your part will make some hesitant to speak and cause others to feel hurried.

Be broad-minded and able to see all sides of a question. Remember that all thinking people pride themselves on being flexible enough to change their minds when convinced there is good reason to do so.

Be friendly and informal, yet maintain the dignity of your position. Do not try to cover up embarrassment or ineptitude by giggling, wisecracking, or trying to entertain. Stay in the background, yet maintain control by such methods as tactfully discouraging timewasters and monopolizers and encouraging the quieter campers to participate, for they have often been spending their time thinking instead of talking and so will have worthwhile contributions to make. Give each the feeling that you *want* to hear what *he* has to say; then listen to him respectfully and intently and thank him when he is finished. Don't assume the role of judge or critic, and avoid taking advantage of your position by sneering, belittling, using sarcasm, or making light of any idea expressed in sincerity. Avoid embarrassing a person or making him lose face before others, and if you feel it necessary to reprimand him, do it tactfully. Bear in mind that your gestures and facial expressions convey impressions just as much as your words. If necessary, protect the members of the group from each other, immediately squelching rudeness, bickering, or derogatory remarks made by anyone to or about another or his ideas. Your own example of showing respect for each individual and your attitude of courtesy and fairness to all will help to set the tone for the group.

Figure 8-7 What Do You Think?

Like a good basketball referee, a good discussion leader controls the situation while keeping himself in the background. You are entitled to express your opinions like anyone else, but you should never take advantage of your position by talking overtime, forcing your ideas on the group, or overruling majority opinion unless camp safety or policy demands it. This little saying expresses it well and briefly:

> Silent prayer of the old preacher:
> "Lord, fill my mouth with wonderful stuff,
> Then nudge me when I've said enough."
>
> —AUTHOR UNKNOWN

OF COURSE THERE WILL BE PROBLEMS

As in every other camp activity, you will encounter problems in a group discussion. There will always be at least one who talks too much, apparently enamored with the sound of his own voice or with the sense of importance that "sounding off" gives him. Although he sometimes has good ideas, he often buries them in verbiage, merely repeats what others have said, or just chatters on with words which apparently come from his mouth without benefit of having passed through his brain. Group members should refrain from garrulousness for, as George Eliot said, "Blessed is the man who, having nothing to say, abstains from giving in words evidence of the fact." For those who don't abstain, we would like to recommend the "South African treatment," which limits a speaker to what he can say while standing on one foot, with his speech automatically ending the instant he touches his other foot to the ground. Other ways to correct such tendencies are to discuss the importance of equal sharing of speaking time during one of your general sessions on good discussion techniques or to assign him some special task, such as acting as blackboard recorder, to keep him occupied and feeling important. You may occasionally have to be even more direct, asking someone to keep a record of each person who speaks and the amount of time he consumes, or you may need to discuss the problem personally with the individual.

The opposite of the excessively talkative camper is the retiring type who talks too little and listens without contributing. Ask yourself why he doesn't enter in, since you know that one of the normal fundamental needs is to belong and fit in with the group and establish oneself as an individual. Perhaps he may lack interest or fear making a mistake, being laughed at, or incurring the ill will of others; maybe the answer lies in your own leadership methods, which may inadvertently cause embarrassment or hurt feelings. Work hard to gain his participation, and then work even harder to maintain it.

There will usually be at least one unpopular camper who is the butt of camp jokes, whose every opinion is scoffed at just because it is his, and who

Figure 8–8 It Takes All Kinds.

isn't even permitted to finish what he is saying. Unless you hasten to change matters and keep others from throwing cold water on his efforts, he will soon stop trying to fit in and contribute.

Some will want their specific, individual problems solved, apparently feeling that the discussion group is like an automat, making it possible to drop in a question or problem, push a lever and receive an immediate answer. Group discussion can only open up various lines of thought and help each member to evaluate them and arrive at his own decision.

Every group is likely to contain biased, opinionated persons or "know-it-alls." These people look upon a discussion as merely a sounding board for displaying their own pearls of wisdom before the admiring multitudes of the ignorant. Such is the intolerant camper or counselor who "only listens when *he* speaks" and furiously attacks any persons who dare to differ with him. He should be reminded of the Chinese saying that getting angry is a sign that one has run out of arguments.

OTHER TYPES OF DISCUSSIONS

The Circular Response or Circular Discussion Method. In an effort to overcome some of the limitations of the usual discussion method, Hillsdale

College has promoted the Circular Response or Circular Discussion Method.* It is based on a technique originated by Dr. Eduard C. Lindeman of the New York School of Social Work, which consists of arranging the group in the usual circle, and choosing someone at random to start the discussion. Then, proceeding clockwise around the circle, each is given a certain amount of time, for instance, one minute, to express himself. No one may talk out of turn or speak again until the discussion gets around to him on the next "go-around." Someone acts as timekeeper (a good job for one inclined to talk too much) and signals when the time is up, and, as usual, one person is assigned to record on the blackboard and another to take permanent notes. Continue around the circle as many times as seems profitable and then summarize the discussion as usual.

When a person's turn comes, he may use his allotted time to (1) add new thoughts or opinions; (2) comment on previous remarks; (3) add to or elaborate upon previous remarks; (4) "pass" with the understanding that he will be given another chance when the discussion returns to him again; or (5) ask that his time be devoted to a period of silence to give each person time to summarize his thoughts.

Before the first go-around, give each from one to three minutes to think about the subject and decide what he wants to say, then devote an additional minute to let him condense it into brief or "telegram" form. He may then, of course, use his allotted time to elaborate as he wishes.

The leader acts in his usual capacity, seeing that the rules are observed (no one interrupts or speaks out of turn, no one exceeds his time limit), summarizes points made, and so on.

The Hillsdale bulletin suggests that, even though the group is already familiar with the method, it is a good idea to go over the ground rules briefly before each session.

Brainstorming. *Brainstorming* is a method often used successfully to solve a problem or plan an activity. It is based on the belief that certain problems can best be solved by allowing the freest exchange of ideas possible. It usually works best with groups of from six to ten, with each person being encouraged to share his thoughts on the subject at hand. Nothing is rejected as being too "far out," for although the suggestion may have little value in itself, it may well stimulate someone else to come up with something of a more practical nature. Write down all ideas as given, and then go back and select for further exploration those which seem most promising.

ADVANTAGES OF THE DISCUSSION METHOD

Although the discussion method is slow and sometimes inefficient, it has the advantage of being democratic, because it gives everyone a chance to express his own thoughts and feelings as well as hear those of others and it minimizes the danger of letting the outspoken or more dynamic members exert undue influence. It also gives each an opportunity to ask questions and obtain more information about points not clear to him. The very act of participating gets people involved, keeps them aware of exactly what is going on and why, and makes them more willing to accept the decisions that result. This is particularly important with older campers who are becoming increasingly unwilling to be

*Described in a four-page bulletin, *For Those Who Must Lead,* "The Hillsdale College Leadership Letter," Volume I, No. II, April, 1963, Hillsdale, Michigan.

dictated to. Increased understanding and appreciation will result as campers learn to respect the opinions of others, even though not necessarily endorsing them, hopefully in the same spirit as Voltaire, who said, "I disapprove of what you say, but I will defend to the death your right to say it." Through discussion, you will often find that your campers have more insight and wisdom than you imagined, and sharing thoughts and ideas will help both you and your campers to gain a better understanding of each other.

ADDITIONAL READINGS

(For an explanation of abbreviations and abbreviated forms, see page 25.)

Beal, George M., et al.: *Leadership and Dynamic Group Action.* Iowa State U., 1962, $2.95, paper.
Breed: *Good Grooming for Teenagers.* Burgess, 1969, $3.25.
Carnegie, Dale: *How to Win Friends and Influence People.* Pocket Books, 50¢, paper.
Convention Highlights:
Andress, Charlotte F.: "Techniques to Achieve a Democratic Meeting." p. 92.
Frederiksen, Nancy: "Leadership With Domination," p. 46.
Hill, Robert: "Camp, the Child's World," p. 70.
Cushing, Luther S.: *Modern Rules of Order.* Fawcett, 1972, 95¢, paper.
Detweiler: *How to Stand Up for What You Believe.* Ass'n Press, 1966, $2.95, paper.
Klein, Alan F.: *Effective Groupwork.* Galloway, 384 pp., $9.95.
Knowles, Malcolm and Hulda: *Introduction to Group Dynamics.* Galloway, rev., 96 pp., $4.50.
Landers, Ann: *Talks to Teen-agers About Sex.* Fawcett, 1970, 60¢, paper.
Ledlie and Holbein: *Camp Counselor's Manual.*
Lifton, Walter M.: *Working With Groups.* Wiley, 2nd ed., 1966, 292 pp., $9.25.
Loeb, Robert H., Jr.: *He-Manners.* Ass'n Press, rev., 1970, $4.95.
Loeb, Robert H., Jr.: *She-Manners.* Ass'n Press, rev., 1970, $4.95.
MacKay: Creative Counseling for Christian Camps, ch. 4.
Nolan, W.I.: *A Guide to Parliamentary Practice.* (Order from N.R.P.A.) 110 pp., $3.95.
Reichert, Richard: *Self-Awareness Through Group Dynamics.* Pflaum/Standard, 38 West Fifth Street, Dayton, Ohio, 1970, 120 pp., $1.95.
Rodney and Ford: *Camp Administration,* ch. 6.
Simon, Sidney B., et al.: *Values Clarification.* Hart Publishing Company, Inc., New York, New York, 1972, 379 pp. $3.95.
Staley, Edwin (Ed.): *Leisure and the Quality of Life.* A.A.H.P.E.R., 1972, 275 pp., $6.95, paper.
Strean: *New Approaches in Child Guidance.*
Todd: *Camping for Christian Youth,* pp. 137–140.
Youth Forums (No. 3013). Boy Scouts, 1971, 32 pp., 45¢, paper.

MAGAZINE ARTICLES

Camping Magazine:
Haskell, Helen L.: "Factors to Consider in Stimulating and Motivating Campers." Mar., 1970, p. 12.
Hunter, D. Bruce: "Don't Use Food as Punishment." Nov./Dec., 1969, p. 18.
Smith, DeWitt: "How Counselors Use Authority." Apr., 1972, p. 12.
Wilson, Don: "Both Schools and Camps Can Offer a Place to Learn." Jan., 1973, pp. 11–13.

Camping For Special Groups

Adams, Ronald C., Alfred N. Daniel, and Lee Rullman: *Games, Sports and Exercises for the Physically Handicapped.* Lea & Febiger, 1972, 254 pp., $11, paper.
Ayrault: *Helping the Handicapped Teenager Mature.* Ass'n Press, 1971, $6.95.
Bogardus, LaDonna (Ed.): *Camping With Retarded Persons.* (Order from ACA) 1970, 46 pp., $1.10, paper.
Camping for Emotionally Disturbed Boys. Compiled by the Depart. of Recreation, Indiana University, (Order from ACA) 50¢, paper.
Camping Opportunities for Disadvantaged Youth. Published by the President's Council on Youth Opportunity. Supt. of Documents, 1971, 79 pp., 75¢, paper.
Carlson, Bernice Wells, and David R. Ginglend: *Play Activities for the Retarded Child.* Abingdon, 224 pp., $4.
Carlson, Bernice Wells, and David R. Ginglend: *Recreation for Retarded Teenagers and Young Adults.* Abingdon, 320 pp., $4.95.
Ford, Dr. Phyllis M.: *Your Camp and the Handicapped Child.* ACA, 1966, 16 pp., 50¢, paper.
Ginglend, David R., and Winifred E. Stiles: *Music Activities for Retarded Children.* Abingdon, 140 pp., $4, paper.
Herbert, W. L., and F. V. Jarvis: *Dealing With Delinquents.* Emerson, 1961, 207 pp., $4.95.
Loughmiller, Campbell: *Wilderness Road.* Hogg Foundation for Mental Health. (Order from ACA) 1965, 139 pp., $2, paper.
Nesbitt, John A., et al.: *Training Needs and Strategies in Camping for the Handicapped.* U. of Ore., 1972, 242 pp., $3.50.
Nesbitt, John A., Paul D. Brown, and James F.

Murphy: *Recreation and Leisure Service for the Disadvantaged.* Lea & Febiger, 1970, 593 pp., $12.50.
Pomeroy, Janet: *Recreation for the Physically Handicapped.* Macmillan, 1964, 382 pp., $8.95.
Robins, Ferris and Jennet: *Educational Rhythmics for Mentally and Physically Handicapped Children.* Ass'n Press, 1968, 224 pp., $9.95.
The Easter Seal Directory of Resident Camps for Persons With Special Health Needs. (Order from ACA) rev., 1971, $1, paper.
Van Krevelen: *Children in Groups: Psychology and the Summer Camp,* ch. 8.
von Hilsheimer, Rev. George: *How to Live With Your Special Child—Handbook for Behavior Change.* Acropolis, 1970, 272 pp., $7.50.
Weber, George H.: *Camps for Delinquent Boys.* Supt. of Documents, 1960, 25¢, paper.
Zweig, Franklin M.: *Research Monograph No. 1 (Therapeutic Camping).* ACA, 1962, 14 pp., 50¢, paper.

MAGAZINE ARTICLES

Camping Magazine:
Bavley, Fred: "New Horizons for Disadvantaged Youth," Feb., 1970, p. 16.
Ford, Dr. Phyllis M.: "Two Modern Challenges for Every Camp Director." Sept./Oct., 1969, p. 18.
Frey, Louise A.: "Real Camping for Handicapped Children." Jan., 1961, p. 8.
Kronick, Doreen: "You CAN Make Exceptional Children Part of Your Regular Summer Camp." Feb., 1972, p. 14.
Rawson, Harve E.: "Research Attests to Behavior Change in Programs Geared to Specialized Camping." May, 1973, p. 16.
Spinelli, Antonio J., and James E. Earley: "Dual Nature Trails Use Both Braille and Printed Markers for Use of Visually Handicapped Campers." Mar., 1972, p. 19.
Wentworth, Samuel, M.D.: "What You Should Know About Regular Camping Programs for Diabetic Children." Mar., 1973, p. 10.
Ziegler, Virginia: "To Love Ugliness." Jan., 1974, p. 12.

Camping For Older Adults

Ammon, George B.: *Adventures With Older Adults in Outdoor Settings.* United Church Press, (Order from ACA) 1972, 60 pp., $1.80, paper.
Cagan, Maxwell S.: *There's Gold in Your Golden Age.* (Order from N.R.P.A.) 293 pp., $6.95.
Corbin: *Recreation Leadership,* ch. 13.
Feehery, James M.: *Camping for Senior Citizens.* ACA, 1966, 75¢, paper.
Kubie, Susan H., and Gertrude Landau: *Group Work With the Aged.* (Order from N.R.P.A.) 214 pp., $9.50.
Vickery, Florence E.: *Creative Programming for Older Adults.* Galloway, 320 pp., $2.95.

MAGAZINE ARTICLES

Camping Magazine:
Glascock, Martha McClain, and E. A. Scholer: "Two Experts View Camping for Older Adults." Mar., 1969, p. 15.
Guerard, Ed: "Steps in Organizing a Senior Citizen Camp." Sept./Oct., 1973, p. 26.
Margolin, Lillian: "What Your Camp Can Do for Older Adults." Jan., 1972, p. 10.

Chapter 9

The Counselor's Role in Guidance

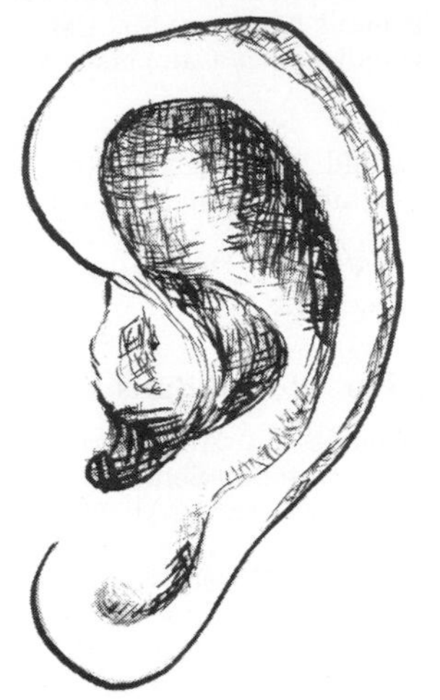

Figure 9-1 Learn To Listen.

It is said that man will work 8 hours a day for pay, 10 hours a day for a boss, but 24 hours a day for a cause.

—AUTHOR UNKNOWN

WILL THERE REALLY BE A "MORNING"?*

Will there really be a "Morning"?
Is there such a thing as "Day"?
Could I see it from the mountains
If I were as tall as they?

Has it feet like water lilies?
Has it feathers like a Bird?
Is it brought from famous countries?
Of which I have never heard?

Oh, some Scholar! Oh, some Sailor,
Oh, some Wise Man from the skies!
Please to tell a little Pilgrim
Where the place called "Morning" lies?

—EMILY DICKINSON

THE COUNSELOR'S ROLE IN GUIDANCE

POSSIBILITIES

The daily informal contacts of camp life give you an unlimited opportunity to objectively study each of your campers in a variety of situations, and by seeing him as a whole person and evaluating his individual strengths and weaknesses, you can gain a better understanding of him and why he is the way he is. After you have done this, you may hope to find ways to guide

*Reprinted by permission of the publishers and the Trustees of Amherst College from Thomas H. Johnson, Editor, *The Poems of Emily Dickinson,* Cambridge, Mass.: The Belknap Press of Harvard University Press, Copyright, 1951, 1955, by the President and Fellows of Harvard College.

him in developing his potentials and becoming a better person through his contacts with you and the camp, but be careful not to attempt the impossible or overestimate your capabilities in this area. When dealing with personalities, it is especially important to remember that "a little learning is a dangerous thing," and if you do not use sound judgment and lack adequate training and experience in the field of guidance, you can do much harm through misguided attempts to help a youngster during these very important formative years. In order to interpret a camper's behavior, you must have an understanding of not only the normal processes of growth and development, but also the specific background conditions that have contributed to make him the sort of person he is. Under favorable conditions, camp offers a fine setting for giving positive guidance and helping a boy or girl to develop and grow.

LEARN TO BE A GOOD LISTENER

As a counselor, you will not only be acting as a camper's temporary parent, teacher, and leader, but will often be regarded by him as a sort of big brother and trusted older friend. It often enhances this warm, personal relationship if you are only a few years older, for he will feel that, since you have so recently gone through the same stage of growth, you can better understand his feelings and problems. This sense of closeness encourages him to chat with you informally, sometimes pouring out his innermost thoughts and emotions. If this occurs, do not become irritated or impatient with him, but encourage him and treasure his confidences, realizing that, like everyone else, he needs a sympathetic, kindred spirit with whom he can communicate and talk freely. A person who trusts no one and so lacks such a confidant tends to bottle up his thoughts and emotions within himself until tensions build up, which may eventually explode.

By thus serving as his safety valve, you gain an unparalleled opportunity to learn more about him as he reveals a side of himself that he may never have fully disclosed to anyone before. Learn to listen carefully, and be observant as you listen, for his facial expressions, mannerisms, and gestures may tell you even more than his words if you have the sensitivity and wisdom to interpret them properly. Develop the ability to sense when to be quiet and let the other person talk and when to enter into the conversation yourself. Good listeners are rare, and thus are deeply appreciated, and by developing this trait, you acquire a skill which will serve you faithfully and prove of inestimable value all your life.

His thoughts are slow, his words are few;
He doesn't jell or glisten.
He has a multitude of friends, for
You should hear him listen.

—RUSSELL NEWBOLD (in *Together*)

These informal contacts and conversations will provide some of your greatest opportunities to influence others. Since there is already a congenial feeling between you and the other person, both of you are in a proper frame of mind to listen eagerly to what the other has to say. Such a favorable climate is hard to achieve in the more formal appointment or interview created specifically to counsel him, for their very formality usually make him cautious and wary of expressing himself freely and hence less receptive to your comments or advice.

SELF-CONCEPTS

Each camper comes to camp with a pre-formed opinion of himself as a person, which is largely dependent upon the way he has been accepted by others in the past. If parents, teachers, or his peers regard him as sloppy, lazy, or a trouble-maker, he will usually consider this to be a true characterization and will probably expect his new associates to feel the same way about him. His *self-concept* will have become so ingrained that he will probably try to live up to his reputation and may nearly drive you crazy with the irksome things he does. However, if he has been praised and considered a good child who is courteous, pleasant, and cooperative, he will probably behave that way at camp.

When a camper demonstrates unacceptable traits, do not punish, nag, or try to bribe him, for this will do little good and may only make him worse, and he is probably so used to being blamed and scolded that he may not even hear you and will almost certainly pay no attention to you. Instead, try to discern how he feels about himself and what his true self-concept is; you will then be in a position to try to alter his behavior by giving him a new and different self-concept. Remember that beneath his facade of indifference and orneriness, he is probably longing to be admired and accepted as a respected member of the group. Try to reward him with a sincere smile and some token of approval each and every time he does something commendable. When occasions do not occur naturally, you may have to purposely create them in order to give him an opportunity to do something praiseworthy. Nothing succeeds like success, and each time he wins approval, it will tend to encourage him to try to win it again. Eventually, he may begin to think of himself as a "good" person rather than a "bad" one, and hopefully his new self-concept will carry over into his life after camp.

CHANGING HABIT PATTERNS

Habits are action patterns which have been repeated so many times that we follow them automatically, finding it easiest to just drift along in our customary ways that require little conscious thought—let's face it, most of us are somewhat lazy and prefer to follow the line of least resistance. This tendency to become "set in our ways" starts at an early age, and even a young camper is likely to prefer to maintain the status quo, unless something important or even catastrophic happens to jar him from his lethargy and make him really want to change. Altering a pattern of life in even minor ways makes us uncomfortable and requires the expenditure of some mental, emotional, and perhaps even physical effort, and our egos cause us to resist change, because we hate to admit to any imperfection in ourselves. We also hesitate to change because the well-worn path provides security, whereas the venture into the unknown produces fear.

You must bear these things in mind when trying to influence others to change and must fortify yourself with large quantities of patience, insight, empathy, and understanding and be prepared for occasional backsliding and delays. Don't expect miracles overnight, for even when a person sincerely wants to change, he is sure to suffer periods of discouragement and impatience that tempt him to give up. This

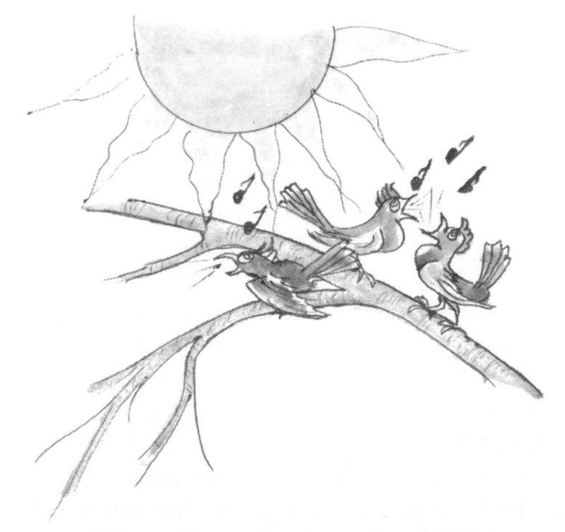

Figure 9–2 This Is a Good Life!

is when he needs you to step in with encouragement and a pat on the back, reminding him of the progress he has already made (even though you may need a microscope to find it). Point out to him that his feelings are common to everyone who tries to change his habits, and it may help to tell him of the setbacks and frustrations you and others experienced on the way to eventual success.

PREPARATION FOR THE GOOD LIFE

One of your basic aims in guidance is to help each camper to respect himself. As we have previously noted at camp, a child can develop such traits as self-confidence, leadership, and followership, and can learn the techniques of group living and of cultivating and keeping new friends. He can also find acceptable ways to satisfy his fundamental needs or wishes by participation and achievement in as many aspects of camp life as possible. The average camp offers opportunities in many areas, such as acquiring or improving physical skills in such activities as swimming, learning to use simple tools, boating, riding, hiking, lashing, tying knots, and cooking. A youngster can also improve and expand his aesthetic tastes through participating in such activities as dramatics, music, arts and crafts, camp improvement, making his own equipment, or helping with the camp newspaper, a vesper service or the production of a skit or camping program. Hopefully, no matter what specific activities a child engages in, his camping experience will teach him skills and ways of living which will provide present satisfaction and lay the groundwork for a well-balanced, happy, adult life, physically, mentally, emotionally, and socially.

A camper lives in a child's world in which children occupy the center of the stage and each is fairly free to determine the role he will play. He can establish his own goals and must then provide the momentum and drive to achieve them, setting his own course and deciding on the speed at which he will travel along it. This encourages the development of the self-reliance, personal adjustment, good mental health, and emotional maturity that any person involved in guidance or counseling strives for. You, his counselor, play an important role in this development as you apply a push in one direction or a restraining hand in another, as the occasion demands. You must encourage him to be as independent and self-reliant as he can, while you remain more or less in the background, ready to discreetly give him assurance, advice, and encouragement. Doing your job well requires tact and skill, for you must know when and how to assist, admonish, or help, and do it so unobtrusively that he is scarcely aware of your participation.

SUGGESTIONS FOR OBSERVING GROUP BEHAVIOR

NOTING INDIVIDUAL DIFFERENCES

As you observe your group in their daily activities, you will note marked differences in individual reactions to the group and in the amount of interest and enthusiasm shown toward participation in group activities. You will also detect similar differences in group response to various individuals. At home, a child is usually accepted and loved just as he is, but at camp, his welcome will most likely depend on what he can contribute and the general acceptability of his personality to others. A few lucky, outgoing newcomers are greeted with open arms and quickly assimilated, for they have customarily been well accepted in the past and so have acquired enough self-confidence to approach a new group with friendly self-

Figure 9–3 Everybody's Friend.

assurance and an easy, relaxed manner. These fortunate individuals seemingly never know a stranger, and so do not understand the pangs of loneliness and rejection experienced by others. The large majority, however, do not stand out in any particular way, remaining more or less on the borderline while the group sizes them up and eventually decides what group status to accord them. There are usually several unfortunate souls who will remain on the fringe for a long time before being accepted, and then only with certain reservations, and a few others will be permanently branded as unacceptable. It is seemingly not always how much time a child spends with the group or the amount of effort he exerts to try to fit in that determines the ultimate outcome: rather it is some more or less intangible factor, which is very difficult for either the child or an observer to pinpoint.

INTERPRETING THESE DIFFERENCES

A camper's reactions to his peers can often reveal much about how he feels about himself to one with the training and insight to interpret the message correctly. If unsure of himself and afraid the group may ignore him, a camper may react in various ways. He may try to cover up his discomfort by adopting an "I-don't-care" attitude or by demanding the spotlight and showing off. He may assume an air of bravado and brag about himself so much that he seems insufferably forward and conceited. Another tactic is to retire into the background and try to make himself as inconspicuous as possible, using every excuse he can think of to avoid having to undergo the painful experience of making contacts with others. He may go around with a chip on his shoulder and quickly take offense where none was intended, or become extremely sensitive and frequently get his feelings hurt. He may adopt an apologetic manner and constantly belittle himself, or he may attempt to get the attention he needs by telling tales of woe to anyone who will listen. Most of these reactions tend to repel others, and this further rejection only intensifies his feelings of inadequacy and self-doubt.

An insecure youngster sometimes tries to win acceptance and approval by becoming subservient and willing to serve as everybody's "doormat," eagerly running errands or performing little services for them. In so doing, he apparently is abandoning all efforts to establish his own identity and win approval and respect by his own accomplishments; he is willing instead to settle for any small crumbs of appreciation and attention he can get, no matter what it costs him.

A youngster who reacts in any one or a combination of these ways may do so because of a lack of previous experience with peer groups in informal situations or because he is trying to protect himself from a repetition of his painful experiences in the past. He may be trying too hard in an attempt to cope with

Figure 9–4 "I'm Not Just Isolated; I'm 'Ice'-olated."

a situation he doesn't understand or lacks the skill to control, and this in itself may cause others to shy away from him. No matter whether he reacts with aggression and assertiveness or surrender and withdrawal, you can be sure that he feels frustrated, unhappy, and lonely, perhaps even wanting to give up and go home because of his innate desire to belong and be accepted. When you encounter a child like this, hurry to the rescue, for he desperately needs someone to help him to find a way out of his misery. If he gives up and runs away now, it will only deepen his sense of inadequacy and make it even harder for him to gain acceptance in the future, if he can ever summon up the courage to try again.

Such an individual may have certain personality traits or habits which repel others, such as selfishness, bossiness, or personal uncleanliness. The possible reasons for his dilemma are legion, and it is indeed a challenge to try to discover what they are and lend a hand in helping him to overcome them. Stay constantly on the alert to discover what forces are really at work behind the scenes, since an individual's outward behavior is often merely a camouflage to conceal from himself and others his true underlying feelings and problems. What appears on the surface often bears surprisingly little resemblance to the turmoil boiling underneath.

COUNSELING WITH YOUR CAMPERS

OPPORTUNITIES FOR THE COUNSELOR

Every association you have with a camper is a potential counseling situation, for everything you do, every word, action, gesture, or facial expression, sets a pattern or expresses an attitude which may influence him far more than you suspect. Each contact with your group or its individuals gives you an opportunity to know them better and perhaps influence them to some degree, and these contacts serve as important learning and growing situations for campers. In our increasingly complex world, each person is forced to make choices and decisions to an extent never dreamed of by past generations, and this applies even to youngsters of camp age. A sensible and well-balanced camp counselor can do a great deal to give campers the knowledge and judgment they need to make the right choices.

GETTING ACQUAINTED

The foundation of your relationship with your campers must rest upon a real concern for each individual and an understanding of and readiness to accept him as he is. You should constantly seek to know him better, exploring his personality, his relationships with others, and his problems, and possibly helping him to realize and examine his true feelings and ideas. With continued contact, you should come to recognize him as a unique individual who differs from every other human being and whose individual patterns of thinking and feeling deserve your respect and acceptance.

DISCUSSIONS WITHOUT NUMBER

Individual counseling or guidance is an integral part of your job as camp counselor, for in addition to exerting influence through group associations, you will also have many personal encounters with campers. These will occur as you find occasion to seek out an individual or are sought out by him for a private chat or discussion.

When the two of you are together, he may often bring up topics that seem trivial to you, but loom as life and death matters to him in his child's world. In order to establish a friendly rapport, it is essential that you give him your undivided attention, so avoid interruptions if at all possible and do not preoccupy yourself with other matters or let your mind wander. Put him at ease and make him feel that you want to hear everything he has to say, and encourage him to express himself freely and honestly.

Observe his choice of words and the way in which he expresses himself, his body movements, facial expressions, and any other indications of his underlying emotions. These will often help you to "read between the lines" and discern what he fails to find words to express or perhaps is unconsciously trying to hide, sometimes even from himself. Even a moment's lapse of attention on your part may cause you to miss some important key to understanding him and what he is trying to tell you.

Listen! Avoid talking too much, for you are trying to learn as much as you can about *him,* and you learn most when *he* talks. Let him occupy the stage, for everyone likes to talk about himself and verbalizing may help him

(Courtesy of Camp Kooch-I-Ching, International Falls, Minnesota.)

to organize his own thinking or see things more objectively. Your main function is to help him to think things through and eventually work out possible ways to handle whatever situation is bothering him.

Offer your own opinions and insights sparingly, and refrain from expressing either approval or disapproval of what he is saying until you are sure you have a fairly complete picture of the entire situation. Try to avoid the common mistake of telling him exactly what to do; this will only delay the process of helping him to learn to face up to his own problems and arrive at his own conclusions.

Ordinarily, you can and should assure him that you will hold what he tells you in strict confidence. However, there may come a time when you feel that, as a camper talks, he seems to be on the verge of divulging something of such a nature that your position may require you to reveal it to a higher camp authority. Under these circumstances, fairness requires that you warn him of this possibility, so that he will not continue unless he is willing to take this risk.

SEE IT FROM THE CAMPER'S VIEWPOINT

When an upset, perplexed, or worried youngster comes to you, or when you, realizing his need, make the overtures, try first of all to get a picture of the problem or situation as *he* sees it. This is not at all simple, for in discussing a situation, it is very easy to falsely assume that we start on common ground with the other person and that his view of the problem is identical with our own. On the contrary, it is much more likely that each person will have a different view, which is determined by such factors as his past and present experiences, his physical health, his mood of the moment, his personality, his general attitudes toward life, and even his own self-concept.

An important point to remember is that each of us has a tendency to see what he is looking for or wants to see in a situation. When we meet Susan for the first time and note how much her looks or mannerisms resemble those of Rebecca, whom we greatly dislike, we are apt to take an immediate dislike to Susan, and if we ever fully come to accept and like her, it will be only after a long and consistently favorable association. If Harry is thrown and painfully injured while riding a horse, he is likely to invent a dozen excuses for never attempting to ride again. If Mary comes from an environment where she was consistently misused and mistreated, she will most likely trust no one and rebuff every effort you make to be kind and helpful. If Jack's school course in nature study was presented in a bookish, boring fashion, the nature counselor will find it hard to stir up even a flicker of enthusiasm in him; in fact, he may be so preoccupied with his thoughts of how much he hates nature study that he will be completely deaf and blind to the fascinating things the nature counselor is doing and saying. When two people are confronted with an identical situation, they may each interpret it so differently that, if you could read their minds, you would not even recognize it as the same situation at all. This is why it is so important for you to try to see a problem through the eyes of the camper, for you cannot otherwise hope to understand his reactions or be of any real help to him.

CHANGING HIS VIEWPOINT

You may find that you will need to help a camper to look at a situation from a different perspective. For instance, if camper John comes to you incensed because Sharkey, the swimming counselor, won't let him practice diving off the dock after dark, can you help him to see the situation through Sharkey's eyes? Sharkey isn't just a "mean old so-and-so" who delights in spoiling campers' fun; indeed, he wouldn't be in camp at all if he weren't devoted to youngsters and interested in helping them to have all the *safe* fun they possibly can. Sharkey is probably pleased at John's interest in perfecting his diving techniques, but because his thorough training has grounded him in the necessity of preventing campers from taking undue risks, he has to veto hazardous proposals that campers make. When John realizes this, he will surely see that Sharkey is only doing his duty as a conscientious swimming counselor.

In trying to broaden a camper's viewpoint, it may help to encourage him to consider various aspects of a problem or situation, such as why it happened, the motives or thinking of the others involved, and any additional factors which have been influential in some way. He may want to consider alternative solutions to the dilemma and the probable consequences of each; this may often cause him to conclude that things actually happened for the best after all. By teaching a camper to examine a problem from every possible angle (including others' viewpoints), you will help him to avoid hasty decisions and to choose a solution that will prove most satisfactory in the long run. This is the thinking process practiced by those who act with maturity and good judgment.

Figure 9-5 A Desire For Affection.

BE AWARE OF YOUR LIMITATIONS

Again, let us emphasize the importance of remaining humble and realistic about your own abilities to completely understand situations and guide people, for this is an area filled with potential danger, and you must exercise extreme caution. You cannot and must not put yourself on a par with a professional guidance counselor, who after college graduation has studied extensively for two or more years in such fields of counseling as mental health, group behavior, and psychology.

In these chapters, we have merely tried to present some common-sense procedures to use when facing everyday situations. The aim has been to help you to effectively solve those problems that you are able to handle and to recognize those which are beyond your capabilities. Confine your efforts to the commonplace happenings and problems of normal camp life and those occasions when a youngster mainly wants guidance and advice or someone to listen to him as he unburdens himself of the tensions and pressures which have built up inside him.

In your close daily contacts with campers, you may be the first to note individual behavior problems or symptoms which seem to point to a possible need for referral to the proper person. The following are examples of such indications:

Confusion as to one's identity or

extreme forgetfulness about common happenings and facts.
Extreme muscle tremors and spasms, especially facial tics (twitches).
Frequent absent-mindedness or disorientation to time and place.
Uncontrolled or unusual homosexual or heterosexual practices or interests.
Continued refusal to eat or being extremely "picky" about one's eating.
Persistent *enuresis* (bed-wetting).

Do not be an alarmist or overemphasize the normal quirks that we all have, but if convinced that there is real need for concern, go immediately to the proper authority, such as your unit leader, head counselor or camp director. Under no circumstances should you discuss the situation freely with other campers or unqualified staff members; this could be quite harmful to the camper or could seriously hamper the efforts of someone in an official capacity who later tries to deal with the situation.

CASE STUDIES IN CAMP

Some camps use the case study method to help campers who have problems, but this should be done only when they have personnel trained in counseling who are capable of conducting and supervising it and counselors who have or are receiving special training in this area. A camp case study provides a method of studying a child or children to bring about a better understanding of them and eventually help them to make a better adjustment to camp and to society in general. It consists of gathering available data about a specific boy or girl, then assembling, organizing, and studying it to discover the nature and causes of whatever difficulty he has, and eventually deciding how best to help him to overcome it. The material gathered should present as complete and objective a picture as possible, but of course, the data alone will not provide an interpretation or pinpoint the problem facing the camper at the moment. Keen insight, knowledge, and intelligence are needed to assemble the material properly and then interpret it. Case studies should therefore not be undertaken except under professional supervision, and we should bear in mind that *treatment* is not usually the basic purpose in a camp situation. Rather, the study can, under certain circumstances, indicate a need for referral, or it can help to solve an immediate problem or provide constructive assistance in promoting the growth and adjustment of a camper or group of campers.

Imaginary case studies are often used with prospective counselors during precamp and in-service training sessions, in order to make them aware of the importance of their role in leadership and to orient them to problems they may meet and various possible approaches toward solving them. Such studies usually prove quite helpful and interesting, as each counselor examines the situation and presents what he considers the best way to handle it, and then all participate in a general discussion and evaluate the various viewpoints presented.

When properly conducted, case studies can broaden and deepen the participant's standing of individuals and their underlying motivations and can provide them with ways to analyze and deal with problems. However, a word of caution is necessary for everyone involved. Although the use of case studies in camp seems exciting and challenging, no individual or group should undertake it without the approval of the camp director and the supervision of adequately trained personnel. When otherwise carried on, much harm may result and both the counselor and the camp may become involved in unpleasant situations, and possibly even legal difficulties.

ADDITIONAL READINGS

(For an explanation of abbreviations and abbreviated forms, see page 25.)

Adams, Jay E.: *Competent to Counsel.* Baker, 1973, 287 pp., $4.50.

Barksdale, L. S.: *Building Self-Esteem.* The Barksdale Foundation, Idyllwild, Cal., 1972.

Blanchard, Howard L., and Laurence S. Flaum: *Guidance: A Longitudinal Approach.* Burgess, 1969, 338 pp., $5.95, paper.

Bloom, et al.: *Camper Guidance—A Basic Handbook for Counselors,* pp. 7–8, 19–23.

Budd, William C., Ph.D.: *Behavior Modification: The Scientific Way to Self Control.* Galloway, 96 pp., $5.

Forrer, Dr. Gordon R.: *Psychiatric Self Help.* Galloway, 71 pp., $5.

Kemp, C. Gratton: *Perspective on the Group Process, A Foundation for Counseling With Groups.* Houghton Mifflin, 2nd ed., 1970, 388 pp., $7.95.

MacKay: *Creative Counseling for Christian Camps,* ch. 4.

O'Banion, Terry, and April O'Connell: *The Shared Journey.* Prentice-Hall, 1970, pp. 3–184.

Otto, Herbert: *Group Methods Designed to Actualize Human Potential.* Stone-Brandel Center, Chicago, Ill., 2nd ed., 1967.

Shivers: *Camping,* ch. 8.

Strean: *New Approaches in Child Guidance.*

Van Krevelen: *Children in Groups: Psychology and the Summer Camp,* ch. 3.

MAGAZINE ARTICLES

Camping Magazine:

Bavley, Fred: "Camp Can Change Campers' Attitudes." Sept., 1972, p. 18.

Campbell, Barry: "Focus on the Camper." Sept./Oct., 1973, p. 13.

Rabban, Dr. Meyer: "What Camps Can Do to Meet Individual Camper Needs and Still Maintain Group Effectiveness." Mar., 1973, p. 8.

"Research Shows Campers Improve Self-Concept." Nov. 1972, p. 12.

Van Krevelen, Alice, Ph.D.: "Stop, Look and Listen if You Want to Be Heard." Mar., 1969, p. 17.

Chapter 10

Some Problems You May Meet

Figure 10-1 Problems! Problems! Problems!

> He drew a circle that shut me out—
> Heretic, rebel, a thing to flout.
> But Love and I had the wit to win,
> We drew a circle that took him in.*
>
> —EDWIN MARKHAM

> Rudeness is a weak man's imitation of strength.
>
> —Quoted from *Newsweek*

PEOPLE ARE HIGHLY INDIVIDUALISTIC

As you note the many similarities among people whom you know well, you are at the same time struck by the even more numerous ways in which they differ. First, they differ physically in such aspects as height, weight, musculature, hair coloring and texture, bone structure, complexion, facial features, and expressions. They also vary in body carriage, speed and way of moving, voice tone and pitch, favorite expressions and word choice, and even ways of laughing, so that you can recognize each when you see him at a distance or hear him talking in the next room. If someone recounts Jack's remarks or actions to you, your immediate reaction is likely to be "that is (or isn't) just like Jack," for you have come to identify him with certain characteristic attitudes, emotional reactions, wishes, ways of thinking, likes and dislikes, abilities, and ideals that make up his particular personality. Human traits are so numerous, and each exists in such varying degrees, that the countless possible permutations and combinations rule out any chance of finding exactly the same combination in any

*Reproduced by permission of Virgil Markham.

two individuals; this is why each of your friends and loved ones occupies a special niche in your heart, which no one else could ever fill.

At the same time these differences are adding variety to your associations with others, they are also increasing the difficulty of always understanding an individual and of establishing a mutually satisfactory relationship with him. Though modern study and research in human behavior have made tremendous strides, providing us with generalities and probabilities which *usually* hold true, each person still remains a unique entity that can always prove the exception to the rule. Since even those who have studied extensively in this area confess their inability to classify a person with assurance or fully explain what he is, how he got that way, what he will do in a certain situation, or how he will respond to a certain type of treatment, it certainly behooves a person with relatively meager training and experience to refrain from setting himself up as an expert and attempting to diagnose and prescribe in complex cases. Fortunately most youngsters in camp are perfectly normal, healthy individuals with many good and a few bad qualities and who seldom present serious problems. Therefore, if you have some training, supplemented with large doses of common sense, you should have little difficulty coping with most of the problems you will meet. However, at the risk of undue repetition, let us again caution you to adopt a policy of "hands off" and referral to the proper person when you note signs of serious trouble, for bungling attempts to help, no matter how well meant, can do irreparable harm during these important formative years in a youngster's life. It is far beyond our ability or purpose in this discussion to give more than general and nontechnical information designed to help you to better understand and meet common problems and situations.

In men whom men condemn as ill
I find so much of goodness still,
In men whom men pronounce divine
I find so much of sin and blot,
I do not dare to draw a line
Between the two, where God has not.

—JOAQUIN MILLER

WHO OR WHAT IS NORMAL?

Society has set up types of behavior which it considers normal or acceptable for given situations. These are not always the same, however, for they change with the passage of time, and each individual stratum of a society or community has its own mores, or customs, so that what one considers as good or normal may be deemed just the opposite by another.

When a person's conduct follows pretty much along the accepted lines in his particular situation, he receives the stamp of approval and is called "normal." It seems that conformity or doing what his particular environment expects is the acid test, and if he strays very far from the norm, he will be classified as exceptional, a genius, antisocial, an underachiever, a failure, a misfit, or whatever other terms happen to be in vogue at that particular time and place. If his behavior bothers others, they will be likely to dub him a "problem child."

Such terms as good mental health and normal behavior are much bandied about today. Most people have a general understanding of what they mean, but would probably be at a loss if asked to give an exact definition of them. Although measurable human traits vary in degree, if you rated a group of people by means of these traits by plotting them on a "normal curve," the majority of people would be clustered about a center, which is known as the normal area or zone and the relatively few found outside this area on either side would be classed as abnormal or deviate. Obviously, the exact point at which the abnormal begins would not be universally agreed upon, since its location is a matter of opinion, and hence would differ with each individual.

GOOD MENTAL HEALTH

A person with good mental health adjusts well to others and finds ways to solve his problems and meet his needs that are mutually acceptable to both himself and society. This places him in a happy state of mind called *euphoria,* in which he is at peace and on good terms with himself and others. This state is hard to steadfastly maintain, however, since the world is made up of individuals, each intent on satisfying his own particular wishes and needs; this makes conflicts and disappointments inevitable. Studies have also revealed that a person's moods vary for seemingly unexplainable reasons, carrying him cyclically from a phase of depression to one of exhilaration in which he is floating blissfully on "cloud nine."

A person with emotional maturity and good mental health has learned to adjust his own wishes to those of his associates and is willing to give as well as receive, taking his disappointments and changing moods in stride without being unduly upset or reacting in extreme ways. We must be realistic, however, and admit that even the most exemplary person cannot always have the wisdom and fortitude to exercise perfect control and to act as others would like. As we have seen, our associates do not always agree on what they want or expect from us, and consequently each of us probably becomes, at some time or another, a "problem child" to someone else.

Figure 10–2 Euphoria Makes You Want to Sing.

WE WANT WHAT WE WANT WHEN WE WANT IT

A newborn baby is entirely selfish and thinks only of himself. He cries when he wants something and is encouraged to continue the practice when it proves successful. Fortunately, as he grows older, those around him are usually wise enough to realize that, unless he is occasionally denied and taught to consider others and be willing to sometimes yield to their needs and wishes, he will never lead a happy life; society has effective and often painful ways of expressing its disapproval of those who remain self-centered and insistent on always having their own way. Occasionally, however, we find someone who has lived among people who gave in whenever he showed his displeasure by crying, throwing a temper tantrum, wheedling, cajoling, bargaining, blackmailing, begging, bullying, threatening, or just making himself generally disagreeable in order to get what he wanted. Parents often react in this way out of a desire to keep peace or in a misguided attempt to show their love for their child, but whatever the parents' motivation, they have effectively taught their child that he can successfully employ these tactics to get what he wants.

When such a child comes to camp, he will usually continue to use these tactics to obtain a material possession, to attain status, to gain recognition or attention from some individual or group, or to get anything else he wants. His methods may have become so habitual that he is scarcely aware of it when he uses them and is therefore greatly astonished when his new camp associates give him the cold shoulder when he exhibits these extremely immature traits.

Though you find his conduct reprehensible and annoying, try not to censure him too much, but instead look upon him as a child with a problem which is largely the result of mishandling by others and which he is too immature to recognize and solve for himself. You will need to help him to understand this problem and to realize that if he continues his present conduct, others will resent it more and more as he grows older and will shun him, making him even more miserable, unless he learns to respect and comply with their rights and wishes.

A COUNSELOR MUST DEVELOP INSIGHT

A child often has urgent wishes and needs which he has found no easy and direct way to satisfy; in desperation, he may flounder about using methods that are so counterproductive and seemingly so unrelated to his desires that neither he nor others understand exactly what he is trying to accomplish by them. For instance, a bullying, loudmouthed braggart may be unconsciously trying to cover up his need for status and attention by his splutter and noise. Your natural reaction to his obnoxious, irritating behavior will probably be to "cut him down to size" and "put him in his place" by giving him a good bawling-out or otherwise belittling him in public. This, you feel, will not only take care of him, but will discourage others from engaging in similar conduct and will also establish you as a forceful leader who can maintain control in any situation.

As you begin to look at the problem more rationally, however, you realize that any such actions on your part would only be treating the symptom, not the underlying cause, and though it might cause him to change temporarily his outward behavior, the net result would only be to intensify the cause: his deep and painful doubts about himself and his worth as an individual. Unless you can find some healthy way to bolster his ego, his misgivings will continue to fester and grow, eventually breaking out again in a new direction. This points up an extremely important principle: misbehavior is quite often merely an outward sign of underlying dissatisfaction which is rarely overcome by direct treatment of the behavior. Repressing it in one area will only cause it to break out later with renewed vigor. You must probe behind the symptoms until you can find the underlying cause and try to remedy it; only then will the symptoms subside. Treating only symptoms is like carelessly brushing a mosquito away from your face; it will soon be back, hungrier than ever and bringing all its cousins with it.

A camper seldom understands why he misbehaves or creates problems. Although he may be aware of vague feelings of unrest and unhappiness, self-diagnosis is notoriously fallible. You might as well tell him to stop his tooth from aching than tell him to stop showing off or being homesick, for his behavior difficulties have a basic cause which is just as real and deep-rooted as the decayed tooth which is causing his physical pain, and willpower alone avails but little in either case. Everything he does is for the purpose of meeting some need, and when his conduct is objectionable to himself or others, you must have the wisdom to size up his problems and help him to find acceptable ways to solve them.

This presents a real challenge, for emotional pains are even harder to diagnose and eliminate than physical ones. (Incidentally, as you become more adept at observing and understanding others, you will be better able to understand and solve your own problems.)

So-called "problem" campers are usually the products of problem environments or associates, and many arrive in camp with cases already full-blown. Conscientious but overdoting parents may have spoiled the child so that he expects the same undue attention in camp, where he is surrounded by others, each entitled to his own share of recognition. A child accustomed to living in a household of adults who center all their attention and affection on him is often at a loss when placed with others of his own age. We may also find his counterpart in the child who is suffering from lack of love, who may be jealous of the family's esteem for a brother or sister, or who feels that his parents sent him to camp just to get rid of him while they enjoy a trip or other exciting adventures. Such a child will understandably demonstrate an abnormal craving for the love denied him elsewhere. A camper's difficulties sometimes arise for the first time in camp, or if already present, get worse when he is subjected to unwise camp procedures which fail to recognize and meet the real issue. Camps sometimes carry on a rigid, strenuous program, requiring each camper to participate in every part of it. Some individuals react badly to such a regimen, becoming sensitive, irritable, quarrelsome, or rebellious, as feelings of resentment and frustration build up. This creates misbehavior in the child and produces discipline problems for his counselors, the entire unit, or even the whole camp.

Figure 10-3 Loneliness Is a Problem Too!

Emotionally stable persons can usually face their problems and disappointments honestly and work out satisfactory solutions. The emotionally unstable meet them by (1) evasion or withdrawing, or (2) aggression or fighting back. The strategy and cunning exhibited by the subconscious mind in attempting to cover up the real trouble, even from the person himself, make it hard to get at the source and help the person in a realistic way.

Even after the true cause is determined, there is no such thing as a never-failing remedy or magic recipe, for each situation is complex and individual in itself. Consequently, an unskilled counselor is likely to be mistreating instead of treating the camper.

Better to build boys than mend men.

—BOYS' CLUBS OF AMERICA

THE CAMPER WHO WITHDRAWS OR EVADES

The timid, apologetic, retiring camper's need for help often goes unrecognized, for he causes little disturb-

Figure 10-4 The Mousey Type.

ance and is overshadowed by those who act with aggression and create problems which clamor for the counselor's attention; this is an example of the old saw that "It's the axle which squeaks the most that gets the grease." However, those trained in psychology realize that a child's very failure to demand attention and his apparent happiness in pursuing his solitary way often indicates a quite serious, developing trend. In contrast, the aggressive person makes himself so obnoxious that he cannot be ignored, and under wise leadership, is likely to bring down upon his head the very treatment he needs to help him to understand his difficulties and start overcoming them while they are still in the early stages.

The evading camper's actions, like those of the aggressor, are usually due to an inner feeling of dissatisfaction, insecurity, or inadequacy, and his behavior may take one of many forms. Instead of meeting his problems head-on, he has retreated into a little world all his own and may adopt any of several automatic, unconscious mechanisms to protect himself from hurt and rebuff.

Daydreaming consists of retreating into the land of make-believe to temporarily escape the stresses of everyday life. When kept under control it affords pleasant relaxation and is often beneficial, for a great doer is usually a great dreamer whose dreams furnish the stimulus to make him jump up and start doing something about them. When his dreaming becomes an end in itself and provides complete satisfaction, it is a waste of time, for no one can keep himself warm and well fed in an air castle.

Wishful thinkers persist in believing what they want to believe despite all the evidence to the contrary; they escape having to face unpleasant facts by simply ignoring them. *Sweet lemons* or *pollyannas* likewise close their eyes to all unpleasantness and difficulty by simply refusing to worry about anything, expressing confidence that everything is predestined to turn out for the best. If any calamity befalls, they shrug it off by saying, "It might have been worse" or "It is God's will." This frees them from guilt feelings or responsibility for neglected work or failure to recognize and correct their own faults. Though often happy and carefree themselves, their unwillingness to do their share leaves others with a disproportionate amount of work to do and responsibility to assume.

Sorry-for-themselves retreat into a self-centered sanctum where they can dwell moodily upon how misunderstood and mistreated they are, until they often become literally obsessed with the idea. They may even go so far as to picture themselves as cold and silent in death, while those who have wronged them stand by in sorrow and contrition, or they may even morbidly play with the idea of suicide. Some want to run home to mother to have their aches and bruises kissed away when faced with the cold fact that others expect them to stand up to life instead of demanding childhood favors and pampering. Others develop a convenient *illness* to avoid unpleasant tasks, while still others become *self-worshipers* to compensate for their lack of status in the eyes of others. Some youngsters who have failed to secure affection and recognition from those of their own age become abnormally attached to an adult who has been kind or at least tolerant of them. They claim to be completely bored with those of their own age group.

Others crowd out the unhappiness caused by inability to fit in with their peers by becoming *loners* and turning to such strictly solitary pursuits as reading, drawing, or boating. Thus they eliminate the necessity of having to tailor themselves to group standards.

Those who have had their suggestions and remarks jeered at or ignored may avoid further hurt by degenerating into *yes-men* who need show no initiative and can retire into the background and avoid calling attention to themselves.

Rationalizers try to avoid blame from either their own consciences or the accusations of others by thinking up plausible excuses to make everything they do seem right and reasonable. A favorite form is *alibiing* or *projecting* the blame (*passing the buck*) for what happens to other people or things. A camper claims that he was late to breakfast because his counselor failed to rouse him, that his team lost because the umpire was partial, or that he lost the tennis match because of his inferior racket. He is afraid to face facts and admit that he, like all humans, has faults and weaknesses. Another form of rationalization is found in the *sour grapes attitude* of the fox who couldn't reach the grapes and so pretended they were so sour that he didn't want them anyway. Thus the uncultured person calls those who like good music or literature "highbrow" and the nonathletic student speaks of "brainless wonders"; the poor student sneeringly refers to good students as "greasy grinds," and those with ambition and initiative are "eager beavers" to the lazy.

Self-repudiators are people whose feelings of insecurity about some trait make them fish for compliments by running themselves down with such remarks as "Oh, I'm terribly dumb" or "I'm awfully plain-looking." They, of course, are hoping that you will heartily reassure them that just the opposite is true.

Some, failing to achieve success in a desired field, *compensate* by redirecting their efforts into another. Thus the girl who is not blessed with physical beauty may work extra hard to become an outstanding student, a corporate executive, or a professional tennis player. The boy without the coordination and physical stamina to gain athletic prowess may become a skilled violinist, a great scientist, or a famous writer. Obviously, *substitution* or *compensation* at its best can be a great force for good, and a study of the lives of some of our foremost Americans shows that disappointments or feelings of inferiority in some area have spurred them on to achieve great distinction in another. But when such feelings distort the personality and cause the person to retire from human companionship or strive to be the biggest troublemaker, liar, gang leader or hoodlum, it is an equally potent force for evil.

THE CAMPER WHO RESPONDS WITH AGGRESSION

Instead of trying to retire into obscurity, those with unmet needs sometimes try desperately to draw attention to themselves. The *braggart,* the *bully,* the *smarty,* and the *tough guy* who swagger about in an attitude of pretended fearlessness and assurance are examples; they are, in reality, covering up a feeling of insecurity because of their failure to attract attention and gain status by legitimate means. The bully usually attacks those younger or weaker than he or those who won't retaliate. The boasting camper is trying to convince himself or others that he is actually the great guy he inwardly fears he isn't; instead, his attitudes repel others and cause them to ridicule, dislike, ignore, or shun him, which only intensifies his problem.

The youngster who *smokes* or *drinks* to excess or who *swears* and

Figure 10–5 Aggressive Behavior.

uses *foul language* may be indulging in a misguided effort to relieve his pent-up emotions and gain status and recognition. *Bossy, domineering* people exercise power in the only way they know how—by making themselves so unpleasant that others would rather give in than resist.

A physically or emotionally handicapped child sometimes takes out his frustrations by wearing a chip on his shoulder, being antagonistic, or resorting to acts of cruelty or vindictiveness.

The *boisterous,* the *show-offs,* and the girls or boys who go to *extremes in dress* would actually prefer to find their niches by other means if they knew how. The antics of the *mimic,* the *cut-up,* and the *practical joker* have at one time brought the attention desired, but so far unattained in other ways, and so have been adopted as standard conduct.

The *constant babbler* who monopolizes the conversation subconsciously envies his quiet, more socially acceptable companion who can feel secure of his place without constantly having to occupy the limelight. People *who eat the fastest, most,* or *least* and those with numerous *food dislikes* or *idiosyncrasies* are in the same category with those who bask in the "individuality" of *poor health,* an *unusual ailment,* or an *artistic temperament.*

The person who *cries* at the drop of a hat or becomes *hysterical* and throws a *temper tantrum* has probably found these methods effective in getting his own way in the past and so continues his tactics.

The *quarrelsome, stubborn,* or *rebellious* person is so unsure of himself that he uses loud words and violent action to drown out his own misgivings and discourage others from questioning him.

The *intolerant* person who "knows all the answers" is, in spite of his dogmatic statements, really distrustful of his own beliefs and is loath to listen to others lest they show up his inferior reasoning. The *overcritical* person calls attention to little flaws in others in hopes that this will make him seem superior by comparison.

Campers who form little *cliques* of two or more are seeking comfort from each other for their inability to make a place for themselves in the larger group. Forcibly breaking up the alliance may cause acute misery as the disapproval forces their egos down still further; a better solution is to lead them gradually into general group participation, so that they will no longer need the consolation of their little band. Some resort to *regression* or reverting to behavior of an earlier period, such as baby talk or complete dependence, hoping to be sheltered and excused for childish behavior and shortcomings as they were at that age.

Other annoying ways of trying to draw attention are noisiness, getting in the way, asking innumerable questions, refusing to eat, deliberately running away, or constantly complaining of injuries and ailments. Although normal children and even adults sometimes use attention-getting devices, immature methods and excessive use should gradually disappear as a youngster grows older and eventually acquires more mature and satisfactory ways to meet his needs.

Thumbsucking, nailbiting and facial *tics* are all nervous symptoms which act as "tension-reducers" and usually result from failure, frustration, or harsh disciplinary measures.

CAMPERS WHO ARE HOMESICK

Many campers feel a sense of loneliness and homesickness upon first coming to camp, but fortunately most of them adjust well and are soon having a fine time and joining enthusiastically in camp activities. However, an occasional camper will remain teary-eyed and aloof, resisting any efforts to make him part of the group and insisting that he wants to go home. Before you can help him, you will need to try to determine just what the root of his problem is.

A child who has never been away from home before may be overwhelmed by the strange faces and unfamiliar surroundings. He may have had little experience in associating with others of his own age outside of school and may be so painfully shy that it is hard for him to seek out or even accept friendships, and having to wash and dress before others may be excruciatingly embarrassing. He may feel a vague uneasiness at the quiet strangeness of the woods, particularly at night when his unaccustomed ears magnify the rustlings of animal life a hundredfold.

This situation sometimes results from an overly dependent parent-child relationship, which may be of a mutual or one-sided nature. Parents, without realizing it, have sometimes come to depend upon the child to satisfy their own need to feel loved and important and therefore do everything they can to encourage his dependency. They may actually enjoy having him express unhappiness at being away and long to have him clamor to come back to them. Their letters may dwell upon how everyone, including his pals and pets, misses him and how much fun they are having doing the things he used to enjoy, and they show their love and concern by frequent letters, telephone calls, and boxes of goodies. It is for these reasons that camps often counsel parents on the type of letter to write and ask them not to send packages or call (except in an emergency) or visit the camper until after the first two weeks of a long-term camp session; by that time the camper will most likely be smiling and enthusiastic about what he is doing.

An opposite problem is the occasional camper who feels that his parents do not love him and have sent him to camp just to get rid of him, so that they can go on a trip or enjoy an uninhibited social life without him. This feeling of rejection often leads him to believe that no one at camp will want him either. He may try to get even with his parents by complaining and bucking everything in the camp where they have placed him.

Another type of trouble comes with the camper who has learned to manipulate his parents by screaming, coaxing, flattering, cajoling, or throwing temper tantrums. When he finds that these formerly successful methods do not work at camp, it seems only natural that he will find fault with the camp and everyone connected with it and will want to return home where he knows how to get his own way.

Spells of homesickness normally reach their peak about the third or fourth day of camp and are strongest at mealtime, in the evening around bedtime, or on Sundays. (Note that these are relatively inactive times when the camper has a good deal of time to think about himself.) Homesickness has its basis in fear, such as fear of strangers, of unfamiliar surroundings, or of not being accepted, and is best fore-

Figure 10–6 I'm So Homesick!

stalled by the methods previously suggested to make the camper feel welcome and at home. It may enlighten *you* and help *him* to let him "talk it out," assuring him that such feelings are perfectly natural and are experienced by nearly everyone when they first stay away from home. It may also help to let him spend some time with an adult to whom he seems naturally attracted; this may, to some degree, provide a substitute for his missing parents. Keep him busy in cabin- or unit-planned activities or ask him to do something he excels at, such as drawing some pictures for the camp paper, helping with an outdoor fireplace, or decorating the tables in the dining room to give him a feeling of being important and needed. Don't just ignore him, for his misery is very real and will probably only get worse if positive steps are not taken. Homesickness sometimes manifests itself as a real or imaginary physical ailment, such as a stomachache or earache. If the nurse is sympathetic and gives him the attention he needs, it may result in a series of excuses to go to the infirmary; a little of this is enough, and then some other satisfying substitutes need to be found.

Sometimes a challenge to his pride to stick it out for a certain number of days with the promise that he may go home then if he still wants to appeals to him. Realize that you are fighting for more than just another camper on the camp roster; you are, in reality, making an important contribution to speed a youngster on his way toward emotional maturity and gradual emancipation from overly close home ties.

Sometimes the best efforts fail, however, and if it seems that the camper is being helped very little, the director may want to consider letting him go home, since homesickness is sometimes contagious and may spread to others who would adjust nicely if not exposed to it.

ENURESIS

Nearly every child is said to suffer from *enuresis* (bed-wetting) at some stage of his growing up, and since there may be a physical cause, those experiencing repeated occurrences should be referred to the camp doctor or nurse. Many cases, however, are simply manifestations of a child's inability to satisfy his emotional needs, resulting in anxiety and worry to which he responds by reverting to regressive behavior. Failure to get enough sleep or relax properly may be contributing causes, and the child with enuresis may have other symptoms of anxiety or emotional unrest, such as nervousness, hyperactivity, defiant behavior, excessive daydreaming, exaggeration, lying, or stealing. His excessive state of anxiety may cause him to be tense and poorly coordinated and consequently accident-prone.

If the health staff finds no physical cause and gives you the go-ahead, you should first set out to determine what is worrying or bothering him and eliminate it if possible. Above all, do not add to his already wounded ego by shaming him. Instead, be especially friendly and understanding, assuring

Figure 10–7 Night Can Be a Frightening Thing.

him that his trouble is not at all unique and that, with his cooperation, you feel sure that the two of you can overcome the difficulty. In the meantime, use such precautionary measures as providing him with rubber sheets, limiting his fluid intake after 5 o'clock, seeing that he goes to the latrine just before retiring and awakening him for another trip three or four hours later until a dry bed becomes habitual. See that he has a flashlight and companionship on night trips to the latrine.

SEX PROBLEMS

ROLE OF CAMP

Since camps are interested in educating the whole child and meeting his physical, mental, emotional, and social needs, you may be called upon to aid with some phase of sex education. Although every child has a normal and growing interest in sex, present-day social pressures and practices sometimes push him into an exaggerated or premature interest in sex and dating. (Bear in mind in this respect that girls mature approximately two years ahead of boys.) Unless children can receive the information they seek from some legitimate source, such as the home or school, they will seek it elsewhere, which unfortunately often turns out to be some equally uninformed or misinformed associates, alley acquaintances, or smutty literature, photographs, movies or television programs produced mainly for financial gain and now so readily available. Only a very naive or poorly informed person remains unaware of the presence of such interests and questions in every individual or group of young people, and instead of ignoring it in hopes it will go away, it is usually better to recognize it and face it openly.

WAYS OF HANDLING

Group discussions are sometimes helpful, since they give each camper a chance to ask questions and learn that his own anxieties and problems are common to others. When sponsored by qualified, wise leaders, they provide a means to substitute sound information for the half-truths and misinformation so commonly present. Unless someone in authority asks you to, do not voluntarily launch out on a planned program in this area unless you detect a real desire or need for it, and then only after you have carefully examined your own qualifications for the task. Is your information sound and sufficiently broad to handle such an assignment, and are your attitudes healthy and your sense of values well-balanced? Have you satisfactorily solved your own sex problems and is your conduct such that you need offer no apologies for it?

One of the best ways to keep growing sex interests and impulses under control is to see that every camper gets plenty of vigorous, whole-body exercise each and every day, even though it may take special planning when the weather is inclement. Young bodies are restless and full of vigor and need an outlet to expend excess energy. This need can be satisfied through an overall camp program which challenges and stimulates and thus keeps both body and mind occupied, leading to a healthy fatigue and sound restful sleep. A person involved in this type of living is less likely to become preoccupied with thoughts of sex or undesirable sex practices.

If you note some individual or group with a seemingly morbid interest in sex or engaged in unwholesome practices, take a frank and positive attitude toward it and view the situation calmly. Do not become unduly suspicious or let your imagination run away with you, but if convinced that there is a real and serious problem which you cannot handle, seek the help of someone better able to cope with it.

FRIENDSHIPS, HERO WORSHIP AND CRUSHES

I do not love thee, Dr. Fell.
The reason why I cannot tell;
But this I know, and know full well
I do not love thee, Dr. Fell.

—THOMAS BROWN (1663–1704)

FRIENDSHIPS

The above quotation expresses a well-known truism; for reasons often not quite clear to us, we are strongly attracted to some people and just as strongly repelled by others. You will find, however, that in order to function as a well-integrated person, you must learn to adapt yourself so that you can carry on pleasant working or social relationships with those you do not particularly care for or may even dislike. Fortunately, to temper the bitter with the sweet, you will probably have the privilege during your lifetime of meeting and enjoying a few kindred spirits with whom you are always attuned, so that almost anything you do with them at any time or in any place is fun. Such mutual relationships are real blessings, for they afford one of life's most satisfying experiences and usually have quite positive benefits, except when allowed to absorb one or both of the participants to the point where they have neither the time nor the desire to carry on normal associations with other individuals or groups.

Friendship is a lovely thing
A gift most freely given—
Not won, not earned, but taken wing
And sent straight down from heaven.

—ELIZABETH ALLEN*

CHANGING SEX PREFERENCES

As previously discussed, it is quite normal at certain stages in a child's development for him to prefer associating with those of his own sex. This gradually changes into an acceptance of and then a preference for those of the opposite sex, finally focusing on some particular individual or a succession of them and eventually culminating in love and perhaps marriage. Although these developments ordinarily take place at approximately the same age in most youngsters, they may be premature or late in a few. This should not be a cause for alarm unless the fixation becomes unduly pronounced at one of the earlier stages. This is most likely to occur at the stage of preference for one's own sex and in extreme cases may involve a strong

*Used by permission of the author.

sexual attraction, sometimes accompanied by abnormal sexual practices.

HERO WORSHIP AND CRUSHES

It is also normal for a youngster to select someone who represents the embodiment of his highest ideals and aspirations and whom he idealizes, cherishes, and holds up as a model or hero. This may prove of inestimable value if the model chosen is a worthy one, for it provides him with a powerful stimulus to try to emulate this person in every detail.

The time at which hero worship is most pronounced often coincides roughly with the period of preference for his own sex, and consequently the one chosen is often a particular pal, a member of his gang or someone of his own sex who is older than he. In camp, it may well be a counselor or other member of the staff. If you are so fortunate as to become the object of your campers' admiration and respect, take pride in the compliment and recognize that it presents one of your greatest opportunities to steer youngsters along the right path as they develop to their full potential.

Figure 10-8 Misery is Having a Camper Catch You Smoking a Cigarette.

An occasional youngster may remain in this stage of preference for his own sex for an unduly long period, sometimes even well into adulthood, and the feeling may become so emotional and intense as to almost exclude normal relationships with other individuals or the group. This is usually termed a *crush*. It is more likely to occur in one who has not received the warmth and affection he needs from his family and friends, and so tries to satisfy his emotional hunger by an abnormally close relationship with someone else. The feelings may or may not be mutual, and when extreme, the relationship may prove detrimental to one or both parties.

As a counselor, you should be aware of the possibility of becoming the object of such adoration, for unless you note its development in the early stages and divert it into healthy channels, it may create a delicate situation for you and others. If you permit it to continue or perhaps even encourage it until it has become full blown and then try to squelch it or turn it off by rough handling or by pointedly ignoring the person, you may do him much harm. Remember that it probably represents only the frantic clutchings of an emotionally starved individual to satisfy his normal and pressing wish for someone to love and admire and to be loved and admired by him in return. Do not be overly suspicious or imagine a developing problem where none exists, but on the other hand, stay alert to the possibility and take timely steps to prevent its development to undesirable stages. If the person is one of your campers, extend him your usual warmth and cordiality, but show him no special attention, keeping him tactfully but firmly in his place as merely one of your group, all of whom share equally in your interest and affection. In time, persistence and understanding will turn your relationship into a perfectly healthy and worthwhile counselor-camper friendship which will bring lasting pleasure and benefit to both of you.

Occasionally an immature counselor or one with unmet emotional needs of his own is flattered by such attention and encourages it to build up his own ego. Such a relationship has a bad effect upon each, for others may shun and criticize them, and the relationship brings neither complete nor lasting satisfaction to either. If the individuals vary in age, as in a counselor-camper relationship, it is most unfair to the younger person, for the older individual is selfishly satisfying his own needs and wishes by taking advantage of someone less experienced.

Beware of the all-too-common error of mistaking a strong, wholesome friendship for a crush or homosexual attraction. Such misinterpretations are extremely unfortunate and produce serious complications which may prove damaging to both the personalities and reputations of the persons involved. Most so-called crushes are simply examples of hero worship, of the universal wish for mutual love and admiration, or of the strong, wholesome friendships which add so much pleasure to life.

Figure 10–9 You're My Ideal.

As previously mentioned, it is humanly impossible to avoid being more attracted to some youngsters than to others, but a good counselor keeps such preferences locked up as deep, dark secrets, staying outwardly objective and impartial at all times. Remember that the child who is unattractive to you probably affects others in the same way, and consequently he, most of all, is likely to be lonesome and in greatest need of your affection and attention.

ADMONITIONS FOR THE COUNSELOR

1. Avoid snap judgments, for human behavior is too complex to understand with a single formula or rule of thumb. Learn all you can concerning a camper who is giving you concern; observe him carefully but without letting him know it. Do not take his previous record too seriously, for a change in environment often produces a change in behavior. The child who has been labeled "bad" at home may completely reverse his conduct when exposed to the new faces, new influences and new activities of camp.

2. Remind yourself again of all the ways to help each camper to satisfy his fundamental desires and to attain a feeling of security in his cabin family. Vary the program so that each child's interests and abilities can be satisfied and recognized in some part of it.

3. Recall that misbehavior is usually a bid for attention or an expression of insecurity or a feeling of being un-

loved and unwanted, and that public reprimand or punishment ordinarily only aggravates the situation. No one is really more miserable, no matter how skillfully he hides it, than the "bad" or "problem" child, and our happiness at helping him to "fit in the groove" is insignificant compared to what he will experience.

4. Inconspicuously try to draw aggressive or retiring campers into activities which afford them a true feeling of success and achievement. Their distress and problems often disappear if they are provided with socially approved ways to satisfy their needs and wishes. It is hard to conceive of any youngster who would willingly continue to "get in peoples' hair" if he could otherwise get the attention, affection, and recognition he craves.

5. Make a particular effort to get close to the camper who seems to be creating a problem for himself or others. This may be tedious, for those most needing help are often too timid or proud to ask for or even accept it when offered. Thus, a casual approach through a seemingly accidental canoe ride or hike is better than a formal conference by appointment. Cultivate the ability to be a good listener, for the problem camper's veneer of bravado usually cloaks an aching hunger for a trusted older person in whom he can confide. Skillful handling soon finds him chatting busily about all his secret hopes and aspirations, and once you have won his confidence and friendship, you are well on the way to your goal.

6. Seldom give advice; instead use discreet questioning and suggestion to enable the camper to work out his own solution.

7. Do not heap coals of fire on a camper's head for his misdeeds. This only produces rebellion or causes him to rationalize or project the blame onto others, further blinding himself to any real insight into his problem. It also kills any possibility of building up the desired friendship and trust between counselor and camper.

8. You may occasionally find it necessary to strongly reprimand or punish a camper who persistently refuses to recognize and accept his share of the responsibility for his difficulties. Use these methods only when all kindlier treatment has failed and never to relieve your own feelings of anger or incompetence.

ADDITIONAL READINGS

(For an explanation of abbreviations and abbreviated forms, see page 25.)

Adams, Jay E.: *Competent to Counsel.* Baker, 1973, 287 pp., $4.50.

Adams, Jay E.: *What to Do About Worry.* Baker, 35¢.

Amos, W. E., and J. D. Grambs (Eds.): *Counseling the Disadvantaged Youth.* Prentice-Hall, 1968.

Barksdale, L. S.: *Building Self-Esteem.* The Barksdale Foundation, Idyllwild, Cal., 1972.

Blanchard, Howard L., and Laurence S. Flaum: *Guidance: A Longitudinal Approach.* Burgess, 1969, 338 pp., $5.95, paper.

Brussel, James A., M.D., and Theodore Irwin: *Understanding and Overcoming Depression.* Hawthorn, 1973, 244 pp., $6.95.

Budd, William C., Ph.D.: *Behavior Modification: The Scientific Way to Self Control.* Galloway, 96 pp., $5.

Corbin: *Recreation Leadership,* ch. 10.

Drug Abuse: Escape to Nowhere. A.A.H.P.E.R., rev., 1970, 104 pp., $2.

Forrer, Dr. Gordon R.: *Psychiatric Self Help.* Galloway, 71 pp., $5.

How Can We Teach Adolescents About Smoking, Drinking and Drug Abuse? A.A.H.P.E.R., 6 pp., 30¢, paper.

Ledlie and Holbein: *Camp Counselor's Manual,* ch. 16.

Menacker, Julius: *Urban Poor Students and Guidance.* Guidance Monograph Series, Houghton Mifflin, 1971, 84 pp.

Rubin, Isadore, and Lester A. Kirkendall: *Sex in the Childhood Years.* Ass'n Press, 1970, 190 pp., $4.95.

Shivers: *Camping,* pp. 149–164.

Strean: *New Approaches in Child Guidance.*

Todd: *Camping for Christian Youth,* pp. 137–140.

Van Krevelen: *Children in Groups: Psychology and the Summer Camp,* chs. 4, 5.

MAGAZINE ARTICLES

Camping Magazine:

Bentley, Bradford M.: "How Tape Recorder Cured Acute Homesickness." Mar., 1965, p. 15.

Colton, Raymond H.: "To Aid a Problem Child, Use His Background Traits." June, 1965, p. 17.

Hill, Robert N.: "Discipline Must Have a Direct Relationship to Action . . ." June, 1963, p. 17.

Huck, Susan C., and Philip A. Denomme: "Checkpoints for Fighting the Drug Menace in Camp." Sept./Oct., 1970, p. 19.

Lainoff, Harold M.: "Help Homesick Campers With Understanding Guidance." May, 1965, p. 26.

Ohlson, Elaine, R.N.: "Handling 'S.S.' in Camp." May, 1969, p. 16. (Homesickness)

Palter, Elsie, Ph.D.: "When Stealing Occurs in Camp." May, 1972, p. 16.

Rotman, Charles B.: "The Problem Camper—To Tolerate, Treat or Terminate." Sept./Oct., 1973, p. 16.

Schlesinger, Mike: "Pot, Pills and People." Mar., 1970, p. 10.

Sohn, David and Sheila: "Drug Abuse—How to Stop It Before It Becomes a Problem." Apr., 1972, p. 18.

Spiegel, Jerry and Eleanor: "Start Treatment for Homesickness Before Child Comes to Camp." June, 1964, p. 20.

Tabeling, Elizabeth Joye: "Homesick—A Word to Avoid." Apr., 1966, p. 24.

Part Three

They've Been Listening to Us! Guess It's Their Turn Now.

Camp Activities

Chapter 11

Planning the Program

Figure 11-1 "Um-m-m . . . What Shall We Do Now?"

Planning is forethought. It pervades the realms of all human action. Whether a man plans a business, a career, a house, or a fishing trip, he is looking into the future in order to arrange his affairs so that they will work out to the best advantage. Applied to our everyday world, planning is nothing but common sense.

—C. EARL MORROW*

Counselors who sit on bottoms never get to top.

Everything has been thought of before, but the difficulty is to think of it again.

—JOHANN WOLFGANG VON GOETHE

WHY PROGRAMS DIFFER

It is very hard to summarize programs, for there are as many different sorts as there are camps. This is not difficult to understand when we realize how many variable factors enter into determining them. The following are prominent among them.

OBJECTIVES OF THE CAMP OR SPONSORING ORGANIZATION

Naturally, the activities chosen for the program will be those which best carry out the objectives of the particular camp. We would expect a church camp to lean heavily toward activities of a spiritual nature, a school camp to emphasize the acquiring of information, and an agency camp to work toward its stated objectives. Special camps, such as those featuring dance, music, or activities for the physically handicapped, will obviously have programs that concentrate mainly on their particular specialty.

PHILOSOPHY AND ABILITIES OF THE CAMP DIRECTOR AND PROGRAM DIRECTOR

A camp program sometimes reflects the particular interests or abilities of the camp or program director. For instance, an avid fisherman will see that poles, tackle, and time on the program are provided for his beloved recreation, a person with a love of music

*From *Planning Your Community*. Reproduced by permission of Regional Plan Association, Inc.

will emphasize related activities, and, a person who likes rather sedentary, "country-club" types of activities will not be likely to promote a strong campcraft and trips program. Superior leaders, however, try not to overemphasize their hobbies and interests, preferring to offer a well-rounded, versatile program, built around the particular needs and interests of the campers.

ABILITIES OF THE STAFF AND RESOURCE PERSONNEL

Some camps hire a large number of specialists, whereas others hire mostly general counselors who bring with them a wide variety of more modest skills and interests. Specialists, of course, may provide better instruction in their fields, but when there are too many of them or if their interests are too limited, each may concentrate on promoting his own activity instead of cooperating as a team member to foster a well-balanced program. This is the exception rather than the rule, however, and often the problem is caused by camp administrators who are so shortsighted as to base monetary rewards, rehiring, and good recommendations on the popularity of the counselor or his activity. A broad-minded specialist not only does his own job well, but also promotes the activities of others. A counselor who is good at tying knots will soon have others joining him and one who sings a merry lilt as he works will be surrounded by happy campers similarly engaged. One who takes time on a hike to watch some squirrels scurrying about will be planting an interest in nature in his followers.

NATURE OF THE CAMP SITE

The nature of the camp site will be influential in determining program. A camp located near a mountain would be foolish not to take advantage of the opportunity for mountain climbing. No one, obviously, will be weaving honeysuckle baskets if it doesn't grow in the camp environment. A remote unit in a decentralized camp can build its own council ring and outdoor kitchen right in its own backyard, whereas a unit in the middle of a centralized camp will need to venture into the wildwood in search of a private nook; this is no hardship, however, since it promotes exploring into regions which otherwise might remain unknown.

EQUIPMENT AND FACILITIES

A camp with an elaborate outlay of backpacking equipment is in a position to sponsor a vigorous trips program. Although, in the minds of some, swimming and boating are almost synonymous with camp, there are camps without such facilities which quite successfully build a program around other worthwhile activities too often neglected in camps where Neptune holds sway. Imagination and a positive approach can turn a lack of equipment into a challenge to campers to master the use of tools to make their own equipment from kits or raw materials or to substitute activities with less elaborate requirements.

LOCATION AND TERRAIN

When interesting historical sites abound in the vicinity, a camp should capitalize on this and plan to study and visit them. Paul Bunyan country will call for storytelling and special events built around this favorite character. A seaside camp may plan visits to fish-processing plants and fishing vessels. In one camp with a fairly steep hillside, enthusiasm over skiing and tobogganing on pine needles reigned, spurred on by a local neighbor who had enjoyed these activities as a boy. In another, there was a meandering, babbling brook where campers loved to wade and search out the secrets of the animal and plant life within and around it.

WHERE FIRES ARE NOT PERMITTED

Camp sites in areas where wood fires are not permitted will have to find substitute methods of cooking and conducting traditional campfire programs. Many are doing this successfully, and youngsters who have never seen a real campfire may scarcely notice the difference.

CLIMATE

Camps in hot areas wisely plan campfire programs without benefit of fire and schedule an extra long siesta and quiet activities for the hottest part

(Courtesy of Camp Mary White, Zia Girl Scout Council, Mayhill, New Mexico.)

of the day. Camps with cool mornings and evenings will, on the contrary, lean toward vigorous activities, with swimming scheduled toward the middle of the day.

THE CAMPERS

The ages, previous experiences, skills, financial status, and social backgrounds of the campers are very influential in determining program. A camper who has seen his grandparents do a lively Lithuanian dance can teach it to the others, while another may contribute a German folk song, and still another demonstrate the art of pottery making, taught to him by his art-teacher mother. Farm boys and girls may be far ahead of their city cousins in nature lore, but may lag far behind in executing fancy dives and swimming strokes.

LENGTH OF THE CAMPING PERIOD

Campers who come for only a week or two will need fairly simple projects which they can complete in a short time; others in short-term agency camps may attempt more advanced projects, since they are putting into practice skills and knowledge already acquired under the sponsoring organization in the city. In short-term camps, planning the program involves deciding on the number and types of activities that can be accomplished in the time available.

Eight-week camps can approach program in a more leisurely fashion and formulate more complicated plans which build up to a climax at the end of the season. One group of campers built a log cabin to shelter their arts and crafts equipment (with the help of some older men on the heavy, technical work); another group undertook to clear a vista and path through the underbrush down to the lake. A group of girls planned a collection of dolls dressed in their native costumes and displayed on papier-mâché relief maps of their native lands.

RATIO OF COUNSELORS TO CAMPERS

A high ratio of counselors to campers permits a more or less ideal situation in which campers can be divided into small groups with each person receiving more personal attention.

CHANGING PROGRAM EMPHASES

Early camps felt that the best way to keep a camper out of mischief and prevent homesickness and boredom was to keep him busy every moment of the day. Almost every instant was planned, and the camper was registered in a number of activities, selected because they were "good for him" or because his parents had requested them. If he found himself in one he heartily disliked, it was just too bad, for the schedule and rules were rigid and permitted no deviation, so that there often seemed to be a grim death struggle going on to see whether he or the summer would come to an end first. Activities were scheduled like school classes, with attendance carefully checked each day, and motivation was supplied by achievement charts, testing programs, intense competition between individuals and groups, and elaborate systems of awards. In some cases, regimentation and scheduling were carried to a degree which almost obliterated the two things the camper most wanted—to have fun and to make new friends.

As with most trends, this period of regimentation was followed by a movement in the opposite direction; this was toward permissiveness, and when carried to extremes, the camp scheduled no activities at all, leaving

Figure 11–2 I'd Druther Go Fishin'.

the camper free to do whatever he chose the entire day. This practice was apparently based on the assumption that the best way to teach a child to make choices and to govern himself is to loosen the reins and let him learn by the trial-and-error method, but actually, children are often unhappy when left entirely to their own resources. In addition, when children learn solely by trial-and-error, they often acquire misinformation and bad habits. Programs planned exclusively by campers, or unplanned programs which "just grow," often lack continuity and are likely to degenerate into mere busy work and eventual boredom. The best results come from a tempering of the impetuosity and daring of youth with the sobering influence of experience and greater maturity, as occurs when campers and counselors plan the program cooperatively.

THE NEW CONCEPTION OF PROGRAM

The essence of "program" was once considered to be only the so-called activity periods, such as archery, swimming, storytelling, woodcraft, and dramatics, which children attended without question. This type of activity planning is termed a *structured program.* We now realize that program is much more, for Mary's development certainly does not begin with arts and crafts at 8:30, stop for lunch at 11:30 and continue again at 2:30 with nature study, to then cease entirely after her 4:30 horseback-riding period. In reality, program is everything that happens to Mary throughout the day, for each single incident, no matter how trivial, is a potential influence for good or bad. Even bedtime hours from taps to reveille have importance, for Mary is learning (we hope) to remain quiet out of consideration for others and because she herself realizes her need for adequate sleep. Can we argue convincingly that archery, weaving, campcraft, or canoeing will be of

Figure 11–3 And Goes Happily to His Doom.

more ultimate worth to her than forming habits of orderliness, cooperativeness, punctuality, or friendliness? We can be sure that Mary is constantly learning something, be it desirable or undesirable, from every experience that comes her way; she cannot be closed up like a book and placed on the shelf at 4:30 to remain unopened until 8:30 the next morning.

Program and activities are not ends in themselves but provide the means through which camping objectives can be achieved. Although learning to play tennis may bring Tommy hours of pleasure throughout life, we cannot ignore the equal or greater importance of his concomitant learning of persistence in mastering a difficult task, good sportsmanship and respect and admiration for someone who can play better.

HOW A CAMP PROGRAM IS PLANNED

The new trend in camping is to let campers and staff cooperatively plan their own activities in what is known as an *unstructured program*. This allows enough flexibility to permit altering it as seems fit as the days pass and needs and wishes change. This flexible program satisfies youth's craving for variety and the need to be up and doing, yet it is by no means haphazard and unplanned, for it indeed requires superior planning to avoid conflicts over facilities, equipment, and the services of the specialists on the staff.

Certain hours, as for rising, going to bed, eating, resting, and swimming, which affect the whole camp must be scheduled or at least definitely arranged for in order to prevent groups from interfering with each other. Beyond that, individuals and groups are left pretty much on their own to choose from the possible activities offered by the camp, according to what seems exciting and worthwhile to them.

The program for the entire camp is usually coordinated by one person, either the program director, assistant camp director, or head counselor. Occasionally, particularly in small camps, the director himself serves in this capacity, but he more commonly acts as an advisor to someone else to whom he has delegated this particular responsibility.

In long-term private camps, each camper may be allowed to decide upon his own activities irrespective of what others in his unit are doing, and various methods for implementing this may be used. One is to have the program director announce at the end of a meal, such as breakfast, what activities are available for the morning; campers then indicate by a show of hands those in which they wish to participate. Duplicate lists are made up, one for the staff member in charge of each activity and the other for the camp office, where the location of each camper and counselor must always be known. It makes for better instruction when participants are classified according to degree of skill, such as sailing for beginners or advanced horsemanship for those who

Figure 11-4 Let Campers Decide Their Own Program.

have passed their preliminary tests. Another method of programming offers still more freedom of choice. Here, the program director simply opens the field for suggestions, and when Jack requests an activity such as fishing, the program director asks how many would like to join him in it.

This freedom of choice is usually more prevalent in long-term camps. Advocates claim as advantages that it: (1) focuses on the individual rather than the activity; (2) widens a camper's circle of friends as he participates with different people in each activity; (3) allows each camper to do what interests him instead of being coerced into following what is voted on by his living group; and (4) prevents the possible animosities which may occur when the same individuals eat, sleep, and do everything else together over a long period of time.

Short-term camps usually find unit programming more useful, feeling that each camper will become better acquainted and feel more at ease if he spends most of his time with only a small group of his peers. In this small "family," he can gain recognition as an individual and have a better opportunity to voice his opinions.

Under either plan of programming, it is customary to hold several all-camp events during the period, their number and character varying with the particular camp. Most camps sponsor some sort of *camp council,* which consists of counselor and camper representatives from each unit who meet with the program director to plan such all-camp events. Care must be exercised to see that the group is not dominated by older people, lest youngsters hesitate to speak up in front of them.

As wide a variety of activities as the camp facilities and talents of the staff permit should be offered to give each child a chance to determine his interests and abilities in several fields. Who knows but that the little camp orchestra may fire the spark of a future Leonard Bernstein who had never before experienced the thrill of being on the producing end of music? One of the finest things a camp can do is to introduce youngsters to a variety of hobbies which may become lasting sources of joy or even financially profitable vocations or avocations.

A hobby is one means for escaping institutional life.

—WILLIAM G. VINAL

HOW PROGRAM DEVELOPS

A day is a wonderful thing. It is like a great doorway flung wide for you to pass through into all manner of adventure.

—ST. NICHOLAS

When staff and campers join democratically in program planning, counselors act as consultants and advisors, not dictators, and must be able to guide and control the situation so that wise choices are made, without forcing their ideas on the group.

Your ability to see opportunities, to select or reject, encourage or discourage, suggest, counsel, and use skill in changing directions will largely determine what all of you will receive as your summer's rewards. Younger campers need many ideas and suggestions, particularly during their first few days in camp, for many of them have unknowingly been so dependent on their parents and on radio, movies, and television for entertainment that they are almost at a complete loss when called upon to make decisions on how to spend their time. Even older campers will often not be able to suggest what they *really* want to do. They are inclined to choose what they have already done, even if they have become somewhat bored with it, because they have too little experience or imagination to see other possibilities. This represents an opportunity for you as their counselor to tactfully broaden their interests and point out new vistas by throwing out a hint or merely picking up and encouraging one of their own ideas. Suggestions from others will follow, and even when one is not accepted in its entirety, it may stimulate others until one idea finally "catches fire" and the group is off to an exciting experience. It is often possible to turn an impractical or unacceptable suggestion into a more suitable variation.

> It's better to get set up before you go ahead and get upset.
>
> —Hal Cochran

Make a big calendar and enter on it the fixed dates for the season, such as all-camp activities and other special events. Within this framework, you can then plan your own particular unit activities, adjusting them and adding details as the season advances.

When youngsters feel at ease and free to express themselves, proposals literally fly back and forth, and it then becomes your job to help them to separate the wheat from the chaff and settle on those things which really hold priority with them. Encouraging them to look ahead and evaluate as they go along, forseeing obstacles and planning how to overcome them, gives valuable experience. You may, on rare occasions, have to come out with a flat "no" if what they are proposing is against camp policy or actually dangerous, but at other times, you may want to let them go ahead and learn by experience, if the consequences will not be too serious.

Figure 11–5 Keep a Schedule of Coming Events Posted.

One of youth's tendencies is to leap breathlessly into anything that sounds new and exciting and then to drop it without ceremony as soon as the newness has worn off or another attraction appears on the horizon. Point out that good workmen never leave an assortment of half-finished undertakings behind them.

Above all, get them involved in all your planning, for forcing preconceived ideas on them from higher up just won't work—it brings only half-hearted compliance and may even cause downright rebellion. When the plan is really theirs, they become so excited they can scarcely contain themselves, and your worries about discipline problems, program, and problem campers will largely disappear.

Develop keen ears and deep insight to spot possible program leads; often just listening to your group's chatter will furnish a clue. If Jim is describing how his uncle worked on landscaping his house, a general discussion may lead to a plan to landscape your own surroundings. If Susan complains about the brush and rough stones on the way to the waterfront, who can better remedy the situation than her unit group? Promote a trip to see the new Adirondack shack the Limberlost Unit has constructed at their outpost camp; soon you may be in the midst of planning a bigger and better one for yourselves.

Several books and stories center on camping experiences; why not read from one during story hour to see if any of the ideas catch on? Post step-by-step directions for a project on the bulletin board or make a sample or model of it. Take the campers on a walk and discuss conservation problems; per-

Figure 11-6 "Wonder If He Likes Peanut Butter and Jelly Sandwiches."

haps they will want to return to fill in a low place or plant cover crops to control erosion. Get a kit or raw materials to make yourself a poncho or make a No. 10 tin can cooking outfit and suggest that they join you. After a canoeing trip has been ruined by a sudden rainstorm, the stage is set for learning to predict the weather to prevent such a catastrophe in the future. Read selections from your poetry notebook or show them some of your nature sketches and watch the interested eyes and eager minds that come to learn. Encourage their interests, even if they lie in a field unfamiliar to you, for research in the camp library will help you, and your fellow counselors, unit leader, or camp specialist will be flattered if you seek their help.

DECIDING UPON PROJECTS

Some projects arise spontaneously, such as a decision to devote the afternoon to cabin clean-up and decoration after rain has spoiled a proposed supper hike. Others, such as a five-day horseback trip, the camp birthday party, or the cabin presentation for the All-Camp Stunt Night, require long-term planning. Such undertakings bring triple enjoyment: (1) planning for and dreaming about them; (2) actually doing them; and (3) reminiscing and basking in the pride of accomplishment.

Facts which in themselves are dry as a bone come alive and become fascinating when learned for a definite purpose. A child is justifiably reluctant to learn the technical jargon of sailboating, knowing full well that it will be months or even years before he can pass the tests and be allowed to even set foot in one. His attitude will change completely, however, if he is learning a nautical vocabulary while actually helping to manipulate the vessel.

THE INDIGENOUS PROGRAM

Most camps now favor what is known as an *indigenous program*. This is one that is strictly personal to the camp and is based upon materials found in or near it. In arts and crafts, native woods are used for whittling, native vegetation for dyeing, and local grasses and reeds for weaving. Nature specimens are the flowers, trees and insects found on the camp grounds. (These projects are done, of course,

Figure 11-7 Get Authentic Information About the Indians Who Inhabited Your Area.

only in accordance with good conservation practices.) The folk songs and ballads of the region find a place in singing, and the dances are those of the early settlers. Stories, dramatics, pageants, and original songs are based upon local folklore and legends, and information is obtained from local residents and the clippings, files, and other resources of the local librarian. It is evident that no two indigenous programs are ever quite the same, since no two communities offer identical natural resources and historical backgrounds.

THE TEST OF A GOOD PROGRAM ACTIVITY

Teach campers to evaluate their program by asking themselves such questions as: What went well and what didn't? What did we learn from the experience and how can we use it in planning for the future?

Activities that bear up well under the following tests are likely to be good ones that make a real contribution to the objectives of camping:

1. Is the activity in accord with the idea of simple outdoor living? Does it further understanding and love of the out-of-doors and is it in line with good conservation practices?
2. Does it develop the ability to live harmoniously with others, respecting their individual personalities and potentialities?
3. Are individuals sometimes given the chance to go off on tangents of their own, or is everything *always* decided by the vote of the majority?
4. Does it answer youth's longing for fun and adventure? Do campers *want* to do it or are they merely acceding to the wishes of some adults? Is it interesting in itself without outside motivation such as awards or special privileges?
5. Does it challenge campers' initiative, resourcefulness, and creative expression, or is it merely a cut-and-dried process in which they follow instructions to cut along the dotted line, then join part A to part B?
6. Does it broaden interests and appreciations and help youngsters to see with Robert Louis Stevenson that:

> The world is so full of a number of things.
> I'm sure we should all be as happy as kings.

7. Is it free from actual physical danger? Does it contribute to the greater health and vitality of the campers?
8. Could they do it just as well or better in their own home communities? (This is one of the most important tests and largely rules out the "city" type of arts and crafts and such organized sports as basketball and baseball.)
9. Does it have carry-over value for use at home or in later life?
10. Does it fulfill fundamental wishes and contribute to the camper's overall mental health?
11. Is it truly a group project to which each camper can feel he has made a real contribution, or do a few of the more aggressive and talented usurp all the positions of importance and claim an undue amount of credit?
12. Is some recognition given to those who make great efforts or develop better-than-average skills? (Keep this in balance, however, remembering that it can be easily overdone, for "every time there is a winner you also pick several losers.")

POSSIBLE PROJECTS

CONSTRUCTION WORK

Among possible projects are making a:

Rustic entrance for unit, cabin, or camp
Totem pole
Outdoor kitchen
Outdoor theater
Campfire circle

Figure 11-8 Let Harmony Ring.

Log cabin
Nature exhibit
Rock garden
Campcraft exhibit
Rustic bulletin board
Nature aquarium
Green cathedral—outdoor chapel
Improvised camping equipment (either from kits or raw materials)
Repair of boats, riding tack, tennis courts, trailways, etc.
Weathervane, weather flags, and instruments for forecasting the weather
Outpost camp
Council ring
Clearing a path
Sundial
Bridge across the creek
Tepee or Adirondack shack
Soil erosion control
Pottery kiln
Nature trail
Fernery
Cleaning up the campsite
Terrariums

EVENING ACTIVITIES

Program of customs, costumes, and dances of other cultures
Potpourri
Informal dramatics
Folk, square, or round dancing
Parties—hard times, pioneer, gypsy, plantation, masquerade, etc.
Old-fashioned singing school
Spelling matches
Progressive games
Village night (invite the camp neighbors in)
Barn dance
Amateur night
Hay ride
Camp banquet
Moonlight hike
Star study
Lantern party
Poetry, stories, good music
Shadow plays
Torchlight or candlelight parade while singing
Quiz show
Discussion groups
Liar's contest (see who can tell the biggest whopper)
Come-as-you-are party

In many camps an occasional evening campfire program is a tradition dear to the hearts of the campers. Make it varied enough so that it goes beyond mere routine and becomes one of the most meaningful events of the summer. It is more romantic and inspiring when conducted in some secluded, special place of beauty reserved for such events, and many camps have worked out elaborate fire-lighting ceremonies for such occasions. Physical comfort warrants attention too, for no one can sit in rapt attention during a fierce bombardment by voracious mosquitoes. Evening programs should taper off to a quiet, sleep-inducing conclusion and should end on time even though it means omitting some part. Symbols, no matter how simple, mean much to campers and serve to stimulate their imaginations and loyalties. Hammett and Musselman* suggested having a "Town Crier" summon campers to a program instead of letting them saunter in, and crowning a winner with a wreath of "laurel leaves" instead of just announcing that he won.

---

*Hammett, Catherine T., and Virginia Musselman: *The Day Camp Program Book.* Ass'n Press, 1963.

SPECIAL DAYS

Woodcrafter's day—hold demonstrations or contests in such skills as building fires, using knife and axe, and erecting a tent.
County or state fair conducted at camp
Camp birthday
Mardi Gras
Gypsy day
Dude ranch rodeo
Circus day
Holiday of a foreign country (costumes, food, dances, games, songs and so on)
Staff day (when campers and staff interchange roles)
Western barbecue day
Regatta day
Water pageant
Local history day
Birthday of a famous person
Clean-up, paint-up day
Storybook day (theme of Robin Hood, Paul Bunyan, Robinson Crusoe or other story carried out through the day)
Village day (when neighbors from the village visit)
Gift day (when campers or groups present gifts, perhaps self-made, to the camp)
International day
Pioneer day
Guest day for another unit or camp
Free choice day

RAINY-DAY ACTIVITIES

Bad weather always looks much worse through a window.

—JOHN KIERAN,
Footnotes on Nature, Doubleday.

Rainy days will often present a problem to the unimaginative counselor, and a steady downpour of several days duration is enough to tax the ingenuity and resourcefulness of even the doughtiest leader and reduce his spirits to a state of drippy dilapidation. Nevertheless, it is essential to keep campers busy and happy, for spells of homesickness are especially likely to sail in with the storm clouds. An "A-1" counselor helps his charges to turn such an occasion into a satisfying and enjoyable experience. A wise leader will keep the threat of rain ever in the back of his mind so that he is ready for those inevitable rainy days. Here are some possibilities:

Figure 11–9 "Let It Rain, Let It Pour!"

Plan a carnival or puppet show
Take a slicker hike in the rain; note the rainy day activities of wildlife
Compose a cabin or unit yell, song, symbol, slogan, or the like
Learn new songs and sing the old
Work on scrapbooks or snapshot albums
Make candy or popcorn or serve "tea"
Play charades and other indoor games
Plan an open house with simple refreshments for another cabin or unit
Plan stunts for the next all-camp program
Hold discussions
Read or tell stories
Write letters
Listen to recorded music
Plan a future trip, a nature trail, or outpost camp
Toast marshmallows
Hold a contest to determine the Biggest Liar
Compose a cabin or unit newspaper to be read at supper
Organize a harmonica, comb, kitchen, or kazoo band or other musical group
Have folk or square dances and singing games
Plan a banquet (with candles or some little extra item of food and a program)
Organize Fireside Clubs with small groups gathered in front of available fireplaces to pursue special interests
Arrange a hobby show or other exhibit
Plan a stunt night (keep it on a high level)
Make posters for the bulletin board
Have a pet show—display stuffed animals
Make puppets or work on a play

(Courtesy of Camp Manito-Wish, YMCA, Boulder Junction, Wisconsin.)

Practice campcraft skills such as knots, tincan-craft, and so forth
Make a model campsite or one of the entire camp layout
Do plaster casts or nature crafts
Carve or paint soap objects
Do string art or bead work
Work on arts and crafts, plan an exhibit
Whittle or carve objects
Mend clothing and get the cabin in apple-pie order
Work on costume box in readiness for the next play
Hold a spelling bee or quiz program
Read or write camp poetry
Make up indoor games and play them
Write a dramatic production and prepare to produce it
Make improvised camping equipment such as trench candles and waterproof matches
Study weather, make weather flags and other weather instruments
Study clouds as they change and move about with the storms
Play active games to relieve tension and get exercise
Mark tools and put them in good repair—sharpen knives, axes, etc.
Work on riding tack, archery tackle, and so on
Get extra sleep or rest
Fish, boat or swim in the rain (if no lightning)
Beautify living quarters by block printing curtains, using natural dyes for materials or adding other decorations
Practice Red Cross first aid techniques
Have a talent show
Play indoor nature games or prepare for your next nature hike
Study rules or techniques of such activities as tennis and horseback riding

You will find other suggestions for programs throughout various chapters of this book, as well as in the sources listed at the ends of several chapters.

*THE BIRTHRIGHT OF CHILDREN**

All children should know the joy of playing in healthful mud, of paddling in clean water, of hearing birds sing praises to God for the new day.

They should have the vision of pure skies enriched at dawn and sunset with

*From Proceedings for 1946 of the National Education Association of the United States; reproduced by permission.

unspeakable glory; of dew-drenched mornings flashing with priceless gems; of the vast night sky all throbbing and panting with stars.

They should live with the flowers and butterflies, with the wild things that have made possible the world of fables.

They should experience the thrill of going barefoot, of being out in the rain; of riding a white birch, of sliding down pine boughs, of climbing ledges and tall trees, of diving headfirst into a transparent pool.

They ought to know the smell of wet earth, of new mown hay, of sweet fern, mint, and fir; of the breath of cattle and of fog blown inland from the sea.

They should hear the answer the trees make to the rain and the wind; the sound of rippling and falling water; the muffled roar of the sea in storm.

They should have the chance to catch fish, to ride on a load of hay, to camp out, to cook over an open fire, tramp through a new country, and sleep under the open sky.

They should have the fun of driving a horse, paddling a canoe, sailing a boat. . . .

One cannot appreciate and enjoy to the full extent of nature, books, novels, histories, poems, pictures, or even musical compositions, who has not in his youth enjoyed the blessed contact with the world of nature.

—HENRY TURNER BAILEY

ADDITIONAL READINGS

(For an explanation of abbreviations and abbreviated forms, see page 25.)

Archery

Archery (No. 3381). Boy Scouts, 1964, 36 pp., 45¢, paper.

Archery—A Planning Guide and Individual Instruction. A.A.H.P.E.R., 1972, 64 pp., $3.25.

Burke, Edmund: *Archery Handbook.* Arco, rev., 1964, 142 pp., $3.50.

Campbell, Donald W.: *Archery.* Prentice-Hall, 1971, 76 pp.

Forbes, Thomas A.: *New Guide to Better Archery.* Collier, 1967, 352 pp., $1.50.

Gillelan, G. Howard: *Complete Book of the Bow and Arrow.* Stackpole, 1971, 326 pp., $9.95.

Gillelan, G. Howard: *Modern ABC's of Bow and Arrow.* Stackpole, 1969, 192 pp., $4.95.

Klann, Margaret L.: *Target Archery.* Addison-Wesley Publishing Co., Inc., Reading, Mass. 01867, 1970, 162 pp., $3.25.

Kujoth: *The Recreation Program Guide,* pp. 38–43.

Lewis, Jack (Ed.): *Archer's Digest.* Digest Books, 1971, 320 pp., $5.95, paper.

McKinney, Wayne C.: *Archery.* Brown, 1971, 95¢, paper.

Niemeyer, Roy K.: *Beginning Archery.* Wadsworth, rev., 1968, $1.65, paper.

Outdoor Tips, pp. 172–177.

Pszczola, Lorraine: *Archery.* Saunders, 1971, $2.25.

Selected Archery Articles. A.A.H.P.E.R., 1971, $1.50.

Shivers: *Camping,* pp. 302–310.

Sigler, Howard T.: *Pocket Guide to Archery.* Stackpole, 1967, 96 pp., $2.95.

MAGAZINE ARTICLES

Camping Magazine:

Wadsworth, Bill: "Add Action to Your Archery Program." Feb., 1969, p. 14.

Fishing

Bale: *What on Earth,* pp. 57–88.

Bates, Joseph D., Jr.: *Streamer Fly Tying and Fishing.* Stackpole, 1966, 368 pp., $7.95.

Bauer, Erwin A. (Ed.): *Fisherman's Digest.* Digest Books, 8th ed., 1971, 320 pp., $5.95.

Blaisdell, H.: *Tricks That Take Fish.* Holt, Rinehart, 1954, 299 pp., $5.95.

Cardwell: *America's Camping Book,* ch. 26.

Crowe, John: *Modern ABC's of Fresh Water Fishing.* Stackpole, $2.95, paper.

Decker, Maurice H.: *How to "Take" Fresh Water Fish in Lake, Pond and Stream.* Sentinel, 1958, 127 pp., $1.50, paper.

Evanoff, Vlad: *A Complete Guide to Fishing.* Crowell, 1961, 206 pp., $4.50.

Evanoff, Vlad: *1001 Fishing Tips and Tricks.* Harper & Row, 1968, 247 pp., $6.95.

Evanoff, Vlad: *Another 1001 Fishing Tips and Tricks.* Order from N.R.P.A., 206 pp., $5.95.

Fichter George S., and Phil Francis: *Guide to Fresh and Salt Water Fishing.* Golden, 1965, 160 pp., $1.25, paper.

Fieldbook for Boys and Men, pp. 320, 420–435.

Fishing (No. 3295). Boy Scouts, 1954, 104 pp., 45¢, paper.

Goldberg, Howard: *The Angler's Book on Fly-Tying and Fishing.* Scribner's, 1973, 192 pp., $8.95.

Kenealy, James P.: *Better Fishing for Boys.* Dodd, Mead, 1968, 64 pp., $3.50.

Knight, John Alden and Richard Alden: *The Complete Book of Fly Casting.* Putnam, 1964, 129 pp., $6.95.

Langer: *The Joy of Camping,* pp. 278–286.

Learn and Tallman: *Backpacker's Digest,* ch. 13.

McClane, A. J.: *The "Field and Stream" International Fishing Guide.* Scribner's, 1973, 224 pp., $3.95.

McNally, Tom: *Fishermen's Bible*. Follett, 1970, 322 pp., $4.95, paper.
Migdalski, Edward C.: *Angler's Guidc to the Fresh Water Sport Fishes of North America*. Ronald, 1962, 431 pp., $8.
Moore, E.: *Fresh-Water Fishing*. Macmillan, 1965, 95¢, paper.
Ormond: *Outdoorsman's Handbook*, part 2.
Outdoor Tips, pp. 76–112.
Ovington, Ray: *Introduction to Bait Fishing*. Stackpole, 1971, 192 pp., $5.95.
Parsons, P. Allen: *Complete Book of Fresh Water Fishing*. Harper & Row, 1963, 322 pp., $6.95.
Power, John, and Jeremy Brown: *The Fisherman's Handbook*. Scribner's, 1972, 192 pp., $7.95.
Shaw, Helen: *Fly-Tying: Materials, Tools, Technique*. Ronald, 1963, 281 pp., $ 7.
Shivers: *Camping*, pp. 356–361.
Slaymaker, S. R. II: *Simplified Fly Fishing*. Harper & Row, 1969, $4.95.
Tacklebox Library. Harper & Row, 1971, $5.95. (five volumes, slipcased)
Wood: *Pleasure Packing*, ch. 13.

MAGAZINE ARTICLES

Issues of *Boys' Life* contain many articles about fishing.

Camping Magazine:
Metcalf, Harlan G.: "Approaches to Nature Recreation and Interpretation." June, 1968, p. 15.

Games and Other Activities

Berger: *Program Activities for Camps*.
Borst, Evelyne, and Elmer D. Mitchell: *Social Games for Recreation*. Ronald, 2nd ed., 1959, 348 pp., $6.50.
Buskin, David: *Outdoor Games*. Lion Press, 1966, 64 pp., $3.95.
Campcraft Instructors' Manual.
Corbin: *Recreation Leadership*.
Donnelly, Richard H., William G. Helms, and Elmer D. Mitchell: *Active Games and Contests*. Ronald, 2nd ed., 1959, 672 pp., $8.
Eisenberg, Helen and Larry: *The New Pleasure Chest*. Abingdon, 1972, 160 pp., $3.95; $1.95, paper.
Eisenberg: *Omnibus of Fun*.
Fowler, H. Waller, Jr.: *Kites—A Practical Guide to Kite Making and Flying*. Ronald, 1965, 95 pp., $5.
Garrison: *Outdoor Education*, ch. XIII.
Harbin: *The Fun Encyclopedia*.
Harris, Jane A.: *File O'Fun, Card File for Recreation*. Burgess, 2nd ed., 1970, $4.95.
Hartley, Ruth E., and Robert M. Goldenson: *The Complete Book of Children's Play*. Apollo, 2nd ed., 1970, $3.95, paper.
Harty: *Science for Camp and Counselor*.
Hunt, Sarah E.: *Games and Sports the World Around*. Ronald, 3rd ed., 271 pp., $6.
Kohl, Marguerite, and Frederica Young: *Games For Children*. Cornerstone, 1968, 184 pp., $1.50, paper.
Kohl, Marguerite and Frederica Young: *Games For Grownups*. Cornerstone, 1951, 176 pp., $1, paper.
Kraus: *Recreation Leader's Handbook*.
Macfarlan, Allan A.: *Boy's Book of Rainy-Day Doings*. Stackpole, 1969, 160 pp., $4.50.
Mason, Bernard S., and Elmer D. Mitchell: *Party Games*. Barnes and Noble, 1946, 193 pp., $1.75, paper.
Mulac: *Fun and Games*.
Mulac, Margaret E.: *The Game Book*. Harper & Row, 1946, 385 pp., $6.50.
Pelton, Barry C.: *Badminton*. Prentice-Hall, 1971, 82 pp.
Permin, Ib: *Hokus Pokus*. Sterling, 1969, 120 pp., $3.95. (magic tricks)
Reeves, Robert: *Make It Yourself Games Book*. Emerson, 1964, 108 pp., $4.95.
Richart, Genevieve: *The Master Game and Party Book*. Order from N.R.P.A., 253 pp., $4.95.
Smith, Robert G.: *The Boys' Entertainment Book*. Denison, 1957, 367 pp., $4.95.
van der Smissen, Betty, and Helen Knierim: *Fitness and Fun Through Recreational Sports and Games*. Burgess, 1968, 122 pp., $4.
Vinton, Iris: *The Folkways Omnibus of Children's Games*. Stackpole, 1970, 320 pp., $8.95.
Wackerbarth Marjorie, and Lillian S. Graham: *Games For All Ages and How to Use Them*. Denison, 1959, 122 pp., $3.95.

Horses and Riding

Anderson, C. W.: *Complete Book of Horses and Horsemanship*. Macmillan, 1963, 192 pp., $6.95; 95¢, paper.
Ball, Charles E.: *Saddle Up!* Lippincott, 1970, 224 pp., $5.95.
Corbin, Don E.: *Get A Horse*. Order from ACA, 1966, 48 pp., $1.50, paper.
Disston, Harry: *Know About Horses*. Devin-Adair, 1961, 216 pp., $7.50.
Ensminger, M. E.: *Horses and Horsemanship*. Interstate, 1969, 583 pp., $14.35.
Froud, Lt. Col. "Bill": *Better Riding*. Scribner's, 1973, 96 pp., $5.95.
Haley, Neale: *How to Have Fun With a Horse*. Arco, 1973, 119 pp., $8.95.
Johnson, Patrica H.: *Horse Talk*. Funk and Wagnalls, 130 pp., $4.95.
McTaggart, Lt. Col. M. F.: *The Art of Riding*. Arco, 1963, 128 pp., $4.50; $1.95, paper.
Mellin, Jeanne: *Ride a Horse*. Sterling, 1970, 128 pp., $4.95.
Molesworth, Roger: *Knowing Horses*. Arco, 1962, 215 pp., $5.
Nissen, Jasper: *The Young Horseman's Guide*. Barnes, 1965, $4.95.
Price, Steven D.: *Teaching Riding at Summer Camps*. Greene, 1971, $1.95, paper.
Selected Riding Articles. A.A.H.P.E.R., 1969, $1.25.
Shivers: *Camping*, pp. 318–322.

Sports Illustrated Book of Horseback Riding. Lippincott, 1971, $3.95; $1.50, paper.
Wright, Gordon: *Learning to Ride, Hunt and Show.* Doubleday, $5.95.

MAGAZINE ARTICLES

Camping Magazine:
Hirn, Doris D.: "Your Riding Program—Do You Work and Plan to Keep It as Safe as Your Waterfront?" May 1969, p. 31.
Loew, Franklin M.: "Planning and Managing Camp Riding Programs." May, 1964, p. 21.
Shepard, Alexander L., and Alan M. Beck: "The Role of Riding in Camp." Apr., 1966, p. 23.
Shires, Thomas E.: "50 Checks for Safe Riding Program." June, 1961, p. 14.

Indians

(See also the bibliography in the chapter on "Arts and Crafts.")
Baity, Elizabeth Chesley: *Americans Before Columbus.* Viking, 1961, 224 pp., $4.50.
Berger: *Program Activities for Camp.*
Brandon, William: *The American Indian.* Random, 1963, 200 pp., $6.95.
Cody, Iron Eyes: *Indian Talk—Hand Signals of the American Indians.* Naturegraph, 1970, 112 pp., $3.95; $1.95, paper.
Collier, John: *Indians of the Americas.* Norton, 1947, $8.50.
Curtis, Natalie (Recorder and Ed.): *The Indian's Book.* Dover, 1969, 548 pp., $4.50, paper.
Dorian, Edith: *Hokahey! American Indians Then and Now.* McGraw-Hill, 1957, 112 pp., $4.33.
Driver, Harold E.: *Indians of North America.* U. of Chicago, 2nd ed., 1969, 668 pp., $6.85, paper.
Giplin, Laura: *The Enduring Navaho.* U. of Texas, 1968, 264 pp., $17.50.
Grant, Bruce: *American Indians, Yesterday and Today.* Dutton, 1960, $5.95.
Hofsinde, Robert: *The Indian and the Buffalo.* Morrow, 1961, 96 pp., $3.78.
Hofsinde, Robert: *Indian Fishing and Camping.* Morrow, 1963, $3.78.
Hofsinde, Robert: *Indian Hunting.* Morrow, 1962, $3.78.
Hofsinde, Robert: *The Indian and His Horse.* Morrow, 1960, $3.78.
Hofsinde, Robert: *Indian Picture Writing.* Morrow, 1959, 96 pp., $3.78.
Hofsinde; Robert: *The Indian's Secret World.* Morrow, 1955, 94 pp., $4.81.
Hofsinde; Robert: *Indian Sign Language.* Morrow, 1956, $3.78.
Hunt: *The Golden Book of Indian Crafts and Lore.*
Indian Lore (No. 3358). Boy Scouts, 1959, 96 pp., 45¢, paper.
Kujoth: *The Recreation Program Guide,* pp. 165–179.
La Farge, Oliver: *The American Indian.* Golden, 1960, 216 pp., $5.95.
Laubin, Reginald and Gladys: *The Indian Tipi.* U. of Oklahoma, 1971, 208 pp., $6.95.
Macfarlan, Allan A.: *Boy's Book of Indian Skills.* Stackpole, 1968, 160 pp., $4.50.
Mason: *The Book of Indian Crafts and Costumes.*
Mason, Bernard S.: *Dances and Stories of the American Indian.* Ronald, 1944, 269 pp., $7.
Rachlis, Eugene: *Indians of the Plains.* American Heritage, 1960, 152 pp., $5.95.
Raphael, Ralph B.: *The Book of American Indians.* Arco, 1959, 144 pp., $3.50.
Rosenfelt, Willard E.: *The Last Buffalo.* Denison, $4.95.
Squires, John L., and Robert E. McLean: *American Indian Dances—Steps, Rhythms, Costumes and Interpretation.* Ronald, 1963, 132 pp., $5.50.
Stember, Sol: *Heroes of the American Indian.* Fleet, 1971, 124 pp., $5.
Sun Bear: *At Home in the Wilderness.* Naturegraph, 90 pp., $3, paper.
Tomkins, William: *Indian Sign Language.* Dover, 1969, 180 pp., $1.25, paper.
van der Smissen and Goering: *A Leader's Guide to Nature-Oriented Activities,* pp. 193–196.
White, Anne Terry, and William Brandon: *The American Indian.* Random, 1963, 200 pp., $6.95.

MAGAZINE ARTICLES

Camping Magazine:
Congdon, LeRoy: "Indian Tepee Accents Program Activities." Feb., 1963, p. 14.
Red Dawn (Stephen S. Jones, Jr.): "Emphasize Indian Lore in a Program for Girls." June, 1965, p. 15.
Wagener, Lloyd: "Indian Ceremonials Spark Entire Camp Program." Feb., 1965, p. 52.

Miscellaneous

Berger: *Program Activities for Camps.*
Corbin: *Recreation Leadership,* chs. 13–29.
Duran, Dorothy B. and Clement A.: *The New Encyclopedia of Successful Program Ideas.* Ass'n Press, 1967, 511 pp., $9.95.
Eisenberg: *Omnibus of Fun,* ch. 9.
Kujoth: *The Recreation Program Guide,* pp. 353–367.
MacKay: *Creative Counseling For Christian Camps,* ch. 7.
Rodney and Ford: *Camp Administration,* ch. 9.
Shivers: *Camping,* chs. 9, 10, 13, 15, 16.
Smith et al.: *Outdoor Education,* chs. 5, 6.
Thurston, LaRue A.: *Good Times Around the Campfire.* Ass'n Press, 1967, 128 pp., $1.75, paper.
Todd: *Camping for Christian Youth,* chs. 16, 17, 18.
Webb: *Summer Camps—Security in the Midst of Change.*

Magazine Articles

Camping Magazine:

Harrison, Gerard A.: "Camping Needs Revival of the Fundamental Ethic," June, 1970, p. 9.

Silva, Bernard J., and Brent Jackson: "Camping's Third Dimension." Jan., 1969, p. 12.

Photography

Cardwell: *America's Camping Book,* ch. 24.

Feininger, Andreas: *The Complete Photographer.* Prentice-Hall, 1965, 400 pp., $9.95.

Ferguson, Robert: *How to Make Movies.* Viking, 1972, 88 pp., $3.25, paper.

Gillelan, G. Howard: *The Young Sportsman's Guide to Photography.* Nelson, 1964, 96 pp., $2.75.

Hattersley, Ralph: *Discover Your Self Through Photography: A Creative Workbook for Amateur and Professional.* Ass'n Press, 1970, $14.95.

How to Make Good Pictures. By the editors of Eastman Kodak Co., Amphoto, New York, New York 10010, 1972, 192 pp., $1.50, paper.

Johnson, James R.: *Photography for Young People.* McKay, $5.50.

Kinsey, Anthony: *How to Make Animated Movies.* Viking, 1970, 95 pp., $7.95.

Kujoth: *The Recreation Program Guide,* pp. 75–83 and 299–302.

Langer: *The Joy of Camping,* pp. 292–299.

Learn and Tallman: *Backpacker's Digest,* ch. 12.

Maye, Patricia (Ed.): *Fieldbook of Nature Photography.* Scribner's, 1973, 256 pp., $6.95, paper.

Ormond: *Outdoorsman's Handbook,* Part 6.

Parsons, Christopher: *Making Wildlife Movies (A Beginner's Guide).* Stackpole, 1971, 223 pp., $7.95.

Photography (No. 3334). Boy Scouts, 1960, 96 pp., 45¢, paper.

Photography. Golden, $1.50, paper.

Webb: *Light From A Thousand Campfires:* Haskell, Douglas: "The Camper With a Camera," p. 290.

Zarchy, Harry: *Photography.* Order from Galloway, 48 pp., $1.98.

Magazine Articles

Backpacker:

Mensinger, Bruce: "You and Your Gear—Camera Care." *Backpacker-5,* Spring, 1974, p. 18.

Porter, Eliot: "Reflections In Nature." *Backpacker-2,* Summer, 1973, p. 52.

Smiley, Ruth: "Seashore Photography." *Backpacker-1,* Spring, 1973, p. 32.

Boys' Life:

Pryce, Dick: "Stalking With a Camera." Nov., 1970, p. 66.

Wagner, Glenn: "Take Better Camp Pictures." July, 1973, p. 32.

Wagner, Glenn: "Explore the Universe with Sky Photography." May, 1970, p. 56.

Camping Journal:

Grant, Ken: "Cameras." Sept., 1972, p. 30.

Grant, Ken: "Care for the Camping Camera." Oct., 1972, p. 29.

Grant, Ken: "Your Guide to Better Outdoor Pictures." Sept., 1970, p. 31.

Haddon, E. P.: "Tips on Taking Trophy Photos." Sept., 1971, p. 24.

Ormond, Clyde: "On the Trail." Sept., 1970, p. 10. (Best type of cameras for outdoor trips)

Park, Ed: "Improve Your Scenic Photos." Sept., 1973, p. 19.

Camping Magazine:

"Campers Get Better Pictures When Basic Rules are Set." June, 1965, p. 17.

Czura, Pete: "Camper's Camera Afield." Apr., 1967, p. 42.

Riflery and Target Shooting

Chapel, Charles E.: *The Boy's Book of Rifles.* Coward-McCann, 274 pp., $6.95.

Kujoth: *The Recreation Program Guide,* pp. 321–326.

O'Conner, Jack: *The Rifle Book.* Knopf, 4th ed., 1964, 332 pp., $10.

O'Conner, Jack, et al. *Complete Book of Shooting.* Popular Science, 1965, $5.95.

Rifle and Shotgun Shooting (No. 3311). Boy Scouts, 1967, 96 pp., 45¢, paper.

Shivers: *Camping,* pp. 310–314.

Stebbins, Henry: *Teaching Kids to Shoot.* Stackpole, 1966, 96 pp., $2.95.

Magazine Articles

Camping Magazine:

"How to Construct a Camp Rifle Range." Sept./Oct., 1963, p. 20.

"Riflery Programs." June, 1966, p. 20.

Stolz, Alan J.: "Camp Rifle Program Offers Skills, Safety and Fun." May, 1965, p. 24.

Tennis

Hopman, Harry: *Better Tennis for Boys and Girls.* Dodd, Mead, 1972, 95 pp., $4.50.

Ideas for Tennis Instruction. A.A.H.P.E.R., 50 pp., $1.

Jaeger, Eloise, and Harry "Cap" Leighton: *Teaching of Tennis for School and Recreational Programs.* Burgess, 2nd ed., 1963, 142 pp., $3.95, spiral.

King, Billie Jean, and Kimi Chapin: *Tennis to Win.* Harper & Row, 1970, 157 pp., $5.95.

Mason, R. Elaine: *Tennis.* Allyn and Bacon, 1973, 96 pp., paper.

Metzler, Paul: *Advanced Tennis.* Collier, rev., 1972, 192 pp., $1.50, paper.

Murphy, Bill, and Chet Murphy: *Tennis for Beginners.* Ronald, 1958, 116 pp., $5.50.

Scharff, Robert: *Quick and Easy Guide to Tennis.* Collier, 1972, 94 pp., $1.95.

Tennis Group Instruction. A.A.H.P.E.R., rev., 1972, 64 pp., $2.50.

Chapter 12

Spiritual Life, Flag Ceremonies and Special Programs

Figure 12-1 "The Heavens Declare the Glory of God. . . ."

LISTEN, CAMPERS. . . .

Listen to God as He speaks to you:
Through the wind in swaying trees and waving grasses.
Through the silence of the deep forest.
Through the ripple of small waves on a lake shore and thundering breakers on a boulder strewn beach.
Through a sunset when "morning stands tip-toe on the frosty mountain top."
Through the soft radiance of a full moon that quiets the spirit and soothes the heart.
Through a diamond studded sky—the borderland of an unfathomable immensity of space.
Through the "music of the spheres" as they move unerringly in their orbits.
Through the wood thrush's twilight love call, rivaling the notes of the finest flutist.
Through beauty without blemish which abounds in a perfect harmony of colors in birds, flowers, insects, crystal and gems.
Through the laughter of innocent children, the sweetest of all music.
Through the self-sacrificing love of wild creatures for their young.
Is not such love more than instinct? They are God's creatures, too.

God speaks to you not only through nature. You may hear His voice:
As you look meditatively into the campfire "when the ashes start to whiten 'neath the embers' crimson glow."
When your soul is stirred by a worship service that gives life a new dimension for you.
When you are moved to do someone you dislike a kindness—when you are suddenly inclined to return good for evil.
When, during one of those high moments of inspiration, you gain a new awareness of God and His will for you.

Yes, campers, God speaks to you. Listen!

—C. Walton Johnson
(Used by permission from Mr. Johnson.)

SPIRITUAL LIFE

"Although camps have different practices in regard to the spiritual life of campers, they almost without exception feel deeply their obligation along this line and have as an important aim the furthering of spiritual growth through an appreciation of the higher values of life."* Most camps have daily

**Camp Leadership Courses for Colleges and Universities*, ACA, p. 9, IIB.

Figure 12–2 Music Speaks to All.

or weekly all-camp periods of devotion, supplemented by various cabin or unit endeavors to highlight a deeper sense of spiritual values as expressed in all phases of daily living.

Such supplementary experiences ordinarily consist of some combination of the following: (1) grace before meals (oral, spoken in unison, sung, silence during an appropriate musical selection, or a period of silent prayer); (2) outdoor vespers or inspirational programs of some sort; (3) sunrise services or morning watch; (4) cabin devotions or meditations just before taps; (5) attendance at religious services in a neighboring church of the individual's choice or at services conducted by visiting clergymen or camp personnel on the campsite in an indoor or outdoor chapel; (6) group discussions on religion, morals, and ethics; (7) singing of hymns and other appropriate songs.

INTERDENOMINATIONAL CAMPS

Interdenominational camps often make it a point to include both counselors and campers of different faiths in the camp community. This provides an opportunity for living together in broad-minded acceptance of those of different faiths, as well as of those who profess no particular faith; in other words, with respect for the right of each person to worship as he pleases. If you accept a position in such a camp, be sure you can wholeheartedly support this attitude without trying to indoctrinate or unduly influence anyone else. Rather, your efforts should be directed toward helping each individual to become the best possible member of his own particular faith. Care should be taken not to force any child, either through rules or group pressure, to attend any particular religious services.

In various ways, many camps now actively try to foster this spirit of understanding and brotherhood. Camp directors sometimes invite local priests, rabbis and ministers to take part in joint discussions of their faiths, with counselors' and campers' comments and questions encouraged. Many worthwhile pamphlets and other materials of aid in furthering such interaction within the camp family are available at nominal cost from the National Conference of Christians and Jews, Inc., 43 West 57th Street, New York, New York 10019.

Encourage each of your campers to observe such practices as he is accustomed to, such as a moment of silent grace before meals or an individual prayer before retiring.

Your personal conduct toward your fellow man and your consistent observance of kindliness, tolerance, fairness to and respect for every individual in camp will best express your own spiritual convictions and their influence on your relationships with others.

What is Christianity? In the home, it is kindness; in business, it is honesty; in society, it is courtesy; in work, it is thoroughness; in play, it is fairness; toward the fortunate, it is congratulations; toward the unfortunate, it is pity; toward the weak, it is help; toward the wicked, it is resistance; toward the strong, it is trust; toward the penitent, it is forgiveness; and toward God, it is reverence and love.

—DOUGLAS HYDE

In a large camp, it is customary to arrange separate services for the three major religious groups, Catholic, Jewish, and Protestant.

Catholic. Each Catholic child is expected to attend Mass on Sundays and Holy Days. (The only Holy Day falling within the usual camp season of June to September is the Feast of the Assumption of the Blessed Virgin Mary on August 15.) A priest should be summoned in case of serious accident to a Catholic camper.

Camps usually take their Catholic campers and staff to the nearest Catholic church for Mass, but arrangements are sometimes made to celebrate it at the camp if a priest is available and the bishop of the diocese approves. Arrangements should be made for Catholics to go to confession and receive Holy Communion at least once a month. Catholics may attend non-Catholic services with the approval of the local Catholic Diocese.

Jewish. Those of the Jewish faith observe Saturday, the seventh day of the week, as Sabbath, the day of rest. The Jewish Sabbath begins twenty minutes before sunset on Friday evening and ends about thirty minutes after sunset on Saturday. Sabbath candles should be lit at or before the beginning of the Sabbath, and the service usually follows immediately. Campers and staff may attend a nearby synagogue, or the services may be conducted by a counselor or other lay leader who understands the spirit and mode of Jewish worship.

Campers of the Jewish faith who come from homes that follow traditional observances will want to adhere to the Jewish dietary laws. No pork in any form should be served; if meat or fowl is on the camp menu, there should be an alternate menu of vegetables, salads, eggs or fish (not shellfish) for those who wish it.

The Jewish Holy Day *Tishoh B'ab* usually falls during the camp season; the date varies each year. Those from homes where there is strict traditional observance will wish to observe it as a fast day and will refrain from swimming and festive activities.

Protestant. There are three ways of providing Sunday worship services for Protestant campers: (1) taking them to a nearby Protestant church which meets with the approval of their parents; (2) inviting local ministers of various denominations to conduct services at camp; or (3) having a worship service conducted by a lay person or by staff and campers.

Few Protestant denominations observe dietary restrictions, although some abstain from eating meat on Fridays. There are no Protestant Holy Days during the camp season.

Informal Worship. Spiritual experiences, of course, are not always confined to formally arranged times or places. Instead, we might think of them as times of the day when our thoughts and very souls rise to unusual heights as we contemplate the way in which some power beyond human comprehension has arranged this wonderful

Figure 12–3 Some Power Up Yonder.

(Courtesy of Cheley Colorado Camps, Estes Park, Colorado.)

universe. Sometimes it may be simply a deep and abiding appreciation of the real goodness and kindliness of our fellow men as we see a companion do a truly noble and unselfish deed or a perfect stranger extend a helping hand to someone younger, weaker, or "down on his luck." Occasions for sharing with others our deeper and more serious thoughts sometimes come unexpectedly, while sharing a brief time off with a fellow counselor, looking out over the countryside from a vantage spot high on a hill, or when a small camper slips his hand trustingly into yours and confides some inner thought or small trouble (but big to him). Other experiences may come in quiet periods of meditation while you enjoy the beauties of a sky full of stars or the call of a lone whippoorwill in the distance. How true that "The Heavens declare the Glory of God; and the firmament showeth His handiwork."

CAMP SERVICES

Most camps hold at least one inspirational service during the week, which may or may not substitute for the regular weekly worship service. This time provides a respite from the regular busyness of camp life and provides an opportunity to ponder on the deeper meanings of life and the things that are all too often simply taken for granted. The most appropriate place for these services seems to be in God's great out-of-doors where His miracles abound unmarred by the tinkerings of man. Some special "Retreat," "Wilderness Cathedral," or "Woodland Chapel" is usually set aside for these occasions, since it seems quite a lot to expect campers to adopt a mood of awe and reverence in a spot where they frolicked hilariously about a campfire just the night before. Enlist their help in selecting some site on a hilltop with

(Courtesy of Camp Mishawaka, Grand Rapids, Minnesota.)

a commanding view of the valley below, a natural amphitheater beside a gently flowing stream, or a sequestered nook surrounded by the majestic trees of the forest. Campers can add seating and other refinements as they wish.

Programs planned jointly by campers and staff are usually most meaningful. Build the service around some central theme of general interest, such as friendship, going the extra mile, what harmonious camp living means, tolerance, patriotism and love of country, beauty, the wonders of nature, the high ideals and motives of the organization sponsoring the camp, humility, walking in the other fellow's shoes, personalities who achieved greatly in spite of difficulties, or the application of the Golden Rule to camp life. There are so many references to nature and matters of conduct in the Bible that you should have little difficulty in selecting passages appropriate to your chosen theme.

Attune the language and nature of the service to those attending it. Adopt an informal spirit of sincerity, dignity, and reverence but avoid sanctimoniousness or undue piousness. Unless there is an outside speaker, let some staff member or camper give a short talk, bringing out the main thought of the service; a short story or anecdote usually promotes interest and understanding.

Set the stage for the proper mood as the audience enters the area. Appropriate recorded music helps, and having campers meet at a distance and file silently down to their seats is also effective; there should be no chatting as they approach and enter the area.

Encourage all participants to use their creative abilities to furnish poetry, prose, songs, and art for the occasion. Music should play an important part, with individuals and groups furnishing vocal and instrumental numbers. Antiphonal singing, dramatization of Bible stories, special prayers and choral readings also furnish variation. There are many hymns that deal with God's handiwork in nature and other topics fitting to camp and the outdoor setting.

To avoid the midday heat in summer, you may prefer to hold the service in the early morning or evening. A blazing campfire will provide light for a night meditation, which also lends itself nicely to an impressive candle-lighting service. Counselors and older campers can be stationed along the path with flashlights, lanterns, or lighted candles to show the way.

Plan the service to last only 30 to 45 minutes, for youngsters tend to get restless and let their attention wander if they have to sit still much longer than that.

Here is a suggested order of service:

Procession—audience
Choir enters singing, approaching through the woods from a nearby meeting place
Scripture reading or opening remarks
Prayer
Hymn
Poem, choral reading, or special number
Musical selection by choir, soloist, or special group
Thought for the day (sermonette)
Hymn
Prayer or closing remarks
Recessional—program participants, choir, then the audience

SUNDAY IN CAMP

Sunday is the golden clasp that binds together the volume of the week.

—LONGFELLOW

For those who observe Sunday as their special day of worship, the regular daily program is dispensed with and campers are given much free time to engage in quiet, restful activities, although tennis courts, boats, waterfront and other facilities are available to those who want to use them. Breakfast is ordinarily served a little later than usual and some extra touch may be added, such as eating in a special place,

Figure 12–4 Visitors' Day.

eating in pajamas, or being served cafeteria style. It is a day for dressing in best camp clothes and for spending time together as a cabin group, listening to music, singing, holding discussions, telling stories, or writing letters. It is often designated as Visitors' Day, with the camp playing host to parents and friends. A cold supper or cookout for small groups is customary to give the kitchen staff extra time off; this also provides an opportunity for small groups to take their meals to a secluded spot of beauty.

Sunday can and should be the most cherished day in the week. In planning for it, we must remember to look at it through the eyes of youth, for, if we fill it with taboos, stuffy pursuits, unnatural quiet and lengthy talks, we will build up rebelliousness, distaste, and even anti-religious attitudes. Campers should know it as a change-of-pace day to renew strength of mind and spirit for the coming week.

God of the open air, we kneel reverently in this temple not made with hands. The tall pines lift our thoughts above us to the Source of all this beauty. The singing of the feather-throated choir puts a melody in our hearts, a song of joy and praise and trust. All the discordant notes of the world are muted; all the problems of life are forgotten. We are filled with an inner peace and know that here we have found Thee. As we leave this hallowed spot, may the reality of Thy presence go with us to give us courage and strength for our daily tasks. Amen.

—DOROTHY WELLS PEASE.
From *Meditations Under the Sky*.
Abingdon, 1957.
Permission by Abingdon Press.

O God, Thou hast given so much to us, give one thing more—a grateful heart. Amen.

—GEORGE HERBERT

To be closer to God, be closer to people.

—KAHLIL GIBRAN.
Permission by the Citadel Press.

When praying, do not give God instructions—report for duty.

—AUTHOR UNKNOWN

Real religion is a way of life, not a white cloak to be worn only on Sundays and then tossed aside into the weekday closet of unconcern.

—WILLIAM A. WARD.
Permission by the Methodist
Publishing House.

God give me a task too big,
Too hard for human hands.
Then I shall come at length
To lean on Thee;
And leaning, find my strength.

—WILBUR HUMPHREY FOWLER,
Guideposts, March, 1966.
Permission by Guideposts.

God of the sea, the winds, the tides, we praise thee for the greatness of thy power and the certainty of thy laws. We see careless picnickers throw their litter to be carried far out into the sea by the outgoing tide, but the next morning it lies stranded on the beach where the high tide has left it.

So it is, our Father, in our lives. We throw out a careless word, an unkind thought, and it comes back to us in resentments and friendlessness. A selfish act, a yielding to temptation, or a deed left undone comes back as a haunting memory, another's failure, or a missed opportunity.

Help us, our Father, to cast only good upon the waters that good may come back with the tide. Amen.

—DOROTHY WELLS PEASE.
From *Meditations Under the Sky*.
Abingdon, 1957.
Permission by Abingdon Press.

WE THANK THEE
For flowers that bloom about our feet;
For tender grass so fresh and sweet;
For song of bird and hum of bee;
For all things fair we hear and see,
Father in Heaven, we thank Thee!

—RALPH WALDO EMERSON

SPECIAL EVENTS

THE CAMP BANQUET

Camp banquets are festive dress-up occasions, with special menus and a candlelighting service: the director lights the candles of the staff and unit heads, who in turn pass the light on to the campers. A unit or committee plans a program of songs, poems, short talks, skits, or other activities around a central theme. There may also be inspirational talks, the presentation of awards and certificates, and the reading of selected poems, plays, and stories written by campers.

DEDICATION CEREMONY

A dedication ceremony may be arranged to recognize some new camp acquisition, especially a project campers have completed, such as a newly laid trail, a site for an outdoor chapel selected and furnished by them, or a new outpost camp. Plan a serious and impressive but brief program with appropriate songs and a special speech of dedication, with sincere praise for those who donated their time and efforts to create something of benefit both to present and future campers.

FOURTH OF JULY (INDEPENDENCE DAY)

Hold a special flag ceremony and stress the day's history and traditions, as well as our reasons for celebrating it. Serve special food, with table decorations in a patriotic motif of red, white, and blue.

BIRTHDAY PARTY

Campers appreciate having some notice taken of their birthdays. A monthly party for those having birthdays within the month with a special "unbirthday party" for the rest handles the situation nicely. Seat the celebrants together and serve them a special lighted birthday cake, with cake and ice cream for everyone. Use favors, sing a birthday song, and hold a brief program. Some camps also set aside a special day to celebrate the camp's birthday.

CLOSING CAMPFIRE

The last campfire should be a memorable event, starting with a processional to the fire, which may be lighted by one of the special methods discussed later on in the chapter. Plan to start off in a light mood, gradually progressing to one more serious and impressive. End on a note of beauty and sentiment, but avoid the type of "tear-jerker" that causes weeping and wailing and badly upset emotions. If the philosophy of your camp sanctions awarding honors, badges, and certificates, this is a good time to present them.

MacKay* suggests putting the blue of the lake, the green of the forest, the violet of the distant mountain, and the red of the sunset into the fire to save for next summer. Symbolize them by casting in, one at a time, a paper cupful of each of the appropriate chemicals to produce these colors. (This is discussed in detail later on in this chapter.) Camps sometimes make a ceremony of

---

*MacKay: Creative Counseling for Christian Camps, p. 84.

saving some of the partially burned wood and ashes from this last campfire to use when lighting the first campfire of the next season.

If your program is held near water, a nice closing event consists of having each unit bring a "boat" fashioned from a piece of cardboard or other material which will disintegrate quickly; it can be tastefully decorated with pretty leaves and flowers. After a brief ceremony, each unit affixes a small lighted candle to their boat, and as it is set afloat, each camper makes a wish and watches it disappear into the distance. All then form a *friendship circle* (each crosses his hands to clasp the hand of the person one either side of him) and sing *Taps* or a goodnight song or repeat a prayer or quotation in unison, perhaps ending with your own special camp or unit hand squeeze. They then file silently away to their cabins, just in time to get ready for bed. At some time early in the season, you may well spend a little time with your campers in thinking about the meaning of the words to *Taps* and why they serve so effectively as a closing prayer just before going off to sleep.

FLAG CEREMONIES

A flag raising ceremony usually starts off the camp day, taking place

Figure 12-5 "Please Let Me Come Back Next Year!"

even before breakfast; in many camps, there is also a flag lowering exercise. Such occasions offer a chance for campers to learn proper demeanor around the flag, as well as how to handle and care for it. They also provide an opportunity both to learn about the history of the flag and its importance as a symbol of our way of life and the principles under which our nation functions and to develop patriotism and a sense of gratitude for the privilege of living in our wonderful country, for, as President John F. Kennedy so aptly said, our attitude should be "Ask not what your country can do for you. Ask rather what you can do for your country."

CONCERNING THE FLAG

Our flag has a field of blue, studded with 50 stars, which represent the 50 states of the Union. There are also 7 red and 6 white stripes, arranged with red stripes at both the top and bottom; these represent the 13 original colonies. The blue of the flag stands for Justice, the red for Courage, and the white for Purity. The blue starred section is called the *Union* or *canton;* the stick to which the flag is attached is called the *staff* and the cord which attaches it is the *halyard.*

The complete rules and customs for the care and display of the flag are contained in a Flag Code, which is readily available from many sources. We will touch on only a few of the main points here.

1. The flag may be flown on any day when the weather is satisfactory, especially on holidays and historic occasions. It should never be left out in rain, sleet, or snow.

2. The flag may be raised at any time after sunrise and should be taken down before sunset.

3. It should be handled and displayed with the greatest respect at all times and should never be placed where it will be soiled or allowed to touch anything below it, such as the ground or water.

4. The flag should always be displayed aloft and free and should be maintained in good condition, mended when torn and cleaned when dirty.

5. Flying the flag at half-mast signifies a period of mourning. First raise it to the peak, then lower it to a position halfway down the pole. Later, when lowering it, again raise it to the top, then bring it down.

6. When the flag is approaching, a boy stands bareheaded and at attention, with his eyes on the flag. He gives a military salute if in uniform; if not, he places the palm of his right hand, holding his hat or cap if he has one, over his heart until it has passed by. A girl stands at attention with her right palm over her heart. Although it seldom creates a problem in the average camp, you must bear in mind that recent court decisions have forbidden forcing anyone to salute the flag.

Figure 12-6 Honoring the Flag.

CAMP FLAG CEREMONIES

Some camps use only the briefest of ceremonies for flag raising and lowering, while others sponsor more or less elaborate services in an attempt to educate as well as inspire. At least two persons are needed to handle and raise a flag properly, but most camps use a Color Guard of at least five, one of whom acts as Color Bearer to carry the flag. These positions of honor are usually rotated among campers on a day-to-day or week-to-week basis. The Color Guard dresses in a distinguishing uniform, such as wearing red or blue sashes around their waists. A group should practice until they can perform their duties with snap and precision. In a flag raising ceremony, the flag is raised at the beginning of the program; in lowering, it remains aloft until everything else has taken place.

Suggested program for flag raising and lowering ceremonies:

1. Color Guard enters the area, followed by those participating in the program, and finally by the campers, who form a horseshoe about the flagpole. Campers and Guard maintain complete silence during the program.

2. Color Guard unfolds the flag and the Color Bearer attaches it to the halyard and raises it *briskly* to the top of the pole as all others stand at attention, saluting it and keeping their eyes on it.

3. Maintaining the salute, all repeat the Pledge of Allegiance:

I pledge allegiance to the Flag of the United States of America and to the Republic for which it stands, one Nation under God, indivisible, with liberty and justice for all.

4. If desired, have a short talk, read a poem or sing a patriotic song.

5. Everyone salutes during the flag lowering ceremony. The Color Guard advances to the flag and the Color Bearer lowers it *slowly* and *ceremoniously* into the hands of the rest of the

(Courtesy of Camp Summer Life, Taos, New Mexico.)

Color Guard, who fold it lengthwise, first into halves, then into fourths. The two Guards at the end away from the stars then begin to fold it into triangles, starting with a triangular fold across the end and continuing with triangular folds back and forth until it is completely folded into one triangle with stars on both sides. They then hand it to the Color Bearer to carry.

6. Color Guard leaves the area, followed by the other participants in the program, and finally the campers, who drop their salute and fall into line.

EVENING OUTDOOR PROGRAMS

Although, in the interest of ecology, many camps have ruled out the traditional campfire of wood, most of them still hold at least one outdoor program for the entire group each week, with additional ones for the smaller groups in between, using some type of simulated campfire. When well-planned, such programs are quite impressive and tend to be remembered by campers long after camp days are over, influencing their attitudes and characters more than almost any other event of the summer. These programs are usually held in an area reserved especially for this purpose. There is a certain magic about sitting closely with friends in a muted light which shuts out the surrounding fringe of darkness and night sounds and makes even the most timid feel, "I belong." Most camps have developed certain traditions and customary ways of doing things which returning campers have come to love and eagerly look forward to each new season; traditional campfire programs fall into this category. Although certain phases are repeated year after year, each year some different touches should be added, for youngsters tend to become bored when they know exactly what will happen next. Like any program, superior evening outdoor programs don't just happen. They come from careful planning, down to the last detail.

SITE FOR THE PROGRAM

The site for the program should be secluded and free from outside distractions, but not too far from the main camp in case of a sudden downpour or if props have to be carried. This also prevents campers from having to travel long distances over rough trails at night. However, try to avoid a seating arrangement which brings camp buildings into view, for this makes it hard to produce the mood of getting away from everyday surroundings. A position on high ground with adequate mosquito control helps campers to concentrate. If a wood fire is used, there should be some sort of windbreak to help control it and to create a vacuum to draw the smoke away from participants.

The site itself should be from 24 to 50 feet in diameter, depending on the number to be accommodated. Keep it as compact as possible, with seats arranged in tiers if necessary and with taller people in the back so that all can see and hear well. A good arrangement calls for seating in horseshoe form with the entrance and exit at the open end, the source of light inside, and the stage toward the rounded end where the audience sits (Fig. 12–7). The Program Director or Master of Ceremonies occupies a seat of honor near the closed end of the area. Campers may simply sit on the ground on ponchos, blankets, situpons, planks laid across short lengths of logs, or wooden benches.

Clear the whole surface of protruding roots, stones, and rubble, and keep it free from all litter to minimize the danger of tripping, which is especially hazardous around an actual wood fire.

There are several successful alter-

Figure 12–7 Program is *By* the Campers, *For* the Campers.

native methods of providing light if your conscience or the law prohibits building a traditional campfire of wood. One method consists of the familiar device of using crepe paper in shades of orange, yellow, or red to camouflage such sources of light as camp lanterns, flashlights, or electric light bulbs. Plumber's or church candles placed upon flat stones produce a surprisingly cozy and pleasant atmosphere, although you may need to place some sort of fireproof windscreen about them if there is enough breeze to blow them out. Even the direct light from flashlights, electric lights, or camp lanterns may be used, although it is usually more effective to at least partially conceal them.

WOOD CAMPFIRES

> Kneel always when you light a fire!
> Kneel reverently,
> And grateful be
> To God for His unfailing charity.
>
> —JOHN OXENHAM

If you decide to build a wood campfire, prepare a safe fire site as usual and place fire tools and a pail of water or sand nearby, but where they won't be tripped over and spilled. There should also be a blanket or other heavy material at hand in case someone's clothing should catch fire.

If for some reason you can't build the fire on the ground at your program site, insulate a wheelbarrow or big metal drum by placing an inch or two of sand or gravel in it and build the fire on top. You can also build it out on a raft, covering it with dirt and anchoring it close to shore or placing it out in the water with the participants coming out to it in canoes.

Since a large part of the effectiveness of your program depends on the success of your fire, pay strict attention to every detail in constructing it so that it will go off at the touch of a match and burn briskly with a minimum of smoke. Lay it well ahead of time and arrange it to feed itself without undue attention and refueling, but keep a reserve supply of wood handy in case of need. Keep the fire small to conserve fuel, to make it less hazardous, and to keep from roasting everyone with excess heat.

Campers usually regard it as an honor to be selected for the fire committee, which is headed by a Chief Fire Keeper under counselor supervision. They select the wood, tend the fire, put it out after the program, and clean up the debris around the site.

A log cabin fire, as discussed in Chapter 27, is usually best since it is long-lasting and less dangerous than many other types of fires. Build it as usual, using medium-sized sticks and filling the spaces in between with plenty of kindling and small-sized split wood. At the fifth or sixth layer of large sticks, lay a platform of small sticks across them and build a small teepee fire on it; continue with a few additional layers of large sticks. When you light the teepee fire, it immediately bursts into flame to ignite the surrounding structure, which soon burns down to embers, setting fire to the loose structure below. For an especially spectacular effect, soak the materials with a little kerosene well ahead of time. NEVER, NEVER apply kerosene to a fire which has already been lighted.

Figure 12–8 Cheerful, If the Wood Supply Permits.

Lighting the Fire

The actual lighting of the fire usually occurs after the campers have assembled and there has been some special opening ceremony. Someone may simply step up with a torch to light the fire, or it may be done by a costumed runner, a person on horseback, a delegation coming across the lake in a canoe, or four persons with lighted candles approaching from the four quadrants of the compass.

"Magic methods," which seemingly create fire without the aid of human hands, provide even more spectacular ways to light the fire. When choosing one of them, use only responsible people and test the method several times to make sure it works satisfactorily and isn't unduly hazardous. Even then, it is always best to provide an alternate method, since the whole program will get off to a bad start if the fire lighting is delayed.

Fire From Heaven. Using this method, someone releases a "ball of fire," which slides down a wire suspended from a tree to the bottom of a kerosene-soaked fire lay and sets it instantly ablaze. Make the "ball" by soaking a bag of sawdust, loosely wrapped gauze, or part of an old burlap bag wrapped around a stone in kerosene. Make the wire taut and keep the "ball" on course by fastening it to an old spool or loop of wire threaded on the wire. The person stationed in the tree holds onto the "ball" by an attached handle of wire until ready to release it. Alter the weight of the "ball" and the angle of the wire until the descent takes place with just the right amount of speed and without endangering anything or anybody.

Spontaneous Combustion. Fasten a piece of black fishline or wire to the bottom of a buddy burner or can with its top and one side cut out and a plumber's candle fastened in the bottom. Place the burner or can opposite a hole in the fire lay big enough to admit it and on the side away from the campers. Extend the wire through under the kerosene-treated fire so that you can inconspicuously draw the can or burner into it when ready.

Color in Your Campfire

Although you can use the chemically treated chips and logs produced commercially to give color in an indoor fireplace, it is usually somewhat cheaper and more challenging to make your own, using chemicals you can purchase at your drug store. Only adults should attempt this and they should work carefully and protect their hands with rubber gloves. Do not mix the chemicals together. Use them only in a crockery or wooden container, since most of them are corrosive to metal. The usual proportion calls for a half pound of chemical to a half gallon of water.

You may use pine cones, bits of wood, sawdust in a bag, or slick magazine pages, rolled tightly into one-inch "logs" and tied at both ends. Place them in a mesh or coarsely knit bag and submerge them in the solution, weighing them down with stones to keep them in place. Leave them at least a day or two to insure thorough saturation, then lift them out and suspend them over the container to drip briefly before placing them on thick newspapers and leaving them for three or four days to dry out thoroughly. Here are some colors and the chemicals which will produce them:

blue	copper sulfate
yellow	common salt
red	strontium
purple	lithium chloride
vivid green	borax
apple green	barium nitrate
orange	calcium chloride
lavender	potassium chloride
emerald green	copper nitrate

ENTERING THE CAMPFIRE AREA

A flashlight parade down a winding trail provides an impressive entrance to the campfire area. Each unit may assemble separately, uniting at the trail entrance on a signal that all is ready. They may sing an appropriate song or approach silently to the rhythm of a tom-tom and file into their assigned seats in the area.

Unit counselors should then collect flashlights or each camper should place his at rest beside him to avoid the distraction of having them flashed off and on during the program.

THE PROGRAM

The Council Chief, who functions as Master of Ceremonies, wearing a special costume and operating from his seat of honor, is responsible for the tenor of the whole affair. Since he may well make or break the whole undertaking, he must be thoroughly acquainted with everything that is to take place and must keep things moving, coordinating the program to run like a well-oiled piece of machinery. He needs showmanship, tact, a well-developed sense of humor and a ready wit, together with an ability to adapt or cover up when things do not go just as anticipated. He or some other responsible person should have previously reviewed all proposed numbers and activities to screen out any which are ineffective, cheap, crude, in poor taste, or likely to embarrass or hurt someone.

The Council Chief uses hand signals to quiet and control the audience and insists that everyone display good manners and courtesy at all times, especially toward the performers. He holds up his hand to signal for attention and doesn't start talking until he has it. Campers may indicate approval by politely clapping their hands or uttering the Indian word "How." Two or even three "Hows" indicate enthusiasm for a number; silence indicates indifference to it. Catcalls, Bronx cheers, and other raucous acts are taboo.

In the long run, a leader gains much more respect and genuine affection when he insists on courtesy and decorum and refuses to accept bad behavior. Campers secretly feel much better inside when they behave in an acceptable manner.

As always, let the campers accept a major role in planning and carrying out the program, for it should indeed be entertainment *by* them, not *for* them. Plan it to last not longer than an hour or an hour and a half and stop on time, even if you have to cut out something, for attention spans are short and bedtime and adequate sleep are necessary. A good Master of Ceremonies can perform wonders in speeding things up or slowing them down to finish in the allotted time.

Make variety the keynote and provide for active audience participation to relieve the tedium and cramped muscles resulting from an excess of sitting still.

After lighting the fire, follow with lively, fun things and gradually taper off into more serious and quieter activities. End on a restful, quiet note, such as singing lullabies and other peaceful songs, reading poetry, or having discussions and storytelling. This calms campers and puts them in a mood for sleep, greatly simplifying counselors' problems in getting them quietly into bed.

Choose your main events from such activities as the following:

Singing
Games, contests
Challenges by individuals or group representatives
Short plays
Shadow plays
Quizzes, short riddles
Amateur or talent nights
Pantomimes
Tall stories—see who can tell the biggest whopper
Stunts, skits
Indian dances and activities
Short talks—humorous or serious
Announcements
Reading of the camp paper by the editor
Honors and awards
Musical numbers
Storytelling
Special theme such as Indians, pioneers, and so on

Always anticipate that old bugaboo, rain, and plan how to adjust to it when it comes. You can often transfer much of the program indoors, turn off the lights, and build a fire in the fireplace or construct a mock campfire with logs, colored light bulbs, and red or orange crepe paper.

ADDITIONAL READINGS

(For an explanation of abbreviations and abbreviated forms, see page 25.)

Barnes, Johnnie: *The Royal Rangers Leader's Manual.* Gospel Publishing House, Springfield, Mo. 65802, 1962, 122 pp., $1.95, pp. 91–122.

Bays, Alice A.: *Worship Services For Life Planning.* Abingdon, 1953, 256 pp., $2.50.
Berger: *Program Activities for Camp,* ch. 9.
Bogardus, LaDonna: *Outdoor Living.* (See *Additional Readings* for Chapter 1.)
Camping Is Education, pp. 17–21.
Convention Highlights:
Johnson, C. Walton: "Techniques of Integrating Spiritual Growth of Campers." p. 91.
Edgar, Mary S.: *Under Open Skies.* Clarke, Irvin, 1955, $2.50.
Ensign: *Camping Together As Christians.*
Kelsey, Alice Geer: *Seven-Minute Stories For Church and Home.* Abingdon, 1958, 128 pp., $2.50.
Klein, Ernst E.: *God Speaks—To Me!* Judson, 1960, 135 pp., $1.75, paper. (Counselor's Guide)
MacInnes, Gordon A.: *A Guide to Worship in Camp and Conference.* Westminster, 1965, 96 pp., $1.50, paper.
MacKay: *Creative Counseling For Christian Camps,* ch. 5.
Messinger, C. F.: *Church Camping For Junior Highs.* Westminster, 1965, 96 pp., $1.50, paper.
Messinger, C. F., J. E. Simpson, and G. F. Ulrich: *Seeking Meaning With Junior Highs in Camp.* Westminster, 1966, $1.85, paper.
Pease, Dorothy Wells: *Inspiration Under the Sky.* Abingdon, 1963, $2.
Schiechen, Samuel J.: *Wonder in God's Wilderness.* Augsburg, $3.75.
Schroeder, Ruth: *Youth Programs on Nature Themes.* Abingdon, 1959, 192 pp., $2.75.
Springer, James C.: *Boys, Girls and God.* Vantage, 1971, 82 pp., $3.75.
Todd: *Camping For Christian Youth.*
Webb: *Light From A Thousand Campfires:*
Baker, Edna Dean: "Religion in Camp." p. 251.
Hazzard, Lowell B.: "Spiritual Values in Camping." p. 45.
Rogers, Mrs. Dwight: "A Prayer for Camp Directors." p. 19.

MAGAZINE ARTICLES

Camping Magazine:
Brown, Stewart A.: "Youth Speaks a New Language at Camp Worship Services." Mar., 1969, p. 46.
Bullock, George: "Encourage Spiritual Awareness." Jan., 1962, p. 38.
Dunbar, David: "Creating Spiritual Awareness in Youth." Dec., 1960, p. 7.
McLarty, Emmett K., Jr.: "Spiritual Values in Camping." Part I, Sept./Oct., 1967, p. 14; Part II, Jan., 1968, p. 18.
Mellinger, Marie B.: "Religion in Nonsectarian Camps." Jan., 1967, p. 22.
Schoonover, Barbara: "And God Created. . . ." Feb., 1962, p. 72.
van der Smissen, Betty: "Camping—The Outdoor Ministry of the Church." Jan., 1964, p. 14.
van der Smissen, Betty: "Nature's Proclamation." Nov./Dec., 1963, p. 32.

Campfire and Council Ring Programs

Berger: *Program Activities For Camps.*
van der Smissen and Goering: *A Leader's Guide to Nature-Oriented Activities,* pp. 179–187.
Webb: *Light From A Thousand Campfires:*
Buchanan, Bruce R.: "Campfire Programs." p. 248.

MAGAZINE ARTICLES

Camping Magazine:
Macfarlan, Allan A.: "Campfires Can Be Memorable—With Wise Guidance and Planning." Nov./Dec., 1963, p. 28.
Nash, Harold W.: "How Campers Share Fun, Responsibility of Planning Campfires." Feb., 1961, p. 14.
"Philosophy for Fire Lighting." May, 1962, p. 3.
Schmidt, Ernest F., and W. Chester Frisbie: "'Sure-Fire' Methods for Starting Campfires." Mar., 1962, p. 18.

Chapter 13

Music, Rhythm, and Dramatic Activities

Figure 13-1 Ears for Music?

Music is a wonderful and lovely gift of God. Next to theology, music is God's finest gift to man. It is a soothing and refreshing balm for every troubled soul, it dispels gloom and drives away our worries and it makes man cheerful and contented.

—MARTIN LUTHER

How monotonous the sounds of the forest would be if the music came only from the Top Ten birds.

—DAN BENNETT, in *Reader's Digest,* September, 1970.

It is probable that from man's earliest existence some form of rhythm has played an important part in his life. Nearly all studies of primitive peoples show that each had its chants and ceremonial dances to use in times of deep emotion. Some expressed joy, as after a successful hunt or encounter with the enemy, while others lamented a misfortune such as the death of a loved one. Still others were used to entreat their gods to supply the people's wants such as rain, a bountiful food supply, or the speedy recovery of an ill or injured person. Throughout history, workers have sung to relieve the tedium of their long hours of labor, and armies have had songs as well as bands and drum and bugle corps to lessen marching fatigue and to raise their morale and patriotism to the highest possible pitch. Humans are, and always have been, lovers of rhythm of all types, and campers are no exception to the rule.

SINGING IN THE CAMP PROGRAM

It is the most natural thing in the world for happy campers to sing at any time and place they happen to be; conversely, campers who sing can scarcely avoid being happy. Song should burst forth as spontaneously as mushrooms after a rain, for the miles fly by while hiking, dishes seem almost to dry themselves, and even mediocre paddlers swing into a space-covering rhythm when there's a song in the air. Good music is a great leavening agent; few fail to succumb to a catchy tune, a strong rhythm, or the sheer beauty of a lovely melody. No camper or counselor should return home without a complete repertoire of good, new (to him) songs, as well as fond memories of frequently singing his old favorites.

TYPES OF SONGS

Most songs can be divided roughly into three types, each having a definite place in the camp program.

Folk Songs. *Folk songs,* such as "Weggis Song" and "Walking at Night," cannot be traced to any one composer; rather, they originated at some time in the past and were passed down orally from generation to generation, no doubt with some modification along the way. These old folk songs seem to have come straight from the emotions and everyday experiences of those who sang them, and they now serve as lasting tributes to them. Fortunately for us, we are now experiencing a revival of interest in these songs, and are finding many of great value. However, we must bear in mind that many so-called folk songs are actually of recent origin and by a known composer and so are not true folk songs at all. This is not meant to belittle them, for some are quite excellent and well worth singing.

Many of the old true folk songs have now been written down. *Ballads,* such as the "Deaf Woman's Courtship,"* tell a story which campers may enjoy acting out as they sing. *Sea chanteys,* such as "Down the River," originated as sailors sang along with their work on the vast and lonely seas. There is a story behind all folk songs, be they singing games, spirituals, plantation songs, cowboy songs, or mountain ballads. Although it is sometimes difficult to trace their origins, the search is well worth the effort, for such knowledge makes them much more meaningful aod enjoyable for both singers and listeners.

> Folk songs are not made; they grow. They fall out of the air; they fly over land like gossamer, now here, now there; and are sung in a thousand places at the same time. Our own actions and our life we find in these songs. It is as if we all had helped make them.
>
> —THEODOR STORM, (1817–1888) *Immensee.*

Rounds or Canons. *Rounds* or *canons* are sung with the group divided into two or more sections, each singing the same melody, but starting at different times. "Harmony Greeting" and "Dona Nobis Pacem" are familiar camp songs of this type.

Art Songs. *Art songs,* such as Bach's "Now Let Every Tongue Adore Thee" and Sibelius' "Song of Peace" ("Finlandia"), were composed by the masters and merit a special place in the camp program. Their sheer beauty makes them a pleasure to sing as well as a help in developing a taste for good music. A few of these art songs are based on old folk songs.

Figure 13–2 Campers Love Singing.

*This as well as other songs mentioned here can be found in "Sing," available from the American Camping Association.

THERE ARE SONGS FOR EVERY OCCASION

There are songs appropriate for almost any time or place. They serve well as "ice breakers" to thaw out a group of new acquaintances or a group and new leader. They are helpful in soothing the ruffled feathers of people at odds because of a minor misunderstanding or difference of opinion. Singing in front of a blazing fire in an indoor fireplace banishes gloom on a cold, rainy day. Singing in close harmony develops a spirit of camaraderie and togetherness as each blends his voice to produce the total effect.

Well-chosen songs will put a group into a receptive mood for almost any activity, be it a serious campfire program, a discussion group, or an evening of pure fun and frolic. There are appropriate songs to welcome newcomers, to express regret at someone's leaving, or even to quiet hunger pangs while waiting in front of the dining room for the signal to "come and get it." Music relieves tension and jangled nerves, and singing during a rest break on the trail helps to reduce fatigue. Singing a pretty lullaby or listening to soft, soothing music on a record player calms restless, boisterous campers and induces an appropriate mood for a siesta or quiet after taps. Music furnishes a background for writing letters, reading, readying equipment, or working on an arts and crafts project. There are appropriate songs to help with rowing, canoeing, horseback riding, hiking, or almost anything else on the agenda. Songs help to maintain campers' spirits when a temporary blackout or a balky campfire disrupts activities or when an outbreak of homesickness threatens.

Figure 13–3 There's Music for Every Occasion.

Music combines well with many other camp activities. Learning native songs and dances helps campers to understand the culture and ways of life of another people. No vesper or other worship service is complete without including some of the many beautiful hymns which glorify God's handiwork as seen in nature. Arts and crafts combine with music when campers design costumes and stage sets for operettas and musical skits, or construct such simple musical instruments as shepherd's pipes, tom-toms, bongo drums, or rattles.

WHO SHOULD LEAD SINGING?

Although camps usually designate one or more staff members as official song leaders, this should in no way discourage others from participating at appropriate times and places; those who try it usually find it a very rewarding experience. Almost everyone has a sense of rhythm; if you doubt it, just watch a group listening to a catchy rhythm and note how many unconsciously sway their heads or bodies or tap their feet. After a little instruction and some practice, almost anyone with a good sense of rhythm can do a creditable job of song leading. Formal musical training undoubtedly helps if you do not let it curb your spontaneity or make you too insistent upon a "concert performance." Although perfection is a worthy objective in many endeavors, the main aim in camp singing should be providing enjoyment and satisfaction. Maintaining reasonably high standards of performance for really worthwhile songs is a major stepping stone toward achieving this goal. Of course it helps when a leader can sing well and has a strong voice to set the pace and keep the group together and on pitch, but many excellent leaders have quite ordinary voices and some don't even sing at all, merely "mouthing" the words as they lead. In fact, a superior singer can actually inhibit youngsters by making them hesitant to join in with their own more average voices.

USING SONGBOOKS

There are now many good song collections on the market, including some inexpensive paperbacks, with songs selected especially for their appropriateness to the camp setting and their appeal to those of camp age. Campers and leaders sometimes compile and mimeograph copies of their own favorites for use in camp and as souvenirs to take home so campers can refresh their memories as time dims the once familiar words and tunes.

Figure 13-4 All Can Take Part.

If you have no songbook, but want to place the words and music before the singers, print large characters on a blackboard or a large piece of wrapping paper which you can roll up to store. At night or in a darkened room, you can use an opaque projector to show the words and music on a screen, a white wall, or a taut bed sheet.

Some song leaders prefer not to use songbooks, especially when teaching a new song; they prefer to maintain eye contact to allow the singers to concentrate more on their hand signals as well as on the melody and meaning of the words. This type of teaching is called *rote* teaching.

PLANNING FOR A SONG SESSION

As previously mentioned, singing may just spring forth spontaneously at any old time and place; at other times, you may want to plan a special song fest or use singing as a part of another program. Plan to have the singing last no longer than ten to fifteen minutes, for it is better to stop while everyone is still enthusiastic and wanting more.

As with any successful program, a good singing session doesn't just happen. It comes about because a leader has planned it so well and prepared it so carefully that his presentation seems almost spontaneous. Such preparation brings confidence and an ability to be relaxed and informal.

Find out all you can about the background of each song. Of what nationality were the people who sang it and what were their occupations and general mode of living? When did it originate and on what occasions did they sing it? If the song was written by a composer, what interesting facts can you tell about his life? Little anecdotes about him or the song add great interest, and as is almost always the case, the more you know about a subject, the more interested you become in it. When you can convey to your group the mood of the people who sang the song, they will enjoy it more and sing it with more meaning and spirit.

When you encounter a group with poor taste in music or with poor singing habits, improving these may tax your patience and ingenuity to the utmost. It may sometimes even be best to go along with them and let them sing some of their old inferior songs while you try to bring about gradual improvements, for as in any type of teaching, we must start where the learners are.

You may sometimes want to start a program with rollicking "fun" or "action" songs, gradually passing on to those more serious and thoughtful, and perhaps finally ending with a hymn, a patriotic song, or your own special camp song.

INTRODUCING NEW SONGS

Before introducing a new song, be sure that you know it thoroughly. Practice singing it until you no longer have any qualms about it. For your first presentations, choose songs with lively tunes, short verses, and oft-repeated choruses. It is often best to teach the chorus first so that the group has something familiar to return to after each new verse. It sometimes helps to teach the song first to a small group, such as a cabin group, who can then serve as leaders for the rest. Rest hour is a good time to do this.

When leading, sing the song through once to show its general tempo and character. Then go back and sing the first phrase, asking them to sing it after you, and then go on to the next. When you have finished this, go back and sing the whole verse and go on to the now-familiar chorus. Repeat the song several times within the next few days until it takes its place as an old familiar friend. When you notice a mistake in timing, phrasing, words, or pitch, correct it immediately before it has had time to become a hard-to-break habit.

TECHNIQUES OF SONG LEADING

Although small groups sometimes sing without a leader, both quality and enjoyment increase when there is one, especially when learning a new song or when the group is large.

Leading camp singing isn't nearly as difficult as it may seem, for only simple movements and techniques are needed. Enthusiasm is a most important quality; let it show through in your facial expression, the sparkle in your eyes, and your whole general attitude. Establishing good rapport with the singers is all-important, so smile often and remain ever-pleasant. Think of the group singers as individuals, each important in himself; this attitude quickly communicates itself to them and enlists their cooperation.

Arrange the group about you in a semicircle to give a feeling of unity, and place yourself where all can see and hear you clearly. Try to sense their mood and adapt your approach to it. Choose a key suitable for the average voice, remembering that children's voices are usually higher than those of

Figure 13-5 Let Those Who Play Instruments Accompany.

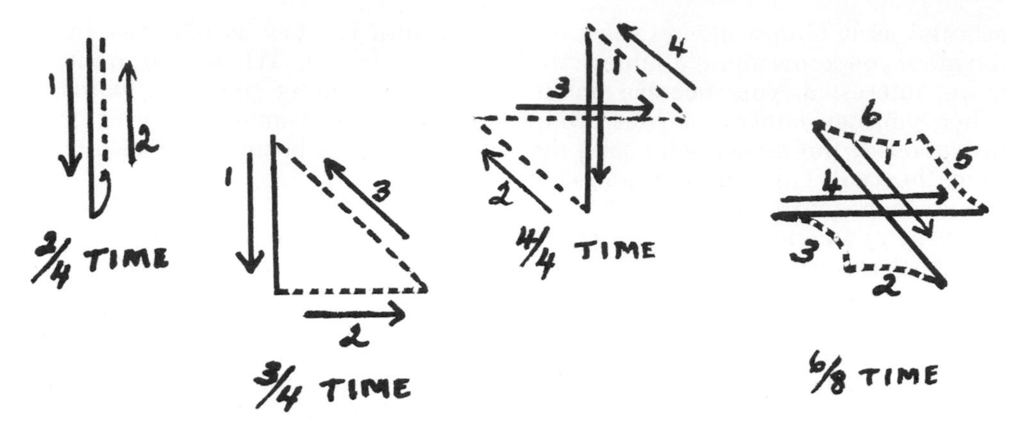

Figure 13-6 Right Arm Movements for Leading Singing.

adults. Use a voice cue, pitch pipe, or tonette to set the pitch.

It is foolish to try to be too fancy or to emulate the complicated movements of a symphony orchestra conductor. Some very successful leaders simply beat out the rhythm with a simple up-and-down or side-to-side movement. However, it isn't at all difficult to master some more meaningful gestures, such as those illustrated in Figure 13-6. Keep the rhythm with your right hand, using an especially vigorous downbeat to emphasize the first beat of each measure and ending it with an upbeat. Keep your right arm swinging like a pendulum and vary the vigor of your movements to indicate the mood or volume you want; strong for spirited, bold singing, less marked for soft, smooth passages. Stop your hand in a fixed position when you want a note held, and cross your hands briskly in front of your body at the end of the song so that all will stop together. Have definite signals for starting and stopping and insist on their being observed, for such niceties add interest and zest to a singing session and foster pride in doing it well.

Regulate volume with your left hand, raising it palm up for an increase and lowering it palm down or placing your finger tips on your lips for a decrease. Beckon or point to a group when you want them to come in, as in a round, or when you want them to sing with more volume. Keep both hands high where everyone can see them clearly. Explain your hand signals to the group and insist that they watch you so they can follow them.

Make your movements clear and decisive, neither exaggerating them nor making them mousy and colorless. Practice by directing your own singing in front of a mirror and keep at it until your movements become confident, easy, and relaxed.

Insist on clear enunciation, bringing out each word clearly so that listeners have no difficulty in understanding them. Aim for good tonal effect with no voices dominating, but all blending in a pleasing manner; tone down those who sing off key or too loudly.

Don't be afraid to compliment a group when they sing well, and encourage them to try for a still better performance by a remark such as, "That's much better; now, let's see if the altos can come in even a little stronger this time."

PLAN FOR VARIETY

Promote friendly, informal competition between groups occasionally, basing it upon superior harmony, depth of feeling, and best interpretation of the song, never on loudness and just plain noise. If they tend to sing too loudly and with little feeling for the song, have them sing it progressively more softly, dying away into a final pianissimo.

Since most songs tell a story, use modulation of tempo and volume to interpret and convey the meaning and to add variety to the program. Never let singing degenerate into a monotonous singsong with each number sounding very much like the others. A pace which is too rapid is preferable to one that drags.

Encourage good part singing, occasionally assigning solo parts to those able to carry them while the rest remain silent, whistle, hum, or "tra-la" in harmony.

Encourage campers who are especially interested to try their hand at leading, or ask them to help you to plan a song session. Always prepare more songs than you think you can possibly use so that you never run short and can do some juggling if things fail to go just as expected. It is also good to sometimes allow time in the program for special requests.

Although the aim of camp singing is enjoyment and the satisfaction that comes from doing it well and tastefully, you need not confine your repertoire to staid, serious numbers. There is a definite place for songs sung just for the fun of it and there are many lighthearted, nonsensical ditties and action songs that are dear to the hearts of live-wire youngsters. Include all types; slow, fast, happy, sad, plaintive, rollicking, thoughtful, sentimental, and just plain lovely. Sing songs such as "Alouette" (a gay Canadian voyageur song) and "Tongo" in which the leader sings a line or two, followed by a group response.

Rounds have been with us for a long time (it is claimed that "Three Blind Mice" appeared in print as early as 1609), and they are usually camper favorites, possibly because they offer a mild form of group competition. When learning a new one, have everyone sing the melody together until it is familiar, then divide them into groups, perhaps appointing a leader for each. Each group then sings the song through a given number of times, usually as many as there are groups.

Descants, as for "Rio Grande," are high-pitched harmonies that accompany the regular melody. Campers may want to try their hand at improvising some for appropriate favorite numbers. *Contra-singing* consists of simultaneously singing two songs whose melodies blend. In *antiphonal singing,* an "echo" group sings from some distant point, as high on a nearby hill or across the lake or out in canoes (music carries particularly well across the water.)

Individuals may want to form duets, trios, or barbershop quartets, singing just for their own amusement or preparing selections for some special occasion. A choir group adds materially to a vesper or Sunday service, especially when they come singing through the woods on their way to the Woodland Chapel or Green Cathedral. A group may sometimes receive special permission to be out after taps to serenade another group or to wake them just before the morning rising signal.

It is often preferable to sing *a capella* (without instruments) so that singers learn to rely on themselves to carry the tune and keep the rhythm. For variation, use simple instruments such as a guitar, handmade shepherd's pipe, harmonica, or accordion to accompany the singing or for a solo part. An Indian tom-tom is effective in opening an Indian song or fading away at its close.

Some camps hold special music appreciation hours for those who want to listen to recorded music. Let camper committees help to plan them, and invite interested parties to submit requests. Plan an occasional program around a central theme, such as the

(Courtesy of National Music Camp, Interlochen, Michigan.)

celebration of some composer's birthday that falls during the camp season.

Unfortunately, campers sometimes become so infatuated with a song that they sing it until it is threadbare and almost unbearable to everyone else. Before condemning them too much for this, examine your program; perhaps there has been a failure to supply enough attractive new songs to alternate with the old. Some camps have successfully solved this problem by gathering everyone for a mock burial service to sing the offending number for the last time, then lay it away in a final resting place and decorate the grave with a bouquet of dandelions.

Encourage groups or units to compose original tunes to accompany favorite poems. This is more challenging and requires more originality than simply borrowing or adapting someone else's tune. Original songs can be made quite personal and can introduce funny little happenings and secret "in" jokes known only to the composers. You may find it fun to compose songs yourself, perhaps making up appropriate words to go with a favorite tune or one of your own creation.

SINGING GAMES AND DANCES

Recent times have witnessed a marked revival of old-time singing games and dances, and they are very popular with campers. Many of them are quite vigorous and serve to let off exuberant steam, especially after youngsters have been cooped up inside for some time because of bad weather; round, square, longways, and folk dances are in this category, along with party games.

As was originally done, the accompaniment can be provided by singing by the participants or bystanders or by simple instruments such as fiddles, guitars, or accordions. You may find adequate callers on your own camp staff or in a nearby community, or you can use records which are available both with and without calls.

Figure 13-7 And Away We Go!

A good way to begin a program is with a few simple "mixers" or "ice breakers" with steps and figures so simple that anyone who can walk can do them. This gets everybody out on the floor and builds up their confidence as you gradually progress to something more complicated. There may be a demand for modern dance forms such as the traditional waltz and fox trot or whatever steps and figures are currently in vogue.

An *International Night* featuring the native costumes and dances of one on more foreign countries is well-received and helps participants to understand people of other cultures. This may be an all-camp project, one sponsored by one or two units, or each unit or cabin may be responsible for preparing one number and teaching it to the others.

Figure 13–8 "Now Swing That Pretty Little Gal!"

RHYTHMICAL INSTRUMENTS

MUSICAL INSTRUMENTS

Many camps encourage campers to bring their own instruments so they can play in combos and other special groups, or perhaps even in an all-camp orchestra or band. Rhythm bands are also popular; most of the instruments are easy to play and are available for rent or purchase at most music stores, together with music and directions for organizing a band.

MAKE YOUR OWN PERCUSSION INSTRUMENTS

Some *percussion instruments* (those for keeping time but not for playing a tune) are easily made and are enjoyable both to make and to use.

For a *drum* (Figure 13–9,A) use a round container such as a No. 10 tin can, an oatmeal box, a round wooden box, the bottom of a plastic bleach bottle, or even a round wooden bowl with the bottom sawed off. Construct drumheads from pieces of inner tube, rawhide, heavy plastic, oilcloth, an animal skin, or some heavy material such as sailcloth or unbleached muslin which has been stiffened by applying a coat of shellac. Draw a drumhead very tightly over each end of the drum, and use strips of leather, inner tube or strong cord to lace them together as shown, or use a rubber band, thumb-

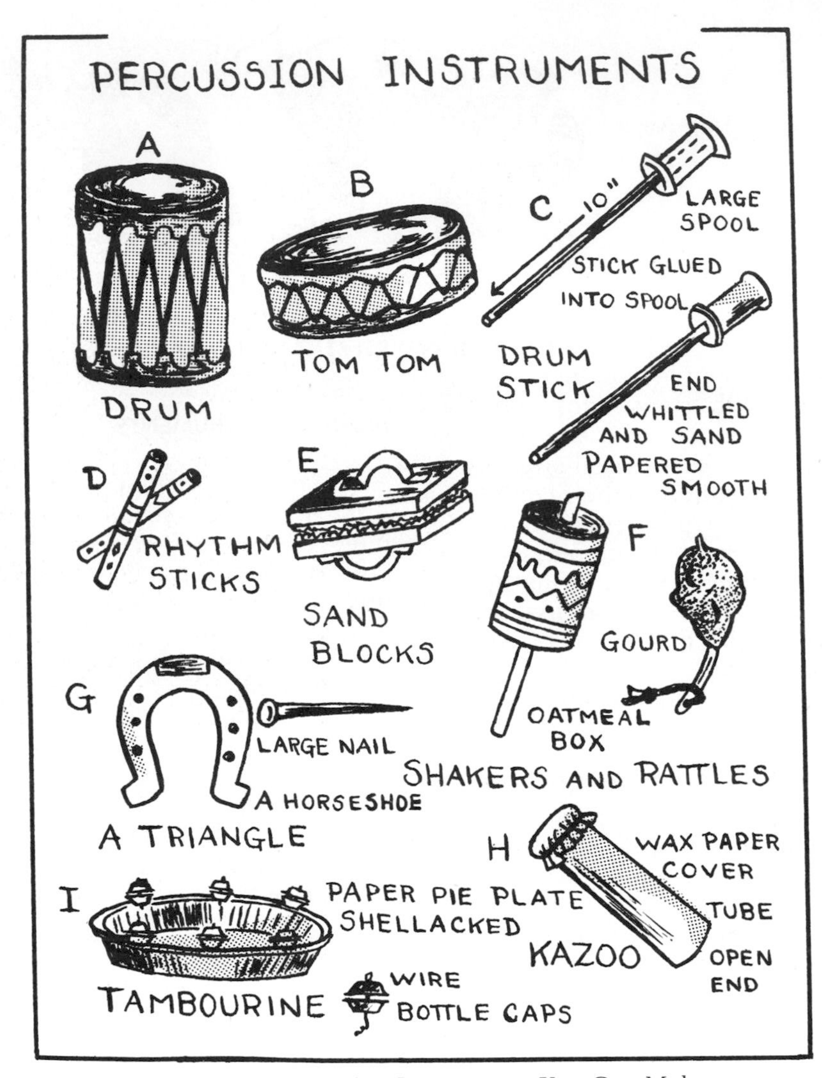

Figure 13-9 Percussion Instruments You Can Make.

tacks, or large-headed tacks to anchor each head separately. To tighten them still more, paint them with shellac after they are in place and let dry; keep working with them until they have a satisfactory resonance. Make a *tom-tom* from a narrower container (Figure 13-9,B), with a drumhead over only one end of it.

Our name "drumstick" for the leg bone of a chicken probably comes from the practice of some Indian tribes of beating their drums or tom-toms with the leg bone of a wild fowl. Certain African tribes beat the drums with their fingers, palms, or fists. You can make a suitable *drumstick* from a piece of wood, experimenting with different varieties until you find one that produces the sound you want. A spool and stick (Figure 13-9,C) or a piece of cloth tied tightly around the mop end of a small dishmop are also satisfactory. Paint the drumsticks and sides and heads of the drum to suit your taste, using bright poster paint or a similar medium. With a tin can drum, glue a piece of brown paper around it to serve as a base for your colors. In making nearly all percussion instruments, the materials used and the manner of finishing them will affect their tonal qualities.

Make *rhythm sticks* (Figure 13-9,D) to beat together by whittling them from round sticks and sandpapering them smooth, then shellacking and painting them.

To make *sand blocks* (Figure 13-9,E) glue or tack heavy pieces of sandpaper to the bottoms of wooden blocks and attach handles of leather, webbing, or wood to hold as you "swish" them together as a rhythmical accompaniment.

Make *shakers* and *rattles* (Figure 13-9,F) from a hollow object, such as a gourd, tin can, cardboard cylinder, or wooden box, partially filling it with pebbles, beans, hard seeds, bottle caps, or small nuts. Make a handle by glueing a stick firmly in place through holes made in the ends. Try varying either the container or the materials inside to get different sound effects. Cover the instrument with paper and decorate it as you wish.

Use a large nail or other metallic object to tap a resonant piece of metal (Figure 13-9,G) for use as a *triangle*. Make a *kazoo* (Figure 13-9,H) by using a rubber band to fasten a piece of waxed paper tightly over one end of a mailing tube. Hum through the open end of the tube.

Marimbas, cigar box violins, shepherd's pipes, and banjos are a little more difficult to make. You will find instructions for making them in some of the sources listed at the end of the chapter.

Music washes away from the soul the dust of everyday life.

—AUERBACH

Music is a philosophy of life, a point of view, a way of living. It can do more to regenerate a sick and weary world than many remedies now put forth by politicians, economists and other weary folk. Through music we can learn what democracy, freedom and happiness are.

—DAVID BARNETT,
in *Living With Music*,
published by W. Stewart.

Music . . . gives tone to the Universe, wings to the mind, flight to the imagination, a charm to sadness and gayety and life to everything.

—PLATO

DRAMATIC ACTIVITIES

Of all people, children are the most imaginative.

—MACAULAY,
Essays on Mitford's Greece.

Children are born imitators, aping everything from the way their mothers and fathers talk to the movements of the patrolman directing traffic on a busy street or a dog, horse, or monkey at the zoo. To them, such imitation isn't really acting at all; they throw themselves so wholeheartedly into their roles that they *become* what they por-

Figure 13-10 The Play's the Thing!

tray. This has the advantage of freeing them from the selfconsciousness and fear of ridicule which assail many of their elders. A child can transfer almost instantaneously from one character to another without losing his sense of reality.

DRAMATICS IN CAMP

Some early camps prided themselves on producing at least one full-blown formal play each season, complete with elaborate and artistic scenery; small participants were decked out in rented costumes and were so well-rehearsed that they delivered their lines faultlessly. The extravaganza was widely publicized, and each participant's relatives—from grandpa and grandma on down to distant cousins—came for the occasion to applaud the young thespians and bring them back for one curtain call after another. Our modern philosophy of good program in a general camp does not look favorably on such finished productions because they violate at least two criteria of good camping: (1) they could be done just as well if not better at home, and (2) they usurp a disproportionate amount of time which the children should be spending in activities indigenous to the outdoor camp environment. Such formalized dramatics should be left to those camps that set themselves up as specialists in that field.

However, there are several types of informal dramatics which fit in with the spirit of general camping and provide children with an outlet for their natural instincts to pretend and imitate.

Sources of Plays. Only short, informal productions are recommended. You can cut long plays or use some of the one- or two-act plays and skits available for campers which can be worked up quickly so that they become *one of many,* not *the* activity of the summer. If you don't want to take the time to learn parts, use an offstage narrator or let the players familiarize themselves with their lines and act them out as they read them.

Most thoroughly enjoyed, however, are the homespun variety concocted by staff and campers. It is as much fun to write them as to produce them. Use either the whole group or a committee for planning, and as soon as the general theme has been decided upon, ideas and suggestions will probably come so fast that the chore will be to sort them out and weave them into a reasonable production.

Since children love all kinds of animals, you may want to work several into the script, giving them anything from walk-on parts to starring roles. Incidentally, shy children often lose their timidity when concealed behind a mask or walking about on all fours under the "fur" of some animal. Don't be afraid to exaggerate, both as to action and plausibility. Build up to a climax, ending on a happy note with all the "good" characters living in eternal bliss while the "bad" ones grovel in the discomfort of their just deserts. Incorporate appropriate dances and songs if you wish, letting the audience join in on any chorus that is familiar. After all, the main purpose of drama is enjoyment and the true measure of the results is what happens to the participants. This last, of course, rules out anything smacking of poor taste, slapstick, or just plain giggling and silliness.

Ideas for plays can come from many sources, such as nursery or Mother Goose rhymes, or well-liked stories such as those of Winnie the Pooh or Uncle Remus. Other possibilities are historical or current events, Bible stories, or the local history of the community or camp.

Play each character to the hilt, with a hero who is the wisest, most charming and honest person imaginable in contrast to a villain who is the

Figure 13-11 Have Plenty of Action.

most underhanded, despicable creature that ever drew a breath. Virtue of every sort must be lavishly rewarded and evil as unfailingly punished.

Make the action brisk and colorful and end each act with a semiclimactic bit of humor, excitement, or grandeur while the audience hisses the villain, applauds the hero, or collapses in laughter. Such audience reactions are good in moderation but shouldn't be allowed to get out of hand.

With somewhat serious plays, mimeograph enough copies of the script to give one to every participant from actors to those responsible for sound effects, lighting, and properties.

Stage, Sets, and Properties. Some camps provide a well-appointed stage with such conveniences as dressing rooms, backdrops, scenery, and curtains. These, however, are not at all necessary with such informal productions as we are discussing. For indoor staging, use a corner of the room with the chairs arranged diagonally across it, or place the audience in a circle around the actors to create a theater-in-the-round. However, an outdoor setting is more in keeping with the camp ideal. Look for a natural amphitheatre with the stage below and a gentle slope for seating the audience, or seat them on level ground with the stage located above on a flattened elevation. Since children's voices do not carry well, place the audience close to the action, and avoid locating the stage in front of a body of water, for it will absorb sound and make hearing difficult.

You are fortunate if your outdoor setting has a natural backdrop of trees and shrubbery to serve as a screen for behind-scenes activity and actors awaiting their cues. If you have no foliage, you may want to plant or transplant some to provide a screen in the future. Scenery is not at all indispensable, but, if used, can be extremely simple, for the youngsters' imaginations will supply details. Indeed, they may find it hilariously funny when you use only token props, such as packing boxes for buildings and cardboard silhouettes for mountains, birds, or the sun, labeling them if necessary. A little resourcefulness does wonders as an inverted tablespoon serves for a telephone, a large towel or blanket for a rug, and a cardboard crescent-shaped moon dangles from a fish pole held by someone standing on a ladder behind the scenes. Colored sheets, tent halves, tarps, or blankets can be fastened over ropes or wires to serve as curtains. Lanterns, strong flashlights, or spotlights furnish adequate stage lighting, and Figure 16-6*D* shows how to make footlights by inserting candles in tin can holders.

Costuming. Here again, odds and ends will do and the children's imaginations will fill in all necessary details. Many camps have a costume box in which to accumulate discarded apparel for use when the need arises. Campers' personal gear will provide such possibilities as berets, camp hats, rain hats, raincoats and boots, pajamas, bathrobes, washcloths, towels, bandanas, hiking boots, bed sheets, blankets, and pillow slips. Burlap bags, old curtains, draperies, dish towels, and bits of remnants can also be pressed into use. Crepe paper comes in a large variety of shades and is helpful for costume-making and other purposes.

Figure 13–12 Fierce Pirates.

Paper bags just large enough to fit over the head make good animal or human masks when ears and noses are pasted on and holes are cut for eyes and mouth. You can improvise beards and false wigs from pipe stem cleaners, frayed rope, shrubbery, or an old mop head, and feathers, grasses, or branches make good hat decorations. You can fashion buckles from cardboard, pieces of wood, or tin cans; bits of metal, shells, nuts, or seeds produce attractive jewelry. A painted piece of metal or wood will serve as a shield, or one can be fashioned from the lid of a large cooking pot or an old wash boiler.

Sound Effects. Use recorded music before the show, between acts, or to set moods during the action.

Here are a few suggestions for sound effects:

Hoof beats—clap soft drink caps or wooden blocks on wood, varying the intensity to indicate whether the horse is approaching or disappearing.

Dog barking, cock crowing, cow mooing—use human voices.

Thunder—shake a piece of sheet metal with one edge resting on the floor.

You get the idea; now use your ingenuity to invent what you need.

Everyone Has a Part. Some children may not have parts in the play, either because they don't want them or because there aren't enough to go around. Nevertheless, there are many non-acting chores to keep everyone occupied. The following are suggested:

Director
Prompter
Properties
Programs
Sets
Costumes
Lighting and sound effects
Seating
Ushers
Superintendent of Clean Up (give him a fancy title to compensate for his unpleasant task).
Publicity (issue invitations and publicity and write a story for the camp newspaper).

An Audience Is Not Always Necessary. Productions need not always be for an audience. Some of the most successful and enjoyable dramatic activities are those which arise spontaneously, simply to pass the time on a rainy day or programless night. However, the initial effort often proves so successful that it stimulates the group to put a little more work into the production and to stage it on some special

Figure 13–13 Colorful Patches on a Burlap Bag Make a Costume Fit for Any Old Crone.

occasion such as a council fire or visitors' day.

Camp Spoofs and Take-offs. Most popular of all are the productions built around camp personalities and local happenings, as when campers lampoon their terrible, tyrant counselors or the staff depicts the campers as seen through counselors' eyes. Campers can usually see the funny side of their own experiences when viewed in retrospect—that long, long trip when the rain came pattering down every day and night or their gruesome first experience at cooking out-of-doors.

ACTIVITIES RELATED TO DRAMATICS

Several activities, although not really dramatics, are related in that they contain some elements of make-believe and dramatizing.

Reading Plays. Play reading may serve as a satisfying substitute for those who like plays but don't want to go into them extensively enough to memorize lines and actions.

Stunt Night. Stunt night is a traditional fun night when campers and staff display their talents in almost any area, such as roping a "broncho," demonstrating feats of magic, putting on a skit or play, or performing on a musical instrument. Let a counselor or responsible camper act as master of ceremonies and hold a preview of the numbers to see that they are suitable.

Pantomime With Reading. Actors take parts as someone reads a ballad, story, poem, folk song, or original skit. In one version, each camper takes a part, such as a horse, crow, or freight train, and whenever a camper's character is mentioned, he makes the appropriate noise for his role (the horse "neighs," the crow "caws," etc.).

Charades. Charades is an old game in which one team or individual selects a word such as "dandie-lyin" or "eye-doll-a-tree" and pantomimes the syllables while the others try to guess the word. You may wish to substitute such categories as Mother Goose rhymes, book titles, folk songs, story book characters, advertising slogans, famous people of today or yesterday, or different professions.

In one variation, a team chooses a word which it whispers to the first member of the other team who must then act it out for his team to guess. Measure the time it takes and then give the other team its turn. Continue, alternating teams until each player has had a chance to act out a word. Time each and add the total time consumed by each team in successfully guessing the other's word. The team with the least total time wins.

New Orleans. This variation is an old childhood favorite. Each team has a base line which it must stay behind while the other team takes a turn at coming close and acting out a chosen occupation, such as pushing a lawn mower, chopping wood, or rowing a boat. The team behind the line tries to guess the occupation and, as soon as successful, tries to tag as many of the acting team as possible before they can scurry back to safety behind their own baseline. Any member tagged must transfer to the other team, which then takes its turn at acting.

Paper-Bag Dramatics. Each group receives a bag of simple properties which they must use in presenting a skit for the other group.

Sealed Orders. A number of humorous or serious situations are written on slips of paper and placed in a hat; each individual or group draws a slip and must then act out the situation while the others attempt to guess what it is. Suggested situations: "timid old lady caught in the middle of a busy street with the traffic light changing"; "Uncle Neddie coming home late and trying to sneak up to his room without being heard"; "the little camper who is afraid to get into the pool for his first swimming lesson." Categories such as those mentioned previously in regard to charades may also be used, or each group may be given a list of characters to work into a skit.

Burlesques. These are take-offs on camp life (or any other desired topic). Subjects might be "the camp unit's first overnight trip"; "cabin cleanup"; "a camper's version of a camp staff meeting" or "visiting day at camp." Again, beware of hurt feelings.

Album of Familiar Pictures. Arrange a "curtain" of blankets and turn off the lights. Have the group behind the curtain pose in a stiff picture (like those in grandmother's album), such as a ladies' bridge club or a bird's-eye view of the camp dining room. Draw open the curtain, turn on the lights, and see what you have. Exaggerate and make it fun.

Shadow Plays. Stretch a sheet (preferably wet) tightly to serve as a transparent curtain with the stage directly behind it and bright lights (auto lights, flashlights, or spotlights) set far enough back to make the actors stand out in silhouette. Turn off all other lights and keep the actors close to the curtain so that their silhouettes will be sharp and clear. Act out a skit, story, ballad, or burlesque. You need use only suggestions of costumes and can cut one-dimensional settings and props from cardboard or old packing boxes and glue them together. Describe the situation briefly or read a whole script as you act it out. Accompany it with "mood music," if you wish.

Marionette and Puppet Shows. These little characters vary all the way from ones fashioned quickly from sacks, socks, or other materials which can be slipped over your hand and manipulated with your fingers (puppets) to elaborate creatures manipulated by from one to fifteen strings attached to control sticks which the operator holds (marionettes). The more elaborate shows involve various skills and interests; someone must design and dress the marionettes or puppets, while others are needed to operate them, make stage sets and props, arrange the lighting, write or arrange the script, read the script or story as it is acted out, and furnish musical accompaniment if it is wanted. Children greatly enjoy these shows, and it is well worth the effort to try at least some of the more simple ones.

Figure 13-14 Puppets Are Fun.

ADDITIONAL READINGS

(For an explanation of abbreviations and abbreviated forms, see page 25.)

Music and Rhythm

LEADERSHIP AND GENERAL

Batcheller, John, and Sally Monsour: *Music in Recreation and Leisure.* Brown, 1972, 135 pp., $3.95, paper.

Corbin: *Recreation Leadership,* ch. 19.

Hoffelt, Robert O.: *How To Lead Informal Singing.* Abingdon, 1963, 111 pp., $1.50, paper.

John, Robert W., and Charles H. Douglas: *Playing Social and Recreational Instruments.* Prentice-Hall, 1972, 112 pp., $4.95, paper.

Kujoth: *The Recreation Program Guide,* pp. 225–237.

Tobitt, Janet E. (Revised by Phyllis Ford and Kathleen Mote): *A Counselor's Guide to Camp Singing.* ACA, 1971, 44 pp., $1.95, paper.

Webb: *Light From A Thousand Campfires:* Wagner, Doris: "Let There Be Good Music," p. 296.

Magazine Articles

Camping Magazine:

Badeaux, Ed: "Folk Songs in Camp." June, 1966, p. 12.

Brobston, Stanley Heard: "Good Music—An Enriching Addition to Your Camp Program." Mar., 1971, p. 18.

Nissman, Blossom: "Singing Gives a Camp Spirit." June, 1967, p. 14.

Roberts, Bette A.: "Bring More Singing Into Your Camp." Feb., 1972, p. 22.

Short, Alison: "A Singing Camp is a Happy Camp." June, 1970, p. 11.

Song Collections

Burl Ives Song Book. Ballantine, 1953, 276 pp., 75¢, paper.

Felton, Harold W.: *Cowboy Jamboree* (Western Songs and Lore). Knopf, 1951, $4.99.

Girl Scout Pocket Song Book (#20-1927). Girl Scouts, 1956, 48 pp., 20¢, paper.

Glazer, Tom: *Treasury of Folk Songs For the Family.* Grosset & Dunlap, 253 pp., $5.95.

Handy Songs, Coop. Rec. Service.

Leisy, James F.: *Let's All Sing.* Abingdon, 1959, 176 pp., $2.95; $1.75, paper.

Let's Sing Together. Westminster, 1965, 96 pp., 35¢, paper.

More Burl Ives Songs. Ballantine, 1966, 224 pp., 75¢, paper.

Nye, Robert, Neva Aubin Vernice, and George Kyme: *Singing With Children.* Wadsworth, 1962, 264 pp., $5.95, spiral.

101 Plus 5 Folk Songs for Camp. Oak, 1966, 152 pp., $3.95.

Scout Songbook (No. 3224). Boy Scouts, 1972, 128 pp., 50¢, paper.

Sing! Coop. Rec. Service, rev., 1966, 95 pp., 50¢, paper.

Sing Together (#20-2051). Girl Scouts, 1957, $1.50, paper.

Tent and Trail Songs. Coop. Rec. Service, 1966, 80 pp., 40¢, paper.

Tobitt, Janet E. (Compiler): *The Ditty Bag* (#23-4606). Girl Scouts, $1.

Making Your Own Instruments

Benson: *Creative Crafts for Children.*

Hunt: *Golden Book of Crafts and Hobbies.*

Hunt: *Golden Book of Indian Crafts and Lore.*

Kettelkamp, Larry: *Drums, Rattles, and Bells.* Morrow, 1960, 47 pp., $4.32. (ages 8–12)

Mandell, Muriel, and Robert E. Wood: *Make Your Own Musical Instruments.* Sterling, rev., 1959, 128 pp., $3.95.

Magazine Articles

Boys' Life:

Cohen, Saul M.: "An Electric Organ." Apr., 1964, p. 36.

"Instruments for the Music of South America." Dec., 1960.

Waltner, Willard and Elma: "Horn Bugle." May, 1964.

Wheeler, Alan: "Pioneer Musical Instruments." Oct., 1970, p. 67.

Rhythmic Activities

Burchenal, Elizabeth: *Folk Dances and Singing Games.* Order from N.R.P.A., $3.50.

Davis, Buleah, and Fran Riel: *Happy Dancing.* Burgess, 1966, 45 pp., $1.25.

Flood, Jessie B., and Cornelia F. Putney: *Square Dance, U. S. A.* Brown, 120 pp., $2.50.

Gilbert, Cecile: *International Folk Dance At a Glance.* Burgess, 1969, 171 pp., $4, paper.

Handy Folk Dance Book. Coop. Rec. Service, $1.25.

Handy Square Dance Book. Coop. Rec. Service, $1.25.

Harris, Jane, Anne Pittman, and Marlys S. Waller: *Dance A While.* Burgess, 4th ed., 1968, 386 pp., $6.95; $4.95, paper.

Jensen, Clayne R. and Mary B.: *Beginning Square Dance.* Wadsworth, 1966, $1.65, paper.

Jensen, Mary B. and Clayne R.: *Beginning Folk Dancing.* Wadsworth, $1.25, paper.

Kirkell, M., and I. Schaffnet: *Partners All, Places All: Forty-Four Enjoyable Square and Folk Dances for Everyone,* Dutton, $4.95.

Kraus, Richard G.: *Folk Dancing.* Macmillan, 1962, 221 pp., $8.75.

Lunt, Lois: *Mix 'Em and Match 'Em.* Denison, 109 pp., $4.95.

Mulak: *Fun and Games,* chs. 12, 15, 16.

Tobitt, Janet E. (Compiler): *Promenade All* (#23-4697). Girl Scouts, 75¢, paper.

Vick, Marie, and Rosann McLaughton Cox: *A Collection of Dances for Children.* Burgess, 1970, $4.95. (Card File)

Magazine Articles

Camping Magazine:

Pasvolsky, Richard L.: "Square Dancing at Camp." Jan., 1966, p. 15.

Dramatic Activities

Marionettes and Puppets

Ackley, Edith Flack: *Marionettes: Easy to Make! Fun To Use!* Lippincott, 1939, 118 pp., $5.95.

Adair, Margaret W.: *Do-It-In-A-Day Puppets for Beginners.* Day, 1964, 89 pp., $4.62.

Alkema, Chester Jay: *Puppet-Making.* Sterling, 48 pp., $2.95.

Cummings, Richard: *101 Hand Puppets: A Guide for Puppeteers of All Ages.* McKay, 1962, 147 pp., $3.95.

French, Susan: *Presenting Marionettes.* Van Nostrand, 1964, 112 pp., $6.95.

Goaman, Muriel: *Judy and Andrew's Puppet Book.* Plays, 48 pp., $3.95.

Hopper, Grizella H.: *Puppet Making Through the Grades.* Davis Mass, 64 pp., $5.60.

Howard, Vernon: *Puppet and Pantomime Plays*. Sterling, 108 pp., $2.95.
Kampmann, Lothar: *Creating With Puppets*. Van Nostrand, 1972, 76 pp., $5.95.
Kujoth: *The Recreation Program Guide*, pp. 306–309.
Lewis, Shari: *Making Easy Puppets*. Dutton, 1967, 86 pp., $4.95.
Mulholland, John: *Practical Puppetry*. Arco, 1962, $4.95.
Richter, Dorothy: *Fell's Guide to Hand Puppets: How To Make and Use Them*. Fell, 1970, 202 pp., $5.95.
Slade, Richard: *You Can Make a String Puppet*. Plays, 1957, 46 pp., $3.95.
Stahl, Leroy, and Effa E. Preston: *The Master Puppet Book*. Denison, 390 pp., $4.95.

PLAY PRODUCTION

Alberts, David: *Pantomime: Elements and Exercises*. U. of Kansas, 1971, 69 pp., $5.50.
Alkema, Chester Jay: *Masks*. Sterling, 1971, 48 pp., $2.95.
Alkema, Chester Jay: *Monster Masks*, Sterling, 1973, 48 pp. $2.95.
Berger: *Program Activities for Camps*.
Brown, Andrew: *Drama*. Arco, 1962, 160 pp., $4.50; 95¢, paper.
Carson, Bernice Wells: *Play A Part*. Abingdon, 1970, 240 pp., $5.95.
Convention Highlights: Kovner, Albert: "Techniques in Creative Dramatics." p. 82.
Corbin: *Recreation Leadership*, ch. 16.
Crosscup, Richard: *Children and Dramatics*. Scribner's, 1966, $5.95.
Franklin, Miriam A.: *Rehearsal*. Prentice-Hall, 5th ed., 1972, 288 pp., $8.95, paper.
Goodridge, Janet: *Creative Drama and Improvised Movement for Children*. Plays, 1970, 158 pp., $5.95.
Hacker, Fred, and Prescott Eames: *How to Put on An Amateur Circus*. Order from N.R.P.A., 112 pp., $3.50.
Kujoth: *The Recreation Program Guide*, pp. 84–105.
Lounsbury, Warren C.: *Theatre Backstage From A to Z*. U. of Washington, 1967, 172 pp., $9; $4.95, paper.
McGee, Cecil: *Drama For Fun*. Broadman, 1969, 175 pp., $4.95.
Olfson, Lewy: *You Can Act!* Sterling, 128 pp., $2.95.
Purdy, Susan: *Costumes For You To Make*. Lippincott, 1971, 121 pp., $4.95.
Stahl, LeRoy: *Simplified Stagecraft Manual*. Order from N.R.P.A., 218 pp., $5.98.
Theater (no. 3328). Boy Scouts, 1968, 88 pp., 45¢, paper.
Webb: *Light From A Thousand Campfires*:
Booth, Judy: "Camp Dramatics—A Performance for Stars—Or a Creative Experience for All?" pp. 292–295.
Winslow, Barbara Brown: *Spotlight on Drama*. ACA, 1962, 26 pp., 60¢, paper. (Also in *Camping Magazine*, Apr., 1962.)

Magazine Articles

Boys' Life:
"Arms and Armor." Feb., 1973, p. 50.
"Big Top Makeup." Mar., 1970, p. 44.
Costumes." Sept., 1972, p. 57.
Stenzel, Al: "Masks From Paper Bags." Dec., 1969, p. 63.
Camping Magazine:
Gudgel, Jeanette A.: "How To Use Drama Effectively." Sept./Oct., 1968, p. 16.
Jackson, Marni: "Drama In Camp." Nov./Dec., 1967, p. 20.
Kase, Judith B.: "Informal Theatre: An Any Place, Any Time, Anybody Camp Activity." Mar., 1970, p. 16.
Telleen, Robert: "Informal Dramatics Can Provide the Means." May, 1971, p. 12.

PLAYS

Ames, Marilyn, and Jane MacDonald: *Easy Skits For Youngsters*. Order from N.R.P.A., 48 pp., $2.50, paper.
Haney, Germaine: *Five-Minute Plays For Children*. Order from N.R.P.A., 45 pp., $2.50.
Kamerman, Sylvia E.: *Dramatized Folk Tales of the World*. Plays. 1971, 575 pp., $8.95.
Murray, John: *One-Act Plays for Young Actors*. Order from N.R.P.A., 336 pp., $4.98.
Siks, Geraldine Brain: *Children's Literature For Dramatization—An Anthology*. Harper & Row, 1964, 332 pp., $7.50.
Thane, Adele: *Plays From Famous Stories and Fairy Tales*. Plays, 1967, 463 pp., $7.95.

STUNTS AND SKITS

Brings, Lawrence M.: *The Master Stunt Book*. Denison, 470 pp., $4.95.
Brings, Lawrence M.: *Rehearsal-Less Skits and Plays*. Denison, 318 pp., $4.95.
Carlson, Bernice Wells: *Do It Yourself!* Abingdon, 1952, $2.95; $1.95 paper.
Chalmers, Van, and LeRoy Stahl: *Laugh Hits*. Denison, 250 pp., $4.95.
Deason, Myrna Reeves, et al.: *The Modern Skit and Stunt Book*. Denison, 314 pp., $4.95.
Eisenberg, Larry and Helen: *Fun With Skits and Stunts*. Ass'n Press, 1953, 254 pp., $3.95.
Eisenberg, Larry and Helen: *The Handbook of Skits and stunts*. Ass'n Press, 1953, 254 pp., $3.95.
Howard, Vernon: *Pantomimes, Charades and Skits*. Sterling, 124 pp., $2.95.
Mulak: *Fun And Games*, ch. 9.
Preston, Effa E.: *Fun With Stunts*. Denison, 351 pp., $4.95.

Chapter 14

Literature in Camp

Figure 14-1 "Yes, Virginia, There Really Is a Bookworm! See Him?"

Nothing is more natural than the desire to own a useful or delightful book; to keep it on a private shelf; to mark it up if need be. The habit of buying and reading books is the clearest indication of an educated person, whether in or out of college.

—MARK VAN DOREN

Books are the treasured wealth of the world, the fit inheritance of generations and nations.

—HENRY DAVID THOREAU

A man learns only by two things: One is reading and the other is association with smarter people.

—WILL ROGERS

THE CAMP LIBRARY

Among its many and varied possessions, a camp should have a good collection of books available to both campers and staff members. First, there should be books for pure enjoyment, about Indians, animals, legends, folk tales, travel, biography, science, or almost anything under the sun that interests people. These books are for leisure reading, alone or to a group, during rest hour, under a shady tree by the brook, on rainy days, in the evening while the corn's a-popping and there's a campfire blazing merrily, or for tucking in with other duffle for use at odd moments on a trip.

There should also be an ample supply of what might be called "how-to-do-it books." To these a counselor can turn for general enlightenment or to consult a group of experts on any problem he has, be it constructing a bridge across the brook, identifying raccoon tracks, making a tent or wigwam, portaging a canoe, or braiding a lanyard. To these also a camper can turn to find a recipe for ring-tum-diddy or to learn how to improve his water skiing, waterproof his tent, or make some plaster casts.

To best serve when and where they are wanted, books should have a home base with a card file listing what is available. When the collection is well-chosen and functional, however, the books won't remain on the shelf long enough to need dusting, but will become part of a true "traveling library," available right on the job, when and where they are needed. As in any public or school library, each book should have a book pocket and a card for the borrower to sign when he takes the book out. In this way, no book will be as good as lost for the camp season because someone carelessly left it at the swimming area or tossed it into the bottom of a closet on the second day of camp. Usually one counselor, perhaps with camper help, assumes responsibility for the library.

Camps use various methods to build up their libraries, usually starting by purchasing a basic selection covering the major areas of camping and outdoor life. It is often possible to borrow others for a whole or part of the summer from the local, county, or state library. Some camps suggest in an early pre-camp letter to campers and counselors that each bring along a favorite book or two to read or exchange with others during the summer; they often leave the books behind when they go home. Parents may be urged to bring or send books instead of gooey, unneeded treats. You may want to recognize a donor by placing a book plate with his name on it in each book given. An appeal through the local press or radio may bring in worthwhile contributions. You must use discretion, however, in determining which books to make a permanent part of your camp library, for it is better to have only a few really worthwhile volumes than whole shelves of unopened books and odds and ends from other peoples' attics.

THE WONDERFUL WORLD OF LITERATURE

Far too many people of all ages have never learned to appreciate the delights of good literature. It is not only a depository of all the accumulated wisdom of mankind, but it also serves to transport the reader into a fantasy world of entertainment, excitement or sheer beauty that helps him to temporarily escape from the cares and worries of his work-a-day world. A well-stocked camp library, judiciously used, may well be the launching pad to start campers on a lifetime of enjoyment, as they come to know literature as a source of knowledge, adventure, and

(Courtesy of Camp Manito-Wish, YMCA, Boulder Junction, Wisconsin.)

fun instead of merely an irksome chore to complete for a required school assignment. Discriminative reading is a habit which may well prove contagious when a few demonstrate their enjoyment of it. The wise reader keeps a notebook and pencil handy for jotting down particularly meaningful passages or bits of information he wants to preserve for future use.

Literature fits in harmoniously with many phases of camp program, and some camps even schedule reading as one of the choices available during an activity period, especially on bad-weather days. Of course, no one should be encouraged to become a bookworm to the exclusion of the many unique outdoor opportunities camp offers, but reading provides a wonderful way to enjoy oneself in front of a blazing fireplace on a chilly, gloomy day or in a group that gathers for story telling, reading aloud, or simply curling up individually, each with a favorite book. There are literary selections that can add immeasurably to an evening program or a vesper or spiritual service or can even constitute a whole program in itself when selected and arranged by a group or committee with each person contributing a selection of his choice or something original he has written. Banquets and ceremonial occasions are scarcely complete without some form of literature. A brief, appropriate "Thought for the Day" may be posted on the bulletin board or read at a set time as before or after the morning or evening meal, at the beginning of rest hour, or in a cabin gathering just before taps.

STORYTELLING

You cannot tell a good story unless you tell it before a fire. You cannot have a complete fire unless you have a good storyteller along.

—G. STANLEY HALL

AN ANCIENT HERITAGE

The art of storytelling is probably almost as old as man, for history reveals that from the advent of speech, primitive peoples loved to cluster about one of their most esteemed and beloved members, the storyteller. From about 800 B.C., when the blind bard Homer was recounting the Iliad and Odyssey, down through the minnesingers, troubadours, and traveling minstrels, men have loved to gather to listen again to the oft-repeated tales of courage and adventure which doubtless lost nothing in the telling under the golden tongue of the skilled narrator. The American Indian likewise made much of storytelling, their legends serving to entertain, pass on traditions, and instruct the younger members of the tribe in geography, history, and biography. What golden spells they must have woven with their tales of bravery and daring!

To this day, the fat, the lean, the dark, the fair, in fact everyone, from the toddler to grandfather and grandmother, loves a well-told tale. Though television, radio, movies and comic books may have somewhat lessened the interest and ability of both "teller" and "listener" in the home and other gathering places, this is not the case in the summer camp, where "Tell us a story" is just as frequent and fervent a plea as ever. True, you may need to encourage some campers to participate the first few times since it may be an entirely new experience for them, but a few sessions will usually convert them into as avid listeners as the old-timers.

No counselor worthy of his hire will fail to have a few good stories up his sleeve for that inevitable moment when nothing else quite fills the bill, and none worth his salt will meet a request by saying, "Oh, I can't tell stories." Almost anyone can learn to be a "good" storyteller, even though not all of us may become supercolossal spinners of yarns.

THE WHY

There are numerous reasons for telling stories; here are four of the most important:

Enjoyment. Hearing a *good* story is fun and that is important enough in itself to warrant its inclusion. It is hard to think of anything we can do that could bring boys and girls more lasting happiness than implanting in them an enjoyment of good literature, for it is foolish to content oneself with trash when so much worthwhile writing exists that we could never read all of it if we devoted a lifetime to the task.

Reliving Great Moments. Who among us does not thrill to the adventures of the pioneers and the doings of such heroes as Paul Bunyan, Robin Hood, Johnny Appleseed, John Henry, or Robinson Crusoe? Campers also become much more interested in and appreciative of their camp community after learning of the customs and daily lives of the Indians and early settlers who once lived there, of famous battles which took place nearby, or the founding of the towns and cities of the area. You can usually gather such information from local historical associations or the clipping files and catalogued books of the local library. The old W.P.A. State Guide Books are also valuable sources of information and may lead to enthusiastic planning for a gypsy trip to a nearby locality to visit what the campers have just been learning about.

Figure 14-3 Our Friend, Skunkie.

Figure 14-2 Reading's Fun.

Gaining New Friends. Though we were not privileged to know Juliette Low, John Muir, Lord Baden-Powell, or Abraham Lincoln in person, we can form an intimate acquaintance with them through the storyteller. What child can fail to develop a kinder feeling toward animals as he sees them through the eyes of Albert Payson Terhune, Ernest Thompson Seton or Uncle Remus?

Moral and Character Values. Since youth is the age of hero worship, there is no better way to teach that "Virtue has its own reward" and "Crime does not pay" than through the stories of the great and good of all ages. Fortunately, this can come about in a perfectly painless way if we avoid sticky sentimentality and over-moralizing which may create resentment and rebellion instead of the good qualities we want to develop.

THE WHEN AND WHERE

Almost any time can be "story time" but there are occasions which literally seem to beg for a story. A campfire, a lovely hilltop at sunset, or a peaceful dell are "naturals" and a circle of blanket-rolled listeners under a starlit sky forms a perfect setting for studying the stars and retelling the same star myths heard by Indian, Greek, and Roman boys and girls many centuries ago. A rainy day seems less dreary when there's an open fireplace and an exciting tale. Camp disappointments and minor tragedies fade under the spell of a Kipling adventure and dishwashing and other chores seem almost to do themselves when there's a good yarn in the spinning. A well-chosen story will often keep restless youngsters relaxed during the rest hour or put them in a mood for going to sleep quickly at night. Here, also, a counselor may find a happy way to resolve unsocial attitudes or problems he may have detected in his cabin. Storytelling also provides pleasant entertainment for restless infirmary inhabitants.

THE WHO

Though everyone likes to hear stories, not everyone likes the same story, for the teenager is bored beyond words with the adventures of Billie Goat Gruff or Jimmie the Jumping Frog; consequently, it is best to have listeners of approximately the same age. If there are age differences, select a story appropriate for the older ones in the group, for being "talked down to" is particularly obnoxious to everyone.

All should understand from the very start that there is to be no disturbance of any sort until the story is finished; therefore, "it's all right to sit with your pal as long as you don't bother anyone and you must save any questions and comments until the story is finished." Encourage campers who "don't like stories" to sample them a few times. Then be sure to choose appropriate ones and tell them well; it's a good bet that few will fail to come back for more.

THE WHAT

There are a few sure-fire stories which appeal to almost everyone but, in general, "the group dictates the story" and what would be adored by one assemblage may fall perfectly flat with another. You must learn to size up your group and pick your story for *them*. Suit it to their general intelligence, background, and personalities.

Boys and girls ordinarily like the same stories until they are about ten, when boys usually begin to prefer real he-man stories and disdain "kid" or "sissy stuff." Tales of Indians, cowboys, pioneers, pirates, airplanes, sports, and science now appeal. In general, girls are not quite so exclusive and still enjoy many of the stories they previously liked as well as some of those now chosen by boys. Small children, six to ten, like stories containing alliteration and nonsensical jingles, as well as those about animals and people like those they know. They are particularly fond of the ludicrous and illogical, such as "Corabelle Cow Who Goes Shopping on Roller Skates" or "Dulcimer Duck Who Carries a Pink Silk Umbrella and Wears Green Spats When She Goes to the Beach." They revel in fantasy and make-believe and so are particularly fond of folk tales, fairy tales and such. They especially like to hear stories a counselor has "spun out" of his imagination and which involve the antics of such characters as Wooly, the caterpillar, Honey, the bear or Porky, the porcupine.

Older children, 10 to 14, demand something which challenges their developing judgments a bit more. They prefer to draw their own morals and conclusions from well-constructed but more subtle plots. Stories of Indians, animals, and legendary heroes still interest them.

Still older campers are even more discriminating and present a real challenge to the storyteller, for their tastes are now approaching, but not yet quite ready for, adult literature. Youngsters of all ages have a good sense of humor, though what strikes them as funny may seem silly or flat to adults and vice versa.

For the novice at choosing stories, many lists are available which classify stories according to type and age appeal; you will find some in the sources given at the end of the chapter. Another safe way to pick a story is to recall one of your own childhood favorites, and you can add to your collection by noting stories which would be good for telling as you read for your own pleasure.

You may tell several very brief stories at one sitting, particularly if they vary in style and subject matter but a single long story may be enough, since the story period should never exceed 20 to 30 minutes for small children and 45 to 60 minutes for older ones. An expert can successfully condense a book or long story but it is risky business for an amateur; it is better for him to divide it into parts to tell in successive sittings like a serial, ending each at a natural break which temporarily satisfies his listeners, yet leaves them curious about what will happen next. Recall how Scheherazade prolonged her life 1001 nights as she kept her fickle husband, Sultan Schariar, entranced and anxious to find out what would happen next as she purposely abandoned her story each night at some extremely exciting spot. That is really storytelling! Books, long stories, or stories depending on the style of the author for their effectiveness are more successfully read than told. To read a story effectively, however, you should so familiarize yourself with it that you know it well enough to read with real expression, using appropriate gestures, and frequently glancing up at your listeners.

Not every story that makes good reading is equally good for telling. Rapidly moving action stories without long descriptions of people or situations are usually best. Despite popular opinion to the contrary, children enjoy well-chosen poetry, particularly that

Figure 14–4 Reading To Work By.

which has been written especially for them. The Bible, especially some of the versions presented in modern, everyday language, is an excellent source of good stories that are beautifully written and full of action and general interest. In keeping with the spirit of camping, it is well to choose from the vast quantity of material pertaining to the out-of-doors, animals, tales of high adventure and our natural heritage and the people responsible for preserving it. Stories involving such positive attributes as love, beauty, wholesomeness, honesty, and altruism are especially appropriate.

The inevitable cry, "Tell us a ghost story," sometimes poses a problem, for there are bound to be some campers in almost any group who want nothing else. Certainly no one can question the mental indigestion possible from a steady diet of gruesomeness and horror and it may prove seriously upsetting to more sensitive campers. There are *some good* ghost and mystery stories which may be used to quench the thirst for the mysterious and supernatural. The best procedure to use with those who clamor for nothing else may be to gradually wean them away by a persistent diet of carefully chosen selections with only an occasional *good* ghost story interspersed. You should, of course, never tell scary or exceedingly exciting stories just before bedtime. Omit off-color stories and those which are overly sentimental or in poor taste, especially stories which tend to belittle or degrade occupations, races, or creeds.

THE HOW

After you have selected your story, read it carefully for general plot and action and decide upon the best method of presentation. Then read it again several times, even as many as 10 or 15, until you have almost memorized it, for there is much more danger of failing through not knowing your story well than of going "stale" through knowing it too well. Nothing is so disconcerting to listeners as a faltering "er" interjected to give you time to recall what comes next or an "Oh, I forgot to tell you," as you go back to insert something you should have told five minutes before. Practice telling the story to yourself until you are positive of every character and bit of action.

When the fateful moment arrives, gather your group of not more than 25 to 30 about you. See that all are seated comfortably to minimize squirming and wiggling, and seat yourself where all can see and hear you clearly; a semicircle is usually best. Place yourself in the firelight or suspend a lantern on a post or tree so that all can clearly see your facial expressions and gestures. Many people lip read without realizing it and so find it difficult to understand when they cannot see your face.

If the setting is around an open fire, use hardwood and build it sufficiently early to let it die down to coals. Appoint one person to inconspicuously take charge of it and keep it going steadily, for a spluttery, smoky fire or one throwing out alarming sparks provides too much competition for any storyteller.

If your listeners are excited or full of pent-up energy, try playing a quiet game or two to put them in an attentive

Figure 14-5 Telling a Whopper!

frame of mind. Arouse interest by pausing a moment before you begin and choose a first sentence which compels immediate attention and curiosity as to what will follow.

Since your voice is the center of attention, make it pleasant, enunciate clearly, and avoid mumbling. Keep your tone low to demand close attention yet loud enough to be audible to those on the outskirts; check by asking if they can hear you. Talking too loudly is irritating and tends to encourage listeners to be restless or to create disturbances. Avoid straining your voice, shouting, or using poorly chosen words and trite phrases.

Vary your tone and rate of speed, for a sing-song manner is monotonous and tends to lull listeners to sleep. Get excited when the story calls for it, and talk in a tired or dispirited tone if that best expresses the mood of the action or character in the story. Appreciate the value of a pause in arousing anticipation. Elicit active participation from your listeners by asking them to guess "what will happen next" or "what would *you* do in this situation." Pick a story you thoroughly enjoy and let yourself get involved in it until you actually feel you are a part of it. Your enthusiasm, facial expressions, and gestures then come naturally and make it much more enjoyable for your listeners. Change your voice or turn your head to indicate a change in characters and pause subtly for effect or change your timing to suit the action of the story. Mimicry and dialect, where indicated, add much if you can do them without sounding stilted or forced. Keep your story moving, for a dragging pace kills interest. Avoid over-dramatizing and such mannerisms as dandling something in your hands or slicking down your hair, for they divert attention from the story to you. You may substitute names of campers for those of the characters in the story to make it seem more real to them.

Look at your listeners and talk to *them* instead of mumbling down your shirt collar. Watch their faces for reactions, making a mental note for future use of those techniques which are most effective. If one or two of your audience seem inattentive, look at them and talk directly to them to bring them back into the fold. Quell disturbers with a sharp glance.

A good storyteller paints a vivid mental picture of what is happening in the story and of the locality and surroundings in which the action takes place. He must deal, therefore, in what is already familiar to his listeners or must take time to familiarize them with what he is talking about. If a listener is to actually "feel" the story and enjoy it to the utmost, he must be drawn into the action, visualizing in his mind's eye each character and the environments in which the action occurs. Add realism by dressing in costume, using simple props, or having someone cued to blow a bugle, give an Indian war whoop, or beat a tom-tom at the appropriate time. Where locations and lay-outs are important, draw a map in the dirt, use a crayon on a large piece of wrapping paper, or use cut-outs from construction paper on a flannel board to show the locations of the homes of the characters and other scenes.

If your story has a moral, do not overstress it; ask your listeners to point it out or let each draw his own conclusions. When you reach the climax, end the story quickly. If they ask, "Is it true?" answer them honestly. Pause for a moment before dismissing the group or end with an appropriate "Thought for the Day," selected by you or your campers.

Encourage your campers to read for themselves by telling or reading well-chosen excerpts from a book and suggesting that it is available for those who want to read more of it. It is often enjoyable to read or tell a long story to a small group, setting aside a certain time for it each day. Each member of the group can take a turn at telling or reading it, and the group may also want to act the story out. It is good fun, too, for the group to write a story or play. Another too-seldom appreciated activity is the reading of a play by a group, with each member reading a part and perhaps following the stage directions for it.

There is no secret formula for telling stories; each good storyteller develops his own techniques. Observe skilled performers and practice whenever you can, for you learn from each experience. You will find that the technique of telling stories is like a piece of good leather; it improves with use.

CHORAL READING

This activity was popular in the past and is well worth reviving. It consists of reciting in unison poetry, Bible quotations, stories, or other types of literature. Group the voices according to pitch and volume and arrange the performers in a semicircle around the leader who gives inconspicuous signals for starting, stopping, emphasis, pauses, and such. Participants should know the selection well enough to be able to pay close attention to the leader. Add variety by assigning solo parts or by having groups recite alternately, as in antiphonal singing. Poems which the group enjoys and which swing along with marked rhythm and are full of repetition are most effective. Choral reading is particularly good for devotions or a campfire program.

CREATIVE WRITING

WRITING CREATIVELY

I would rather be the author of one original thought than conqueror of a hundred battles.

—W. B. CLULOW

To be creative you must take some old material and fashion it, through your own imagination and personality, into an entirely new and unique product. If you would foster creative work in others, you must use a cautious and sensitive touch, for dictatorial methods and too many unwanted suggestions soon crush the spark of originality. Your role as a counselor is one of encouraging, giving aid where needed and, in general, setting the yeast which, in the hands of the camper, will foam and bubble over into a true creative product. Hammett and Musselman* emphasize that writing is simply putting words together to show how you think and feel and that there are just three steps to it: (1) see it, (2) feel it, (3) write it down. Instead of talking, you are writing, so put it down just as if you were saying it.

Campers are often inclined to dismiss with a shrug the suggestion that they compose a poem or do a piece of creative writing, for some of them have been discouraged by insistence in school upon such mechanical details as neatness, legibility, and exact diction, spelling, and punctuation. Though these things are admittedly important, original thought and self-expression are the paramount objectives in creative work. Do not expect youngsters to attain adult standards, though, as always, they should do their best. Mrs. Cumming tells of a seven-year-old who, after insisting that he could not write anything, chattered on in the following soliloquy which she, unknown to him, recorded as he talked.

I hear echoes when I walk around hiking.
All the pretty voices I hear in places I go.
I see all the pretty flowers around the lake,
    in the forest and the mountainsides.
You have a good time in camp.
I wish I could stay at camp a long time,
And see all the pretty trees around with
    pretty leaves on them,

*Hammett and Musselman: *The Camp Program Book*, Ass'n Press, 1951.

(Courtesy of Star Lake Camp, Bloomingdale, New Jersey.)

And see the tadpoles in the lake.
I have a good time going in swimming, and have a good time horseback riding.
All these things I have fun doing.
I like the cute birds in the trees;
They whistle at me, and I whistle at them.
The bees are funny things;
They sting some children, but not me.
Sometimes they sting me!
There are very funny things around camp.
Some voices sound hummy, and people act very funny sometimes.
The mountainside sometimes just sings by itself, and no one else makes a noise.
The falls make a pretty noise;
There are rocks at the bottom of the falls.
Then you sit down and think about it, and you want to write a poem about it.*

Encourage every camper to jot down his thoughts, for his own benefit if not for sharing with others, and give him recognition by posting an especially good achievement on the bulletin board, reading it at the campfire, or publishing it in the camp newspaper. Encourage him to write poems, plays, pageants, diaries, letters, and accounts of things seen and done, and to illustrate them with simple line drawings.

*Conversation of Charles Mitchell, recorded by Mrs. Ely C. Cumming of Mary Gwynn's Camp, Brevard, North Carolina.

THE CAMP PAPER

It is advantageous to have a camp paper, for it (1) serves to encourage and recognize creative writing; (2) keeps campers and staff, as well as parents and friends, informed of doings of the whole camp; (3) fosters good camp morale; and (4) serves as a souvenir to recall many pleasant memories of the summer.

Camp papers vary greatly in fre-

Figure 14-6 "What'll I Write?"

quency of publication. Some camps put out a page or two every day, while others go to the opposite extreme and publish only one or two papers during the entire summer, with an occasional "extra" to celebrate some special camp event. A few camps print their papers but most mimeograph them and this process gives satisfaction to many campers, since many different talents are needed to write and edit copy, make up the dummy, do the artwork, type, cut stencils, run off the pages, and assemble and staple them. Colored inks and paper add variety and allow artistic expression. Some camps type only one copy which is read at a campfire or other gathering, but most supply each camper with a copy to send home or place among his souvenirs.

The staff is usually assisted by an interested counselor with an appointed or elected camper editor-in-chief. Other staff writers act as reporters for units or activities such as waterfront, riding, riflery, campcraft, and arts and crafts. Encourage those not officially on the staff to submit contributions.

Prepare and cut the stencils for materials which do not need to be current and run them off ahead of time to minimize inaccuracies, sloppy appearance, and last-minute rush. Hold a staff meeting soon after the issue appears to make a critical evaluation and plan for the next issue. Follow up by posting written assignments for future issues and carry on the project in a business-like fashion appropriate to a juvenile newspaper office. Include poems, jokes, news flashes, honor achievements, stories, editorials, special features, puzzles, interviews, gossip columns, or other items as you and the campers wish.

Make it a point to include each camper's name frequently in some connection for nearly everyone likes to see his name in print. Use "by-lines" for those who write good articles; this stimulates future contributions and gives recognition where it is due.

Keep the staff representative of the whole camp instead of letting it fall under the control of a little clique. Wholesome, kindly humor adds immeasurably, but anything which might hurt or serve as a personal "axe to grind" is strictly taboo. Although working on the camp paper is a very worthwhile activity, again, do not encourage campers to become so engrossed in it that they fail to take advantage of the wonderful opportunity for outdoor living available only in camp.

THE CAMP LOG

The Camp Log is a sort of camp annual put out at the end of the summer. You may mimeograph or otherwise reproduce it, or it may be in the form of a scrapbook, compiled by a central staff or by each individual on his own. In it go photographs, programs, invitations, pressed flowers or leaves, place cards, a few pages for autographed messages, poems read at special events, or almost anything else he wants to take home to show friends and relatives and to look over in future years. The cover may range from a simple mimeographed sheet to a leather or wooden portfolio form, constructed and decorated in the arts and crafts shop.

ADDITIONAL READINGS

(For an explanation of abbreviations and abbreviated forms, see page 25.)

Choral Reading

Breeding, Mrs. Lonnie H.: *Let's Play a Story.* Order from N.R.P.A., 133 pp., $3.95.

Brown, Helen A., and Harry J. Heltman (Eds.): *Choral Readings for Teenage Worship and Inspiration.* Westminster, 1959, $1.

Brown-Azarowicz, Marjorie: *A Handbook of Creative Choral Speaking.* Burgess, 1970, $3.95.

Enfield, Gertrude: *Verse Choir Technique.* Drama Bookshop, $2.

Gullan, Marjorie: *Speech Choir.* Harper & Row, 1937, $8.75.

Lists of Books Recommended for Children

American Library *Booklist.*

Good and Inexpensive Books for Children. Childhood Education International, 3615 Wisconsin Ave., N.W., Washington, D.C. 20016, $2.

Library Journal.

Reader's Choice Catalogue. Scholastic Book Service, free.

Reading (No. 3393). Boy Scouts, 1965, 32 pp., 45¢, paper.

Recommended Paperbacks. Horn Books, Inc., 585 Boylston Street, Boston, Mass. 02116, 30¢.

School Library Journal.

Materials for Reading or Telling

Arbuthnot, May H. (Compiler): *The Arbuthnot Anthology of Children's Literature.* Scott Foresman, 1961.

Berg, Jean Horton: *Mr. Koonan's Bargain.* Nautilus, 1971, 48 pp., $3.95. (ages 6–10)

Botkin, B. A.: *A Treasury of New England Folklore.* Crown, 1965, $7.50.

Carrighar, Sally: *One Day on Beetle Rock.* Knopf, 1944, 196 pp., $5.95.

Carrighar, Sally: *One Day at Teton Marsh.* Ballantine, 220 pp., 95¢, paper.

Cathon, Laura, and Thusnelda Schmidt (Compilers): *Perhaps and Perchance Tales of Nature.* Abingdon, 1962, 260 pp., $3.50.

Chase, Richard: *American Folk Tales.* Dover, 1971, $2, paper.

Chase, Richard: *Grandfather Tales.* Houghton Mifflin, 1948, $5.50.

Chase, Richard: *The Jack Tales.* Houghton Mifflin, 1943, $4.95.

Child, George G.: *Child's Book of Folk Lore.* Dial, $4.50.

De Angeli, Marguerite: *Bright April.* Doubleday, 1946, $3.50.

De La Mare, Walter: *Animal Stories.* Scribner's, 1940, 420 pp., $5.95.

Dorson, Richard M.: *Buying the Wind.* U. of Chicago, 1964, 573 pp., $8.95.

Feurlicht, Roberta Strauss: *The Legends of Paul Bunyan.* Macmillan, 1966, $3.95.

Fischbach, Julius: *Story Sermons for Boys and Girls.* Abingdon, 1947, 192 pp., 95¢, paper.

Foster, Laura Louise: *Keer-Las, The Life Story of a Young Wood Duck.* Naturegraph, 1965, 80 pp., $3.50; $1.50, paper.

Gagliardo, Ruth: *Let's Read Aloud.* Lippincott, 1962, 256 pp., $5.95.

George, Jean: *My Side of the Mountain.* Scholastic Book Service, 1959, 208 pp., 75¢, paper.

Grahame, Kenneth: *The Wind in the Willows.* Scribner's, 1953, $1.45; Dell, 95¢, paper.

Gruenberg, Sidonie M. (Ed.): *Favorite Stories Old and New.* Doubleday, rev.

Harris, Joel Chandler: *Uncle Remus: His Songs and His Sayings.* Grosset & Dunlap, $2.95.

Hazeltine, Alice I.: *Hero Tales From Many Lands.* Abingdon, 1961, $5.95.

Hollowell, Lillian (Ed.): *A Book of Children's Literature.* Holt, Rinehart, 1966.

Johnson, Edna, Carie Scott, and Evelyn R. Sickels: *Anthology of Children's Literature.* Houghton Mifflin, 1970, $19.95.

Kane, Henry B.: *The Tale of a Meadow.* Knopf, 1959, 110 pp., $4.79.

Kane, Henry B.: *The Tale of a Pond.* Knopf, 1960, 110 pp., $3.50.

Kane, Henry B.: *The Tale of a Wood.* Knopf, 1962, 120 pp., $3.50.

Kipling, Rudyard: *The Jungle Books.* Doubleday, 1964, $3.75; Signet, 50¢, paper.

Kipling, Rudyard: *Just So Stories.* Doubleday, 1952, $3.25.

Lang, Andrew (Ed.): *The Red Book of Animal Stories.* Tuttle, 1972, $3.25, paper.

Leach, Marie: *The Rainbow Book of American Folk Tales and Legends.* World, 1958, 319 pp., $7.71.

Maxwell, Gavin: *A Ring of Bright Water.* Dutton, 1961, $6.95. (grades 8–9)

Morrow, Betty: *See Up the Mountain.* Harper & Row, 1958, 47 pp., $3.95. (ages 8–10)

Murphy, Robert: *The Pond.* Dutton, 1964, $5.50; Avon, 60¢, paper.

North, Sterling: *Rascal.* Dutton, 1963, 189 pp., $4.50.

O'Dell, Scott: *Island of the Blue Dolphins.* Houghton Mifflin, 1960, 184 pp., $3.95, paper.
Olson, Sigurd F.: *Runes of the North.* Knopf, 1963, 255 pp., $5.95.
Olson, Sigurd F.: *The Singing Wilderness.* Knopf, 1956, 245 pp., $5.95.
Parnall, Peter: *The Great Fish.* Doubleday, 1973, $3.50.
Parnall, Peter: *The Mountain.* Doubleday, 1971, $4.50.
Rawlings, Marjorie Kinnan: *The Yearling.* Scribner's, 1939, $2.45, paper.
Reynolds, Barbara Leonard: *Pepper.* Scribner's, 1952, $2.58.
Rush, William Marshall: *Duff: The Story of a Bear.* McKay, 1950, 149 pp., $3.50. (ages 11–14)
Salten, Felix: *Bambi.* Grosset & Dunlap, 1929, 293 pp., 75¢, paper.
Seredy, Kate: *The White Stag.* Viking, 1937, $3.95.
Seton, Ernest Thompson: *The Biography of a Grizzly.* Grosset & Dunlap, 1958, 167 pp., $1.95.
Seton, Ernest Thompson: *Two Little Savages.* Dover, 1903, 206 pp., $2.50, paper.
Seton, Ernest Thompson: *Wild Animals I Have Known.* Scribner's, $3.63.
Shephard, Esther: *Paul Bunyan.* Harcourt, 1941, $4.50.
Simley, Anne: *Folk Tales To Tell or Read Aloud.* Burgess, 1963, Vol. II, 112 pp., $2.75.
Smith, Helen R. (Ed.): *Laughing Matter.* Scribner's, 1949, 166 pp., $2.95.
Stanger, Margaret A.: *That Quail, Robert.* Fawcett, 1966, 60¢, paper.
Viereck, Phillip: *The Summer I Was Lost.* Day, 1965, $4.50.
Wadsworth, Wallace: *Paul Bunyan and His Great Blue Ox.* Doubleday, 1964, $4.50. (ages up to 12)
Ward, Jane Shaw: *Tajar Tales.* Order from ACA, rev. 1967, 36 pp., $1, paper.
Webb, Kenneth and Susan: *The Boy Who Could Sleep When the Wind Blew.* ACA, 1963, 51 pp., $1, paper.
White, E.B.: *Charlotte's Web.* Dell, 1952, 184 pp., 95¢, paper.

Miscellaneous

Kujoth: *The Recreation Program Guide,* pp. 188–197. (Journalism)
Walter, Nina Willis: *Let Them Write Poetry.* Holt, Rinehart, 1962, 179 pp., $3.40, paper.

Poetry

Arbuthnot, May Hill: *Time for Poetry.* Scott Foresman, rev., 1965, 228 pp., $5.25.
Edgar, Mary S.: *Once There Was a Camper.* Welch, 222 Evans Ave., Toronto 18, Ontario, 1970, 48 pp., $1.75, paper.
Fisher, Aileen: *In the Middle of the Night.* Crowell, 1965, 40 pp., $3.95.
Frost, Frances: *The Little Naturalist.* McGraw-Hill, 1959, 47 pp., $2.96.
Frost, Robert: *You Come Too.* Holt, Rinehart, 1959, 94 pp., $4.50.
Gregory, Horace, and Marya Zaturenska: *The Crystal Cabinet.* Holt, Rinehart, 1962, 225 pp., $3.50.
Hughes, Rosalind: *Let's Enjoy Poetry.* Houghton Mifflin, 1958, 278 pp., $6.20. (ages 7–9)
McDonald, Gerald D.: *A Way of Knowing: A Collection of Poems for Boys.* Crowell, 1959, 288 pp., $4.95. (ages 12 and up)
Ward, Herman M. (Ed.): *Poems for Pleasure.* Hill and Wang, 1963, 137 pp., $3; $1.25, paper.

Storytelling

Anderson, Paul S.: *Storytelling With a Flannel Board, (Books One and Two.)* Order from N.R.P.A., 260 pp., $6.95, each.
Corbin: *Recreation Leadership,* ch. 21. (Contains lists of materials to use.)
Cundiff, Ruby Ethel, and Barbara Webb: *Story Telling For You.* Kent State U. Press, 1957, 103 pp., $2.
Dorson, Richard M.: *American Folklore.* U. of Chicago, 1959, $8.50; $2.95, paper.
Goodreds, V.S.: *Good Stories and How To Tell Them.* Order from N.R.P.A., 281 pp., $4.95.
Kujoth: *The Recreation Program Guide,* pp. 374–380.
Sawyer, Ruth: *The Way of the Storyteller.* Viking, rev., 1962, $1.85, paper.
Shedlock, M. L.: *The Art of the Story-Teller.* Dover, 1951, 320 pp., $2.50, paper.
Smith, Helen Reagan: *Basic Story Technique.* U. of Oklahoma, 1967, 253 pp., $5.95.
Tooze, Ruth: *Story Telling.* Prentice-Hall, 1959, 268 pp., $7.50.
Webb: *Light From A Thousand Campfires:*
Goellner, William A.: "Revive the Art of Storytelling," p. 300.

Magazine Articles

Camping Magazine:
Brown, Ruth: "What Would Camp Be Without Books," Jan., 1972, p. 16.
MacRae, Roderick: "Johnny and the Goblins," May, 1964, p. 11.

Chapter 15

Arts and Crafts

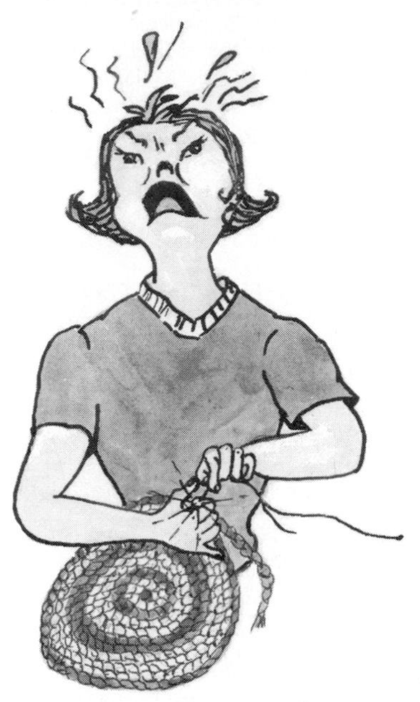

Figure 15-1 Ouch!!!

> One is never tired of painting because you have to set down, not what you knew already, but what you have just discovered. There is a continual creation out of nothing going on.
>
> —WILLIAM HAZLITT (1821)

THE CAMP PROGRAM

GENERAL CHARACTERISTICS

Camps now recognize the importance of their arts and crafts program, for it not only broadens their program as a whole but also makes unique contributions toward the accomplishment of major camp objectives. The camp program need not and should not duplicate the child's city crafts activities, which are often carried on in an elaborately equipped room under the direction of a highly trained specialist and are sometimes geared mainly to those of unusual talent and interest. Instead, it should include something for everyone, from the gifted to those who claim to be too inartistic to even draw a straight line. There are many possibilities, including such utilitarian activities as repairing or making your own camping equipment or recycling scrap lumber by building tables, chairs, shelves, and other comforts for your living quarters and decorating them to suit your own particular tastes and personality. There are a multitude of things to do, ranging from making souvenirs to wear, take home, or give as gifts to activities carried on just because of the satisfaction creating something brings or because you find the end results interesting or beautiful.

Good programs can be conducted without any special Crafts Center at all, but it is more common to have some sort of central area with at least one staff member especially trained and skilled in this field who acts as consultant or instructor. The center may be quite simple, with only a well-lighted room, comfortable chairs, tables, workbenches and improvised storage cabinets, bins and shelves, and a few simple tools and raw materials. Some camps, however, feature elaborate quarters with a relatively expensive and complete outlay of tools and raw materials.

Programs are conducted in a variety of ways. In a more formal programming setup, each living unit is scheduled to come to the Crafts Center at a designated time, or individuals may choose to come during a regular activity period or in their free time. In informal programming, living units may be supplied with basic materials and have the privilege of checking out special tools and materials to work with in their living units. The Arts and Crafts Center is kept open for those who want to work there with the staff either being present there to give help and advice or available on call wherever they are needed. This latter arrangement makes sense, since many activities, such as whittling a lapel pin or name tag or sandpapering and waxing a piece of driftwood, require painstaking, time-consuming work which can be done at odd moments in living quarters, during stops along the trail, or while attending story hour, taking part in a cabin discussion, or as the soup is simmering over the fire.

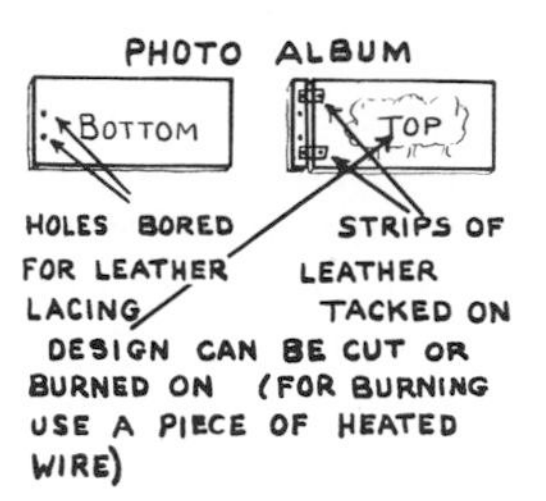

Figure 15-2 A Photograph Album.

Activities carried on with native materials, gathered and prepared on the camp site, constitute what is called an *indigenous* program, as distinguished from the type of program in which the materials are purchased from a supply house in a prepared or semi-prepared state. The participant in an indigenous program may supplement his native findings with odds and ends of waste materials, such as bottle caps, old purses, boxes, and such, as well as inexpensive things readily available at neighborhood stores such as pipe cleaners, paste, glue, crayons, and cord. An indigenous program is in line with the "do-it-yourself" idea of modern camps and is the one usually practiced in the better camps.

AN INDIGENOUS PROGRAM

Like all phases of camp program, arts and crafts should supplement rather than duplicate the camper's winter activities by utilizing to the fullest the uniqueness of the camp setting and the raw materials and inspiration from nature available there. This pretty much rules out such activities as craft strip braiding or fitting part A into B in an already prepared model where the youngster merely follows someone else's ideas instead of using his own imagination and creativeness to the utmost to give him the satisfaction of producing something strictly his own with the ideas coming out of *his* head, carried on by *his* hands, with materials *he* has gathered and prepared.

ADVANTAGES OF AN INDIGENOUS PROGRAM

Nearly everyone agrees that one of the prime objectives of the summer camp should be to better acquaint campers with and make them more appreciative of nature, but past efforts in this direction have often been conducted in such bookish, uninteresting ways that the very name "nature study" or "nature program" makes a youngster shudder. However, when he becomes absorbed in searching for materials to weave into a basket for his mother, plants or flowers to provide natural dyes for the grass mat he has woven for Aunt Nell, or wood suitable to cut and sand into a tie rack for dad or a photograph album for grandma, he almost unconsciously learns a great deal about nature but in a completely absorbing and enjoyable way.

Not only must he become sharp-eyed and alert to locate and recognize possibilities, but he must also acquire skill in judging textures and qualities as he surveys his assembled assortment and decides how best to use it. This develops his true creative ability, and he acquires manual skill as well as hand-eye coordination as he gathers, prepares, and constructs what his mind has pictured.

Such a broad program as we have in mind exposes him to a whole panorama of possibilities and encourages him to dabble in many activities and thus learn where his true abilities and preferences lie. He is free to explore and experiment as much as he likes, expanding his knowledge of nature and the arts as he goes. This not only provides present enjoyment but may also lead to a vocation or a lifelong hobby so desperately needed in our modern culture to counteract tension and boredom and solve the problem of what to do with our ever-increasing free time. An additional advantage is that he learns the relative unimportance of money in achieving true relaxation and entertainment, for indigenous materials are free and the other necessary ingredients cost but little.

Many projects require patience and "stick-to-it-iveness" to carry them through to completion, and these are certainly desirable qualities to cultivate. The camper also learns to make judgments and solve problems, for these are necessary when deciding what to use and how to use it.

Figure 15–3 Painting from Nature.

CONDUCTING THE PROGRAM

As a general counselor, you will want to work with your campers in this area as in all other phases of their program. You, too, will learn how much fun it is and will profit from it just as much as they. In searching for the beautiful in color and design, there is no more promising source than nature. However, many of us have never learned to recognize these things when we see them. A good way to start off with campers is to take them on an observation tour, proceeding slowly and pausing at likely spots so each camper can look about and point out interesting things he sees, such as pleasing contrasts and blendings of colors, graceful curves and shapes found in grasses, trees, or shrubs, the contours of hills, valleys, and water lines, the movements, formations, and coloring of clouds, and the speed and grace of animal, bird, and insect movements as each creature demonstrates how his individual physical makeup, even down to his protective coloring, fits him for his particular mode of life and natural habitat. With practice, you will develop a true awareness and sensitivity, so that whenever you feel yourself going stale again, you can return to native haunts, varying the type of terrain and season to "recharge your battery" and acquire renewed enthusiasm. Take along a sketch pad or notebook to jot down details you want to recall.

Encourage each camper to be original in his work and to reproduce what *he* sees as it appears to *him* rather than copying from his neighbor or a book. However, don't minimize the importance of books and examples of all sorts, for they often point up possibilities, furnish inspiration, and enable the beginner to profit by the experience of others to save time and avoid disappointment and wasted materials. They can also help him to learn such things as the essentials of design, the choice and use of tools, and the possibilities of various media in constructing and finishing products.

In presenting new information, a new technique, or the use of a new medium, such as papier mâché or tincancraft, it is best to demonstrate by using the actual materials as you explain what you are doing and why.

If campers tend to imitate rather than use a creative approach, put your point across tactfully by commenting favorably so others can hear when you find someone who is being original and creative and weight these qualities heavily when giving ratings or choosing items for display.

You will need to use a great deal of discretion in determining just how much help to give an individual and when and how to give it. Some prefer to be left pretty much alone and are frustrated and irritated when someone stands over them, giving unsought suggestions and advice. Others may lean on you too much to the detriment of their own creativeness and originality.

The type of program we are advocating is indeed time consuming, and an occasional camper may become so engrossed in a project that he is reluctant to lay it aside to participate in other phases of camp life. Indeed, why should he have to, if your camp program is flexible and truly geared to meet individual camper needs and preferences as long as his failure to show doesn't adversely affect others or interfere with general camp routines or policies? Of course, it would be undesirable to have him become so involved that he becomes uninterested in other things.

CARRYING ON THE PROGRAM

COLLECTING MATERIALS

Almost every camp site has a wealth of possible materials if you are able to recognize them. Therefore, one of your first tasks may well be to make a general survey to learn what your particular locale offers.

When you are ready to start out with your campers to collect materials, equip each with a good-sized bag to carry back his "haul." Let each gather anything he sees that he feels may be useful as long as he does not violate the principles of good conservation. This means that he must never needlessly destroy or damage any living thing, especially if it would deplete the supply so that not enough remains to quickly replenish it. Only a selfish, unthinking individual would take nature's creations when it would deprive those following of their rightful heritage. To prevent this, campers sometimes plant and cultivate a continuing supply of such treasured natural materials as honeysuckle and Virginia creeper for basket weaving and seeds or nuts for making jewelry, model animals, and such. Before starting out on your expedition, make sure that everyone knows how to recognize and avoid such hazards as poison ivy, oak, and sumac.

Here are examples of some native materials which may prove useful:

Native clay
Seashells

Fallen birch or other bark

Cattails
Bones
Bird feathers
Dead animal skins and fur
Fish scales
Acorns
Fungus
Nuts
Horns
Corn husks
Hickory and other nuts
Moss
Sand
Gourds
Growths of bamboo
Ears of corn
Weeds and interesting grasses
Interesting seeds
Discarded birds' eggshells
Pine cones and needles
Lichen
Dried pods

Vary the types of locale you visit, because, be it deep woods, swampy territory, a meadow, the beach, or a river bank, each area offers unique natural materials.

Alert both staff and campers to watch for and save such commonly discarded things as:

Straws
Pocketbooks
Chicken wish-bones (fine for making bow-legged cowboys)
Cans and can lids
String
Old boards
Moccasins
Linoleum or rugs
Corks
Paper cups
Oilcloth
Bits of cardboard
Old inner tubes
Bags and sacks
Milk bottle caps and cartons
Discarded tooth-brushes
Corrugated card-board
Empty cereal boxes and other cartons
Cellophane wrappings
Egg cartons
Sewing scraps
Bottles, (glass or plastic)
Discarded clothing
Cord and rope
Feathers
Old drapes and sheets
Old furniture
Newspapers
Coat hangers and odd bits of wire
Mop and broom handles
Buttons
Magazines
Spools
Lollypop and ice cream sticks
Coconut shells
Bottle caps
Old felt hats
Toothpicks
Aluminum foil
Eggshells

Supplement the above with such readily available supplies as:

Pins
Pipe cleaners
Stapler and staples
Rubber bands

(Courtesy of Barbara Ellen Joy and Marjorie Camp.)

Inks
Shellac
Enamels
Needles
Wallpaper samples
Unshelled peanuts
Wax crayons
Construction paper
Marking pens
Cellophane tape
Compass
Brayer
Craft foam (Styrofoam, etc.)
Oil paints
Gumdrops
Popcorn
Thread
Colored thumb-tacks
Poster paints
Ribbon
Dowel sticks
Paper clips
Brushes
Various types of paper
Paste and glue
Rubber cement
Colored toothpicks

Trips to nearby factories will often yield waste scraps of leather, suede, cotton and other cloth, plastic, linoleum, metal, rubber, and wood. Stores, salesmen, or factories will sometimes donate outdated samples or sample books.

Let each individual use what he has gathered or put everything together for common use, sorting it into piles of related items and placing them on shelves or in boxes and bins where all can see what is available. Alert everyone to save useful scrap materials and take frequent forays into the wilds to find what new things the advancing season or another terrain will provide. This will keep your store of raw materials growing in both amount and variety.

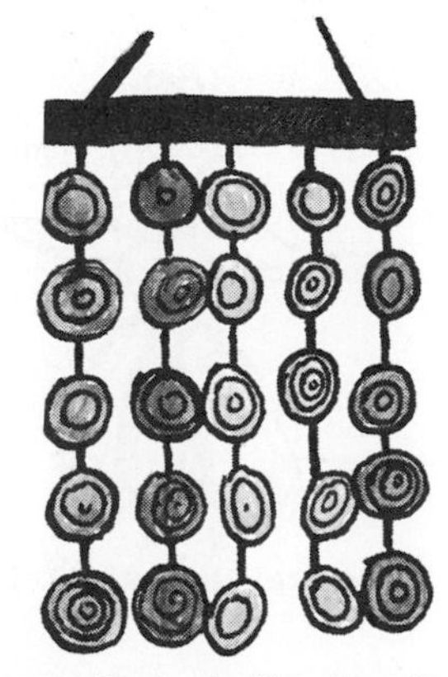

Figure 15-4 A Tin Can Jingle.

WHAT TO MAKE

Although we can discuss only a very few of the possibilities in this chapter, you will find other suggestions for projects in Chapters 13, 16, 17, 20, 21, 22, and 24.

The following list of projects may prove helpful:

Wall plaques
Doorstops
Tie racks
Lapel pins
Coin purses
Toys
Vases
Lamps
Book ends
Paper knives
Trinket boxes
Knot boards
Fishing equipment
Table decorations
Winter bouquets
Plant boxes
Camping furniture and equipment
Nature displays and trails
Musical and rhythm instruments
Potholders and hot plate pads
Costumed dolls
Coasters
Wooden buttons
Games
Mobiles
Bookmarks
Candle holders
Wooden buckles
Party favors and place cards
Indian costumes, rattles, tom-toms
Outdoor campsites and other structures
Model campsites
Birdhouses and feeders
Candles
Bookbinding
Relief maps
Letter trays
Yarn animals and dolls
Belts
Mosaics
Wastebaskets
Picture frames
Soap sculpture
Rustic signs
Scrapbooks and memory books
Katchina dolls
Photography (develop own films and prints)
Curtain pulls
Greeting cards and stationery
Paperweights
Napkin rings
Murals
Baskets
Masks
Totem poles
Bows and arrows
Whistles
Hiking sticks
Marionettes and puppets
Jewelry

BASKETRY

Basketry is an ancient art common to nearly every country, and its true origin is lost in antiquity. In the United States, we can use such native materials as willow branches (cut in the spring when the sap is running), cattail leaves from low damp places, flags, rushes, straw, wire grass, sweet grass, sedge, broom wheat, rye, and corn husks. Honeysuckle and Virginia creeper vines, when peeled and allowed to dry for two years, work up fast and make an even coil. Using wood splints from hickory, ash, oak, and maple trees requires more experienced hands than those of the average camper.

PIXIES AND OTHER THINGS

The dictionary defines a "pixie" as an elf or fairy, but campers often apply the term to all sorts of two- and four-

Figure 15–5 Some Pixies You Can Make.

legged creatures which their hands and imaginations create from the materials they have.

NUTS

A hike in season will disclose such nuts as acorns, hazelnuts, walnuts, and buckeyes, which you can use for making lapel pins, buttons, bracelets, and tops. To make a lapel pin, use either a half or a whole acorn or other nut and paint on a face (Fig. 15–5*D*), remembering to place the eyes halfway between the top and bottom and the mouth halfway between the chin and eyes. Use epoxy or glue to attach a safety pin on the back and add such details as hair, earrings, and hats. Make the bug (Fig. 15–5*A*) by painting half a walnut or other shell and gluing on antennae of vines or pipe cleaners. Place a marble on the bottom to make it movable. With a few additions, the shell can become a rabbit or a turtle (*B* and *C*); paint spots on the turtle or cut them from colored construction paper and paste them on. You can make a sailboat (Fig. 15–6*E*) from a lightweight half shell such as a pecan. Make the sail from construction paper and run a toothpick mast through it.

You can convert coconut shells into many things. Figure 15–5*E* shows a monkey mask made from a half shell. Sandpaper off the "hair" to smooth an area for the face and drill small holes for the nose, paint on the mouth, and glue on buttons for eyes and small shells for ears. Arrange it to hang as a wall ornament as shown. Figure 15–6*F* shows how to convert coconut shells into bird feeders and baths.

PINE CONES

Pine cones are beautiful in themselves and come in many sizes and forms which make them quite versatile. Large ones make lovely wall or Christmas tree ornaments when you paint the tips and attach a string between the scales or into a small screw eye inserted at the top to hang them. You can also convert big cones into candlestick holders by slicing off the bottom to provide a flat base and inserting a candle in the top.

Cones also serve as a base or body for all sorts of animals, and the possibilities are limited only by your imagination, as shown in the story of the woodcarver whose artistic output ran heavily to horses. He carved them swiftly and unerringly from almost any sort of wood, and rough and crude though they were, each had its own remarkable individual "horsishness." He explained his gift for carving them so easily and quickly by saying, "I jest look at the piece of wood till I see the horse and then I carve away the wood and there's the horse."

Make a woodpecker (Fig. 15–6*A*) from a cone, adding a maple seed or acorn head and a maple seed or feather tail. Glue on twig or matchstick legs and whittle a beak from a match, toothpick, or bit of wood. Glue the woodpecker in position on a "hollow tree" and mount it on a base. You can also perch birds by gluing on pipe cleaner feet and legs and gluing them to the limb of a branch "tree" or you can make them stand upright by embedding their feet in a large "glob" of clay and letting it dry.

Figure 15–5*G* is a turkey with a large cone for its body, a small cone for its head and pipe cleaner feet, neck and bill. Glue on discarded bird feathers for wings and tail and paint on the eyes or glue on seeds to represent them.

Make the fish (Fig. 15–6*B*) by painting the large end of a pine cone a light color, adding eyes and a maple wing tail, and mounting it on a slab of wood or a flat stone. Use it as a decoration or paperweight.

Make the bird feeder shown in Figure 15–6*C* by inserting a mixture of

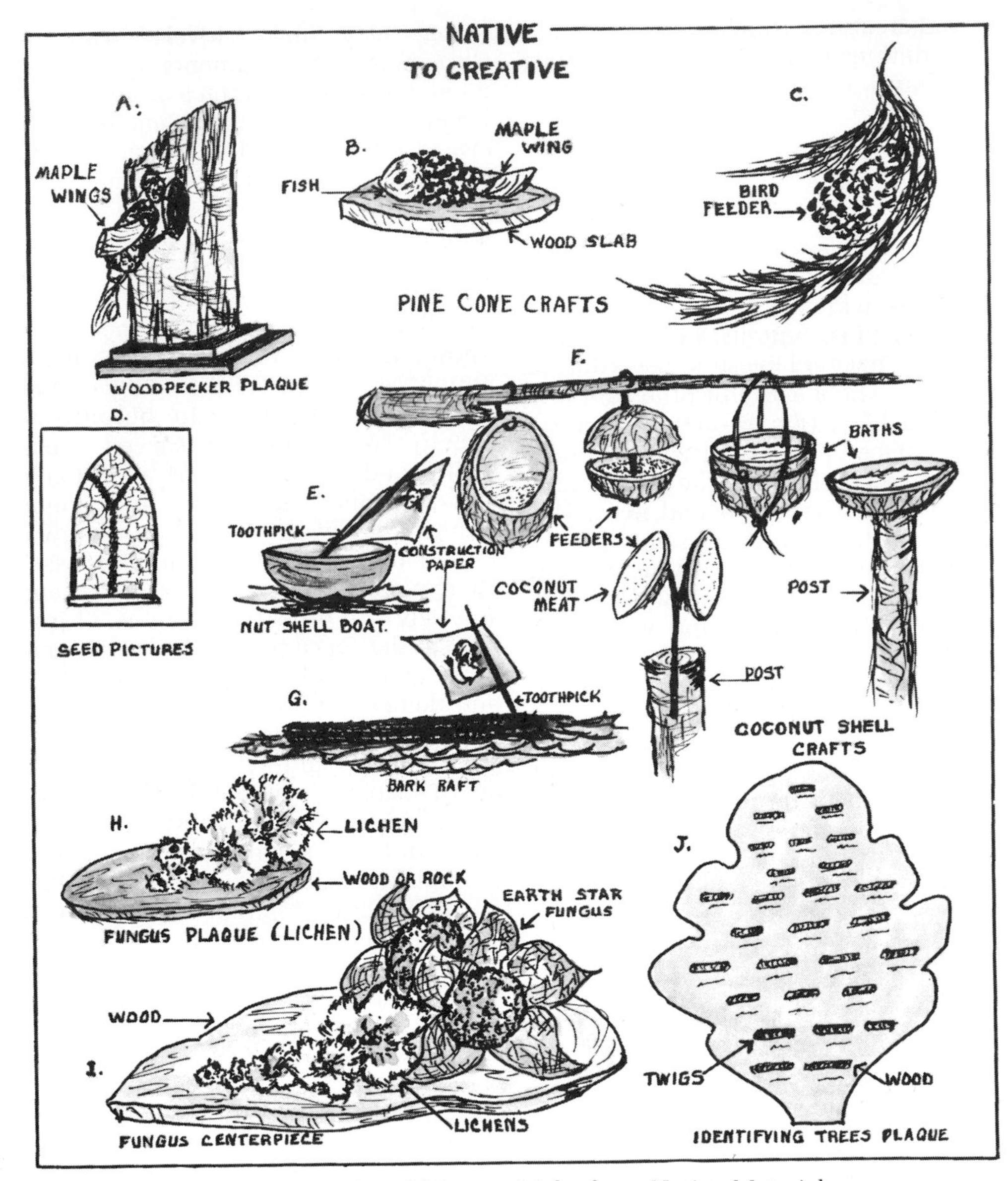

Figure 15–6 More Things to Make from Native Materials.

honey and bird seed into a pine cone and hanging it on a tree or other convenient place not too near people.

Make an armadillo with a small chestnut burr head, a pine cone body and twig tail and feet.

SHELLS AND OTHER WATERFRONT FINDINGS

Shells, bits of sponge, coral, dried seaweed, sharks' teeth, or fish fins, when combined with pipe cleaners and liquid glue, can be made into many beautiful and useful objects, such as earrings, pins, brooches, hairpins, and decorations for such things as boxes and place cards. You can create animals and dolls by using various kinds and sizes of shells for heads, bodies, and legs.

SEED PICTURES

You can produce artistic pictures by gluing seeds of assorted sizes and colors onto a suitable background (the stained glass window in Figure 15-6*D* is an example). If you can't find seeds of the color you want, you can, of course, dye or paint them.

MILKWEED PODS

Milkweed pods are also versatile. To convert them into birds (Fig. 15-5*F*), select partly open, dried pods which resemble bird bodies, then insert a toothpick bill and black seed eyes and make legs and feet from pipe cleaners. Paint the pods in gay bird colors.

FUNGUS OR LICHEN

You can often find lichen or fungus in attractive natural colors or you can paint them any color you want. They make very attractive centerpieces, paperweights or wall plaques (Fig. 15-6*H* and *I*).

TWIGS

The wall plaque (Fig. 15-6*J*) shows one of many ways to use twigs. This plaque is made by gluing or tacking twigs from many varieties of trees onto a large "leaf" cut from a piece of wood. Place the correct label for each twig below it or give each a number and hold a contest to see which camper can identify the most correctly.

MOBILES

These fascinating creations are made by suspending a number of objects from a solid support so that even a slight breeze keeps them in constant motion. Use very light objects and hang the mobile fairly high to take full advantage of air currents. Tie or glue a heavy dark thread or light thin wire to the object to suspend it from the support. Use varied shapes and colors to add interest. You may use objects related to a central theme or motif such as Indian or pioneer life, trees, flowers, animals, storybook heroes, or geometric forms. Another possibility is to feature various nature specimens, such as berries, pine cones, leaves, dried flowers, pods, or seeds. You may also cut out interesting folded paper designs or construct three-dimensional objects, such as an Indian tepee or tom-tom. You can also use such items as paper cups or plates, papier-mâché figures, bits of bright cloth or plastic, beads, feathers, buttons, pipe cleaner figures, thin bits of metal, shapes whittled from light wood such as balsa, cardboard, bits of ribbon, or designs cut from wallpaper. The mobile will not work

Figure 15-7 Some Mobiles.

well unless everything is exactly balanced, so begin by suspending and balancing the framework and then add objects to maintain an exact balance. Avoid monotony by balancing several small objects with a heavy one. Try to select light objects which will appear to dance or float gently in the air.

A NAVAJO LOOM

With a Navajo loom you can weave mats, rugs, mattresses, or sit-upons out of broom grass (also called sedge grass or sage grass) or any other long grass which is fairly straight and does not have greatly enlarged joints. Wheat straw, cattails, or suitable reeds will also serve. Gather the grass when it is mature, cutting it close to the ground to get as much length as possible. Hang it up to dry and when it has dried, remove the leaves by giving them a sharp pull. Soak the dried grass in water to make it more flexible and easier to handle and lay it on newspapers to soak up excess moisture.

CONSTRUCTING THE LOOM

1. Measure the length of your grass in inches and make two sticks, "A" and "B" (Fig. 15-9), somewhat longer than the grass and about 1 to $1\frac{1}{2}$ inches thick.

2. Divide the length of your grass by 3 and drive that number of "Y" stakes, 16 inches long, into the ground, spacing them slightly less than 3 inches apart (Figs. 15-8 and 15-9).

3. Make two 16-inch long "X" stakes (Fig. 15-9) and drive them in opposite the two outside Y stakes and slightly farther from them than you want the length of your mat to be.

4. Use square lashing to attach stick B to the X stakes (Fig. 15-8).

5. Cut as many heavy "C" strings (carpet warp, twine, or light rope) as you have Y stakes, making them long enough to reach between the X and Y stakes with enough left over so that you can tie clove hitches to attach one end of the string to a Y stake and the other to the B stick (Fig. 15-9).

6. Cut the same number of "D"

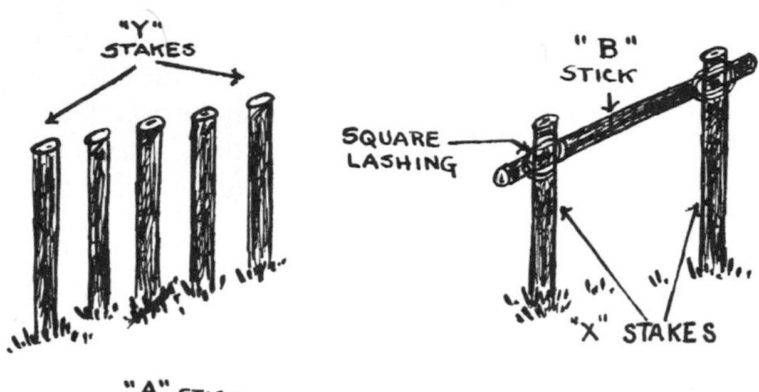

Figure 15-8 Starting a Navajo Loom.

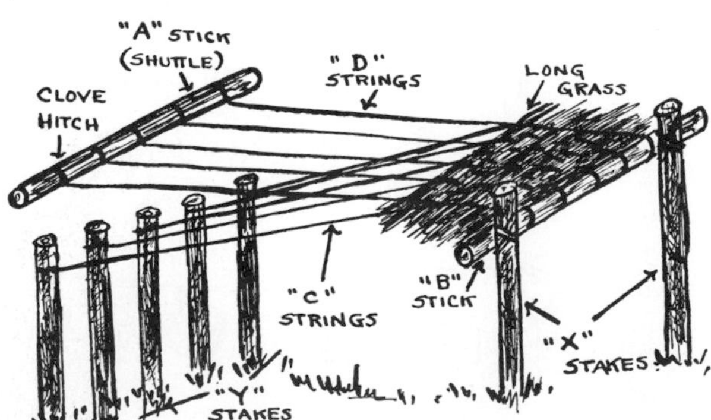

Figure 15-9 Weaving with a Navajo Loom.

strings, making them at least 6 inches longer than the C strings, and use clove hitches to attach one end to the A stick and the other to the B stick (Fig. 15-9). In weaving, the A stick acts as a shuttle, which you manipulate up and down between the Y stakes. Therefore, the D strings must be long enough to allow the A stick to fall well beyond the Y stakes when you lower it to the ground.

WEAVING WITH THE LOOM
(Figure 15-9)

Use heavy reeds singly or divide fine materials such as grass into bundles. Raise the A stick or shuttle, push a bundle of grass tightly up between the C and D strings and lower the A stick to bring the D strings over the top of the bundle. Insert another bundle of grass between the C and D strings, push it up tightly into place, and bring the shuttle (stick A) up with the D strings under the bundle. The shuttle is now back in its original position and you are ready to repeat the process, inserting new bundles of grass as you lower and raise the shuttle to bind them securely into place with the D strings.

Continue until you have a mat of the length you want. Untie the C and D strings at one end of the mat and tie them together (Fig. 15-10) and repeat at the other end.

When weaving wide mats from long lengths of grass it is easier if two people help, stationing themselves on opposite sides of the loom to place the bundles in position and push them compactly into place. A third could assist by lowering and raising the shuttle.

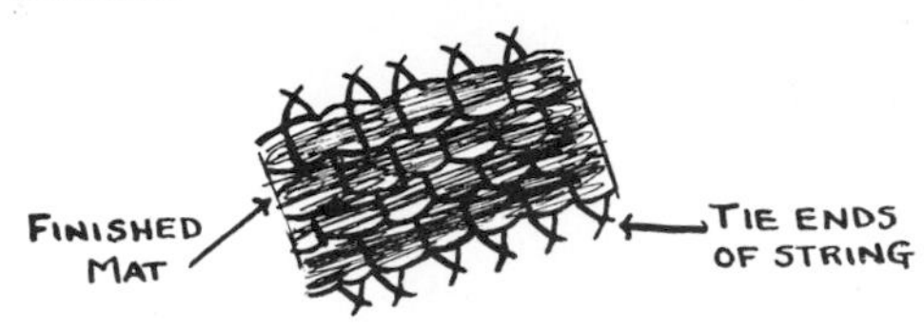

Figure 15-10 Finishing the Mat.

VARIATIONS

Although many native materials come in quite attractive colors, you can get other colors by using native or commercial dyes. You can weave with single colors or work out interesting patterns by combining them into stripes or other designs. You can also add a touch of color by using colored C and D strings (or dyeing your own), using multiple strands together to intensify the effect. This method produces attractive place mats when used with fine grasses.

To convert a mat into a *carry-all* fold it in half lengthwise and sew the sides together with heavy thread or cord. Braid together heavy rope, webbing, or fine cord to make handles.

DRIFTWOOD

If you walk along a seashore, you will frequently find pieces of driftwood which are interesting in themselves. They become especially fascinating when you realize that they may have been drifting around for years and may have come originally from some country thousands of miles away or some romantic ship long buried at sea. The constant erosion by salt water may have eaten away the bark and soft spots in the wood and the soaking has preserved the wood and given it an attractive silver-gray color, while constant buffetings by tides have rounded off rough corners and protrusions. You can also find similar pieces of wood near inland lakes or rivers, as well as in deserts, open fields, or forests where constant exposure to sun and changing weather conditions produce similar effects. Driftwood pieces exist in all imaginable shapes and sizes and offer you a challenge to determine how best to capitalize on their particular "personalities."

POSSIBLE USES FOR DRIFTWOOD

What does your piece of wood look like? Would it make a good tree if you stood it on end, sprayed it green or brown, and added bits of felt, gum drops, or moss for foliage (Fig. 15–11*A*)? Does it resemble the body of a fish, animal, or bird, so that by adding small pieces for a tail, feet, legs, ears, and so forth you can make it into a good caricature? Could you convert it into a sign for your camp or cottage (*B*) by flattening it on one side and incising letters with a wood burner and painting them in a contrasting color or by whittling letters from other wood and gluing them on? *C* shows an attractive decoration for the table, sideboard, or mantel or for use as a background for a bouquet of flowers. *D* is a lamp and *E* is a jewelry tree, sprayed with gold or other metallic paint. *F* shows a piece of driftwood used as the base for a mobile. *G* is a planter made by hollowing out an oval-shaped depression in the wood and lining it with plastic or gluing a watertight clam shell into place.

PREPARING YOUR DRIFTWOOD

Select only firm, solid pieces without dry rot, and if they are water soaked, set them aside for three to six months to dry out thoroughly. When you have decided what you want to make from a piece, saw off unwanted parts or projections and use sandpaper to round off the sawed ends to make them blend in with the rest of the piece. The best way to attach a small piece is to drill a small hole in both it and the main piece and glue a small stick or dowel of appropriate size into the holes.

Use a wire or very stiff brush to remove all loose particles. There are several methods of finishing your piece and you may want to experiment with them on waste portions or inconspicuous places such as the bottom of the piece. Some woods, particularly hard woods, have a naturally beautiful grain which you may want to make the most of; if so, use rough sandpaper to get down to the grain and finish off with fine sandpaper to produce a satin smooth finish. If you prefer to keep the natural gray finish, use very fine sandpaper to sand it lightly, for the gray layer is thin and easily destroyed. Conceal sawed-off places with a matching shade of gray.

Apply a coat of white shellac first to keep later treatments from sinking into the wood and eventually darkening it. To produce a pleasing rich, deep

Figure 15–11 Some Ways to Use Driftwood.

luster, rub in successive coatings of linseed oil, protecting them with a coat or two of wax rubbed in well.

Another possibility is to apply a thin coat of paint in one or more pastel shades, blending them into each other to give a light tinted effect. A pleasing finish results if you apply a light coat of white to the main parts, then add touches of black to recessed areas and use your fingers to blend them in while still wet. Add metallic touches by placing a small amount of metallic powder on a piece of paper and blend it in sparingly with your finger while the black and white are still wet. Rubbed-in oil paint also gives a pleasing tint. Apply metallic finishes of gold, copper, bronze, or aluminum from a spray can.

Protect these finishes with a coat or two of good quality, hard-drying varnish or shellac, topped off with a coat or two of wax rubbed in well. Use outdoor paint or varnish if the object will be exposed to the weather.

PIPE CLEANER FIGURES

Pipe cleaners are inexpensive and are so flexible that you can easily twist them into figures of people, animals, birds, trees, or almost anything else you want. You can paint or dye them any color desired. Use two cleaners to make a human figure (Fig. 15–12). Bend one in half for the body, rounding off the top into a head and turning back the ends for feet. Wind the second cleaner several times around the first to round out the body and extend the ends outward for arms and cut them off to the proper length. Insert a small nut, round button, or wad of tissue paper or cloth to fill in the hollow framework of the head. Use crepe paper or other materials to fill out the body, and wind overlapping, narrow strips of skin-colored tissue paper over the whole figure and paste down the loose ends. Draw features on the face with India ink, crayons, or water colors or cut them out of paper and paste them on.

Figure 15–12 Pipe Cleaner Figures.

Make hair from fringed crepe paper, bits of frayed rope, yarn, or fur and add hats of felt or cardboard, trimming them with feathers, ribbons, or small flowers. Fashion clothing from crepe paper, construction paper, or bits of cloth.

Make the figures stand upright by gluing the "shoes" to large flat buttons, pieces of stiff cardboard, or a flat piece of wood or cardboard.

Convert the figures into lapel ornaments by inserting a safety pin in the back or use them for favors, table decorations, or for figures in model campsites or woodland scenes.

COLLAGES

Collages are made by pasting or gluing a large assortment of materials to some sort of background to produce a picture or design. Since a large variety of textures, surfaces, and materials are used, making collages provides valuable experience in recognizing and appreciating the individual qualities and characteristics of many media.

SAND PAINTING

Painting pictures with colored sand is an interesting activity which brings pleasing results. Builders' sand gives better results than regular beach sand, which is too fine. First design the picture (flowers, seascape, landscape, house, or whatever) on a piece of paper with water colors or wax crayons; then outline it roughly on a piece of thin board or heavy cardboard which will serve as a background. Mix vegetable or other dyes in water, placing the colors you want in available containers such as bottles, cans, cups, or shallow dishes. Estimate the amount of sand you will need for each color and place it in the proper container of dye, stirring or shaking it to see that each grain of sand is dyed. Remember that wet sand is darker than it will be when dry and mix your colors accordingly. Spread out each batch of sand on newspapers to dry. Cut off enough lengths of string to cover the outlines of the areas of the picture and dip each in the appropriate dye bath and let dry. Use a small stick or paint brush to outline each area of the picture with glue and press a piece of string of the right color into it. Be sure to make all applications while the glue is still damp and let it dry thoroughly each time. Apply glue to one area and spread it uniformly with a bit of cardboard or a brush and sprinkle it thickly with the proper color of sand. Let dry and repeat until all areas of the picture are covered. If you wish, you can add another layer of glue and sand to produce a deeper texture. Spray a coat of clear plastic or varnish over the picture to preserve it, then frame and hang it.

MAKING FLOUR PASTE

There are many ways to make your own paste. One method is to mix a half cup of flour (rye is preferable to wheat) with enough water to form a creamy mixture and then heat it over a low flame for about five minutes, stirring it constantly to prevent lumping. If you want to preserve it for future use, add a few drops of glycerine, oil of wintergreen, or alum.

PAPIER-MÂCHÉ

Papier-mâché is a very inexpensive and versatile medium for constructing useful and decorative objects. You will need only paper (newspapers, tissues, or paper toweling), fine wire or string, and some sort of paste or glue, such as ordinary school paste, flour paste, or wallpaper paste, mixed as directed on the package.

STRIP METHOD

This is a simple method which consists of wrapping layers of damp paper strips around a frame and applying some adhesive substance to hold them together.

To make a plate, bowl, tray, or similar object, choose some form such as a bowl, bottle, can, or half of an orange or apple which is the appropriate size and shape. Tear, rather than cut, narrow strips of paper an inch or less in width on the bias and soak them in water until they are pliable but not too weak to handle; this may take up to 24 hours or more. Cover the outside of the form with a light coating of petroleum jelly or grease to keep the finished product from sticking to it. If you want added strength and body, wrap a layer or two of cheesecloth over the form either before you begin or after you have applied the first two or three layers of paper. Wrap a layer of paper strips horizontally around the form, overlapping each slightly, and use a brush to cover it lightly with a coat of paste. Next apply a layer of paper strips vertically, overlapping them as before, and again cover them with paste. Continue with additional layers, applying them in alternate directions or crisscrossing the strips in each layer, until you have built up a shell at least $\frac{1}{8}$ inch thick. Let the object dry thoroughly, allowing as much as two or three days if the weather is damp. Slip the product off the form, sand it smooth, and paint or otherwise finish it as you wish, adding a top layer or two of shellac to protect it and make it semi-waterproof. A coat of wax on top will give even more sheen and protection.

To make large papier-mâché figures, such as people or animals, rough shape the body from crumpled newspapers, chicken wire, or lengths of straight wire. Fasten on additional crumpled or rolled pieces for neck, arms, and legs. Bend and shape the frame or armature as you wish and wind string or fine wire around it to hold it in place. Tie on wads or rolls of paper or cloth for noses, ears, and tails. Then cover the armature with strips of paper narrow enough to follow the contours closely, alternating the directions and using paste as before. For a really smooth finish, allow each layer of paper to dry thoroughly, then sand it smooth before you apply the next. Paper toweling on the outside layer provides an excellent surface for painting. Add strands of yarn or twine to the wet papier-mâché to simulate fur or hair.

PULP METHOD

Though slightly more complicated, the pulp method provides a medium of finer texture which will produce a smoother and more "finished" product. Tear newspapers into tiny, confetti-sized pieces and soak them in water overnight or as long as necessary to get a smooth, fine gray pulp or mâché. If you want to use white rather than gray mâché, scoop the pulp up in a sieve and run clear water through it until the ink is removed. Squeeze out excess water and knead in enough commercial or flour paste to produce a mixture that has the consistency of heavy cream and is sticky enough to adhere well yet not too sticky to handle. Add color to the mixture if you wish. For a still smoother medium, mix 2 cups of powdered modeling clay, 1 cup of calcimine (any color), and 2 cups of water and stir as you gradually add bits of toilet or cleansing tissue until you have the same heavy-cream consistency. Let it stand 24 hours before using it.

Apply the mixture to an armature or over a form such as a bowl, bottle, or piece of wood. If you want to model figurines or other objects as you would with clay, start with a large enough mass to complete the entire figure and pull out portions for the arms, legs and head. Etch in details with a sharp instrument such as a knife, and use a flat knife or spoon to smooth the surface. Use fur, rope, or yarn to add hair, manes, tails or eyebrows while the mâché is still damp. When the object is quite dry, sandpaper it smooth and decorate it with colored paper, poster paint, oil paint, or water colors; use crayons, India ink, or colored inks to draw in details. Add a coat of shellac for protection and a coat of wax on top to give a high gloss. Some raveled burlap will provide a shaggy coat for an animal, and construction paper, crepe paper, or pieces of fabric may be used for clothing for human figures. Construct hats from felt or cardboard and trim them with such things as wild bird feathers, small colored stones, beads, or sequins.

OTHER PAPIER-MÂCHÉ PROJECTS

You can use papier-mâché to make many other attractive items, such as jewelry, table decorations, wall plaques, puppet heads, doll heads, favors for parties, or models of circuses, towns, or camps. Glue on sequins, beads, snips of metal, or glitter to add sparkle and shine. Papier-mâché relief maps are lovely and lighter than clay maps, and you can also insert pins or thumb tacks into them. When making

(Courtesy of Girl Scout Camp Wiedemann, Wichita Area Girl Scout Council, Kansas.)

masks, start with a layer of cheesecloth as a base.

CLAY MODELING

Clay that can be used for modeling exists in all parts of the world and may be colored white, yellow, green, gray, or even black or blue. You will probably be able to find a satisfactory type right on your own camp site. The bibliography at the end of the chapter lists sources that tell how to construct a potter's wheel and kiln at little cost.

Figurines, animals, pendants, plaques, tiles, and bowls are quickly made and bring out the creative imagination of even the most inhibited. As one child ungrammatically said, "I closed my eyes and seen an angel and made one like I seen it."*

*Cole, Natalie Robinson: *The Arts in the Classroom.* John Day Co., 1940, p. 39.

MARBLEIZING PAPER

Even a novice can turn out lovely marbleized paper. Use any kind of paper which is not too absorbent. Pour kerosene, turpentine, or other oil into a large pan of water and add a little oil paint in one or several colors; since water and oil won't mix, both the oil and the oil paint will remain floating on top. Breathe on the mixture or stir it slightly to make it swirl, then marbleize the paper by laying it on top of the mixture. You can add further decoration with wax crayons after the paper is dry.

CHIP CARVING

Chip carving requires precision and patience, and therefore may not be suitable for younger campers. Most chip carving designs are based upon geometrical patterns which are usually laid out with the aid of a ruler and compass. The "chips" are triangular pieces of wood, removed with a slicing knife (a razor blade will do in an emergency). Slope the chips gradually rather than gouge them out. Basswood (linden) is best because it is soft and workable, is fine-grained, and takes a nice finish, but pine or apple wood is also satisfactory.

Trace your design on an object such as a box, album, scrapbook, coaster, tray, letter knife, checker, belt buckle, costume pin, or carved button. Dye or stain the chips or use chips from different kinds of wood to bring out the design and glue them on. Finish as you would any other wooden object.

DYEING WITH NATURAL DYES

When tied and dyed, silk, chiffon or cheesecloth can be made into beautiful cabin curtains, bedspreads, scarves, costumes, and similar items. Natural dyes from berries, bark, or plant roots produce soft, attractive shades, though they are usually less brilliant than those obtained from commercial dyes.

You must first treat the material with some sort of mordant to increase the brilliance of the dye and set it permanently. For cotton, linen, rayon, or other vegetable fibers, use $\frac{1}{4}$ ounce of plain washing soda combined with 1 ounce of alum and a gallon of water. For animal fibers, such as silk or wool, substitute $\frac{1}{4}$ ounce of cream of tartar for the soda. First wash and rinse the material thoroughly, squeeze out excess water, place it in the mordant, and bring it to a boil, letting it boil gently for an hour. Replace the water as it evaporates to maintain the right proportion. Then rinse the material thoroughly.

To prepare the dye bath, break, crush, or cut into small bits about 1 peck of plant materials for each pound of material to be dyed. Place them in a steel, copper, or enamel container and cover them with water (rain or soft water if at all possible) and let them soak overnight or until your dye is of the intensity you want. Run the dye through a strainer to remove solid materials and add hot water to produce enough lukewarm mixture to easily cover the material. Place the material in the dye and stir it around with a wooden paddle. Slowly bring the solution to a simmer (just below the boiling point) and add $\frac{1}{2}$ cup of salt for cottons or $\frac{1}{2}$ cup of vinegar for wools about five minutes after the simmering begins. Stir the material occasionally to assure even dyeing and continue to simmer for from a half hour to an hour or until the material is somewhat darker than you want it to be when dry. If water boils away, lift out the material and add boiling water to restore its consistency.

Rinse the material several times, starting with boiling water and gradually reducing the temperature each time until the rinse water is clear. Squeeze out excess moisture and dry in the shade. You can use the dye water several times but it will give a somewhat lighter shade after each use.

The following are indigenous sources of the principal colors:

Blue:

- Blackberry—berries
- Blue ash (boiled with copper sulphate)
- Hazel—roots
- Larkspur—flowers
- Red maple—bark (boiled with copper sulphate)
- Sunflower—seeds

Black or Dark Brown:

- Alder—bark
- Butternut—bark
- Coffee bean—inside kernel
- Hemlock—bark
- Hickory—bark
- Onion—skins (boil them)
- Red oak—bark
- Sumac—leaves, roots, or bark
- Black walnut—hulls and shells

Purple:
Barberry—berries
Blueberry—berries
Cedar—tips of branches
Elderberry—berries
Maple—rotted wood
Pokeweed—berries
Purple flag—petals
Juniper (Red cedar)—rootlets
Sumac—berries
Wild cherry—roots

Gray:
Bayberry—leaves
Blackberry—young shoots
Butternut—hulls
Red maple—bark (use mordant of copperas)
Rhododendron—leaves
St. John's wort—flowers (pick in July)
Sumac—leaves (use mordant of copperas)
Willow—bark

Green:
Elderberry—leaves
Giant arbor vitae—twigs and leaves
Laurel—leaves
Plantain—roots and leaves
Spinach—leaves
Water scum (algae)—whole plant

Red:
Alder—inner bark
Amaranth—seeds
Beets—boiled with alum (red violet)
Bloodroot—root
Calliopsis—flowers
Cedar—inner bark
Dahlia—flowers
Dandelion—roots
Hemlock—bark
Lady's bedstraw—roots
Pokeberry—berries (boil with alum)
Raspberry—berries (dark red)
Red dogwood—inner bark
Red sumac—berries
Strawberry—berries
Sycamore—old, half-rotten roots

Yellow:
Alder—inner bark or leaves
Apple—bark
Balsam—flowers
Bayberry—leaves
Black oak—inner bark
Broomsedge—stalks and leaves
Coreopsis—flowers
Cottonwood—seed vessels or leaf buds
Dock—roots
Elderberry—leaves
Goldenrod—flowers
Holly—boiled with alum
Lady's bedstraw—flowering tops
Gray lichen (from oak and pine trees)—whole plant
Marigold—flowers
Peach—leaves
Pear—leaves (dull yellow)
Pignut hickory—inner bark
Privet—branch tips or clippings
Saffron—dried stigmas
Sassafras—bark
Shiny sumac—roots
Smartweed plant (use mordant of alum)
St. John's wort—flowers (pick in August)
Sumac—roots
Thistle—flowers
White mulberry—roots and leaves
Zinnia—flowers

Orange:
Lombardy poplar—leaves (use mordant of chrome)
Mountain ash—berries
Onion—papery brown skins (steep them)

Magenta:
Dandelion—tap root

Khaki:
Juniper (Red cedar)—berries

WEAVING

Weaving, which consists of lacing one set of threads or strips of material in and out of another to form a solid material, is a very old craft, long used for both utilitarian and decorative purposes. The colonists brought weaving with them to America, although the Indians had developed their own weaving techniques long before. Weaving is quite popular in many camps, some of which have elaborate table or floor looms and competent instructors to show campers how to use them. Some looms are simple to construct and with them you can make such things as mats, trays, belts, scarves, sit-upons, and book marks.

COMMONLY USED TERMS

Loom—the frame which holds the raw materials.

Warp—the stationary threads, placed lengthwise on the loom to provide a base through which to weave the woof.

(Courtesy of Gnaw Bone Camp, Nashville, Indiana.)

Weft or *woof*—the cross threads which are laced in and out of the warp.

Shuttle—an implement used to hold the woof while weaving it through the warp. It may be a needle with an eye through which the woof is threaded or a flat piece of plastic, wood, or other material around which it is wound. Heavy materials, such as reeds, grasses, or large strips of cloth or plastic can be manipulated by hand instead of with a shuttle.

Beater—an instrument used to press the woof tightly up into place to keep the weaving tight and even. A round stick, an ordinary comb, or a coarse comb of plastic or whittled wood is commonly used.

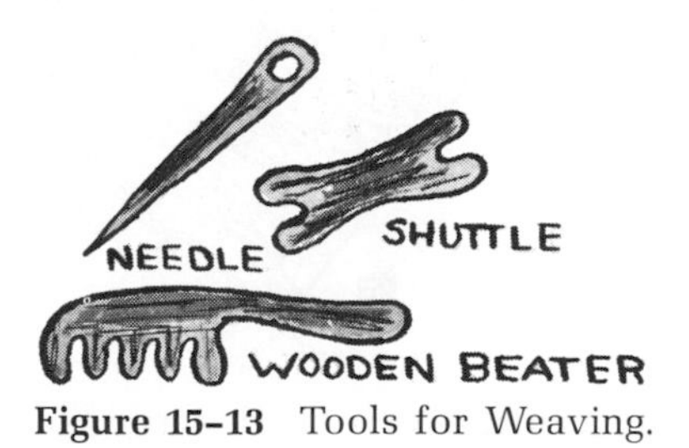

Figure 15-13 Tools for Weaving.

DARNING STITCH WEAVING ON A WOODEN LOOM

The loom shown in Figure 15-14 can be used to weave such things as small doormats, sit-upons, place mats, or decorative wall mats. Use four sticks long enough to form a rectangle somewhat larger than your completed mat is to be. Flatten each stick on two opposite sides, and use square lashing to join them together in a rectangle with the flattened sides of the sticks on the top and bottom. Drive in an even number of brads or nails about 1/8 to 1/4 inch apart across the top and bottom sticks of the rectangle.

Use a clove hitch to anchor the end of the warp to the first nail on the bottom stick and then wind it back and forth between the nails on the top and bottom sticks to form the warp. Fasten the end to the last nail with another clove hitch. If you want to add extra strength or intensify the color effect of the warp, wind multiple thicknesses of the string between each set of nails before going on to the next. Now lace

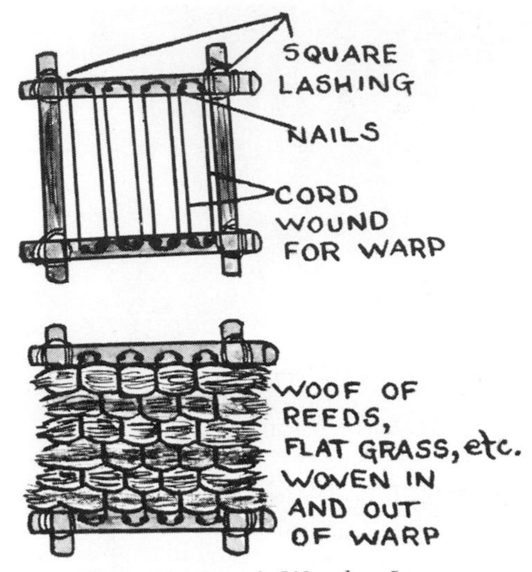

Figure 15-14 A Wooden Loom.

the woof alternately in and out of the warp, pressing it tightly up into place to keep it compact and even.

Use ribbon, strips of cloth, heavy string, rope, craft strip, or strips of leather for the warp, and use these or native materials such as broad-leaved grasses, long pine needles, sedges, rushes, twigs, corn husks, honeysuckle, or willow for the woof.

To prepare native materials, cut them as long as possible and hang them up to air dry thoroughly. When you are ready to use them, soak them in water until they are soft and pliable and then lay them on newspapers to remove excess moisture. Lace them singly or in uniform bundles in and out of the warp, placing the butt ends at alternate sides for a uniform appearance. Alternate each row so that the woof goes over the warp thread it previously went under, and continue until you have a mat as long as you want. You can use native or commercial dyes to dye the warp and woof and weave it in uniform colors or in stripes, checks or any other patterns desired.

DARNING STITCH WEAVING ON A CARDBOARD LOOM

Figure 15-15 shows a cardboard loom that is used to weave square or rectangular pieces. Use a piece of corrugated or other heavy cardboard to make a loom somewhat larger than you want your finished article to be. Cut notches $\frac{1}{8}$ to $\frac{1}{2}$ inches apart across both the top and bottom. Wind the warp lengthwise on the loom, crossing it over behind the cardboard projections at each end to reach the next notch. Use any thin material desired for the woof and fasten it to the warp at one side. Use a flat shuttle or your hand to lace it alternately under and over the warp, using a beater to press it tightly up into place as you proceed.

Make a turn around the warp at the end of the row and come back through the warp, passing under the thread you went over before, and fasten the end of the woof securely at the end of the last row. Remove the piece by slipping the loops in the warp off the projections in the cardboard. You can tie lengths of materials through the loops to add fringe. Work out a design by using various colors of warp and woof

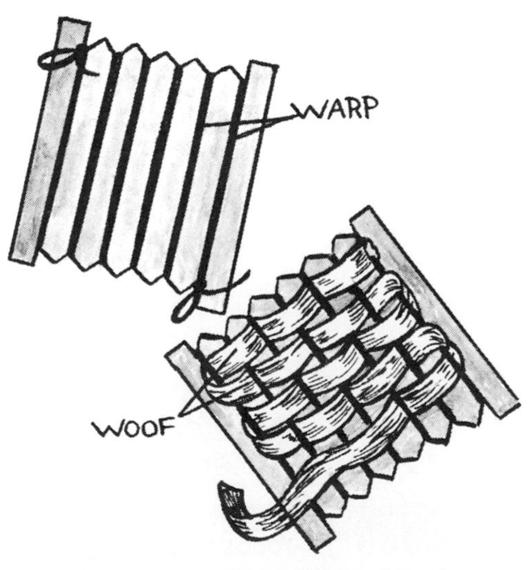

Figure 15-15 A Cardboard Loom.

Figure 15-16 Loom Designs.

(Fig. 15-16). When trying to work out a pattern, it is usually wise to first draw it to scale in color on paper.

To construct a cardboard loom for making a circular or oval mat, use a compass or trace around a bowl or other object of appropriate size and shape. Then cut it out and notch it. Lay down your warp as shown in Figure 15-17 and weave the woof in and out as before.

MAKING A MAT WITHOUT A LOOM

Figure 15-18 shows a circular or oval mat made from native materials without using a loom. Prepare bunches of long pine needles, long grass, or other materials, and weave them into a long rope or strand about the size of your finger, introducing new materials to replace the old as they run out. Hold them in place by means of buttonhole stitches as shown. Weave a mat with the strand as shown, fastening each row firmly to the previous one by means of frequent buttonhole stitches. Such mats can be used as rugs, hot dish mats, or decorations.

Figure 15-17 A Circular Loom.

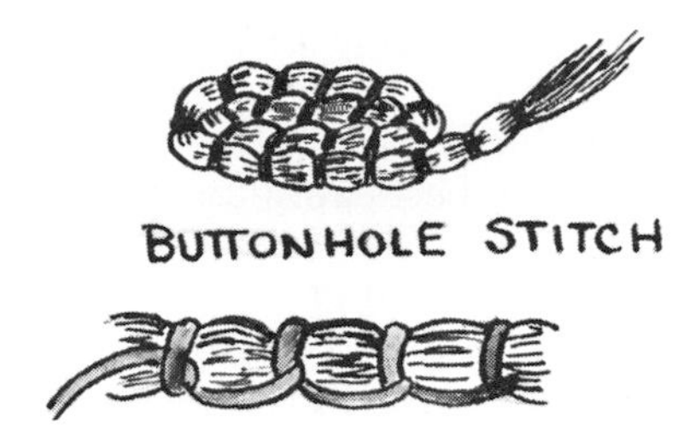

Figure 15-18 A Pine Needle Mat.

MAKING A MODEL CAMPSITE

An interesting project for an individual or group consists of constructing small-scale models of such things as a campsite, Indian village, pioneer village with stockade, early settlement, or farm. It provides many hours of challenging work, for imagination, creativeness, and ingenuity are required to determine what to use and how to use it to create something as decorative and realistic as possible. Youngsters often become intensely interested in such an undertaking and do much reading and research in an attempt to make it authentic.

This technique may be used to display various types of tents, fires, or other camp "fixin's," each labelled with its name, use, and other pertinent information. Campers can make a model campsite to demonstrate their knowledge of camp construction and layout and good camping practices by properly locating the tent, campfire, and other facilities with respect to the terrain (freedom from danger of insects, flooding, winds, convenience to water, and so forth). You may give the group a model or drawing of a terrain with certain inherent hazards which they must be able to recognize so they can construct the best camp for that particular terrain.

When beginning a project, carefully plan it and draw it to scale on a large piece of wrapping paper. Build the model outdoors or indoors on a table top or a platform of boards, wallboard, or plywood.

Build up the terrain with earth, sand, dyed sawdust, or gravel, or model it from papier-mâché or plaster of Paris which can be painted when dry. Give variety to the contours by including such features as hills and cliffs and making depressions for lakes and rivers. Most of us have very little actual knowledge of the exact details and formations of various terrains; therefore, it may be quite worthwhile to go out for a detailed study, observing such things as the varying slant of the rocks in a hill or rock ledge, the slope, composition, and vegetation of the bank of a stream or lake, and similar characteristics. You will note that in large supposedly homogeneous areas such as a meadow, a field of oats, or a grassy plot, there are a great variety of tints and shades instead of the uniform coloration you would expect. Take a sketch pad along for taking notes and making rough sketches of what you see. It also helps to study good photographs and realistic drawings and paintings.

You may want to place a backdrop or painted landscape behind your model to give depth and to allow you to show distant waterfalls, mountains, and other features. Conceal the juncture between the backdrop and your model with some device such as a woods, hedge, fence, line of buildings, or range of hills.

Scatter gravel or pebbles loosely on top of your ground surfaces, embed them in wet papier-mâché or plaster of Paris, or spread them over a light coating of glue or paste on top of a dry surface. Paint on grass or use shades of green, yellow, and brown flock moss or bits of sponge painted green. Spray or dip small plants, branches, grasses, or weeds into paint and use them for landscaping.

Make trees from evergreen branches or from thorny or multi-branched twigs or bushes with "leaves" of dyed sponges, green construction paper, or green gumdrops. Embed them, as well as other things you want to stand upright (cranes, small flowers, tents or tepee stakes), in wet papier-mâché or plaster of Paris or in small lumps of moist clay painted an appropriate color.

Make Indian tepees by whittling lodge poles from twigs and covering them with cloth or cardboard. Use small sticks, matches, or toothpicks for buildings and make tripods and other useful camp devices from twigs, using appropriate knots and lashing to join them together with twine, string, or strong thread. Soak the completed structures in water for about an hour so that the knots and lashings will tighten as they dry.

Make the borders of rivers and lakes realistically ragged and uneven and place characteristic animals and natural vegetation along them. Use real water or simulate it with blue cellophane, clear cellophane over blue paper, or aquamarine paint with touches of white. Include a model dock or marina with canoes, rowboats, and sailboats fashioned from soft wood or flexible cardboard. Use melted paraffin to waterproof them if you use real water.

Lash a rustic bridge across a river or marshy area. Construct a covered wagon from a wooden box, block of wood, or strong cardboard with wire hoops over the top to support a paper or cloth covering. Whittle wagon wheels out of soft wood or use bottle caps, small pieces of tin can, or cardboard. Make people and animals using one of the techniques already discussed and glue their feet to the surface or embed them in bases as described for trees and shrubs.

Make buildings out of construction paper, soft wood, small boxes, or pieces of cardboard, gluing them together or joining them with masking tape. Paint them and add windows and other details. Make a log cabin from small twigs (willow is usually readily available and easy to whittle) or glue them over a box or other base. Notch them at the corners and join them log-cabin style, using glue or small nails to fasten them together. Construct rafters from twigs and cover them with a roof of reeds, small twigs, or overlapping whittled "shingles." Construct a fireplace by using papier-mâché or plaster of Paris to cement small pebbles together. To make a more modern building, glue on pieces of sandpaper for siding or "clapboards" or draw lines on brick-colored construction paper to represent bricks. Add windows of cellophane, outlining panes with toothpicks or whittled sticks.

Add bunks, duffle bags, storage compartments, and other paraphernalia in or about the buildings (Adirondike shacks display these particularly well since they have one open side. Add such touches as a flag and flagpole, a woodpile near an outdoor firesite, a Chippewa kitchen, a rustic table, a grease pit, cooking utensils, and cranes. Then post a "legend" or explanation nearby with labels to explain what you are showing.

These models can be used for many purposes. They can provide an introduction to various phases of camp life for visitors or inexperienced campers. They can be used to increase campers' appreciation and knowledge of nature, good camping techniques, or almost anything else desired. You can use them to test the qualifications of those wanting to go on trips or participate in other advanced activities. They also make attractive displays as table centerpieces for camp banquets or other festivities.

A token award, such as honorable mention in the camp paper or a citation at a recognition ceremony, may be given to persons or groups producing the most ingenious, interesting, authentic, or decorative display.

ADDITIONAL READINGS

(For an explanation of abbreviations and abbreviated forms, see page 25.)

Basketry

Basketry (No. 3313). Boy Scouts, 1968, 32 pp., 45¢, paper.

Christopher, Frederick J.: *Basketry.* Dover, 1952, 108 pp., $1.25, paper.

Braiding and Knotting

Graumont, Raoul M.: *Handbook of Knots.* Cornell Maritime, 1954, $3; $2, paper.

Graumont, Raoul M., and Elmer Wenstrom: *Square Knot Handicraft Guide.* Random, 1971, $3.95, paper.

Phillips, Mary Walker: *Step-by-Step Macramé.* Western, $2.50, paper.

Shaw, George Russell: *Knots: Useful and Ornamental.* Collier, 1972, 194 pp., $2.95, paper.

Strom, Nils, and Anders Enestrom: *Big-Knot Macramé.* Sterling, 48 pp., $2.95.

Bookbinding

Bookbinding (No. 3378). Boy Scouts, 1969, 24 pp., 45¢, paper.

Ceramics and Pottery

Andrews, Michael F.: *Sculpture and Ideas: For School and Camp Programs.* Prentice-Hall, 1965, $9.95.

Hofsted, Jolyon: *Ceramics.* Golden, $2.50.

Hyman, Richard: *Ceramics Handbook.* Arco, 1959, 144 pp., $3.50.

Isenstein, Harald: *Creative Claywork.* Sterling, 96 pp., $3.95.

Kampmann, Lothar: *Creating With Clay.* Van Nostrand, 1972, 77 pp., $5.95.

Kujoth: *The Recreation Program Guide,* pp. 67–71.

Leeming, Joseph: *Fun With Clay.* Lippincott, 1951, $4.75.

Pottery (No. 3314). Boy Scouts, 1969, 64 pp., 45¢, paper.

Priola, Joan B.: *Ceramics—and How to Decorate Them.* Sterling, 144 pp., $6.95.

Rhodes, Daniel: *Clay and Glazes for the Potter.* Chilton, rev., 1973, $12.50.

Supensky, Thomas G.: *Ceramic Art in the School Program.* Davis, 1968, 111 pp., $8.25.

Zarchy, Harry: *Ceramics*. Knopf, 1954, 171 pp., $5.19.

Design

Ballinger, Louise Bowen, and Thomas F. Vroman: *Design: Sources and Resources*. Van Nostrand, 1965, $7.95.
Guyler, Vivian Varney: *Design in Nature*. Davis, 1970, 124 pp., $9.95.
Moseley, Spencer, et al.: *Crafts Design: An Illustrated Guide*. Wadsworth, 1962, 436 pp., $19.90.
Wolchonok: *Design for Artists and Craftsmen*. Dover, 1953, 224 pp., $3, paper.

Drawing and Painting

Art (No. 3320). Boy Scouts, 1968, 48 pp., 45¢, paper.
Bogerad, Alan D.: *It's Fun to Draw*. Tudor, $3.95; $1.95, paper.
Brandt, Rex: *Watercolor Technique*. Van Nostrand, 1963, 160 pp., $8.50.
Brooks, Leonard: *Oil Painting: Basic and New Techniques*. Van Nostrand, 1971, $5.50; $2.95, paper.
Gollwitzer, Gerhard: *Express Yourself in Drawing*. Sterling, 1960, $3.50.
Guptill, A. L.: *Pencil Drawing: Step by Step*. Van Nostrand, 1959, 147 pp., $3.95.
Hawkinson, John: *Collect, Print and Paint From Nature*. Whitman, 1963, 40 pp., $3.95.
Hawkinson, John: *More to Collect and Paint From Nature*. Whitman, 1964, 40 pp., $3.95.
Hawkinson, John: *Our Wonderful Wayside*. Whitman, 1966, 40 pp., $3.95.
Hill, Adrian: *Beginner's Book of Oil Painting*. Emerson, 1959, 76 pp., $3.95.
Hill, Adrian: *Beginner's Book of Watercolor Painting*. Emerson, 1959, 78 pp., $3.95.
Kujoth: *The Recreation Program Guide*, pp. 106–113.
Painting (No. 3372). Boy Scouts, 1954, 56 pp., 45¢, paper.
Williams, Guy R.: *Paint Now, Learn Later*. Emerson, 128 pp., $4.95.

Driftwood

Ishimoto, Tatsuo: *The Art of Driftwood and Dried Arrangements*. Crown, 1951, 143 pp., $4.50.
Thompson, Mary E., and Leonid Skvirsky: *The Driftwood Book*. Van Nostrand, 1966, 216 pp., $6.95.

Indian Crafts

D'Amato, Janet and Alex: *Indian Crafts*. Lion, 1968, 65 pp., $3.95.
Hofsinde, Robert: *Indian Games and Crafts*. Morrow, 1957, 127 pp., $3.95.
Hunt, Ben, and J. F. "Buck" Burschears: *American Indian Beadwork*. Bruce, 1951, 64 pp., $3.95, paper.
Hunt, Ben: *Ben Hunt's Big Indiancraft Book*. Bruce, 1969, 188 pp., $7.95.
Hunt, Ben: *The Golden Book of Indian Crafts and Lore*. Golden, 1954, 112 pp., $4.45.
Minor, May Nono: *The American Indian Craft Book*. Popular Library, 1972, 416 pp., $1.25, paper.
Norbeck, Oscar E.: *Indian Crafts for Campers*. Order from Galloway, rev., 1974, 260 pp., $8.95.
Salomon, Julien H.: *Book of Indian Crafts and Indian Lore*. Harper & Row, 1928, 418 pp., $7.95.
Seton, Julia M.: *American Indian Arts: A Way of Life*. Ronald, 1962, 246 pp., $6.
Sides, Dorothy Smith: *Decorative Art of the Southwestern Indians*. Dover, rev., 1962, 101 pp., $1.50, paper.
Turner, Alta R.: *Finger Weaving: Indian Braiding*. Sterling, 1973, 48 pp., $2.95.
Whiteford, Andrew H.: *Indian Arts*. Golden, 160 pp., $3.95; $1.95, paper.

Leathercraft

Cherry, Raymond: *General Leathercraft*. McKnight, 4th ed., 1955, 144 pp., $2.64, paper.
Ginnett, Elsie: *Make Your Own Rings: Working With Leather*. Sterling, 1974, 88 pp., $6.95.
Grant, Bruce: *Leather Braiding*. Cornell Maritime, 1950, $3.50.
Groneman, G.: *Leathercraft*. Bennett, 1963, 151 pp., $6.48.
Kujoth: *The Recreation Program Guide*, pp. 211–224.
Leatherwork (No. 3310). Boy Scouts, 1970, 56 pp., 45¢, paper.
Leeming, Joseph: *Fun With Leather*. Lippincott, 1941, 91 pp., $5.50.
Petersen, Grete: *Leathercrafting*. Sterling, 1973, 48 pp., $2.95; 95¢, paper.
Sunset Things to Make With Leather. Lane, $1.95, paper.
Williams, Guy R.: *Working With Leather*. Emerson, 1967, 128 pp., $4.95.

Metal Work and Jewelry Making

Clegg, Helen, and Mary Larom: *Jewelry Making for Fun and Profit*. McKay, 1951, 162 pp., $4.95.
Ginnett, Elsie: *Make Your Own Rings and Other Things: Working With Silver*. Sterling, 1974, 88 pp., $6.95.
Kramer, Karl and Nora: *Coppercraft and Silver Made at Home*. Chilton, 1959, $5.50.
Maryon, H.: *Metalwork and Enameling*. Dover, 4th ed., 1971, 374 pp., $3.50, paper.
Metalwork (No. 3312). Boy Scouts, 1969, 36 pp., 45¢, paper.
Quick, Lelande: *Gemcraft—How to Cut and Polish Gemstones*. Chilton, 1959, 182 pp., $7.50; $3.95, paper.
Shoenfelt, Joseph F.: *Designing and Making Handwrought Jewelry*. McGraw-Hill, 1960, 170 pp., $4.95; $1.95, paper.
Untracht, Oppi: *Enameling on Metal*. Chilton, 1957, 191 pp., $7.50; $3.95, paper.

Zarchy, Harry: *Jewelry Making and Enameling*. Knopf, 1959, 120 pp., $4.39.
Zechlin, Katharina: *Creative Enameling and Jewelry-Making*. Sterling, 1965, 100 pp., $3.95.

Miscellaneous

Abell, Vivian: *Don't Throw It Away*. Meredith, 1974, 180 pp., $7.95.
Bachert, Russell E., Jr.: *Outdoor Education Equipment*. Order from Galloway, 197 pp., $7.95, paper.
Bale: *What On Earth*.
Benson, Kenneth R.: *Creative Crafts for Children*. Prentice-Hall, 1958, 106 pp., $7.25.
Carlson, Bernice Wells: *Make It and Use It*. Abingdon, 1958, 160 pp., $2.95.
Carlson, Bernice Wells: *Make It Yourself!* Abingdon, 1950, 160 pp., $2.95; $1.95, paper.
Corbin: *Recreation Leadership*, ch. 14.
Di Valentin, Maria and Louis, et al.: *Practical Encyclopedia of Crafts*. Sterling, 1973, 600 pp., $20.
Exploring the Hand Arts. Girl Scouts, 1955, 118 pp., $1.25, paper.
Facklam, Margery, and Patricia Phibbs: *Corn-Husk Crafts*. Sterling, 1974, 48 pp., $3.50.
Family Book of Crafts. Sterling, 1973, 576 pp., $20.
Frankel, Lillian and Godfrey: *Creating From Scrap*. Sterling, 128 pp., $2.95.
Grimm, Gretchen: *Creative Adventures in Arts and Crafts*. Bruce, 1962, 96 pp., $2.75.
Griswold, Lester and Kathleen: *The New Handicraft: Processes and Projects*. Burgess, 10th ed., 1969, 462 pp., $9.95; $4.95, paper.
Hellegers, Louisa B., and Anne E. Kallem (Compilers): *The Family Book of Crafts*. Sterling, 1973, 608 pp., $20.
Horn, George F.: *Posters: Designing, Making, Reproducing*. Davis, 1964, 96 pp., $6.30.
Howie, Olive: *Handy Crafts From Scraps*. Order from N.R.P.A., 76 pp., $3.68.
Hunt, Ben: *The Golden Book of Crafts and Hobbies*. Golden, 1954, 112 pp., $4.45.
Ickis, Marguerite, and Reba S. Esh: *Arts and Crafts*. Dover, 1965, 309 pp., $2, paper.
Jaeger, Ellsworth: *Easy Crafts*. Macmillan, 1947, 129 pp., $4.95.
Kampmann, Lothar: *Creating With Printed Materials*. Van Nostrand, 1969, 76 pp.
Kujoth: *The Recreation Program Guide*, pp. 44–58.
Liebers, Arthur: *Fifth Favorite Hobbies*. Hawthorn, 1968, 188 pp., $4.95.
Lindbeck, John R., et al.: *Basic Crafts*. Bennett, 1969, 274 pp., $7.12.
Mann: *Outdoor Education*, ch. 5.
Mattil, Edward L.: *Meaning in Crafts*. Prentice-Hall, 3rd ed., 1971, 201 pp., $8.50.
Portchmouth, John: *Creative Crafts for Today*. Viking, 1970, 190 pp., $8.95.
Reed, Carl, and Joseph Orze: *Art From Scrap*. Davis, 1960, 89 pp., $4.25.
Reeves, Robert: *Make-It-Yourself Games Book*. Emerson, 1964, 108 pp., $4.95.
Stevens, Harold: *Ways With Art: 50 Techniques for Teaching Children*. Van Nostrand, 1963, 224 pp., $3.95.
Sunset Crafts for Children. Lane, 1968, 96 pp., $1.95, paper.
Things to Make for Children. Lane, 1964, 96 pp., $1.95.
Turner, G. Alan: *Creative Crafts for Everyone*. Order from Galloway, 263 pp., $7.95.
Yates, Brock: *Plastic Foam*. Order from Galloway, 128 pp., $4.95.
Young, Jean: *Woodstock Craftsman's Manual*. Praeger, Vols. 1 and 2, $10 each; $4.50 each, paper.
Zarchy, Harry: *Here's Your Hobby*. Knopf, 1957, 337 pp., $4.99
Zechlin, Ruth: *Complete Book of Handicrafts*. Branford, 1968, 347 pp., $9.50.

MAGAZINE ARTICLES

Camping Magazine:
Bale, Robert O.: "How Crafts Programs Can Serve Campers." May, 1962, p. 31.
Brandon, T. Edmund: "A Pioneer Theme Enhances Camp Arts and Crafts," Jan., 1975, p 11.
Prentice, Charlotte Kramer: "Use Local Resources to Find Materials for Creative Crafts." Jan., 1973, p. 15.

Mosaics

Argiro, Larry: *Mosaic Art Today*. Int'l Textbook, rev., 1968, $10.
Timmons, Virginia Gayheart: *Designing and Making Mosaics*. Davis, 1971, 112 pp., $8.85.
Unger, Hans: *Practical Mosaics*. Viking, 1965, 80 pp., $6.95.

Nature Crafts

Alkema, Chester Jay: *Crafting With Nature's Materials*. Sterling, 1972, 48 pp., $2.95.
Bale: *Creative Nature Crafts*. Burgess, 1959, 120 pp., $3.95.
Bauzen, Peter and Suzanne: *Flower Pressing*. Sterling, 48 pp., $2.95.
Benson, Kenneth R., and Carl E. Frankson: *Creative Nature Crafts*. Prentice-Hall, 1969, 97 pp.
Jaeger, Ellsworth: *Nature Crafts*. Macmillan, 1950, 128 pp., $3.95.
Kujoth: *The Recreation Program Guide*, p. 66.
Musselman, Virginia: *Learning About Nature Through Crafts*. Stackpole, 1969, 128 pp., $3.95.
Nagle, Avery, and Joseph Leeming: *Fun With Naturecraft*. Lippincott, 1964, 80 pp., $4.75.
Plummer, Beverly: *Earth Presents: How to Make Beautiful Gifts From Nature's Bounty*. Atheneum.
Stinson, Thelma: *Native 'N Creative*. Cokesbury, 1957, 29 pp., 40¢, paper.

MAGAZINE ARTICLES

Camping Magazine:
Hager, Gwen: "A Potpourri of Nature Crafts for Your Summer Use." May, 1972, p. 22.

Paper

Alkema, Chester Jay: *Creative Paper Crafts in Color.* Sterling, 1973, 168 pp., $8.95.
Johnson, Pauline: *Creating With Paper.* U. of Wash., 1966, $8.95; $4.95, paper.
Johnston, Mary G.: *Paper Sculpture.* Davis, 1965, 82 pp., $5.30.
Murray, William D., and Francis J. Rigney: *Paper Folding For Beginners.* Dover, 96 pp., $1, paper.
Rainey, Sarita: *Ways With Paper: Construction and Poster.* Order from N.R.P.A., 35 pp., $1.95.
Rottger, Ernst: *Creative Paper Design.* Van Nostrand, 1961, 96 pp., $5.95.

Papier-Mâché

Anderson, Mildred: *Papier-Mâché and How to Use It.* Sterling, 96 pp., $3.95.
Betts, Victoria Bedford: *Exploring Papier-Mâché.* Davis, rev., 1966, $6.50.
Johnson, Lillian: *Papier-Mâché.* McKay, 1958, 88 pp., $4.95.

Sculpture

Lewis, Roger: *Sculpture (Clay, Soap and Other Materials).* Knopf, 1952, 44 pp., $3.59.
Leyh, Elizabeth: *Children Make Sculpture.* Order from N.R.P.A., 96 pp., $5.95.
Sculpture (No. 3322). Boy Scouts, 1969, 24 pp., 45¢, paper.

Silk Screen

Biegeleisen, J. I., and Max A. Cohn: *Silk Screen Technique.* Dover, 1963, 187 pp., $2, paper.
Eisenberg, James, and Francis J. Kafka: *Silk Screen Printing.* McKnight, rev., 1957, 55 pp., $1.60.

Special Techniques

Belfer, Nancy: *Designing in Batik and Tie Dye.* Davis, 1972, 116 pp., $9.95.
Conroy, Norma M.: *Making Shell Flowers.* Sterling, 1972, 48 pp., $2.95.
Fletcher, Edward: *Pebble Collecting and Polishing.* Sterling, 1973, 96 pp., $3.95.
Fressard, M. J.: *Creating With Burlap.* Sterling, 1970, 48 pp., $2.95.
Goodman, Stuart and Leni: *Art from Shells.* Crown, $7.95.
Janvier, Jacqueline: *Felt Crafting.* Sterling, 1970, 48 pp., $2.95.
Krauss, Helen A.: *Shell Art.* Hearthside, 1965, 160 pp., $6.95.
Kujoth: *The Recreation Program Guide,* pp. 426–430. (woodworking)
LaCroix, Gretha: *Creating With Beads.* Sterling, 1969, 48 pp., $2.95.
Leeming, Joseph: *Fun With Fabrics.* Lippincott, 1950, $4.95.
Leeming, Joseph: *Fun With Shells.* Lippincott, 92 pp., $3.50.
Leeming, Joesph: *Fun With Wire.* Lippincott, 1956, 96 pp., $4.50.
Lynch, John: *How to Make Collages.* Viking, 1961, 136 pp., $5.95; $2.95, paper.
Lynch, John: *How to Make Mobiles.* Viking, 1953, 96 pp., $3.95.
McDowall, Pamela: *Pressed Flower Pictures: A Victorian Art Revived.* Scribner's, 1970, 78 pp., $12.50.
Maile, Anne: *Tie and Dye.* Ballantine, $2.95.
Marks, Mickey Klar: *Sand Sculpturing.* Dial, 1963, 40 pp., $3.50.
Olson, David F.: *Stone Grinding and Polishing: Make Your Own Gems.* Sterling, 1974, 48 pp., $3.50.
Priolo, Joan B.: *Ideas for Collage.* Sterling, 48 pp., $2.95.
Randall, Reino, and Edward C. Haines: *Bulletin Boards and Displays.* Davis, 1961, 64 pp., $4.25.
Saeger, Glen: *String Things You Can Make.* Sterling, 1973, 48 pp., $2.95.
Schegger, T. M.: *Make Your Own Mobiles.* Sterling, 96 pp., $2.95.
Van Rensselaer, Eleanor: *Decorating With Seed Mosaics, Chipped Glass and Plant Materials.* Van Nostrand, 1960, 214 pp., $6.95.
Villasenor, David and Jean: *How to Do Permanent Sandpainting.* Order from ACA, 1972, 32 pp., $2.
Williams, Guy R.: *Making Mobiles.* Emerson, 1969, 94 pp., $4.95.
Yates, Brock: *Plastic Foam for Arts and Crafts.* Order from Galloway, 128 pp., $3.50.

Weaving

Coates, Helen: *Weaving For Amateurs.* Viking, 2nd ed., 1946, $5.
Lawless, Dorothy: *Rug Hooking and Braiding for Pleasure and Profit.* Crowell, rev., 1962, 286 pp., $5.95.
Rainey, Sarita R.: *Weaving Without a Loom.* Sterling, 132 pp., $8.95.
Tidball, H.: *The Weaver's Book.* Macmillan, 1961, 173 pp., $5.95.
Znamieroski, Neil: *Weaving.* Golden, $2.50.

Chapter 16

Tincancraft

First the thought, and then the act,
Before the dream becomes a fact.

—H. S. WALTER*

Figure 16-1 Tin Cans Serve Many Purposes.

THE VERSATILE TIN CAN

A tin can is one of the most versatile objects in existence. It can serve as a cup or cooking utensil; it can be made into an efficient little oriole cache (Fig. 29-6), a hobo stove (Figs. 16-5*F* and 29-7), or a buddy burner (Figs. 16-5*G* and 29-8); flattened out and shaped, it becomes a tray (Fig. 16-6*C*, *H*), a shade (Fig. 16-6*G*), or anything that your creative mind designs. You will be surprised to discover how easy it is to convert tin cans into useful or decorative objects.

Tin cans are light and easy to work with and are easy to solder. Working with them also provides preliminary practice in using tools and patterns preparatory to working with such relatively expensive metals as copper, pewter, aluminum, brass, and silver. If you make a mistake, you can simply throw the can away and begin again with the loss of nothing more serious than a little time.

*Published by permission of The Indianapolis News.

MATERIALS NEEDED

It is possible to purchase sheet tin at a hardware store, but it is simple to get your own free by cutting and straightening out a tin can of suitable size. (Incidentally, tin cans are really misnamed for they consist of only about 2 per cent tin, placed as a thin covering on both sides of a layer of steel.) Scrap wire for handles is free for the picking up around the house, camp, or in nearby scrap heaps.

The tools you need for making simple things are few and inexpensive and so common that most homes or camps already have them (Fig. 16-2). Tin snips, cotton gloves, pliers, hammer, hack saw, flat file, three-cornered file, and nails or nail sets are all that are really essential.

After you progress to more complicated or decorative items, you may want to add *duck bill tin snips* (Fig. 16-2*F*) for cutting curved surfaces neatly and a *jeweler's saw* (Fig. 16-2*I*) for cutting out intricate designs or orifices in metal, as when making letters of the alphabet. The thin blade of the

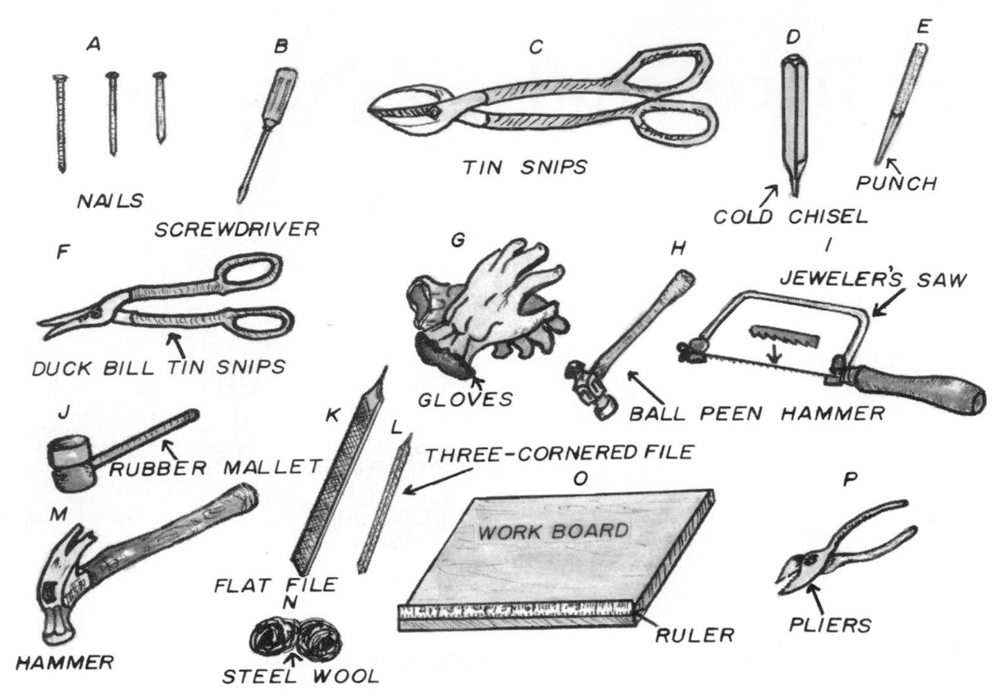

Figure 16–2 Tools For Working With Metal.

jeweler's saw is removable so that you can insert it into the metal by making a hole just large enough to admit it, then reinserting the blade in the handle and fastening it in place with wing nuts. Point the teeth downward toward the handle and cut by pulling downward. Keep the blade straight up and down and work slowly and carefully, especially when turning corners or working in tight spots, for it is easy to break the thin blade.

Use a hammer and *cold chisel* (Fig. 16–2*D*) to cut through metal which is too heavy to cut with tin snips. A screwdriver can be used for this but it won't do as neat a job. A *hard rubber* or *wooden mallet* (Fig. 16–2*J*) or *ball peen hammer* (Fig. 16–2*H*) will enable you to pound metal without scarring and denting it as the metal head on a regular hammer would. You will need *steel wool* (Fig. 16–2*N*) if you want to polish the metal. A work board (Fig. 16–2*O*) is a great convenience, and a ruler or tape measure attached to one side by means of wire nails will permit using it to measure as well as to lay off angles with a T-square and triangles. You will need an *eggbeater drill* if you want to make small, neat holes.

For soldering, you will need a can of soldering paste, a tube of wire solder, and an alcohol lamp. Follow the directions that come with them. Use fine wire such as lightweight stovepipe wire to hold the parts together while you solder.

PREPARING TIN CANS

Tin cans are available in almost any shape and size desired, varying from small tobacco tins to large oil cans. The standard sizes used for canning fruits and vegetables are as follows:

No. 1—large evaporated milk can
No. 2—most canned vegetables
No. 3—canned tomatoes
No. 5—twice the size of a no. 3 can

No. 10—gallon size, available from restaurants, school or camp dining rooms, etc.

Always wear cotton or canvas work gloves when working with metal; the sharp, jagged edges can easily cut you, or your unaccustomed work with heavy tin snips and other tools may cause blisters.

Some cans are used just as they are or are merely cut down in height. When you want to convert a can into a flat sheet of metal, use an ordinary wall can opener to cut off both ends, then cut down on both sides of the side seam with your tin snips and remove it. Place the resulting circular piece of metal on your work board or a sturdy work table, hold one side with one hand and press it out flat with the other. Complete the flattening process by rolling over it with a stick or use the head of your hammer.

WORKING WITH METAL

When making something rather complicated, it is best to make a paper pattern, shaping and reshaping it until you are sure it is just right. If some sections are to be cut out for decorative purposes, it will help you to visualize the finished product if you color them dark on the pattern. Use a pencil to trace the pattern on the tin and cut along the marked line with your tin snips, resting the bottom of them against your work board or table as you cut. Take your time so that you won't injure yourself or do a jagged job of cutting.

There are several ways to make the cut edges more attractive and safer to handle. You can simply smooth them off with a file, but this leaves them still somewhat sharp and hazardous to handle. A better way is to turn the edge over with your pliers, then place the object over a post or the butt of a log and mash the edge flat with a regular or ball peen hammer or a mallet. If the surface is curved, you will need to cut out a series of small V-shaped pieces along the edge before turning it over. The best method of all is to make small cuts in the tin, each $\frac{1}{8}$ to $\frac{1}{4}$ inch deep, then fit a piece of wire right at the base of the cuts and use your pliers to turn the edge over and tuck it in around the wire. Keep working at it until the edge is smooth and well-rounded.

When you need to bend a piece of metal at a right angle, bend it over the edge of a work table or place it between two boards in a vise (Fig. 16–3) and flatten it over the tops of the boards.

Holes can be used for decoration, for inserting a wire handle, or for suspending the object from a nail. To make them, place the article over a tree stump or block of wood and use a hammer and nail set, ice pick, or other sharp object of appropriate size. As mentioned previously, you can make neater holes with a hand drill, resting the object on a soft piece of wood for the drill to enter after piercing the metal. When possible, flatten the other side of the holes you have punched out.

To convert a flat piece of metal into a cylinder, choose some round object such as a nail, an empty spool, a wooden dowel, or other item of the size you want, then place the piece of metal over it and use your hand or a narrow board to fit the metal around it.

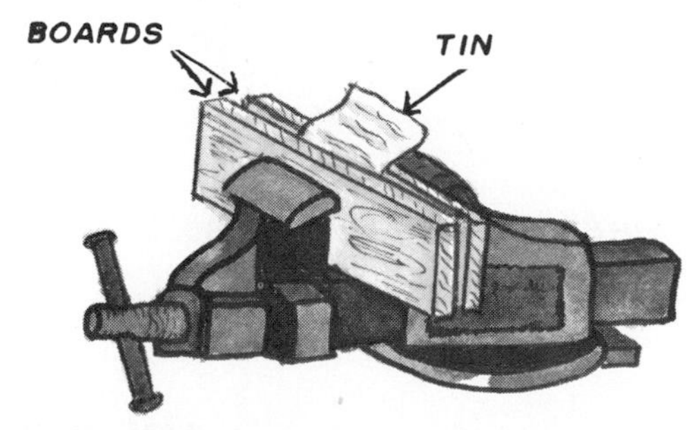

Figure 16–3 Using a Vice To Make a 90° Turn in Metal.

You can join pieces of metal by riveting, nailing, soldering, or leaving tabs on one piece to insert into slits in the other and then bending the tabs over.

ADDING HANDLES

There are a number of ways to add handles. Figure 16–4*A* shows a tin can with a strip left on both sides of the seam which can then be bent around a wooden handle and fastened with nails and wire lashing (*B*) or made detachable by fastening it with wing nuts (*C*). Figure 16–4*D* shows a wire handle held in place with tight wire lashing; *E* shows a wire handle inserted through two holes in the tin can; and *F* shows a snap-on handle made from wire coat hangers (X and Y).

SOME THINGS TO MAKE

Figure 16–5 shows a variety of useful things fashioned from tin cans of appropriate size. Figure 16–5*A* is a well-perforated can with a handle to use for dipping your silverware into hot, sterilizing water; *B* is a spatula; and *C* shows several types of forks made from wire coat hangers. Figure 16–5*D* is a scoop for dry foodstuffs such as sugar or flour; use a screw to attach the wooden handle. A weatherproof holder for toilet paper to place near an outdoor latrine is shown in Figure 16–5E. Suspend it on a crossbar between two forked sticks as shown.

You can make a complete set of nested cooking utensils by choosing tin cans of appropriate sizes as shown in Figure 16–5*H*. Be sure to equip them with detachable handles (Fig. 16–4) so that they will nest compactly.

Other useful camp "fixings" are also shown in Figure 16–5. Kettles, stew pots, plates, and frying pans are best made from number 10 or gallon tin cans cut to appropriate depths. Cups are made from number 2 or number 2½ cans, while number 2½ or number 5 cans are about right for cereal bowls. (Before using tin-can cooking or eating

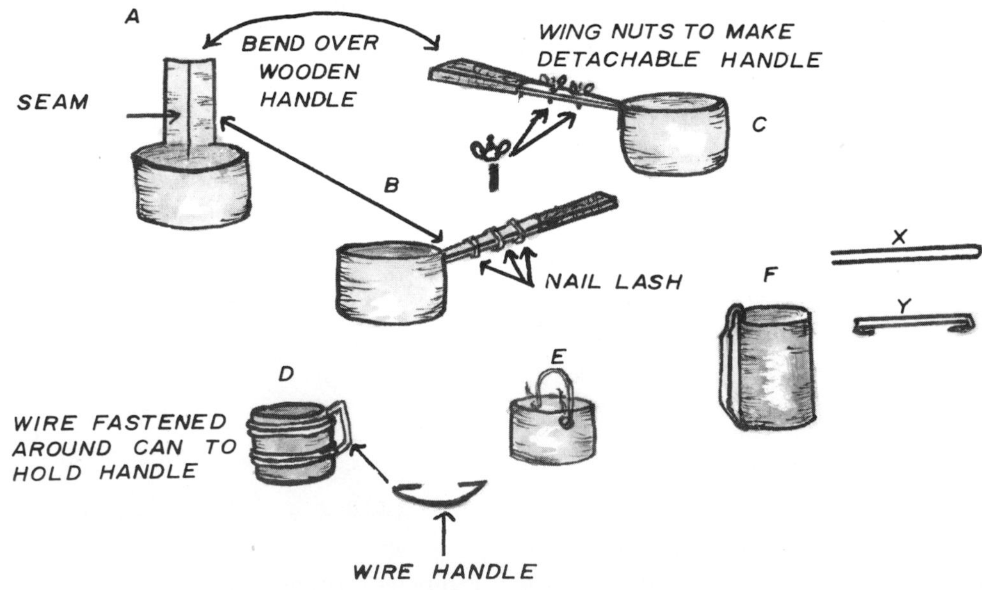

Figure 16–4 Ways To Attach Handles.

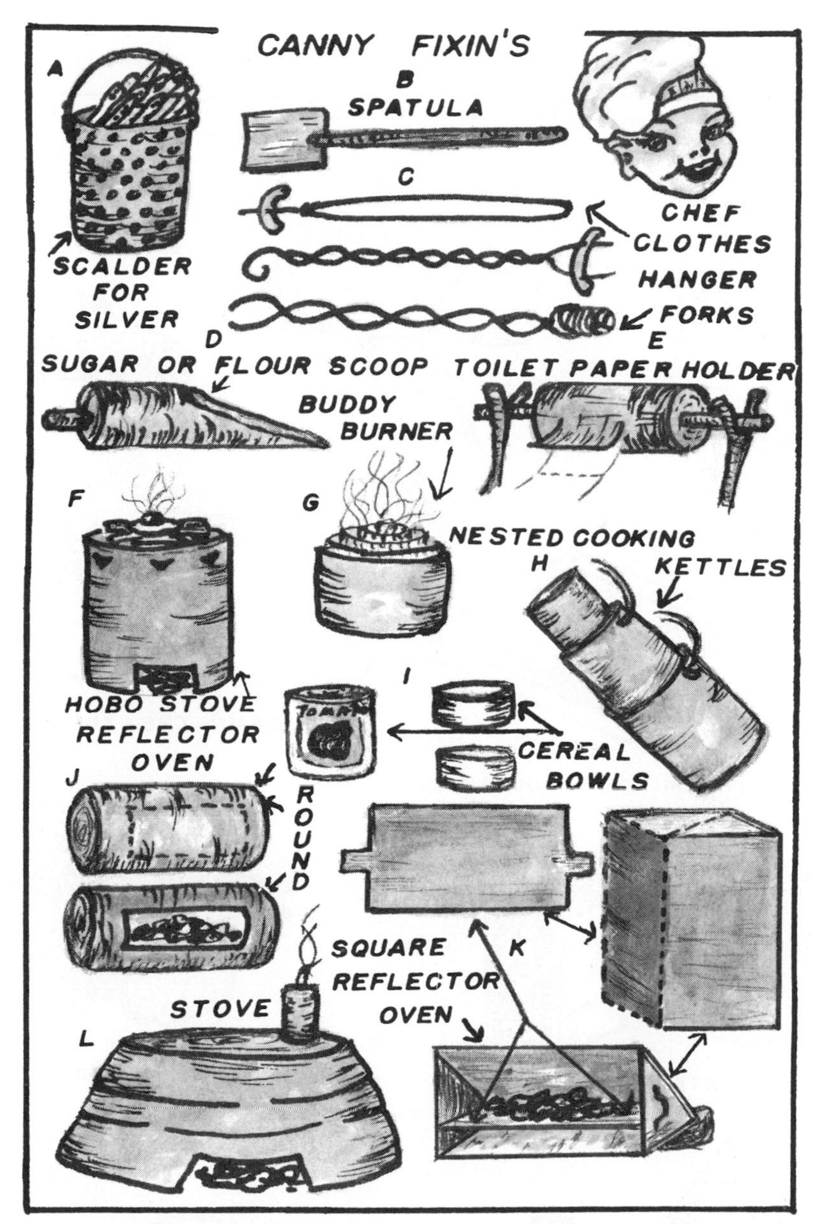

Figure 16–5 Useful Things To Have Around Camp.

utensils, heat them and scrub them thoroughly with hot water and a good scouring powder to remove the lacquer that is usually present on them.) Use only cans that have contained food, not paint or oil, for cooking utensils. Make a ditty bag of denim or other strong material with a drawstring at the top to carry your nested cooking outfit. Always be sure to dry out tin utensils thoroughly immediately after using them, for they rust very quickly. Use a plastic scouring pad rather than steel wool to clean them.

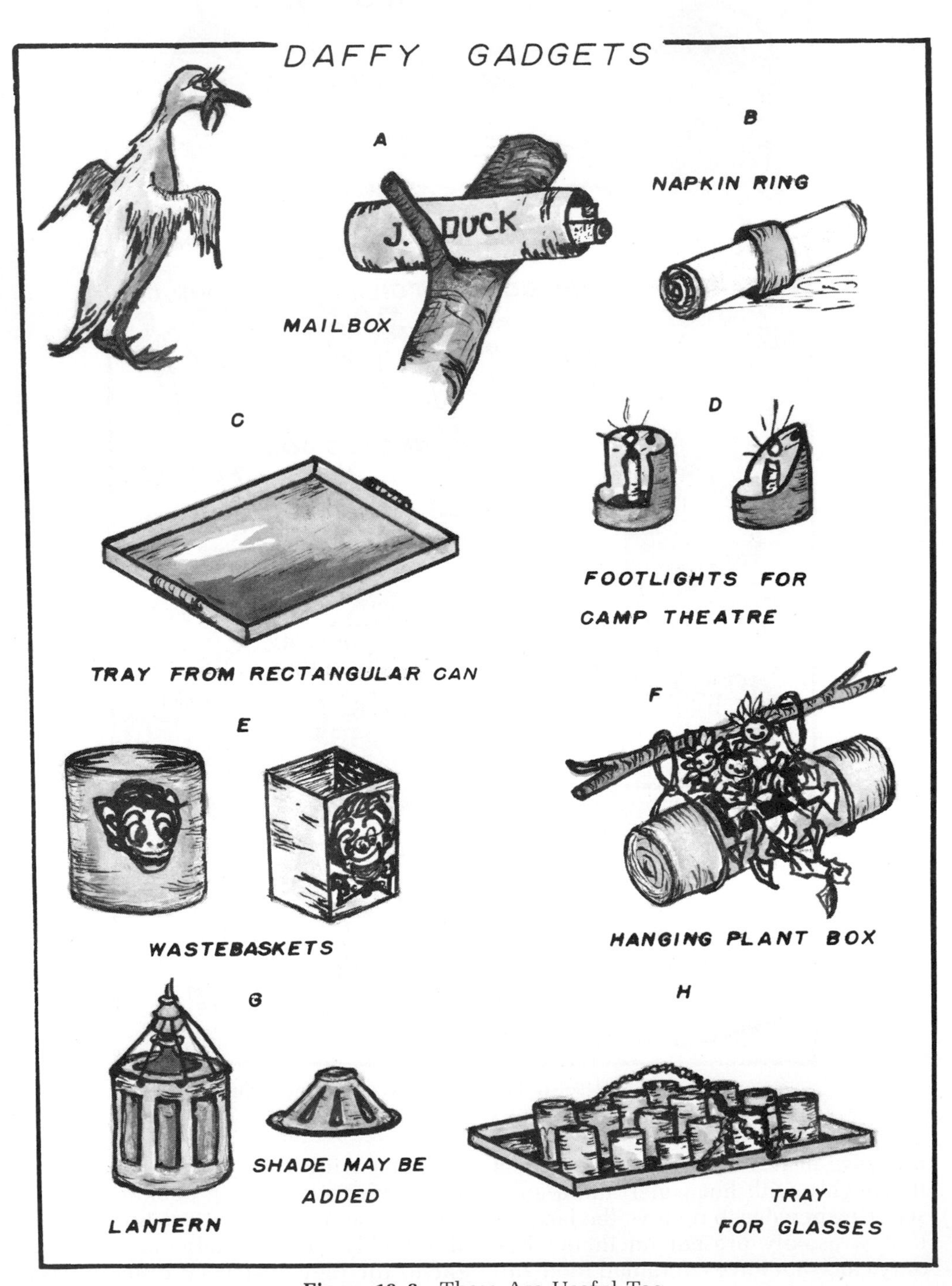

Figure 16-6 These Are Useful Too.

Hobo Stoves

Hobo stoves (Fig. 16–5*F*) are handy little cooking devices that will heat up in no time at all with just a handful of twigs for fuel. If you want to cook directly on the top, heat it to remove the lacquer and then scrub it thoroughly.

To make a hobo stove* which can be disassembled and packed into a flat, compact bundle, cut off the top of a number 10 tin can and slice the sides into three or four strips and flatten them; when ready to use the stove, merely stick the sides solidly into the ground and balance the top over them. Make a ditty bag to fit your hobo stove.

An excellent stove, large enough to support several pots and pans, can be made from an old washtub or wash boiler (Fig. 16–5*L*).

Reflector Ovens

Figure 16–5*J* and *K* are reflector ovens which can be propped up in front of the fire and will do a fine job of baking almost anything you want. The shelf or baking sheet is suspended in the middle so that the heat is reflected onto the surface from both above and below. The stove in Figure 16–5*J* is made from a round can; *K* is one made from a rectangular can cut diagonally across, with a shelf made from one side of the can. Perhaps you can devise a way to make the sides detachable so that you can pack it flat like commercially made reflector ovens. Make a ditty bag to carry it in.

**Suggestions for Improvising Camping Out Equipment.* Camp Publications.

Other Articles

To make a useful and decorative set of kitchen canisters, select tin cans of the right size and enamel them (two coats for permanence) in any color scheme desired. Paint the name of the contents on the outside and add further decoration with your own free-hand painting or with decalcomania designs. You can buy glass or wooden knobs at the variety or hardware store or you can make your own wooden ones to fasten on with a screw. Figure 16–6 shows other things to make and your own inventive mind can devise still others.

To leave a bright metal finish, burnish the outside with steel wool. Another method of finishing consists of holding the object over the fire until it assumes a cloudy dullness, then quickly burnishing it with a brush and a good scouring powder.

To make an anchor for the candle in a candle holder (Fig. 16–6*D*), cut an "X" in the bottom of the tin can and bend the edges up until they fit snugly around the candle.

ADDITIONAL READINGS

(For an explanation of abbreviations and abbreviated forms used, see page 25.)

Note: Additional helpful references may be found in the bibliography in Chapter 15 on Arts and Crafts.

Howard, Sylvia W.: *Tin-Can Crafting.* Sterling, 1960, 64 pp., $3.95.

Jaeger: *Wildwood Wisdom.*

Mason: *The Junior Book of Camping and Woodcraft.*

Richardson, Nancy: *How to Stencil and Decorate Furniture and Tinware.* Ronald, 1956, 186 pp., $7.00.

Skibness, Edward J.: *How to Use Tin Can Metal in Science Projects.* Denison, 1960, 120 pp., $4.50.

Chapter 17

Nature and Ecology

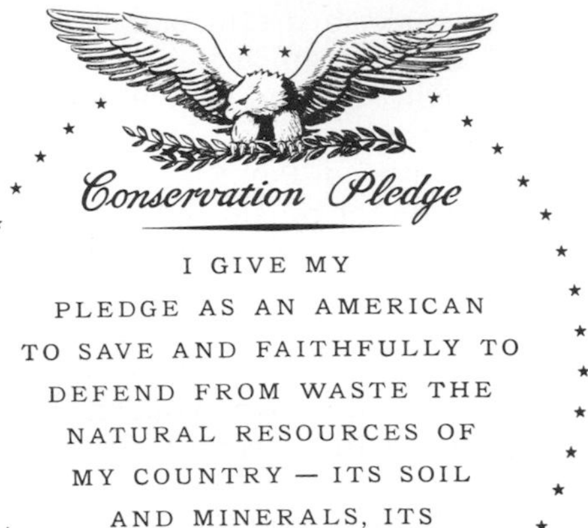

Figure 17-1 This pledge originated in a national competition conducted in 1946 by *Outdoor Life Magazine* and is reprinted through their courtesy.

The old log in the woods will never be a great tree again—things never go back—yet lying there —covered with moss—it is creating new life —which in turn will be great and beautiful . . . .

The fish eats the insect—the bird the fish —the mammal the bird—and—the insect the mammal—as each—in a universal rhythm is creating new life—for there is no life except life which comes from life . . . .

Waters flow where daisies grew—
Trees grow where swans once swam—

All things upon this earth are developing into new things—from what is here must come what is to be . . . there is no other material . . . .*

—GWEN FROSTIC

CHANGING EMPHASES IN CAMP NATURE PROGRAM

A return to the simple life and its intimate contact with nature has always been a recognized purpose of camping, but the methods used have not always brought the appreciation and love of nature hoped for. Campers have victoriously displayed badges and ribbons won by learning the scientific names of 20 insects or mounting 20 flowers, and have returned to the city bearing such live pets as squirrels, turtles, grasshoppers, snakes, and even skunks to foist upon long-suffering parents or to let die of neglect and mistreatment. Only an occasional camper acquired enough interest in nature to make it a lifelong hobby, for, like human friends, plants and animals become truly cherished only after long and personal acquaintance. Learning a name or viewing a still, cold corpse impaled upon a mounting pin will never bring about such a result.

It may bolster one's ego to identify a giant dragonfly as *Epiaeschna heros*, but it cannot compare with the enchantment of watching this evil-looking, blood-thirsty creature zoom and bank through the air, using its basketlike undercarriage of legs to scoop up flies, mosquitoes, and other insects, which it later crams into its capacious mouth. Its appetite is enormous, and it has been known to bolt down 42 flies topped off with large quantities of its own tail, which had

*Reprinted by permission of the author and publisher from Gwen Frostic "These Things Are Ours," 1960, Presscraft Papers, Benzonia, Mich., 49616.

been bent around and fed into its mouth. Its needle is only an elongated stomach, and its huge eyes have 30,000 facets, which enable it to see in all directions. These, with its fierce expression, give it a truly sinister look, but it is helpful, not harmful, to man and does not merit its common names of devil's darning needle, horse killer, and snake feeder. Perhaps it is unfortunate that its long "darning needle" does not have its reputed power to sew up the lips of liars.

Figure 17-2 "Who Are You?"

NEW CONCEPTIONS OF NATURE STUDY

One frog in the pond is worth five in formaldehyde.*

Nature study in camp should not be conducted in a bookish, school manner, with formal methods and highly technical terms. Instead, it should find a niche in many camp activities, making use of teachable moments as they arise and capitalizing on a youngster's curiosity and his desire to know the how, why, where, when, and what of anything not familiar to him. When you can't answer a question, your response may well be, "I don't know, but let's see if we can find out."

A group should seldom be in too big a hurry to stop and watch the antics of a venturesome squirrel or listen to a noisy blue jay as he performs his mission of warning his camp neighbors about a possible dangerous intrusion. Instead of acquiring knowledge in order to pass tests or to pose as a walking encyclopedia, a camper learns by personal observation and, in so doing, develops a genuine feeling for nature as it seeps in pleasantly and unconsciously as he uses eyes, ears, noses, touch, and even taste to satisfy his inquisitive mind about the world of nature around him. Van Matre terms such a feeling for the environment *acclimatization.** Specimens are not the smelly laboratory variety nor the foreign imports of zoo and circus but what the campers find as they venture forth to look at whatever lies beside the path, under rocks or old logs, in trees, or at the bottom of a creek or pond. How much more interesting nature's creatures are as we see them carrying on their normal activities in their natural habitats, than when we study their dead, dried-up skeletons. With the aid of such inexpensive pieces of equipment as a homemade butterfly or dip net and a little pocket microscope, the field of exploration is unlimited.

A night of restless slumber under a quaking aspen creates a real interest in noting how the flat, wide stem is set "on edge" against the broad leaf so that the least breeze keeps it stirring to produce the very disturbing rainlike patter of the previous night. Like opportunity, nature experiences often knock but once, and each should be seized upon when it appears. We cannot schedule happenings for a definite time and place, for Mother Earth's children are

*van der Smissen, Betty, and Goering, Oswald H.: *A Leader's Guide to Nature-Oriented Activities.* Iowa State University Press, 1965, p. 8. By permission.

*Van Matre, Steve: *Acclimatization.* ACA, 1972, p. 10.

too busy carrying on their daily activities to be amenable to man-made schedules. Let us not emulate the poor misguided nature counselor who said, "Now, children, come away from that porpoise washed up there on the beach! Remember, we're studying birds today, and we won't get around to porpoises until two weeks from Tuesday."

A child's feeling of confidence and security in the out-of-doors increases as he becomes familiar with it and learns that the fierce beasties heard last night or read about in his story books just don't exist in a modern camp. He learns that nearly all these creatures are quite timid and that they want most of all just to stay out of his way. They will not attempt to harm him unless teased, cornered, or otherwise frightened. Although he should retain a healthy respect for any which might prove unfriendly, he can sometimes make friends with chipmunks, squirrels, toads, and birds, since many woodland creatures readily respond to kindly overtures. His appreciation makes him enjoy doing a good turn for smaller, weaker woodfolk instead of tormenting or killing them just for the fun of it. His spiritual self gets an uplift as he views the indescribable wonders and beauties of nature, and since love comes from the heart, rather than the mind, the result is a genuine and abiding love for all living creatures.

Tests and ranks depend on information secured by firsthand observation rather than learned from a book. Though not used as springboards to nature study as they once were, a well-selected supply of nature books serves as the backbone of a good camp program. First should come an assortment of handbooks on all topics, each small and light enough to be slipped into a pocket or knapsack and used for identification on the trail. When divided among the parties in a group, they do not prove a burden to anyone. Back in camp are all sorts of pamphlets and larger resource books, well illus-

(Courtesy of U. S. Forest Service.)

(Courtesy of U. S. Forest Service.)

trated, preferably in color, and complete enough to give full information as well as interesting anecdotes about what has been seen. Bulletin boards, pictures, slides, film strips, photographs, and movies are valuable supplements.

ECOLOGICAL AND CONSERVATION APPROACHES

The dictionary defines *ecology* as "that branch of zoology which deals with the relationship of living things to their environment and to each other." This, of course, includes man. The topic proves fascinating as one notes how the individual members of a nature community interact to further the welfare of the whole just as the members of a human community. Information about this subject is available from many sources such as Storer: *The Web of Life,* which is listed in the bibliography at the end of this chapter.

Life histories are also interesting. How does an oak tree start? What determines where trees will grow? Where and how does a young sapling get the food to nourish itself? What are its enemies, and how do they harm it? What defense does it have against them? Do other members of the bird or

Figure 17-3 Safe in the Arms of a Tree.

animal world help? For what does it furnish food and shelter? Of what use are oak trees to man?

Ultimately, all living things are dependent upon plants, for every animal, including man, either dines directly upon some form of plant life or upon some other animal which, in the final analysis, does so. Everything looks like a delectable dietary tidbit to something else, so that each is simultaneously engaged in a struggle to secure its own food and to avoid becoming the food of another. Each has its own means of securing food, some of them unique and interesting. The opposite leaves of the teasel are joined into a small cup at the stem, which catches water to drown minute ants for its banquet dish. The rare Venus's-flytrap has a hairtrigger mechanism that causes the sharp teeth along the edges of its leaves to interlock instantly and trap any insect unlucky enough to merely brush against them.

Everything has a way of protecting itself. Deer can outrun most of their enemies, and cats climb trees to evade dogs. Porcupines pursue their leisurely way, secure in the knowledge that their barbed quills will deter most attackers; skunks make amiable and affectionate pets, but nature has given them the power to exact a fiendish revenge on whatever frightens or attacks them. The chameleon changes color, the rabbit "freezes," the rosebush has thorns, and the thistle has prickles to help protect it against its enemies. Camouflage also provides an effective means of protection.

Nature provides each variety of life in abundance, so that, though some may become food or succumb to disease, wind, flood, or unfavorable climatic conditions, there will always be enough left to carry on the species. The female frog lays 20,000 eggs, but only 200 develop into adult frogs, while the other 19,800 lose their lives by accident or become food for fish and water insects. Nature, if left to her own devices, will usually keep all species in balance, so that they neither die out nor become so numerous as to overrun the earth, and every single form of life has its own role in maintaining this equilibrium, which is called the *balance of nature*.

Figure 17-4 "I Guess I Outsmarted That Old Snake."

Enough birdlings are created to spare a few for the snake, just as enough lettuce and green beans grow to supply our needs. We must erase from our minds once and for all the idea that certain forms of life are more worthy than others, for man's previous efforts to kill out what he considered to be unworthy species sometimes backfired in a most unfortunate way. A concentrated drive to eradicate "chicken-killing" hawks, for instance, may bring about a huge oversupply of rats, mice, snakes, and frogs, which really constitute over 90 per cent of the hawks' diet in contrast to the occasional chicken that they might eat.

Almost everything we do affects plant or animal life in some way. Picking berries in the fall cuts down on the supply of winter food for some bird or animal as well as the number of seeds that might sprout and grow into new plants. Squirrels lose out when we gather nuts. Draining a swamp to provide more farm land kills thousands of plants and animals which cannot survive without a wet environment. Spraying of trees kills the insects and grubs which provide food for certain birds, and it may leave residues harmful to bird and animal life, including man. Killing squirrels will eventually mean fewer trees, for dead squirrels cannot bury nuts to sprout and grow into future forest monarchs.

Man, in his greediness to sell beaver pelts, thinned out these little animals until no more beaver dams were built in certain areas. When hard rains came, water rushed down the open streams, causing floods to destroy both property and life; between rains, the creek beds dried out so that water life could not survive, and land animals went thirsty.

Man has used the rivers as garbage tanks and open sewers and as drains for the various chemicals and waste products of manufacturing; as a result, they are no longer fit for swimming, and even plant and fish life often cannot survive in them.

Man has cut down the trees and shrubs and cleared the fence rows that used to provide food and shelter for animals and birds. He has shot and trapped so many animals for food, furs, or sport that some, such as the buffalo and grizzly bear, are scarce, and others, including the great auk and passenger pigeon, are extinct.

Conservation is the appreciation, understanding, and wise use of natural resources for the greatest good for the most people for the longest time.*

Forest preserves, mandatory hunting and fishing licenses, open and closed seasons, bag limits, and the nurturing and "planting" of young birds, fish, animals, and trees are feeble strides toward preservation of what little remains of our once great heritage, but the understanding and loyal

Figure 17–5 "Is Breakfast Ready?"

support of millions are necessary to make our efforts effective. Camp provides an ideal climate for instilling in young people an appreciation of ecology and a deep love and appreciation for all nature's wildlife. These campers will go home to cooperate in an all-out effort to protect what we have left of our natural environment for future generations. After all, they are the voters of tomorrow, who will determine the policies of the future.

One of man's most myopic perspectives has been with regard to the conservation of the soil, upon which all plant and animal life depends. Topsoil, consisting of a mixture of minerals and the decaying remnants of animals and plants, is admirably suited for plant growth. It lies above the non-fertile subsoil and varies from a depth of a few inches on hilltops to several feet in the valleys.

When our ancestors came to America, they were delighted with the rich topsoil produced by many years of undisturbed natural processes. They hastened to clear the land to plant crops, but after several years of repeatedly planting the same crop with no efforts made to replenish what was taken from the soil, the land became less and less productive. This concerned them little, however, for so much new land was available that they simply moved on to repeat the process in a new spot. Progressive farmers now plant crops in rotation so that one crop can partially restore what the other depleted, and they judiciously apply fertilizers and other top dressings to keep their topsoil in good condition.

Vegetation keeps soil porous and

* *You and Conservation*, ACA.

loose, enabling it to absorb and hold large quantities of water, which is gradually absorbed by the plants and returned to the air by evaporation. Without plant growth, rains quickly run off down sloping surfaces, forming ever-enlarging gullies and carrying away large quantities of topsoil. When the farmer makes his plow lines straight up and down the hillsides, he adds to this wastage. To avoid this problem, the careful farmer uses contour plowing. However, every year 25,000,000 cubic feet of our richest topsoil is washed away and eternally lost for cultivation. This is not a cheering picture, when we stop to think that from 500 to 1,000 years are required to create a depth of one inch of fertile topsoil. Rapidly draining slopes cause swollen streams and eventually floods, which carry away still more topsoil and destroy the plant and animal life along the banks.

Topsoil in dry areas, without roots of vegetation to hold it in place, blows away as dust, leaving behind whole areas of infertile and desolate dust bowls. Some ill-informed farmers still burn off their land each year in a misguided attempt to kill off weeds and get the ground "ready" for spring crops, but this practice actually does irreparable damage to their precious topsoil.

Testing of the soil and supplying needed chemicals, rotation of crops, planting of cover crops to hold moisture and prevent erosion, and use of terraced and contour plowing on hillside areas are valuable steps in soil conservation.

True conservation is based upon an appreciation of the value of each living thing in maintaining the balance of the whole. It tells us that it is prudent to use the surplus which nature lavishly supplies but that we must always carefully leave enough of everything to insure its continuance for our own future use and that of coming generations. We may liken this to an investment at the bank, where the interest always continues to accumulate as long as we leave the principal intact. When man, in his infinite shortsightedness, sets himself up to decide which varieties of life are worthy to continue, he is likely to upset nature's nicely poised balance in ways difficult to foresee. It is much wiser to take the attitude that any wanton destruction of wild life is extremely undesirable.

Figure 17–6 "Hello, World."

CONSERVATION BEGINS AT HOME

One of the best ways to familiarize campers with nature and good conservation practices is to involve them in projects of their own choosing to improve their camp. Try to develop in them a sense of proprietorship about the camp so that each feels a glow of accomplishment when he has helped to do something to improve it. Be sure to discuss any plans with your Camp Director before going ahead. It is also wise to confer with such experts as your camp caretaker, county agent, conservation officer, park superintendent, or forester, since ill-advised efforts by amateurs sometimes do more harm than good. Here are some possibilities:

1. Take your group on a leisurely tour of the camp, noting spots that show the results of violations of good conservation practices. Make a list of what needs to be done and arrange it in

the order of priority. Let each group decide which, if any, it would like to undertake, keeping always in contact with the director and being guided by his wishes. Involve your campers in all proceedings; remember, do *with,* not *for,* them; their eager minds and willing hands contribute observations, suggestions, and accomplishments that may surprise you

2. Plan to make your camp a bird and animal sanctuary and seek ways to further their welfare and safety. Plant shade, fruit, or nut trees, berry bushes, sunflower seed, commercial bird seed, sweet corn, beans and other vegetables, small grain, and so forth. Make brush piles and plant shrubbery and other forms of cover along fencerows, camp roads, and wagon trails.

3. Make and erect birdhouses; you may get occupants this summer, or at least they will be ready for next year's nesting. Short bits of string and cord are appreciated at nesting time. Suspend a hummingbird feeder (they can be purchased commercially) and fill it with a 50-50 solution of sugar and water with a bit of food coloring added; you'll enjoy their grace and beauty while feeding. Attract birds and other creatures that eat mosquitoes; this is preferable to using poisonous sprays, which kill helpful insects.

4. Make a bird center near camp and where there is ample foliage to provide hiding places. Keep bird baths and food handy. Construct a bird blind to hide behind to give you a better look at birds. If the light is right, take photographs. Groups can adopt a bird family as their own to watch through the summer.

5. Construct an animal sanctuary with food and fresh water in constant supply. Make it a practice never to hurt

(Courtesy of Barbara Ellen Joy and Marjorie Camp.)

or frighten any creatures, and note how tame they get.

6. Help forest development by thinning out places where trees are too thick for any to grow well. Weed out those that are less desirable or are crooked or diseased. Prune off dead or diseased limbs, painting over the wounds (green or black blend in nicely) to prevent sap from bleeding and to keep diseases and insects out. Clear out any brush or vines that are choking young trees. Remember that it is sometimes wise to let dead trees stand. They furnish homes and nests for certain birds and animals and will eventually rot away, returning their substance to enrich the soil as nature intended.

7. Locate beds of poison ivy, poison oak, or poison sumac, particularly those near camp and trails. Spray individual plants to kill them. Proceed with care, for highly susceptible people may be accidentally poisoned.

8. Promote a Conservation, Anti-Litter, Earth, or Ecology Day with appropriate posters, films, slides, filmstrips, pamphlets, and books, and bring in outside resource personnel. Plan special projects to carry out.

9. Hold a scavenger hunt, awarding varying points for bringing in such unwanted debris as pieces of glass, bottles, bits of loose paper (we hope, not left by camp personnel, who should always use waste cans and keep their camp ground so neat that periodic clean-up crusades are unnecessary). Make a wire enclosure to display the haul, and recycle when possible.

10. Volunteer for community service in cleaning up adjoining roads, a public beach, or park, always, of course, under the direction of those in charge.

11. Keep your camp grounds neat, but avoid overdoing it, for too much neatness can be harmful to wildlife, as when fencerows are kept so clean that there is no food or cover, or when you sweep the floor of your campsite so thoroughly that you damage vegetation, remove decaying twigs and humus that would replenish the soil, uncover roots, and set the stage for erosion. Keep paths narrow and avoid clearing more campsite area than you actually need for comfort and safety.

12. Clean up the banks of a lake or other body of water and improve living conditions for its surrounding wildlife. If erosion is taking place, it is carrying away topsoil, which makes the water muddy so that it is not pleasant to look at or do anything in. In addition, erosion may make it uninhabitable for fish and other inhabitants and may eventually fill in the body of water until it no longer exists. Take steps to stop the erosion by filling in gullies, planting brush and other cover along the shore, and building conversion dams and canals to distribute the water over the area so that it sinks in instead of running off.

13. Keep a close watch over your trails. If one begins to show signs of wearing through or becoming so impacted by the passage of many feet that things can't grow in it, direct traffic to a new one and set out to repair the old one as described above. Zigzag trails up and down slopes to prevent erosion. To prevent unthinking individuals from using the old ones, post a sign, such as: "Stop! Your feet are killing me."

14. Let each child or unit plant its own bed of tree "seeds," such as acorns, nuts, maple wings, or fruit pits, watering and caring for it and watching the tiny treelets sprout and grow. In future summers, he or other campers can transplant seedlings to permanent homes.

15. Small trees and shrubs, if taken with plenty of dirt, can be transplanted at almost any season of the year. Water them well weekly until the roots have had time to become well established. Spare trees can sometimes be found where not needed on the campsite; they may be purchased from nurseries; or

Figure 17–7 Plan a Camp Reunion to Plant Trees.

they are often available free or at nominal cost from state and federal nurseries. Plan your own Arbor Day as an annual event, with an appropriate dedication ceremony and with each child marking his planting by a stake with his name on it. He'll be proud to watch it grow, especially if he comes back in succeeding summers or can point it out to his children as he brings them to their first camp session. Some camps promote a camp reunion for early spring or late fall for this purpose.

16. Make "Stay on the Path" your camp motto to avoid wanton destruction of outside tender vegetation. Campers may outline main paths with small painted rocks to make them easier to follow, especially at night.

17. Stress good principles of conservation, such as cutting no living trees unless absolutely necessary (the same toasting sticks and lug poles will serve repeatedly) and choosing wisely when you cut. If you build wood fires, prepare safe fire sites and put out fires completely. Seriously consider using stoves instead of wood fires. Choose materials for arts and crafts judiciously, and use sparingly. Avoid ditching tents. Replace all sod removed and leave a trip campsite in better condition than you found it.

18. Plant or transplant materials for future use in arts and crafts projects (grow your own).

19. Organize camp and unit Fire Brigades, using older campers especially. Ask your local conservation agent or other official to help you set it up and to pick out those areas in camp which are especially hazardous. Set up fire stations in strategic locations, equipped with axes, shovels, stirrup pumps, buckets, and fire brooms. See that staff and campers know where fire stations are and how to use them. See that everyone in camp knows exactly what to do if he is the first to spot a fire or when he hears the sound of the fire siren. Hold frequent fire drills at unexpected times and when campers are in various locations.

20. Make a tour of the camp to note what food Mother Nature is growing for future use by her star boarders. What can you do to help?

21. Discuss what conservation progress is being made on a local, state, and national level. What still needs to be done? What regulatory laws exist, and how do they help? Who is harmed when people cheat on the regulations? How are conservation efforts financed? How can you, as John Q. Citizen, contribute in camp and in your own home community?

22. Restock your fishing area. Ask for help and advice from your state hatchery or other sources. Don't take fish you won't use, and return little ones to the water unharmed so that you can catch them again when they've grown up.

23. Study the helpful roles played by such commonly despised creatures as bats, ants, skunks, insects, worms, spiders, snakes, bees, and wasps. Since all of them play an important role in nature's master plan, develop an attitude of living and letting live instead of torturing and murdering them indiscriminately.

24. Discuss the harm done by in-

Figure 17-8 Peter 'Possum.

discriminate weed spraying killing off *all* growth, and so on). Sprays that kill flies and mosquitoes also kill off helpful insects. Use good practices in camp.

25. Collect in a glass jar water from a spot where erosion is taking place. Let it sit for 24 hours, and note the good topsoil that it carried.

26. Take a wildlife census of the camp with groups or individuals designated to watch for certain varieties, such as birds, insects, butterflies, animals, and snakes. Post colored pictures to help in identification. Keep a scrapbook or use a file card for each type seen, noting name, date, place spotted, occupation when seen, and the name of the spotter. Detailed information and photographs or colored pictures can be added.

27. Make a compost pile at some distance from the main camp, placing on it grass cuttings, excess leaves, vegetable parings, and the like. Place some lime between each layer to hasten disintegration, and add fertilizer if you wish. Keep it damp, and stir it up occasionally. Next summer you will have some excellent humus to mix with soil in your garden or other area where you want luxuriant growth to occur. You can plant a border of trees and shrubbery around your compost pile to make it less conspicuous.

28. Keep a diary of things you do to make life more comfortable and safer for wildlife. Take before-and-after photographs and add new photographs next summer.

29. In what ways do the camp and campers use natural resources unnecessarily (gasoline, water, paper, electricity, etc.)? What can you as individuals and as a group do to stop this waste?

30. Consider the environmental effect of some camp activities such as campfire rings, cookouts, games and sports, trips, fishing, arts and crafts, and hiking. Do you need to change any procedures?

31. Set up and operate a camp weather station.

NATURE COUNSELING

Each counselor must, in a sense, be a nature counselor. This does not mean that he is expected to be an authority on nature lore but rather that he will be interested and willing to start with whatever meager knowledge he has and add to it as he learns with his campers. He need not be ashamed to admit that he doesn't know all the answers, for even a specialist starts out knowing absolutely nothing about his subject. The counselor will gradually need to say, "I don't know, but let's find out," less and less often as he explores with his campers and consults the camp naturalist and source books about what he cannot learn by observation.

Nature, like happiness, lurks in unexpected places, more often disclosing itself to those alert enough to notice rather than to those who go out consciously seeking it. A hike may end up a hundred yards from the cabin as a fascinated group watches a spider weave its web, or a trip to gather materials for arts and crafts may turn into a study of different woods and their uses; who can say that these side excursions are not more valuable than the original objectives?

The qualities you need most to further a good program are curiosity, enthusiasm, and an insight into the possibilities for integrating nature with many camp experiences. Most important of all is an interest in and love of *human* nature. Don't let the program degenerate into a boresome, tedious thing. Your attitude is all-important, so show enthusiasm and an eagerness to learn. Cloak every undertaking in a spirit of fun and adventure, sometimes going out with a specific purpose in mind, such as catching minnows to fish with, finding wild strawberries or blueberries for a pie or cobbler, visiting an old lumber mill, or learning what measures a neighboring farmer takes to prevent loss of soil by erosion. A leisurely pace and a receptive attitude can turn an excursion into a vibrant answer to youngsters' How? When? Where? and Why?

Figure 17-9 He'll Be Home for Christmas—Maybe.

A trip offers a wonderful opportunity to acquire information about the world in which we live. What camper would fail to be interested in nontechnical information about different terrains and soils and their effect upon flora and fauna, and about watersheds, rivers, drainage, currents, water life, and the hundreds of displays Dame Nature has set up along the way? When conducted with naturalness and enthusiasm, nature study becomes one of the most interesting activities in camp. Carry it on in the out-of-doors under the sun, skies, winds, and rain of nature's own laboratory whenever possible.

Such pieces of equipment as microscopes, pocket magnifying glasses, butterfly nets, binoculars, and attractive nature books stimulate youngsters to want to use them. Hands and imaginations occupied in making cages, arranging bulletin boards, mounting displays, and planning museums and nature trails produce interested, happy campers.

LEARNING TO USE YOUR SENSES

To learn what nature is all about, you must first develop your five senses to the greatest extent possible. Early

(Courtesy of Camp Wapalanne, New Jersey School of Conservation.)

settlers did this to a degree seldom seen today, for their livelihood and even their lives depended upon it. Like the Indians, they were instantly aware of anything unusual in their surroundings—a new smell, a new sound, a broken twig, crushed blades of grass, animal droppings, or a track or claw marks in mud or soft ground. It is only through a long period of training and experience that you can hope to emulate them, although trips with experienced persons furnish short cuts as they give you tips and show you the possibilities.

Sight. Although you may pass your vision test with a 20/20 rating, you may be perfectly oblivious to many things you should see along a trail. To illustrate just what is possible, stop and concentrate upon the trees around you. How do they vary in size, shape, limb arrangement, and leaf structure? How many can you identify? Do any show signs of disease or pests? Are there birds' nests or signs of animal homes? Now take a good look around you—up, down, close, and as far away as you can see. Make a mental note of everything you see. Compare it with what others see. Which areas look worthy of further investigation?

Have each camper use four twigs and a string to mark off an area three feet square, then have him observe it carefully as he makes a list of everything he sees in a given time (pebbles, insects, vegetation, movement, soil texture, a feather, leaf, and so forth). Try the same project in different types of terrain.

Go slowly along the trail, looking for signs of other inhabitants, such as those mentioned in the first paragraph of this section. Turn over a rock to see what is underneath it; be sure to re-

Figure 17-10 "I Never Realized I Had So Many Neighbors."

place it as you found it in order to avoid disturbing the natural environment.

Play some of the tracking and trailing games described in Chapter 23.

Smell. Takc a deep breath; what odors can you detect? How does the smell of outdoor camp air differ from that of the city? Why? As you walk along the trail, note any change in odors. Try to find out what causes them. Many animals have a much keener sense of smell than you do and thus detect your presence long before you are even in their sight. They can often detect your reactions of fear of them. For this reason, you will need to keep an animal downwind when trying to approach him. Select some familiar substances such as an onion and a crushed mint leaf and pass them along in front of a blindfolded person to see how many he can identify. Does smell have anything to do with the fact that food is tasteless to you when you have a bad cold?

Taste. Beware of indiscriminate tasting of things with which you are unfamiliar, but try out such items as a leaf of wintergreen, an Indian turnip, and other substances that you know to be harmless.

Touch. Feel the texture of a great many things and note the differences. Try this with a circle of blindfolded persons to see how many each can identify.

Hearing. Sit down, close your eyes, and really listen. Make a mental note of everything you hear in a period of five minutes. Compare with other individuals. Listen for grunts, rubbings, rustlings, chirps, squeaks, and similar noises. How many can you identify? Try to locate the source of the noise to better enable you to connect the animal with the sound. Many birds and animals can communicate with each other to convey feelings, such as contentment, anger, fear, and pain, and to give mating calls and warnings of danger. Try to learn some of these.

WATCHING WILDLIFE

Patience and the ability to glide silently along a path or remain still for long periods of time are essential for meaningful nature viewing. The best time depends somewhat upon the weather and other factors, but in general most birds and animals tend to be most active and out searching for food during the early morning hours and just before dusk, preferring to seek shade and a secluded spot to rest during the hot part of the day. Many seem to have built-in barometers warning them to seek shelter at the coming of bad weather. However, it is said that birds will continue eating during a rain if it is going to last for a long period of time but will refrain if the shower will be brief. What are your observations about this?

A quiet wait near a body of water is often rewarded, since nearly every

Figure 17–11 A Tree House (Lash, Don't Nail It).

creature seeks water at customary times once or twice a day. As you approach your vantage point, you can be sure that almost every living thing is aware of your coming, since their senses are so superior to yours. Make yourself comfortable, lying down or sitting on a convenient stump or rock, cushioned by a piece of foam rubber, or even bring your own folding chair. You may want to construct a natural-looking blind, complete with mosquito netting, for closer watching and better photography. Be prepared to wait at least 15 to 30 minutes to give your fellow inhabitants time to resume what they were doing. People sometimes learn to imitate certain animals and birds to call them nearer.

You may want to construct a bosun's chair, a tree house, or an observation tower to give you a different view.

NIGHT TRIPS

Night trips furnish an interesting variation, since the viewer will find an entirely different type of life out hunting for its supper. A revealing way to start out is simply to sit quietly outside your cabin door. Then you can progress to careful trips along the trail, made less conspicuous by wearing dark clothing and streaking your face with charcoal (it is easy to wash off). Move quietly and smoothly, pausing now and then to listen, smell, and look. Ordinarily, you will not need a flashlight, for the stars give enough illumination even on a moonless night. However, few creatures will notice your flashlight if you cover the end of it with piece of lightweight red cloth, plastic, or crepe paper. Allow at least 45 minutes for your eyes to become accustomed to the darkness.

NATURE RAMBLES

Nature walks are not hikes but leisurely rambles, allowing enough time to look, listen, smell, taste, touch, and investigate. Keep the group small (three to eight) and travel slowly and quietly to avoid scattering your wild friends in terror. Proceed with your back to the sun so colors will show up more brightly.

Take pocket magnifying glasses, binoculars, sacks or boxes for bringing back unusual "finds," a few good identification books, and a notebook and pencil to jot down matters of interest. Cameras for snapping pictures of unusual finds and a tape recorder for capturing sounds are handy. Face masks, which can be used to just break the water, are helpful for the study of aquatic life.

Wear sturdy, high-topped shoes and clothing with long sleeves and legs to avoid poisoning from poison ivy and scratches from surrounding shrubbery. Work out signals for such instruction as "freeze where you are" and "come closer for a better look." Stay about a yard apart on the trail and move slowly and as quietly as possible. Incidentally, most animals are colorblind, so it doesn't matter what colors you wear, but they are sensitive to black and white, so it is as well to blend in with your background as much as possible.

COLLECTING

Though making collections still has its place, it does not occupy the pinnacle it once did. One reason is that previous collectors, in their zeal to get "just one more specimen," all but annihilated some of our rarer species of flora. Before picking a flower or other specimen, apply good principles of conservation by glancing about to see that there are ample quantities left to carry on the species.

Collections also sometimes become ends in themselves, with the collector heaving a satisfied sigh each time he has corralled another specimen, fastened it on paper, and labeled it with a polysyllabic title. He neither knows nor cares anything about Exhibit X beyond having a mere nodding acquaintance with its name; in fact, he may completely overlook it the next time he pursues his one-track search for some new victim to add to his store. This sort of collecting becomes busy work, contributing nothing whatsoever toward furthering a real love of nature.

When properly regarded, collections of rocks, minerals, flowers, leaves, seeds, insects, shells, ferns, mosses, and the like add to a nature program. Accompany each mounting with its name, date, place found, your name as collec-

(Courtesy of Missoula Council Camp Fire Girls, Inc., Missoula, Montana.)

tor, and chatty data concerning its life and place in the balance of nature and its commercial value to man.

Reproducing specimens by painting, sketching, or photographing them rather than collecting them is much more meaningful and more in accordance with good conservation practices, since it leaves the specimen intact for others to enjoy.

> Take nothing but pictures; leave nothing but footprints.
>
> —Wilderness Society, *Off on the Right Foot*

PRESSING PLANTS

It is easy to make a press to prepare leaves, ferns, and flowers for mounting. A 10 by 12 inch press will meet ordinary needs and should be constructed so as to simultaneously dry and flatten specimens. Two pieces of board, approximately 10 by 12 inches and about ½ inch thick, are needed for the outside covers. Cut a dozen or more sheets of blotting paper (or newspaper) and half as many sheets of corrugated cardboard from packing boxes to fit, and complete the outfit with two web or leather straps.

Place each plant between sheets of blotting paper and separate from the others by a sheet of corrugated paper. Place the covers on the top and bottom, draw the straps tight, and leave for several days while the plants dry and flatten. If desired, a weight can be placed on top of the press. Beware of picking rare specimens or large quantities of even the plentiful; a hundred campers make a serious inroad if each picks only one leaf.

You can mount pressed specimens on such things as lamp shades or album covers and shellac or place a sheet of plastic over them.

NATURE MUSEUMS

Camp museums may be located in the nature house, under a tree near camp, or along a nature trail. Use them to display such camper activities as a nature bulletin board, mounted specimens, indigenous arts and crafts projects, trail maps, writings about nature topics, papier-mâché relief maps, live pets, weather predictions and equipment, knot display boards, friction sets made from camp materials, mats and baskets woven of native materials, and articles fashioned from local clay.

The craft house should be supplied with guide books, displays, tools, storage facilities, and working space at tables. A fireplace provides a cheery environment for indoor work on damp days. Campers should plan and maintain all exhibits themselves, keeping an eye out for new and different materials. Maintain a "What Is It?" shelf or corner for unidentified curios, placing the name of the person who first correctly identifies it in a place of honor on the bulletin board. Change the display frequently so that campers do not pass it by because "it's just the same old thing."

USEFUL PLANTS

Collect samples of medicinal plants, those which can be eaten, and others which are useful and label them with their names and uses. It is inter-

Figure 17-12 "Look What's Going By."

esting to gather and serve a meal composed exclusively of wild foods, but be sure to get expert help to avoid eating something harmful or poisonous. Use native dyes, and make elderberry jelly, blueberry pie, or wild strawberry shortcake. Consult listings in the Additional Readings section on "Wild Foods" in Chapter 28 for help.

KEEPING WILD THINGS IN CAMP

A fernery or wild flower garden, an insect cage, an aquarium for water life, or a terrarium for things that live on land may be made if you know how to care for them properly.

Even though your state may be one of the few in which it is not illegal to keep wild animals in captivity, it is usually much wiser not to do so. Many of them die from fright and lack of proper food and care, and those successfully kept for some time lose their ability to fend for themselves when turned loose. Many wild parents such as deer, rabbits, and even birds will not accept their young if they detect the odor of man upon them. Often seemingly deserted babies have only been left temporarily while their parents go out searching for delicious tidbits for them to eat. It is much better to leave them in the wilds as nature intended and watch them in their normal pursuits.

MAKING A NATURE TRAIL

LAYING OUT THE TRAIL

Laying out a nature trail teaches much to those who do it and also furnishes entertainment for other campers and incoming visitors. It may be the undertaking of a single unit, or the whole camp may cooperate on various phases of it. A trail about one-half to a mile long, arranged as a loop or figure-of-eight, takes about an hour to wander through and brings the traveler back to where he started without having retraced any of his steps. Short side trips can be indicated to show interesting things off at the side, such as an unusually large tree or a deserted bee's nest. Ideally, it should go through several varieties of terrain (woods, meadow, streams, marshland, ponds, and brushy areas) to show differences in flora and fauna.

A winding trail is more interesting than a straight one. Clear it just enough to permit passage single file, Indian style. This will preserve a woodsy look and avoid destroying more wild growth than is necessary. Some advocate putting wood chips on camp paths, because they improve the footing and eventually disintegrate to enrich the soil. Lay flat stones or build a "corduroy road" of sticks across damp places and build rustic bridges across streams. Zigzag up and down slopes to avoid causing erosion.

LABELING

A nature trail is actually a conducted tour with signs and labels instead of a human guide. Pick out the things you want to show along the way and ask for volunteers to look up information about each. Have a committee to select what is to be told and exactly how to express it. In general, brevity should be the keyword, for few will take the time to read long messages. If more information seems desirable, put the most pertinent first, following with other details on separate tabs, stacked so that the reader must lift one to get to the next.

Use "down-to-earth" language, bits of information with human interest quality, little poems, and touches of humor. Invite people to touch, taste, smell, or listen, as the characteristics of the specimen dictate. Point out relationships, telling why this environment is particularly appropriate for the subject. Ask a provocative question on one side of a card, which the reader must turn over to find the answer. Add a colored picture, arrows, or cues in puzzle form to help the person find what he is looking for. Strategically placed bulletin boards and a bench for adults to rest on also contribute. Another project may be to prepare trail guides, containing a map, a key to what will be seen, and additional information about it. Give the guide to each person starting out on the trail.

There may be a bird sanctuary somewhere along the way with protective cover and other items to attract our feathered friends and a bulletin board with identifying pictures. Construct bird houses and hang them in the area to increase the bird population from year to year. A nearby blind to hide behind helps watchers see more action.

Changes will be in order as the summer progresses and new flowers or other seasonal changes appear. Let a maintenance committee take care of changes as well as see that the trail is kept in good condition.

Never nail labels to trees. Fasten them to ropes or wire between trees,

(Courtesy of Camp Wapalanne, New Jersey School of Conservation.)

tied loosely about the tree so that they won't cut into the bark, or nail or gun-staple them to stakes placed nearby. You can make temporary labels to last through a summer by printing with India ink on filing cards or pieces of poster board and painting both sides with two or three coats of clear shellac or varnish. For more permanent signs, use paint or enamel in contrasting colors on pieces of wood or metal, again protecting them with coats of clear shellac or varnish.

You can sharpen the campers' observations by giving them sheets to fill out as they move along the trail.

BIRDS*

Bird study has a larger following than any other phase of nature, and these projects for carrying it on are suggested.

Birdwalks—best in early morning or late evening, when the birds are most active. Learn to identify by nest, color, sound, and manner of flight.

Collect feathers. Collect old nests (no birds except hawks use them a second time) and dissect them to see what materials were used in their construction. Place modeled eggs painted the proper colors in whole nests and display them on branches arranged to resemble trees.

Contrast the bills and feet of birds to see how they are adapted to their diet and habits. Listen to the bird's song and watch its pattern of flight.

Make a bird scrapbook of pictures, stories, anecdotes, and poems.

Make plaster casts of tracks in mud or at the beach.

*Write to the National Audubon Society, 1130 Fifth Avenue, New York, N.Y. 10028, for information about the Audubon Junior Clubs for Summer Camps.

PLANTS

Make a wild flower garden or fernery. (Ferns and wild flowers will grow only with soil and other conditions similar to those of their natural habitat.)

Draw or paint pictures of wild flowers, adding name, date, where found, and such information as native country, seeds and their dispersal, pollination, and uses (medicinal, dyes and so on). In mounting specimens, use small pieces of Scotch tape or dip the specimens in a mixture of glue and vinegar spread evenly on glass, and transfer them to heavy paper.

Study seeds and their dispersal by barbs, parachutes, wind, animals, and other means. Collect seeds and keep them for making a wild flower garden. Glue some specimens on mounting boards and label them.

Make a plant gall collection.

Study lichens, mosses, and ferns. Look at them through a microscope.

Identify nut-bearing bushes and trees. Learn when the nuts ripen and what animals eat them.

Study flower arrangement for indoor decoration.

Identify poison ivy, poison oak, and poison sumac.

Figure 17–13 "Elementary, My Dear Watson."

Identify different types of mushrooms, particularly the morels, which are safe to eat. Do not trust other kinds, for even experts have difficulty in distinguishing the poisonous ones.

Which flowers open at different times of the day? Could you devise a flower clock?

TREES

Identify trees by contour, color, leaf, bark, flower, seed, and wood structure. Learn all you can about them: what they are used for, how they burn, and so on.

Press and mount leaves, using methods suggested for flowers.

Photograph trees; make sketches or watercolors of them.

Learn how individual trees serve for shade, beauty, soil conservation, firewood, or commercial products. Do you realize that a single large tree in full leaf during summer furnishes moisture to the air and has the cooling effect of ten room-sized air conditioners operating 20 hours a day? They also serve as windbreaks, and they cushion noise, provide protection for birds and animals, and convert carbon dioxide to oxygen for us to breathe. Learn about their early uses by the Indians and pioneers. Identify the kinds found in camp furniture, walls, and so forth.

Study stumps to learn the life history of the tree, such as its age, injuries, insect damage, favorable and unfavorable seasons, and the like.

Learn the uses of different kinds of woods in fire-building (tinder, kindling, heat, light, fire dogs, and others). Which ones are best for whittling? Notice how the growth of a tree is affected by those surrounding it.

INSECTS

There are over 900,000 varieties of identified insects in the world. Learn the distinguishing characteristics of insects, spiders, bees, wasps, grasshoppers, bugs, beetles, flies, moths, butterflies, and others. Identify the various sorts and learn their habits, food, life cycles, and use or destructiveness. Watch them in their native habitat.

Make sketches of common varieties.

Prepare and mount specimens, adding pertinent information about them.

Raise families of butterflies, moths, ants, and other insects.

Lay a large piece of butcher's paper under a bush. Shake the bush gently and note what insects fall out of it.

Watch an ant colony at work.

Stay long enough to watch a spider weave his web. Take a photograph of it.

ROCKS AND MINERALS

Distinguish between minerals and rocks.

Visit a quarry, a fresh road cut, a dried-up stream bed, or a mine opening.

Gather specimens, using a geology hammer (an ordinary hammer will serve) to prepare uniform sizes (about $1\frac{1}{2}$ by $2\frac{1}{2}$ inches) for collections. Wash carefully and label. Keep the specimens in boxes with compartments of cardboard; mount small samples on a mounting board or in plaster of Paris. Enter dates, places, and interesting facts about each find.

Study the characteristics of rocks, determining which are best for use in fireplaces, as kettle supports, and so on.

FISH

Make your own poles, baits (flies and lures), and lines. Catch or dig your own live bait.

Learn to recognize the different species and learn their life histories.

Mount an especially good specimen.

Learn to clean fish and study their structures as you clean them.

ANIMALS

Take close-up photographs. Use a portrait attachment.

Make plaster casts of tracks.

Play stalking games.

Look for traces of animals, such as droppings, tracks, dens, burrows, bits of fur, and homes.

Find out which animals can see, hear, smell, or taste more acutely than man.

Stalk animals with a camera (takes patience and skill). Lie or sit still and watch them. If you wait long enough, you may be able to discover where they live.

STARS

It is best to study stars on a clear evening when there is no moon to detract from their brightness.

Use the beam of a focusing flashlight to help point them out.

Learn the folklore regarding the stars and constellations.

Figure 17–14 Caught in the Act.

Paint diagrams of the heavens on dark blue or black paper with luminous paint so you can use them at night.

Take time exposures of stars with your camera.

Binoculars make the observation of stars more interesting. You will also need a simple telescope and a star map for the current month.

MAKING PRINTS

There are several methods of printing feathers, flowers, leaves, and ferns. Better results are obtained if you first press the specimens flat. Use the prints to decorate your memory book, place cards, invitations, stationery, handkerchiefs, or cabin curtains.

OZALID AND BLUE PRINTS

These give beautiful results but are slightly more expensive than other prints and require some skill to make well.

CRAYON PRINTS

Place a leaf, vein side up, on a flat surface, cover it with a sheet of unlined paper, and, holding leaf and paper firmly in place, rub a soft crayon over the paper with parallel strokes until the edges and veins stand out clearly. Outline the edge with a firm black line and cut out the print and mount it, or use it for decorating menus or stationery.

INK PAD PRINTS

Lay a leaf, vein side down, on an ink pad, cover with a layer of newspaper cut to fit the ink pad, and rub thoroughly. Transfer the leaf, inky side down, onto a piece of paper, cover it with a fresh newspaper, hold it firmly in place, and rub until the ink pad print appears clearly on the paper.

PRINTER'S INK PRINTS

Spread a small quantity of printer's ink of any desired color on a piece of glass and run a rubber photographic roller through it until it is thinly and evenly spread. Place the leaf, vein side up, on a newspaper and rub the inky roller over it, transferring a uniform coating of ink. Reverse the leaf, place it on a fresh sheet of paper, cover with newspaper, and, holding it firmly in place, rub over it with a clean roller until the transfer is completed.

SMOKE PRINTS

Many consider smoke prints to be the most attractive of all. Candles (plumber's are best) and some grease such as lard or petroleum jelly are necessary. Spread a small quantity of grease evenly over one fourth of a sheet of newspaper and pass it through the candle flame (being careful not to let it get close enough to burn) until it is uniformly coated with carbon. Then lay it on a flat surface, place the leaf vein side down on it, cover with a clean piece of newspaper, and rub over the newspaper, holding the leaf firmly in place. Transfer the leaf, carbon side down, to a fresh sheet of paper, again cover with newspaper, and rub until the smoke print is transferred.

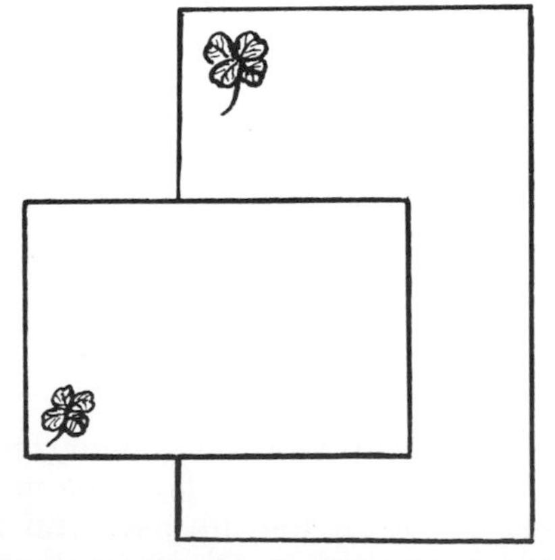

Figure 17-15 Smoke Print Stationery.

SPATTER PRINTS

An old toothbrush and some India ink or diluted poster paint are necessary for this method of printing. Protect the scene of operation by spreading newspapers about, and place the leaf on a plain sheet of paper. Pin the edges flat so that no paint can get under them, and slant the heads of the pins slightly toward the center of the leaf. Dip the toothbrush into the paint to get a thin but uniform coating on it. Holding the brush at a 45-degree angle and about 2 inches from the paper, use a knife, nail file, or thin, flat stick, to scrape *toward you* across the toothbrush. Continue the process until a sufficiently heavy "spatter" has been deposited around the leaf. Do not remove the leaf until the paint is dry. You can also make spatter prints with a spray gun or with an aerosol can of paint (see Fig. 17-16).

PLASTER CASTS

Inexpensive plaster casts of flowers, animal tracks, leaves, and the like are simple to make and are quite attractive when used as paper weights, book ends, or wall plaques. They may be tinted in natural colors if desired. Plaster of Paris may be purchased at the hardware or drugstore and should be mixed in an old container such as a tin can, using a stick for stirring. (It is practically impossible to remove the plaster from anything with which it has come in contact.) Estimate the amount

Figure 17–16 Making Leaf Prints With a Spray Gun.

of plaster needed for the cast desired and place three fourths of that amount of water in the container. Pour in as much plaster of Paris as will sink to the bottom, then add a trifle more for good measure. Put in a pinch of salt to hasten setting and stir thoroughly. A good mixture has the consistency of pancake batter.

If an animal track is to be cast, dust it lightly with talcum powder and press a circular or rectangular collar of cardboard of the size desired for the finished cast into the earth around it. Pour in the plaster of Paris slowly and let it harden for about 30 minutes. Then lift the cast carefully, remove the cardboard collar, and scrub it well with water. Plaques should have a screw eye or paper clip for hanging inserted in the edge before they are dry. Paint them in natural colors.

To make a positive cast (with the track in relief), powder the negative cast lightly, place a collar about it, and pour in more plaster of Paris. When dry, carefully separate the two casts.

To make casts of leaves, ferns, flowers, seeds, and so forth, pour the plaster of Paris into a mold, dampen the specimen, and place it on the plaster of Paris, brushing it with a paintbrush to make a tight contact over its entire surface. When about half dry, remove the leaf and let the plaster continue to harden.

Obviously, superfluous plaster of Paris should never be poured down the drain.

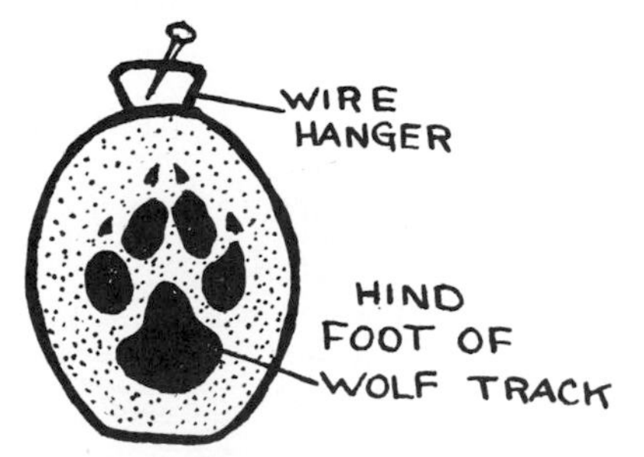

Figure 17–17 Plaster of Paris Wall Plaque of an Animal Track.

NATURE GAMES

Starvation Hike. Go out and cook a meal, using only things found growing in the woods. Be sure you *know* what is safe to use.

Nature Quests. See who can bring in and identify a square-stemmed plant; a lady beetle; a piece of wood that is shaped like an animal; and such. Be careful not to cause harm or destruction.

Nature Treasure or Scavenger Hunt. Give each group, person, or pair a list of from 10 to 20 nature objects to bring in, such as leaves of certain trees, common flowers, certain kinds of rocks, discarded birds' nests, discarded feathers, and so forth. The first back with the correct and complete list wins. Some of the items should be easy to find, others hard. Avoid poor conservation practice; do not tramp over or collect items that are not in such plentiful supply that a few will not be missed.

Nature Quiz Programs. Conduct these like television quiz programs, with small prizes for winners.

Leaf Relay. Give each team a list of trees. The first one in line runs to get a leaf of the first tree on the list, returns, and gives the list to the second in line, who then reads the second kind of tree and runs to get a sample, and so on. The first group through wins.

Identification. Have pictures of animals, trees, birds, insects, and the like, pasted on cards. Flash them. The first person to identify the picture correctly receives the card. The person with the most cards at the end of the playing time wins.

Touch, Taste, Smell Identification. Blindfold players and pass around objects for them to identify, designating whether they are to do so by tasting, smelling, or feeling.

Tree Identification. Make a tour, stopping at various trees, so that each person can fill in the name of the tree on his numbered chart. The person with the greatest number of correct identifications wins. When first learning, participants may take their tree identification books along and be given three or four minutes to identify the tree with the assistance of the book. Ferns, flowers, birds, sea shells, animals, or any other kind of wildlife desired may be identified in this game.

Trailing. The person chosen to be "It" walks carelessly through the woods, making no effort to conceal his footprints or avoid breaking branches. Ten minutes later, a small group or an individual tries to follow his trail and spy him where he is hiding beside it. A variation is to have two persons walk in single file through the woods. At a given signal, they reverse, and the one originally in the rear tries to lead the way back over the same trail. He may be given a start of 25 points, with 2 points deducted each time he wanders off the trail and 1 each time he hesitates more than a minute in determining the correct course.

Nature Sounds. Each participant listens for five minutes, listing all the nature sounds heard and identified. This is a particularly good game to play at night.

Upside Down Hike. Turn over rocks, decaying logs, and large sticks to see what is living underneath them. Be sure to restore them without harming any living inhabitants.

What Is It? Have a number of clues describing a nature object written on a card, with the least well-known first. Read them one at a time until someone is finally able to guess the object and receives the card as his reward. A variation is to let campers take turns giving oral clues until a fellow camper is able to guess what he has in mind.

What's Wrong with This Picture? Announce that a certain nature object

Figure 17-18 Sounds of the Night.

is to be described and that, although most of the characteristics given will be true, a few erroneous ones will be included. See how many can detect the incorrect ones.

Quiet, Please! The members of one group sit blindfolded with some designated object located about 6 feet in front of them. The idea is for the second group to creep stealthily in and steal the object without being detected. When members of the blindfolded group hear an opponent approaching and point directly at him, he is eliminated. A variation is to have only one member blindfolded while the others are scattered in various directions and at different distances from him. They take turns whistling, rustling leaves, stamping a foot, and so forth. If he can judge the direction and point directly to the person, the two exchange places.

Sign in a park: "May it be said of these flowers that they died with their roots on."

ADDITIONAL READINGS

(For an explanation of abbreviations and abbreviated forms, see page 25.)

Conducting the Program

Bale: *What On Earth,* pp. 91–156.
Boy Scout Handbook, pp. 274–316.
Brown, Vinson: *The Amateur Naturalist's Handbook.*
Brown, Vinson: *How to Explore the Secret World of Nature.* Little, 1962, 174 pp., $4.95.
Brown, Vinson: *Knowing the Outdoors in the Dark.* Stackpole, 1972, 192 pp., $6.95; $2.95, paper.
Brown, Vinson: *Reading the Woods.* Stackpole, 1969, 160 pp., $5.95; $2.95, paper.
Buck, Margaret Waring: *Small Pets From Woods and Fields.* Abingdon, 1960, 72 pp., $3.95; $1.75, paper.
Cardwell: *America's Camping Book,* ch. 23.
Corbin: *Recreation Leadership,* ch. 26.
Ecology Workshop Instructor's Guide (No. 4158). Boy Scouts, 1972, 72 pp., $3.60.
Elman, Robert: *Discover the Outdoors.* Lion, 1969, 224 pp., $6.95.
Fieldbook for Boys and Men, pp. 386–403, 414–419, 443–447, 456–463, 481–493.
First Aid to Animals (No. 3318). Boy Scouts, 1963, 56 pp., 45¢, paper.
Forestry Activities. Supt. of Documents, 31 pp., 20¢, paper.
Hammerman and Hammerman: *Teaching in the Outdoors.*
Harty: *Science for Camp and Counselor.*
Headstrom, Richard: *Adventures With a Hand Lens.* Lippincott, 1962, 220 pp., $5.95.
Hillcourt: *New Fieldbook of Nature Activities and Conservation.*
Hoke, John: *Terrariums.* Watts, 1972, 90 pp., $3.45.
Hussong, Clara: *Nature Hikes.* Golden, rev., 1973, 48 pp., $1.50.
Invite Birds to Your Home (#0100). Supt. of Documents, 1971, 16 pp., 20¢, paper.
Kohn, Bernice: *The Beachcomber's Book.* Viking, 1970, 96 pp., $3.75.
Langer: *The Joy of Camping,* pp. 271–277.
Mand: *Outdoor Education.*
Nature Hobbies and Activities (No. 26-094). Boy Scouts, 35¢, paper.
Nickelsburg, Janet: *Field Trips—Ecology for Youth Leaders.* Burgess, 1966, 120 pp., $3.95.
Schramm, Wilbur: *Classroom Out-of-Doors—Education Through Camping.* Sequoia, 1969, 192 pp., $3.25, paper.
Shivers: *Camping,* ch. 10.
Shuttlesworth: *Exploring Nature With Your Child.*
Smith and others: *Outdoor Education,* ch. 4.
Snediger, Robert: *Our Small Native Animals: Their Habits and Care.* Dover, 1963, 248 pp., $2.50, paper.
Swan, Malcolm D. (ed.): *Tips and Tricks in Outdoor Education.* Interstate, 1970, 184 pp., $4.50, paper.
van der Smissen, Betty, and Oswald H. Goering: *A Leader's Guide to Nature-Oriented Activities.*
Van Matre, Steve: *Acclimatization—A Sensory and Conceptual Approach to Ecological Involvement.* ACA, 1972, 138 pp., $3.25, paper.
Van Matre, Steve: *Acclimatizing—A Personal and Reflective Approach to a Natural Relationship.* ACA, 1974, 225 pp., $3.75, paper.
Vinal: *Nature Recreation.*
You and Conservation—A Check List for Camp Counselors. ACA, rev., 1971, 12 pp., 25¢, paper.
Zehnpfennig, Gladys: *Ecology for Young People.* Denison, 1972, 92 pp., $3.50, paper.

MAGAZINE ARTICLES

Boy's Life:
"Save Trees By Trimming." Feb., 1973, p. 69.
Shaman, Diana: "Start a Rock Collection." Mar., 1972, p. 44.
Spencer, Billie: "Insect Collections." Apr., 1973, p. 7.
Taylor, John: "Anti-Litter Kit." Aug., 1972, p. 58.

Camping Journal:
Farmer, Charles G.: "Close to Nature." Aug., 1974, p. 33.

Camping Magazine:
Abraham, Eugene, and Ronald James Moglia: "Let's Study Our Environment in its Natural Setting." Jan., 1973, p. 14.
Bacon, E. M.: "Make Your Woodlands Work for You." Jan., 1971, p. 13.
Fenn, Roger C.: "Achieving Relevancy in Nature Programming." Apr., 1971, p. 24.
Fluckel, Robert W., and Charles A. Gregory: "Ecology Goes to Summer Camp—An Experimental Itinerate Approach to Environmental Education." Nov., 1972, p. 13.
Hammerman, William M.: "ACA Sets Up Criteria for Counselors to Teach Ecology at Camp." May, 1973, p. 14.
Katsanis, Andrew: "Good Conservation Pays." Apr., 1968, p. 28.
Mooney, Bill: "How to Meet the Challenge of a Limited Budget When Planning a Nature Program." Mar., 1973, p. 18.
Neely, Dan: "Tree Problems Need Early Diagnosis in Order to Save Our Wooded Camp Areas." Part I, May, 1973, p. 18; Part II, June, 1973, p. 16.
Olsen, Margaret E.: "How Campers Can Help Improve Your Camp's EQ." Mar., 1972, p. 9.
Seed, Allen H., Jr.: "Campers vs. Litter—Practical Ecology in Camp." June, 1971, p. 13.
Stahr, Elvis J.: "Camp—The Ideal Place for Teaching Environmental Urgencies." Mar., 1971, p. 20.
Stinson, Thelma: "FIRST to Stimulate Campers' Interest in Nature Find Out What Interests Them!" Sept./Oct., 1969, p. 16.
Stinson, Thelma: "More Ways to Build Nature Interest." Nov./Dec., 1969, p. 15.
Stinson, Thelma: "To Build Nature Interest Use What You Have!" Jan., 1970, p. 13.
Van Matre, Steve: "Acclimatization—A Vital Part of Your Camp Ecology Program." June, 1971, p. 8.
Wadsworth, William H.: "Camp Environment Checklist." June, 1971, p. 11.

National Wildlife:
Adams, Marjorie Valentine: "Have You Started Your Life List?" June/July, 1975, p. 14. (A discussion of the sport of "birding")
Harrison, George H.: "How People Are Planting for Wildlife." April/May, 1975, p. 24.

Conservation and Ecology

Alexander, Taylor R., and George S. Fichter: *Ecology.* Golden, 1973, 160 pp., $1.95, paper.
Allen, Durward L.: *Our Wildlife Legacy.* Funk & Wagnalls, 1962, $8.95; $3.95, paper.
Asimov, I.: *ABC's of Ecology.* Walker & Co., 720 Fifth Ave., New York, N.Y. 10019, 1972, $4.95.
Bridge: *America's Backpacking Book,* ch. 26.
Caldwell, Lynton Keith: *Environment: A Challenge to Modern Society.* Natural History Press, 1970, 292 pp., $7.95.
Callison, Charles H.: *America's Natural Resources.* Ronald, 1967, 220 pp., $6.95.
Cardwell: *America's Camping Book,* ch. 52.
Conservation of Natural Resources. Boy Scouts, 1967, 80 pp., 45¢, paper.
Conservation of the Campsite. ACA, 1960, 48 pp., 75¢, paper.
Day, Albert: *Making a Living in Conservation.* Stackpole, 1971, 96 pp., $3.95.
DeBell, Garrett (ed.): *The Environmental Handbook.* Ballantine, $5.95; 95¢, paper.
Environmental Science (No. 3363). Boy Scouts, 1972, 64 pp., 45¢, paper.
Fieldbook for Boys and Men, chs. 20, 21.
Forestry (No. 3302). Boy Scouts, 1971, 84 pp., 45¢, paper.
Frome, Michael: *Battle for the Wilderness.* Praeger, 1974, 246 pp., $8.95.
Gabrielson, Ira N.: *Wildlife Conservation.* Macmillan, rev., 1965, 244 pp., $5.95.
Gibbons, Euell: *Stalking the Good Life.* McKay, 1971, 248 pp., $7.95.
Grossman, Shelly and Mary Louise: *The How and Why Wonder Book of Ecology.* Grossett & Dunlap, 48 pp., $1.50.
Guggisberg, C.A.W.: *Man and Wildlife.* Arco, 1970, 224 pp., $12.50.
Hoke, J.: *Ecology.* Watts, 1971, $3.95.
Jennings, Gary: *The Shrinking Outdoors.* Lippincott, 1972, 181 pp., $5.50.
Klein, Stanley: *A World of Difference.* Doubleday, 1971, 63 pp., $4.95.
Kolbas, Grace Holden: *Ecology: Cycle and Recycle.* Sterling, 1972, 168 pp., $7.95.
Lapedes, Daniel N.: *Encyclopedia of Environmental Science.* McGraw-Hill, 1974, 754 pp., $24.50.
Laycock, George: *America's Endangered Wildlife.* Grosset & Dunlap, 1970, $4.95.
McHenry, Robert and Charles Van Doren (eds.): *A Documentary History of Conservation in America.* Praeger, 1972, 422 pp., $13.50.
Mand: *Outdoor Education,* ch. XI.
Manning: *Backpacking One Step at a Time,* ch. 20.
Nickelsburg, Janet: *Ecology, Habitats, Niches, and Food Chains.* Lippincott, 1969, $4.43.
Nobile, Phillip, and John Deedy (eds.): *The Complete Ecology Fact Book.* Doubleday, 1972, 472 pp., $10.
Olsen, Jack: *Slaughter the Animals, Poison the Earth.* Simon & Schuster, 1971, $6.95.
Olson, Sigurd F.: *Open Horizons.* Knopf, 1969, 230 pp., $5.95.
Parnall, Peter: *The Mountain.* Doubleday, 1971, 32 pp., $4.50. (A copiously illustrated account of what happened when a mountain was in-

undated by people after being made a National Park.)
Passmore, John: *Man's Responsibility for Nature: Ecological Problems and Western Transactions.* Scribner's, 1974, 213 pp., $7.95.
Pearson, John: *The Sun's Birthday.* Doubleday, 1973, 111 pp., $5.95, paper.
Reed, Keith: *Nature's Network: The Story of Ecology.* Natural History Press, $6.95.
Riviere: *Backcountry Camping,* chs. 10, 14.
Schoenfeld, Clay: *Everybody's Ecology: A Field Guide to Pleasure in the Out-of-Doors.* Barnes, 1971, 316 pp., $7.95.
Shepard, Odell (ed.): *The Heart of Thoreau's Journals.* Dover, 1961, 228 pp., $2, paper.
Simon, Noel, and Paul Geroudet: *Last Survivors.* World, 275 pp., $19.95.
Soil and Water Conservation (No. 3291). Boy Scouts, 1968, 96 pp., 45¢, paper.
Storer, John H.: *The Web of Life.* Devin-Adair, 1972, 128 pp., $2.75, paper.
Turk, Amos, Jonathan Turk, and Janet T. Wittes: *Ecology, Pollution, Environment.* Saunders, 1972, 217 pp., $3.95, paper.
Warner, Matt: *Your World—Your Survival.* Ablelard, Ltd., 257 Park Ave., New York, N.Y. 10010, 1970, 128 pp., $4.25.

MAGAZINE ARTICLES

Boys' Life:
Laycock, George: "Their Time Is Running Out." Nov., 1970, p. 8.

Backpacker:
'Directory of Leading Conservation Organizations." *Backpacker-6,* Summer, 1974, p. 64.
"The Need for Water Conservation." Nov., 1969, p. 58.

Camping Journal:
"Man's Best Friend, the Tree." Feb., 1971, p. 32.
Steindler, Gerry: "Wagon Tongue." Nov., 1968, p. 4.

Edible Wild Plants

See the bibliography in Chapter 28.

Identification

ANIMALS

Breland, Osmond P.: *Animal Life and Lore.* Harper & Row, 1972, $10.
Burt, William H., and Grossenheider, Richard B.: *A Field Guide to the Mammals.* Houghton Mifflin, 2nd ed., 1964, 284 pp., $7.50.
Caras, Roger: *North American Mammals.* Hawthorn, 1967.
Carrighar, Sally: *Wild Heritage.* Houghton Mifflin, 1965, 276 pp., $5.95.
DuPuy, William Atherton: *Our Animal Friends and Foes.* Dover, 1969, 276 pp., $2, paper.
Fieldbook for Boys and Men, pp. 405–407, 465–479.
Mammals (No. 3271). Boy Scouts, 1972, 48 pp., 45¢, paper.
Musselman, Virginia: *Learning About Nature Through Pets.* Stackpole, 1971, 128 pp., $3.95.
Ormond: *Complete Book of Outdoor Lore,* pp. 345–481.
Orr, Robert T.: *Mammals of North America.* Doubleday, 1971, 250 pp., $9.95.
Rood, Ronald: *Animals Nobody Loves.* Green, 215 pp., $7.95; Bantam, 1971, 75¢, paper.
Rue, Leonard Lee, III: *Sportsman's Guide to Game Animals.* Harper & Row, 1968, 655 pp., $6.50.
Shuttlesworth, Dorothy: *Animal Camouflage.* Doubleday, 1966, 63 pp., $3.95.
Zim, Herbert S., and Dr. Donald F. Hoffmeister: *Mammals.* Golden, 1955, 160 pp., $1.50, paper.

BIRDS

Adler, Helmut E.: *Bird Life for Young People.* Sterling, 1970, 155 pp., $6.95.
Armstrong, Edward A.: *The Way Birds Live.* Dover, rev., 1968, 98 pp., $1.50, paper.
Austin, Oliver L.: *Families of Birds.* Golden, 1971, 200 pp., $1.95, paper.
Austin, Oliver L.: *Water and Marsh Birds.* Golden, 1967, 224 pp., $4.95.
Bird Study (No. 3282). Boy Scouts, 1967, 72 pp., 45¢, paper.
Blachly, Lou, and Randolph Jenks: *Naming the Birds at a Glance.* Knopf, 1963, $5.95.
Bosiger, E., and P. Faucher: *Birds That Fly in the Night.* Sterling, 1973, pp. 80–112, $3.95.
Chapman, Frank M.: *The Warblers of North America.* Dover, 1968, 308 pp., $3, paper.
Cruickshank, Alan: *A Pocket Guide to Birds.* Pocket Books, 1972, 216 pp., $1.25, paper.
Davids, Richard: *How to Talk to Birds.* Knopf, 1972, $6.95.
DuPuy, William Atherton: *Our Bird Friends and Foes.* Dover, 1969, 330 pp., $2, paper.
Fieldbook for Boys and Men, pp. 449–463.
Peterson, Roger Tory: *A Field Guide to the Birds.* Houghton Mifflin, 1968, 290 pp., $5.95; $3.95, paper.
Peterson, Roger Tory: *A Field Guide to Western Birds.* Houghton Mifflin, 2nd ed., 1961, 366 pp., $5.95; $3.95, paper.
Rand, Austin L.: *Birds of North America.* Doubleday, 1971, 256 pp., $9.95.
Robbins, Chandler S., Bertel Brunn, and Herbert S. Zim: *Birds of North America.* Golden, 1966, 340 pp., $5.95; $3.95, paper.
Schultz, Walter E.: *How to Attract, House and Feed Birds.* Collier, 1974, 196 pp., $7.95; $2.95, paper.
Stefferud, Alfred, and Arnold L. Nelson (eds.):

Birds In Our Lives. Arco, 1970, 447 pp., $5.95, paper.
Thomas, Arline: *Bird Ambulance.* Scribner's, 1972, 130 pp., $2.65, paper. (Caring for injured birds)
Zim, Herbert S., and Ira N. Gabrielson: *Birds.* Golden, 1956, 160 pp., $1.50, paper.

MAGAZINE ARTICLES

Reader's Digest:
George, Jean: "The New Art of Bird 'Reading'," Mar., 1973, p. 136.

BUTTERFLIES AND MOTHS

Clarke, J. F. Gates: *Butterflies.* Golden, 1964, 25¢, paper.
Dickens, Michael, and Eric Storey: *The World of Butterflies.* Macmillan, 1973, 127 pp., $5.95.
Dickens, Michael, and Eric Storey: *The World of Moths.* Macmillan, 1974, 128 pp., $6.95.
Ehrlich, Paul: *How to Know the Butterflies.* Brown, 1961, 262 pp., $5.75; $4.25, paper.
Hogner, Dorothy Childs: *Butterflies.* Crowell, 1962, 68 pp., $3.95.
Hogner, Dorothy Childs: *Moths.* Crowell, 1964, 71 pp., $4.50.
Klots, Alexander B.: *A Field Guide to the Butterflies.* Houghton Mifflin, 1951, 349 pp., $5.95.
Werner, Alfred, and Bijok, Josef: *Butterflies and Moths.* Viking, rev., 1970, $7.95.
Zim, Herbert S., and Robert Mitchell: *Butterflies and Moths.* Golden, 1964, 160 pp., $1.50, paper.

FISH

Eddy, Samuel: *How to Know the Freshwater Fish.* Brown, 2nd ed., 1970, 253 pp., $4.50, paper.
Fieldbook for Boys and Men, pp. 421–435.
Herald, Earl S.: *Fishes of North America.* Doubleday, 1972, 256 pp., $9.95.
Walden, Howard T.: *Familiar Freshwater Fishes of America.* Harper & Row, 1964, 324 pp., $6.95.
Zim, Herbert S., and Hurst H. Shoemaker: *Fishes.* Golden, 1956. 160 pp., $1.50, paper.

FLOWERS AND OTHER PLANTS

Botany (No. 3379). Boy Scouts, 1964, 64 pp., 45¢, paper.
Cobb, Boughton: *A Field Guide to the Ferns.* Houghton Mifflin, 1956, 281 pp., $5.95; $3.95, paper.
DuPuy, William Atherton: *Our Plant Friends and Foes.* Dover, 1969, 292 pp., $2, paper.
Durand, Herbert: *Field Book of Common Ferns.* Putnam, rev., 1949, 219 pp., $4.95.
Fieldbook for Boys and Men, pp. 335–341, 347–353, 360–371.
Hardin, James W., and Arena, Jay M., M.D.: *Human Poisoning From Native and Cultivated Plants.* Duke, 1973, 167 pp., $6.75.
Harty: *Science for Camp and Counselor,* ch. 6.
Hausman, Ethel H.: *Beginners Guide to Wild Flowers.* Putnam, 1955, 384 pp., $4.95.
Hylander, Clarence J.: *Flowers of Field and Forest.* Macmillan, 1962, 231 pp., $5.95.
Martin, Alexander C.: *Weeds.* Golden, 1973, 160 pp., $1.95, paper.
Mathews, F. Schuyler: *Field Book of American Wild Flowers.* Putnam, 1966, 601 pp., $5.95.
Peterson, Roger Tory, and Margaret McKenny: *A Field Guide to Wildflowers of North-Eastern and North-Central North America.* Houghton Mifflin, 1968, 448 pp., $5.95; $3.95, paper.
Selsam, Millicent E.: *Plants That Heal.* Morrow, 1959, $4.32.
Shuttleworth, Floyd S., and Herbert S. Zim: *Non-Flowering Plants.* Golden, 1967, 160 pp., $1.50, paper.
Taylor, K., and Hamblin, S. F.: *Handbook of Wild Flower Cultivation.* Macmillan, 1962, 307 pp., $7.95.
Zim, Herbert S., and Alexander G. Martin: *Flowers and Plants.* Golden, 1950, 156 pp., $1.50, paper.

INSECTS

Barker, Will: *Familiar Insects of America.* Harper & Row, 1960, 236 pp., $6.95.
Borror, Donald J., and Richard E. White: *Field Guide to the Insects of America North of Mexico.* Houghton Mifflin, 1970, 404 pp., $5.95; $4.95, paper.
Clausen, Lucy W.: *Insect Fact and Folklore.* Macmillan, 1962, 95¢, paper.
Fieldbook for Boys and Men, pp. 409–419.
Headstrom, Richard: *Adventures With Insects.* Lippincott, 1963, 221 pp., $4.50.
Hylander, Clarence J.: *Insects On Parade.* Macmillan, 1967, $5.95.
Insect Life (No. 3348). Boy Scouts, 1963, 64 pp., 45¢, paper.
Klots, Alexander and Elsie: *Insects of North America.* Doubleday, 1971, 252 pp., $9.95.
Parenti, Umberto: *Insects: World of Miniature Beauty.* Golden, 1972, 80 pp., $5.50.
Snodgrass, Robert Evans: *Insects: Their Ways and Means of Living.* Dover, rev., 1967, 362 pp., $3, paper.
Sterling, Dorothy: *Insects and the Homes They Build.* Doubleday, 1954, 125 pp., $3.95.
Zim, Herbert S., and Clarence Cottam: *Insects.* Golden, 1951, 160 pp., $1.50, paper.
Zim, Herbert S., and George S. Fichter: *Insect Pests.* Golden, 1966, 160 pp., $1.50, paper.

MISCELLANEOUS AND GENERAL

Berman, Lucy: *Nature Thought of It First.* Grosset & Dunlap, 97 pp., $4.95.
Borland, Hal (ed.): *Our Natural World.* Lippincott, 1969, 849 pp., $10.

Brown, Vinson: *The Amateur Naturalist's Handbook.*
Collins, Henry H., Jr.: *Complete Field Guide to American Wildlife: East, Central & North.* Harper & Row, 1959, $9.95.
Comstock, Anna Botsford: *Handbook of Nature Study.* Comstock, 24th ed., 1939, 937 pp., $15.
Laun, H. Charles: *The Natural History Guide.* Alsace, rev., 1970, 530 pp., $5.50, paper.
Martin, Alexander C., Herbert S. Zim, and Arnold L. Nelson: *American Wildlife and Plants.* Dover, 1961, 500 pp., $5.50; $3.50, paper.
Milne, Lorus and Margery: *Invertebrates of North America.* Doubleday, 1972, 252 pp., $9.95.
Nature (No. 3285). Boy Scouts, 1952, 96 pp., 45¢, paper.
Ormond: *The Complete Book of Outdoor Lore,* pp. 287–481.
Watts, May Theilgaard: *Reading the Landscape.* Macmillan, 1966, 230 pp., $5.95.

MUSHROOMS

Bigelow, Howard E.: *Mushroom Pocket Field Guide.* Macmillan, 1974, 117 pp., $3.50.
Christensen, Clyde M.: *Common Edible Mushrooms.* U. of Minn., 1969, 124 pp., $6.75; $2.95, paper.
Kleijn, H.: *Mushrooms and Other Fungi.* Doubleday, $12.95.
Krieger, Louis G. C.: *The Mushroom Handbook.* Dover, 1967, 560 pp., $3.95.
Smith, Alexander H.: *The Mushroom Hunter's Field Guide.* U. of Mich., rev., 1963, $9.95.

REPTILES AND AMPHIBIANS

Barker, Will: *Familiar Reptiles and Amphibians of America.* Harper & Row, 1964, 220 pp., $6.95.
Cochran, Doris M., and Coleman J. Goin: *The New Fieldbook of Reptiles and Amphibians.* Putnam, 1970, $5.95.
Conant, Roger: *A Field Guide to Reptiles and Amphibians.* Houghton Mifflin, 1958, 366 pp., $5.95.
Fieldbook for Boys and Men, pp. 437–442.
Leviton, Alan: *Reptiles and Amphibians of North America.* Doubleday, 1972, 252 pp., $9.95.
Morris, Percy A.: *Boy's Book of Turtles and Lizards.* Ronald, 1959, 229 pp., $6.75.
Reptile Study (No. 3342). Boy Scouts, 1971, 64 pp., 45¢, paper.
Schmidt, Karl P., and R. F. Inger: *Living Reptiles of the World.* Doubleday, 1957, $4.95.
Villiard, Paul: *Reptiles As Pets.* Doubleday, 1969, $4.95.
White, William, Jr.: *A Frog Is Born.* Sterling, 1972, 80 pp., $3.95.
White, William, Jr.: *A Turtle Is Born.* Sterling, 1973, $3.95.
Zim, Herbert S., and H. M. Smith: *Reptiles and Amphibians.* Golden, 1956, 160 pp., $1.50, paper.

ROCKS, FOSSILS, MINERALS, ETC.

Collins, Henry Hill, Jr.: *The Wonders of Geology.* Putnam, 1962, 129 pp., $3.64.
Fay, Gordon S.: *Rockhound's Manual.* Harper & Row, 1972, $7.95; $3.50, paper
Fieldbook for Boys and Men, ch. 21, pp. 495–500.
Geology (No. 3284). Boy Scouts, 1953, 88 pp., 45¢, paper.
Harty: *Science for Camp and Counselor,* ch. 5.
Pearl, Richard M.: *How to Know the Minerals and Rocks.* New American Library, 1965, $1.25, paper.
Pough, Frederick H.: *A Field Guide to Rocks and Minerals.* Houghton Mifflin, 3rd ed., 1960, 349 pp., $7.95.
Rhodes, Frank H. T.: *Geology.* Golden, 1971, 160 pp., $4.95; $1.95, paper.
Zim, Herbert S., Frank H. T. Rhodes, and Paul R. Shaffer: *Fossils, A Guide to Prehistoric Life.* Golden, 1962, 160 pp., $1.50, paper.
Zim, Herbert S., and Paul R. Shaffer: *Rocks and Minerals.* Golden, 1957, 160 pp., $1.50, paper.

SHELLS

Abbott, R. Tucker: *How to Know the American Marine Shells.* New Am. Library, 1961, 222 pp., $1.25, paper.
Abbott, R. Tucker: *Seashells of North America.* Golden, 1968, 280 pp., $5.95; $3.95, paper.
Johnstone, Kathleen Yerger: *Collecting Seashells.* Grosset & Dunlap, 1970, 198 pp., $5.95.
Melvin, A. Gordon: *Gems of World Oceans, How to Collect World Sea Shells.* Naturegraph, 1964, 96 pp., $5.95; $2.95, paper.
Murray, Sonia J.: *Shell Life and Shell Collecting.* Sterling, 96 pp., $4.95.

SPELUNKING

Anderson, Jennifer: *Cave Exploring.* Association Press, 1974, 126 pp., $4.95, paper.
Cardwell: *America's Camping Book,* ch. 28.
Harrison, D.: *World of American Caves.* Henry Regnery, $5.95.
McClurg, David R.: *The Amateur's Guide to Caves and Caving.* Stackpole, 1973, 191 pp., $5.95; $2.95, paper.
Sterling, D.: *Story of Caves.* Doubleday, 1956, $1.98.

SPIDERS

David, E.: *Spiders and How They Live.* Prentice-Hall, 1973, $4.95.
Dupree, R.: *Spiders.* Follett, $1.25.
Levi, Herbert W., and Lorna R.: *Spiders and Their Kin.* Golden, 1969, 160 pp., $1.50, paper.
Shuttlesworth, D.: *Story of Spiders.* Doubleday, 1959, $5.95.

STARS

Adler, Irving: *The Stars: Stepping Stones Into Space.* Day, 1956, $3.69.

Astronomy (No. 3303). Boy Scouts, 1971, 80 pp., 45¢, paper.
Fieldbook for Boys and Men, ch. 23, pp. 513–529.
Harty: *Science for Camp and Counselor,* ch. 4.
Jennings, Gary: *The Teenager's Realistic Guide to Astrology.* Association Press, 1971, 222 pp., $5.95.
Joseph, Joseph M., and Sarah L. Lippincott: *Point to the Stars.* McGraw-Hill, rev., 1972, $4.72.
Kals, W. S.: *How to Read the Night Sky: A New and Easy Way to Know the Stars, Planets and Constellations.* Doubleday, 1974, 155 pp., $4.95.
Levitt, I. M., and Roy Marshall: *Star Maps For Beginners.* Simon & Schuster, 1969, 47 pp., $4.50; $1.95, paper.
Mayall, R. Newton, Margaret W. Mayall, and Jerome Wyckoff: *The Sky Observer Guide.* Golden, 1965, $1.50, paper.
Mundt, Carlos: *Stars and Outer Space Made Easy.* Naturegraph, 1963, 80 pp., $5.50; $2.50, paper.
Rey, H. A.: *The Stars, A New Way to See Them.* Houghton Mifflin, 3rd ed., 1967, $7.95.
Zim, Herbert S.: *Stars: A Guide to the Constellations.* Golden, rev., 1957, 160 pp., $1.50, paper.

TREES, SHRUBS, ETC.

Brockman, C. Frank: *Trees of North America.* Golden, 1968, 280 pp., $5.95; $3.95, paper.
Fieldbook for Boys and Men, pp. 354–359, 372–385.
Grimm, William Carey: *Recognizing Native Shrubs.* Stackpole, 1966, 319 pp., $7.95.
Grimm, William Carey: *Home Guide to Trees, Shrubs, and Wildflowers.* Stackpole, 1970, 320 pp., $9.95.
Hepting, George H.: *Diseases of Forest and Shade Trees of the United States.* Supt. of Documents, 1971, 658 pp., $4.
Martin, Alexander, and Herbert S. Zim: *Trees.* Golden, 1956, 160 pp., $1.50, paper.
Mathews, F. Schuyler: *Field Book of American Trees and Shrubs.* Putnam, 1915, 465 pp., $5.95.
Ormond: *Complete Book of Outdoor Lore,* pp. 287–344.
Petrides, George A.: *A Field Guide to Trees and Shrubs.* Houghton Mifflin, 2nd ed., 1973, 431 pp., $5.95; $3.95, paper.
Platt, Rutherford: *A Pocket Guide to Trees.* Pocket Books, 1972, 256 pp., $1.25, paper.
Symonds, George W. D.: *The Shrub Identification Book.* Morrow, 1963, $15; $5.95, paper.
Viertel, Arthur T.: *Trees, Shrubs and Vines.* Syracuse, 1970, $3.95, paper.

WATER LIFE (SEE ALSO FISH)

Amos, W. H.: *The Life of the Seashore.* McGraw-Hill, 1966, $3.95.
Bartsch, Paul: *Mollusks.* Dover, 1968, 112 pp., $2, paper.
Buck, Margaret Waring: *Along the Seashore.* Abingdon, 1960, 72 pp., $3.95; $1.95, paper.
Buck, Margaret Waring: *In Ponds and Streams.* Abingdon, 1955, 72 pp., $3.50; $1.95, paper.
Goetz, Delia: *Swamps.* Morrow, 1961, 63 pp., $4.14.
Golden Nature Guide to Pond Life. Golden, 1967, 160 pp., $1.50, paper.
Hausman, Leon A.: *Beginner's Guide to Fresh-Water Life.* Putnam, 1950, 128 pp., $3.50.
Hofmann, Melita: *Trip to a Pond.* Doubleday, 1966, 64 pp., $4.95.
Klots, Elsie: *New Field Book of Freshwater Life.* Putnam, 1966, 398 pp., $5.95.
Reid, George K.: *Pond Life.* Golden, 1967, 160 pp., $1.50, paper.
Vogt, D., and H. Wermuth: *The Complete Aquarium.* Arco, 1963, $7.50.
Zim, Herbert S., and Lester Ingle: *Seashores, A Guide to Animals and Plants Along the Beaches.* Golden, 1955, 160 pp., $1.50, paper.

Learning to Observe

Bridge: *America's Backpacking Book,* ch. 24.
Brown, Vinson: *Reading the Woods.* Stackpole, 1969, 160 pp., $5.95; $2.95, paper.
Elliott, Charles: *The Outdoor Observer.* Dutton, 1969, 119 pp., $4.50.
Gregg, James: *The Sportsman's Eye: How to Make Better Use of Your Eyes in the Outdoors.* Backpacker Books, 1971, 210 pp., $6.95.
Van Matre, Steve: *Acclimatization.* ACA, 1972, 138 pp., $3.25, paper.
Van Matre, Steve: *Acclimatizing.* ACA, 1974, 225 pp., $3.75, paper.

Nature Crafts

See Chapter 15.

Nature Games

Cassell, Sylvia: *Nature Games and Activities.* Harper & Row, 1956, 91 pp., $3.27.
Frankel, Lillian and Godfrey: *101 Best Nature Games and Projects.* Order from Galloway, 128 pp., $4.95.
Hillcourt: *New Fieldbook of Nature Activities and Conservation.*
Musselman, Virginia W.: *Learning About Nature Through Games.* Stackpole, 1967, 128 pp., $3.95.
van der Smissen and Goering: *A Leader's Guide to Nature-Oriented Activities,* ch. III.

MAGAZINE ARTICLE

Boy's Life:
Wheeler, Alan: "Camping Games." June, 1971, p. 42.

Photography

See the bibliography in Chapter 11.

Tracks and Trailing

See Chapter 23.

Chapter 18

The Waterfront

I wish that I'd been born a fish
So I could swim whene'er I wish.
Then mother would not have to say
It is too cold for you today.
—*The Eavesdropper*

Figure 18–1 "Aw C'mon It's Easy."

Water holds a certain fascination for almost everyone and camp aquatic activities rank high in popularity. All types of swimming and boating are enjoyable and nearly every other camp activity can be integrated at one time or another with the waterfront. For instance, a beautiful waterscape provides an almost perfect setting for a campfire or spiritual program, storytelling, sketching, discussions, painting, or photography. Singing is particularly beautiful when performed by a group on the opposite shore or out in boats, for the sound is especially resonant over water; rounds, antiphonal singing, and answer and response and echo songs are especially appropriate.

Near water, one can study an entirely different assortment of plants and animals. Water goggles are helpful in studying underwater life and some camps provide glass-bottomed boxes and boats for this purpose. Almost any type of boat, from a canoe to a raft, will furnish transportation to get away from the humdrum of familiar camp surroundings.

Children find fun things to do in bodies of water no larger than a small brook, for they can wade, study wildlife, search for pebbles, try to catch minnows with their hands, construct bridges and dams, and make and sail miniature boats. Beachcombing is a favorite activity in camps located near a seashore.

WATER SAFETY

THE PROBLEM

From 7000 to 8000 deaths by drowning occur each year and many of them are needless, for had the victims used more common sense or had even a minimum of instruction in proper water skills and safety procedures, they might still be alive today.

Figure 18–2 "Hold On Tight!"

SOME SAFETY PRECAUTIONS

Since it is likely that activities in or near water will continue to grow in popularity and since most people at some time in their lives will venture into or near water, it seems obvious that it is almost as important to give everyone instruction in correct swimming and boating techniques as it is to teach them to read. Although good swimmers occasionally drown, it is quite true that safety as well as pleasure increases in direct proportion to the skill and confidence of the participant. The following safety precautions will help to minimize hazards and prevent accidents:

1. Teach children to swim and feel confident in the water at the earliest age possible; approximately 29 per cent of drownings occur in children under 15 years of age. The old scare technique of filling them with the idea that "water is dangerous, so stay away from it" never did work very well and certainly won't help to prevent the many deaths that result from accidentally falling into the water or from falling out of a boat or having it capsize. More important than learning to do fancy swimming strokes and dives is developing the ability to do one or two dependable strokes. Still more essential is developing a sense of at-homeness in the water, so that you can relax and be secure in the knowledge that you can stay afloat for hours by treading water, doing a face or back float, or, best of all, using the technique of *drownproofing* or the *bobbing jellyfish float* with its accompanying travel stroke, which will keep you afloat indefinitely and eventually get you to shore without becoming at all fatigued. By far the greatest cause of tragedies is that people tend to panic in an emergency and become tense and struggle frantically, so that they soon wear themselves out or dip below the surface, ingest water, and become even more frightened.

Figure 18–3 Don't Be a Dock Sitter.

A human body with air in the lungs simply can't sink. If you swim, you are probably aware of this because of the difficulty you encounter when trying to lower yourself to the bottom of a pool to pick up a coin. Camps should join the American Red Cross, youth organizations, schools, recreation and park departments, and other organizations that are endeavoring to teach everyone how to swim and observe proper safety precautions. One difficulty lies in the scarcity of people qualified to offer instruction in these areas. If you are interested, inquire about the 10-day aquatic, small craft, and first aid instructor schools conducted each year by the American Red Cross. The classes (there were 22 in 1974) are offered at various locations and at minimal cost to the participants, who must be at least 17 years old and have good swimming ability. Most are held in early June in time to qualify for positions in summer aquatic programs such as those carried on in camps. They offer instruction in first aid, swimming, lifesaving, boating, canoeing and sailing. For further information, contact your local area office of the American Red Cross.

Figure 18–4 This Is a No-No in Deep Water.

2. Parents and others responsible for children should never leave them unattended near water.

3. We need to dispense with the idea that just anyone can rent or own a boat and go out in it. Those unskilled in handling boats should practice in safe water and receive instruction before taking them out.

4. Swim only at patrolled beaches or swimming pools and never go swimming without a companion. If your group consists of four or more swimmers, use a buddy system. This is important, even in the most informal groups—remember how often drownings occur at family and other social outings.

5. Those without good swimming skills should not go out in water over their heads while depending on such artificial supports as water wings, inner tubes, plastic animals, swimming boards, or air mattresses. Many deaths result from slipping off them or having them slip out of the person's grasp.

6. Perfect your own lifesaving and water safety skills, not only to benefit yourself but also so you can help someone else in trouble.

7. Walk, don't run, on pool docks, and never engage in horseplay or take chances in or near water.

PROGRAM TRENDS

Paralleling the increased public interest of the last few decades in all sorts of water activities, camps have shown a corresponding increase in their offerings. In addition to the usual forms of swimming, diving, lifesaving, and boating, there is increasing use of such accessories as flutter boards, water skis, swim fins, and surfboards. Some camps now include such activities as snorkeling and skin and scuba diving, although most rightfully hesitate to make them available to any but older campers and counselors who are expert swimmers, and then only if truly competent supervision is available. Increased participation has brought more emphasis on such related events as water pageants and water carnivals, synchronized swimming, competition in swimming and diving (sometimes with other camps), tilting from boats and canoes, using war canoes, water polo, water basketball, and a large assortment of other water games and contests.

Rowboats are still as popular as ever and are sometimes used with outboard motors for lifesaving and water skiing and for transportation for fishing and camping trips. The ever-popular canoe is more than holding its own, and canoe trips lasting from one night to several weeks are now standard in many camps. Sailing, too, is showing a decided upswing with such exciting events as sailing regattas on the agenda. Many camps, though possessing natural bodies of water, are turning to swimming pools as a solution to pollution and other problems with natural bodies of water.

Waterfront activities are naturally popular and little artificial motivation is needed to enlist the wholehearted participation of campers. The aquatic program ordinarily consists of these divisions: (1) swimming (instructional and recreational); (2) diving; (3) lifesaving, water skiing, scuba diving, surfing; (4) boating (canoeing, sailing, kayaking, rowing, and the like); and (5) trips by water.

THE WATERFRONT STAFF

THE WATERFRONT SUPERVISOR

The waterfront supervisor is in charge of all waterfront activities, and, according to ACA standards,* should be at least 21 years old and should be currently certified as an American Red Cross Water Safety Instructor, a YMCA Leader Examiner, or a Boy Scouts of America National Aquatic Instructor. If the small craft area is separate from the swimming area, it should be under the supervision of a currently certified American Red Cross Small Craft Instructor. The waterfront supervisor is responsible for assigning duties to his staff of assistants and for seeing that they are used to best advantage in carrying out a well-planned program which must also be coordinated with the entire camp program. All activities using the waterfront, such as boat trips or fishing, must be cleared by him.

The waterfront supervisor also sees that campers are tested and classified for a well-planned program of instruction. He trains and supervises his staff, which may include instructors in such waterfront activities as swimming, diving, lifesaving, scuba and skin diving, water skiing, canoeing, rowing, outboard boating, and sailing. He assigns duties, checks on their successful completion, and makes sure that suitable reports on the progress of his department and that of individual campers are made. He sees that all equipment is adequate in quantity and quality and that safety precautions are invariably observed. He also makes appropriate seasonal reports and recommendations for the following season.

Although his many duties usually

Camp Standards with Interpretations for the Accreditation of Organized Camps, p. 30.

(Courtesy of Camp Mishawaka, Grand Rapids, Minnesota.)

exempt him from cabin responsibilities, he should be a trained camper and in sympathy with all phases of camp life so that he sees the waterfront in its proper relation to the total program. He must know his subject matter thoroughly and must constantly strive to learn while on the job, for he has one of the most demanding jobs in camp and is at one time or another likely to be responsible for the safety of every person there. He must have presence of mind, sound judgment, and the ability to remain calm, even when faced with an emergency.

He is also responsible for staff use of the waterfront. Usually during precamp training he tests and classifies all staff members according to their swimming and boating abilities and sets up procedures and schedules for their instruction and use of equipment. He also acquaints them with swimming hazards and safety measures and the general rules and procedures for camper and staff use of the waterfront.

WATERFRONT ASSISTANTS

According to ACA standards, in addition to the waterfront supervisor, there should be a minimum of one person with at least a Senior Red Cross Life Saver, YMCA Senior Lifesaver, or Boy Scout Lifeguard Certificate on duty for each 25 campers in the water. These persons may be supplemented by others who hold Red Cross Junior Life Saver Certificates or their equivalent. There must be a total of one guard for every 10 persons in the water; some of these guards may be responsible persons without lifesaving training. These members of the waterfront staff may or may not have cabin responsibilities, and their waterfront duties are determined by the waterfront supervisor in accordance with their abilities in swimming, diving, or boating. All waterfront personnel should be trained

Figure 18–5 Over the Bounding Main.

and interested in the whole camp program and should consider their activities as integral parts of it. All should cooperate willingly in helping out with general camp program on rainy days and as their duties at the waterfront permit.

GENERAL COUNSELORS' DUTIES AT THE WATERFRONT

A cabin counselor is usually expected to accompany his campers during their periods at the waterfront and may be asked to assist in any way needed. He should look upon this as still another opportunity to observe his campers in a different situation and thus understand them better. Since waterfront activities are favorites with many campers, they appreciate it when their cabin counselor shares their interest. Cabin counselors with appropriate skills may be asked to help out during the peak periods of the day or when their group is participating.

Waterfront rules must be obeyed immediately and without question and counselors should set a good example themselves as well as make sure that their campers follow the rules.

Counselors who wish to participate in waterfront activities will be asked to take classification tests, just as the campers do. Though it is sometimes

(Courtesy of National Music Camp, Interlochen, Michigan.)

possible for staff to receive instruction from waterfront personnel, they must bear in mind that this is a privilege which can be granted only when it does not interfere with their regular duties or those of the waterfront staff.

THE SWIMMING, DIVING, AND LIFESAVING PROGRAM

Early in the camp season, all campers are tested and classified as nonswimmers, beginners, intermediates, swimmers, or lifesavers. Two swimming periods (ordinarily a half-hour in length) are scheduled during the day, one in the late morning for instruction, and the other in the late afternoon for recreation and informal practice of what was learned in the morning. In decentralized camps, campers usually go to the swimming area as a unit and separate according to classification upon arrival at the dock, each going to his respective area for instruction.

WATER SAFETY DEVICES

Vigilance at every single moment is necessary, for one accident during a summer can cause untold grief, seriously damage the reputation of the camp, and even do a great disservice to the whole field of organized camping. Three special safety devices are in common use.

The Buddy System. The buddy system provides each camper with a companion of similar ability. The two enter and leave the water together and stay near each other at all times; thus, it is impossible for one of them to disappear or get into difficulty without its immediately being known to the other. When the signal for "buddy call" is

(Courtesy of Camp Mishawaka, Grand Rapids, Minnesota.)

given (about every ten minutes), they quickly join hands and raise them in the air. Failure to stay close to and watch over a buddy means prompt banishment from the water for the rest of the day or even longer.

The Check Board System. As each swimmer enters the water, he turns over a tag bearing his name on the check board so that the red side is uppermost. As he leaves the swimming area, he turns it back to expose the white side again. A counselor should be stationed near the board to see that no one forgets. Some camps use pegs with the camper's name on them to insert into a peg board in a similar manner.

Colored Caps. Each swimmer wears a colored cap denoting his swimming ability so that waterfront staff can immediately spot a camper out of his proper area or one engaging in activities too hazardous for his ability. The following color system is suggested:

Nonswimmer—red (danger)
Beginner—yellow (caution)
Intermediate—green
Swimmer—blue
Lifesaver—white

HINTS FOR THE USE OF THE WATERFRONT

Waterfront counselors must keep their eyes and attention on swimmers at all times; knitting, chatting, reading, or basking in the sun are definitely out of place. When on duty, they never enter the water except to rescue a swimmer (and this is recommended only as a last resort) or when necessary for some particular phase of teaching.

Docks are not lounging places; use them only as directed by the waterfront staff.

Sunburn is even more of a danger for waterfront staff than for others, since they must spend long hours exposed to the sun's rays; they should apply a good sunscreening lotion and wear long trousers and long sleeves, at least during a portion of the hours on duty. See that campers also take precautions. Recent studies indicate that constant exposure to the sun and heavy tanning can cause premature aging of the skin, permanently damage it, or even predispose to cancer.

As in all camp activities, informality and fun are of great importance, but waterfront rules must be rigidly enforced, for there is too much at stake to brook even minor breaches of the rules. Campers will readily respond if shown the importance of this requirement. Waterfront staff must be businesslike when on duty and see that every instruction is obeyed immediately and without quibbling.

Wait for at least an hour after eating before going into the water. Never swim when tired or overheated.

Campers and counselors should never go swimming alone or at times when the waterfront staff is not on duty. On trips they should swim only in approved areas and when at least one Senior Lifesaver is on guard. Never dive into unknown waters which have not been thoroughly investigated for sufficient depth and hidden hazards. Visitors should use the waterfront only under the same regulations as staff and campers.

Figure 18–6 "Gee, Look at Me!"

Campers enter the water only on signal and come out promptly on signal. You can lessen their natural resentment at mandatory orders by giving some preliminary warning such as "one more dive and out" instead of a "sudden death" blast of the whistle meaning "Come out *now*."

All wear shoes and robes to and from the bathing area and do not loiter in wet suits, but hurry back to their cabins for a brisk rubdown to avoid chilling. Dry between the toes and sprinkle with talcum to discourage athlete's foot. Hang wet suits and towels out to dry immediately.

Thunderstorms are a particularly serious menace to those near water. Everyone in swimming or out in boats must immediately head for shore.

For sanitary reasons, no one takes soap and water baths in the swimming area or permits such animals as horses or dogs to swim or drink there.

A night swim of 5 to 20 minutes is sometimes permitted on hot nights if there is enough lighting to make the entire area clearly visible and it is carried on under the careful arrangement and supervision of the waterfront staff. Powerful, focusing-beam flashlights and white swimming caps help to reduce hazards.

Overestimating one's own ability and taking chances are among the major causes of swimming catastrophes. Unexpected fatigue and muscle cramps can incapacitate even experienced swimmers.

A short before-breakfast dip of 3 to 5 minutes may be permissible, but it should be optional because some people react badly to it.

Distance swimming is allowed at the discretion of the waterfront staff

(Courtesy of Camp Mishawaka, Grand Rapids, Minnesota.)

and only if each swimmer is accompanied by his own rowboat, oarsman, and senior lifesaver.

Whereas swimming in moderation is one of the best forms of exercise known, too frequent or long periods are debilitating and lay the foundation for colds, sinus infections, and other ailments. Two half-hour periods a day, even less if the water is cold, are usually enough. Campers with open sores, skin infections, or colds should not go into the water, and those who develop blue lips or nails, a pale face, or shivering or whose teeth chatter must come out immedately.

BOATING

(See also the section on Canoe Trips in Chapter 31.)

The popularity of boating almost equals that of swimming. It not only gives pleasure in itself but also provides transportation to outlying regions for fishing or camping out and a means of rescuing those in distress.

Contrary to popular opinion, properly constructed and maintained boats do not capsize when used with common sense and some degree of skill. Most catastrophes result from using boats in poor condition or from such misuses or indiscretions as improper loading or overloading, traveling in dangerous or rough water, fooling around, standing up, rocking the boat, or changing positions improperly. All small craft should be tested for seaworthiness and steadiness, and they should be used only by those persons who have passed appropriate tests (including actual practice in shallow, safe water) in recovering from capsizing and swamping.

The Federal Boating Safety Act of 1971 requires that, after April, 1972, *every* passenger in *any* boat on Federal

(Courtesy of Girl Scout Camp Seikooc, Wichita Area Girl Scout Council.)

waterways must have a U.S. Coast Guard approved life preserver (technically known as a personal flotation device or PFD), and since that time, most states have wisely passed similar legislation. New types of safety equipment are now available which are quite comfortable and in no way interfere with the wearer's activity. Children quickly become accustomed to them and regard wearing them as a normal part of small-craft boating.

Always keep the center of gravity low in a canoe; to this end, remove the seats and kneel on a light kneeling pad at the bottom. Some prefer to kneel on the paddle-side knee, resting their back against a thwart and stretching the other leg out in front, braced against a rib of the canoe. Sit on the floor or even lie flat in the canoe to further increase stability if you should inadvertently be caught in rough water. Step, sit, or kneel in the exact center of the canoe to keep your weight balanced. In two-man paddling, the bowman uses a straight stroke while the stern man, who is responsible for steering, paddles on the opposite side with a "J" stroke.

Of all small craft, rowboats are least likely to upset, canoes rate second, and sailboats are trickiest of all. Tipped boats, even if submerged, will not sink to the bottom and a canoe will support several and a rowboat, up to a dozen people. Therefore, if you are thrown out into the water, instead of striking out for shore, swim to the boat and hang on until help comes. This explains why demonstrations of endurance and the ability to tread water and float occupy such a prominent place in boating tests.

Before venturing far from shore, boaters should learn to interpret weather signs, for it is imperative to head for the nearest land at the first signs of an approaching storm. Stay near shore on trips, even though it means traveling greater distances. To change positions in a small boat, do not stand up, but instead, keep your body low and grasp the gunwales with both hands to keep your weight in the center and to avoid losing your balance. It is safest to pull over into shallow water before attempting the transfer.

Neither visitors, counselors, nor campers should use boating equipment until they have passed appropriate tests and secured specific permission from the waterfront staff and given their

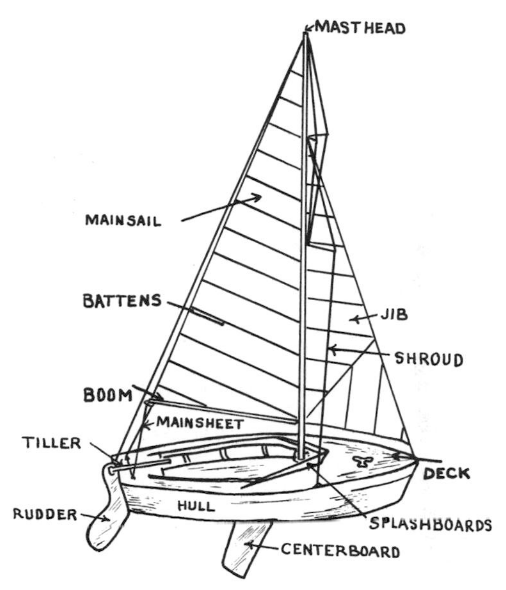

Figure 18-7 Sailboat Nomenclature.

exact departure time, destination, and expected time of return. Boating after dark is permissible only in an emergency or for an occasional moonlight cruise under the immediate supervision of the waterfront staff.

Those who do not swim well enough to qualify as boaters often find the waterfront a tantalizing but forbidden temptation. To appease them, camps sometimes permit an occasional excursion under careful surveillance of the waterfront staff and with one senior lifesaver and a life preserver for each nonswimmer.

Stow all waterfront equipment neatly away; never carelessly leave it lying about to be stumbled over or misused. Keep it in good repair and teach campers to respect it as they do fine tools, repairing any damage themselves or instantly reporting it to the proper person. Train campers thoroughly in the care of boats, giving practice in launching them and taking them from the water, entering and disembarking, and so forth. Never drop or drag canoes over the ground when launching them or removing them from the water. Carry them when on land, and wade out into shallow water to launch them so they don't drag on the bottom. Real boaters are not satisfied to just splash about haphazardly but pride themselves on neat and exact manipulations, performed with perfect timing and skill.

ADDITIONAL READINGS

(For an explanation of abbreviations and abbreviated forms, see page 25.)

Boating, Canoeing, etc.

Andrews, Howard L., and Alexander L. Russell: *Basic Boating—Piloting and Seamanship.* Prentice-Hall, 1964, 359 pp., $9.95.

Angier, Bradford, and Zack Taylor: *Introduction to Canoeing.* Stackpole, 1973, 191 pp., $5.95; $2.95, paper.

Basic Canoeing. ARC, 1965, 67 pp., 35¢, paper.

Basic Rowing. ARC, 1964, 80 pp., paper.

Berger: *Program Activities for Camps,* pp. 81-82.

Blandford, Percy W.: *Canoes and Canoeing.* Grosset & Dunlap, 1968. (also contains plans for building)

Boats and Canoes (no. 26-038). Boy Scouts, 35¢, paper.

Bohannan, John: *Your Guide to Boating: Power or Sail.* Barnes and Noble, 1965, 400 pp., $2.50, paper.

Canoeing (No. 3308). Boy Scouts, 1968, 56 pp., 45¢, paper.

Cardwell: *America's Camping Book,* chs. 45, 46.

Clark, Alice and Lincoln: *The ABC's of Small Boat Handling.* Doubleday, 1963, 225 pp., $1.45, paper.

Consumer Reports, 1974 Buying Guide Issue, p. 357.

Corbin: *Recreation Leadership,* ch. 28.

Fieldbook for Boys and Men, ch. 12.

Gabrielson et al.: *Aquatics Handbook,* chs. 16-19.

How to Repair Fiber Glass Boats. Ferro Corp. (C. M. Magarian), Fiber Glass Div., Fiber Glass Road, Nashville, Tenn. 37211, 1969, 38 pp., $3.

Kenealy, James P.: *Boating From Bow to Stern.* Hawthorn, 1966, 327 pp., $4.95.

Lane, Carl D.: *The New Boatman's Manual.* Norton, 1964, 643 pp., $8.95.

Langer: *The Joy of Camping,* pp. 147-185.

McNair, Robert E.: *Basic River Canoeing.* ACA, 1969, 104 pp., $2.

Merrill: *The Survival Handbook,* ch. 13 to p. 237.

Miracle and Decker: *Complete Book of Camping,* ch. 16.

Motorboating (No. 3294). Boy Scouts, 1962, 80 pp., 45¢, paper.

Ormond: *Complete Book of Outdoor Lore,* ch. 3.
Rodney and Ford: *Camp Administration,* p. 233.
Rowing (No. 3392). Boy Scouts, 1964, 44 pp., 45¢, paper.
Sea Exploring Manual (No. 3229). Boy Scouts, 8th ed., 1974, 448 pp., $6.95.
Scharff, Robert: *The Collier Quick and Easy Guide to Motor Boating.* Collier, 1963, 123 pp., $1.95, paper.
Shivers: *Camping,* pp. 332–347.
Smith, Hervey G.: *The Small Boat Sailor's Bible.* Doubleday, 1964, 147 pp., $2.50, paper.
Wells, George S.: *Happier Family Boating.* Stackpole, 1966, 96 pp., $2.95.
Whitney, Peter Dwight: *White-Water Sport: Running Rapids in Kayak and Canoe.* Ronald, 1960, 120 pp., $5.50.
Zarchy, Harry: *Let's Go Boating.* Knopf, 1962, $4.49.

MAGAZINE ARTICLES

Camping Journal:
"Boats." Feb., 1973, p. 41.
McKeown, William: "Boat Camping." Apr., 1970, p. 23.
McKeown, William T.: "Boat Camping." Sept., 1972, p. 15. (life preservers)
Miller, Stephen: "So You Want to Own a Canoe." June, 1971, p. 32.

Camping Magazine:
Cooper, Richard E.: "Camp Water Safety Aided by Red Cross Courses." Mar., 1972, p. 42.

Journal of Health, Physical Education and Recreation:
Holtz, Doris D.: "Safe Boating." May, 1966, p. 38.

Reader's Digest:
Carper, Jean: "Boating Safety Is No Accident." May 1973, p. 57.

Wilderness Camping:
Burrell, Bob: "Canoe Backpacking." July/Aug., 1973, p. 20.
"Canoe Shopper's Guide." May/June, 1973, p. 45.
Harrison, David: "Wood and Canvas Lives." May/June, 1974, p. 33.
Lange, Richard H.: "The Beginning Kayak—Getting Started." Sept./Oct., 1973, p. 18.
Ruhl, James R.: "A Canoe in Your Future." May/June, 1973, p. 40.
Trevor, John B., Jr.: "Abenaki Canoe Lift." May/June, 1974, p. 55.
Walbridge, Charles: "Reading White Water." May/June, 1974, p. 36.
"Wilderness Camping's Canoe and Kayak Shopper." May/June, 1974, p. 56.

Sailing

Aymar, Gordon C.: *Start 'Em Sailing.* Ronald, 2nd ed., 1959, 128 pp., $5.50.
Basic Sailing. ARC, 1966, 122 pp., paper.
Carter, Samuel, III: *How to Sail.* Sentinel, 1967, 127 pp., $1.50, paper.
D'Alpuget, Lou: *Successful Sailing.* Sterling, 80 pp., $6.95.
DeFontaine, W. H.: *The Young Sportsman's Guide to Sailing.* Nelson, 1961, 96 pp., $2.75.
Drummond, A. H., Jr.: *The Complete Beginner's Guide to Sailing.* Doubleday, $5.95.
Farnham, Moulton H.: *Sailing For Beginners.* Macmillan, 1967, 272 pp., $8.95.
Gabrielson et al.: *Aquatics Handbook.*
Henderson, Richard: *Hand, Reef and Steer: A Practical Handbook for Sailing.* Reilly & Lee, 95 pp., $5.95.
Knights, Jack: *Sailing—Step By Step.* Arco, 1966, 160 pp., $4.50; 95¢, paper.
Marchaj, Czeslau: *Sailing Theory and Practice.* Dodd, Mead, 1964, $15.
Mitchell, Leeds: *Introduction to Sailing.* Stackpole, 1971, 192 pp., $5.95.
Pearson, Everett A.: *The Lure of Sailing.* Harper & Row, 1965, 328 pp., $7.95.
Sailing. Golden, $1.50, paper.
Small-Boat Sailing (No. 3319). Boy Scouts, 1965, 96 pp., 45¢, paper.
Smith, Rufus G.: *Sailing Made Easy.* Dodd, Mead, 1964, $4.
Sports Illustrated Book of Junior Sailing. Lippincott, 1964, 85 pp., $3.50.

MAGAZINE ARTICLES

Camping Magazine:
Frederickson, Bruce E.: "Selecting Sailboats for Your Camp." Apr., 1970, p. 18.
Gidwitz, Betsy: "Plan a Safe Sailing Program." Apr., 1963, p. 23.
O'Day, George D.: "Basic Ingredients For Camp Sailing." Mar., 1962, p. 25.

Skin and Scuba Diving, Water Skiing, etc.

Allen, Barry: *Sports Illustrated Skin Diving and Snorkeling.* Lippincott, 1973, 96 pp., $3.95; $1.50, paper.
Anderson, Glen E.: *Water Skiing Skill.* Macmillan, 1968, 128 pp., $1.95, paper.
Bergaust, E., and W. Eoss: *Skin Divers in Action.* Putnam, $3.49.
Borgeson, Lillian, and Jack Speirs: *Skin and Scuba Diver.* Arco, 1962, 144 pp., $3.50.
Clifford, William D., and Thomas C. Hardman: *Let's Go Water Skiing.* Hawthorn, 1969, 157 pp., $4.95.
Counsilman, James and Barbara Drinkwater: *Beginning Skin and Scuba Diving.* Wadsworth, 1964, 52 pp., $1.65, paper.
Dixon, Peter L.: *The Complete Book of Surfing.* Ballantine, rev., 1969, 220 pp., 95¢, paper.
Floherty, J., and M. McGrady: *Skin Diving.* Lippincott, $4.50.
Frey, Hank and Shaney: *Diver Below.* Collier, 1969, 182 pp., $2.95. (skin and scuba diving)

Gabrielson et al.: *Aquatics Handbook,* chs. 13, 14, 18.

Joseph, James: *Better Water Skiing for Boys.* Dodd, Mead, 1964, $3.95.

Sand, G.: *Skin and Scuba Diving.* Hawthorn, $4.95.

Scuba Diving. Golden, $1.50, paper.

Shivers: *Camping,* pp. 347–351.

Sullivan, G.: *Teen-Age Guide to Skin and Scuba Diving.* Fell, $3.95.

Tillman, Albert A.: *Skin and Scuba Diving.* Brown, 1966, 160 pp., $1.95, paper.

Tinker, Gene and Barbara: *Let's Learn to Snorkel.* Walker & Co., 80 pp., $4.95.

Water Skiing (no. 3357). Boy Scouts, 1969, 64 pp., 45¢, paper.

MAGAZINE ARTICLES

Boy's Life:
"Water-Skiing Signals." July, 1972, p. 42.

Camping Magazine:
"Water Skiing Hand Signals." June, 1967, p. 13.

Journal of Health, Physical Education and Recreation:
Vickers, Betty Jane: "First Lessons in Synchronized Swimming." Apr., 1963, p. 32.

Swimming, Diving, Lifesaving

Aquatics Guide. AAHPER., 1973–1975, $1.75, paper.

Armbruster, David A., Robert H. Allen, and Herbert S. Billingsley: *Swimming and Diving.* Mosby, 6th ed., 1974, 290 pp., $10.25.

Barone, Marian: *Beginning Diving.* National Press, 1973, 90 pp., $2.95.

Batterman, Charles: *Techniques of Springboard Diving.* MIT Press, 1968, $5.95.

Berger: *Program Activities for Camps,* pp. 97–103.

Billingsley, Hobie: *Diving Illustrated.* Ronald, 1965, 245 pp., $6.

Cardwell: *America's Camping Book,* chs. 29, 30.

Clotworthy, Robert: *The Young Sportsman's Guide to Diving.* Nelson, 1962, 96 pp., $2.75.

Collis, Martin, and William Kirchhoff: *Swimming.* Allyn and Bacon, 1973, 120 pp., paper.

Corbin: *Recreation Leadership,* ch. 28.

Counsilman, James E.: *The Science of Swimming.* Prentice-Hall, 1968, 457 pp., $9.50.

Fairbanks, Anne Ross: *Teaching Springboard Diving.* Prentice-Hall, 1963, 208 pp., $7.25.

Ferinden, William: *Teaching Swimming.* Remediation Associates, Inc., Box 318, Linden, New Jersey 07036, 1970, 89 pp., $3.95.

Fieldbook for Boys and Men, ch. 11.

Gabrielson, M. Alexander (Ed.): *Swimming Pools—A Guide to Their Planning, Design and Operation.* Hoffman Publications, 1972, 2nd ed., 266 pp., $12.50.

Gabrielson et al.: *Aquatics Handbook.*

Higgins, John, Alfred Barr, and Ben Grady: *Swimming and Diving.* Arco, 3rd ed., 1962, 329 pp., $4.95.

Howes, Gordon T. ("Mike") (Ed.): *Lifeguard Training—Principles and Administration.* AAHPER, rev., 1974, 124 pp., $8.95.

Kiphuth, Robert: *Basic Swimming.* Greenwood, 125 pp., $9.25.

Lanoue, Fred: *Drownproofing, a New Technique for Water Safety.* Prentice-Hall, 1963, 112 pp., $5.90.

Lifeguard Training: Principles and Administration. A Project of the Council for National Co-operation in Aquatics. Ass'n Press, 2nd ed., 1973, 223 pp., $8.95.

Lifesaving (No. 3278). Boy Scouts, 1965, 56 pp., 45¢, paper.

Life Saving and Water Safety. ARC, 1956, 248 pp., paper.

MacKenzie, Marlin M., and Betty Spears: *Beginning Swimming.* Wadsworth, 1965, 88 pp., $1.50, paper.

McAllister, Evelyn D.: *Easy Steps to Safe Swimming.* Barnes, 4th ed., 1969, 128 pp., $3.95.

Merrill: *All About Camping,* pp. 365–367.

Merrill: *The Survival Handbook,* pp. 237–242.

Midtlyng, Joanna: *Swimming.* Saunders, 1974, 130 pp., $2.25.

Newman, Virginia Hunt: *Teaching Young Children to Swim and Dive.* Harcourt, 1969, 86 pp., $4.50.

Rodney and Ford: *Camp Administration,* pp. 231–233.

Roy, Harcourt: *Beginner's Guide to Swimming and Water Safety.* Drake, 1972, 159 pp., $5.95.

Ryan, Jack: *Learning to Swim Is Fun.* Ronald, 1960, 80 pp., $5.

Scout Handbook, pp. 346–355.

Shivers: *Camping,* pp. 323–332, 351–356.

Silva, Charles E.: *Lifesaving and Water Safety Today.* Ass'n Press, 1965, 175 pp., $1.95, paper.

Smith, Hope M.: *Water Games.* Ronald, 1962, 95 pp., $5.

Spears, Betty: *Fundamentals of Synchronized Swimming.* Burgess, 3rd ed., 1966, 130 pp., $3.75.

Sports Illustrated Book of Diving. Lippincott, 1961, 96 pp., $3.50.

Sports Illustrated Book of Swimming. Lippincott, 1961, 96 pp., $3.50.

Swimming (No. 3299). Boy Scouts, 1960, 48 pp., 45¢, paper.

Swimming and Diving. A Project of the Council for National Co-operation in Aquatics. Ass'n Press, 1969, 264 pp., $12, paper. (bibliography of books, periodicals, films, etc.)

Swimming and Water Safety. ARC, 1968, 142 pp., paper.

Swimming and Water Safety Courses (Instructor's Manual). ARC, 1968, 97 pp., paper.

Vickers, Betty J.: *Teaching Synchronized Swimming.* Prentice-Hall, 1965, 170 pp., $5.50.

Vickers, Betty J., and William J. Vincent: *Swimming.* Brown, 2nd ed., 1971, 61 pp., 95¢, paper.

Water Fun for Everyone. Ass'n Press, 1965, 191 pp., $5.95.

Waterman, Frank: *Learn to Swim*. Funk & Wagnalls, 1968, 160 pp., 95¢, paper.
Yates, Fern, and Theresa W. Anderson: *Synchronized Swimming*. Ronald, 1958, 164 pp., $7.50.

MAGAZINE ARTICLES

Boys' Life:
Smyke, Ed: "Keeping Afloat With Drownproofing." Aug., 1966.

Camping Journal:
Martenhoff, Jim: "Make Yourself Drownproof." July, 1968, p. 36.

Camping Magazine:
Beck, Albert W.: "A Refreshing Change in the ARC Swimming Program." Feb., 1970, p. 18.
Berlyle, Milton K.: "Planning Waterfront Facilities." Part I, Sept./Oct., 1965; Part II, Nov./Dec., 1965.
Bredamus, James C.: "Swimtime is When a Camp Director Needs a Friend." Apr., 1971, p. 23.
Buchanan, Ernest T., III: "The Reluctant Swimmer." June, 1969, p. 14.
Cooper, Richard E.: "Camp Water Safety Aided by Red Cross Courses." Mar., 1972, p. 42.
Gidwitz, Betsy: "Waterfront Safety Check." Feb., 1963, p. 12.
Hainsfeld, Harold, and Irv Simone: "Teaching Aids for Water Sports." June, 1961, p. 12.
Lent, Arnold D.: "New Buddy Plan Aids Waterfront Safety." May, 1970, p. 14.
Melamed, Monte: "New Recreational Spray-Shower Aids Camp Swimming Programs." Jan., 1972, p. 28.
Nelson, Henry: "Proper Painting for Camp Swimming Pools." Feb., 1973, p. 24.
Price, Fern E.: "Water Pageants Build Creativity." Feb., 1968, p. 17.
Santoro, Joel T.: "Training of Waterfront Personnel." Apr., 1967, p. 19.
"Waterfront Equipment Inventory Check List." Nov./Dec., 1963, p. 19.

Part Four

Camping and Trail Skills

CAMP SMOKE

There's a ripple on the water,
There's a frost tang in the air,
Now the maple trees are red beside the stream.
And I see our empty campground,
With the spruce trees for a background
And the birches bending o'er it, in my dream.

On the ridge the bucks are pawing,
Where the beeches spread their branches,
And the brush above is all fresh hooked and clean of bark.
There are doe tracks in the valley,
Made where moonbeams dance and dally,
When the waxing hunter's moon drove back the dark.

There's an old cock partridge drumming
In the black growth thicket yonder,
Where old bruin left his foot prints in the moss,
Where he reached and scratched the highest,
Scratched the spruce bole much the highest,
Just to tell the thicket dwellers he was boss.

There's a snowshoe rabbit sitting
Where my fir bough bed was piled,
And a "quilley-pig" is grunting round the spot
Where the cook fire mulled and glimmered
And the tea pail slowly simmered
While the bacon in the fry pan sizzled hot.

From the blackness of the spruces,
Where the shadows fall the thickest,
Comes a hoot owl's mournful calling through the night;
And the balsam laden breezes,
Stealing softly through the reaches,
Soothe the drowsy woodland camper in their flight.

Ah, the woodland trails are calling!
Load the old canoe with duffle,
I must pitch my tent again beside the spring.
Bring the pole and six-foot paddle,
Far up river we will travel
To the campground where the yellow birches swing.

To that same old sheltered campground,
With the spruce trees in the background,
Where the hoot owl breaks the silence of the night.
Where the snowshoe rabbit crouches
We will make new balsam couches,
In the shadows of our campfire's smoky light.

There's a ripple on the water,
There's a frost tang in the air
And the maple trees are red beside the stream.
All the old wood trails are calling,
While the browning leaves are falling,
Where I see the camp smoke curling, in my dream.

—HERMAN H. HANSON*

*By permission of Mr. Hanson.

Chapter 19

Some Camp Pests You May Meet

Figure 19–1 After All, Who's Invading Whose Home?

Black bugs in the water
Red ants everywhere,
Chiggers round our waistline,
Sand flies in our hair—
But the dust of cities
At any cost we shun,
And cry amid our itchings,
"Isn't camping fun?"

—ALICE ARMIGER SKEEN

. . . having now secured my supper, I looked out for a suitable place to amuse myself in combating mosquitoes for the balance of the evening.

—MERIWETHER LEWIS

DANGERS IN OUTDOOR LIVING

Tommy and Tina Tenderfoot often forego the pleasures of outdoor adventure because of the horrible tales they have heard of dangers lying in wait for the unwary. However, conversations with a sampling of the thousands of people who now engage in some type of camping indicate how groundless such forebodings are. There are now few if any dangerous animals roaming about in areas of the United States where campers are likely to go. Although many of nature's creatures can prove bothersome or possibly even dangerous on occasion, most merely want to live and let live as far as humans are concerned. The smart camper respects their right to privacy and minds his own business, leaving them free to do the same. However, he is wise to learn something about them and their habits.

A person in a good organized camp is probably much safer than he would be at home, dodging traffic and other city hazards. The probabilities are that you will spend weeks or even months around camp without ever so much as seeing a poisonous snake or dangerous animal, since, even if present, they are usually shy and afraid of outsiders and are even less anxious than you to foster a close acquaintance. Since a wild creature's very life depends upon his ability to hunt and to escape being caught by something hunting him, he is very alert and his senses are usually much keener than yours. This makes him aware of your presence long before you have detected his, and he will be off and away so fast that you may never know he was there. An animal will not usually bite or otherwise harm you unless you have frightened him by slipping up on him when he was asleep or have made him feel trapped or cornered; then, like any living thing in similar circumstances, he may fight back in self-defense.

Throughout the text, we have stressed safe practices when using tools and equipment. In this chapter, we will briefly discuss certain kinds of wildlife which might cause concern, feeling that, as in many things, it is better to be aware of some possible dangers and ways to avoid them, rather than to wait until something happens and then give first aid and curative measures. We have not attempted to give extensive information about treatments and remedies, feeling that they are quite adequately treated in the references listed at the end of the chapter. Training in first aid is helpful for all camp personnel. Every group taking a trip out of camp should have at least one member qualified in first aid and should carry a suitable first-aid kit and instruction manual to take care of possible emergencies. The camp nurse and/or physician usually supervises the first-aid training and the assembling of the first-aid kit.

POISON IVY, POISON OAK, AND POISON SUMAC

SOURCE OF THE POISONING

Poison ivy, poison oak, and poison sumac cause much distress, for it is estimated that at least two out of three people are allergic to at least one of them, and they are so common and widespread that you always run the danger of encountering them, even in your own backyard. Since all three have common characteristics, we will discuss them together.

The allergic reaction results when an oily substance from these plants comes in contact with the skin; susceptible persons vary in the severity of their reaction. Although poisoning is ordinarily caused by direct contact with the leaves, it is also possible from contact with the stems, roots, or even soot and smoke from burning plants in a brush fire or campfire. You can also get the oil on your skin indirectly by contact with things on which the oil has been deposited, such as clothing, tools, or even the hair of dogs or other animals which have been running through the brush. Poisoning is possible at any time of the year, but it occurs most commonly in spring and summer when the sap is more abundant and people are more likely to be outdoors. Individuals differ greatly in their susceptibility, some apparently being quite immune while others need only be in proximity to the plants. No one can ever be sure of immunity, however, for, as with certain other allergies, one previously immune can suddenly become susceptible.

IDENTIFYING THE PLANTS

Poison Ivy. *Poison ivy* is probably the most widespread of the three, with some variety being found in almost every area of the United States, except certain southwestern states. Although there are many varieties, they all have the same characteristic arrangement of leaves, which always grow in clusters of three on a single stem, as shown in Figure 19–2. Thus the old saying, "Leaflets three, let be" is still a good rule to follow, although it may make you unduly suspicious of certain harmless plants.

The leaves are roughly oval, from

Figure 19-2 Poison Ivy and Virginia Creeper.

1 to 4 inches long, and vary somewhat in appearance, even on the same plant, for some are quite irregular, sometimes even lobed like oak leaves. They are a glossy, bright green in summer and turn to attractive shades of red or russet in the fall (the uninformed have been known to gather them to use in fall decorations). The inconspicuous greenish-white flowers are borne in loose clusters on slender stems and are followed by waxy white or ivory pea-sized fruit which are segmented somewhat like a peeled orange. *Poison ivy* is often confused with harmless *Virginia creeper* or *woodbine* but it is quite easy to distinguish between them since the latter has five leaflets (the friendly hand) whereas poison ivy has only three leaflets (the maimed hand).

The plant growth takes many forms, most commonly appearing as a vine twining about trees, fences, houses, and even rock piles; it may also appear as a low, leafy shrub, growing out in the open. As it matures, it sometimes resembles a small tree with a trunk several inches thick. It sometimes grows along the ground, blending with other plants to form an attractive green carpet.

Poison Oak. *Poison oak* is a misnomer, for it is not a member of the oak family at all, but simply another form of poison ivy whose characteristic three leaves are lobed somewhat like oak leaves. It is most commonly found in the states of California, Washington, and Oregon and ordinarily grows as an upright shrub, although it sometimes climbs on other objects like a vine. The leaves are usually glossy and uneven with a somewhat leathery appearance. The greenish-white flowers are about $\frac{1}{4}$ inch across and are followed by greenish-white berries in mid-October.

Poison Sumac. *Poison sumac* is found chiefly in swampy areas east of the Mississippi River. It never grows as a vine, but rather as a coarse, woody shrub or small tree from 5 to 25 feet tall that is frequently asymmetrical, often leaning to one side. It is commonly confused with certain harmless varieties of sumac which serve such useful purposes as furnishing tannin for treating leather, controlling erosion on waste hillsides, or growing as ornamental plants. The classification in Table 19-1 should help you to distinguish between them.

Figure 19-3 Poison Oak.

Figure 19–4 Some of the Sumacs.

PREVENTION OF POISONING

Prevention is far better than treatment in the case of these noxious plants, and it is wise to eradicate them from frequently used areas by using a good chemical preparation to kill them, following up as necessary to curb new growth. Only adults should participate in this procedure, however, and they should get complete information from such sources as the United States Department of Agriculture* before attempting it.

Since it is usually impractical to try to eradicate the plants over all areas where campers hike, they should learn to recognize them and keep an eye out to avoid direct contact. When hiking, protect skin areas by wearing long sleeves, long trousers, and even gloves. It also helps to cover exposed skin surfaces with such protective ointments as those recommended by the United States Department of Agriculture* or with a thick lather of strong yellow laundry soap, which you can later wash off. Upon returning to camp, immedi-

**Poison Ivy, Poison Oak and Poison Sumac.* Farmers' Bulletin No. 1972, Supt. of Documents, U.S. Govt. Printing Office, rev. 1963, 30 pp., 15¢.

Table 19–1 Characteristics of Three Varieties of Sumac

	Poison Sumac	Smooth Sumac	Staghorn Sumac
Branches	Smooth.	Smooth.	Covered with fuzz.
Leaflets	7 to 13, arranged in pairs; oval-shaped with smooth or untoothed margins. Mid-ribs are scarlet.	Many leaflets; slender, lance-shaped leaves with toothed margins.	Many leaflets; slender, lance-shaped leaves with toothed margins.
Berries	White or greenish; arranged in loose clusters 10 to 12 inches long at the *sides* of the branches.	Red; arranged in seed heads at the *ends* of the branches.	Red; arranged in seed heads at *ends* of branches.
Location	Usually in bogs or swampy areas.	Dry uplands.	Dry uplands.

ately remove your clothing and avoid touching it again until after it has been laundered; this is to prevent contact with any oil which may have gotten on it. Scrub your skin with several applications of strong laundry soap, rinsing well after each, then apply rubbing alcohol. This is designed to remove any oil which may have accidently adhered to your skin.

Several methods have been tried to produce immunity to these plants, but so far none has proved entirely successful. Don't let anyone persuade you to try the old folk remedy of eating some of the leaves to acquire immunity, for it is wholly ineffective and may give you a severe case of poisoning.

SYMPTOMS

Symptoms may appear from within an hour or two up to seven days after exposure, beginning with redness, burning, and itching in a localized area which may then spread. This is followed by a breaking-out or rash, swelling, and watery blisters, with possible fever, major itching, and general discomfort.

TREATMENT

Consult a doctor for severe cases. Do not scratch, for although it may not spread the poison, it will increase the discomfort and can cause a dangerous secondary infection. Although there is no quick cure, certain measures may relieve the itching and intense discomfort. Recommended are applications of compresses of very hot or very cold water, followed by a drying agent such as calamine lotion or compresses dipped in a solution of Epsom salts or cornstarch in water or in a solution of one level teaspoon of boric acid mixed with two glasses of water.

SNAKES

FACT AND FANCY

There are probably no more feared or despised creatures in the world than snakes, yet of the several hundred varieties in the United States, only four are poisonous—the corals, the rattlers, the copperhead, and the cottonmouth. It is estimated that only about 1500 of the approximately 200,000,000 people in the United States are bitten by poisonous snakes each year and, of these, not more than one in a hundred will die from the effects. For instance, for every person in Missouri who dies from snake bite, there are 3100 who die from falls, 735 from drowning, and 5975 from automobile accidents.* It therefore seems ridiculous to let fear of snakes keep us from taking to the woods.

A snake wants most of all just to be let alone to pursue his snaky business and will almost never bite you unless you come upon him by surprise or tease or frighten him. His usual reaction upon detecting human presence is to slither away to safety or to lie still and hope you will not notice him. Hence, for every snake you see, there are probably countless others that detected you first and crept silently and unobtrusively away.

Snakes play an important part in the balance of nature and are especially useful to campers and farmers, since they eat large quantities of such bothersome creatures as certain insects and rats and mice which would soon overrun the countryside if not curtailed by their natural enemies. The large majority of snakes are non-poisonous and so useful that they should be greeted with a welcome mat and protected rather than killed. They are another example

*Keefe, Jim: "Snakebite," *Missouri Conservationist.*

Figure 19-5 Get Him While He Sleeps.

of how even commonly disliked creatures have a role to play in keeping nature in balance.

Snakes have long been the subjects of high-powered imaginations and unfounded folk tales which attribute to them such uncanny powers as the ability to charm animals and birds, to milk cows, or to grasp their tails in their mouths and roll along the ground to inject poison into a victim through the "stingers" in their tails. They don't swallow their young to protect them from threatened danger, they are not vicious by nature, and they don't chase people about in order to bite them.

Snakes are not slimy and cold to the touch but acquire their temperature from the atmosphere around them. Their skins, with a covering of scales, feel almost like soft kid leather. Most of them lay eggs, although a few bear their young alive. They have no legs but draw themselves along by means of the sharp edges of the scales on their undersides; this enables them to move quite rapidly over rough ground (one variety is called "racers"). Some in particularly smooth areas, such as deserts, propel themselves along by throwing loops of their bodies forward, first on one side, then the other, and so are called "side-winders." Some can swim, others can climb trees and shrubbery, and most have a protective coloration which makes them blend in with their native haunts. Snakes have long, slender tongues which are forked near the end and serve as sensory organs or antennae. By darting them in and out rapidly, they can detect ground vibrations and movements near them. They swallow their food whole, having jaws which unhinge so that they can ingest and swallow almost unbelievably large prey.

Figure 19-6 Common Garter Snake (Non-Poisonous).

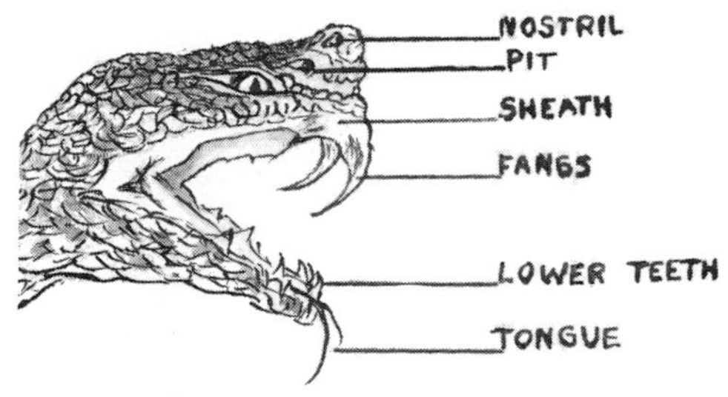

Figure 19–7 Head of a Pit Viper.

THE PIT VIPERS

Three of the four poisonous snakes (rattlesnakes, copperheads and cottonmouth moccasins) are known as *pit vipers* because of the deep pits located on each side of their head about halfway between nostril and eye (Fig. 19–7). The pits are sensitive organs which detect temperature changes and so warn them of an approaching warm-blooded animal and guide them to strike it accurately to kill or immobilize it. Their two sharp, hollow fangs are located in the upper jaw and normally lie flat against the roof of the mouth. When the snake strikes, it erects its fangs which pierce the flesh and act like hypodermic needles to inject poison or venom. If a snake's fang is extracted or broken off, it will be replaced by another within a few days.

The other variety of poisonous snake, the coral snake, has no pits and differs in other important ways, so it will be discussed separately. Distinguishing characteristics of the pit vipers are given in Table 19-2.

Miraculous tales abound as to the ability of some snakes to leap through the air and fasten their fangs into their victims but a snake's tail always remains on the ground and, even from a coiled position, it cannot strike for more than one-third to one-half of its length. When not coiled, it cannot strike even that far or with any degree of accuracy. A snake's strike is so rapid that it appears as a blur and it is doubtful that any creature is quick enough to dodge it.

Although, as mentioned previously, there are only four main types of poisonous snakes in the United States, there are several varieties of each, bringing the total to 30 or 40 different kinds which are so widespread that there is probably no state without at least one kind.

Water or Cottonmouth Moccasin. The *water* or *cottonmouth moccasin* is usually found in swampy territory or

Table 19–2 Distinguishing Characteristics of Pit Vipers

	Pit Vipers (Poisonous)	Non-Poisonous Snakes
Pits	Have characteristic pits.	Have no pits.
Head	Triangular, when viewed from above. It is broader than the neck and so makes a definite angle where they join. (See the diamondback rattler in Figure 19–8.)	Head not angular and not much broader than the neck so that it tapers off to join it smoothly.
Pupil of Eye	Upright and elliptical.	Round.
Underside of Tail	Scales in uninterrupted rows around the snake for all or most of its length.	There is a line which goes up the middle on the underside of the snake and divides the scales into two rows.
Teeth or Fangs	Have both teeth and fangs.	Have teeth but no fangs.

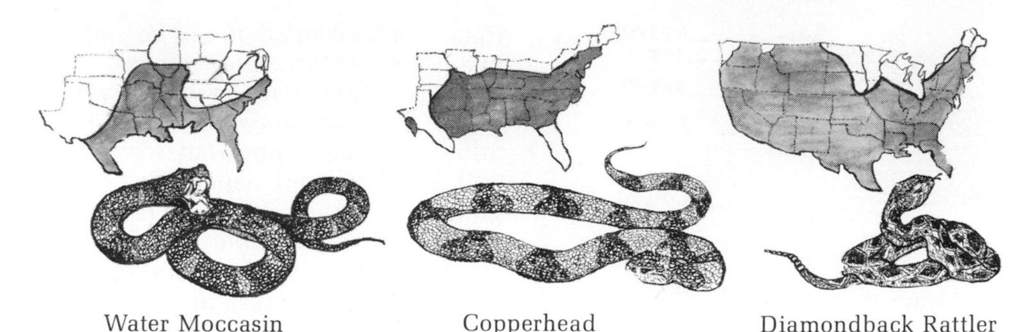

Figure 19–8 The Pit Vipers.

in the trees and bushes overhanging streams and marshes in southern states, as indicated in Figure 19–8. It is 3 to 6 feet long and has a dark muddy or olive-brown color with 11 to 15 inconspicuous darker bars on its short, thick body. It is somewhat pugnacious and inclined to stand its ground and fight back when threatened. There are several varieties of harmless water snakes which resemble it and are often mistaken for it. It usually threatens before striking by opening its mouth wide to show its ugly white interior; this explains its name, "cottonmouth."

The Copperhead. The *copperhead* (also called the *Northern moccasin* or *pilot snake*) is found chiefly in the eastern and southern states as indicated in Figure 19–8. It is usually 2 to 4 feet long and of a hazel or pinkish-brown color, with cross markings of darker reddish-brown blotches which are shaped somewhat like an hourglass or a short-handled dumbbell. A copperhead has the *narrow* part of the hourglass on its back, unlike several harmless varieties which somewhat resemble it but have the *broad* part of the hourglass on their backs. The name "copperhead" comes from the distinctive copper coloring of its head. It usually prefers rocky, wooded terrain.

Rattlesnakes. It is estimated that there are 16 to 26 varieties of rattlesnakes in the United States, distributed so that there is at least one variety in nearly all of the 50 states. They range in size from the little eight-inch pygmy rattlers to the giant diamondbacks. They are variously marked and colored, but all have one common characteristic—the rattles on the end of their tails with which they usually warn their victims before striking. The tail and rattles vibrate so rapidly that you

Figure 19–9 Misery Is Finding Out the Copperhead You Chopped Up in Front of Your Campers Was Really Miss Patty's Pet King Snake!

can scarcely see them and they make a unique sound somewhat like the ticking of an alarm clock or the sound of a locust. A rattler sheds its skin as many as two to five times a year, leaving a bit of skin each time to harden into another "rattle." Some of the rattles are subsequently lost through wear and accident, so it is not true that you can tell the age of the rattler by counting the number of rattles.

THE CORAL OR HARLEQUIN SNAKE

The *coral snake* is southern, as indicated on the map in Figure 19–10, and exists in several varieties, each potentially quite dangerous, since their venom is even more toxic than that of the pit vipers. Fortunately, coral snakes prefer darkness and so tend to stay burrowed beneath the soil in daytime. You are not likely to encounter one except at night or after a flood or hard rain. Their heads resemble those of non-poisonous snakes in that they have no pits and are not angular but taper off gradually to join their necks. They have short fangs which are permanently erect. Instead of striking to inject their poison in one or a few quick jabs as the pit vipers do, they try to catch hold and hang on to chew and thus inject their venom in a number of places. The venom affects the nervous sytem and tends to paralyze the victim, instead of traveling through the circulatory system as does that of the pit vipers.

The coral snake is long, slender, colorful, and attractive. It closely resembles some harmless varieties of king and milk snakes and the only sure way to distinguish between them is to note the color of the nose and the exact arrangement of the red, yellow, and black bands, as indicated in Table 19–3.

PREVENTING SNAKE BITE

Since snakes are ordinarily shy and prefer to avoid contact with anything as potentially dangerous as a human, they present little danger as long as you carefully avoid coming upon them while they sleep or frightening or threatening them. With proper

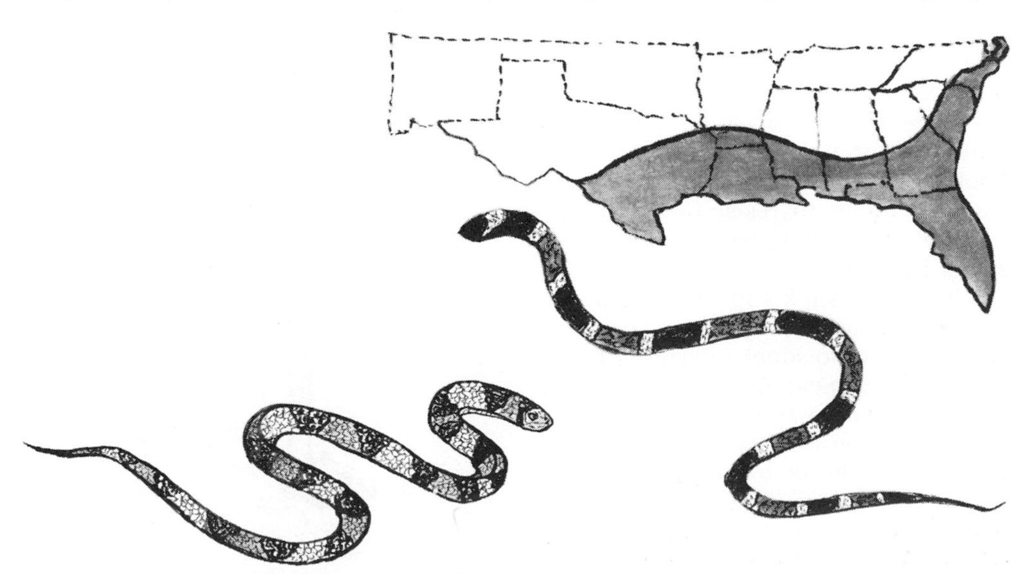

Figure 19–10 Coral Snake and Scarlet King Snake.

Table 19–3 Distinguishing Characteristics of the Coral Snake

	Coral Snake	Harmless Varieties
Nose	Black.	Pink or yellow.
Bands	Broad red bands lie next to narrow yellow bands. It may help you to remember this to recall that red, symbolizing danger, touches yellow, which symbolizes caution. The black bands lie between the yellow bands.	The red bands are broader and are separated from the narrower yellow bands by the black bands. Thus the red and yellow never touch each other.

precautions, you may well camp in many areas for days or even weeks without ever meeting a single poisonous snake or even one of the much more plentiful harmless varieties. Watch where you step, sit, and place your hands. Be especially careful when stepping over logs or reaching into holes or underbrush where you cannot see clearly, and be cautious when placing your hands and feet while climbing ledges, for snakes frequently hide out or sun themselves in crevices or on rock surfaces. Although they have no ears and so cannot hear you, they are quite sensitive to ground vibrations. Therefore, some people advocate carrying a hiking stick and tapping it gently on the ground as you go along to apprise the snake of your coming so that he will move out of your way. Since 98 per cent of snake bites are on the extremities, with 68 per cent on the foot or leg, it may be advisable to wear boots 10 or more inches high that are sturdy enough to resist fang penetration when in country known to be snake infested.

A hiking stick can also serve as a snake stick, especially when you want to trap a non-poisonous variety for further study. You can fashion a rough one from a branch 4 to 6 feet long with a fork at the bottom, whittled down to about 2 inches in length (Fig. 19–11). Directions for making more sophisticated snake sticks can be found in Hillcourt's *Field Book of Nature Activities and Conservation* or in the Boy Scout *Reptile Study* booklet (see the bibliography at the end of this chapter). To use a snake stick, place the forked end over the snake's head to trap it tightly against the ground, then pick it up, grasping it firmly just back of its head so that it can't reach around to bite you and using your other hand to control its body. Do not attempt to pick up poisonous varieties, for only experts should risk such close contact with them.

TREATMENT OF SNAKE BITES

Not many cases of poisonous snake bite are reported each year in America, and few of these prove fatal. The

Figure 19–11 A Snake Stick.

American Red Cross* reports a mortality rate of only 10 to 15 per cent, even when the bite goes *untreated,* and the rate drops to only one in a hundred with proper treatment. The poison is somewhat slow to act so that there is always time to get medical treatment in ordinary situations. Someone has said that there is more danger of choking to death from eating popcorn in a movie than of dying from snake bite, and many more people die annually from the stings of bees and wasps than from snake bite. Nevertheless, any group hiking through "snaky" territory far from a doctor should take along a snake-bite kit and perhaps some antivenom and know how to use them. The kit consists of rubber tubing, a rubber suction pump, and an antiseptic. The seriousness of the bite depends upon such factors as the size and kind of snake, the potency and amount of venom present in the snake at the particular time, the size and physical condition of the victim, and whether or not the venom was injected into or near a vital organ.

If someone is bitten, try to identify the snake or at least determine whether or not it is poisonous. The bite of a non-poisonous snake appears as two rows of teeth marks and should be treated like any other puncture wound. If the snake is one of the pit vipers, there will be one or two deep fang marks or punctures and an immediate painful, burning sensation, quickly followed by discoloration and swelling, with later symptoms of general weakness, nausea, breathing difficulty and possibly unconsciousness. This bite calls for immediate action.

If medical aid can be obtained within an hour, hurry to get it, for the most helpful treatment is a prompt injection of antivenom to counteract the poison and minimize pain and discomfort. Transport the victim by vehicle or on a stretcher which you can improvise from a blanket, some safety pins, and two poles, as shown in Figure 19–12. Keep the victim quiet and at rest, for any physical activity will speed up his circulation and spread the poison more rapidly. Fright and shock often do almost as much harm as the actual bite, so try to reassure him and prevent him from seeing his injury or the treatment given.

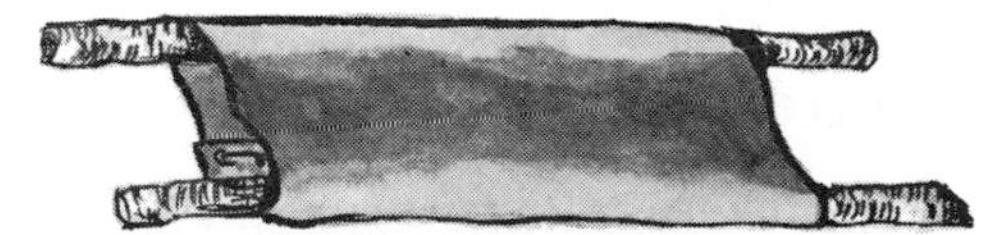

Figure 19–12 An Improvised Stretcher.

In the meantime, direct your efforts toward (1) slowing down the spread of the poison, and (2) treating the victim for shock. Start these measures immediately, even while waiting for medical attention, for every second counts. Apply a constricting band, using the rubber tubing from your snake-bite kit or a bandana or strip of cloth folded to about a two-inch width, around the limb a couple of inches above the wound. Do *not* twist the band with a stick, for you are *not* trying to apply a tourniquet to *stop* circulation, but are merely trying to *slow it down.* It is tight enough when you can just manage to wedge a finger under it and too tight if the patient's foot or hand becomes numb. Loosen the band for about 90 seconds every 10 minutes. If the swelling moves up, advance the bandage ahead of it. Do not give stimulants of any sort, particularly alcohol, for they do no good whatsoever and are actually likely to do harm by speeding up the circulation and thus spreading the poison faster.

You can use the same treatment for the bite of a coral snake, but it is less effective. Here, the most important thing by far is to get medical treatment and an injection of antivenom as soon as possible.

---

*American Red Cross *First Aid Textbook,* Doubleday and Co., 4th Edition, 1957, p. 149.

INSECTS AND OTHER UNWELCOME GUESTS

Discourage unwelcome animal visitors by choosing your campsite carefully, as discussed elsewhere, and avoid dropping crumbs and keeping food about to tempt them. Place your food in covered containers and burn your garbage immediately, burning out tin cans so that they will not attract wild animals during the night.

Many insects are quite obnoxious and their poisons can cause discomfort; more serious complications can occur in persons who are particularly allergic to them or who receive a number of bites at one time. A few insects are especially dangerous since they may carry such diseases as tularemia or Rocky Mountain spotted fever.

BITE PREVENTION

Fortunately, it is no longer necessary to resort to such unpleasant, old-fashioned repellents as smudge fires and "dopes" containing citronella and creosote. A number of commercial products are quite effective, smell better, and do not irritate the skin or stain and damage clothing, except for certain man-made fabrics such as rayon. The United States Department of Agriculture* recommends repellents containing adequate amounts of "deet" (diethyltoluamide) as best for all purposes, since they protect effectively for several hours against a large number of pests, such as leeches, spiders, ticks, chiggers, biting flies, gnats, and mosquitoes. Such repellents can be sprayed on your skin and clothing and around your tent and camping area for sleeping comfort, as well as for protection when on the move.

When travelling where insects are plentiful, cover yourself well with clothing and perhaps even wear a head net of cheesecloth or nylon fabric (Fig.

***U.S. News and World Report*, July 5, 1965.

Figure 19–13 Don't Invite Company You Don't Want.

Figure 19–14 A Head Net.

19–14) which you can tuck into your shirt or fasten at your neck with a drawstring. Apply a good repellent as directed to all exposed skin areas and to the edges of such openings in your clothing as cuffs, waistbands, collars, and the tops of your socks. Avoid breathing its fumes or getting it into your eyes or on such plastic equipment as eyeglass frames, pens, fishing rods, and watch crystals. When you return to camp, scrub yourself thoroughly several times with generous applications of soap, rinsing well after each. This will help to remove many of the tiny insects which otherwise might wander over your body for as long as an hour or more before settling down to bite.

If "buzzed" by such insects as hornets or bees, walk slowly away from them. Avoid moving rapidly or slapping at them frantically, for this frightens them and makes them more likely to bite.

TREATMENT OF INSECT BITES

When insects bite or sting, they usually inject an acid which causes redness, itching, swelling, and pain. Avoid scratching the bite and apply an antiseptic to minimize the danger of infection. A compress of some neutralizing agent such as a solution of household ammonia, baking soda, or vinegar in water will help to relieve local symptoms, and cold applications in the form of ice or ice water may minimize the pain. When a bee stings, it often leaves its stinger in the wound where you can see it as a dark speck or dot. Use your finger nail or a knife blade to carefully scrape it out. The stinger is a hollow tube which may still contain poison so avoid squeezing it lest you force the poison into the wound.

Figure 19–15 Zoom! Zoom! Zoom!

CHIGGERS (CHIGOES, JIGGERS, OR RED BUGS)

These orangish-red, spider-like creatures are the larvae of a tiny mite and are so small that you will probably be unable to see them without a microscope. They usually get on you while you walk through grass, and they often wander about for an hour or more until they find a suitable place to bite, injecting a substance which breaks down the tissue so that they can suck it up. You can best avoid them by the methods previously mentioned.

WOODTICKS

These blackish or reddish-brown insects cling to tall grass or shrubs and transfer themselves to people and animals as they pass by. They cause much discomfort and are sometimes even dangerous, since certain varieties can transmit Rocky Mountain spotted fever and other serious or even fatal diseases. Preventive injections are effective, and those going into tick-infested areas should get them. Fortunately, ticks do not ordinarily burrow under the skin until six to eight hours after they get on you, giving you an opportunity to find and remove them before they have done any harm. Have regular tick inspections (each examining someone else) twice a day. If you find a tick, do not try to pull it off if it has already started to burrow in, for the head will probably remain embedded and this can cause irritation and possibly infection. Do not crush a tick between your fingers lest you get some of the infective material on you. Try to make the tick detach itself by applying a bit of alcohol, kerosene, gasoline, a strong nicotine solution made from tobacco, a heated wire, or a lighted match to its hind end. If this is unsuccessful, cover the tick with a thick oil such as butter, lard, grease, or petroleum jelly to smother it.

SPIDERS

The bites of several spiders are quite painful but few are actually dangerous. One bite that is dangerous is that of the female *black widow spider* (Fig. 19–16). She can be identified by her shiny black body which has a bright red hourglass-shaped spot on the underside of the distended, round, oversized abdomen. She is about one-half inch long.

If you are bitten, seek professional medical treatment just as soon as possible for, although only about one bite in a hundred proves fatal, bites can cause severe illness which can be minimized by prompt medical attention. You may not even feel the bite, or it may cause severe pain. Although the result may be only a local redness and swelling, some victims have severe systemic reactions, including shock (paleness, weakness, rapid pulse, cold skin, anxiety, and sometimes unconsciousness), nausea, vomiting, labored breathing, great thirst, and cramps, especially in the abdominal region. While waiting for medical attention, use the same measures recommended for snake bite.

Another dangerous spider is the *brown recluse spider* (Fig. 19–17) which you can recognize by the dark brown fiddle-shaped area on the front portion of its back. Its body varies in color from a light grayish to dark reddish-brown and it is about one-fourth of an inch long. As its name implies, the brown recluse tends to hide during the day in

Figure 19–16 Underside of a Black Widow Spider.

Figure 19-17 Brown Recluse Spider.

obscure places, such as under rocks, in woodpiles, in decayed logs, or in dark closets or other dry remote areas in buildings, coming out only at night to feed. Its bite causes severe pain which may be delayed for as long as one-half to two hours. The bite area grows red and warm and a white spot appears over the bite and later becomes indented as the tissues eventually die and slough off after about a week or so. The patient becomes restless and feverish and may break out in a rash with weakness, numbness, and a tingling sensation in the limbs. In rare cases, jaundice occurs with bloody urine and convulsive seizures. Get professional help as soon as possible to prevent serious complications and minimize scarring.

CENTIPEDES AND SCORPIONS

These are particularly dangerous in the Southwest. The scorpion stings with its poisonous tail and the centipede bites with its poisonous fangs. Be sure to thoroughly inspect your bedding before retiring and your shoes and clothing before putting them on. If someone is bitten, give first-aid treatment as for a spider bite and get the patient to a doctor as soon as possible.

CATERPILLAR (LARVA) OF IO MOTH

This beautiful, showy specimen can be identified by its light green coat with two pink and white stripes zigzagging down each side. Its back is a wilderness of spines which give off a substance poisonous to the touch. The sting causes pain, irritation, and swelling.

ADDITIONAL READINGS

(For an explanation of abbreviations and abbreviated forms used, see page 25.)

Camp Pests

Angier: *Survival With Style,* ch. 12.
Arnold, Robert E., M.D.: *What To Do About Bites and Stings of Venomous Animals.* Collier, 1973, $1.95, paper.
Better Homes and Gardens Family Camping Book, ch. 16.
Boy Scout Handbook, pp. 138–143.
Cardwell: *America's Camping Book,* ch. 33.
Hillcourt: *New Field Book of Nature Activities and Conservation.*
Johnson: *Anyone Can Camp in Comfort,* pp. 79–82; chs. 9, 10, 11.
Langer: *The Joy of Camping,* pp. 242–250.
Learn and Tallman: *Backpacker's Digest,* chs. 14, 16.
Manning: *Backpacking One Step at a Time,* ch. 5.
Miracle and Decker: *Complete Book of Camping,* ch. 29.
Reptile Study (No. 3311). Boy Scouts, 1967, 96 pp., 45¢, paper.
Riviere: *Backcountry Camping,* ch. 14.
Riviere: *The Camper's Bible,* ch. 13.
Shockey and Fox: *Survival in the Wilds,* ch. 2.
Sunset Camping Handbook, pp. 76–77.
Whelen and Angier: *On Your Own in the Wilderness,* ch. 15.
Winnett: *Backpacking For Fun,* ch. 8.

MAGAZINE ARTICLES

Boys' Life:
Pryce, Dick: "Living With Insects." July, 1971, p. 24.
"World Famous Snakes." Aug., 1972, p. 50.

Camping Journal:
Laycock, George: "Beat the Bugs." July—Aug., 1966, p. 49.
Rutherford, Jim: "Coping With the Camp Bugs." July, 1970, p. 26.

Camping Magazine:
Hamessley, Mary Lou, R.N.: "The Hazardous Brown Recluse." Apr., 1974, p. 14.
"Rid Camp of Poison Ivy." June, 1966, p. 23.

First Aid, Health and Safety

Angier: *How to Stay Alive in the Woods,* chs. 21–25.

Better Homes and Gardens Family Camping Book, ch. 20.

Boy Scout Handbook, pp. 121–147.

Bridge: *America's Backpacking Book,* chs. 15, 16.

Brower: *Going Light—With Backpack or Burro,* ch. 8.

Camp Physicians's Manual. Thomas, 1967, 192 pp., $8.50.

The Camp Nurse. ACA Health and Safety Committee, ACA, 26 pp., 50¢, paper.

Cardwell: *America's Camping Book,* Part IV; p. 347; chs. 32, 33.

Corbin: *Recreation Leadership,* ch. 9.

Emergency Preparedness (No. 3366). Boy Scouts, 1972, 64 pp., 45¢, paper.

Fear, Gene: *Surviving the Unexpected Wilderness Emergency.* Survival Education Ass'n, Tacoma, Wash. 1972, 196 pp., $3.95.

Fieldbook for Boys and Men, ch. 13.

First Aid. ARC.

First Aid (No. 3276). Boy Scouts, 1972, 64 pp., 45¢, paper.

Hafen, Brent O., Alton L. Thygerson, and Ray A. Peterson: *First Aid—Contemporary Practices and Principles.* Burgess, 1972, 214 pp., $3.50, paper.

Hamessley, Mary Lou, R.N.: *Handbook for Camp Nurses and Other Camp Health Workers.* Tiresias, 1973, 159 pp., $3.95.

Henderson, John, M.D.: *Emergency Medical Guide.* McGraw-Hill, 2nd ed., 1969, $8.95.

Johnson, Loren A., M.D.: *Survivit Manual.* Survivit Company, Lake McQueeney, Tex., 1973, $1.

Kodet, Dr. E. Russel, and Bradford Angier: *Being Your Own Wilderness Doctor.* Stackpole, 1968, 127 pp., $3.95.

MacInnes, Hamish: *International Mountain Rescue Handbook.* Scribner's, 1972, 218 pp., $10.

Merrill: *All About Camping,* chs. 23, 24.

Merrill: *The Hiker's and Backpacker's Handbook,* ch. 11.

Merrill: *The Survival Handbook,* ch. 10.

Miracle and Decker: *The Complete Book of Camping,* ch. 30.

Mitchell, Dick: *Mountaineering First Aid.* The Mountaineers, Seattle, Wash., 1972, 92 pp., $2.20, paper.

Nourse, Alan E.: *The Outdoorsman's Medical Guide.* Harper & Row, 1974, 128 pp., $3.95.

Rethmel: *Backpacking,* ch. 7.

Rodney and Ford: *Camp Administration,* Appendix A.

Safety (No. 3347). Boy Scouts, 1971, 64 pp., 45¢, paper.

Schmidt, Ernest F.: *Camping Safety,* ACA, 1971, 44 pp., 50¢, paper.

Shivers: *Camping,* pp. 247–256.

Suggested Policies and Standing Orders for Camp Nursing Services. ACA, rev., 1968, 25¢, paper.

Wilderness Pocket n' Pak Library. Life Support, 1969–1972, $4.95 per set: booklets $1 each. (Pocket-size, accordian-fold vinyl package of 5 booklets: "Survival in the Wilderness," "Edible Plants in the Wilderness" (Vols. I and II), "Poisonous Plants in the Wilderness," and "Primitive Medical Aid in the Wilderness.")

Wood: *Pleasure Packing,* ch. 11.

Magazine Articles

Camping Journal:

Kowalski, Julius M., M.D. and Pete Czura: "First Aid for Campers." Sept., 1971, p. 26.

Camping Magazine:

Andzel, Walter: "How to Handle Heat Illnesses." June, 1973, p. 25.

"14 Camp Accidents Which Could Have Been Avoided." Jan., 1970, p. 16.

Means, Elizabeth, R.N.: "Helpful Hints From a Camp Nurse." Apr., 1970, p. 20.

Putt, Arlene M.: "The Most Important Element in Camping Must Be Our Concern for Camper's Health and Safety." Feb., 1973, p. 20.

Stevenson, Dr. Jack L.: "Safety Is a Never-Ending Job." Apr., 1972, p. 22.

Chapter 20

Knots and Lashing

> The healing fragrance of the wood; the beauties of the lake and of coastline; the open air; the clean blue skies—these belong to all people, and the right to enjoy them is the heritage of every child.
>
> —*Camping for Crippled Children**

Figure 20-1 All Tied Up in Knots.

Man has, no doubt from his earliest existence, wanted to fasten things together, and he has used such natural materials as vines and thin strips of bark or hide to fulfill this need. Some American Indians used thongs or dried strips of leather from the skins of animals, applying them wet so that they would contract into tight fastenings as they dried.

ROPES

Until recent years, rope was made of such natural materials as jute, cotton, sisal, manila, or hemp. It is interesting to note that our native marijuana is a form of hemp; its seeds were probably broadcast as the hemp was being transported across the country to rope factories. It early became a problem when it sprouted and grew among the grass in pastures; ranchers called it "loco weed" because it made the mustangs and livestock "loco" and useless after they ate large quantities of it.

*Published by permission of The National Society for Crippled Children and Adults, Inc.

These original sources of rope have now been largely replaced by such synthetic or man-made materials as nylon, Dacron, and polyethylene which, although more expensive, are improvements. They have these points of superiority: (1) they are as much as 50 to 100 per cent stronger for their size and weight; (2) they are easier to handle and do not swell and kink when wet; (3) they suffer little if any damage from mildew and moisture; (4) they float on water; and (5) they add color since they are available in a variety of shades. Their one major disadvantage is that they are often more or less slick and therefore fail to hold well in some knots. However, a few extra turns or a combination of two knots usually gives security.

YOUR CAMP ROPE AND ITS CARE

Ropes are useful in dozens of ways around camp, as when pitching your tent, flying your flag, hanging your laundry out to dry, or mooring your boat. For ordinary camp use, a rope 5

Figure 20-2 Carry Your Rope Like This.

to 6 yards long and $^3/_8$ inch in diameter is most useful.

If your rope is made of a non-synthetic material dampness will greatly weaken it, so avoid getting it wet whenever possible and dry it out quickly and thoroughly if it does get wet. These ropes also shrink and swell when wet, so you will need to loosen tent guy ropes and other ropes under stress if rain seems imminent or a heavy dew is expected, for otherwise, they may break under the extra strain.

Avoid walking on a rope or otherwise grinding dirt into it for the particles will gradually cut the fibers. Sharp bends and kinks weaken it so untie knots when you are through with them. When your rope is not in use, arrange it as shown in Figure 20-2 by gathering it up in even loops, circling the loops with an end, then passing the end through one of the loops (called *hanking* it); then hang it up or wear it strung on your belt.

Like axe handles, canoe paddles, or oars, ropes collect salt from hand perspiration which may attract such animals as porcupines. They may gnaw the rope to get the salt, so store it where they can't get to it, especially when on trips.

ROPE TERMS

End—short part of the rope.
Standing Part—remainder or long part of the rope.
Bight—made when an end is laid back parallel to its standing part.
Underhand Loop—made by crossing one end *under* its standing part.
Overhand Loop—made by crossing one end *over* its standing part.
Overhand Knot—made by pulling an end through a loop.
Hitch—used to fasten a rope to something, such as a post or ring.

WHIPPING THE END OF A ROPE

The ends of a rope will untwist unless you fasten them in some way, and several different methods can be used. If the rope is made of synthetic material, you can fuse the fibers at each end by applying heat from a match or trench candle. Two simple methods of fastening the ends of a rope made of non-synthetic material are tying an overhand knot in each end or wrapping the ends with adhesive tape. The best method, however, is whipping each end with a two-foot length of string, twine, or thin nylon cord, as shown in Figure 20-4.

Step A. Lay a length of string in an overhand loop (Y) back along the end of the rope and wind the standing part (Z) back along the loop.

Step B. Continue winding end Z back along loop Y and pass end Z through loop Y.

Step C. Pull end X to bring loop

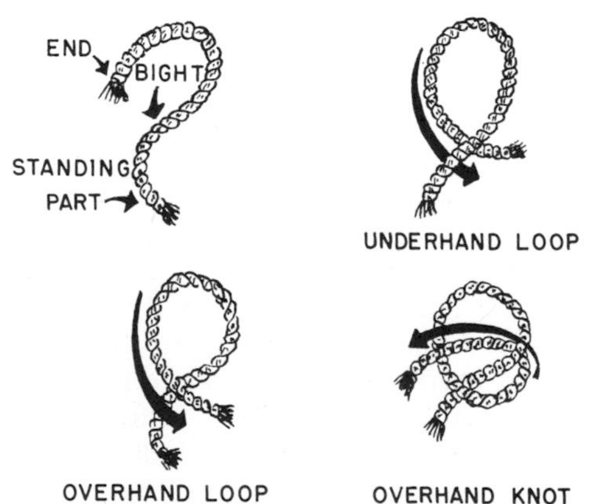

Figure 20-3 Basic Terms Used in Knot Tying.

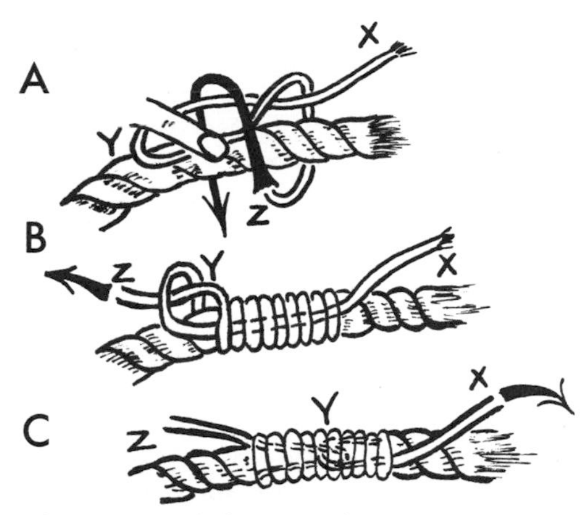

Figure 20-4 Whipping the End of a Rope.

Y back midway under the circular turns. Now cut off the excess string on ends X and Z.

KNOTS

There are literally hundreds of types of knots, but you will find that you need know only a few to meet your ordinary needs in camp. Learn to tie these knots so well that you can even do it in the dark, and know what each is used for and why. You may want to learn others to meet special needs or even to use mainly for decoration or for such projects as knotting belts or lanyards.

You will need two ropes of the same or different size to practice some of the knots, but most of them can be tied with the ends of the same rope. It will help you to follow the directions and diagrams or to teach others if you give each end a different appearance by dipping one or both in ink of contrasting colors or by painting them. You can then say, "Now cross the red end over the white," or "Pass the blue end under its standing part." It also helps you to teach others if you fasten to a knot board samples of the progressive steps in tying a knot, labelling them as needed.

CHARACTERISTICS OF A GOOD KNOT

1. It is simple and easy to tie.
2. It performs well in the job for which it is intended.
3. It will not jam and is easy to untie. This is particularly important around camp where rope is usually scarce and must be used over and over.

TO ENLARGE THE END OF A ROPE

Stopper or *end* knots are used to enlarge the end of a rope to keep it from pulling through a ring, such as a

(Courtesy of Forty Knots.)

tent grommet, or to provide a good hand grip on the end of the rope.

Overhand Knot (Fig. 20-3). This knot tends to jam after stress has been applied so that it is hard to untie. To make it larger, double the end or pass it through the loop several times before tightening it.

Figure-of-Eight Knot (Fig. 20-5). This knot is slightly larger and easier to untie. Among other uses, you can attach a fishhook to a line with it. Make an underhand loop and bring the end over around the standing part and pull it up through the loop. Now pull it tight.

Figure 20-5 A Figure-of-Eight Knot.

TO JOIN TWO ROPES

Square or Reef Knot (Fig. 20-6). This is used to join together two ropes of equal size or the two ends of a rope.

Form a bight with rope A and bring end B up through it, around behind both the end and standing part, and down through the bight again. Pull it tight. To untie it, give a hard pull sideways on both the end and standing part of A and pick it apart.

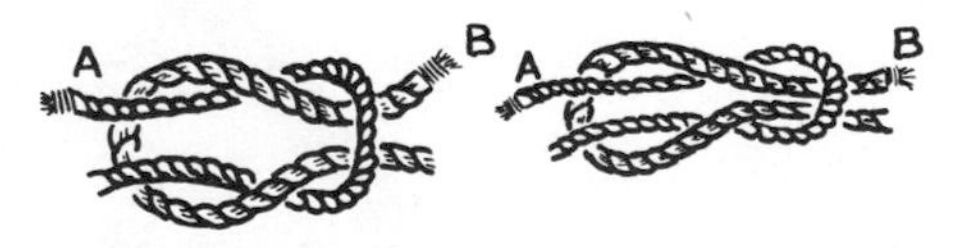

Figure 20-6 A Square or Reef Knot.

It is easy to tie a *granny* (Fig. 20-7) instead of a square knot, but it is not effective since it will pull apart when stress is applied. Note that this knot

Figure 20-7 A Granny Knot.

results from bringing end B around in such a way as to have the end and standing part on *opposite* sides of the bight in A instead of on the *same* side as in the square knot in Figure 20-6.

Sheet Bend (Weaver's Knot or Becket Bend) (Fig. 20-8). A square knot will not hold when joining two ropes of unequal size, but a sheet bend will. Make a bight A in the larger rope and bring end B of the smaller rope up through it, around behind both the end and standing part of A, across and around under its own standing part and pull it tight. Be sure to leave both ends A and B somewhat long so that the knot will hold. For greater security, after bringing end B across under its standing part, take two or more turns around the bight in B and pull it under its standing part again (not shown).

Figure 20-8 A Sheet Bend.

To untie it, pull on both end A and its standing part to loosen the knot and then pick it apart.

TO ATTACH A ROPE TO AN OBJECT

Taut Line Hitch (Fig. 20-9). This knot can be used to anchor a tent guy rope, to secure a rope to a ring, or for lifesaving purposes. This knot will not slip, yet you can tighten or loosen the

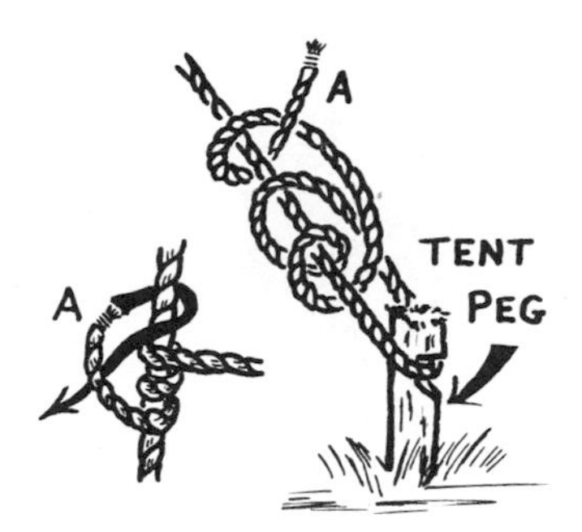

Figure 20-9 A Taut Line Hitch.

rope merely by pushing the knot up or down on the standing part. This makes it particularly appropriate for a nonsynthetic tent guy line, for you can quickly slide the knot toward the peg to loosen it when rain threatens, then slide the knot back up the standing part to tighten it again after the rope has dried.

Pass end A around the peg, and, starting away from the peg and working back toward it, take three turns around the standing part and finish with an overhand knot around the standing part above the turns. Pull it tight.

Clove Hitch (Fig. 20-10). This knot is used to start and finish lashing, put up a clothesline, or anchor a rope to a tree or other object. Do not use it for anything which moves about, such as a horse or boat, for movement may loosen it.

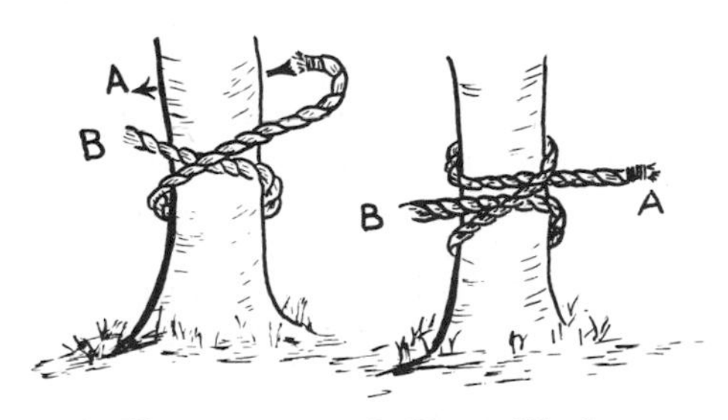

Figure 20-10 A Clove Hitch.

Bring end A around the post in an overhand loop and continue around the post again and tuck it under the turn just made. Pull it tight.

Half Hitch and Two Half Hitches (Fig. 20-11). This knot is used to attach a rope to a post, as when stringing a clothesline, or to a ring, as in the painter of a boat. Use two or more hitches for greater security.

Figure 20-11 A Half Hitch and Two Half Hitches.

Bring the end of the rope around the post in an overhand loop and tuck it up through the loop (one half hitch). Then make a second half hitch by making an overhand loop and bringing the end up through.

Slippery Hitch or Highwayman's Hitch (Fig. 20-12). This is a novelty or "fun" knot that provides a temporary fastening which you can *cast off* (untie) in a hurry.

Step 1. Gather up the standing part of the rope and bring it around behind the post to make bight A.

Step 2. Gather up the standing part again and bring it in front of the post and up through the bight just made to make bight B.

Step 3. Pull on the end to tighten.

Step 4. Now gather up the end and bring it around in front of the post and up through bight B to make bight C.

Step 5. Pull the standing part to tighten all; the hitch will now hold.

To untie it in a jiffy, give a quick jerk on the end.

The name *Highwayman's Hitch* supposedly came from the fact that in olden days a highwayman could use it to tether his horse and make a quick getaway after staging a hold-up.

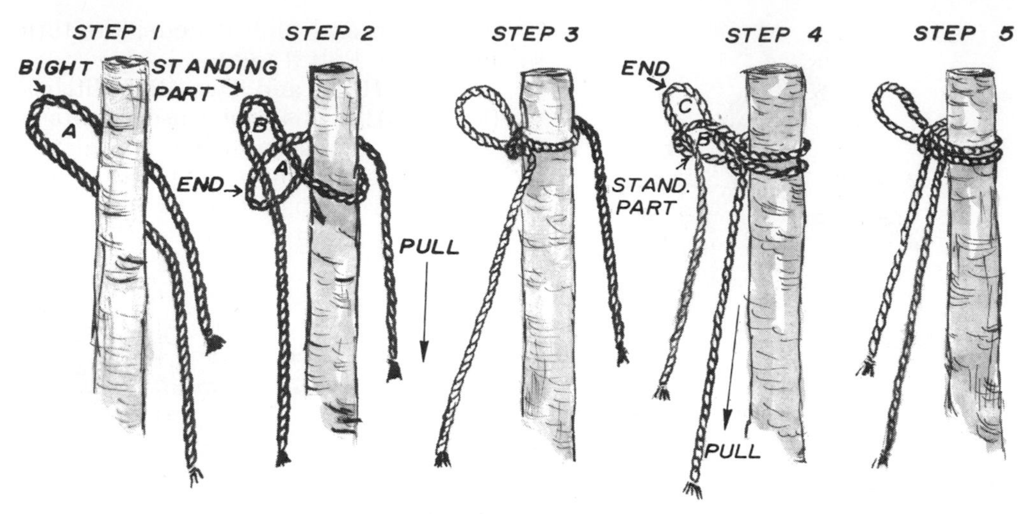

Figure 20-12 A Slippery or Highwayman's Hitch.

TO MAKE A LOOP IN A ROPE

Bowline* (Fig. 20-13). This is used to make a permanent loop in a rope which will stay the same size even when stress is applied. It is useful for anchoring a boat, when tied in the end of its painter or bowline (hence the name) and slipped over a post, for emergency use as when lowering a person during a fire, and also for making a bedroll, tying around the waist of a mountain climber, leading or tethering an animal, or throwing out in the water to someone in trouble.

This little saying may help your campers to remember how to tie this knot:

> The rabbit jumped out of his hole,
> Ran around the tree and
> Jumped back in his hole again.

Make a small overhand loop with the standing part far enough down to allow for the size noose you want. Bring end A up through the loop (rabbit jumped out of his hole), around behind the standing part (ran around the tree), and down through the loop again (rabbit jumped back in his hole again). Hold onto the end as you pull the standing part to tighten the knot.

*Pronounced bō′-lin.

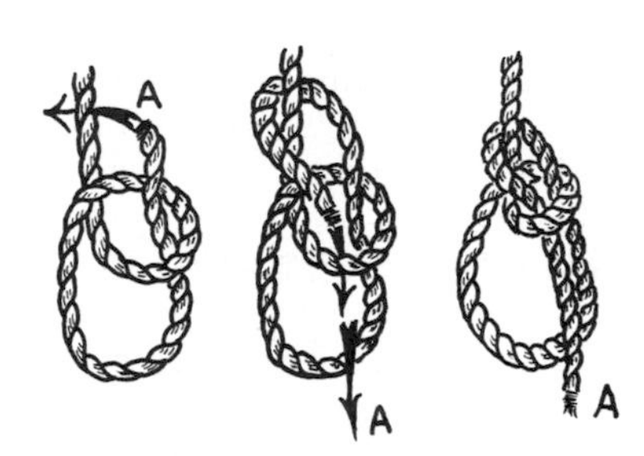

Figure 20-13 A Bowline.

Sailors learned to tie this knot with one hand while clinging to the rigging with the other. Could you do it?

Running Bowline or Slip Knot (Fig. 20-14). This forms a noose which pulls tight when stress is applied and, therefore, it should never be used on a living person or animal. Use it to retrieve an object floating in water, tie up a package or bedroll, suspend an object from a tree, or whenever you need to fasten a rope tightly around an inanimate object.

Step 1. Use the end to tie an overhand knot around the standing part.

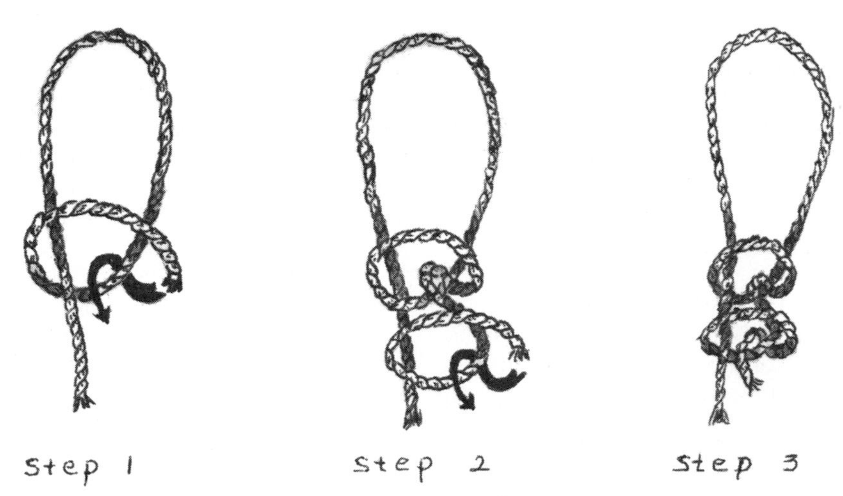

Figure 20-14 A Running Bowline or Slip Knot.

Steps 2 and 3. Use the end to tie a second overhand knot around the standing part and pull the knot tight. Note that since both overhand knots are tied around the standing part, they will slip up and down on it and so adjust the noose tightly about the object.

TO SHORTEN A ROPE OR BY-PASS A WEAK SPOT

Sheep Shank (Fig. 20-15)

Step 1. Fold the rope twice as shown to get the length you want or to by-pass the weak spot.

Step 2. Use each end to tie an

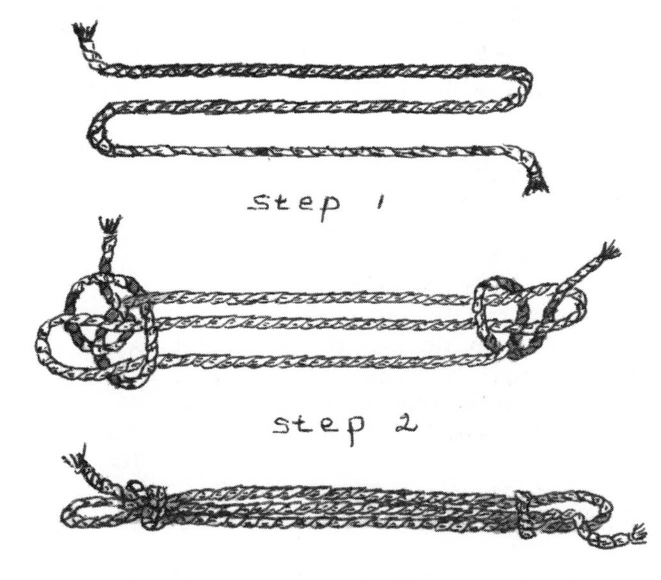

Figure 20-15 A Sheep Shank.

overhand knot around the folded portion adjacent to it.

Step 3. Tighten the knots and, for more permanency, pass each end down through the loop next to it as shown.

TO SUSPEND AN OBJECT

Barrel Hitch (Fig. 20–16). This can be used to suspend a handleless object.

Step 1. Place the object on the rope, leaving end A long enough to complete the hitch. Bring end A and standing part B up above the object and complete a half knot, C and D.

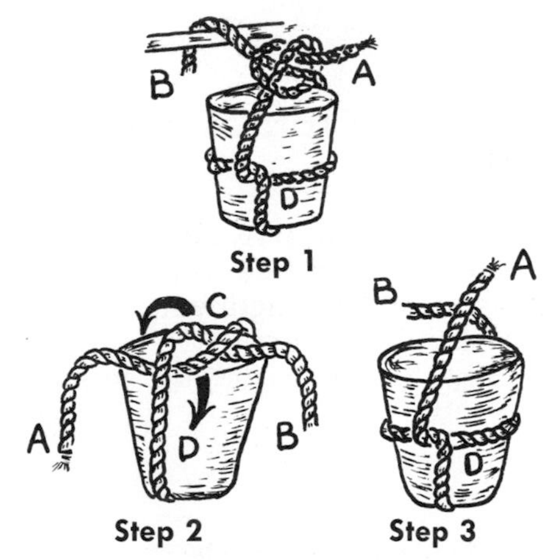

Figure 20–16 A Barrel Hitch.

Step 2. Pull the half knot open sideways to form two bights and pull them halfway down on opposite sides of the object.

Step 3. Bring both end A and standing part B up above the object and use end A to tie a slip knot about standing part B. Draw the slip knot tight around the object and suspend it by standing part B.

LASHING

Lashing is used to join sticks or poles together, using cord, light rope, or *binder twine* which is cheap, strong, and readily available at most hardware or farm supply stores. Lashing is quite secure when properly done and can be applied and removed without damaging either poles or cord. It looks "campy" and substitutes well for nails, which can inflict permanent damage if driven into living trees and which often are unavailable during trips.

Lashing is useful in many camp projects, such as constructing tables, benches, racks to hold cooking gear or tools, rustic bridges, tripods for supporting a washpan, or drying racks for bathing suits or towels. If wood from trees is unavailable at your campsite, you can substitute old broom and mop handles, metal bars, and such.

Practice in lashing, using grocery string and lead pencils or small sticks, provides good "program" for use on rainy days or at night, and campers can later transfer the skills mastered to actual camp situations.

Though it is not absolutely essential, a more workmanlike and sturdier result is achieved when you use your knife or hand axe to notch the pieces being lashed to make them dovetail together where they join (Fig. 20–22). Use enough cord to make as many turns as are necessary to do a solid, neat job.

The secret of a tight, solid job of lashing is found in the final step, *frapping* (Figs. 20–17 and 20–19). This is done by winding the cord tightly between the sticks and the turns of lashing you have previously made.

It is customary to use the standing part of your cord when lashing instead of the end as you do when tying knots.

TO JOIN STICKS AT RIGHT ANGLES

Square Lashing (Fig. 20–17)

Step 1. Cross two sticks at right angles and use the end of the cord to make a clove hitch around one of them,

(Courtesy of Camp Nahelu, Ortonville, Michigan.)

leaving enough of the end to complete a square knot when you have finished.

Step 2. Bring the standing part down across the horizontal stick, around behind the vertical stick, up across the horizontal on the other side, and then around behind the vertical stick again.

Step 3. Continue this process until you have made at least four or five

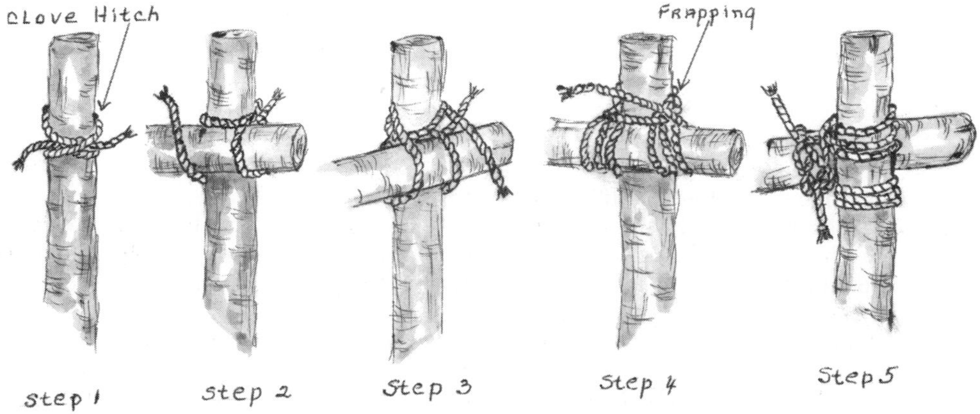

Figure 20-17 Square Lashing.

complete turns around both sides of each stick.

Step 4. Frap with four or five tight turns between the lashing and the sticks.

Step 5. Tie a square knot or clove hitch with the two ends, then cut off any excess twine and tuck the ends in under the lashing.

TO JOIN TWO STICKS AT AN ANGLE

Diamond or Diagonal Lashing (Fig. 20–18)

Step 1. Anchor end A with a clove hitch around both sticks, leaving enough of end A to complete a square knot when finished.

Step 2. Use the standing part to make three to five turns around both sticks and repeat across in the opposite direction.

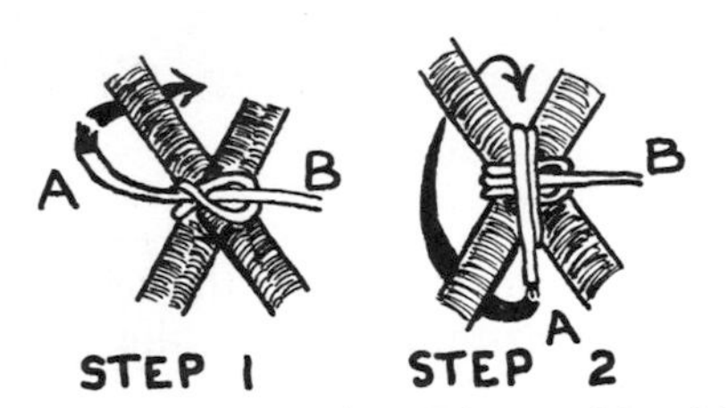

Figure 20–18 Diamond or Diagonal Lashing.

Step 3. Frap tightly and finish with a square knot (not shown) with the ends of A and B.

TO JOIN STICKS INTO A BASE

Tripod Lashing (Fig. 20–19). This type of lashing is used to join three sticks which can then be spread apart and stood upright to form a base.

Step 1. Lay the three sticks parallel and tie them together with a clove hitch.

Step 2. Weave the cord over the first stick, under the second, over the third, etc., until you have made four or five turns around them.

Figure 20–19 Washstand Made With Tripod Lashing.

Step 3. Frap somewhat loosely between the sticks, allowing enough slack to stand the sticks up and spread them apart as a base. Finish with the usual square knot or clove hitch.

TO JOIN POLES PARALLEL WITH EACH OTHER OR TO LENGTHEN A POLE

Round or Shear Lashing (Fig. 20–20). This is used to join two poles together side by side or to make one long pole by lashing two poles together. To lash two poles together:

Step 1. Place them parallel and anchor the rope to one of them with a clove hitch, leaving the end long enough to make a square knot when completed.

Step 2. Take at least five tight turns around the poles.

Step 3. Frap tightly between the poles.

Step 4. Finish off by tying a square knot with the two ends. Lash in at least two other places along the joining.

To lengthen a pole by splicing another to it, lay poles with their ends overlapping and do shear lashing with tight frapping at three or four places along the overlapping parts.

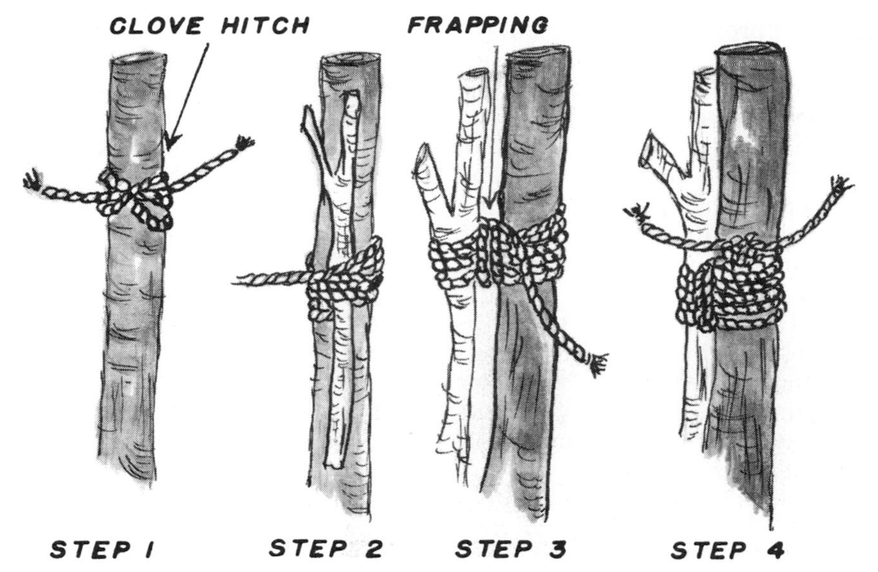

Figure 20-20 Round or Shear Lashing.

TO MAKE TABLE TOPS AND OTHER OBJECTS

A Malay Hitch (Fig. 20-21). This is used to join sticks or boards together to make a shelf or table top. You can also use it to convert wisps of long grass, straw, or other suitable materials into a mattress, a mat for your cabin floor, a fence, or a "screen" in front of a latrine or outdoor shower.

Step 1. Use a cord slightly over twice as long as your completed object is to be. Space out the sticks or portions

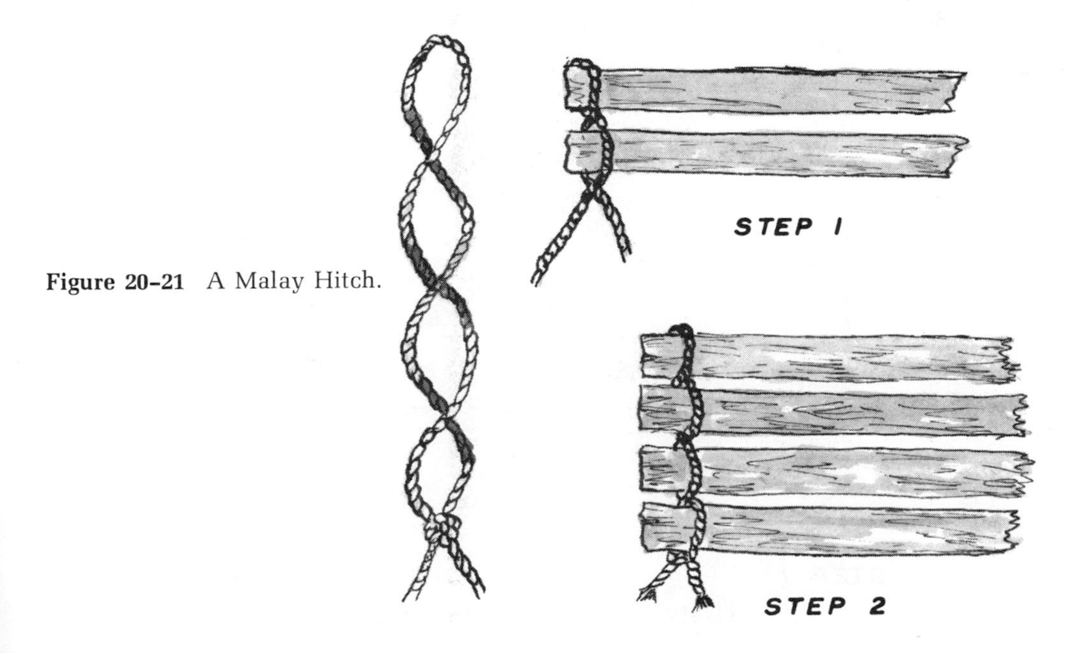

Figure 20-21 A Malay Hitch.

of grass at appropriate distances. Loop the middle of the cord around the stick and continue by tightly bringing one end of the cord alternately over and under each succeeding stick or wisp of grass. Then circle the top stick and bring the cord down again, passing on the opposite side of each stick until the end is down where you started. Join the two ends with a square knot.

Step 2. Repeat this process as many times as you wish at various places along the length of the sticks. You can gain extra security by circling each stick with the cord before going on to the next one.

Continuous Lashing (Paling Hitch) (Fig. 20-22). This is used to lash several small sticks, lengths of bamboo, or laths along one long stick or pole or between two or more sticks. You can use it for making a table top which can be rolled up for easy storing or transporting, a tie or belt rack, or a ladder for a climbing plant.

Step 1. Although not absolutely necessary, it will add more stability if you notch both long poles and crosspieces to make them dovetail snugly together. Elevate the long poles by resting their ends on objects such as rocks or chair seats so that you can work freely.

Step 2. Use a piece of string or cord about four times as long as one of the long poles and use a clove hitch to fasten the middle of the cord near the end of one of the long poles.

Step 3. Place the crosspieces at desired intervals along the long pole, then bring both ends of the cord tightly across the top of the first crosspiece, then around behind the long pole, and bring them up over the next crosspiece. Continue on to the top. Keep the cord just as tight as possible. Now make a few turns with each end around the long pole and join them with a square knot.

Step 4. Fasten the other ends of the crosspieces to the other long pole in the same manner.

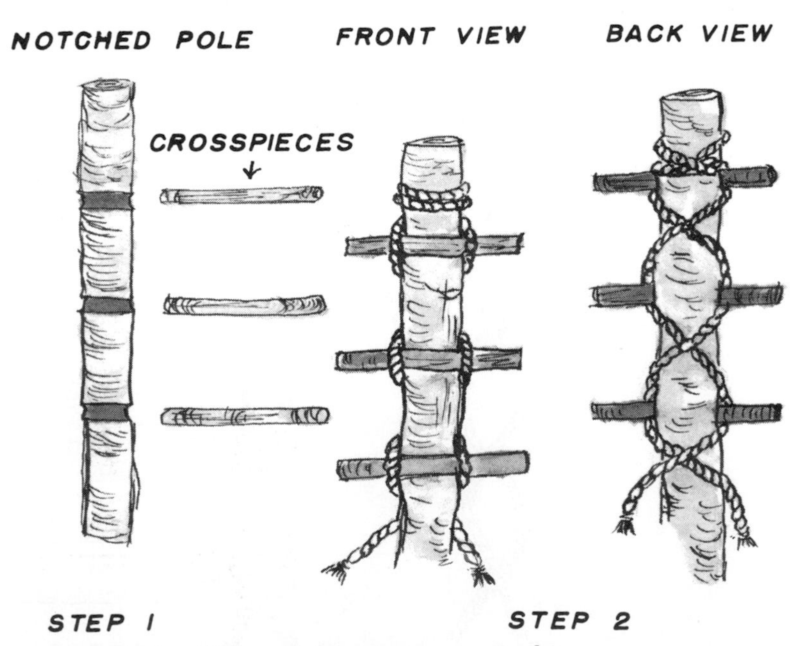

Figure 20-22 Continuous Lashing.

Figure 20-23 "Serves Her Right! I Told Her Not to Tie a Granny."

ADDITIONAL READINGS

(For an explanation of abbreviations and abbreviated forms used, see page 25.)

Ashley, Clifford W.: *The Ashley Book of Knots.* Doubleday, 1944, $16.95.

Boy Scout Handbook, pp. 225-229.

Cardwell: *America's Camping Book,* Part VIII, chs. 36-41.

Day, Cyrus L.: *The Art of Knotting and Splicing.* U. S. Naval Institute, 2nd ed., 1955, 224 pp., $5.00.

Fieldbook for Boys and Men, ch. 7, pp. 84-111.

Gibson, Charles E.: *Handbook of Knots and Splices.* Emerson, 1963, 152 pp., $4.95.

Glass, Walter: *The Key to Knots and Splices.* ACA, 1959, 94 pp., $1, paper.

Graumont, Raoul M.: *Handbook of Knots and Splices.* Cornell Maritime Press, 1954, $2.50; $1.75, paper.

Harvey, Virginia I.: *Macrame: The Art of Creative Knotting.* Van Nostrand, 1972, 128 pp., $8.50; $3.95, paper.

Hensel, John: *The Book of Ornamental Knots.* Scribner's, 1973, 160 pp., $9.95.

Knots and Lashing. Girl Scouts, rev., $10. (Flip Charts)

MacFarlan, Allan and Paulette: *Knotcraft: The Art of Knot Tying.* Ass'n Press, 1967, 186 pp., $5.95.

Mason, Bernard S.: *Roping.* Ronald, 1940, 138 pp., $5.

Merrill: *All About Camping,* pp. 322-329.

Miracle and Decker: *Complete Book of Camping,* ch. 31.

Montgomery, Edward: *Useful Knots for Everyone.* Scribner's, 1973, 128 pp., $4.95.

Ormond: *The Complete Book of Outdoor Lore,* ch. 12.

Pesch, Imelda M.: *Macrame.* Sterling, 48 pp., $2.95. (Creative knotting)

Pioneering (No. 3382). Boy Scouts, 1967, 64 pp., 45¢, paper.

Sea Exploring Manual (No. 3229). Boy Scouts, 1966, 448 pp., $2.45.

Severn, Bill: *Rope Roundup.* McKay, 1960, 237 pp., $3.95.

Shaw, George Russell: *Knots: Useful and Ornamental.* Collier, 1972, 194 pp., $2.95, paper.

Smith, Hervey Garrett: *Arts of the Sailor.* Van Nostrand, 1953, 233 pp., $5.95.

Strom, Nils, and Enestrom, Anders: *Big-Knot Macrame.* Sterling, 48 pp., $2.95.

Chapter 21

The Weather

Figure 21-1 Raining Cats and Dogs.

"Whatever the weather may be," says he,
"Whatever the weather may be,
It's the songs ye sing, an' the smiles ye wear,
That's a makin' the sun shine everywhere."

—JAMES WHITCOMB RILEY*

THE IMPORTANCE OF WEATHER

Although it is easy to see why the weather was so important to the largely outdoor people of early America, it seems of only casual interest to most of us today, except when some spectacular phenomenon such as a blizzard brings it to our attention. We are ordinarily content to carelessly flip on the radio or television or consult a daily newspaper to determine how to dress or whether to go ahead with our plans for a picnic or trip to the golf course. However, the weather is of vital interest to you as a camper, since you will be spending most of your time in the out-of-doors with only a minimum of rather primitive equipment to shelter you, and almost every activity you engage in will be influenced by its whims. When away from the main camp, you will have no official Weather Bureau report to rely on, and if you pride yourself on being a real outdoorsman and camper, you won't even want one, for you will prefer to depend on your own knowledge and powers of observation to tell you what is in store. You will indeed need such foreknowledge to prevent wasting valuable time and effort preparing to cook out, take a nature hike, or hold an evening campfire program, only to have it rained out by the brief but violent summer thunderstorms so common in many areas. It assumes even greater importance when you are out on a trip because, in the

*From *Pipes O' Pan at Zekesburg.* The Bobbs-Merrill Co.

face of an approaching storm, you will want to select the most suitable site available and make camp, pitching your shelter, stowing your gear, and gathering a fuel supply to cheer you and enable you to cook a warm, satisfying meal. Such preparedness will probably determine whether your experience is a pleasant or perfectly miserable one. If you are on the water, your very life, as well as the safety of your boat and gear, may depend on an early start for shore to beach your boat and establish yourself comfortably. Many lives are needlessly lost each year because of lack of weather knowledge and proper respect for the hazards of rough water, mountain storms, lightning, and flash floods.

Studying the rudiments of weather prediction and the conditions which cause and foretell weather changes is interesting in itself, and it also deepens your knowledge of nature and the world around you. Most of us become so involved in our daily rush from hither to yon that we keep our noses straight ahead, completely oblivious to the everchanging patterns of the sky and atmosphere around us. How often do you take time to just relax and enjoy the calmness and beauty of a blue, cloudless sky? Have you paused recently to observe the spectacular pageant as the clouds undergo a complete metamorphosis in the building-up of a storm? Have you watched "scud" clouds scurrying across the sky in a wild, turbulent scramble and wondered what force was driving them and where they were going and why? And have you watched lazy, occasional clouds gradually build up into high, spectacular mountains of a grandeur unsurpassed by the land mountains that tourists drive hundreds of miles to see?

WEATHER FORECASTING

As an amateur weathercaster, you cannot hope to equal the long-range forecasts of the United States Weather Bureau, with its highly trained personnel and elaborate equipment for observing and measuring conditions and collecting data. The Bureau maintains some 750 weather stations throughout this country, as well as in neighboring ocean and land areas. Each observes and reports conditions in its own area which, when combined with the data from other stations, airplanes, ships at sea, and cooperating foreign countries, make it possible to construct a huge worldwide weather map as it would appear from a point high enough to look down on the whole world. Since weather travels from one place to another, this master picture enables the Bureau to predict with considerable accuracy what is coming and when it will arrive; however, many of the forces affecting the weather interact in unpredictable ways, necessitating constant revisions and liberal sprinklings of "probablies" or "possibilities."

You may find it interesting to learn more about the operations of the Bureau as it constantly tries to improve its instruments and better its performance, and you will find sources for further study in some of the references listed at the end of this chapter. You can get Daily Weather Maps from the Bureau,* and although they may arrive a day late, you will find them quite informative as to the workings of the Bureau and their weather predictions based upon their own observations and information about what is happening as far as thousands of miles away.

The Bureau's forecasts are for periods of 24 to 36 hours or longer and cover large areas. Although you cannot match this scope, you can, after some study and with the aid of a few simple instruments, do a creditable job of forecasting for your own immediate

*To subscribe, contact the Superintendent of Documents and ask for further information, including the modest fee required.

Figure 21-2 He Doesn't Give a Croak.

area on a short-term basis of from 2 to 12 hours. Although an occasional summer storm may surprise you by giving as little as an hour's warning of its approach, your predictions should be accurate enough to meet your ordinary camp needs, for even young campers often attain an accuracy of from 60 to 80 per cent. However, you will first need to learn something about atmospheric conditions. Weather is "made" by the interaction of such factors as temperature, pressure, moisture, and wind, and you must observe all of these and be able to interpret the combinations properly to arrive at worthwhile predictions.

THE ATMOSPHERE

The study of the air or atmosphere is called *meteorology* and those professionally trained in this area are known as *meteorologists.*

COMPOSITION OF THE ATMOSPHERE

The earth is a globe suspended in space which extends outward for countless miles in all directions. The *atmosphere* or that portion of space which exerts an appreciable amount of pressure occupies an area approximately 50 miles wide around the earth. Invisible gases fill this space, gradually thinning out away from the earth until they eventually become so thin and scattered as to approach "nothingness." Gases constantly try to expand in all directions as much as the outward pressure on them will allow and, of course, they are also subject to the laws of gravity. Consequently, each layer of air presses down on all the layers below until almost 97 per cent of all the gases are concentrated within 18 miles of the earth, 50 per cent within the last 3½ miles. The atmosphere near the earth consists of about 20 per cent *oxygen* (necessary for animal life), 0.3 to 0.03 per cent *carbon dioxide* (necessary for plant life), some 78 per cent *nitrogen,* 0.5 per cent water in the form of vapor, and minute quantities of other gases.

The clouds and what we call "weather" are contained in the comparatively narrow band 5 to 8 miles above the earth. This explains why an airplane can often escape bad weather by flying above the clouds and turbulence we are experiencing on earth.

AIR CURRENTS

The sun's rays pass through the atmosphere without heating it appreciably until they meet the earth's surface, which they do heat. The earth then reflects this heat back to warm the air immediately above it. When the gases in the air are heated, they expand and become lighter and less dense, and hence rise. The cooler air above these gases rushes in to take their place and be warmed in turn. As the warm air rises into the increasingly thinner air, it comes under less and less pressure and so continues to expand and rise as more cool air comes down to take its place. This process of expanding and rising cools the gases at the rate of about 5 degrees for each 1000 feet of altitude, so that the temperature is about 50 degrees 2 miles above sea level and 20 degrees below zero 5 miles up. This explains why high mountains are always capped with snow regardless of the season.

The motion of the earth on its axis and the constant up-down movements of the warm and cool air exchanging places cause what are known as *air currents* or *updrafts* and *downdrafts*. Since gases under increasingly less pressure are able to expand in all directions, the rising air also expands sideways, producing horizontal movements we know as *breezes* or *winds*. We note the effect of these air currents in the capricious antics of a piece of paper, thistle-down, or winged seed which has been picked up and borne aloft. Spiders on their silken threads have been observed as high as 5 miles up where air currents have carried them. These air movements, however, are unpredictable for, in addition to other variable factors, the earth, and consequently the air above it, is not warmed uniformly. For instance, dark, plowed soil absorbs heat from the sun's rays much more readily than does a grassy meadow, and almost any sort of land absorbs it faster than does a body of water; consequently, the air above is correspondingly heated to different temperatures and at different rates. At night, when there are no longer any sun's rays to warm it, the earth continues to heat the air above from its retained heat, but again at different rates; bodies of water and meadows retain their heat longer and consequently heat the air above them less rapidly. These variations in heating cause the air to expand and move at varying speeds so that while the air is almost motionless in one spot, it may be a seething froth of activity in the form of a good breeze or stiff gale only a short distance away.

AIR PRESSURE

The familiar expression "light as air" would lead us to believe that air is weightless, but such is not the case. Air becomes more and more compressed and consequently heavier as it nears the ground owing to the continuing attempt of the gases to expand, the pull of gravity, and the weight of all the air above pressing downward. Consequently at sea level the air ordinarily exerts a downward pressure of 14.7 pounds per square inch. This is what makes it possible to drink liquid through a straw, as illustrated in Figure 21-3. As you suck upward on the straw, you draw the air out of it, creating a *vacuum*. The air, pressing downward on the liquid, then forces a column of it into the straw and up into your mouth.

HUMIDITY

Air contains moisture in the form of invisible *vapor*. Although you are ordinarily unaware of it, you have noted it as steam rising from a pan of boiling water or as your warm breath condensed in the cold air of a winter morning. The amount of moisture in the air is expressed as its *humidity*. Most of the moisture comes by evaporation from rivers, lakes, oceans, soil, and trees and other forms of vegetation. A perpetual interchange of moisture

Figure 21-3 Drinking Through a Straw.

takes place between the earth and the atmosphere: the air draws or evaporates moisture in the form of vapor from the earth's surface; this vapor forms clouds and the moisture is eventually returned to the earth as rain, snow, or some other type of precipitation.

On a hot muggy day, the air is so full of moisture that it has almost reached the *saturation point* (has absorbed all the moisture it can hold at its present temperature). Consequently, it cannot adequately evaporate the perspiration from your skin, and since that is one of the best ways to rid yourself of excess body heat, you feel uncomfortable. We speak of such a day as a *humid* one. A *barometer* is a device for measuring the humidity, or amount of moisture in the air, by determining the amount of weight or pressure it exerts. By taking successive readings, we can note not only the amount of humidity but also whether it is increasing or decreasing and how rapidly. All three of these factors are quite important in weather prediction. Dry air (low humidity) is heavier and hence exerts more pressure than moist air (high humidity).

Although several types of barometers are available, the commonest is the *aneroid barometer* (meaning "without liquid"). It consists of a box which is sensitive to air pressure and a needle which moves around a marked dial to register changes in pressure. It is relatively inexpensive and is convenient in that you can easily move it about; however, it is not the most accurate type of barometer.

Figure 21-4 An Aneroid Barometer.

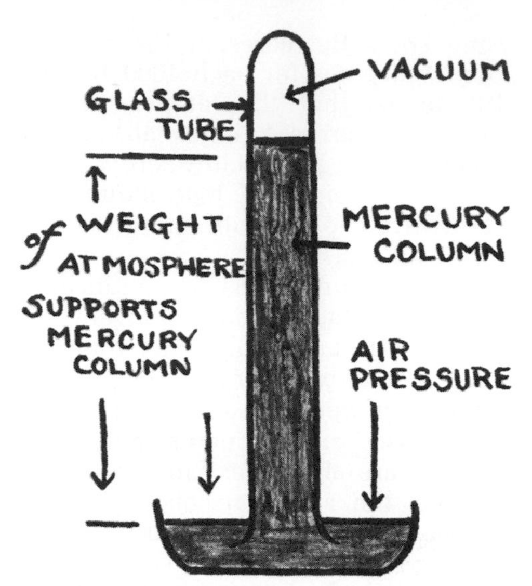

Figure 21-5 A Mercury Barometer.

A *mercury barometer* acts on the same principle as drawing liquid through a staw. It consists of a graduated tube of mercury, closed at the top with an open bottom that rests in an open container of mercury. There is a vacuum above the mercury in the tube. When the air presses down on the surface of the mercury in the vessel it forces some of it up into the tube, just as the liquid was forced up into the vacuum you created in the straw. A graduated scale on the tube registers the height of the column of mercury. A square inch of air of average humidity weighs 14.7 pounds at sea level and will support a column of mercury 30 inches high. Very dry air is heavier and consequently pushes the mercury up higher; this indicates fair weather. Moist air is lighter and so lets the mercury drop; this is usually a sign of bad weather. In general, the higher the barometer reading, the finer the weather.

At higher altitudes above sea level, the air is thinner and lighter, as we have noted, and the normal or average barometer reading is therefore lower. At 3000 feet above sea level, the average reading is about 27. In areas below sea level, the readings are correspondingly higher. In order to use barometer readings for weather prediction, you will need to learn what the average readings are for your particular area.

TEMPERATURE

Air temperature is measured by the familiar *thermometer*. The usual variety consists of a closed tube of mercury which expands when heated and so rises in the tube; you read its height on the graduated scale. Conversely, cooler air causes the mercury to contract, resulting in a correspondingly lower reading on the scale.

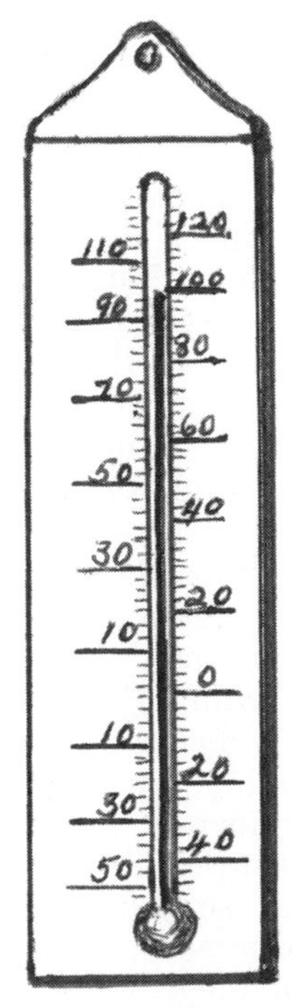

Figure 21–6 A Thermometer.

WATER CONDENSATION

The warmth of the air causes the moisture from the earth to evaporate or change into *water vapor,* and invisible gas which is light enough to be picked up and carried about in the air. The amount of moisture air can absorb and carry varies with its temperature and, in general, the warmer the air, the more it can carry. Thus, a 20 degree rise in temperature at ground level approximately doubles the amount of moisture the air can bear. When it is carrying all it can at its present temperature, we say the air has reached its saturation point or its humidity is 100 per cent. A change in temperature thus alters the saturation point. When the amount of moisture is below the saturation point, it is called the *relative humidity,* expressed as a percentage of the saturation point. Thus, theoretically, humidity could range from 0 to 100 per cent.

We have noted that as the warm air near the earth expands and rises, it gradually cools. Its saturation point becomes lower and lower and its ability to hold moisture in the form of vapor decreases correspondingly. When the air passes the saturation point at its current temperature, it reaches what is known as *dew point,* and since it is also contracting as it cools, it squeezes out the excess moisture it can no longer hold in the form of minute droplets. These droplets are so tiny and light that they continue to be airborne and, under certain conditions, join together into larger and larger droplets and finally become visible as *clouds. Fog* is similar to a cloud near the earth; we have difficulty in seeing through fog because our eyes cannot penetrate these millions of droplets. The droplets reflect back automobile lights or the rays from a flashlight as effectively as millions of tiny mirrors. *Smog* results when fog is combined with smoke or other airborne particles found near industrial or otherwise polluted areas.

When the humidity is high as night comes on, the moist air is cooled as it comes in contact with the rapidly cooling trees and grass and, if it reaches dew point, its excess moisture condenses on them as *dew*. We observe this same phenomenon on a warm day when the dampness in the air condenses as beads of moisture on a pitcher of ice water.

PRECIPITATION AND OTHER WEATHER PHENOMENA

You have no doubt noticed minute bits of dust floating about in the air when a ray of sunshine strikes them in a certain way. Similar dust particles are distributed throughout the atmosphere and on a clear day they make the sky look blue; when especially numerous, they give the sky a gray or hazy appearance. These dust particles are the nuclei about which moisture collects as droplets when the ascending air cools to dew point. As the air continues to rise and cool, it squeezes out more and more moisture in the form of droplets that eventually take on electrical charges that attract them to each other. As they unite into larger and larger droplets, they eventually become too heavy to be airborne and fall to earth as raindrops, each consisting of from one to seven million droplets.

Snow results when the droplets freeze into tiny ice crystals in the cold, upper regions of the atmosphere, with hundreds or thousands of them uniting into the beautiful designs of single snowflakes.

Sleet occurs when snow partially melts as it falls through a layer of warmer air just above the ground. If the half-melted snow freezes just as it hits the ground, it is called *glaze*.

Hail results when rain from a rather low-lying cloud is caught in a strong updraft of air and tossed back up into a high, freezing area where it is coated with snow and ice. It then falls back down through the low-lying cloud, acquires more moisture, and again falls down into the strong updraft which may throw it back up to acquire another layer of ice and snow. This process may be repeated several times until the ice-covered pellet finally becomes so heavy that it pierces the updraft and crashes to earth as hail. It is claimed that hailstones as big as baseballs, with 25 layers of ice and snow, fell at Annapolis, Maryland on June 22, 1915. Hail is a freakish weather phenomenon which can occur even in balmy surface temperatures if other conditions are right, for as we have seen, there are always freezing temperatures high in the atmosphere. In fact, hailstorms are said to occur most frequently in June.

Frost occurs when the temperature drops below freezing under conditions which would ordinarily produce dew.

We see a *halo* or *ring* around the sun or moon when we see its light shining through ice crystals in the atmosphere.

Mythology explained *lightning* as bolts of fire sent by the War God, Thor, to paralyze the earth's people, but since the observations of Benjamin Franklin, we have known that it is actually a form of electricity. Electrical charges in the atmosphere usually pass harmlessly from one cloud to another, but a bolt of lightning occasionally comes down to earth with enough power to kill men or animals, start fires, or uproot trees. Lightning follows the line of least resistance as it leaps from one handy electrical conductor to another on its way to the ground. Therefore, to prevent it from striking you, you must avoid becoming the most convenient conductor in its path by taking care not to be the most prominent object in the area or near something else that is. Some of the most dangerous places to be are near a fence or clothesline, at the top of a hill, in a boat, on the beach, riding a horse or bicycle, on a golf course or meadow, or under an especially tall tree or one standing alone. Among the safest places are in an automobile (the metal body conducts the bolt to the ground), in a cave, in a ravine between two hills, or in a grove of trees. If you are caught out in the open, lie flat on the ground or in a ditch. If you are indoors, stay away from plumbing and electrical appliances and don't use the telephone or take a bath. Since water is a good conductor of electricity, anyone swimming or boating should get on land as quickly as possible.

Thunder, although often alarming, is perfectly harmless; it is believed to be caused by the rapid expansion of the air as it is heated by the passage of lightning through it. To roughly estimate the distance of lightning in miles, count the number of seconds between the time you see the bolt and hear the thunder and divide by five. (You can roughly estimate seconds by counting a-thousand-and-one, a-thousand-and-two, etc.) This method is based on the fact that, while light travels at 186,000 feet per second, sound travels only about 1100 feet per second. Since there are 5280 feet in a mile, sound travels at approximately $\frac{1}{5}$ mile per second; therefore, an interval of 5 seconds would indicate that the lightning was about a mile away.

A *rainbow* occurs when we see the sun's rays through rain which is falling opposite the sun. The water, like a prism, breaks the rays into the colors of a rainbow.

CLOUDS

The sky, nature's roof, forms a backdrop for the clouds. Cloud names are of Latin derivation and there are four basic types of clouds, with nine combinations of these four types.

BASIC FORMS OR FAMILIES OF CLOUDS

1. *Cirrus* are the "lock" or "curl" clouds and are the highest of all (5 to 10 miles) (Fig. 21-7). They are always white, being composed entirely of ice crystals, and are sometimes called "witch's broom" or "mare's tail." If the sky is bright blue above and the wind is from the north or northwest, cirrus clouds indicate fair weather for 24 to 48 hours. However, if the sky is gray-blue and the clouds are moving swiftly, especially from the west, they will likely turn to *cirrostratus* clouds (Fig. 21-10) and rain or snow may follow.

Figure 21-7 Cirrus Clouds—U. S. Weather Bureau—R. H. Curtis.

2. *Stratus* or "spread sheet" clouds (Fig. 21-8) are a horizontal overcast of

Figure 21-8 Stratus Clouds—R.A.F.

"fog" high (about 2100 feet) in the air. These clouds are always a shade of gray and are sometimes dark enough to practically conceal the sun or moon. Rain usually but not always follows.

3. *Cumulus* (Fig. 21-9) are the billowy, puffy "heap" or "wool pack" clouds with flat, grayish bottoms which rise to a high, dome-shaped mass of white. They are the lowest clouds of all, being only about a mile above the earth. They are often quite active and usually indicate fair weather, except on a hot, muggy day when, if massed near the horizon or increasing in size, they may indicate rain.

Figure 21-10 Cirrostratus Clouds—U. S. Weather Bureau.

Figure 21-9 Cumulus Clouds—U. S. Weather Bureau—ANSCO.

4. *Nimbus* clouds are the low-lying "umbrella" clouds. They are dark, with ragged edges and no definite shape, and usually indicate steady rain or snow. *Scud* clouds are the small, ragged pieces frequently seen traveling rapidly across the sky below the nimbus clouds.

Variations and Combinations*

5. *Cirrostratus* clouds (Fig. 21-10) are very high (about 5½ miles up). They are whitish and film-like and form a milky, tangled-web sheet over the sky. They sometimes mean nothing in the morning, but when they persist or appear in the afternoon, they are likely to be a forerunner of rain or snow within 24 hours, particularly if they started as *cirrus* clouds and are coming from the west.

6. *Cirrocumulus* clouds ("mackerel" sky) have a rippled appearance somewhat like sand on the seashore (Fig. 21-11). They are very high, puffy clouds about 4 miles up. They usually indicate fair weather, but may bring high winds.

Figure 21-11 Cirrocumulus Clouds—U. S. Weather Bureau—R. H. Curtis.

**Alto* means high; *fracto* means ragged or broken by the wind.

7. *Altocumulus* (Fig. 21-12) are small, high, white clouds which may lie close together in rows or lines, giving a dappled appearance to the sky. They are also called "sheep" clouds and they usually indicate fair weather.

Figure 21-12 Altocumulus Clouds—U. S. Weather Bureau.

8. *Stratocumulus* (Fig. 21-13) are the dark-colored twist-shaped clouds (about 1 mile up) which ordinarily thin to cumulus or *fractocumulus* (Fig. 21-15) later on and seldom bring the rain they threaten. They are likely to be accompanied by high winds, especially in the fall.

9. *Altostratus* (Fig. 21-14) are thin, gray, curtain-like clouds (about 3 miles

Figure 21-13 Stratocumulus Clouds—U. S. Weather Bureau.

Figure 21-14 Altostratus Clouds—U. S. Weather Bureau.

up) that often show a bright patch when the sun or moon hides behind them. They are sometimes followed by squally weather.

10. *Fractonimbus* clouds follow nimbus and generally break up to disclose patches of blue sky indicating clearing weather.

11. *Fractostratus* clouds follow on the heels of fractonimbus and commonly clear into a blue sky with cirrus tufts scattered about.

Figure 21-15 Fractocumulus Clouds—U. S. Weather Bureau.

12. *Fractocumulus* (Fig. 21-15) are cumulus clouds which have been broken up into somewhat thinner clouds of irregular appearance. They usually indicate clear weather.

Figure 21–16 Cumulonimbus Clouds—U. S. Weather Bureau.

13. *Cumulonimbus* (Fig. 21–16) are the "thunderhead" clouds which are the most spectacular of all. They have dark bases and light tops and tower into the air like mountains. When they appear in the west, a storm will likely occur within a few hours, often accompanied by thunder and lightning.

Clouds moving in different directions at various levels foretell rain.

WEATHER INSTRUMENTS YOU CAN MAKE*

There are several weather instruments that campers can make. It is advisable to have at least one good commercially made instrument of each kind by which to check their accuracy.

A CLIPPER SHIP BAROMETER

A *clipper ship barometer* works on the same principle as a mercury barometer and will roughly indicate rises and falls in the humidity and how rapidly they are taking place. Fill a bottle two-thirds full of colored water and fit it with a tight cork or rubber stopper. Drill a hole through the stopper and insert a 10-inch length of rubber tube through it so that one end extends into the water as shown in Figure 21–17. Use melted paraffin or candle wax to make a seal around the tube so that it is air- and water-tight. Invert the bottle carefully so that no air enters and anchor it securely in the shade and out of direct winds. Turn the outer end of the tube up as shown and support it in place. Some of the water will run down into the tube, leaving a vacuum in the top of the bottle above the water line. Watch the bottle for a few days to determine what the normal water level is, then mark it on the bottle and extend a graduated scale on either side of it for recording changes in the water level and, consequently, changes in the humidity or air pressure. (Water may even drip out of the end of the tube when it is rainy.)

A WEATHER VANE (WIND VANE)

Make a weather vane as shown in Figure 21–18. Use light wood or a large tin can flattened into a sheet and cut into any form desired, such as an arrow, rooster, fish, or boat. Make the tail large and broad enough to catch the wind so that it will always keep the longer, lighter head pointing directly into the wind. Place a pole out in the open where the wind has free access to it. Place one end securely in the ground and fasten direction indicators on the other end as shown, lining them up with true, not magnetic, north. Find the balance point of the vane and drill a hole just in front of it and glue one end of a round shaft or dowel into it. Drill another hole in the top of the pole deep enough to hold the other end of the dowel securely and large enough to

*Further directions for making weather instruments are contained in sources listed in the bibliography for this chapter, such as Harty's *Science for Camp and Counselor* and the Boy Scout booklet, *Weather.*

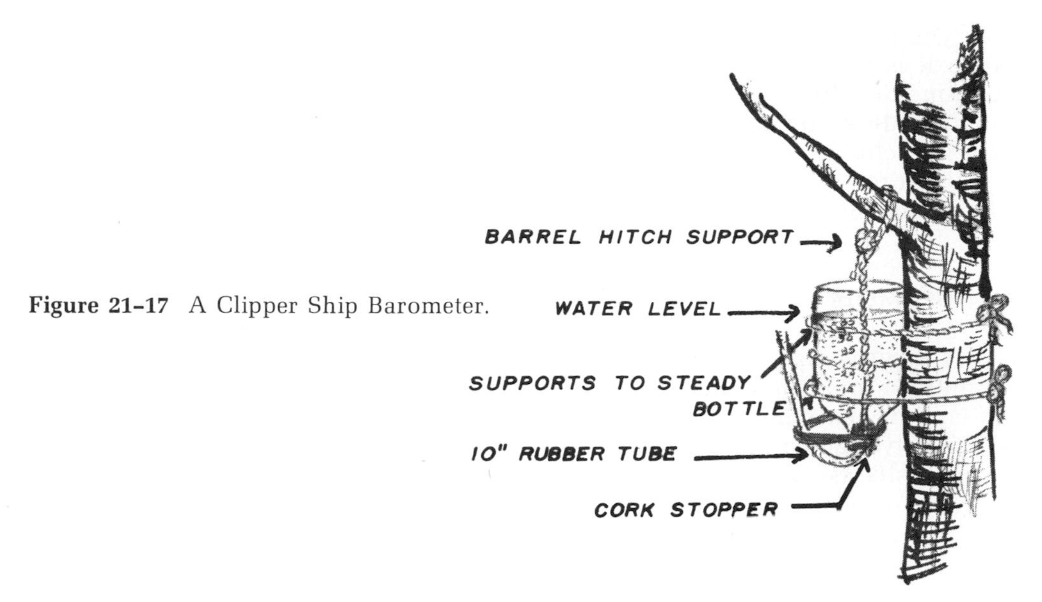

Figure 21-17 A Clipper Ship Barometer.

let it turn freely when used with a pair of washers.

A NEPHOSCOPE

A *nephoscope* lets you watch cloud movements without having to look directly into the sun. Mark the compass directions on a flat piece of cardboard, wood, or metal and fasten it in a convenient spot out in the open, orienting it with true, not magnetic, north (Fig. 21-19). Paint the back of a fairly large mirror or piece of glass with black, shiny enamel and place it on top of the direction indicator. The glass will reflect the sky so that you can watch the clouds and their movements in the mirror.

NATURE'S THERMOMETER

Although you may prefer the conveniences of a commercial thermom-

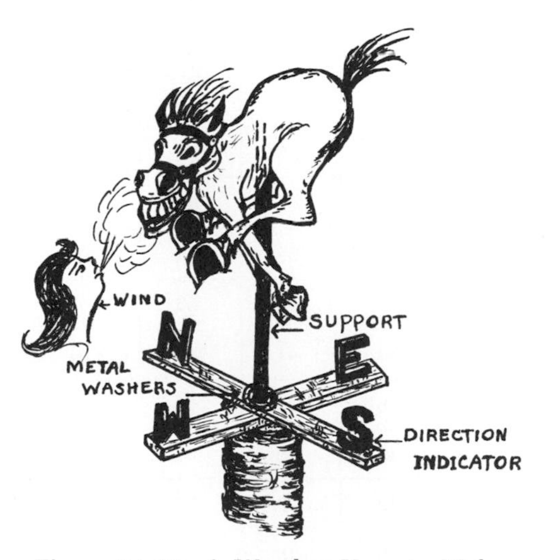

Figure 21-18 A Weather Vane to Make.

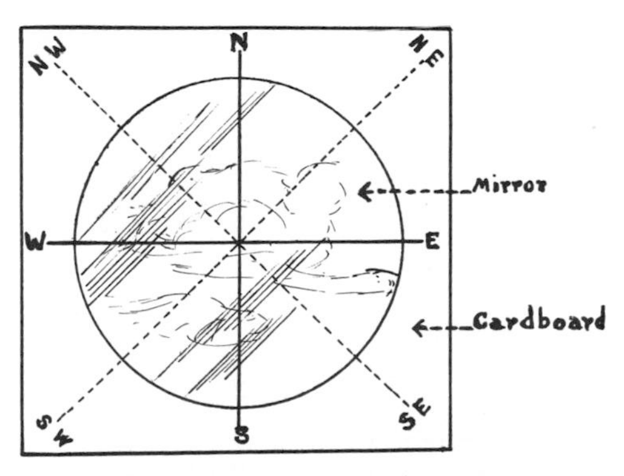

Figure 21-19 A Nephoscope.

eter, you can estimate the temperature when it is between 45° and 80° F. by counting the chirps of a cricket. Count them for 15 seconds and add 35. The sum will closely approximate the true temperature, for a cricket varies his rate of chirping with the temperature.

A HYGROMETER

A *hygrometer* measures relative humidity. You can make one of the wet-and-dry bulb thermometer type by placing two identical thermometers side by side on a board (Fig. 21-20). Convert one to a wet bulb thermometer by wrapping one end of a cloth, a shoelace with the plastic or metal tip removed, or a piece of lamp wicking around the bulb and extending the other end down into a vessel of water so that it will draw up enough moisture to keep the bulb constantly damp. As the water evaporates around the bulb,

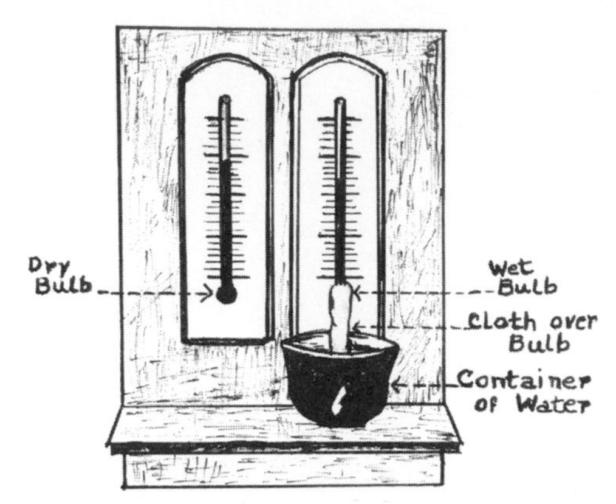

Figure 21-20 A Wet-and-Dry Bulb Hygrometer.

Table 21-1 Hygrometer Readings and Relative Humidity

Degrees of Difference between Wet and Dry Bulb Readings	Dry Bulb Reading (°F.) 30°	40°	50°	60°	70°	80°	90°	100°
	(The figures below indicate the relative humidity in per cent.)							
1°	90	92	93	94	95	96	96	97
2°	79	84	87	89	90	92	92	93
3°	68	76	80	84	86	87	88	90
4°	58	68	74	78	81	83	85	86
6°	38	52	61	68	72	75	78	80
8°	18	37	49	58	64	68	71	74
10°		22	37	48	55	61	65	68
12°		8	26	39	48	54	59	62
14°			16	30	40	47	53	57
16°			5	21	33	41	47	51
18°				13	26	35	41	47
20°				5	19	29	36	42
22°					12	23	32	37
24°					6	18	26	33

it cools it so that the thermometer registers the temperature at 100 per cent humidity (saturation point). The other dry-bulb thermometer registers the temperature at the true atmospheric humidity level, so that by subtracting the dry bulb reading from that of the wet bulb and consulting Table 21-1 you can learn the approximate relative humidity (percentage of saturation).

AN ANEMOMETER

To make an *anemometer* for measuring wind speed, cross two sticks at right angles (Fig. 21-21) and fasten four lightweight cups or cones across them parallel to the ground. Paper or plastic cups can be used temporarily, but for more permanent cones, plug the ends of small funnels with tight-fitting pieces of cork or whittled wood, or make a paper pattern and cut the cones from flattened tin cans or other light metal and solder them together. Give them a coat or two of paint to protect them, making one a contrasting color to make it easy to count the number of revolutions as they spin around. Mount the crossed sticks on a dowel, then make a hole in a pole deep enough to hold the dowel securely and large enough so that the dowel can turn freely. Insert the dowel into the pole using a pair of washers, then place the anemometer out in the open where even a slight breeze will turn it. To roughly estimate the wind speed in miles per hour, count the number of revolutions in 30 seconds and divide by 5.

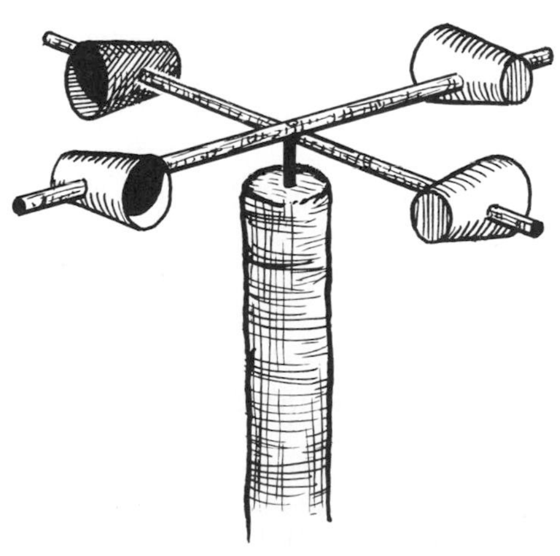

Figure 21-21 An Anemometer.

SETTING UP A CAMP WEATHER BUREAU

INSTRUMENTS YOU WILL NEED

Although you can achieve some success with a minimum of instruments or even none at all, it is desirable to have as many of the following as possible.

1. A weather vane (wind vane) to determine wind direction. Place it on a pole 15 to 20 feet in the air and away from any obstructions, such as hills, woods, or tall buildings. Without a vane, you can observe the direction of smoke or toss a light piece of paper up into the air.
2. An anemometer for determining wind speed. Place it like the wind vane.
3. A barometer for determining humidity. Place it out of the direct sun and wind.
4. A thermometer to determine temperature. Place it facing north and where it will be shielded from wind, sun, and rain. The best way to protect it is to build a shelter with well-ventilated sides and a wide, overhanging, solid top. Paint the shelter white to give further protection from the sun's rays.
5. A hygrometer to determine the relative humidity. Protect it like the thermometer or place it in a similar shelter.

Table 21–2 Beaufort Scale for Estimation of Wind Force*

Beaufort Number	Effects on Land	Miles per Hour	Terms Used by U. S. Weather Bureau
0	Smoke rises straight up.	0–1	Calm
1	Smoke drifts slowly but wind vane does not move.	1–3	Light
2	Wind felt on face; leaves rustle, wind vane moves.	4–7	Slight breeze
3	Leaves and small twigs move constantly.	8–12	Gentle breeze
4	Raises dust and loose paper; small branches move.	13–18	Moderate breeze
5	Small trees begin to sway; whitecaps form on inland waters.	19–24	Fresh breeze
6	Large branches move; wind whistles in telephone wires; hats blow off.	25–31	Strong breeze
7	Whole trees in motion; hard to walk in wind.	32–38	Moderate gale
8	Breaks twigs and small branches from trees; trees in violent motion.	39–46	Gale
9	Small trees knocked down and shingles torn from roofs.	47–54	Strong gale
10	Rare inland; large trees uprooted; walls blown down.	55–63	Whole gale
11	Very rare; telephone poles and houses knocked down.	64–75	Storm
12	Impossible to stand against.	Over 75	Hurricane

*This scale was devised by Sir Francis Beaufort in 1805. The strength of the wind is indicated by numbers from 0 to 12.

6. A nephoscope to watch cloud movements.
7. A poster of cloud forms, in color if possible.
8. A protected outdoor bulletin board on which to post such things as pictures of cloud forms, tables, general weather information, and your observations and predictions.
9. Weather flags to use in flying predictions (Fig. 21–22).
10. Mimeographed or printed forms for recording your observations and predictions (Fig. 21–23).

MAKING OBSERVATIONS

Make your first weather observation as early in the morning as possible and make a second about 12 hours later; a third observation about midway

Figure 21-22 Make and Fly Weather Flags.

Date	Rel. Humid.	Wind		Temp.	Clouds		Other Signs	Forecast	What It Was
		Dir.	Vel.		Type	Movement			
A.M. P.M.									
A.M. P.M.									
A.M. P.M.									
A.M. P.M.									

Figure 21-23 Form for Recording Weather Data and Predictions.

between is desirable if convenient. Record your observations, predictions and what actually happened on a form such as that in Figure 21-23.

INTERPRETING YOUR OBSERVATIONS

There are practially no weather signs which universally hold true for every area of the United States, for many factors, such as the topography of the country and the presence of lakes, hills, and woods, cause variations. To compile a set of reliable relationships and signs for your particular area, make and file careful observations, recording them on forms such as that shown in Figure 21-23; study them over a period of time until you can detect a consistent pattern of causes and results.

Weather forecasters usually consider the relative humidity reading, particularly whether it is rising or falling and how rapidly, as the single most important indicator of the weather. Humidity and information about the wind constitute the most important pair of indicators. Table 21-3 will help you to interpret what you observe about these two factors.

Another fairly reliable combination is wind direction and cloud formations (Table 21-4). It is especially useful when on a trip because the only instrument you need is a compass to determine wind direction.

There are countless proverbs about the weather, some of them based on mere superstition. Others, however, have value since they describe atmospheric conditions which actually "cause" the weather to be whatever it is. The following seem to be somewhat reliable. Can you explain why?

Red sky (or rainbow) in the morning, sailors take warning.
Red sky (or rainbow) at night, sailor's delight.

Evening red and morning gray,
Sets the traveler on his way;
Evening gray and morning red,
Brings down rain upon his head.

A red sky has water in his eye.

(Raindrops are caused by the condensation of water around a grain of dust, and humidity allows the red rays of the sun to pass through and be seen more clearly.)

Rain before seven, clear before eleven.

(Rain seldom lasts longer than five hours anyway.)

When dew is on the grass
Rain will never come to pass.

When grass is dry at morning's light,
Look for rain before the night.

When the stars begin to huddle,
The earth will soon become a puddle.

Table 21–3 Wind-Barometer Relationships*

Wind Direction	Barometer Reduced to Sea Level	Weather Indicated
SW to NW	30.1–30.2, steady	Fair, slight temperature changes for 1 to 2 days
	30.1–30.2, rising rapidly	Fair, followed within 2 days by rain
	30.2 and above, stationary	Continued fair, no decided temperature change
	30.2 and above, falling slowly	Slowly rising temperature, fair for 2 days
S to SE	30.1–30.2, falling slowly	Rain within 24 hours
	30.1–30.2, falling rapidly	Wind increasing in force, rain within 12-24 hours
SE to NE	30.1–30.2, falling slowly	Rain in 12–18 hours
	30.1–30.2, falling rapidly	Increasing wind, rain within 12 hours
	30.0 or below, falling slowly	Rain will continue 1-2 days
	30.0 or below, falling rapidly	Rain, with high wind, followed within 36 hours by clearing
E to NE	30.1 and above, falling slowly	Rain may not fall for several days
	30.1 and above, falling rapidly	Rain probably within 12–24 hours
S to SW	30.0 or below, rising slowly	Clearing within a few hours, fair several days
S to E	29.8 or below, falling rapidly	Severe storm imminent, followed within 24 hours by clearing, colder
E to N	29.8 or below, falling rapidly	Severe NE gale and heavy rain
Going to W	29.8 or below, rising rapidly	Clearing and colder

* *Weather Forecasting.* U. S. Department of Commerce, p. 39.

(Mist forms over the sky and causes the smaller stars to cease to be visible. The brighter ones shine through dimly with a blur of light about them, each looking like an indistinct cluster of stars. This, therefore, indicates an increase in humidity.)

Sound traveling far and wide
A stormy day will betide.

The higher the clouds, the finer the weather.

Mackerel scales and mare's tails
Make lofty ships carry low sails.

When the wind's in the south, the rain's in his mouth.
When the smoke goes west, good weather is past.
When the smoke goes east, good weather is next.

The weather will clear when there is enough blue sky to make a pair of Dutchman's breeches.

The ring around the moon means rain;
The larger the ring, the sooner the rain.

(Cirrostratus clouds are around the moon and are the forerunners of unsettled weather.)

Table 21-4 Wind and Cloud Relationships

Direction Wind Is From	Cloud Forms	Forecast
NE, E, SE or S	Cirrostratus (with halo) coming from SW and becoming thicker	Rain within 24 hours; warmer
NE, E, SE or S	Altostratus (hiding sun), getting lower, darker and thicker	Steady rain within 6 hours; will last 6–24 hours.
S or SW (very gusty)	Cumulonimbus clouds on horizon, approaching from W	Heavy rain showers within 2 hours; last less than 1 hour; cooler
Light, variable wind	Towering, cumulus clouds before noon; sky hazy	Rain showers (or thunderstorms) in late afternoon
NW or W	Scattered clouds	Good weather will continue

INDICATIONS OF STORMY WEATHER

Rainbow in the morning.
Wind lacking to moderate, and from southeast or east.
No dew at night.
Atmosphere muggy and sticky.
Temperature 70° F. or above, especially if rising.
Falling barometer.
Smoke not rising straight up in the air.
Crickets, birds, and other noises seem extra loud.
Odors are especially noticeable.
Breeze causing undersides of leaves to show.
Rapidly moving cirrus clouds, especially from the west.
Dark clouds gathering on the horizon to the west.
Stratus, nimbus, altostratus, cirrostratus, or cumulonimbus clouds.
Clouds moving in different directions at various heights.
Clouds becoming more numerous and nearer the earth.
Red or rosy morning sky.
Gray or dull sunset.
Insects are especially obnoxious and hang about screens, tents, etc.
Smoke beats downward.
Birds fly lower; it is hard for them to fly in the higher rarefied air.

INDICATIONS OF FAIR WEATHER

Rainbow in late afternoon or evening.
Gentle winds, especially from the west or northwest.
Heavy morning dew, fog, or frost.
Temperature below 70° F., especially if falling.
Steadily rising barometer.
Smoke rising straight up.
Cloudless skies or only clouds high in the sky.
Cumulus clouds or stationary cirrus clouds.
Night sky full of bright stars.
Stratocumulus, altocumulus, cirrocumulus, fractonimbus, fractostratus, or fractocumulus clouds.
Red sunset (sun goes down like a ball of fire).
Spiders spin long, widespread webs and scurry busily over them.

No one sign is infallible when predicting the weather; note all and take an average when making a prediction.

ADDITIONAL READINGS

(For an explanation of abbreviations and abbreviated forms used, see page 25.)

Adler, Irving: *Weather in Your Life*. Day, 1960, 122 pp., $5.69.
Angier: *Skills for Taming the Wilds,* ch. 2.
Angier: *Survival With Style,* ch. 5.
Basic Outdoor Boating, pp. 87–89.
Bell, Thelma Harrington: *Thunderstorm.* Viking, 1960, 128 pp., $3.50.
Bonsall, George: *The How and Why Wonder Book of Weather.* Grosset and Dunlap, 1960, $1.
Brown: *The Amateur Naturalist's Handbook,* chs. XII, XIII.
Cocannouer, Joseph A.: *Water and the Cycle of Life.* Devin-Adair, 143 pp., $4.95.
Dalrymple: *Survival in the Outdoors,* ch. 12.
Fenton, Carroll Lane, and Mildred Adams Fenton:

Our Changing Weather. Doubleday, 1954, $2.50.
Fieldbook for Boys and Men, ch. 22, pp. 503–511.
Harty: *Science for Camp and Counselor,* ch. 2.
Laird, Charles and Ruth: *Weathercasting, A Handbook of Amateur Meteorology.* Prentice-Hall, 1955, 163 pp., $6.40.
Langer: *The Joy of Camping,* pp. 251–268.
Lehr, Paul E., R. Will Burnett, and Dr. H. S. Zim: *Weather.* Golden, 1962, 160 pp., $1.50, paper.
Merrill: *All About Camping,* pp. 121–125.
Mooers: *Finding Your Way in the Outdoors,* ch. 13.
Riviere: *Backcountry Camping,* ch. 13.
Sager, Raymond M.: *The Sager Weathercaster,* October House, Inc., 55 West 30th Street, New York, N.Y. 10011, 1969, 26 pp., $5.95.
Scharff: *The Collier Quick and Easy Guide to Motor Boating,* ch. 8.
Schneider, Herman: *Everyday Weather and How It Works.* McGraw-Hill, rev., 1961, 189 pp., $3.95.
Shivers: *Camping,* pp. 217–222.
Shuttlesworth: *Exploring Nature With Your Child.*
Uman, Martin A.: *Understanding Lightning.* Sterling, 166 pp., $6.50.
van der Smissen and Goering: *A Leader's Guide to Nature-Oriented Activities,* pp. 154–158.
Viemeister, Peter E.: *The Lightning Book.* MIT, 1972, 316 pp., $1.95, paper.
Weather (no. 3274). Boy Scouts, 1963, 64 pp., 45¢, paper.

MAGAZINE ARTICLES

Boy's Life:
Jackson, Harold: "Rain or Shine." Mar., 1961. (Directions for making a weather station)

Changing Times:
"A Ring Around the Moon Means Rain," June, 1973, p. 10. (Old-time ways of predicting weather are a curious mixture of fact and fancy)

The U.S. Weather Bureau handles a number of free or inexpensive publications in this field. For a complete listing, write the Superintendent of Documents for a free copy of price list No. 48, *Weather, Astronomy, and Meteorology.* Some of the most useful are (order by numbers and name from Superintendent of Documents and include payment):

The Aneroid Barometer (No. C 30.2: B 26/2). 1957, 10 pp., 15¢.
Cloud and Code Chart (No. C 30.22:C 62/2/11958). 10¢. (Poster suitable for bulletin board.)
It Looks Like a Tornado, Aid for Distinguishing Tornadoes from Other Cloud Forms (No. C30.6/2: T 63). Rev. ed., 1968, 11 pp., 10¢.
Instruments Used in Weather Observing. 4 pp., 5¢.
Lightning (No. C 30.2:L62). 1963, 4 pp., 5¢.
Tornadoes, What They Are and What to Do About Them (No. C 30.2:T 63/4/963). Rev. ed., 1963, 4 pp., 5¢.
Weather Forecasting (No. C 30.28F 76/3). 1952, 39 pp., 25¢.
Weather Science Study Kit (No. C 30.78: W37). 1963, $1.00. (Contains several of the above pamphlets.)

Chapter 22

Finding Your Way in the Out-of-Doors

Figure 22–1 Silly Two-Legged Beasts! They Have to Have a Compass to Tell Them Where to Go.

The buffalo trail became the Indian trail, and this became the trader's "trace"; the trails widened into roads and the roads into turnpikes and these in turn were transformed into railroads.

—F. J. TURNER,
The Frontier in American History (1893).

Maps are truly wonderful things, often beautiful enough to frame, and good ones are so accurate that they tell us exactly where we are, how to get where we want to go, and what we will see along the way. We are used to casually consulting an automobile road map to find roads which will lead us to towns we want to visit, but most of us are completely unaware of how much other information they contain. If you have never carefully studied this type of map, treat yourself to the experience—you will be surprised!

As a camper or hiker, however, you will not find automobile maps too useful, for you will be wandering off the beaten path and travelling on trails and poorly constructed back roads not even shown on road maps, and there will be no road signs to tell you which way to go. Much of the charm of hiking and backpacking is the feeling that you are out where others seldom go, seeing things they do not see. However, for such voyaging, you will need to develop skills in such areas as using a compass and reading a special kind of map called a *topographic* (or *topo*) map.

THE COMPASS

There are two main types of compasses: (1) the *needle compass* which has a fixed dial and a moveable needle, and (2) the *revolving dial compass* where the needle is fixed and the dial revolves under it. Either type can be used for cross-country exploring, but those in organized camping usually prefer the needle compass because it is smaller and weighs less.

THE PARTS OF A COMPASS

There are many types of compasses, but we will describe here the *Silva Jr.-Type 5 Compass,* an inexpen-

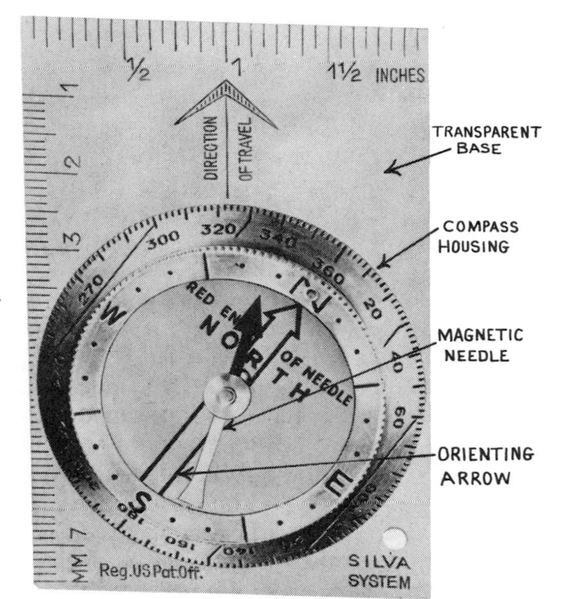

Figure 22–2 A Silva Jr. Compass. (Courtesy of Silva, Inc.)

sive model manufactured by Silva, Inc., which enjoys great popularity for camp use. It has a transparent plastic base with a *direction-of-travel arrow* imprinted on it; the compass can be adjusted so that this arrow points in the direction you want to go. The base also has a metric scale along one side and a scale in inches across one end for measuring distances on maps. Just above the base is a freely moveable circular *housing* containing a circle called the *azimuth circle* on which 360 degrees or *azimuths* are marked in a clockwise direction. The circle is divided into *quadrants* with N (north) at 0° or 360°, E (east) at 90°, S (south) at 180°, and W (west) at 270°. The letters for the quadrants are engraved on the top of the housing and the degrees are on the outer rim.

Printed inside the housing is a stationary *orienting arrow* which points to N (0° or 360°) and a *magnetic needle* which is mounted on a pin so that it moves freely. The end of the needle is painted red and is magnetized so that when you hold the compass level so the needle can move freely, it always points to magnetic north, no matter how you turn the compass.

USING A COMPASS

Since the tip of the compass needle is magnetized, metal or steel near it will deflect it, resulting in an inaccurate reading. Therefore, avoid using the compass near such things as a metal belt buckle, knife blade, hatchet, outboard motor, metal bridge, or telephone or power line.

To read directions from your compass, you must first *orient* it, or turn it so that the magnetic needle is aligned with north as printed on the housing. Hold the compass level about waist high so that the needle will swing freely. Now turn yourself around until the needle lies along the orienting arrow and hence points to N (0° or 360°). You are now facing magnetic north; your right shoulder is toward the east, south is behind you, and west is at your left shoulder.

Now, suppose you want to travel in a certain direction—let's say 60°.

Orient your compass and *set* it by turning the housing to bring the figure 60 directly above the direction-of-travel arrow. Keeping the needle lined up with the orienting arrow and pointing to N, turn yourself around until you are directly behind the direction-of-travel arrow. You are now facing in the direction you want to go. To take a *bearing* or *azimuth reading* on some distant object, do the opposite; point the direction-of-travel arrow toward it, and keeping your compass oriented, read the degrees where the arrow intersects the housing.

To follow a compass direction, pick out two conspicuous landmarks, such as trees or rocks, in line with the arrow and start out, picking out another landmark in line with the arrow as you approach the first so that you always have two landmarks to walk toward. This frees you from having to keep your eyes glued on your compass. Stop occasionally to recheck the compass bearing to make sure you are still on course.

A simple game to test your ability to follow compass directions is called the "Silver Dollar Game." To play it, place some inconspicuous object such as a can lid on the ground. Select a compass bearing of less than 120° and walk 100 feet in that direction; then add 120° to the original bearing and again walk 100 feet; add an additional 120° and walk another 100 feet. Place a marker where you finish; if your readings and measurements have been accurate, you have walked around an equilateral triangle and are back exactly where you started. You can make this into a game for campers by giving each a card with a set number of degrees and distances and seeing who can return nearest to his starting point.

TRUE NORTH AND MAGNETIC NORTH

A compass needle points to *magnetic north,* which over most of the United States is not the same as *true north,* the direction of the North Pole. Magnetic north is the direction of the northern magnetic pole, which is a region about 1400 miles south of the North Pole along the northern edge of Canada. The only place where true north and magnetic north coincide, and where the compass needle will actually point to true north, is along a wavering imaginary line called the *zero* or *agonic line,* which passes diagonally downward across the United States as shown in Figure 22–3. As the map indicates, the needle points increasingly east of north in regions west of this line and west of north in eastern regions. The angle between true north and magnetic north in any given area is called the *angle of declination* and it increases the farther we go from the agonic line, until it is as much as 20° or more in the extreme northeastern and northwestern sections of the United States. It is usually indicated on a map by means of two arrows, one pointing toward the top of the map to true north, the other to magnetic north as you would read it on your compass; the angle of declination is the angle between these arrows. In making a map for your own use around camp, you may want to ignore this difference and draw the map using magnetic north as you read it on your compass, indicating on your map that you have done so. (See Figure 22–6.)

MAPS

SOURCES AND KINDS OF MAPS

A map is a view of an area as it would appear from the air. There are many kinds of maps, ranging from the complicated and detailed road maps issued by the leading oil companies to crude, homemade sketch maps for guiding a person through relatively rough and unsettled country.

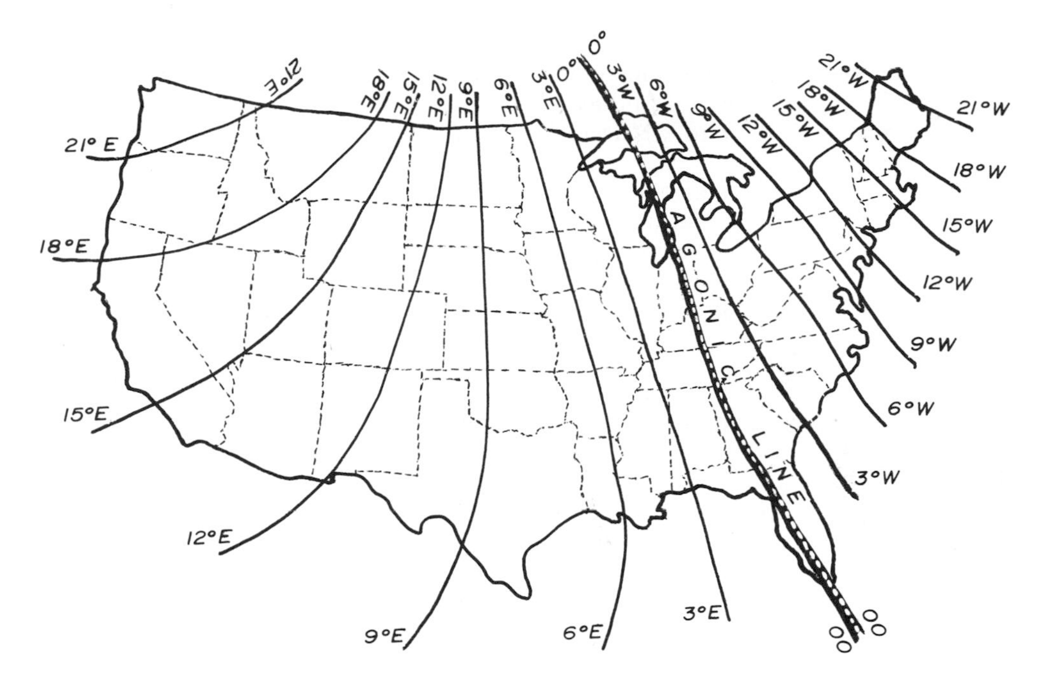

Figure 22-3 The Agonic Line and Compass Declination.

The most useful maps for a hiker or backpacker are the *topographic* (or *topo*) maps that are published by the Topographic Division of the United States Geological Survey. They are inexpensive and are excellent for anyone travelling on foot, on horseback, or by canoe, for they give a graphic picture of what can be seen on a particular trip. Each of these maps covers a relatively small area in great detail. They tell where hills are located and how steep and high they are; they show streams, and you can even determine the direction of their flow since water always flows from small tributaries into larger bodies of water; in fact, by reading the changes in elevation as the stream progresses, you can even estimate how swiftly the water will be flowing. They show canoe routes and places where it will be necessary to portage; marshlands are indicated so that you can avoid camping near them and their mosquito inhabitants. Timber areas and every valley and lake, as well as such man-made "improvements" as houses and bridges, are depicted.

You can sometimes find maps of an area in a local store; if not, write to the Map Information Office, United States Geological Survey, Department of Interior, Washington, D. C. 20242. (If west of the Mississippi, address your request to Geological Survey, Federal Center, Denver, Colorado 82225.) Ask for a free "Index to Topographic Maps" of the state in which the area is located. This will inform you of the various regional maps available, so that you can select the ones you want and send the small sum (usually from 40 cents to a dollar each) necessary to purchase them. Regional maps come on sheets approximately 30 by 38 inches.

The United States Coast and Geodetic Survey* supplies similar maps

*United States Coast and Geodetic Survey, Washington, D. C. 20025.

for water travel, each showing about 40 miles of seacoast. They also have maps of some of the larger inland bodies of water such as the Ohio and Mississippi rivers.

Interesting maps are also available from the United States National Park Service* and the Forest Service,** as well as from state conservation agencies, state parks, and state highway departments.

LEARNING TO READ A MAP

A map usually contains a *legend,* or summary of information, in the lower right-hand corner which includes such items as the following:

1. *Name* or *title* of the region depicted.

2. *Name of the person or firm* who made the map and *date* made. The date is important, particularly for maps of well-settled regions where construction and land use or disuse may entirely change the appearance of a locality within a few years.

3. *Compass direction.* Maps are ordinarily laid out with north at the top, but the particular contour shown or the shape of the area sometimes makes it more convenient to do otherwise. Most maps use two arrows to indicate true north and magnetic north, and the arrows are joined to form the angle of declination.

4. *A scale of distances.* A map is drawn to a certain *scale,* which is the proportional relationship between the distance as represented on the map and the actual distance over the ground. For instance, backpacking maps are usually drawn to large scale, such as letting 1 inch on the map represent 24,000 inches or 2,000 feet on the ground. The scale may be expressed: (1) in words and figures (1 inch = 24,000 inches); (2) as a ratio (1:24,000); or (3) as a fraction (1/24,000). The scale is usually given also as a graphical scale or measuring bar, which is convenient because you can readily measure it off on paper for use in measuring distances between points on the map.

5. A *key* to the meaning of the various symbols used on the map.

*National Park Service, United States Department of Interior, Washington, D. C. 20252.

**Forest Service, United States Department of Agriculture, Washington, D. C. 20250.

FOLLOWING A MAP

When using a map and a compass to plan a trip, first locate your present position and intended destination on the map. Study the symbols of what lies between and try to form a mental picture of the intervening terrain. Remember that a *beeline,* or shortest route, is not always best for it may lead through difficult or even impassable terrain or it may not take you through some of the interesting spots you want to visit. Plan your route carefully, making appropriate *doglegs* around obstacles, and trace on the map or a sheet of paper the exact route you plan to follow. To mark your route without permanently marring your map, use masking tape to fasten a sheet of clear plastic kitchen wrap tightly over it and mark on the plastic with a wax crayon. Calculate compass bearings at each turn and use the map scale to estimate distances between them.

Remember that directions on commercial and government maps are usually given in terms of true north, whereas your compass readings will be in terms of magnetic north. You must take the difference into consideration, especially when in an area where the declination is great, for if it is 14°, for example, you can stray as much as ¼ of a mile off course for each mile you travel. One way to compensate for this difference is to add or subtract the angle of declination each time you take

(Courtesy of Cheley Colorado Camps, Estes Park, Colorado.)

a compass bearing, but it is easier to place a series of magnetic north-south lines across your map, making the first one an extension of the half arrow on the map that indicates magnetic north, and drawing the others parallel to it at 1-inch intervals.

To take an azimuth or bearing on the first leg of your trip, you must first orient your map by laying it flat on a table or the ground, placing your compass above it, and turning the map until the magnetic N-S lines you have drawn lie parallel to N-S as indicated by the needle on your compass. Now place the bottom of the base of your compass at your present location and rotate the base so that the direction-of-travel arrow lies parallel to the path of the first leg of your route. Read off the azimuth or bearing where the direction-of-travel arrow intersects the housing. Measure the length of the line, and using the distance scale on the map, estimate the length of the first leg. Determine the directions and distances of other legs in the same way and record the information on your map. Note which landmarks on the map you can use as check points as you follow the trail.

When you are ready to start out, place the direction-of-travel arrow at the degree reading of the first leg and orient your compass. Then place yourself directly behind the arrow, pick out two distinct landmarks ahead and start toward them, counting your strides or using a *pedometer** so you know when you have completed the first leg and are

*A pedometer (see Figure 23–6), which looks something like a watch, is an instrument which measures the distance you have walked by registering the number of steps you have taken. After adjusting it to the length of your stride, you suspend it freely from your waist so that it will be jostled at each step. It is more accurate on level ground than on rough or hilly terrain.

ready to start the second. Determine the new direction and pick out landmarks to walk toward as before.

Using similar principles, you can use the *triangulation method* to find out where you are on the map when out in the field. Pick out two visible distant landmarks you can locate on the map. Orient the map, take a bearing on the two landmarks, and draw lines through them at these degrees. You are located at the point where the lines intersect.

MAKING A MAP

A person who draws or makes maps is known as a *cartographer*. You may want to make maps just for the fun of it, but there are also several practical reasons for doing so: (1) a map provides one of the best ways to insure returning safely and quickly when venturing into new territory; (2) if you are out rambling about and happen onto a perfect spot for establishing an outpost camp, a map will enable you to find it again; (3) if a member of your party is ill or injured, you can make a map of the spot and leave part of your equipment there to lighten your load while taking him back for treatment; or (4) a map will be needed by members of your group who will be taking different routes or coming at different times to a predetermined campsite or meeting place. Knowledge of mapmaking also allows you to plan and participate in many enjoyable orienteering games.

Rough-Sketching. When making a map, it is more interesting to choose a cross-country route, not more than a mile or two in length, with a variety of things to see along the way. You will need a compass, a pencil, and a notebook or a few sheets of paper on a clipboard to make the preliminary rough-sketch map as you walk along the route. Quadrille or graph paper is convenient since you can let each square represent a certain number of feet or strides. Jot down degrees and distances at every turn and make notes about the terrain and landmarks as you go along so that you can later convert your rough sketch into an accurate and attractive finished map. For convenience, it is suggested that you use magnetic compass readings, ignoring the compass declination in your area; this simplifies the problem for both the person making the map and the one following it. If you prefer to use true north, you will have to adjust each compass reading for declination. For instance, if you are in the West where declination is 12° east, you will have to add 12° to each magnetic bearing; if in the East, with a west declination of 12°, you must subtract 12° from each magnetic reading.

A *stride* consists of two *steps* or *paces*. Therefore, to count your strides you need only take note of how many times your left foot contacts the ground. To determine the length of your stride, use a string or rope exactly 20 or 25 feet long to lay off a distance of 100 yards, preferably over mixed terrain such as you might find on a trail. Start with your toes at the starting line and count each stride as you proceed at your usual cross-country hiking pace; walk it several times and take the average. Now divide 3600 (the number of inches in 100 yards) by the number of strides to determine the length of your stride in inches.

To avoid having to count in high numbers, start with a counted number of pebbles and throw one away at the end of a predetermined number of strides, say 25 or 50. You then need only count the stones you have left to find the total number of strides. You can also estimate distances by the time it takes to cover them if you first time yourself several times over measured distances. In estimating distances, you should allow for travel over difficult terrain, such as steep slopes, where your step normally shortens.

When you are ready to rough-sketch your map, mark your starting point on the paper. Pick out a landmark some distance away, take a compass bearing on it, and start out, counting strides as you go. When you encounter features or landmarks that you want to include, jot them down on your sketch map, making notes as needed. When you reach the first landmark, jot down the number of strides, pick out another landmark, take a new compass bearing and proceed as before.

If you want to show a landmark that is off at one side of the trail, such as an old deserted house (Fig. 22–4*C*), take a compass bearing on it from some distance away (*A*), then count the strides to another point (*B*) and take another bearing. By projecting the two angles on the map and properly plotting distance *AB* to scale, the house will be located at *C* where the lines intersect. If you want to know how far away from the path the old house is, you can measure perpendicular distance *CD* on the map and use the map scale to find the actual distance.

Map Symbols (Fig. 22–5). Certain map symbols are in general use and enable one person to understand maps made by others. These symbols are of four types:

1. *Culture,* or works of man, such as bridges, houses, dams, and so forth are shown in black.

2. *Relief,* or relative elevations and depressions above or below sea level (hills and valleys), are shown in brown. Hills are indicated by *contour lines,* usually explained in the legend in the lower right-hand corner of the map. All points on a single contour line are the same elevation, or height, above sea level so that, if you walked along the line you would not go up or down. Contour lines are often arranged in groups of five with the fifth one somewhat heavier and with the height printed along it. Each line indicates a rise or fall of a certain number of feet (from 5 to 250 feet, as stated in the map legend). Widely spaced lines indicate a gradual slope; those close together, a steep one. Lines falling practically on

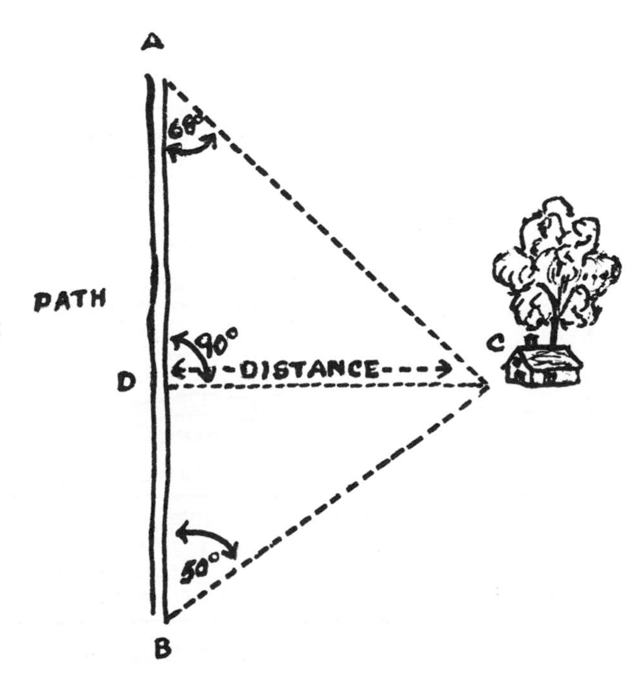

Figure 22-4 Locating an Object at the Side of the Trail.

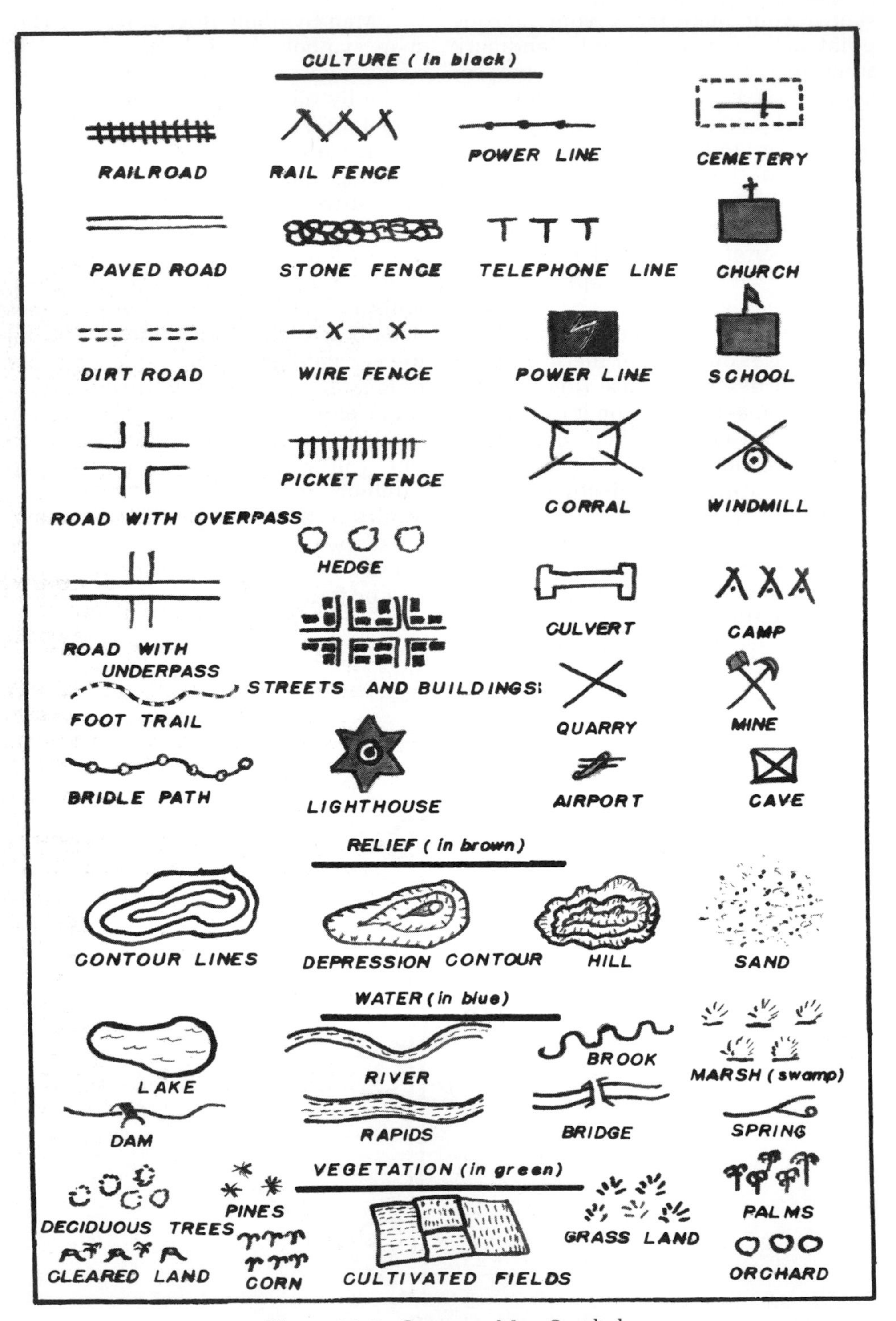

Figure 22–5 Common Map Symbols.

top of each other represent a cliff or steep mountainside. Contour lines spread widely over the countryside signify that the whole region is rolling. It may help you to better visualize the actual appearance of the land if you think of the contour lines as rings left by water which once covered the hill and slowly receded, leaving a ring at each stopping point.

3. *Water features,* such as lakes or rivers, are shown in blue.

4. *Vegetation,* such as woods or crops, is shown in black, blue, or green.

For convenience, maps are often drawn entirely in black instead of colors. Common map symbols are simple and usually roughly resemble what they depict. You may have to invent symbols for unusual objects on your map; make them bear a likeness to what they represent and explain them in your legend. Just for practice, start at Happy Valley Camp in the lower left-hand corner of the map of Happy Valley Camp and Vicinity (Fig. 22–6) and take an imaginary trip around the path indicated. Write out what you would see along the way.

Completing The Map. When you have completed your rough-sketch map, translate it into a completed trail map as soon as possible, while the details are still fresh in your memory. Use a ruler, compass, and protractor to insure accuracy and draw it to scale of between 200 and 2000 feet to the inch. Don't worry if the point where you finish on the map doesn't exactly coincide with your starting point; such deviations are common when using rather crude instruments and measurements and are called *errors of closure.* Keep your symbols small and use black India and colored inks.

Keep the purpose of your map in mind. If others are to use it as a guide, too many details will be confusing. If you want it to be a decorative wall map, make it a gaily colored "romance" or picture map. You can give the map a parchment-like appearance by daubing it lightly with a bit of linseed oil or yellow shellac.

PROTECTING YOUR MAP

Although you can carry a rolled-up map, it is usually preferable to fold it to a convenient size. Fold it once or twice lengthwise and six or eight times across accordion-fashion, like a road map. Turn it so the part you want to travel over is on the outside and place it in a vinyl map case, a plastic sheet such as the refill sheet for a photograph album, or place a piece of plastic kitchen wrap or dry-cleaner bag over it and seal it with masking or plastic tape. If your map is quite large and cumbersome and you are only going to travel over a small part, there is no need to burden yourself with the whole map. Cut out the part you will need, then replace it when you return using plastic tape to seal it back in place.

You can add still more durability by mounting the map. Since the folds are particularly vulnerable to wear, protect them by cutting the map into sections at the fold marks and mounting each piece, leaving a ⅛-inch space between them. Use a warm iron to press the sections onto a special adhesive-backed material called "chartex," available at most art supply stores, or use rubber cement or wallpaper paste to fasten the pieces to unbleached muslin, linen, or sheeting, smoothing them out to eliminate wrinkles and air bubbles. Place the whole map under a heavy weight and leave it overnight.

To waterproof both sides of your map, apply two or more coats of clear shellac or spray it with a clear acrylic.

MAKING A RELIEF MAP

A *papier-mâché* relief map is quite decorative and provides a more realis-

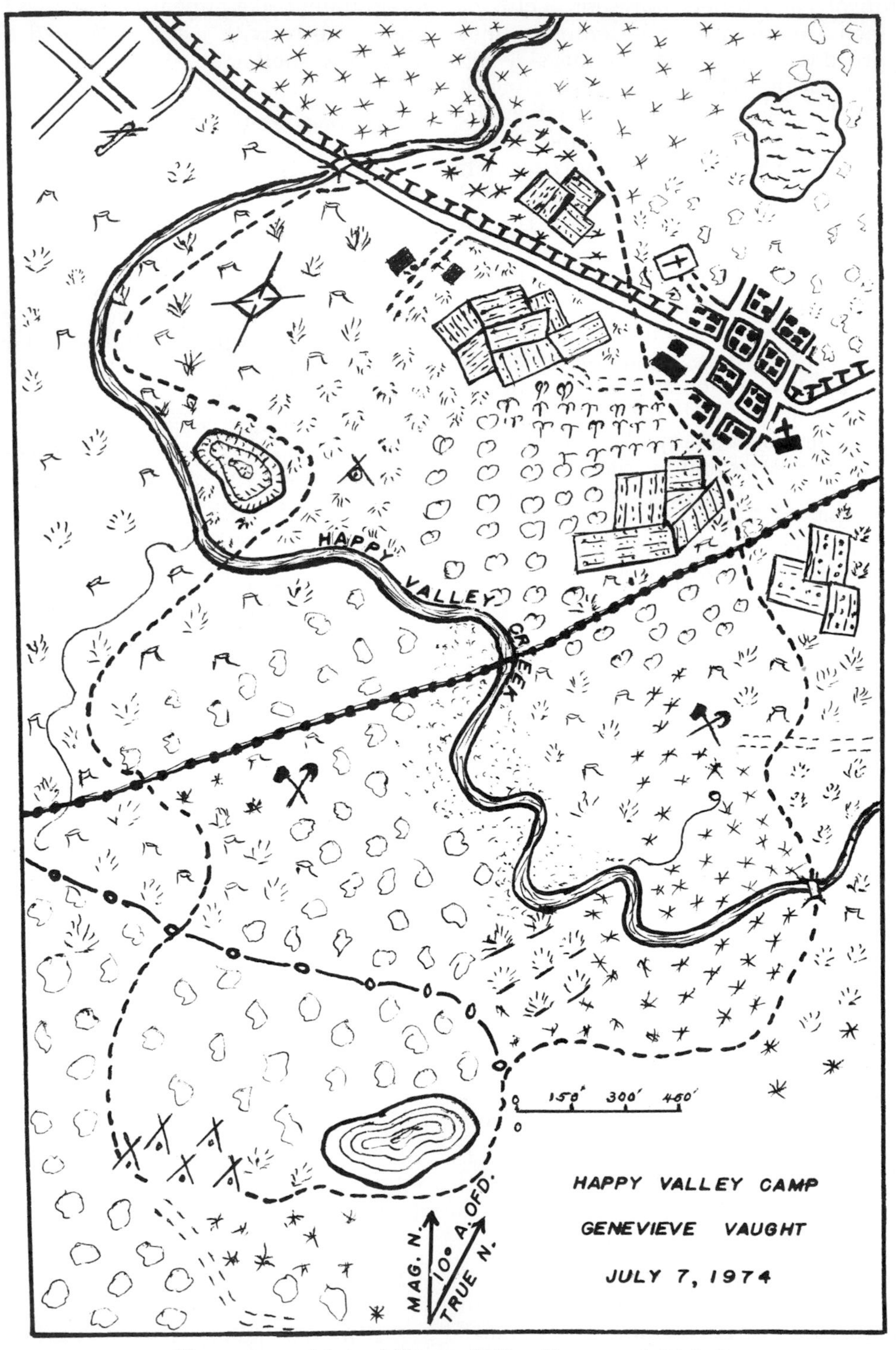

Figure 22-6 Map of Happy Valley Camp and Vicinity.

tic view of an area. Start with a large piece of thin board, plywood, or stiff cardboard and lay off the area to scale, indicating the locations of rivers, woods, houses, and other things you want to show. Tear up a quantity of old newspapers or paper towels into small scraps and soak them for several hours in hot water. Knead and manipulate them until they become quite "gooey"; then press out as much water as possible and mix in a quantity of library paste. Use the mixture to cover the base, building it up to the proper height and contour for hills and scooping it out for rivers, valleys, and other depressions. When it is dry, draw in details and paint it with appropriate shades of tempera paint or colored inks. Make "trees" of twigs and bits of sponge; "grass" of sawdust dyed green and placed on a thin layer of glue. Sand sprinkled over glue makes good bare ground and buildings may be fashioned from twigs or cardboard and finished in appropriate colors. Making such a model of your camp site is a good project and will provide hours of pleasure for your campers.

STAY FOUND

PREVENTION PAYS

Don't be deluded into thinking that you are an expert after studying this brief treatise on compasses and maps. Before you go forth into strange territory, you will need to study carefully some of the excellent sources given at the end of this chapter and then practice many hours with the tools of your trade. A miscalculation of just a short distance or a few degrees can set you up for a truly harrowing experience. Never venture into unfamiliar territory alone and always tell some responsible person where you are going, the exact route you plan to take, who will be in the party, and when you expect to return.

Never start without your compass, and if possible, take along a detailed map of the region on which to mark your path as you go. If you have no map, it is wise to make a rough chart as you progress to use for finding your way back. It is also helpful to jot down walking time as well as distances between various points. Two essential things to do are to *look back* occasionally to see how things will look on your return and to *write things down* instead of relying on your memory. Remember that you must use your compass as you go, for it is of almost no use *after* you are lost. Take an initial reading and jot down additional ones each time you change directions.

Although some people claim to have a "sixth sense" of direction, experiments have shown that it simply is not true, for even experienced explorers, guides, and woodsmen became quite confused when blindfolded and told to walk in a straight line. Their seemingly uncanny ability to find their way without benefit of compass or map can probably be attributed to their

Figure 22–7 This is One Way to Find Your Way Back.

highly developed habits of observation which cause them to unconsciously note such things as the position of the sun, the direction of prevailing winds, details about the terrain, and distinguishing landmarks along the way. You will do well to emulate them.

If you are hiking in a group, stay together. It is wise to provide each member with a whistle to use if he inadvertently strays, for a whistle blast carries a long way through the silent woods.

IF YOU BECOME LOST

If you should suddenly realize that you aren't quite sure where you are, don't panic; stay calm and think it over. There is probably no real emergency, for the chances are that you are not far off route and can reason your way out if you just use your head. Climb a tree (don't take chances if you can't do it safely) or hill to get a long view and to try to spot some landmark which is familiar or which you can locate on your map to give you a general idea of where you are. Try to remember the exact route you traveled since you were last oriented.

If none of these help, it may be best to just sit down, conserve your energy, and wait for someone to find you. Members of your group will soon miss you and come looking and there are always other people available to form a search party if needed. The chances are that you'll be found within a few hours, and even if you have to stay out overnight, the experience will probably not amount to much more than an unpleasant inconvenience. If you have brought a knife, matches, and flashlight along, you can spend several days without coming to any real harm, for people have survived as long as 30 days without food, provided they had water to drink. If you doubt the purity of the available water, purify it as described in Chapter 31. If you have a survival kit and know how to use it, you are in good shape for you can find nourishing food in the wilds. Send out signals of your whereabouts to possible rescuers as described later on in this chapter. In most cases, it is best to stay right where you are for you are probably not too far off route and searchers will therefore know the general area in which to look.

In most civilized areas there are regular air patrol flights which usually will spot you if you choose an open area and spell out SOS in letters 6 to 10 feet high, well-spaced against a contrasting background.

If night is approaching or a potential storm is brewing, prepare to spend the night, by finding the best shelter you can and making yourself comfortable until morning. Clear a space and build a fire for warmth and cheer. Lay in an adequate supply of fuel to keep your fire going as long as you want it, remembering that even warm days are often followed by uncomfortably cool nights. If you leave the site for any reason, such as to look for water or more fuel, be sure to mark your path so that you can readily find your way back.

If it is fairly early in the day and you decide to move on but have no idea where home is, you will find civilization in almost any direction if you travel in a straight line. But there's one catch if you don't have a compass—it is an established fact that every unguided person tends to travel in a more or less circular path, usually to the right but occasionally to the left. You are no exception, and unless you take precautions to prevent it, you will probably travel in a wide circle which will eventually bring you back very close to where you started. It is best to choose one direction, then pick out two landmarks in line with it and start out, picking out another landmark as you near the first, as previously discussed. If you have been a good camper and brought your compass, things will be much simpler, for you can take an azimuth reading and stay with it. If you come to an impassable section such as a swamp, dogleg around it with three 90° turns, counting your strides so that you are sure that you are back on course again.

It is wise to mark your path as you go along so that you can return if you wish and so those searching for you will know they are on your trail. Tear off strips of cloth and tie them about head high at intervals or use one of the methods for marking a trail discussed later on in this chapter. Take a brief rest now and then, and when you come to a steep incline conserve your strength by zigzagging up it or climbing it at a slant as animals do.

If you locate a railroad track, a telephone or electric line, or a wall or fence, follow it for it will eventually lead you to civilization. Go downhill rather than uphill, especially when you find running water. Listen for human sounds and look for signs of smoke.

DANGER OR DISTRESS SIGNALS

Three of anything has been long and widely recognized as a signal of danger or distress. Three rocks placed on top of each other, three clumps of grass tied in knots, three blazes on trees, three smudge fires, three whistle blasts, or three gunshots are examples (Fig. 22-13). Note that the Morse code applies this principle in its call for help, SOS, which consists of three dots, three dashes, and three dots.

Use three smudge fires as signals for help in the daytime, placing them just far enough apart to be distinguishable at a distance. Build a good fire and get it going well, then pile nonflammable materials such as green or rotten wood or wet leaves on it to make it "smudge" or smoke. Use a blanket or coat to smother the smoke momentarily so it collects into larger, more noticeable puffs. A big, bright fire shows up better at night, but be careful not to make it large enough to set the forest on fire. Friends in camp or the ever-watchful fire warden in his fire tower will soon see the signal and send help. Never give a distress signal just for fun, lest it be ignored in time of real need like the plea of the little boy who cried "wolf" too often.

TELLING DIRECTIONS WITHOUT A COMPASS

Some methods of using Mother Nature's signs to tell directions are not very dependable or consume so much time that you would hesitate to use them. However, the following are quite helpful.

TELLING DIRECTIONS BY THE STARS

The stars are our oldest and most faithful guides to direction. When ancient literature speaks of "being guided by a star," it refers to the *North Star* (also called *Polaris* or the *Pole Star*), which is an even more accurate guide to direction than a compass, for it never varies more than one degree from true north no matter where you are in the United States.

To locate the North Star (Fig. 22-8), find the *Big Dipper* and the *Little Dipper* in the sky. The two stars opposite the handle that form the front edge of the Big Dipper are known as the *pointers* because they point directly to the North Star in the tip of the Little Dipper's handle. Although the Big Dipper circles around the Little Dipper every 24 hours, the pointers never cease to point to the North Star. The bowls of the two Dippers constantly face so that they always seem to be pouring into each other.

There are many interesting myths

about the stars. One version tells us that many years ago a tribe of Indians was living happily in the midst of good hunting until the coming of an extremely large mother bear and her cub who frightened away all the small game. This brought famine to the Indians and they decided to send out their best hunters to kill the bears. After being hotly pursued through many miles of wilderness, the bears finally fled to the top of a tall mountain where the mother bear leaped into the sky in desperation and was followed by her cub. The hunters began to shoot and finally pierced the cub's tail with an arrow, fastening it in the northern sky. This arrow is the North Star. The cub began running around its tail, making a complete circuit each day. The mother bear's wounds appear as the seven stars of the Big Dipper and she remains in the sky, making a complete circle each day around her cub. The Indians called the Big Dipper the Big Bear (Ursa Major) and the Little Dipper the Little Bear (Ursa Minor).

USING YOUR WATCH AS A COMPASS

Some people advocate a method of telling directions using the sun and a watch. Here's how to do it. Stand with your left shoulder toward the sun, hold your watch flat in your palm, and point the hour hand directly toward the sun. South is now located halfway between the hour hand and 12 o'clock, using the shorter distance between the two as shown in Figure 22–9. To find the sun on a cloudy or hazy day, stand a knife blade or match up against the watch and adjust it until the shadow of the match lies directly over the hour hand: the hour hand will now be pointing directly toward the sun. If you are on Daylight Saving Time you will have to set your watch back one hour. Many claim this method isn't accurate. Try it

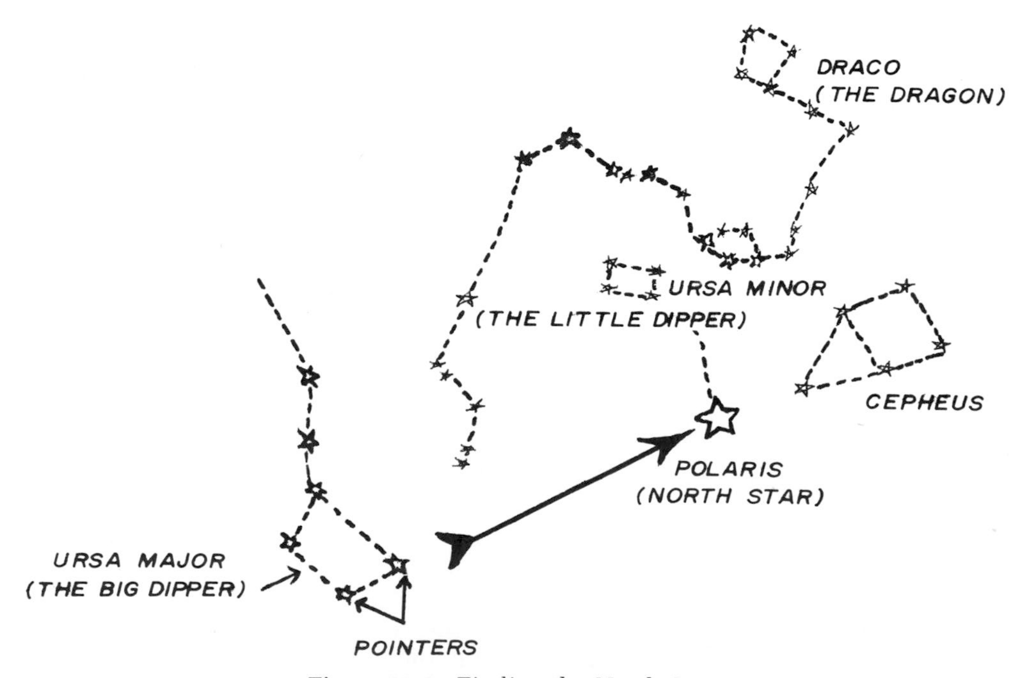

Figure 22–8 Finding the North Star.

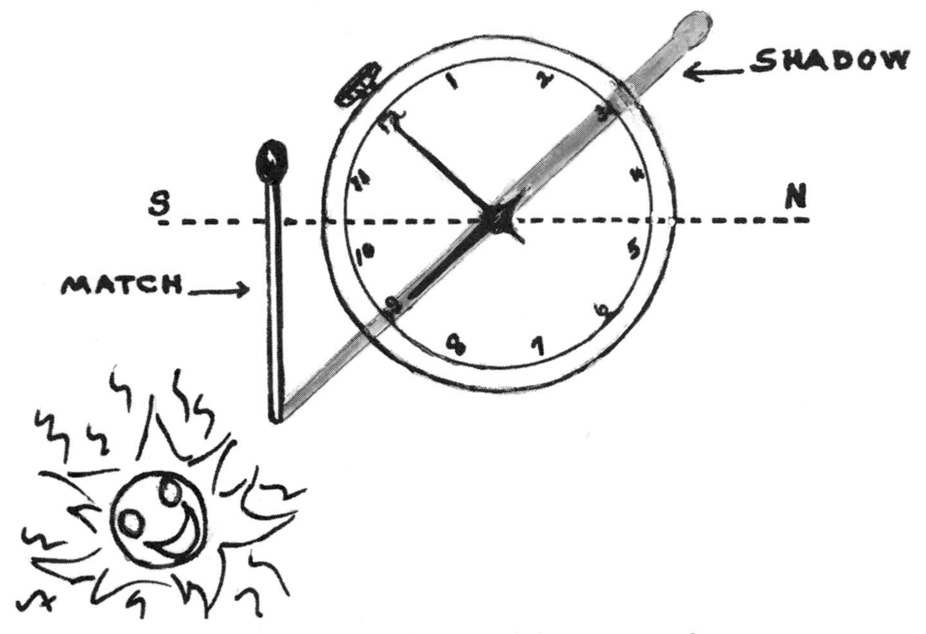

Figure 22–9 Finding South by Your Watch.

and check it with your compass, adjusting for declination, to see what results you get.

*THE SHADOW COMPASS**

Select a place where the sun is shining and drive a stick from 3 to 5 feet tall into the ground and mark the tip of the stick's shadow with a stone or other object. Wait at least 15 minutes, or until the shadow has moved to a new location, and again mark its tip. If you have time, do this several times. Connect the tip marks with a line; it will lie roughly true east-west with the last mark pointing west. A line exactly perpendicular to the east-west line will consequently lie approximately north-south. This method is most accurate around noon and decreases in accuracy the further away from noon the time. Check your directions with your compass to find out how accurate they are, remembering to allow for compass declination. Incidentally, when your own shadow is so short that you can almost step on the tip of it, you can be sure it is about noon.

*This method is attributed to Robert Owendoff. (Robert S. Owendoff: *Better Ways of Pathfinding*. Stackpole, 1964, pp. 73–80.)

MEASURING INACCESSIBLE DISTANCES

Here are some simple principles of geometry to use for measuring inaccessible distances.

ESTIMATING THE HEIGHT OF A TREE, CLIFF, OR BUILDING

Mark your own height prominently on the tree or other object you want to measure or have a friend whose height you know stand against it. If you have a ruler, hold it upright at arm's length

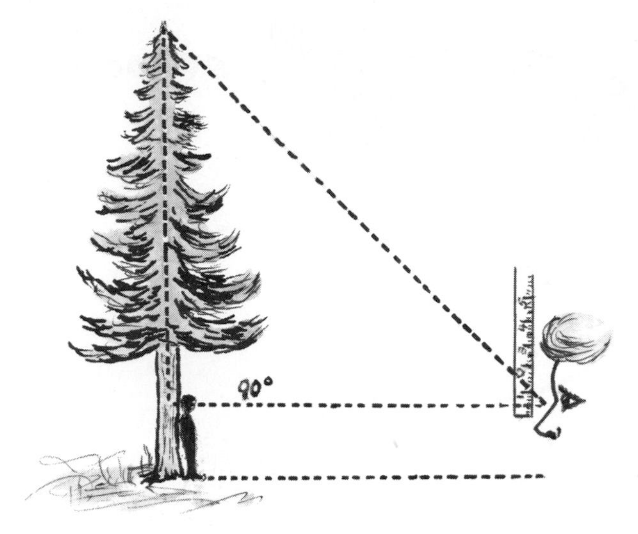

Figure 22-10 Measuring the Height of a Tree.

in front of you with the bottom at eye level. Now sighting with one eye along the ½-inch mark on the ruler, step back until it is just even with the mark on the tree (Fig. 22-10). Now sight the top of the tree across the ruler and note the point at which a line from the top of the tree intersects the ruler. Count the number of half inches to that point and multiply by your height or that of your friend. You can substitute a straight stick for the ruler, using the same principles.

An Indian method (Fig. 22-11), not quite so accurate but giving as exact a figure as is usually needed, is to walk away from the object to be measured until you can just see the top of it when you bend over, clasp your ankles and look through your legs. The height of the object, XY, roughly equals the distance you are from the tree, YZ.

ESTIMATING THE WIDTH OF A RIVER

To measure the width of something such as a river or gorge, select an easily distinguishable landmark on the other side, such as a tree (Fig. 22-12Z), and

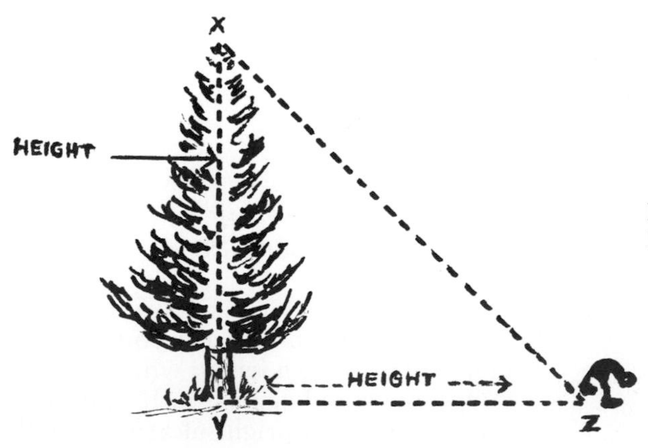

Figure 22-11 Indian Method of Measuring the Height of a Tree.

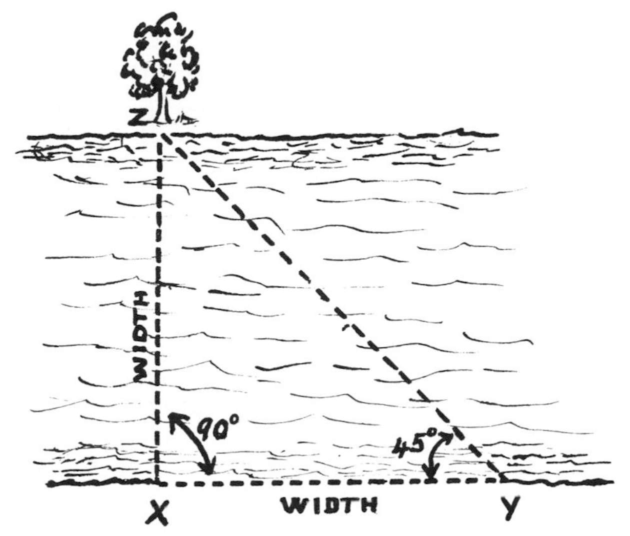

Figure 22-12 Estimating the Width of a River.

mark spot X directly across from it. Now walk down the river bank until you are at a 45° angle with the tree and mark spot Y. You have now outlined an isosceles triangle; since XY equals XZ, you can determine the width of the river by measuring XY.

ESTIMATING DEPTH

To determine the approximate depth of a river, lake, or chasm, drop a rock from just above the water's surface and time it until it hits bottom. Square the number of seconds which elapsed and multiply the result by 16 to get the approximate depth in feet.

LEARNING TO ESTIMATE MEASUREMENTS

Many boys and girls are notoriously poor at judging distances and heights, probably owing more to lack of practice than to any innate inability to do so. Being able to make such estimates often comes in handy and the best way to acquire the skill is to practice estimating objects which you can actually weigh or measure afterward to check your accuracy. With practice, you should be able to get within 10 per cent of the correct answer most of the time.

In judging long distances, it sometimes helps to mentally divide them into short, familiar distances, such as 100 yards, 3 feet, or 12 inches, and then estimate the number of shorter distances in the long one.

In making rough estimates, it is useful to know some of your own measurements, such as:

1. The length of your ordinary hiking pace and stride.
2. The length of your foot in the type of shoe you ordinarily wear.
3. Your exact height and the distance from finger tip to finger tip with both arms outstretched. (These distances are usually about equal so you can use one for measuring heights and the other for widths.
4. A finger joint that is exactly an inch long.
5. The length of your forearm.
6. The length from the ground to the tips of your outstretched hands.

It is handy to mark your hiking stick for measuring by burning short lines on it at one inch intervals.

TRAILS AND SIGNALS

Trails are as old as mankind, for it is impossible for any creature to go through wooded territory without leaving some trace. Such obscure signs as a track in the mud or sand, a branch accidently broken off, or a vine carelessly torn by the foot, though easily overlooked by the tenderfoot, are quite meaningful to one skilled and practiced in woodland ways.

The first trails were made by the big game animals in going to and from their favorite feeding grounds, water holes, or salt licks. The Indians, then pioneer trappers and explorers on foot or on pack horses, and finally covered wagons and stagecoaches followed these same trails, making them ever wider and easier to follow. Many of them became the bases of the routes of our railroads and highways.

Early paths seldom passed through valleys but instead kept to the ridges in hilly or mountainous country where there were few streams to ford and where the traveler could command a wide view of the surrounding countryside, to protect himself from ambush.

METHODS OF LAYING TRAILS (Fig. 22–13)

Blazing. The favorite pioneer method of marking a trail through the wilderness was *blazing,* or using an axe or sheath knife to take a chip out of a tree to expose the white surface which could be easily spotted from a distance. Of course this method is unthinkable today, for trees are far too precious to mutilate. We know that a wound in the bark of a tree is just as serious as a cut or break in our own skin, for it makes an opening for parasites and diseases to initiate their damaging, perhaps even fatal, attacks.

Brush Blazes. The brush blaze was a favorite Indian method of trail marking. It consists of breaking a shrub branch every hundred yards or so, leaving it still attached but with the lighter undersides of its leaves exposed to attract attention. The branch was left pointing in the direction to be taken. To indicate an abrupt change in direction, the branch was completely broken off and supported in a crotched stick with its butt end pointing in the new direction.

This method may still be permissible in regions where the underbrush is very heavy and a few broken branches will never be missed but this is unlikely to be true near any organized camp.

Grass. In prairie regions where fairly long grass is abundant, a wisp of grass can be used as a cord to tie other clumps together, leaving the heads upright when the trail lies straight ahead and lopping them over to point in the direction of any turn made.

Rocks. Use rocks to mark the trail along the seashore or in barren regions. A small rock on top of a large one indicates "this is the trail"; a smaller rock placed to one side means turn in this direction. Pebbles can also be laid out in the form of a "V" to show directions.

Other Methods. Paper weighted down with stones or bits of colored cloth tied to twigs can be used, but since your trail should show no evidence that you have been over it, those following it should gather these up as they come along. You can also scratch direction arrows in bare dirt or use a grease pencil to mark on rocks (the marks will soon disappear).

SIGNALING

THE MORSE CODE (Fig. 22–14)

The most universally used and understood code is the *international Morse code* which uses dots and dashes

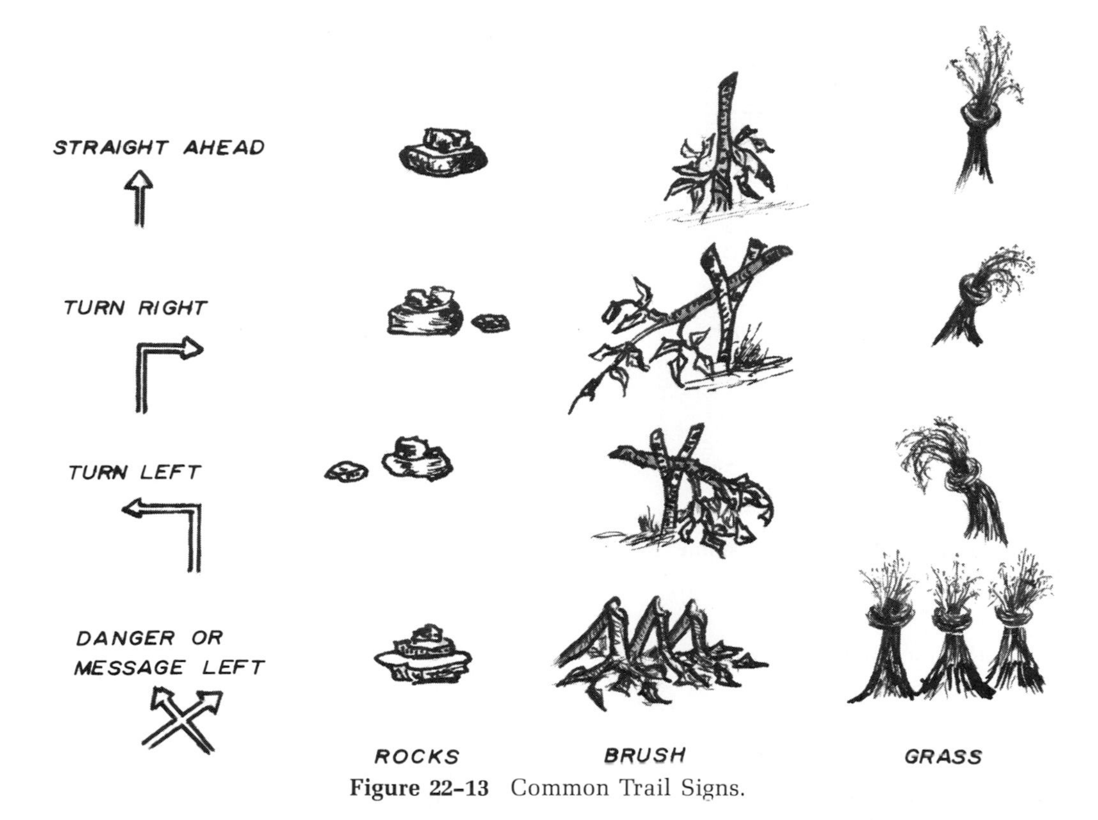

Figure 22-13 Common Trail Signs.

to spell out messages. You indicate a dot by a short flash or sound (held while you count "one") and a dash by a long one (held while you count "one, two, three").

The Morse code is adaptable to many forms of communication; you can use a lantern, flashlight, automobile horn, flag, torch, whistle, drum, or a mirror held to reflect the sun's rays. When using a smudge fire to transmit smoke signals in Morse code, two persons can hold a blanket above the fire, removing it at proper intervals to allow large billows of smoke to rise and spell out the message. At night, hold a blanket in front of a blazing campfire.

Pause and count three at the end of each letter; count five at the end of a word and pause still longer for the end of a sentence. Strive for accuracy and clearness rather than speed. When first practicing at receiving the Morse code, use two persons, one to call out the dots and dashes as received, the other to write them down for later decoding. Practice signaling from short distances at first, then gradually move away until you are finally so far away that you need field glasses to read the message. Morse code is not only fun, but it may save steps or get help in an emergency when you need to communicate with a group far away.

WRITTEN CODES

It is fairly simple to work out a secret code for a cabin or group of campers to use for written messages. Figure 22-15 shows three examples; use your ingenuity to make up your own.

You can use pure lemon juice to write an invisible note to a friend. The paper will look blank but he can bring

Alphabet

A	•–	N	–•
B	–•••	O	–––
C	–•–•	P	•––•
D	–••	Q	––•–
E	•	R	•–•
F	••–•	S	•••
G	––•	T	–
H	••••	U	••–
I	••	V	•••–
J	•–––	W	•––
K	–•–	X	–••–
L	•–••	Y	–•––
M	––	Z	––••

Numerals

1	•––––	6	–••••
2	••–––	7	––•••
3	•••––	8	–––••
4	••••–	9	––––•
5	•••••	0	–––––

Figure 22–14 International Morse Code.

out the message by pressing the paper with a warm iron.

GAMES TO MAKE LEARNING MORE ENJOYABLE

MAP SYMBOL RELAY

Teams of 4 to 10 players line up in relay formation. Each team has a set of cards bearing map symbols stacked in front of it and a similar set with names of what the symbols stand for spread out nearby. On signal, the first player on each team runs forward, picks up the top symbol card, places it on top of its matching name card and runs back to touch off the second player who repeats with the second symbol card, and so forth. The first team placing all of its cards correctly wins.

Variation: Supply each person with a paper and pencil. Hold up the symbol cards one by one and have each player write down what the symbol stands for. The winner is the individual or team with the most nearly correct list.

COMPASS CIRCLE RELAY

Two teams of 8 to 16 players line up in relay formation. Each team has a circle in front of it with N marked conspicuously and straight marks to indicate the positions of the other directions (NE, E, SE, S, SW, W, NW; or NNE, NE, ENE, E, ESE, SE, SSE, S, SSW, SW, WSW, W, WNW, NW, NNW). Stack a set of cards, each bearing a direction, near each circle but not arranged in order. At a given signal, the first player on each team runs up, takes the top card and places it in its correct position in the circle and comes back to touch off the second player who places the second card, and so on. The first team to place all the cards correctly wins.

COMPASS CHANGE

One player is "it" while eight others distribute themselves around the circle in the positions of the different directions (N, NE, E, and so forth). A prominent sign marks N on the circle but no other positions are marked. "It" calls out two directions (as NE and S) and these two players try to change places before "it" can slip into one of their positions. The person left out is "it" and the game continues.

WHAT IS IT?

Each person has his own topographic map. Pick out two base points on the map and give compass bearings from them. Each participant uses his compass to locate the base points and to determine where lines drawn at the compass bearings would intersect and what he would see there. Give several base points and compass bearings. The person with the most nearly correct answer wins.

	1	2	3	1	2		3	1		2	3	1	2	3		1	2	3
Message	S	H	A	L	L		W	E		S	L	E	E	P		O	U	T
Code	T	J	D	M	N		Z	F		U	O	F	G	S		P	W	W

Add one, two or three letters in sequence as indicated to each letter of the real message.

	−1	+1	−1	+1	−1	+1	−1	+1	−1	+1	−1	+1	−1
Message	W	I	L	L	W	E	H	I	K	E	O	U	T
Code	V	J	K	M	V	F	G	J	J	F	N	V	S

Alternately subtract one letter, then add one, to the real meassage.

A B C D E F G H I

J K L M N O P Q R

S T U V W X Y Z

Figure 22–15 Angle Code. (From Gibson, H. W.: *Recreational Programs for Summer Camps,* page 51.)

BEELINE OR CROW-FLIGHT HIKE

Pick out a compass bearing and follow it as closely as possible on a map or outdoors to find out where it will lead and what you will see along the way.

BURIED TREASURE

Give each person a card with a set of directions, such as "Go 25° for 75 yards, then 120° for 100 yards, and 75° for 150 yards." Each participant uses a compass and estimates distances to try to find the correct destination. Sets of directions can vary as long as all end up at the same spot. The person most nearly correct wins the "buried treasure." This can also be a "trip" over a topographic map.

PROGRESSIVE SUPPER HIKE

Half of the group take food and equipment for a cookout and lay a trail, distributing themselves at four spots along the trail. The first group prepares the first course, the second the main dish, the third dessert, and the fourth presents the evening program. The rest of the group follow with their eating utensils and try to follow the trail to get their suppers.

DECODING MESSAGES

Use teams of four players and station one member of each at the four corners of a large building. Give a 100-word message to the first player of the first team to transmit by Morse code (using flashlight, flags, lantern, etc.) to his teammate at the next corner, who then sends it on to the third, and so forth. The last player decodes the message and whispers it to the leader. The second team is given a different 100-word message to transmit in the same way. The team with the most nearly correct decoded message wins.

ORIENTEERING

Orienteering is a sport which originated in Sweden several years ago and still flourishes there, providing fun, good exercise, and valuable experience with map and compass for many thousands of young and not-so-young people who compete annually for proficiency pins. It is also gaining well-deserved popularity in the United States. There are many variations to accommodate everyone from the youngest and greenest beginner to the rugged expert. The object is to cover an unfamiliar route in the shortest possible time, using a map and compass and good judgment to pick out the best way. The route can cover from ½ to 50 miles and includes at least five or more landmarks or *control points* which are prominently marked, by a colorful banner for example, so that they are clearly visible to anyone coming reasonably near. Individuals or buddies (two people working together) start out at 15 to 20 minute intervals, trying to pass all the control points and complete the course in the least possible time. Each is given a direction sheet or key to the route and is allowed a certain amount of time to study the key and to use his compass and a topographic map or a master map to determine the best way to go. To insure that each contestant passes each control point, there may be a judge stationed there or the contestant may be asked to pick up a number or identifying card.

Orienteering games are of two types:

1. *Route Orienteering.* The route is already laid out on a master map which each contestant studies to determine directions and distances for himself.

2. *Point Orienteering.* Each contestant is given only the locations of the finish and control points and he must study the map to pick out what he deems the best and fastest route. This type of orienteering is more challenging since it requires good judgment and a

(Courtesy of Girl Scouts U. S. A.)

knowledge of map symbols to decide whether it would be better to take short cuts involving such obstacles as marshy ground and a high hill or to travel a little farther to enjoy easier going.

Your campers may enjoy the following orienteering games:

Paul Revere's Ride. Lay out one or more routes of equal length and difficulty and provide each player with a compass and map or a key to his route. Use one of the methods mentioned previously to see that he passes all control points, and time him until he crosses the finish line. The winner is the one who completes his route in the least time. If you use only one route, have players start out at intervals.

Bringing Home the Bacon. Lay out separate routes of equal length and difficulty for each team and station one team member at each of its control points. Give the first member of each team a compass and a key to his route. At a given signal, he proceeds as rapidly as possible to his teammate at the first control point and gives him the compass and key sheet to take on to the third teammate at the next control point, and so forth. Players must wait inconspicuously at control points without speaking or giving any other signal to help their teammates to find them. The first team to complete its route wins.

Winning at orienteering games requires several essential skills in pathfinding: (1) ability to follow instructions; (2) skill with map and compass; (3) an understanding of map symbols and how to choose the best route; (4) speed. For further information about orienteering games, maps, and other materials, see the bibliography at the end of this chapter or write to the United States Orienteering Federation, Suite 317, 933 North Kenmore Street, Arlington, Virginia 22201 or the American Orienteering Service, P. O. Box 547, La Porte, Indiana 46350.

ADDITIONAL READINGS

(For an explanation of abbreviations and abbreviated forms used, see page 25.)

Maps, Compass, and Pathfinding

Angier: *How To Stay Alive in the Woods,* chs. 16–18, 20.
Angier: *Skills for Taming the Wilds,* ch. 7.
Angier: *Survival With Style,* ch. 4.
Angier: *Wilderness Gear You Can Make Yourself,* ch. 11.
Bale: *What On Earth,* pp. 37-47, 54–55, 108–111.
Boy Scout Handbook, pp. 204-213.
Bridge: *America's Backpacking Book,* ch. 14.
Brower: *Going Light With Backpack or Burro,* ch. 7.
Brown, L.: *Map Making: The Art that Became a Science.* Little, Brown, $4.95.
Cardwell: *America's Camping Book,* chs. 31, 35.
Compass and Maps. Girl Scouts, rev., $10. (Flip charts)
Dalrymple: *Survival in the Outdoors,* ch. 5, pp. 84–91.
Disley, John: *Your Way With Map and Compass.* American Orienteering, 1971, 61 pp., $2.50.
Fieldbook for Boys and Men, ch. 3, pp. 62–63, 301-307, 530–533.
Fletcher: *The Complete Walker,* pp. 239–248.
Garrison: *Outdoor Education,* ch. X.
Gatty, Harold: *Nature Is Your Guide: How to Find Your Way on Land and Sea by Observing Nature.* Dutton, 1958, $4.95.
Greenhood, David: *Mapping.* U. of Chicago, 1964, 289 pp., $2.95, paper.
Harty: *Science for Camp and Counselor,* pp. 149-150, 259-260, 263–266.
Hathaway, J.: *Maps and Map Making.* Western, $2.95.
Kjellstrom: *Be Expert With Map and Compass.*
Langer: *The Joy of Camping,* pp. 229–241.
Learn and Tallman: *Backpacker's Digest,* chs. 7, 17.
Macfarlan: *The Boy's Book of Hiking,* ch. 7.
Manning: *Backpacking One Step at a Time,* pp. 54–57; ch. 16.
Merrill: *All About Camping,* chs. 18, 19, 20.
Merrill: *The Hiker's and Backpacker's Handbook,* ch. 8.
Merrill: *The Survival Handbook,* chs. 2, 3.
Miracle and Decker: *Complete Book of Camping,* chs. 26, 27.
Mooers, Robert L., Jr.: *Finding Your Way in the Outdoors.*
Ormond: *Complete Book of Outdoor Lore,* ch. 4.
Ratliff, Donald E.: *Map, Compass and Campfire.* Binfords and Mort, Portland, Ore., 1964, 63 pp., $1.50.
Rethmel: *Backpacking,* pp. 8–3 to 8–8.
Rinkoff, Barbara: *A Map Is a Picture.* Crowell, 1965, 40 pp., $3.75.

Riviere: *Backcountry Camping*, ch. 12.
Riviere: *The Camper's Bible*, ch. 12.
Rutstrum, Calvin: *The Wilderness Route Finder*. Macmillan, 1973, 214 pp., $1.95, paper.
Shockley and Fox: *Survival in the Wilds*, ch. 3.
Whelen and Angier: *On Your Own in the Wilderness*, ch. 17.

MAGAZINE ARTICLES
Backpacker-3, Fall, 1973:
Braasch, Gary: "An Orientation to Map Making," p. 32.

Boys' Life:
"Maps and How to Use Them." Dec., 1969, p. 64.
Marshall, Joe: "Compass Skill Games." Aug., 1971, p. 52.

Camping Journal:
Duffey, Dave: "Duffel Bag." June, 1967, p. 14. (How to estimate distances when hiking)
Martenhoff, Jim: "Wilderness Direction-Finders." Jan., 1968, p. 30.
Ormond, Clyde: "On the Trail." June, 1968, p. 14.

Orienteering

Disley, John: *Orienteering*. Stackpole, 1967, 168 pp., $4.95.
Kjellstrom: *Be Expert With Map and Compass*.

MAGAZINE ARTICLES
Boys' Life:
Halter, Jon G.: "Orienteering," Mar., 1973, p. 44

FILMS

These films may be rented or purchased from International Film Bureau, Inc., 332 South Michigan Avenue, Chicago, Illinois 60604:
By Map and Compass
Orienteering
The Invisible Force of Direction

Signaling

Angier: *How To Stay Alive in the Woods*, ch. 19.
Angier: *Skills for Taming the Wilds*, ch. 22.
Angier: *Survival With Style*, ch. 14.
Cardwell: *America's Camping Book*, ch. 34.
Coggins, Jack: *Flashes and Flags: The Story of Signaling*. Dodd, Mead, 1963, $3.50.
Dalrymple: *Survival in the Outdoors*, ch. 11.
Merrill: *The Survival Handbook*, ch. 4.
Shockley and Fox: *Survival in the Wilds*, ch. 4.
Signaling (No. 3237). Boy Scouts, 1940, 56 pp., 45¢, paper.
Zim, Herbert S.: *Codes and Secret Writing*. Morrow, 1948, 154 pp., $3.94. (grades 5–9)

Chapter 23

Hiking, Trailing and Stalking

Figure 23–1 "Hush, Puppies!"

Afoot and light-hearted, I take to the open road,
Healthy, free, the world before me,
The long brown path before me, leading wherever
I choose.

—WALT WHITMAN*

Hiking is fun and almost everyone enjoys it, whether the purpose is reaching a certain destination, exploring a historical or otherwise interesting spot, or just taking a ramble like the bear's trip over the mountain "to see what he could see." It is also one of the best ways to get and keep in condition. The wise hiker wears clothing which is both comfortable and appropriate for the season, time, and place.

HIKING

CARE OF YOUR FEET

Have you ever thought about what the word "tenderfoot" means? Since each of your feet comes down and momentarily bears your weight about a thousand times each mile, they deserve maximum care and attention. Never start on a long hike without having gradually toughened yourself to it by a series of shorter hikes, wearing the shoes and socks you will wear on longer hikes.

Blisters result from friction between your shoes and skin, and they are much easier to prevent than to cure. Avoid wearing darned socks or ill-fitting or new shoes, and put a coating of moist soap on the backs of your heels and inside the heels of your socks and dust your feet and the insides of your socks with talcum or foot powder before you start out. At the first sign of redness or soreness, apply a piece of adhesive tape or moleskin (a thin layer of felt with an adhesive backing, available at drug stores) to absorb the friction and save your skin. However, you should never apply tape *after* a blister has formed. Keep your toenails fairly short and cut them straight across with rounded corners so they won't dig into your skin. If the scree shield on the top of your boot irritates the back of your heel, protect it with a piece of adhesive tape or moleskin or leave the top two holes of your boots unlaced until they are well broken in.

*From *Leaves of Grass*. Permission by Doubleday and Co., Inc.

FOOTWEAR

Nothing is so important to a serious hiker or backpacker as his footwear, for no matter how gay his smile and debonair his farewell, his mouth soon turns down and his enthusiasm wanes as that little hole in his sock or the mildly tight spot in his shoe brings him torture with each step. Soon he lags behind and reaps the displeasure of his companions.

Boots

Types. There are literally hundreds of brands and models of boots from which to choose, many imported from other countries in addition to those made in the United States. We include only a brief discussion here, but more detailed information can be found in the references listed at the end of this chapter.

Many hike in *tennis shoes* which may prove satisfactory for short jaunts over smooth trails with only a light load to carry, but continued use produces sore soles and possibly bruised or sprained ankles. High shoes which reach above the ankle with cleated or corrugated soles are recommended. Although tennis shoes may seem economical they really aren't in the long run, for a pair will last for only about a hundred miles of hiking. Although they provide no protection against moisture and quickly become soaked, they do dry out rapidly.

Well-fitting, sturdy *work shoes* with cleats or corrugated soles give more support and are satisfactory for light hiking over easy forest trails. Such shoes as *waffle stompers* and *campus boots* are light, comfortable, and easy to break in, but although they are currently popular for casual wear about town they prove quite unsatisfactory for serious hiking.

Trail shoes or *trail boots* (Fig. 23-2*B*) are tougher and stiffer and so are preferable for the hiker who follows longer trails or travels cross-country where he will occasionally have to cross running streams or rockslides. Their sturdy construction and thicker soles support the feet well, and they can be made quite water repellent. *Climbing boots* (Fig. 23-2*C*) are specialized boots with soles that are flush with the uppers to provide added security by allowing more foot contact with the climbing surface. A few hikers prefer them for general hiking but most want a thicker sole. *Mountaineer boots* (Fig. 23-2*D*) are heavier and more rugged and have thicker soles. Although they are too heavy and stiff for general hiking, they may be desirable for expeditions into heavy brush or where the user is likely to encounter rocks, ice, or snow. Although *moccasins* (Fig. 23-2*A*) are too light to give sufficient support for use on the trail, many people wear them when in a canoe or for a restful change after making camp. For sloshing around in wet areas, there are boots with rubber bottoms and leather tops.

Which Type For You? It is very important that you select a boot that is suited to the type of travel you will engage in and then see that the pair you buy is exactly fitted to your feet. Tell the clerk in the outfitting store exactly how you expect to use the boots and approximately what price you are willing to pay. Will you need special protection against sharp rocks, stinging insects, cold, snow, or desert sand? Will the toes need to be stiff enough to kick steps in snow and ice while climbing? Will you just be travelling along easy forest trails with only a light pack? As a general rule, the heavier the load, the heavier the boot should be; but choose the lightest shoe that will do the job, for it is estimated that each pound you carry on your foot is equivalent to 5 pounds carried on your back. Therefore, if your shoe weighs a mere pound over what is necessary, you are carrying the equivalent of an extra 10 pounds in your pack. That's a lot of

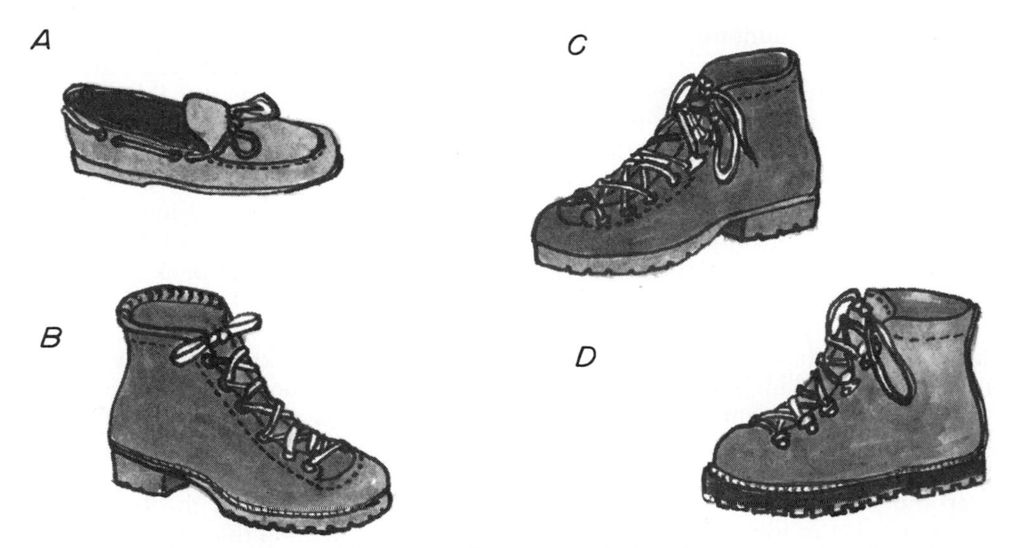

Figure 23-2 Some Types of Shoes. *A*, Moccasins; *B*, Trail Shoes; *C*, Climbing Boots; *D*, Mountaineer Boots.

wasted effort and can take the fun out of hiking. A fairly light, flexible shoe that fits comfortably and is reasonably priced will, for ordinary purposes, give all thc protection the average hiker needs. The important thing is to choose what's right for you and the situation.

Some Features. Leather uppers "breathe" and so are preferable for ventilation and can also be made quite water repellent. Some uppers are made with the smooth side of the leather out, but "rough outs," which can also be made water repellent, are becoming more popular because of their superior resistance to abrasion from rough surfaces and underbrush. Suede leather results when leather has been split, and although it is lighter than regular leather, it naturally will not hold up as well under rough usage. Lined and insulated boots are available for use in extremely cold weather.

Boots which lace to the toe can be tied tightly to keep the feet from sliding about unduly. Boots can lace with eyelets, rings (swivel eyelets), hooks, or a combination of these. Lacing and unlacing is faster with hooks, but they sometimes catch on underbrush or get broken or twisted, making them unusable; this is indeed unfortunate on a trip, but they can later be replaced at a boot repair shop. Leather laces stretch and loosen when wet and have been largely supplanted by nylon laces which wear well and, if made of soft-woven unwaxed material, will not be especially likely to come untied. To tie your shoestrings, moisten them and then pull one loop through the knot a second time before tightening it. This prevents the strings from coming untied along the trail, which can be dangerous as well as annoying.

Soles should be sufficiently thick and hard to protect the feet on rough terrain and are usually made of corrugated synthetic rubber which provides good traction. Vibram is the trade name of a popular type of sole, but beware lest they leave black scuff marks when worn on home floors. Although softer soles may hold more firmly, they offer little protection from rough surfaces and wear out rapidly. Leather soles are not at all satisfactory since they slip on the pine needles and wet surfaces commonly encountered on a trail.

Boots should have as few seams as possible because they are difficult to waterproof, and what seams there are should be double or triple stitched. Boots should reach just above the ankle to give good ankle support and protection from rough underbrush and outcroppings along the path. The average hiker will not want boots higher than this since they are hot, hard to put on and take off, and inclined to bunch and buckle around the ankle, irritating the Achilles tendon along the back of the heel. Some boots have a scree shield to keep out water, rocks, or snow, which is located at the top of the boot and is usually made of some type of elastic fabric. If your boots don't have one or if you want more extensive protection, gaiters are available to slip on as needed. These are waterproof fabric sleeves, usually about 7 to 9 inches high, which zipper closed around the ankle and are held down by a strap or thong which slips under your instep. The toes of your boots should be fairly firm to prevent injury to your toes when banging up against rocks.

Selecting the Proper Size. When trying on boots wear the two pairs of socks you expect to hike in. You will probably need a hiking shoe a size or a size and a half larger than your usual street shoe; this is because your feet spread out owing to the weight of your pack and the extra blood which accumulates as you hike along. In addition, the two pairs of socks, both heavier than those ordinarily worn, take up extra room. If your outfitter seems knowledgeable, solicit his help when making your selection. Since nearly everyone has one foot larger than the other, try the boot on this one first. Everyone's feet are different and shoes are made on different lasts and to different specifications, so you should try on many pairs in the search for one that feels exactly right for you.

Here are some tests for a proper fit. With the boot still unlaced, slide your foot as far forward as possible in it and try to slip one finger down behind your heel as far as the sole of the boot. It should fit snugly; if there is room for two fingers, the shoe is too big. Now kick the back of the heel against the floor to push your foot back in the boot and lace it tightly. There should now be enough room to curl your toes slightly. Do some knee bends; your foot should move about very little in the shoe. Have someone hold your foot down to the floor and try to move your foot sideways inside the boot; if much movement is possible, the boot is too loose. Walk around the store for several minutes with a shoe from each of two pairs on your feet. Remove the shoe which feels least comfortable and substitute another from a third pair; keep repeating this process until you finally locate the pair which feels most comfortable. If possible, try climbing up and down stairs or up and down an incline; this is the acid test for comfort. Some outfitters will let you borrow a pair of boots to wear indoors at home for several hours if you are careful not to scuff them up; other outfitters rent out boots, which is a good way to try out several models and sizes before making a final selection.

It is possible to buy boots by mail, if you are careful to follow the specific directions given by the outfitter for determining the correct size. Although this is probably not as satisfactory as being fitted in a shop, you can usually return them for a new selection if they don't fit.

Some people find that arch supports and/or one or more inner soles improve both fit and comfort.

Children's Boots. Getting good hiking boots for children is sometimes difficult. However, there are now strong work shoe and outing types available in shoe stores, and a few manufacturers now make regular hiking boots in children's sizes. One drawback to buying an expensive pair is that children's feet grow so rapidly that the shoes are likely to be outgrown before they are worn out. Some outfitters will allow a generous trade-in on a new pair if the old ones are still in good condition, and some camps, as well as outfitters, have found a solution by keeping an assortment on hand to rent out.

Breaking In Boots. In caring for boots, bear in mind that they are made of leather which has pores to "breathe" and so ventilate both foot and boot. In order to preserve this quality, strive for water repellency rather than waterproofing, which would necessitate actually plugging up the pores. Also, avoid applying anything which will stretch and soften the leather so that it no longer gives firm support. A new pair of boots needs an application of something to condition the leather and make it water repellent. Among the several good preparations available is one with a silicone dressing and wax base called Sno Seal. Warm it right in the container to liquefy it and use a brush or piece of cloth to paint it on the leather. Then rub it in vigorously with your fingers and work it in especially well around the seams and the welt, for these are the places where moisture tends to enter. Now put the boots on and go for a short walk about town or along an easy trail. Gradually increase the length of your walks as you continue to break in the boots. Some people advocate breaking in boots by soaking them in water and walking about in them until they are dry, but we do not recommend this because of the damage soaking does to the leather.

Boot Care. A good pair of boots represents a sizeable investment, but if properly cared for, they will serve you well for many years. Heat is probably the worst enemy of leather so never place your boots on a radiator, in the oven, or near a campfire, or leave them in the trunk of a car on a hot summer day. If they accidentally get wet, wipe them clean and stuff them with crumpled newspapers, then let them dry out gradually at room temperature. When dry, treat them with a good leather conditioner as previously described.

Occasionally during use, brush the dirt off your boots and use a small brush and a bit of saddle soap with a small amount of water to wash them; then apply a good conditioner. This keeps the leather from drying out and becoming stiff and also restores the water repellency.

Socks

It is customary to wear two pairs of socks when hiking; a heavy pair on the outside and thinner ones next to the foot. Socks absorb perspiration as well as moisture from the outside, cushion the feet, and minimize the blister-causing friction between boot and foot. A new "wick dry" sock is recommended for the inner pair; it claims to "wick" perspiration from the feet and is made of 50 per cent Orlon acrylic, 30 per cent wool, and 20 per cent nylon. An outer pair with padded soles made of approximately 33 per cent each of wool, cotton or Orlon, and nylon is recommended. A blend containing wool is superior because it stays cushiony and warm even when wet but it should be mixed with other fibers for longer wear. If your feet are sensitive to wool, wear a thin pair of part cotton socks underneath. Socks of 100 per cent nylon are too slippery, and those of 100 per cent cotton are not at all satisfactory since they absorb and hold perspiration and outside moisture and then feel clammy and cause blisters. Hiking socks should be a full size larger than those you ordinarily wear.

On a trip, carry several pairs of socks and change to fresh ones at rest stops or at noon, fastening the soiled pair to the outside of your pack to dry out as you go along. Wash out your soiled socks each night so that you have a fresh supply for the next day. Never wear darned socks or those with holes in them and avoid those with a rough texture which might prove irritating.

USING YOUR BODY

Relax your whole body and swing along rhythmically as you walk. Point your toes straight ahead (Indian style) or even slightly inward, but not out like a duck, which is fatiguing and hard on your arches. When you toe out, you shorten your stride by an inch or more; this amounts to several hundred extra steps on a 5 mile hike. Keep your body erect or, if carrying a pack, lean forward slightly from your hips to let the pack push you along. Glide along smoothly with a minimum of sideward and upward movement.

GENERAL HINTS

Do not make a hike a speed or endurance contest; what you do and see along the way is far more important than how far you go. Like a machine, your body works most efficiently at a moderate rate of speed, so strike a steady pace that you can maintain indefinitely, and rest five or ten minutes every hour or so on a long hike. Avoid staying immobile too long lest your leg and back muscles stiffen. Relax completely by sitting against a tree or lying flat on your back with feet propped up to let the blood which has collected in your legs and feet drain away.

Figure 23–3 Walk Like an Indian, Not a Duck.

Three miles an hour is a good speed for maintained hiking. If you really want to hurry, use the *Scout's pace,* which consists of dog trotting for about 50 paces, then walking the same number. This eats up the miles steadily and rapidly and allows you to cover a mile in 10 to 12 minutes without undue fatigue. Although swift Indian runners were said to cover 100 or more miles between dawn and dusk, 15 to 20 will usually be enough for the average hiker in an organized camp. Unless you are really trying to cover a certain distance in a limited time, its more fun to hike at a moderate pace, allowing time to stop and examine anything that looks interesting along the way.

A hiking staff (Fig. 24–5) about $1\frac{1}{2}$ inches around and 4 to 6 feet long is an invaluable companion when hiking. It almost becomes a third leg to prevent crippling falls while you're traveling over rough terrain or climbing up and down hills. You can also use it to push aside branches or thorns and to test the depth and footing in a creek you must cross. It can double as a snake stick if you choose one with an appropriate fork at the top (Fig. 19–11).

A good hiker never steps on anything, such as rocks or logs, which he can step over or go around and thus avoids undue fatigue and sprained ankles. Keep glancing ahead to spot possible hazards and pick your way carefully as you proceed, for you'll really handicap yourself and your companions if you injure yourself and can't continue under your own power. Hold aside low-hanging branches so they won't snap back into the face of the person following you and warn your

Figure 23-4 Don't Forget Your Third Leg.

companions of dangerous holes or other hazards along the way.

When hiking with campers, one counselor should head the line as a pacesetter, striking a moderate pace which all can maintain without undue hardship, and a second counselor should bring up the rear. The most successful hiking groups are composed of individuals of approximately the same age and physical stamina so that the strong do not have to wait for the slow or the latter overdo in an effort to keep up.

WHERE TO HIKE

The importance of providing hiking trails is increasingly being recognized on the city, state, and especially the national level, for over 120,000 miles of footpaths are provided in the national parks and forests alone. The most famous hiking trails are the two located at either side of the North American continent. In the East, the Appalachian Trail* extends over 2,000 miles from Mount Oglethorpe in Georgia to Mount Katahdin in Maine, passing through breathtaking panoramas in the Great Smoky, Blue Ridge, Allegheny, Catskill, Green, and White Mountains as well as the Berkshire Hills. The trail crosses 14 states, 8 national forests, 2 national parks, and 6 major rivers. Fireplaces and lean-tos are placed along the way and occasional offshoot trails lead down to villages where supplies can be replenished. The Appalachian Trail's western counterpart, the Pacific Crest Trail,** covers about 2,250 miles reaching from Canada down through Washington, Oregon, and California to Mexico, passing along the crests of the Cascade, Sierra Nevada, and Sierra Madre Mountains and crossing Yosemite and Sequoia Parks. It also provides fireplaces and lean-to shelters for foot travelers.

Of course, most of us in summer camp will have to find our adventure nearer to home. Stay off main highways whenever possible; country roads or cross-country hiking is safer and much more interesting, and the soft ground and grass of field and forest are less fatiguing to your feet.

If you must travel on a busy highway, divide into twos or threes and spread out in single file or walk not more than two abreast. Stay entirely off the pavement on the left side of the road so that you can see approaching traffic. Walking on a highway at night is particularly dangerous; avoid it except in an emergency and then wear something white or tie a white strip of cloth around your right thigh and carry a lighted lantern or flashlight to alert approaching vehicles. It is dangerous to walk along a railroad track and foolhardy as well as illegal to walk over a railroad trestle.

Hitchhiking is taboo. Not only is riding with strangers extremely dan-

*For more information write to the Appalachian Trail Conference, 1916 Sunderland Place NW, Washington, D. C. 20036.

**For more information write to the Regional Office, Pacific Crest Trail, 729 N.E. Oregon Street, Portland, Oregon 97208.

(Courtesy of Girl Scouts U.S.A.)

gerous, and even illegal in many states, but if you are a red-blooded camper you will want to be independent enough to go the whole way on your own two feet.

When hiking cross-country show due respect for the property of others. Every stick, stone, flower, and fruit tree is someone's property and he may feel about it like the old farmer who said of his wife, "She ain't much, but she's mine!" Respect *No Trespassing* signs; they likely have been put up because of damage done by previous travelers and may be assumed to mean just what they say. Close gates behind you if you found them that way and avoid climbing fences, for it is easy to break them down and do permanent damage. If it is absolutely necessary to climb a fence, do so next to a post where you will cause the least damage and carefully repair any you may have done. Do not walk across cultivated fields but stay close to the edges where no crops have been planted. Pick fruit or flowers only when given express permission to do so.

Fasten a small plastic bag to your waist and stow candy wrappers or bits of debris in it to carry back with you.

PROTECT YOURSELF

Remaining in perspiration-soaked clothing is just as dangerous as staying in rain-soaked clothing insofar as bringing on a cold is concerned. When on a trip of any length, always carry a change of clothing with you and slip into it immediately if you get wet. This applies particularly to wearing wet socks and shoes, for, in addition to inviting colds, they will make your feet sore and tender. If no change is possible, stop to build a fire and dry out thoroughly before proceeding.

THIRST

Thirst is often due to a drying out of the tissues lining your mouth rather than to general dehydration, and consequently this kind of thirst is best relieved by merely rinsing your mouth instead of gulping down large quantities of liquid. If you have been perspiring freely, however, you will need to replace the salt, as well as the fluid, your body has lost, so add some extra salt to your food or put a little in your drinking water. Eating candy bars along the way will make you thirsty, so munch on raisins or other dry fruit or suck on a fruit pit, a piece of hard candy, or a clean pebble instead.

Vigorous hiking soon uses up the fuel readily available in the blood stream, so it is a good idea to take along a snack, such as a plastic bag of "bird seed,"* to eat along the trail. Carry your own canteen of water unless you know there are safe sources on the way. You can refill it at a suitable stream, and by dropping in a purification tablet, you can purify your water as you hike. (See Chapter 31 for details on purifying water.)

*Make "bird seed" by mixing together unsalted peanuts, raisins, small candies, and sugared cereal.

MAKE THE MILES FLY

Think of interesting things to do to make the miles go faster. A continuous round-robin story with each person being unexpectedly called upon to take up the story at a given signal, singing merry hiking songs, marching in strict "military fashion" for variation, and playing hiking games serve this purpose. Sing sweetly and talk quietly; don't annoy others by loud, boisterous conduct.

HIKE VARIATIONS

Even old, familiar trails take on a new glamor when there is a definite purpose for following them. Have a certain objective in mind but do not be in such a hurry that you haven't time

Figure 23-5 Carry a Small Bag to Put Your Trash In.

(Courtesy of Cheley Colorado Camps, Estes Park, Colorado.)

to stop for the unusual. Here are some possible types of hikes:

1. *Orienteering and Map and Compass Hikes.* (These are discussed in Chapter 22.)

2. *Heads and Tails Hike.* Flip a coin at each fork in the road to determine whether to turn right or left.

3. *Carefree Hike.* Hike to some interesting or beautiful spot to cook an outdoor meal, hold a program, sing, or play nature games.

4. *Breakfast Hike.* Go to a good vantage point to watch the sun rise and cook breakfast. Start at daybreak if you want to see and hear the birds at their best.

5. *Star Hike.* Go to a hill on a clear evening to study the stars and their legends. Take blanket rolls or sleeping bags and plan to stay overnight.

6. *Fishing Trip.* Hike out to fish in a nearby stream or lake. Take a lunch to supplement the fresh fish you *hope* to catch.

7. *Historical Hike.* Brief yourself by reading and consulting others about nearby historical spots, then hike out to visit them.

8. *Moonlight Hike.* Go out to note nature's completely different night life.

9. *Camera Hike.* See who can snap the most interesting photographs along the way.

10. *Nature Hike.* Give each hiker a list of nature specimens (flowers, trees, animals, or insects) to collect or identify, or see who can collect the most interesting pieces of driftwood, sea shells, or other items to use in the craft shop or add to the nature display.

11. *Rain Hike.* Waterproof yourselves completely and splash along, watching how animals and plants behave in the rain.

12. *Creek's or River's End Hike.* Follow a creek or river to its origin or mouth.

13. *Overnight Hike.* Find a good place to spend the night; cook breakfast and return to camp.

14. *Sealed Orders Hike.* Give the group a set of sealed directions with a new one to open at each spot along the way or distribute them along the route so the group will find a new one as soon as they have successfully followed the old. Give instructions in compass points and distances such as "Go 50 paces at 75° and look under the three rocks piled below the big pin oak tree; then go straight E and look inside the big hollow oak tree off at the left." For variety, give clues in rhymes, riddles, or codes. Make the clues challenging but not so difficult as to discourage the campers. A group is best limited to five or six.

15. *Trail Clearing Hike.* Find and clear a new trail and establish an outpost camp at the end. Do as little damage as possible in making the trail passable.

16. *Hare and Hound-Hike.* The "hares" lay a trail (see p. 400 for methods) and conceal themselves at intervals within 50 feet of the trail. The "hounds" then follow and try to spot the hares. If a hare can escape being seen until all the hounds have passed him, he gets in free. Use small groups and make the hounds stay on the trail.

17. *Hold the Front.* The participants draw for positions in line and arrange themselves in single file. The object is to get and maintain the head position. As they hike along, the counselor picks out some nature specimen and asks the head player to identify it. If he can, he keeps his place; if not, each person behind him is in turn given a chance to try. The first to succeed advances to the head of the line. The counselor then asks a question of the person behind the one who has just advanced and the question is repeated down the line as before until someone answers it correctly and advances up ahead of the one who first missed it. The winner is the person at the head of the line when the game ends.

18. *Roadside Cribbage.* Give each player 10 to 20 counters (acorns, pebbles, or such) and pass out duplicate lists of objects, such as specific kinds of birds, trees, or flowers. As they hike along, each looks for the specified objects and the first to see one calls "pegs" and drops one of his counters. The object is to be the first to dispose of all his counters. If someone doubts that the one who called "pegs" really saw the object, he may challenge him; if he can prove he was right; he may give the challenger one of his counters; if not, he must retrieve his own counter and also accept one from the challenger.

19. *Hike to Another Camp.* This is done, of course, only by invitation or previous arrangement.

20. *Bus or Camp Truck Hike.* Ride out by bus or camp truck and hike back or let the vehicle meet you at the halfway point on your return. This gives you a chance to venture farther from camp.

21. *Conservation Hike.* Hike out to discover examples of poor conservation such as erosion and, if feasible, plan to return to take corrective measures.

22. *"What Is It?" Hike.* Give each member a list of objects he might see along the way, such as a particular kind of bird, tree, moss, or flower. Assign points to each object according to its

Figure 23-6 Take a Pedometer to Measure Miles.

rarity. The hiker who first sees and correctly identifies an item on the list scores the allotted points for himself or his team. Penalize him in points if his identification is incorrect.

No matter what kind of a hike you take, do not let it degenerate into a prosaic walk or you will have a group of bored, disgruntled campers on your hands. With young children, cloak every hike in an aura of glamor and adventure by encouraging them to pretend to be a band of giants, little elves, colorful gypsies, or bold, swaggering pirates. Whatever their realm of fancy, it is much more fun to hike in the land of "let's pretend." You must, of course, adapt your methods to the age of the group. *Plan* your hike, no matter how short it is. Meet as a group to decide where to go, what to do, what to wear and what equipment to take, how to pack it and how to divide up the jobs on the way and at your destination. Return by a different route if you can. Take along a pedometer (see p. 387) to learn how many miles you hike.

Be on the lookout for interesting places you may want to come back to for a cookout, an overnight hike, or to make an outpost camp. Perhaps you may spot a new source of clay for your pottery kiln, some tall reeds just right for basket weaving, or a high hill ideal for a supper cookout and an overnight bivouac to study stars.

TRACKING AND STALKING

Have you ever seen a whippoorwill sitting lengthwise on a closely matching branch in an effort to make you think he is merely the stub of a rotten limb or seen a possum feigning death in hopes you'll pass him by with only a casual glance? To see such interesting episodes of nature, you must train your five senses to be alert. Learn to move quietly and inconspicuously, for nearly all animals and birds are exceedingly timid and, if you disturb them, they will be gone to the four winds without so much as letting you catch sight of them. If hiking with others, work out signals such as a finger on lips for "freeze where you are" or a beckoning hand for "come closer."

Practice to sharpen your powers of observation. A good game for this purpose is called *Kim's Game*. Group 20 or more objects on a table or have pictures of them mounted on a poster. Let each participant study the array for one minute, then have him turn his back and write down as many as he can remember; score one point for each item named correctly and deduct one for any omitted.

HOW TO TRACK AND STALK

It's great fun to be able to trail some animal through woods or fields and, if the trail is hot, you may be able to creep up close and watch him as he goes about his daily activities. You'll need to become skilled to follow tracks, so start out by studying human tracks along a sandy beach or the edge of a river or lake where they are easy to see. Learn to distinguish whether the person was walking, running, carrying a heavy object, or perhaps even walking backward to fool you. Learn to estimate how fresh the tracks are; those newly made will have sharp edges and no debris will yet have blown into them.

Now try your hand at studying bird or animal tracks, learning to identify them from some of the good source books available. Do not keep your eyes glued down at your feet, but glance ahead for such traces as droppings, bits of hair left on bushes, signs of feeding, or places where branches were displaced or the undersides of leaves turned upward. This lets you follow more rapidly so that you have a better chance of catching up with your quarry. If you lose the trail, mark the last spot where you were sure you were on it and investigate in ever widening spirals until you pick it up again.

Getting near an animal without letting it become aware of you is called *stalking,* and it requires a great deal of ingenuity and skill, for animals have very highly developed senses of smell and hearing (and sometimes sight) and will quickly flee for parts unknown at the least sign of an intruder. Learn to move slowly and silently and avoid stepping on dry twigs which may snap like the crack of a rifle. Be ready to "freeze" if the animal looks your way. Step toe first on grass, heel first on hard ground.

You may want to camouflage yourself so you blend in with the surrounding terrain. Avoid bright colors and belt buckles or other metal which might reflect. Conceal your face with a mask of green branches. Since most animals have a keen sense of smell, approach them by moving *into* the wind, even though it may force you to make a full half-circle.

Conceal yourself behind such natural hiding places as bushes, large

Figure 23–7 Poor Little Innocent!

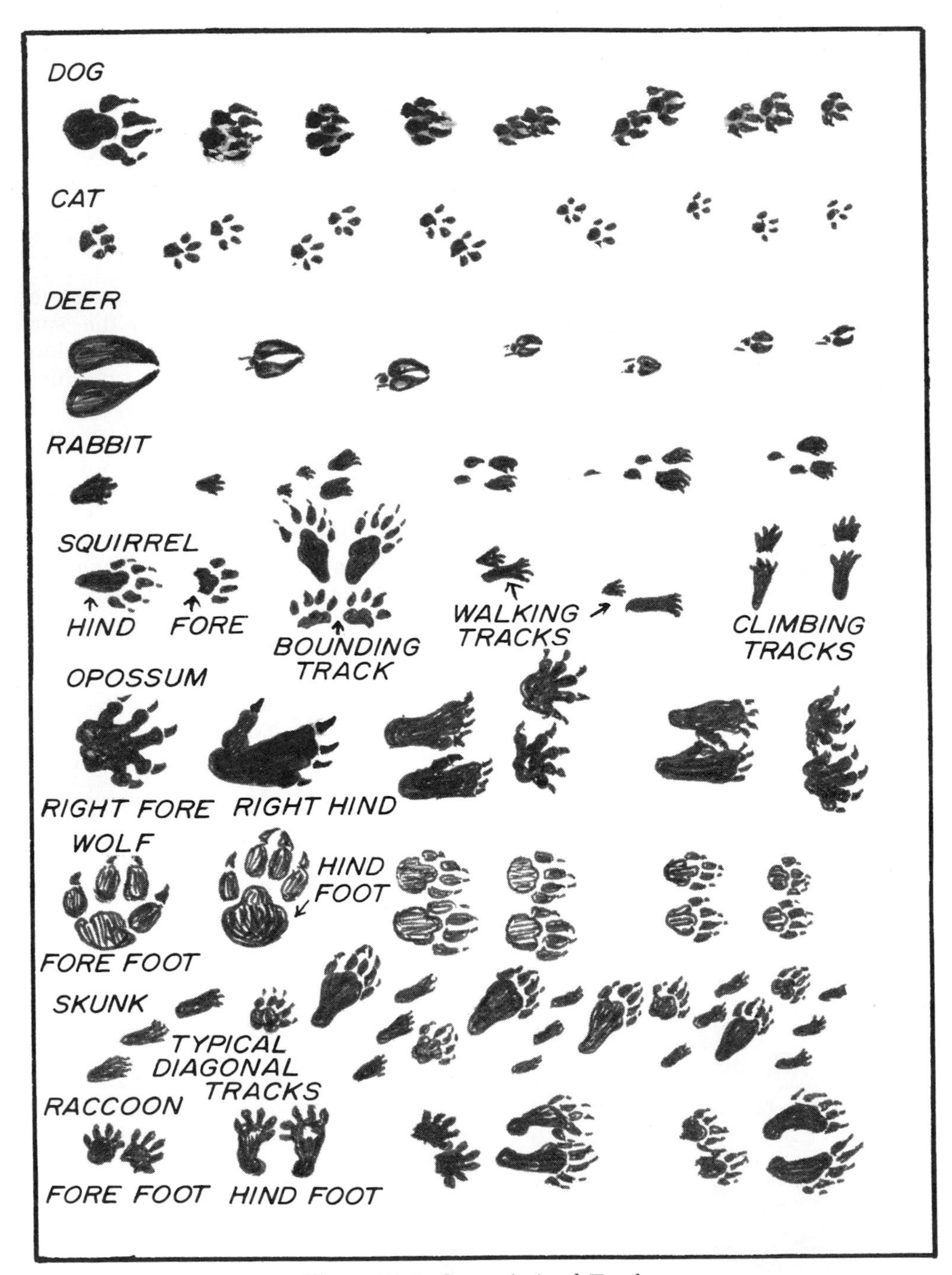

Figure 23-8 Some Animal Tracks.

rocks, and trees. Stay low to avoid being silhouetted against the sky; stoop down, go on all fours, or even wriggle along on your stomach if necessary. Quick movements draw attention so avoid them unless you are sure the animal is looking in another direction. Wild animals must maintain a constant watch for their natural enemies since their very lives depend on it; hence, through instinct and practice they have developed an uncanny wariness and ability to detect the unusual, and *you* are definitely "unusual" in their forest home. You will need infinite patience and skill to study wildlife intimately and to get good close-up photographs but it will be well worth the effort.

TRACKING AND STALKING GAMES

Trail the Deer. A leader, wearing shoes with a peculiar heel plate or arrangement of brads, starts out ahead while the others try to follow his trail. To make your tracks unique, you can insert hob nails or upholstery nails into rubber heels, then remove them later without damage to your shoes.

Deer Stalking. One player, the "deer," places himself in an environment that has some covering such as grass, bushes, or trees. The others scatter out about 100 yards away and each then tries to approach the "deer" without being seen. Anyone seen well enough to be identified is eliminated and the one nearest the "deer" at the end of a designated time wins and becomes the "deer" for the next game.

Freeze. "It" is in front of the others who are lined up about 100 feet away. He turns his back and counts to ten while they move toward him as rapidly as possible. At the end of the count, he shouts "freeze" and quickly turns around and calls out the name of any person he sees making the slightest motion. That person must return to the starting line. The first person to touch "it" or cross the finish line wins and becomes the new "it."

Sleeping Rabbit. "It" sits with his eyes closed while the others gather around in a circle. The leader points to one player who tries to sneak up to "it" and touch him without being detected. If "it" hears him and points directly to him, he must return to his place. Anyone able to come in and touch "it" without being detected becomes the new "it."

Capture the Flag. The field is divided into two halves with a center line marked across it. Each team occupies its own half of the area and has its own flag erected 100 to 200 yards behind the center line. The object of the game is to enter your opponents' half of the field, capture their flag, and return to your own half without being tagged. Any person tagged in enemy territory is "caught" and must remain in prison, an area off at one side about 20 to 30 yards in back of the center line. To "catch" a player, it is necessary to hold him long enough to pat him three times on the back. (If this proves too rough; rule that his opponent need only touch him once.) A prisoner can be released by having a teammate touch him while he is still in prison and both of them can then return home "free." Each team may choose players to act as color guards; they must stay outside of a circle drawn 25 steps around the flag unless they are pursuing an opponent who has entered it. Set a time limit, such as a half hour, and if neither team has captured the other's flag by then, the winner is the team with the most prisoners.

A variation is to widen the area and include trees, rocks, bushes, and natural hiding places which players may use to conceal themselves while approaching to capture the flag or release prisoners. The time may be extended to hours or even a half day without having the players lose interest. Choosing a good terrain is the secret of success in this game.

ADDITIONAL READINGS

(For an explanation of abbreviations and abbreviated forms used, see page 25.)

Footwear

Angier: *Home In Your Pack*, pp. 80–90.
Bridge: *America's Backpacking Book*, ch. 8.
Cardwell: *America's Camping Book*, pp. 94–97.
Colwell: *Introduction to Backpacking*, ch. 4.
Fletcher: *The Complete Walker*, pp. 26–37.
Learn and Tallman: *Backpacker's Digest*, ch. 2.
Manning: *Backpacking One Step At A Time*, ch. 8.
Merrill: *The Hiker's and Backpacker's Handbook*, ch. 7.
Rethmel: *Backpacking*, pp. 3-3 to 3-7.
Riviere: *Backcountry Camping*, pp. 110–117.
Wood: *Pleasure Packing*, ch. 2.

MAGAZINE ARTICLES

Backpacker-4, Winter, 1973:
Barker, James: "Bootery Snobbery." pp. 65–67.
Masia, Seth: "You and Your Gear—Breaking in Boots." p. 16.
"The Best of the Boots." pp. 49–72.

Camping Journal:
"Boots and Rainwear." Feb., 1973. ('73 Buyers' Guide)

Wilderness Camping:
Wood, Robert S.: "Pleasure Packing—Buying Boots." May–June, 1973, p. 12.

Hiking

Angier: *Home in Your Pack*, chs. 1, 8.
Angier: *Skills for Taming the Wilds*, ch. 1.
Berger: *Program Activities for Camps*, pp. 88–92.
Boy Scout Handbook, pp. 191–203.
Bridge: *America's Backpacking Book*, chs. 1, 4, 17.
Cardwell: *America's Camping Book*, ch. 42.
Corbin: *Recreation Leadership*, ch. 25.
Fieldbook for Boys and Men, ch. 2.
Fletcher: *The Complete Walker*, pp. 3–13, 37–52.
Kujoth: *The Recreation Program Guide*, pp. 144–160.
Langer: *The Joy of Camping*, pp. 186–191.
Macfarlan: *The Boy's Book of Hiking*.
Manning: *Backpacking One Step at a Time*, chs. 1, 17.
Musselman, Virginia: *Learning About Nature Through Games*. Stackpole, 1967, 128 pp., $3.95, ch. 13.
Ormond: *Complete Book of Outdoor Lore*, ch. 1.
Ormond: *Outdoorsman's Handbook*, part 5.
Rutstrum: *New Way of the Wilderness*.
Sussman, Aaron, and Ruth Goode: *The Magic of Walking*. Simon and Schuster, 1969, 410 pp., $7.50; $2.95, paper.
Whelen and Angier: *On Your Own in the Wilderness*, ch. 3.
Winnett: *Backpacking for Fun*, ch. 6.
Wood: *Pleasure Packing*, ch. 9.

MAGAZINE ARTICLES

Backpacker-5, Spring, 1974:
Nordstrom, Frank: "Shaping Up." p. 61.
Camping Journal:
Bates, Oren: "Turn Your Toes In." Mar., 1967, p. 48.
Wilderness Camping:
Ross, Robert N.: "The Mechanics of Walking." May–June, 1973, p. 28.
Ross, Robert N.: "The Walking Stick." Mar.-Apr., 1973, p. 30.

Tracking and Stalking

Fieldbook for Boys and Men, pp. 470–479.
Jaeger, Ellsworth: *Tracks and Trail Craft*. Macmillan, 1948, 381 pp., $5.95.
Langer: *The Joy of Camping*, pp. 271–277.
Murie, Olaus J.: *A Field Guide to Animal Tracks*. Houghton Mifflin, 1954, 374 pp., $5.95.
Ormond: *Complete Book of Outdoor Lore*, pp. 345–481.
Pocket Guide to Animal Tracks. Stackpole, 1958, 96 pp., $2.95.
Seton, Ernest Thompson: *Animal Tracks and Hunter Signs*. Doubleday, 1958, 160 pp., $5.95.

MAGAZINE ARTICLES

"Animal Tracks." May, 1967, p. 69.

Where to Go

Bridge: *America's Backpacking Book*, ch. 25.
Fletcher: *The Complete Walker*, Appendix III. (Organizations that promote walking)
Kujoth: *The Recreation Program Guide*, pp. 160–164.
Learn and Tallman: *Backpacker's Digest*, ch. 20.
Macfarlan: *The Boy's Book of Hiking*, chs. 1, 3.
Ryback, Eric and Tim: *The Ultimate Journey: Canada to Mexico Down the Continental Divide*. Chronicle Books, San Francisco, 1973, 207 pp., $7.95.

MAGAZINE ARTICLES

Readers' Digest:
Farney, Dennis: "Walk the Wild Appalachian Trail." Oct., 1972, p. 208.

Chapter 24

Using Knife, Axe and Other Tools

Figure 24-1 Ouch! Or Words to that Effect!

The Yankee boy, before he's sent to school,
Well knows the mysteries of that magic tool,
The pocket-knife. To that his wistful eye
Turns while he hears his mother's lullaby;
His hoarded cents he gladly gives to get it,
Then leaves no stone unturned till he can whet
it;
And in the education of the lad
No little part that implement hath had.
His pocket-knife to the young whittler brings
A growing knowledge of material things.

—John Pierpont

THE CAMP KNIFE

The knife, along with the gun and axe, was an important tool of the pioneer, and the modern camper engaged in campcrafts finds it equally important. It is useful for performing many camp kitchen chores and for making utilitarian items, such as fuzz sticks to start a stubborn fire and handy gadgets to use around the campsite, and decorative articles, such as totem poles and lapel pins. Young children may lack the hand-eye coordination necessary to use a knife skillfully and safely, but older girls and boys (age 11 and and up) soon become quite adept with it when taught carefully and enthusiastically. All of us have been dismayed upon seeing initials and other designs carved in public places, but they do bear mute testimony to the fascination which using a knife holds; therefore, in camp, let us concentrate on teaching youngsters to channel this seemingly irresistible impulse into constructive rather than destructive uses.

SELECTING A KNIFE

A knife with multi-purpose blades, such as a Boy or Girl Scout knife, is usually best for general camp use. It will probably have a cutting blade, a combination screwdriver and bottle-cap opener, an awl or reamer for making holes in leather and other materials, and a can opener (Fig. 24-2). Choose a sturdy model that fits well in your hand. It should have a slightly rough handle to enable you to grip it firmly, but too much roughness may cause blisters. A bright-colored handle makes it easier to find if you mislay it or drop it in the duff on the ground.

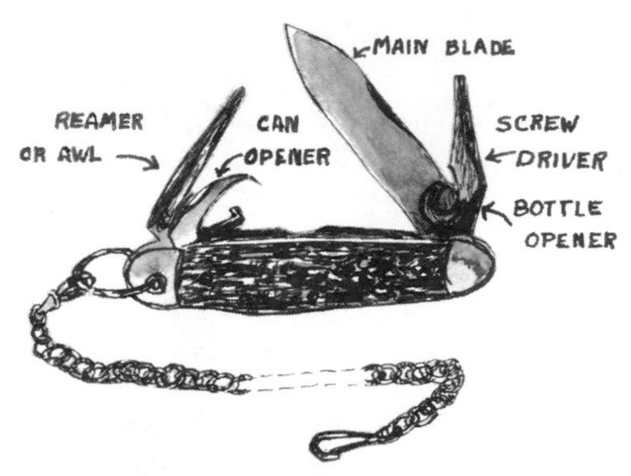

Figure 24–2 A Camp Knife.

Trying to economize on a knife will prove to be poor economy in the long run, since a cheap one is likely to be poorly constructed with a blade composed of such soft material that it won't hold a sharp edge. A blade of good quality carbon steel is best; avoid stainless steel for you can't sharpen it to a keen edge and it won't even hold what little edge you do get.

CARING FOR YOUR KNIFE

Treat your knife like the high-class tool it is. Wipe the blade off after each use and never put it away wet. Remove any rust or stains with fine steel wool, scouring powder, or dampened ashes from your campfire, and occasionally put a drop of oil on the spring and blade joints. When storing it for any length of time, protect the blade by applying a coating of oil or petroleum jelly. Never carelessly leave a knife lying about; stow it away in a safe place or keep it in your pocket, anchored to your belt or pants by a chain, leather thong, or strong cord long enough to permit you to use it without detaching it.

Don't use your knife to stir hot food or to poke around in the fire, for heating the blade excessively destroys its *temper* so that it will never again hold a sharp edge. On a cold day, hold the blade in your hands for a few moments to warm it, for an extremely cold blade chips easily. The *reamer* on your knife should be kept sharp.

OPENING AND CLOSING YOUR KNIFE

To open the blade, hold the knife in your left hand, insert your right thumbnail in the notch in the blade, and pull it open. Never allow the fingers of your left hand to rest across the blade slot at any time lest the strong spring snap the blade shut on them with disastrous results. To close the blade, again hold the knife in your left hand and push the back of the blade with your right, being careful, of course, not to place your fingers across the blade slot.

If the blade of a new knife seems stiff and hard to open, apply a few drops of lubricating oil to the spring and use a metal pry to open and close it several times; it will loosen up with continued use.

SHARPENING YOUR KNIFE

Manufacturers sometimes leave a knife blade dull so the new owner can sharpen it to suit his own particular taste. For general camp use, extend the *bevel* or sharpened area back only a short distance. If thinned back too far, the blade will be weakened and may chip. If left too rounded, it will be dull. A sharp blade cuts fast and clean and with less effort. It is also much safer, since it bites into the wood instead of sliding off and possibly cutting you or a bystander.

When a knife has been neglected and is quite dull, use a file or hand-turned grindstone to rough-shape it. Avoid using a power grindstone unless you are quite experienced, for when improperly used, it cuts away too rapidly, overheating the blade and spoiling its temper and thus damaging it permanently. If you get a nick in the blade, use a file or hand grindstone to cut down the whole edge even with the nick before you try to put a sharp edge on it.

Use an *oilstone* or *carborundum stone* (*whetstone*) for the fine edge. The latter is more convenient since you use water instead of oil to lubricate it to reduce friction and avoid overheating the blade. These stones usually have a coarse side for preliminary fast grinding and a fine one for putting on the finishing touches (*honing* the blade).

If you use a rectangular stone, hold it in your left hand and keep it well lubricated with water or oil. With the knife in your right hand, turn the edge of the blade away from you and elevate the back slightly (about 20°). Using a circular motion, draw the edge of the blade toward you across the stone. Reverse the blade and repeat on the other side, always drawing the blade away from the edge. Continue alternating sides until the blade is sharp. When using a round stone, hold the knife steady and move the stone across the blade with the same circular motion. Now finish by stroking each side of the blade a few times on a piece of leather such as an old belt or leather shoe sole. This removes the *wire edge* or hooked roughness left by the stone.

Test the sharpness of your blade by trying to cut a sheet of paper held between your thumb and forefinger. If the blade is really sharp, it will sever the paper cleanly and easily. If not, repeat the whole sharpening process. You may have to practice a long time before you learn to do a good job in a minimum of time.

Keep your knife in good condition by giving it a few strokes on the fine side of the sharpening stone and on a piece of leather after each use. If you do this, you should never have to use the file or coarse side of the carborundum again, unless you are so unfortunate as to get a nick in the blade. A good camper takes pride in always keeping his knife sharp and observes the unwritten camper law of never lending or borrowing a knife.

USING YOUR KNIFE

Practice whittling on a bar of soap (save the shavings to use later) or a piece of soft wood such as basswood or white pine. Remember that a knife is potentially very dangerous and should never be used carelessly. Always direct your strokes so that you can't possibly cut yourself or anyone else if your knife should slip. Keep your thumb and fingers around the handle, never on the back of the blade where they would close the blade on your fingers if your knife should slide off what you are cutting. Although expert whittlers sometimes violate this rule when doing intricate work, their skill and long practice have given them skill and control which a novice does not possess.

Cut with a sliding stroke *straight* down the wood and away from you; never use diagonal strokes which may carry the blade off the wood to cut you. Take your time, work slowly and deliberately, and pride yourself on being a safety rather than a speed artist. Haste, carelessness, and overconfidence result in accidents.

If you notice that your fingers are becoming red or sore, apply a piece of adhesive tape, an adhesive bandage, or a leather fingerstall to prevent further irritation which would eventually result in a blister.

Close your knife whenever you move about, even for a few steps; serious accidents have occurred from tripping while carrying an open knife. When passing a knife to someone else, close it or hand it to them handle first.

After some preliminary practice,

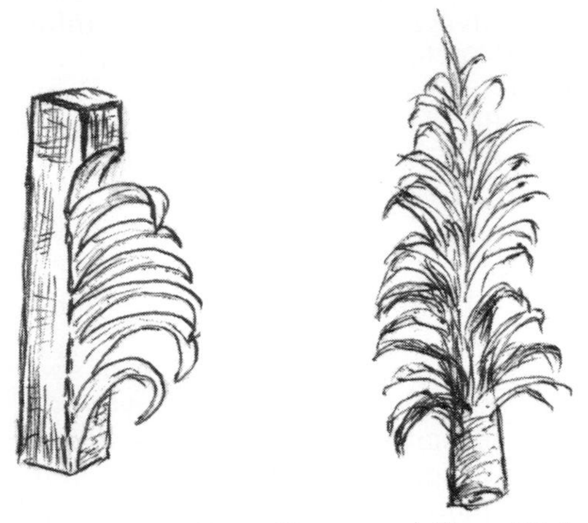

Figure 24-3 Fuzz Clump and Fuzz Stick.

you will be ready to try making such simple, utilitarian items as fuzz clumps and fuzz sticks (Fig. 24-3). These not only provide good practice in using your knife, but also prove quite useful for starting wood fires with damp wood or when there is a scarcity of kindling. As soon as you can turn out specimens with fine, closely spaced "curls," making each just as long as possible without severing it from the stick, you will know that you have really progressed.

WOOD CARVING

GENERAL PROCEDURES

Although advanced whittlers often use such specialized tools as crooked knives, chisels, gouges, special wood-carving knives, jigsaws, coping saws, and eggbeater drills, it is surprising what you can do with an ordinary pocketknife. There are many simple items you can make if you have patience and an average amount of skill.

Many kinds of wood are suitable for carving, but some are better than others. White pine, oak, white ash, white or yellow poplar, red cedar, basswood, butternut, maple, and holly are all recommended, and prunings from such fruit trees as cherry and apple are also good. Choose a well-seasoned piece which has dried for at least a year. If you look carefully, you should be able to find suitable pieces in any wooded area, in the scrap lumber around a building site, or in the odds and ends that carpenters and cabinetmakers collect. If you want an especially fine piece, go to a lumberyard or hobby shop.

Wood for whittling should be straight-grained, fine-textured, and soft enough to cut well, yet with enough "body" to hold together. It should be free from knots and should split straight and smooth ahead of your knife, but not farther than you want it to. Avoid brittle woods and those which will not hold together after large sections have been cut away. Porous woods are usually too coarse-grained for good whittling.

If the piece is much larger than you need, rough-shape it to size with your axe or saw. Use your knife slowly and patiently, for it is very discouraging to make a careless or hasty miscut which completely ruins the result of many laborious hours.

THINGS TO MAKE

Campers and staff members often wear name tags during the first few days of a camp session to help everyone to connect names with faces. The "woodsy" way to make them is to use a small twig or scrap of wood about 2 to $2\frac{1}{2}$ inches long and as big around as your index finger (Fig. 24-4). Use your knife to flatten the wood on one side and then sandpaper it smooth. Print your name or nickname on it with India ink, burn it in with a wood-burning pen, or carve away around it to make it stand out in relief. You can also paint or stain the letters to make them stand out. Gouge out a small groove above center on the back and use tape, plastic wood, or epoxy or household cement to anchor a safety pin in it. Apply a thin coat of wax to the whole pin or rub it well with clean hands until the oil from your skin permeates it; you will find that rubbing your fingers over your nose gives you an especially generous supply of body oil.

Make pins or buttons by using a small saw to cut off thin, cross-section slices from a piece of hard wood that has an interesting grain. Shape them as you wish with your knife and use a small drill to make holes in them or drive a nail through them. Finish them as described later in this chapter.

A hiking staff (Fig. 24–5) is handy to have when traveling over rough or hilly country. Choose a fairly straight, sturdy stick about chest high and an inch or more in diameter. Carve your initials with bark carving (described later in this chapter) and work out special designs to give it personality and make it uniquely your own. It will become dearer to you each time you use it on some pleasant expedition, and you will find it a real help when making your way over difficult terrain.

Make clothes pegs (Fig. 24–6) and lash them to trees or tent poles or fit them into holes bored in dead wood (never a live tree), fastening them in with plastic wood or glue. Many other

Figure 24–4 Try Your Skill at These.

Figure 24–5 A Good "Ole" Hiking Staff.

whittling projects are described elsewhere in this book, and it is even more fun to be original and think up your own.

To get your campers whittling, start some project of your own and casually pursue it at odd moments as during rest hour or while listening to someone read aloud or tell a story. They'll soon get the fever and you'll all be having fun together while producing useful gadgets for camp life or souvenirs to take home.

CARVING TOTEM POLES

Indian totem poles (Figs. 24–7 and 24–8) are fun to make and can vary from large ones to miniatures only a

Figure 24–6 Clothes Pegs.

Figure 24-7 Some Totem Poles.

Figure 24–8 Another Totem Pole.

few inches to a foot or two in height. Carefully lay out the design (including the colors) on paper and then transfer it to your piece of wood. Rough-shape it with large tools and then usc your knife to cut it to shape. To impart a true Indian flavor, avoid intricate detail and don't strive for perfection, for Indian totems were merely rough outlines with the refinements left to the imagination. Glue on such protruding parts as tails and beaks and use paint or enamel to bring out details or use native stains as the Indians did.

FINISHING WOODEN ARTICLES

There are many ways to finish a wooden article. Skillful, experienced whittlers can produce what they want with a minimum of sharp, decisive strokes and often leave their stroke marks showing. As a beginner, however, you may prefer to hide your more inaccurate and indefinite strokes by sanding the surface smooth. Use steel wool or progressively finer sandpaper if you want a velvety smooth surface. When sandpapering a round object, wrap the sandpaper around it to distribute the pressurc evenly over a large area instead of gouging into the wood. Use a whisk broom to remove clinging bits of sand or steel wool that might get onto your skin or remain on the wood where they would interfere with your finishing process.

The modern trend is to retain the natural color of the wood, applying substances only to protect it from moisture and wear or to enhance and bring out the natural beauty of the grain. A soft, velvety glow is preferable to a high sheen.

WAYS TO APPLY A DESIGN

1. Burn the design in with a wood-burning set.

2. Incise the design by cutting it out with a knife or special carving tools, or cut away around it to leave it standing out in relief.

Figure 24-9 Book Ends.

3. Decorate the object with chip carving or inlays.

4. Carve the design out of other types of wood or other materials and glue it on.

5. Use the Indian method to smoke on a design. Rub the object well with grease and hold it over the fire until it becomes dark brown. Then, while it is still warm, burnish it vigorously with a cloth. Now gouge out your design so that it stands out in a pleasing white contrast. You can achieve a similar effect by cutting out the design in adhesive tape and applying it to the wood, then smoking the whole thing. (The tape acts as a mask, leaving the design standing out in the original wood color when you remove it.) To get a dark design on a light background, cut away the bark around the design and smoke the whole thing. When you remove the remaining bark, the design will stand out dark against a light background.

6. Use bark carving, which is best done in the summer or fall when the bark is less inclined to peel off. Cut the bark away around the design or cut the design into the bark (incise it) and apply a coat or two of clear varnish to help anchor the remaining bark to the wood.

METHODS TO ENRICH AND PROTECT YOUR WOODCARVING

Here, too, there are many methods from which to choose, and you may want to experiment with several on pieces of scrap wood before making a final choice. Here are some possibilities:

1. Smooth on melted white candle wax or paraffin with a brush or apply a coat or two of good furniture polish with a cloth, using a circular motion to rub it in well. Allow each coat to dry thoroughly before putting on the next. For a tinge of color, melt colored candles or use wax crayons. These methods will protect the wood, preserve its beauty, and impart a sheen. To melt paraffin, cut it into fine slivers, put them in an old tin can, and place the can in a container of water boiling over a fire. Watch it carefully and take it off the heat as soon as it is melted. Handle it with extreme care for hot paraffin can cause severe and painful burns.

2. Rub in beeswax with the palm of your hand (your body heat causes it to go on properly). You can also mix the beeswax with turpentine or a bit of liquid furniture polish.

3. Use a coat or two of boiled linseed oil, followed by one or two coats of wax, rubbed in well. Although oil will alter the color of the wood to some degree, it helps to preserve it and also imparts a slight polish.

4. Apply one or two coats of white shellac, mixed with an equal volume of alcohol. When using any type of shellac, varnish, lacquer, or paint, you will get better results if you apply several *thin* coats rather than one thick one. Let

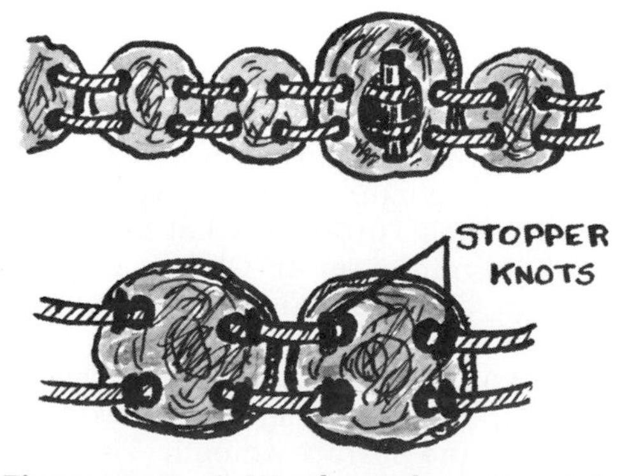

Figure 24-10 A Wooden Belt or Bracelet.

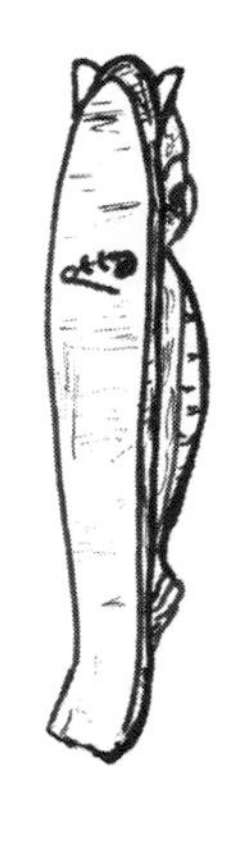
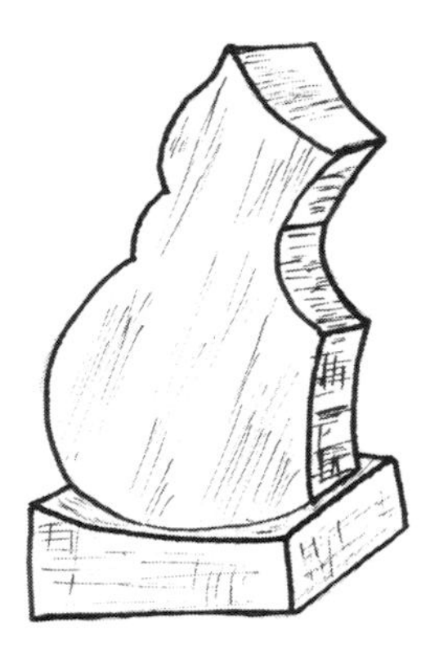

Figure 24–11 Whittle a Pin or Door Stop.

each coat dry thoroughly and sandpaper it smooth before you put on the next.

5. For a soft tint, soak crepe paper in water to produce a transparent dye or paint on a heavy coat of water color which will soak into the wood. Adopt the Indian method of using plant dyes for a real "woodsy" touch.

6. For a dark shade to conceal unwanted blemishes or unattractive wood grains, use paints, enamels, varnishes, or lacquers. Many of these substances, as well as such thinners as turpentine, alcohol, and benzol commonly used with them, are both toxic and combustible, so use them only in a well-ventilated area where you will not inhale the fumes and cleanse your hands thoroughly before proceeding with other activities. Destroy any rags or papers you use for they are also highly flammable. Clean your brushes thoroughly and then wash them out in a good detergent and hang them up to dry. Never leave them standing on end as this will press the bristles out of shape.

7. Spray the wood with a thin coat of clear plastic to protect it. Apply it over a stain or other coloring or alone if you want to maintain a light color.

Occasionally rub down wooden objects with a good quality of oily furniture polish or boiled linseed or other type of oil. This helps to replace the natural oils that are lost as the wood gradually dries out.

THE SHEATH KNIFE

A *sheath* or *hunting knife* (Fig. 24–12) was indispensable to the pioneer and served him in many ways. However, it is not so essential for today's average camper, although he may find it handy for doing heavy carving and for such camp tasks as slicing bread, peeling potatoes, or cutting up meat.

Sheath knives come in many styles, sizes, and shapes, but for ordinary camp use it is best to choose a rather small one with a fairly narrow, thin blade, 4 to 6 inches long, that slopes gradually from the back of the blade to the sharp edge. Such a blade takes a keen edge and is easy to manipulate. Most modern handles are made of some

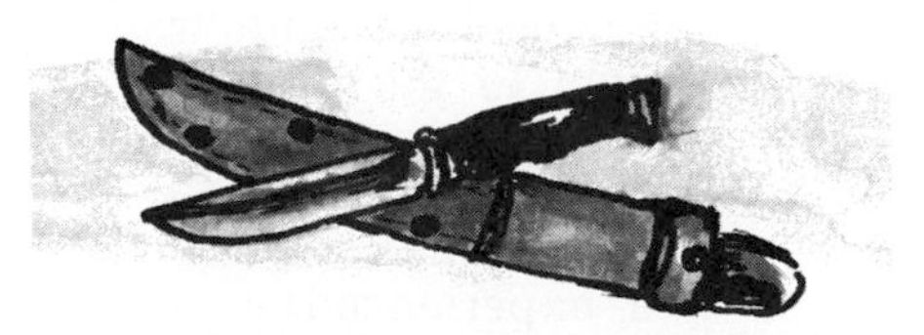

Figure 24–12 A Sheath Knife.

sort of composition material, although the older types made of horn, hair, or leather still exist. The upright guard just back of the blade serves to prevent your forefinger from slipping onto the blade as you use it.

To sharpen and care for a sheath knife, use the same methods described previously for a pocketknife. Place it in its protective sheath when not in use, and when traveling, keep it handy in your pack or wear it on your belt at the side of your hip where it won't be in your way when you sit down or bend over and keep the edge of the blade turned backward (Fig. 24–15). The sheath should have rivets along the sides to keep the blade from cutting through the leather. When handing it to someone else, extend it handle first with the blade turned upward.

AXES

Camp is the smooth grip of an axe handle,
The clean bite and the white chips flying.

—*Our American Heritage*

TYPES OF AXES

The axe was also indispensable to the pioneer and played an important role in the settlement of our country. Nearly every area had its own blacksmith who fashioned his product to suit his own preference or that of his customers. Each type of axe was consequently unique to the particular region it came from and so was known as the Maine axe, the Hudson's Bay axe, the Kentucky axe, and so on. The designs of the several types now available are therefore the result of both tradition and adaptation to the purposes they served in various areas. Axes range in length from the little 10 to 13½-inch scout axe to the 33-inch axe of the lumberjack and experienced woodsman; they vary in weight accordingly.

Figure 24–13 Take a Chip Off the Old Block.

Double-bitted and Pole Axes

There are two basic types of axes. The *double-bitted axe* is usually full size and has a *bite* or *blade* (cutting edge) on each side of the head. One edge is usually ground thin and sharp for felling trees while the other is left thicker and stronger for splitting wood. This type of axe is attributed to that legendary hero of the Northwoods, Paul Bunyan, who of course wasn't content to chop like ordinary people but had to have an axe with which he could chop "both coming and going." The champions of the double-bitted axe claim that it is better-balanced and easier to handle than the single-bladed axe, called a *pole axe*. However, it has little if any place in the usual organized camp, for it is too dangerous for anyone but a mature and experienced person to use.

The head of a *pole axe* has an edge on one side and a flattened area called the *pole* or *poll* on the other. This gives it an advantage over the double-bitted axe, because the flattened area can be used as a hammer for such tasks as pounding in tent pegs. The pole axe comes in a wide variety of styles and weights, but we will confine our discussion to the two types most commonly used in organized camps.

The Scout or Hand Axe

This short 10 to $13\frac{1}{2}$-inch axe weighs from 8 ounces to $1\frac{1}{4}$ pounds and is recommended for general light camp use. It is sturdy and rugged, inexpensive, light, easy to handle, and will meet your ordinary needs in preparing firewood and doing light camp construction.

It is known by a variety of names, such as *scout axe* or *hatchet*, and since it is held in one hand, it is also called a *hand axe*. It has a protective leather sheath which permits you to wear it on your belt; hence another of its names, the *belt axe*.

Selection. Don't try to economize on an axe, for like a knife, a cheap one will likely be poorly balanced and have a blade of inferior steel which won't take or hold a sharp edge. The parts of an axe are indicated in Figure 24–14.

Most handles are made of tough hickory and may be bonded into the eye of the head with epoxy, which usually will hold tight for a long time. Handles can also be secured by (1) a series of screws; (2) a wedge of hard wood; or (3) a wedge of metal driven into the end of the handle to spread it so that it fits tightly in the eye. Another type of handle consists of a thick layer of composition material or leather over a strip of metal which continues on down to form the head; this type has an advantage in that it can never work loose. If the handle is made entirely of wood, the grain should be fine and run parallel with the handle. Hold the axe up and sight along the handle to make sure that it is aligned directly with the head. Avoid choosing an axe with a gaily painted handle, for the paint may conceal flaws in the wood or it may irritate your skin as you use the axe. The bump at the end of the handle is to keep it from slipping out of your hand as you use it.

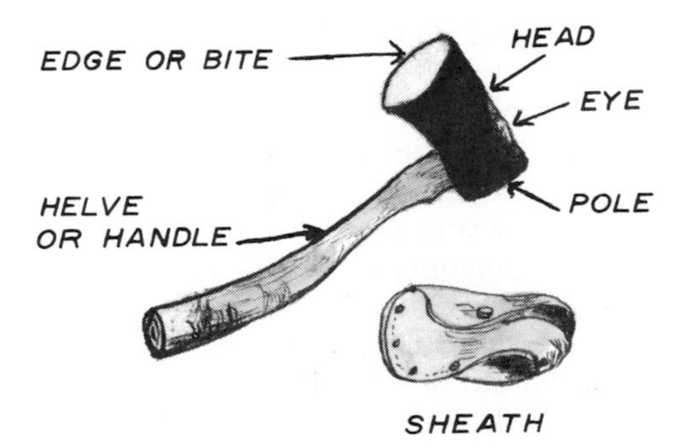

Figure 24–14 A Scout or Hand Axe.

The Camp Axe

A *camp* or *three-quarter axe* is smaller and lighter than a full-sized axe, but is sturdy enough to turn out large amounts of work and so is a favorite with counselors and experienced older campers. It has an 18 to 22-inch handle and a slightly larger and heavier head than that of a scout axe, which gives it more power. It should be fitted with a protective sheath with metal rivets or a tough leather buffer strip that fits across the edge.

The *Hudson's Bay axe* is a slightly longer, heavier model which finds favor with many who have heavy work to do.

TAKING YOUR AXE ON TRIPS

In the interests of conservation, many hikers consider it unnecessary and even inadvisable to take any type of axe along on short trips, for there are usually ample amounts of down wood which you can break by hand or under your foot.

If you want to take a scout axe, place it in its sheath and keep it handy in your pack or wear it on your right hip with the blade pointed toward the rear, as shown in Figure 24–15.

A camp axe turns out so much work with so little time and effort that many prefer to take it on extended trips

Figure 24-15 Wear Your Belt Axe and Sheath Knife Like This.

even though its longer handle makes it somewhat inconvenient to handle. Place it in its sheath and strap it on the outside of your pack with the blade pointed toward the rear.

CARING FOR YOUR AXE

Treat your axe like any other fine tool and always keep it in good condition, sharp and ready to go. As with any prized tool, a good camper neither lends nor borrows an axe; you will learn why after you have once had to go through the painful experience of having to renew the edge on an axe which has been misused.

In cold weather, warm the blade in your hands before using it, since cold metal is brittle and may chip or break.

Inspect the handle of your axe frequently to make sure that it is still tight, for it is easy to see the danger of a loose head on a swinging axe. No matter how tightly a head held in by screws or wedges fits at first, it will probably eventually work loose as the wood dries out. Some may advise you to tighten it by soaking the axe overnight in a pail of water but this will tighten it only temporarily and it will be looser than ever when the handle dries out. Soaking it in oil will tighten it for a somewhat longer period, but the only really satisfactory method is to drive another wedge into the handle to spread it enough to fit tightly again. Use a hacksaw to cut off any portion of the wedge that protrudes.

Never leave an axe lying about where it might cut or trip someone. Drive it firmly into a chopping block, a dead log, or a stump, or replace it in its sheath and put it away.

If you want to paint an identifying mark on the handle, place it away from the area your hands touch, since continued contact with the paint might irritate your skin and cause blisters. Oil softens leather, so do not use it on your sheath; use saddle soap or shoe polish instead.

When carrying an unsheathed axe for even a short distance, turn the blade down and grasp the handle close to the head to keep it from cutting you if you should trip or catch it on underbrush. When handing it to another, hold it by the handle and extend it head first and do not let go until you are sure he has a firm grip on it.

SHARPENING YOUR AXE

Manufacturers often leave an axe dull to allow the new owner to sharpen it to his own taste. If you are inexperienced, you will probably be wise to ask some experienced person to help you at first. If the axe is extremely dull or has a nick in the blade, you may need to rough-shape it with a hand grindstone. Hold the axe so that the stone turns into the blade and keep the stone

Figure 24-16 Using a Flat File.

moist to avoid overheating the blade and ruining its temper.

Follow with the 7 to 10-inch *flat or mill file*. Use a large metal washer or use the reamer of your knife to make a guard to slip over the tip of it (Fig. 24-16) to keep your fingers from slipping down onto the edge of the axe. Clamp the axe in a vise or use your hand, foot, or a peg to hold it firmly against a log or block of wood (Fig. 24-16). Kneel on one knee, hold the file in one hand, and place the fingers of the other near the tip to keep it at the correct angle. Take long strokes away from the edge and extend the edge back about an inch, tapering it enough to produce a sharp edge but not enough to weaken it so that it will chip or break. Leave the corners of the blade a little thicker since they enter the wood first and so must be strong.

After you have finished with one side, turn the axe over and proceed with the other. Now repeat the whole procedure with the fine side of the file. Finish off by holding the axe between your knees or in one hand and using a carborundum or sharpening stone in circular fashion over both sides to *hone* them (remove the *burr* or *wire edge*).

When an axe is sharp, it does a much faster job, biting in to remove sizeable chips of wood instead of chewing it out in small bits. It is also less likely to glance off the wood and injure you or a bystander. Frequently take a few moments to hone your axe and keep it in tip-top shape, so that you will never again need to use the coarse side of the file or grindstone unless you get a nick in the blade.

USING YOUR AXE

Get a solid, broad chopping block, 1 to 2 feet high, and level off the top, making a small depression in the middle to hold the wood (Fig. 24-20). If the block tends to roll, drive stakes in solidly against it on both sides.

Before you begin, look carefully about to make sure there is no one near and no brush or overhanging branches to deflect your axe on the backswing. Wipe the perspiration from your hands frequently, for wet hands are slippery, and keep your hands and legs well out of the way in case your axe should miss or slide off the wood. Chop at a 45-degree angle (Fig. 24-17), never directly across the grain of the wood since this makes little progress and quickly dulls your axe. Aim so that your axe will enter the chopping block after you have severed the stick instead of striking you or the ground where contact with sand or pebbles will dull or chip it.

When using a scout axe, grasp it close to the end of the handle and kneel on one knee. With a camp axe, stand with your feet comfortably spread and solidly planted on ground that has no pebbles or sticks that might cause you

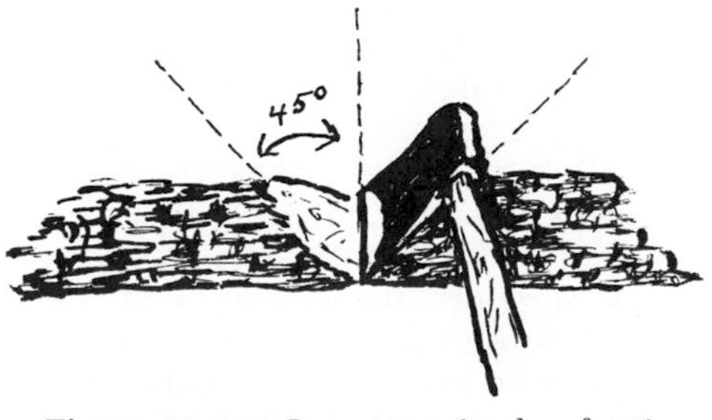

Figure 24-17 Cut at an Angle of 45°.

to slip. Grasp the axe with your left hand up near the end of the handle and your right fairly well down toward the head. Take a good backswing to get momentum and slide your right hand down to join the left as the axe bites into the wood. Slide your right hand back up the handle again to help lift and control the axe on the backswing, then repeat. Learn to coordinate your whole body in a rhythmic swing, using many muscles, especially the powerful ones in your back, shoulders, and hips. Skilled and powerful chopping, however, depends more on skill and timing than on muscle power. A long backswing creates good momentum which, when combined with the pull of gravity and the weight of your axe head, produces power. Work steadily but don't rush; keep your eyes focused constantly on the spot you want to hit and try to score a bull's-eye every time. Rest whenever you get tired, for fatigue lessens coordination and leads to bad accidents. With an axe, a slight miscalculation or a moment of carelessness can result in a very serious, disabling injury, so err on the side of being overly cautious.

Cutting a Log in Two

If the log you want to cut has a tendency to roll, anchor it by driving several stakes in along the sides. If it is small enough to be turned over easily, make a "V" halfway through it on the top side with the top of the "V" as wide as the log is thick. Cut at a 45-degree angle and chop alternately from right and left, using well-aimed, decisive strokes that take out chips frequently. You may need to twist your axe slightly to free them. If your axe sticks in the wood, loosen it by pressing down on the handle slightly. Avoid using a short backswing and timid strokes that merely peck out the wood in fine bits instead of sizeable chips. Remember that "the better the axeman, the fewer the chips." When you have finished the "V" on one side, turn the log over and make another on the other side to meet it. If the log is to be cut into several pieces, complete all the "V's" on one side before turning it over. This leaves the weight and length of the log to steady it as you chop.

If the log is too large to turn over, stand on one side of it and cut fairly wide "V" across from you, keeping the log between you and your axe for protection. Then step across the log and repeat from the other side. Make your "V's" wide enough to almost meet so that you can complete the job with a few well-aimed blows.

Felling a Tree

Never cut a live tree if you can avoid it, but if it is absolutely necessary, choose one that is diseased, crooked, or crowded, for you destroy something it will take nature many years to replace when you cut down a sound, live tree.

To sever a small sapling with one stroke, bend it over until the fibers are strained, then give it a sharp blow on top of the bend. For a larger tree (Fig. 24–18), determine in which direction it can fall with the least danger of getting entangled with other growth. Then cut a small *kerf* (B) on the opposite side. Cut another kerf (A) a little over halfway through and slightly farther down on the opposite side of the trunk. Slope the top of the kerfs downward and cut

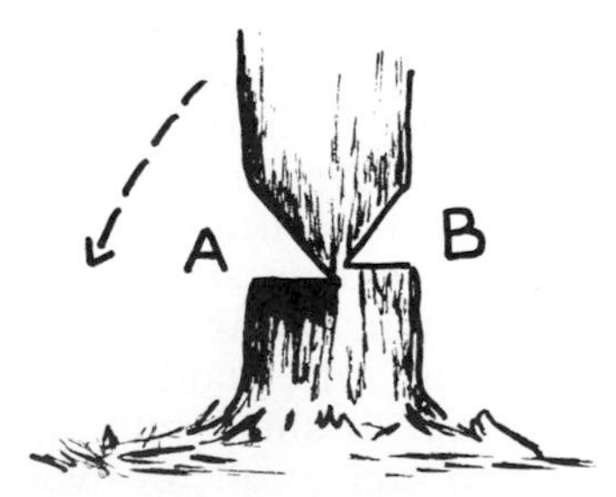

Figure 24–18 Felling a Tree.

them straight across at the bottom so that they will leave a stump which is flat on top. Push gently on side B, and if the tree doesn't fall, take a few more strokes in kerf B and try again.

Kerf A acts as a hinge to pull the tree over in the direction you want and it should keep the butt from sliding back to injure you. Nevertheless, play it safe and step quickly out of the way when the tree starts to fall just in case you have miscalculated.

Felling a tree with a saw is even easier and leaves a perfectly flat stump. Use the same principles to direct the fall, sawing a short slit on side B and a longer, lower one opposite it at A. Then deepen the slit on side B until a slight push will send the tree over.

Figure 24-19 Chopping Small Sticks in Two.

Lopping off Branches

To trim the branches from a fallen tree, stand on one side of it, and starting at the butt end, lop off the lowest branch on the opposite side of the trunk. Sever it as close to the trunk as possible. Continue on up the trunk, always keeping the trunk between you and your swinging axe. Then step across the trunk and clear the branches from the other side.

Cutting Small Sticks in Two with a Scout Axe

When cutting small sticks in two, avoid the dangerous practice of simply laying the stick loose on the block and hitting it. This leaves both ends free to fly dangerously through the air.

The *contact method* is one of the safest methods. Use your left hand to hold the stick crosswise on the block (Fig. 24-19), place your axe on it and bring both axe and stick down simultaneously against the outside edge of the block. If necessary, continue to bring both axe and stick down against the block until the stick is severed. Be sure to direct your strokes so that the axe will enter the block after the stick is severed. With a larger stick, use several strokes, giving the stick a quarter or half turn between each.

Splitting Kindling

Since split wood burns much better than whole sticks with the bark on, it is wise to keep some fine kindling and larger split wood on hand. To use the *contact method*, stand at one side of the chopping block, grasp the piece of wood in your left hand, place your axe on top of it, and bring both wood and axe down simultaneously against the edge of the chopping block (Fig. 24-20*A*). Repeat as many times as necessary to complete a split across the top. Then, turning your axe to face downward in the split, stand the stick upright on the block, remove your left hand and bring both axe and wood down against the chopping block (Fig. 24-20*B*). Repeat as many times as necessary to complete the split. To get still finer kindling, split the segments.

If your stick is too large to split by this method, stand it upright on the chopping block, place your axe on top

Figure 24–20 Contact Method of Splitting Kindling.

of it and drive it into the stick with another piece of wood. Never use another axe for this purpose for it is likely to break one or both of them.

You should never use your foot to hold the stick against the chopping block for it is extremely dangerous.

Sharpening a Stake

To sharpen a stake, hold it upright on the chopping block and sharpen it on four sides (Fig. 24–21). A four-sided point can be made more quickly and will drive into the ground more easily.

Figure 24–21 Sharpening a Stake.

SAWS

Campers often prefer to use a saw to cut large pieces of wood. In comparison with using an axe, it is safer, especially for the inexperienced, wastes less wood, and does the job more quickly and easily. It also leaves the pieces with flat ends, a decided advantage when using them for camp construction or arts and crafts.

A *crosscut* saw or *bucksaw* is an old favorite for use in camp and there are even some folding types so light and compact that they are suitable to take on trips. Figure 24–22*A* shows a collapsible bucksaw which folds into a compact $30 \times 2\frac{1}{2}$-inch package and weighs only about 22 ounces. It has a leather thong instead of the usual metal turnbuckle at the top. Two people use it, one at each side, and each takes a turn at pulling it toward himself; no one ever pushes. Keep the frame per-

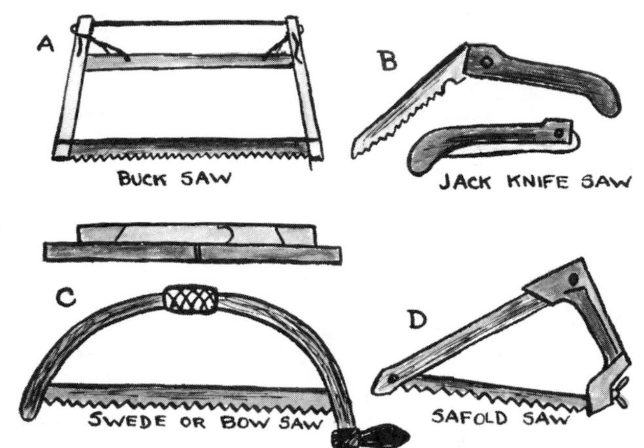

Figure 24–22 Some Types of Saws.

pendicular to the wood and do not bear down on it but let the weight of the saw do the biting.

Figure 24–22*B* is a *jackknife saw* featuring a blade which folds into the handle like the blade of a jackknife and is held in place by a wing nut when in use. It folds to a length of about 12 inches and weighs about 11 ounces.

Figure 24–22*C* is a one-handed *Swede* or *bow saw* with a tubular metal frame curved over the blade like an archer's bow. Several sizes are available, and some weigh as little as 2 pounds and can be dismantled and fitted into a case 12 to 18 inches long.

The *Safold saw* (Fig. 24–22*D*) features a steel blade which folds into the metal handle to form a package $24 \times 13\frac{3}{4}$ inches and weighing only about a pound. It is the favorite saw of most backpackers. The *folding saw,* shown with the sawbuck in Figure 24–23, is another lightweight model that can do a lot of work in short order. The *cable saw* (Fig. 24–23) is the lightest and smallest of all. It consists of a thin, wire-like flexible blade with a handle at each end that can be rolled up into a small coil for carrying. One person can use it for light cutting by holding onto both handles, or two can use it with each holding a handle and standing on opposite sides of the piece to be cut.

THE SAWBUCK

If you expect to do much sawing, it will pay you to construct a *sawbuck* or *sawhorse* (Fig. 24–24). Cut and sharpen four sturdy stakes, about 3 to 4 inches thick and 3 feet long, and drive them firmly into the ground in pairs to form "X's." Steady the joints as shown by lashing them with wire or strong cord. Lash or wire a short stick across the bottom of each "X," placing one end inside and the other outside the crossed sticks.

Figure 24–23 A Cable Saw.

Figure 24–24 Folding Saw and Saw Buck.

Figure 24–24 shows the sawbuck as it would be used by a right-handed person. He lays the stick across the two "X's," stands on the far side, and rests his knee on the stick to steady it. Notice that the piece to be sawed off rests just outside the sawbuck; this keeps the saw from binding in the wood.

OTHER TOOLS

When simple tools are readily available, most campers enjoy using them to repair or construct camp furniture and "fixin's." It is an imposition to ask the caretaker to lend his tools; therefore, each living unit should have its own basic set, each painted with a distinguishing color or design so that straying tools can be instantly recognized. Other special or more expensive tools should be kept available at some central place where they can be checked out when needed.

When many people use the same tools, some will invariably be lost or mislaid. A tool board (Fig. 24–25) helps to prevent this and allows you to arrange them in an orderly fashion so you can quickly locate what you want or spot any that are missing. Use a peg board and pegs or make a tool board

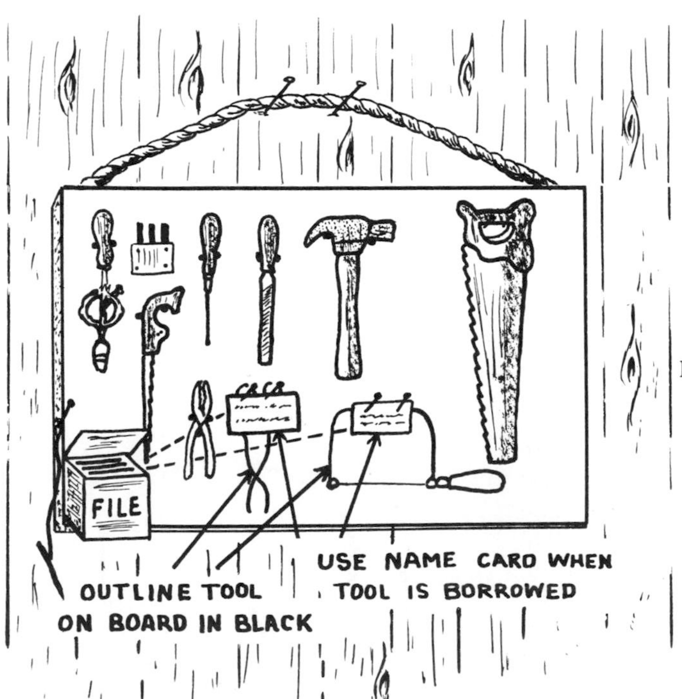

Figure 24–25 A Tool Board.

Figure 24-26 Why Not Construct a Rustic Bridge?

from any suitable piece of lumber. Lay it flat and place your tools on it in desired locations, then trace the outline of each tool on the board and paint it in solid. Insert nails, hooks, or other suitable holders to suspend each tool and stand or hang the board upright and put the tools in place. Make a card for each tool, with its name and a rough drawing of the tool on it. Punch a hole in the card for hanging it on the board, and file the cards in a box near the board. When a person borrows a tool, he removes its card from the box, signs his name on it, enters the date and time, and hangs it on the board in place of the tool. When he replaces the tool, he enters the time and date on the card and refiles it in the box. The outlines of the tools on the board show each person where to replace them and also reveal at a glance which tools are missing. Since people are not always familiar with the correct name of a tool, you may find it advantageous to number as well as name them and file the cards by number.

Bear in mind the old truism that a workman is known by his tools, and keep each tool in A-1 condition at all times. Hold each user responsible for returning a tool in good condition and occasionally set aside a rainy day or other convenient time to thoroughly recondition them. It is valuable for youngsters to learn to respect good tools and to understand the need to keep them in top condition as well as how to do so.

Provide as large an assortment of tools as possible and add to it as finances permit. Remember that cheap tools are usually inferior and prove to be a poor investment in the long run.

Here is a suggested minimum list for a camp:

- Claw hammer
- Shovels
- Saw and saw files
- Cold chisel (5/8″)
- Machine oil in a can
- Camp axes (20″)
- Jigsaw
- Rope and nylon cord for lashing
- Assortment of nails, tacks, screws, brads, etc.
- Strong shoe thread
- Bucksaw and sawbuck
- Plane
- Hand drill
- Files (assorted types)
- Sandpaper (assorted grades)
- Rakes
- Brace and bit
- Screwdrivers (assorted sizes)
- Hand grindstone
- Wheelbarrow
- Thin copper or picture wire
- Tin snips
- Post hole digger
- Plastic wood
- All-purpose cement
- Sharp rasp
- Binder twine
- Pliers with wire cutter (6″ or 8″)
- Ice pick
- Needles (assorted sizes)
- Level
- Square
- Steel tape measure
- Yardstick

ADDITIONAL READINGS

(For an explanation of abbreviations and abbreviated forms used, see page 25.)

KNIFE, AXE. ETC.

Aller, Doris: *Sunset Wood Carving Book.* Lane, 1964, 95 pp., $1.95.
Angier: *Skills for Taming the Wilds,* ch. 8.
Ball, A.: *Wood Carving For Fun and Profit.* Exposition, $3.50.
Better Homes and Gardens Family Camping Book, ch. 15.
Cardwell: *America's Camping Book,* ch. 8.
Jaeger: *Wildwood Wisdom.*

Knife and Axe (no. 19-6318). Girl Scouts, 1953, 40 pp., 30¢, paper.
Mason: *The Junior Book of Camping and Woodcraft.*
Miracle and Decker: *The Complete Book of Camping,* chs. 8, 9.
Riviere: *Backcountry Camping,* ch. 8.
Riviere: *The Camper's Bible,* ch. 6.
Rutstrum: *The New Way of the Wilderness.*

Tools, Whittling, Camp Construction

Anderson, (H. S.) Andy: *How to Carve Characters in Wood.* U. of New Mexico, 77 pp., $1.50.
Beard, D. C.: *Shelters, Shacks and Shanties.* Scribner's, 1972, 243 pp., $4.95.
Carlson, Bernice W.: *Make It and Use It.* Abingdon, 1958, 160 pp., $2.50; $1.60, paper.
Fun With Tools (No. BL-25). Boys' Life. (Articles reprinted from Boys' Life)
Furniture You Can Make. Lane, 2nd ed., 1971, $1.95, paper.
Gottshall, Franklin: *Wood Carving and Whittling Made Easy.* Bruce, 1963, 128 pp., $4.95.
Gross, Chaim: *The Technique of Wood Sculpture.* Arco, 1964, 136 pp., $4.95.
Gross, Fred (Ed.): *How to Work with Tools and Wood.* Pocket Books, 1955, 35¢.
Hoppe, H.: *Whittling and Woodcarving.* Sterling, 1969, 48 pp., $2.95.
Hunt, W. Ben: *Ben Hunt's Big Book of Whittling.* Bruce, 1970, 182 pp., $7.95.
Hunt: *Golden Book of Crafts and Hobbies,* pp. 108–111.
Ickis: *Book of Arts and Crafts,* chs. I, X.
Jeffrey, Harry R.: *Wood Finishing.* Bennett, 1957, 112 pp., $2.96, paper.
Leavitt, Jerome E.: *Carpentry for Children.* Sterling, 1959, 96 pp., $3.95. (Grades 2–6).
Leeming, Joseph: *Fun With Wood.* Lippincott, 1942, 111 pp., $5.50.
Maintenance and Care of Hand Tools (No. WI 35:9-867). Supt. of Documents, $1.
Miracle and Decker: *The Complete Book of Camping,* ch. 10.
Ormond: *Complete Book of Outdoor Lore,* ch. 13.
Ormond: *Outdoorsman's Handbook,* pp. 119–150.
Peterson, Harold A.: *American Knives.* Scribner's, 1958, $6.95. (A history of knives)
Pioneering (No. 3382). Boy Scouts, 1967, 64 pp., 45¢, paper.
Rood, John: *Sculpture in Wood.* U. of Minn., 1950, $6.95; $2.95, paper.
Rowlands, John J.: *Cache Lake Country.* Norton, 1947, $5.95.
Rutstrum, Calvin: *The Wilderness Cabin.* Macmillan, rev., 1972, 194 pp., $2.45, paper.
Sunset Ideas for Building Barbecues. Lane, 1971, 72 pp., $1.95.
Tangerman, E. J.: *Whittling and Woodcarving.* Dover, 1962, 293 pp., $2.00; $1.75, paper.
Toolcraft. Girl Scouts, rev., $10. (Flip Charts)
van der Smissen and Goering: *A Leader's Guide to Nature-Oriented Activities,* pp. 44–49.
Waltner, Elma: *Carving Animal Caricatures.* Dover, 1972, $2.50, paper. (Grades 7–12.)
Woodcarving (No. 3315). Boy Scouts, 1966, 48 pp., 45¢, paper.
Woodcraft Techniques and Projects (by Sunset Editors). Lane, $1.95.
Woodwork (No. 3316A). Boy Scouts, 1970, 64 pp., 45¢, paper.

Magazine Articles

Boys' Life:
Green, Bar Bill: "Time for Pioneering." Oct., 1965, p. 30. (How to construct a monkey bridge)
Wagner, Glenn: "Start a Home Workshop." Aug., 1963.
Wagner, Glenn: "The Adirondack Lean To." Sept., 1962, pp. 72–73.
Wheeler, Alan: "Wilderness Engineering." June, 1972, p. 36.

Camping Magazine:
Cassel, Sylvia: "Make Whittling Worthwhile." June, 1954.
Cassel, Sylvia: "Try Hiking Sticks." Mar., 1952.
Jaeger, Ellsworth: "Making Belts and Necklaces From Twigs." Jan., 1950.
Melamed, Monte: "Easy-to-Make Bench Using Chimney Blocks as Base." June, 1965, p. 27.
Melamed, Monte: "Easy-to-Make Small Parts Bin." June, 1964, p. 13.

Chapter 25

Tents and Shelters

Figure 25-1 Keep Your Tent Taut If You Don't Want Ducks Swimming With You.

Aloft I raise my Shield; the pelting Rain
And rattling Hail assault my Slope in vain.
The burning Sun, the Weight of Winter Snow
Alike I scorn—then rest secure below.

—From *Mottoes**

THE IDEAL TENT

Campers sometimes go on overnight or even longer trips and at night, merely curl up in their jungle hammocks, sleeping bags, or blankets. You may, in fact, prefer to lie out in the open under a star-spangled sky where you can enjoy to the fullest the sounds, sights, and smells of nature. This is fine and dandy in good weather or when there is shelter nearby to flee to when a storm threatens; however, on extended trips or when the forecast calls for possible thunderstorms, you will need to carry some sort of shelter. Don't be misled into thinking that in bad weather you can remain snug, dry, and happy for long with only a "waterproof" sleeping bag and ground cloth for protection. In addition, when working with youngsters, you should remember that they feel great excitement at the mere idea of living in a tent, for to them it is the very essence of camping.

An ideal tent would be quick and easy to set up and take down, be lightweight and compact to carry, offer absolute protection against rain, insects, and forest creatures, provide privacy, and be cool and well-ventilated in summer, yet warm and easy to heat in winter and on cool nights. Unfortunately, such a combination of virtues just isn't possible, for, as the old outlander said after gazing spellbound for several hours at a giraffe in the zoo, "There jest ain't no setch animal." This explains the several hundred varieties of tents now on the market, as each manufacturer attempts to produce one that is superior to those of his competitors.

TYPES OF TENTS

Some modern tents are merely variations on old ideas, while others use refreshing new approaches. Many now utilize lighter, stronger materials and feature telescoping or jointed aluminum poles that combine compactness with strength and lightness. Some

*Published by permission of Western Brick Company.

tents have folding aluminum or plastic frameworks that you can erect in as little as 90 seconds. Others are suspended from a framework, thus eliminating the need for pegs and guy lines, and are stable enough to pick up and move about. *Pop-up tents* usually have a light, collapsible, compact framework of aluminum that springs into an igloo-shaped structure almost as quickly as you can open an umbrella. *Wing tents* give added room through flies that extend like wings from two or more of the corners.

TENTS CLASSIFIED BY SHAPE

In general, we can roughly classify tents into three basic types according to shape, but there are many hybrids which combine characteristics of the various types.

Conical and Pyramidal Tents. These tents (Fig. 25-2), which are usually tall, were formerly erected with a center pole that was always in the way like a sore thumb; however, they now feature other means of support. Their steeply sloped sides shed rain very quickly, which makes them especially well-suited to open-plains country where there are often sudden and severe storms. They are sturdy and serve nicely in a permanent or semi-permanent camp, since, in the large sizes, several campers can bed down, lying with their feet toward the center and their bodies arranged like the spokes of a wheel. However, the bulk and weight of these tents usually make them impractical for light-trip camping.

TEPEE. The *tepee* of the plains Indians has no bothersome pole in the center and features smoke flaps that adjust to let the smoke escape when you want to build a small fire inside for warmth or cooking. Not too much waterproofing is required, since the steep walls quickly shed water.

MINER'S TENT. This tent, once a favorite, is seldom seen now. It is supported by either a center pole or a rope attached to the peak and thrown across a tree limb. It accommodates two or three campers and is tall enough to stand up in.

UMBRELLA TENT. This rather heavy, bulky tent is sometimes used for family camping or for long trips where transportation is not too much of a problem and the occupants expect to

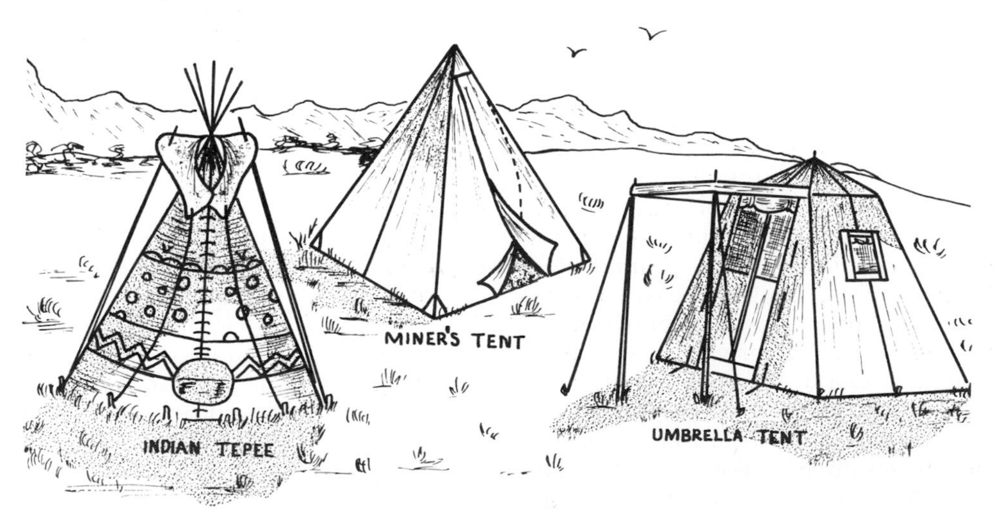

Figure 25-2 Conical and Pyramidal Tents.

stay put for some time. It is easy to erect, has ample headroom, and has a front fly that can be erected to provide a front porch for light cooking. The usual sizes accommodate three to five campers and flaps can be added at the sides of the canopy to house two or three more. Early models were supported by a center pole with side supports that spread out like the ribs of an umbrella, but some of the newer models are suspended from a frame or have side poles that leave the center unobstructed.

Wedge or "A" Tents. *Wedge or "A" tents* (Fig. 25–3) are favorites for light-trip camping, since they are relatively light, are easy to pitch, and furnish adequate shelter for the average summer backpacker. The steep roof sheds rain well and some models are tall enough to permit standing.

PUP TENT. The familiar *pup tent* has long been a standby for short-term camping. It is just large enough to provide a crawl-in type shelter for two people and their duffel. However, the cramped quarters may prove a bit frustrating during a prolonged rainy spell unless supplementary facilities are available. Many modern backpacker tents are variations of the pup tent and, when made of light materials, they may weigh as little as 2 or 3 pounds. When poles are required, collapsible ones made of lightweight aluminum can be used. In wooded country the smaller models need no poles, since they can be supported on a rope strung between two trees or bushes.

EXPLORER TENT. The *explorer tent* is amazingly roomy and has enough headroom to permit standing. You can pitch it by stringing ropes from loops on top of the tent and throwing them across the limb of a tree or by using an inside "T" pole. This tent is easy to pitch and strike and sometimes has a screened window in the rear to improve ventilation. It is well adapted to winter camping, since you can build a fire in front of the open door. It is a favorite for canoe, pack animal, or automobile camping, and a few are even light enough for backpacking. Some types reduce weight and bulk by sloping and narrowing toward the rear.

WALL TENT. This ever-popular tent is most commonly used for permanent sleeping quarters at the main camp or when a party expects to remain in the same place for several weeks. It provides ample headroom and the sides can usually be rolled up for free ventilation. It comes in a variety of sizes, but it is usually too bulky and heavy for light-trip use.

Lean-to Tents. Lean-to tents (Fig. 25–4), which can be used in summer, are also suitable for cold-weather camping, because the canopy over the open front will catch the heat from a reflector fire and reflect it inside onto the sleepers. A small fire for cooking

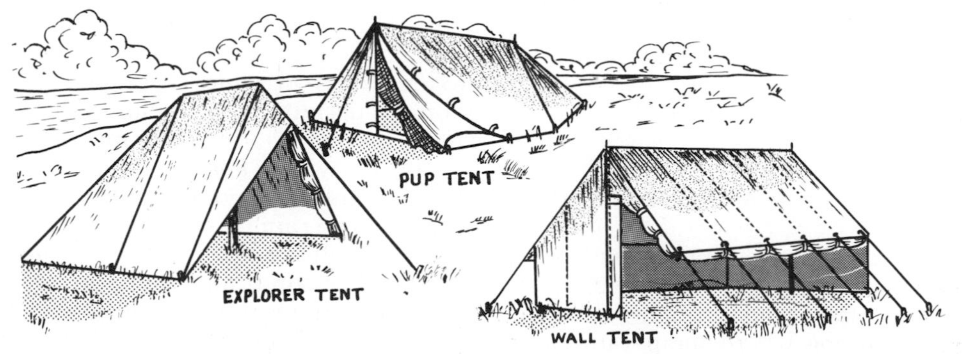

Figure 25–3 Wedge or "A" Tents.

Figure 25-4 Lean-to Tents.

can also be built in front of the opening. Light models are available for mediumweight and even lightweight camping. The walls slope toward the rear to reduce weight and they shed rain well.

CAMPER TENT. The *camper tent* has a short ridge and a front porch, and requires two poles for pitching.

BAKER TENT. This is a great favorite for middleweight camping, and some models are even light enough for backpacking. It is adaptable to both summer and cold-weather use but cannot withstand the high winds characteristic of some areas. It is especially suitable for automobile or station wagon camping, because the canopy can be suspended from the vehicle to provide added privacy and space. It is really like half a wall tent, with a versatile flap that can be used as an awning in sunny weather or lowered over the front to shut out rain.

TENTS CLASSIFIED BY SEASONAL USE

Tents can also be classified by the season for which they are most appropriate. *Forest tents* are suited to summer camping where temperatures are mild and winds are rarely over 20 to 30 miles an hour. Although some have no fly, insect barrier, or floor and so offer no more protection than an old-style pup tent, others have floors and are quite rain- and bug-proof.

Alpine tents (Fig. 25-5), which are also called *timberline* or *mountaineering tents,* are intended for use by mountaineers and explorers who camp in severe weather conditions, such as extreme cold, snow, blizzards, and strong winds up to 100 miles an hour. They must be very rugged and constructed to conserve heat while providing adequate ventilation for living and even cooking. There must be enough room to shelter the people and their gear, yet they must be compact and light enough for backpacking. Figure 25-5 shows one type that features a zippered door at one end and a 42-inch tunnel door at the other that can be extended to provide cross-ventilation and to permit an occupant to crawl inside without admitting much cold, snow, or wind. There is also a high tunnel vent to provide additional ventilation. The rain fly extends well down the sidewalls to keep the tent snug in all weather conditions. Support comes from two pairs of interlocking "A" poles at the front and back that come down through sleeves in the sides of

Figure 25-5 An Alpine Tent.

the tent and pass through grommets at the bottom. The tent is anchored by tent pegs.

TENT FEATURES

SIZE AND WEIGHT

Tents vary in size from the huge summer-cottage varieties intended to be transported by automobile or truck to the small crawl-in types suited only for overnight sleeping or protection during a brief downpour. Campers can usually save both weight and money by buying tents that are large enough for two or more people. A floor size of at least 5 × 7 feet is needed for two or more adults.

Since only the larger outfitters carry a complete line of tents and have enough room to set them up, you may want to consult the catalogues of some of the dealers listed in Appendix E to find out what is available. To help you to visualize the actual size of a tent, use string or rope to make a mock-up of it; then get in it with your sleeping bag and duffel. How does it feel?

WATERPROOFING VS. WATER REPELLENCY

Since one of the most important functions of a tent is to protect its occupants and their equipment from rain and heavy dew, we need to understand the difference between a waterproofed and a water repellent material. A *waterproofed* material is impervious to rain because the individual fibers have been treated with a waterproofing substance or because the material has been coated with one.

Although a waterproofed material may sound ideal, it has certain disadvantages. Waterproofing makes the material heavier and stiffer, and in time the treatment may crack and lose its effectiveness, necessitating a retreatment. In addition, it is obvious that a surface that won't let moisture in won't let it out either. Therefore, in a tightly closed tent, the pint or more of moisture that each occupant gives off during the night through his breathing and perspiration collects around him as a chilly, uncomfortable blanket, which may even have an unpleasant odor. As the evening progresses and the air cools off, this moisture condenses upon contact with the cooler tent walls and ceiling and eventually drops down on the sleepers below, making them and their gear almost as wet as if they had been out in a rain.

Water repellent materials, on the other hand, are made of coated fibers or of fibers that are very closely woven. A tent made of water repellent material may prove satisfactory during a light rain, especially if it has a steep roof to drain the water off rapidly and is pitched tautly, leaving no wrinkles or folds to collect and hold moisture. However, in areas that frequently have heavy or steady rains, water repellent materials alone will not prove satisfactory.

Figure 25–6 Pound That Tent Peg Down.

VENTILATION AND INSECT SCREENING

Another problem with a tightly closed waterproof tent is that it will not freely admit oxygen. As the night wears on, a sleeper uses up much of the available oxygen, replacing it with carbon dioxide; the result may well be a severe headache, nausea, and general malaise. Inadequate ventilation can have much more serious consequences when a camper succumbs to the temptation to avoid foul weather and cooks inside his tent with a portable stove. This is extremely dangerous, because the burning process creates the insidious killer, carbon monoxide, which makes him feel drowsy, and he may eventually fall into a sleep from which he will never wake. Records show that this fatal result has occurred in all too many cases.

Fabrics that do allow the passage of air are said to be "breathable." It is obvious that a tent has breathability in inverse proportion to how waterproof and airtight it is, so that even one which is merely water repellent will need some means of ventilation. There are various ways to provide this.

At one extreme are the tarpaulin shelter and the time-honored pup tent, which, being open at both ends, obviously admit plenty of air, as well as numerous unwanted flying and crawling creatures. Don't consider going on a trip, particularly in malaria country, without adequate protection from blood-thirsty pests, for no trip can be fun with them as tent mates. The better tents have screened doors, which usually open with one or more zippers, as well as vents or windows. There should be rain shields to adequately cover them, preferably ones you can manipulate from inside.

If your tent does not have adequate screening, you will have to rely on insect repellents or a *mosquito bar,* which you can fashion yourself from a few yards of material, preferably black. Sew it together in the shape of a pup tent and tie it or otherwise support it over the top of your sleeping bag. You can make the bar out of finely woven mosquito netting or bobinette, although these are rather fragile. Nylon marquisette is better.

THE TENT FLY

A *tent fly* (Fig. 25–12 *A* and *C*) is a piece of waterproofed material that is suspended above a tent to catch and divert the direct force of the rain. It should be pitched steeply enough to shed water quickly and should extend well out beyond the tent eaves and walls, so that a slanting rain will not blow in and the dripping from the rain will be well outside the tent walls. The fly should never touch the tent wall. A tent sometimes comes with an attached fly, but summer backpackers usually prefer to have the fly separate, so that they can avoid extra weight and leave the fly at home when fair weather is predicted or can take just the fly itself to provide an airy shelter for sleeping and even cooking. A fly keeps a tent warmer in winter and keeps it cooler in summer if the tent is pitched in the sun. When used above a breathable tent, it also solves the problem of condensation and breathability, because the moisture and carbon dioxide that escape through its roof are dissipated in the space between the roof and fly. If the moisture condenses on the inside of the fly, it will run down the sides to the ground outside the tent.

SHELTER FABRICS

Cotton. Prior to World War II, cotton was used in nearly all tents and shelters, usually in such forms as canvas, drill, duck, twill, or poplin. Now, however, it is rarely used except in heavy tents for family or long-term camping or in tents for those who value economy above lightness and compactness. In addition to its heaviness, cotton has other disadvantages: it has a low tear strength and it tends to mildew or rot when exposed to moisture and not promptly dried out. On the positive side, however, cotton is cheaper than most synthetics and can be tightly woven into a water repellent fabric whose fibers swell when wet to further close up the air spaces between them. Its fibers also readily accept and retain waterproofing.

Nylon. Shelters made of some form of nylon are now chosen by most light-trip campers. Although more expensive than cotton, it is ultra-light and can be compressed into a very small bundle for packing. Two forms are common: a smooth fabric called *nylon taffeta* and *ripstop nylon,* which has heavier fibers interspersed at quarter-inch intervals to give it added strength and to prevent tears from spreading farther down the fabric. Nylon has good tear strength, will not rot or mildew, and dries out quickly when wet. Tightly woven nylon is water repellent and will prove satisfactory in a light rain, but in a heavy or continuous downpour, the rain will sift through the material as a fine mist. Since its fibers do not readily take to waterproofing, the only way to actually make it waterproof is to apply a waterproof coating

(Courtesy of Robert E. Smallman, Girl Scouts, U.S.A.)

on the surface. This, of course, adds weight but the nylon will still be lighter than cotton. Unfortunately, the coating may eventually crack and disintegrate, necessitating a retreatment.

You can wash off a piece of nylon with a garden hose or you can put it in the washing machine, using a mild detergent, and leave it out to air dry.

Raw nylon has a tendency to fray, so the edges should be heat-fused or made with deep seams, turned back and well finished. Exposure to open flame damages it, so care must be used around a campfire. Repeated folding or creasing in the same place will eventually cause small leaks.

New Materials. New materials constantly appear under various trade names as manufacturers vie with each other to find the "perfect" material. Investigate these but don't embrace them too enthusiastically until they have stood the test of time, for continued hard usage will often reveal drawbacks that weren't apparent at first.

You can buy various shelter materials from outfitters (see Appendix E) to make a tent or shelter on your own sewing machine. You will find directions in some of the references listed in the bibliography at the end of this chapter. Kits are also available from some outfitters.

COLOR

Tent color is largely a matter of personal preference. White and light colors reflect rather than absorb the sun's rays and so are cooler in summer, but they also soil easily, attract insects, and tend to silhouette the occupants at night to provide an impromptu movie for the neighbors. Although some people prefer the cheery and flamboyant blues, yellows, oranges, and reds now available, true nature lovers are likely to stick to more somber hues, such as khaki, olive-drab, soft brown, or green, which blend in better with woodland surroundings. You can sometimes successfully use a dye to change the color of your tent, but you will have to re-waterproof it afterwards.

FLOORING

Some tents come with a waterproof tent floor already sewn in. This should be a *tub floor,* so called because it extends 6 to 18 inches up the tent wall to form a shallow "tub" that prevents ground water from entering the tent.

Tents without sewn-in floors should have a *sod cloth* (Fig. 25–7), which is a strip of material 6 to 18 inches wide that extends inward from the bottom of the tent wall. You can then overlap it with a waterproof *floor cloth* to produce a floor that is impervious to ground water and things that fly, crawl, and creep. A tarp of waterproof nylon serves nicely, or you can even use a piece of polyethylene, although it won't last long and will soon have to be replaced. Dirt and abrasion are the arch enemies of a tent floor, so take off your hiking shoes before you enter and clean the floor daily (a small whisk broom is ideal for this). One advantage of the detachable floor cloth is that it is easier to clean and replace when necessary.

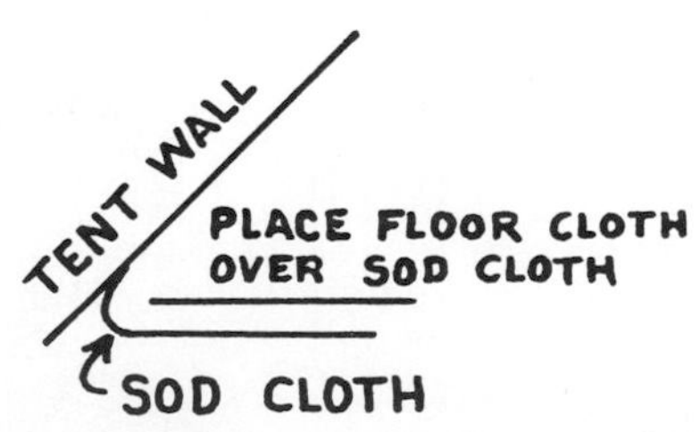

Figure 25–7 Sod Cloth in Place Inside Tent Wall.

TENT POLES

For backpacking, tent supports must be light and simple and quick to erect in case of sudden rain. Some poles telescope; others come apart and nest together for easy packing. Still others come in sections that are held together by *shock cords* (bands of rubber sheathed in nylon running up through the hollow centers), which make the poles easy to assemble and help to prevent loss. Light poles are made of tubular aluminum, duraluminum, fiber glass, or a still lighter material, magnesium, and each weighs 2 ounces or less.

TENT PEGS

Tents often come without tent pegs, so that the owner can select the proper type for the conditions under which he will camp. Because of the urgency of forest conservation, the day is gone and should be forgotten when a camper could simply go out and use his knife and axe to cut and shape his own tent pegs; if his tent needs stakes, he should plan to take them with him.

Figure 25-8*B* shows a twisted skewer type, available in aluminum or chrome moly steel and in 10 or 12 inch lengths. It is strong and drives easily, and so is especially well suited for use in pebbly ground, although it will hold well almost anywhere.

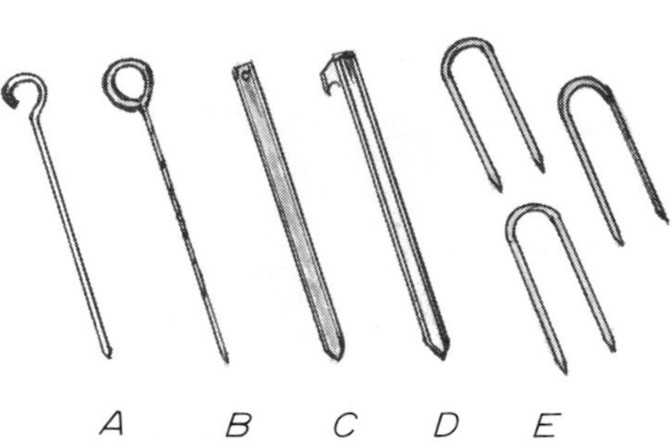

Figure 25-8 Some Tent Pegs.

In Figure 25-8*C* is an aluminum peg that is formed into a half circle at the top with a lip to hold the tent line and to serve as a striking surface for driving it. It will hold everywhere except in rocky terrain. These stakes nest together for compactness and can be held together by a rubber band.

A plastic T-peg (Fig. 25-8*D*) is quite durable and will not bend as aluminum sometimes does. It penetrates readily, holds well, and is especially suitable for use in loose sand or high winds where other stakes may fail to hold. It is very light and inexpensive.

Figure 25-8*E* shows some U-shaped tent stakes or staples that are available from Holubar. (See Appendix E.) Made of duraluminum, they will last for years, will hold securely in any kind of ground, and are especially effective in high winds.

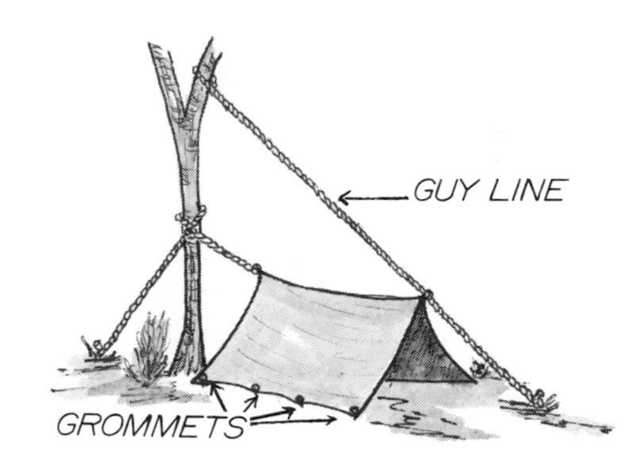

Figure 25-9 Some Ways to Use Trees In Tent or Tarp Pitching.

Figure 25–10 Tent Adjusters.

Modern stakes are inexpensive and extremely light, but of course, in backpacking every ounce counts, so travelers in woodland areas usually take as few as possible, anchoring their tent lines to rocks, trees, or even bushes. Figure 25–9 shows some ways to do this.

Figure 25–10 shows some tent adjusters. These are available in nylon or aluminum and are used to adjust tent lines to the proper degree of tension. Each adjuster has three holes in it and the line is threaded up through one end hole, down through the center hole, around the tent peg, up through the other end hole, and then tied or knotted. To adjust it, pull the guy line slack and slide the adjuster to a new position. The adjuster takes the place of the time-honored taut line hitch which is used for this purpose. Each adjuster weighs only 1 ounce and costs about a dime.

TENT LINES

A roll of 100-pound–test nylon cord provides the best tent lines, for it is quite strong, does not shrink when wet and resists mildew and rotting. Parachute cord, number 5 manila rope, and window sash cord are also acceptable. You can make the lines waterproof by periodically rubbing them with beeswax or melted paraffin. Be sure your rope is strong enough to withstand high winds and storms. A 1 to 1½ inch wide strip of strong automobile inner tube added to your rope and passed through a tarp or tent grommet (Fig. 25–11) will give extra flexibility for protection against damage from high winds.

SELECTING A TENT

When choosing a tent, consider such factors as means of transportation, the duration of your camping trips, how often and how long you expect to use it, what seasons you will be using it in, such climatic conditions as rainfall, winds, and temperatures, the need for protection from insects, and *the state of your finances.*

As with many other purchases, you will usually get just about what you pay for, so buy the best tent you can afford. When properly cared for, a quality tent will give you many years or even a lifetime of satisfactory service. Before making a final choice as to size, shape, and other features, you may want to rent or borrow several models to try out.

Select a tent made of good-quality fabric that is lightweight and closely woven. The tent should have wide felled seams, and all seams should have two rows of double stitching, with at least 8 or 10 stiches to the inch. The thread should be nylon or Dacron. There should be reinforcement at points of friction or strain, such as corners and peaks, where loops are attached, and where poles or pegs come in contact with the material. Be sure

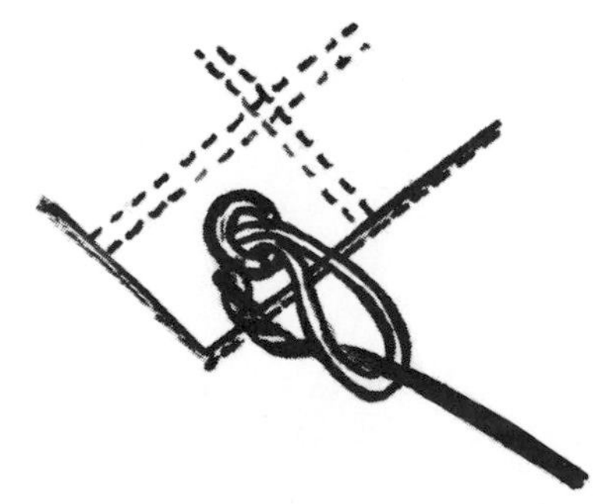

Figure 25–11 A Strip of Inner Tube Gives Elasticity.

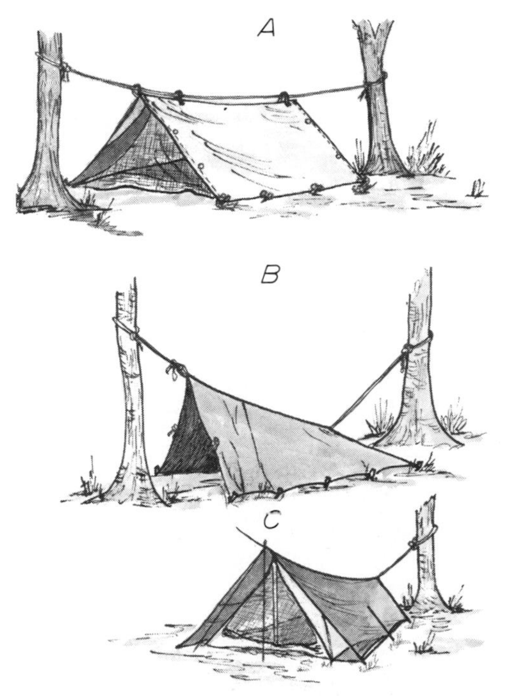

Figure 25–12 Some Backpacker Tents.

there is adequate ventilation and insect protection. Zippers should be heavy duty and made of non-corroding material. If the salesman tells you the tent is fireproof and waterproof, ask him to demonstrate these qualities; he'll welcome the opportunity if his claims are justified. Check to see that all specified pegs, poles, guy lines, and the stuff bag and other extra equipment are actually included in the package.

An extremely inexpensive tent is likely to become an expensive headache in the long run, since it will probably wear out quickly and perform poorly. Such a tent is often made of leaky, nondurable material and is not cut squarely, so that you can never pitch it quite right. The seams may be so poorly constructed that they pull out or fail to brace the material to give it the added strength they should. They may be sewn with that abomination, the "chain stitch," which pulls out completely as soon as you break one thread. *Grommets,* or the metal rings inserted for attaching lines (Fig. 25–9), may be so poorly anchored in the material that they quickly pull out as soon as they are subjected to the strain of strong winds. *Beckets* are the loops along the bottom of the tent walls that are slipped over pegs when pitching the tent; be sure they are well made and strongly reinforced. Although it is occasionally possible to get an inexpensive tent that will fulfill your ordinary camp needs, don't trust your own judgment unless you know tents or can get expert advice. It is wise, if you can afford it, to buy a tent made by a reputable tent maker who takes pride in his product and is willing to stand behind it.

PITCHING A TENT

PICKING THE LOCATION

Observe National Forest and Park regulations, which prohibit camping within 100 feet of lakes and streams. Choose a spot that has good drainage and is well above high-water marks, so that there will be no danger of inundation from a flash flood from a nearby creek or a runoff of water from a neighboring hillside. If possible, find a spot that is slightly higher than the surrounding area with a natural windbreak to shelter you from strong winds and rain. Ditching a tent is, of course, unthinkable today because of our belated recognition of the damage it does to the terrain. The above precautions help to prevent catastrophies and make ditching unnecessary. Avoid pitching your tent directly under trees, and inspect those nearby to see that they are sound and not likely to drop dead limbs or blow over on your tent in a storm. Also, beware of such trees as pine, birch, and maple, which drop substances damaging to tent fabrics.

(Courtesy of the Boy Scouts of America, North Brunswick, New Jersey.)

Select a level area with no sharp rocks, twigs, or other rough objects that may damage your tent floor and disturb your sleep; get down on your hands and knees and go over every inch of the ground carefully to remove pebbles, clumps of grass, or anything else that you could easily trip over in dim light and that can assume the characteristics of a mountain or a bed of thorns during a long night of attempted sleep.

GENERAL CONSIDERATIONS

Pitch the back of your tent toward prevailing high winds and rains and erect it in a neat, workmanlike manner. Your tent should be taut but not overly so, as you sometimes see in the spick-and-span models pictured in equipment catalogues. When there is a high wind, tighten the ropes and close all openings, for wind inside a tent can cause ballooning and possibly severe damage to the tent itself. Fasten down loose flaps so the wind can't catch and tear them or cause loud, booming noises to keep you awake.

USE AND CARE OF TENTS

CARE OF YOUR TENT IN CAMP

Air out your tent thoroughly on sunny days and roll up the flaps with the edges inside where they won't catch and hold dew. Keep your tent floor clean; dirt, leaves, and other debris are messy and can damage the fabric and promote mildew. During wet weather, place a doormat of branches, old burlap, or reeds outside to use as a "shoe scraper." Keep an extra pair of soft shoes just inside the door to slip into as you enter the tent.

PACKING

Your tent will repay you with a longer life and better service if you care for it properly. To pack your tent, fold it neatly, but avoid creasing it repeatedly in the same places or the fabric will eventually break down there. Roll the folded tent into a narrow, compact bundle, using your knee to exert pressure, and shape it to fit into your tent stuff bag. This bag simplifies carrying the tent and also protects it from dirt and wear. For a small tent, you can make your own stuff bag or you can use a gunny, flour, or feed sack with a drawstring at the top.

TARP AND PONCHO SHELTERS

A *tarp* (*tarpaulin*) is a versatile piece of equipment that is almost worth its weight in gold; you can cover your duffel with it, use it as a ground cloth for your tent or bedroll, convert it into almost any type of shelter desired, erect it as a dining porch or cooking area, use it as a fly over your tent, or string it between two trees to serve as a windbreak. You can use it as an emergency stretcher by pinning it with blanket pins or lashing it through its grommets to two long poles (Fig. 19–12) and you can even use a light tarp as a sail.

For summer camping in mild climates, many backpackers prefer a tarp or poncho shelter to a tent. A tarp usually has grommets or tie tapes along all four sides for attaching it to guy lines and tent pegs (Fig. 25–13*A*), and the variety known as a poly tarp has five additional tie tapes strategically located on the center area to offer additional possibilities. Some tarps have snaps along the sides, allowing you to snap two of them together to form one large surface.

Several ways to construct a tarp or poncho shelter are shown in Figure 25–13, and an ingenious camper can devise dozens of others. You can use one end as a ground cloth, stretching the other above you as a shelter. You will not actually need tent pegs since you can weight the edges down with rocks, as shown in Figure 25–13*F*. Since tarp shelters are particularly vulnerable in high winds, keep them low to minimize wind ballooning.

Tarps are available in most tent materials and come in a variety of sizes, weights, and colors. A popular choice is one 9 × 12 feet, made of waterproofed ripstop nylon. This type will shelter two adults, weighs only about a pound, and folds into a small, compact package that you can carry in an outside pocket of your packsack. A tarp should be lap felled and double stitched around the edges with nylon or Dacron thread. Since a tarp shelter is open at both ends, you will have no trouble with condensation or lack of ventilation, but you will need to carry a mosquito bar or other protection in insect country.

A still lighter and cheaper tarp is a sheet of thin, transparent *plastic* or *polyethylene,* such as painters use for dropcloths and farmers use for various purposes. It is available in 2 mil (.002 inch) or 3 mil (.003 inch) thicknesses at paint and hardware stores. Outfitters carry a superior translucent type in a 4 mil thickness. Although easily torn, it is stronger than it looks, is completely waterproof, and is so inexpensive that campers consider it expendable and often take along several sheets to use as a ground cloth, to keep the wood

Figure 25-13 Some Tarp or Poncho Shelters.

for their campfire dry, or to shelter themselves and their gear. It can be converted into an emergency poncho by cutting a hole in the center. The cheapest way to buy it is in rolls of 100 feet, which you can then cut to the size you need. Since exposure to flame will "wilt" or burn it, use care around an open fire.

Ely* suggests reinforcing the sheet by means of a 150 foot length of ½ inch wide adhesive filament tape (sometimes called acetate-backed, glass-reinforced strapping tape). Place strips of tape around the four edges of the plastic and both ways across the center. Add three or four strips across the piece in both directions and finish with two strips running diagonally between opposite corners.

*Ely, Ron: "The Polytarp." *Boy's Life*, Mar., 1967.

Figure 25-14 How to Use a Visklamp.

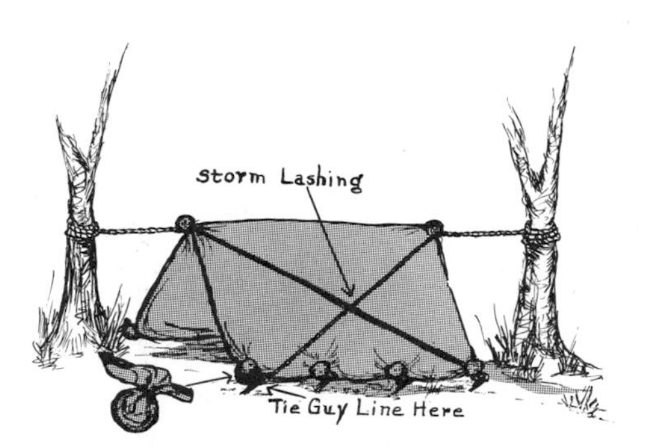

Figure 25-15 A Polyethylene Tent.

Since holes made in plastic will quickly tear out, you will have to devise some other way to attach lines for pegs and guy lines. A special device called a *Visklamp* (Fig. 25-14) works nicely. It consists of a small rubber ball and a clamp with two holes in it. To use it, pick the spot where you want to attach a guy line, gather up the plastic, twist it a few times around the ball to secure it, and pass both ball and plastic up through the larger hole in the Visklamp. Now slide both ball and plastic down to the smaller hole and attach the guy line to the larger hole.

Figure 25-15 shows simple, do-it-yourself "buttons" for attaching guy lines. To make these, place a bit of the plastic around a wad of paper, grass, or dirt, and secure it with a bit of string or twine. Tie these buttons at the corners and at frequent intervals along the edges of the plastic, then use a slip knot to attach the guy lines to the buttons. Since poly tents tend to balloon in the wind, stabilize them by tying ropes diagonally across between the corners, as shown in Figure 25-15.

If you want to add ends to your shelter, use pieces of plastic, or a poncho, tarp, blanket, or raincoat. To make a door in a piece of plastic, place strips of adhesive filament tape along the edges of the opening or turn back the edge around a small stick and fuse the materials together with a little gentle heat.

Figure 25–16 A Plastic Tube Shelter.

Since plastic is so fragile and easily torn, avoid walking on it or laying it over sticks, stones, or rough surfaces. Even with great care, it will probably last only a week or two, but it does provide a cheap emergency shelter. Its very inexpensiveness and expendability, however, have created a serious problem. Travelers now report that the landscape is marred by bits and pieces of plastic discarded by selfish or ignorant campers to clutter up the landscape and create eyesores for all who follow. Never be guilty of this serious breach of outdoor etiquette—take every scrap you brought out back with you and take time to remove fragments left by others.

A *plastic tube tent* (Fig. 25–16) is a popular variation of the plastic sheet shelter and is commonly used by backpackers. You can buy such tents or you can cut your own from rolls of tubing available from outfitters in 3 foot diameters and 3 or 4 mil thicknesses. You can suspend the tent across a line tied between two trees. It provides its own ground cloth and no tent pegs are necessary since the weight of your body and duffel will hold it down. The tent has the same advantages and disadvantages found in the plastic tarp shelter. With care, it will last a week or two. Carry a few plastic spring clothespins with you to keep the tube in place on the supporting line and to pin up the ends to keep out ground water and blowing rain. You can also make a doorsill by propping up a few inches of the plastic across some of your gear. Since plastic is airtight, you must be careful not to completely close off both ends. Tube tents can be erected in just a few minutes, weigh only about a pound per person, and cost very little; these qualities probably account for their popularity. Tube tents are also available in coated nylon, which lasts much longer but weighs and costs more. You can add beckets of doubled-over cloth, adhesive tape, or plain Scotch tape.

BUILDING SHELTERS

Campers often like to construct Indian tepees (Fig. 25–2) by lashing the tops of 5 to 20 poles together and then spreading them out at the bottom in a large circle to serve as a base for a hand-decorated cover of waterproofed canvas or other tent material. (The Indians used birch bark, buffalo hides, or deer skins.) You can find directions for making tepees in some of the references listed in the bibliography at the end of this chapter.

Older campers may find it challenging to build a *lean-to,* an *Adirondack shack* (Fig. 25–17), or a log cabin, and these make welcome additions at outpost camps or other frequently used sites.

Figure 25–17 An Adirondack Shack.

ADDITIONAL READINGS

(For an explanation of abbreviations and abbreviated forms, see page 25.)

Angier: *Home in Your Pack*, ch. 4. (Includes directions for making several types of tents)
Angier: *Skills for Taming the Wilds*, ch. 12.
Angier: *Survival With Style*, ch. 2.
Angier: *Wilderness Gear You Can Make Yourself*, ch. 2.
Better Homes and Gardens Family Camping Book, chs. 6, 7.
Boy Scout Handbook, pp. 230–232.
Bridge: *America's Backpacking Book*, ch. 11.
Camping (No. 3256). Boy Scouts, 1966, 64 pp., 45¢, paper.
Cardwell: *America's Camping Book*, chs. 4, 12. (Includes directions for making your own tent)
Colwell: *Introduction to Backpacking*, ch. 7 to p. 108.
Cunningham and Hansson: *Lightweight Camping Equipment and How to Make It*, chs. I, V.
Dalrymple: *Survival in the Outdoors*, ch. 10.
Fieldbook for Boys and Men, pp. 38–41.
Fletcher: *The Complete Walker*, pp. 137–176.
Johnson: *Anyone Can Camp in Comfort*, ch. 2.
Langer: *The Joy of Camping*, pp. 3–28.
Laubin, Reynold and Gladys: *The Indian Tipi*. Order from N.R.P.A., 208 pp., $6.95.
Learn and Tallman: *Backpacker's Digest*, ch. 15.
Litepac Camping Equipment. Boy's Life, 20¢. (Articles reprinted from *Boy's Life*)
Macfarlan: *The Boy's Book of Hiking*, ch. 10.
Manning: *Backpacking One Step at a Time*, ch. 12.
Mason: *The Junior Book of Camping and Woodcraft*.
Merrill: *All About Camping*, pp. 87–102.
Merrill: *The Survival Handbook*, ch. 5.
Miracle: *Sportsman's Camping Guide*, pp. 15–22 and 46–48.
Miracle and Decker: *The Complete Book of Camping*. ch. 2 and pp. 204–209. (Auto camping)
Olsen: *Outdoor Survival Skills*, ch. 2.
Ormond: *The Complete Book of Outdoor Lore*, ch. 6.
Ormond: *Outdoorsman's Handbook*, pp. 178–181. (Tipis and wigwams)
Rethmel: *Backpacking*, pp. 2–5 to 2–6 and A–4 to A–6.
Riviere: *Backcountry Camping*, ch. 3.
Riviere: *The Camper's Bible*, chs. 1, 2, and 4.
Rutstrum: *The New Way of the Wilderness*.
Shockley and Fox: *Survival in the Wilds*, ch. 11.
Tents and Simple Shelters. Girl Scouts, $10. (Flip charts)
Wood: *Pleasure Packing*, ch. 7.

MAGAZINE ARTICLES

Backpacker-3, Fall, 1973:
"Backpacker's Equipment Section." pp. 57–59.
Bentley, Judy: "You and Your Gear—Care and Repair of Tents." p. 16.
Hastings, Honey C.: "Make and Fix It." p. 18. (How to make a tent)

Camping Journal:
"Buyer's Guide." (Current year)
Clark, Fred: "New Tents and Tarps." July–Aug., 1966, p. 30.
Forshee, John H.: "You Build It Backpack Tent." Jan., 1972, p. 26.
Gibbs, Jerry: "Take a Tarp." Jan., 1973, p. 26.
Laycock, George: "How to Pitch a Tent." June, 1967, p. 26.
Ormond, Clyde: "On the Trail." Feb., 1970, p. 16. (Plastic sheets)
Ormond, Clyde: "On the Trail." Apr., 1970, p. 18. (Tent pegs for different situations)
Ormond, Clyde: "On the Trail." May, 1971, pp. 22. (Emergency shelters)
"Pop and Prairie Schooner Tents." Apr., 1967, p. 66.
Reynolds, Judith L.: "How to Repair Your Tent." Oct., 1973, p. 24. (Cotton tents)
White, Robin: "The Versatile V-Fly." Oct., 1971, p. 26. (Directions for making a fly that pitches 12 ways, sleeps 6, and costs under $30)

Consumer Reports:
Consumer Reports Buying Guide Issue. "Family Camping Tents." 1973, p. 334.
"Tents." May, 1971, p. 296. (Cabin and umbrella tents)

Chapter 26

Sleeping Out-of-doors

Figure 26-1 "Shucks, I Thought Hot Dogs Were Good To Eat!"

> Bed is too small for my tiredness.
> I'll find a hill for my pillow soft,
> with trees,
> Pull the clouds up around my chin.
> God, blow out the moon, please.
>
> —Elizabeth Coatsworth, in *A Desk Drawer Anthology*. Theodore Roosevelt (ed.), 1937.

> Night is a dead monotonous period under a roof; but in the open world it passes lightly, with its stars and dews and perfumes, and the hours are marked by changes in the face of nature.
>
> —Robert Louis Stevenson, in *Treasure Island.*

> With never a thought of danger, he lies in his blanket bed,
> His coat of canvas the pillow supporting his drowsy head
> As he watches the white clouds drifting through limitless azure seas
> Where only the stars can find him as they peep through the sheltering trees.
>
> —James Barton Adams

Since a third or more of a camper's time is spent sleeping, his bed deserves much thought and attention. A good night's rest with at least eight hours of sleep for adults and even more for youngsters is a "must" at any time and especially so when undergoing the rigors of a trip.

If you are "tripping" by covered wagon or have other means of transporting your heavy baggage the bulk and weight of your bedding are not of tremendous importance, but when you are traveling entirely on your own two feet with all your equipment on your back, it really becomes a problem to provide a comfortable bed which is lightweight and not too bulky. Canoe bedding, too, should be light and compact, although it is possible to take a little more than when backpacking.

REQUIREMENTS FOR SLEEPING COMFORT

A good outdoor bed should provide warmth, for even in summer, nights are cool and the ground is always more or less cold and damp. The bed should be light and compact for carrying, should provide a reasonable amount of softness and smoothness with freedom from bumps, and should provide protection from the cold, damp ground.

BEDS

BLANKET BEDS

While at present, most people seem to prefer a sleeping bag, some people like to sleep in blankets. This possibility may well provide the answer for those with limited resources or those who feel that they will sleep out so seldom, and then only in summer months, that they can scarcely justify buying a bag. We should not look down on the idea of sleeping in blankets, for they served adequately for hundreds of years before sleeping bags were even thought of. They even have some advantages, because they are easily altered to suit weather conditions, are easy to wash, and can be dried or aired simply by hanging them on your camp rope stretched between two trees. Dark, strong blankets that won't show soil are preferable.

Cold weather calls for blankets of 100 per cent virgin wool; their loose weave and long nap trap dead air, making one wool blanket equivalent in warmth to several part-wool or cotton ones. Two relatively thin blankets are better than one thick one, since they are easier to manipulate and trap a layer of dead air between them to provide extra insulation. Good wool blankets are expensive, however, and are usually too warm for summer; part-wool blankets are more satisfactory in warm weather despite their tendency to collect moisture. Quilts and comforters are too bulky and fragile to merit consideration.

Making a Bedroll. Some people simply roll up in their blankets and claim to sleep in perfect comfort throughout the night. This seems unlikely, however, since studies show that the average person doesn't go to bed and sleep "like a log" but changes position many times during the night. Consequently, a person who tries to sleep like this would probably feel confined and become irritated as various parts of his anatomy periodically become exposed to the atmosphere. If you want to try it, wrap yourself in an *envelope bed;* spread your blanket on the ground, bring the two sides up over you tucking one edge of the blanket under you, then lift your feet and tuck the blanket under them. To use two blankets, place the edge of one blanket at the center of the other, lie down and proceed as before.

When using two blankets, it is usually best to pin them together in some way. A *Klondike bedroll* (Fig. 26–2) is easy to make. The one illustrated is made from three blankets and four 3-inch horse blanket pins. First place a tarp or ground cloth on the ground and put the blanket you want outside (number 3) on half of it. Add as many blankets as you want, placing the edge

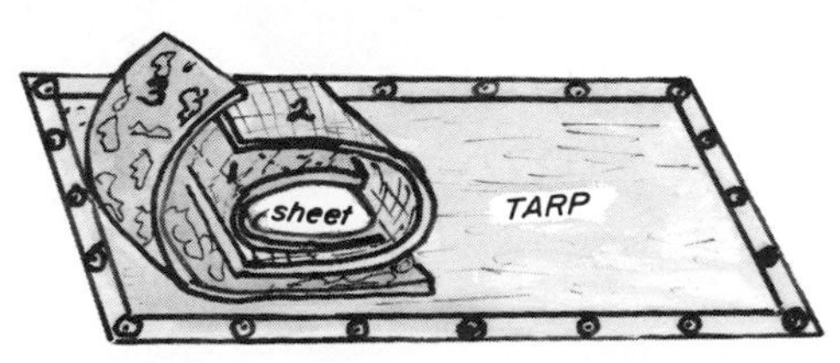

Figure 26–2 Making a Klondike Bedroll.

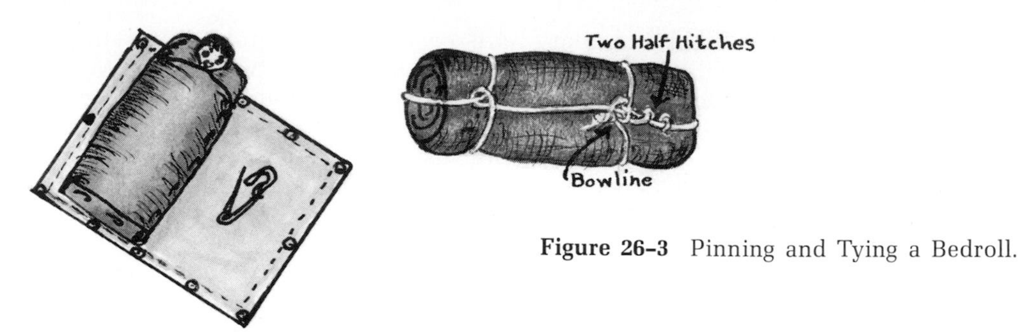

Figure 26-3 Pinning and Tying a Bedroll.

of each at the center of the one below. Finish with a folded sheet or light cotton blanket which will be next to you and will protect your blankets from undue soiling. Now begin folding the blankets over, starting with number 1, then number 2, and so forth. Insert two blanket pins along the outside edge and two along the bottom (make sure that the pins go through all thicknesses). Fold or snap your poncho or ground cloth around the outside and roll and tie it for carrying as shown in Figure 26-3. Be sure to make the bedroll wide enough to allow some movement, for most people dislike a feeling of confinement and find that it interferes with their rest.

SLEEPING BAGS

Most people who expect to do much outdoor sleeping will prefer to invest in some sort of sleeping bag. A good-quality bag, properly cared for, will last for years and will provide convenience, comfort, warmth, and maximum lightness and compactness. In the long run, it may actually save you money, since continued use of home bedding under trip conditions is hard on it and necessitates frequent cleaning.

SHAPES

Sleeping bags come in four basic shapes, and there are many variations since each manufacturer tries to come up with the "perfect" sleeping bag.

Rectangular Bags. These are roomy, square-cut bags (Fig. 26-4*A*) with plenty of room for restless sleepers. They are more expensive than the narrower types and their ample proportions add bulk and weight, making

Figure 26-4 Rectangular and Mummy Sleeping Bags.

them more suitable for car camping than backpacking. They are also not as warm as the other types since there is excess space inside to absorb body heat.

Mummy Bags. Mummy bags (Fig. 26–4*B*) represent the opposite extreme in shape. They follow the shape of the body, and this reduces bulk, weight, and expense and increases warmth. If their tendency to follow you as you turn in the night bothers you, place one hand on each side of the bag as you turn; this habit will probably soon become almost subconscious. Although some find a mummy bag too confining, its advantages so outweigh its disadvantages that most backpackers prefer it, finding that they soon become accustomed to its snug fit.

Barrel Bags. This variation on the mummy bag has, as the name suggests, a rounded portion in the middle to permit bending the knees and maneuvering about a bit more freely.

Semi-mummy Bags. These are a cross between the mummy and the rectangular bag.

For comfort, all bags should have an enlargement or "box" at the foot to permit the sleeper to extend his feet and move them about somewhat.

BAG CONSTRUCTION

A sleeping bag consists of an *inner* and an *outer shell* with a filler (a rather thick layer of insulating material) in between. Neither shell should be waterproof or even extremely water repellent, since it is essential that the bag "breathe" to let the pint or more of moisture your body gives off each night evaporate instead of condense into a chilly, wet blanket around you. Various materials are used for the shells, the commonest being some form of poplin. Bags filled with down require an especially closely woven material (usually nylon) to confine the down, which tends to migrate and drift through ordinary materials. All nylon should be the ripstop kind to keep little rips and holes from becoming big ones.

Manufacturers differ as to the desirability of using a *differential cut* for the shells. (This means cutting the inner shell so that it is smaller than the outer one.) Proponents of the idea claim that it makes the bag warmer because it is impossible for a chance movement of an elbow or foot to force the inner shell against the outer shell, which would, of course, compress the insulating material between the shells and produce a cold spot. Opponents claim that this cut actually causes the bag to be less warm, since it pulls the inner shell away from the body, leaving extra air space to absorb body heat.

Insulation (Middle Layer or Insulation)

Although warmth may seem like the thing you want least as you pack up your gear on a warm sunny day, you must bear in mind that the sun will go to bed long before you do, and that the air will likely become quite chilly before morning in most areas of the United States. This is especially true at high altitudes.

As you drift off to sleep, your muscles relax and your metabolism slows down markedly, causing a corresponding drop in the production of body heat. When you are not warm enough, your muscles automatically contract (perhaps even to the point of making you shiver) to step up heat production, and you sleep fitfully, if at all, and arise stiff, tired, and decidedly unenthusiastic about starting out for another hard day on the trail.

Bedding cannot, of course, supply any heat in itself, but it serves as insulation to keep out cold air and prevent the loss of body heat by conduction and convection. In a sleeping bag, the insulation is provided by the more or less thick filler between the shells, which is usually a loose, fluffy material containing countless minute air pockets that trap and render motionless large amounts of air. This still or "dead" air provides excellent insulation.

Many materials insulate well, but none to date can perfectly meet the backpacker's need for a light, compressible, resilient, "breathable," fireproof, non-allergenic, yet inexpensive material. Of the many materials tried, only three are currently used in modern sleeping bags: the down of waterfowl, polyester fiberfill, and forms of polyurethane foam. However, new materials continue to appear as manufacturers attempt to find a more nearly perfect filler.

The thickness, or *loft,* of the insulation is all important in determining how well it will insulate, and it is customarily measured by zipping up the bag, fluffing it up as full of air as possible, and measuring the height from the floor to the top of the bag. Of course, you must remember that half of the loft will be above you and the other half below when you are in the bag. Therefore, when a manufacturer says that his bag has a loft of 6 inches, the effective amount of insulation around you is actually 3 inches.

Figure 26-5 "Wonder Which One Would Keep My Little Tootsies Warm."

The Army Quartermaster Corps has developed a guide for rating the insulation value of clothing and sleeping bags according to their thickness. However, experienced outdoorsmen say that these figures are only minimums and that you will need more for real comfort.

Temperature in Degrees	Total Loft in Inches
40	3
30	$3\frac{1}{2}$
20	4
10	$4\frac{1}{2}$
0	5
−10	$5\frac{1}{2}$
−20	6
−30	$6\frac{1}{2}$

Materials Used For Insulation

Goose Down. Goose down is the overwhelming choice of the cold-weather backpacker. It is extremely light, can be compressed into a small bundle for carrying, yet is so resilient that it quickly springs back into shape as soon as pressure is released. Ounce for ounce, it provides more insulation than any of the synthetic materials yet devised. The best quality of down is found under the regular feathers on the breasts of mature northern geese and is plucked in the fall or winter when it is most luxuriant.

High-quality goose down is becoming increasingly scarce and expensive, because the geese are being raised commercially for food and are killed at a younger age before the down has reached its prime. The down from northern ducks is sometimes used, and although it is not as soft and warm as goose down, it is often superior to some of the inferior-grade and "reconditioned" goose down on the market. Down bags first came into extensive use after World War II and are now widely used.

A major drawback of down is its tendency to clump together and lose nearly all its insulating value when wet. It is also quite difficult to clean a down bag.

Polyester Fiberfill. Although bags of *polyester fiberfill,* such as Dacron 88, have been on the market for several years, their bulk and weight make them better suited for car camping than backpacking. Recently, however, this has changed with the advent of such improved forms as Dupont's Dacron II, Celanese's Polarguard, and other trademarked products. Although these materials are less compressible and twice as heavy as down of the same insulating ability, 4 to 5 pound bags are now available which can be made up into manageable bundles and will meet the needs of the average backpacker in anything but extremely cold temperatures.

These synthetic fillers are breathable and non-allergenic and insulate much better than down when wet. Cleaning the bag presents no problem since you can simply wash it out by hand and squeeze it almost dry, and some bags are even machine washable. Their most appealing feature, however, is their low cost.

Polyurethane Foam. *Polyurethane foam* is the newest entrant in the field and shows great promise as improvements continue to be made. It is a spongelike material which, although heavier than down, is cheaper and provides much better insulation when wet. It is both breathable and non-allergenic, but, unlike down, it does not drape closely about the body and so leaves air spaces which absorb body heat. It also has a tendency to turn with the body, creating air currents which carry away still more heat. For these reasons, this type of insulation is not too satisfactory for use in extremely cold weather.

Polyurethane foam is not as compressible as either down or polyester fiberfill, so a bag cannot be compressed into a small space but must be rolled up and carried on the outside of the pack. However, this very incompressibility is at the same time an advantage, because it provides a softer cushion and better insulation under the sleeper. It also gives good protection from ground dampness, although you may want to use the customary ground cloth under it to protect it from dirt and abrasion.

Most foam bags open only at the top and have a drawstring to pull them close about the neck; this makes them rather hard to get into and out of. They can be washed out by hand and squeezed almost dry. Like polyester fiberfill bags, their chief appeal lies in their low cost.

Ways of Stabilizing Insulation

Down is composed of thousands of units called *pods,* each consisting of a center with many branching filaments that create numerous small air pockets to trap dead air; this gives down its superior insulating ability. As previously mentioned, down has a tendency to migrate or move about, so that if it is simply placed loose in a large area, such as that between the inner and outer shells of a sleeping bag, it will wander about and eventually collect in a few areas, leaving the rest of the bag devoid of down and, consequently, of insulation. Therefore, some method must be used to stabilize the down and keep it evenly distributed throughout the bag. The simplest method is called *quilting* (Fig 26–6*A*), which is done by stitching straight through the shells and the down. This is not satisfactory for

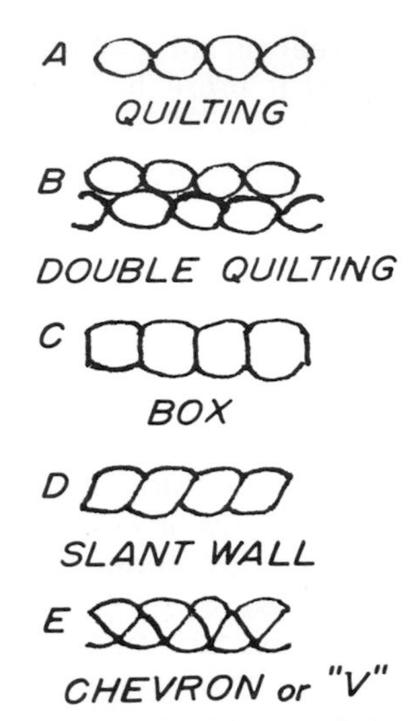

Figure 26-6 Methods to Stabilize Down.

anything but hot-weather bags, since each row of stitching compresses the down to almost nothing, resulting in a series of cold spots. *Double quilting* (Fig. 26-6*B*), is better because it uses two layers of quilted down, placed so that the stitching or thin part on one is opposite to the thick part on the other.

Still better than double quilting are baffles, which are strips of material placed vertically across between the inner and outer shells to form tubes which contain the down. The *box* type of baffle (Fig. 26-6*C*) is inserted at right angles; the *slant wall* baffle (Fig. 26-6*D*) is placed at a 45-degree angle. The *chevron* or *V* baffle is made by sewing a strip of material continuously along between the inner and outer shells and is considered the best method of all.

Various materials are used for the baffles, with ripstop, downproof nylon being best for down. The tubes formed by the baffles usually run horizontally around the bag to counteract the tendency of the down to drift toward the bottom of the bag and there are usually some cross baffles in the tubes to further stabilize the down. Installing the baffles and distributing the down properly in them requires much painstaking, skilled work, and this partially accounts for the high cost of a good down bag.

Polyester fiberfill consists of long, springy fibers which come in the form of batts which can be cut to any desired shape and size. The fibers interlock and so have little tendency to wander or drift, making an intricate system of baffles unnecessary. The filler can be kept in place merely by sewing straight through both it and the shells, although this will, of course, result in the usual cold spots. For this reason, double quilting is usually recommended. With this type of filler, cheaper materials such as nylon taffeta can be used for the shells.

Polyurethane foam needs neither baffles nor quilting, but can simply be cut to the desired proportions and enclosed in appropriate inner and outer shells.

Bag Openings

Some bags, particularly the mummy types, have an opening only at the top or a zippered opening extending part way down one side. Obviously, this makes them less convenient to get into and out of, but the saving in weight and expense makes them attractive to many, particularly young people who don't mind the inconvenience at all. A more convenient arrangement is to have a zipper running all the way down one side and across the bottom. This allows you to open the bag to get any amount of ventilation you want or even to open it flat and sleep on top of it in hot weather. It also simplifies the problem of airing and sunning it as well as making it easier to insert a washable liner or a thick one to give added warmth. You can also zip two bags of this type together, one with the zipper on the right, the other on the left.

Metal zippers are seldom found in modern bags since they transmit cold and are more likely to jam. They have been largely supplanted by those made of nylon or plastic, which are lighter, work more smoothly, and have less tendency to jam. If a zipper does become balky, apply a little wax, light lubricating oil, or Zip-Eaze all along it and work it up and down several times.

Double zippers with slides at both the top and bottom are superior since they permit opening the bag from either the top or bottom to provide a greater choice in ventilation. They should be workable from either the inside or the outside, especially for cold-weather camping.

Since the zipper opening is the prime source of cold from the outside and loss of heat from the inside, it should be completely faced with a good *zipper draft tube,* filled with insulating material and extending all the way to the bottom and slightly beyond. It must be attached so that it can't possibly foul the zipper or cause it to jam.

Head and Neck Protection

Rectangular bags are usually left open at the top or have a drawstring to draw them close about the neck. This makes it necessary to carry some sort of supplementary protection for the head and neck in cold weather. Separate hoods are available for this purpose, and some bags have detachable hoods which can be left at home during warm weather. Mummy bags and their variations usually have an extension at the top which can be pulled tight about the face and neck in cold weather, leaving only the nose and eyes exposed, and some have an extra drawstring around the shoulders to make them fit even more snugly.

Removable Liners

Some bags come with removable liners to protect the inside of the bag from dirt and abrasion, and these can be taken out for laundering. They come in a variety of materials, such as cotton shirting, outing flannel, or ripstop nylon, and are anchored in place with tapes or snaps to keep them from twisting or rolling up as the occupant turns.

If your bag has no such liner, you can easily make one from material of your choice. A twin-bed size sheet or cotton "bed blanket" works well in summer and is about the right size for an adult bag, but you may want a warmer material for cold weather. The problem of fitting the liner to the bag is simplified if your bag is the type which opens down one side and across the bottom. Open the bag and measure the length along one side, across the bottom, and up the other side, and buy a piece of snap tape of this length. This is a strong twill tape which comes in the form of two tapes snapped together. To fit the liner into the bag, separate the two strips of tape and carefully sew one strip flat along the inside of the bag opening, just inside the zipper where it won't foul it or interfere with opening or closing it. Attach the other half of the tape to the liner, sewing along one side, across the bottom, and up the other side. You are now ready to snap the liner in place inside the bag.

THE USE AND CARE OF A DOWN BAG

A down bag usually comes with its own *stuff bag* into which you literally stuff it, handful by handful, being sure to work at least half of it down into the bottom half of the stuff bag. As soon as you arrive at your campside, remove the sleeping bag from the stuff bag (handle it carefully to avoid damaging the delicate system of baffles inside). With the zipper closed, pick up the bag by the edges and shake it with a sort of whip-like motion to get as much air as possible into the down. Do this at least an hour before retiring to give the down time to attain its full loft. Leave the zipper closed until you are ready to crawl into the bag to discourage "wild critters" from entering and to prevent the down from collecting moisture. Always keep your bag well away from any open flame, for a stray spark can burn a hole in it or even set it on fire in a matter of seconds.

Air out your bag every day if possible, turning it inside out and placing it outside on sunny days. This will prevent mildew and odors.

Before storing it, fasten a plastic dress bag such as cleaners use around it and suspend it in a dry, clean room or otherwise store it loosely so the down can maintain its loft.

Make every effort to keep it clean, both inside and outside, for it is difficult to satisfactorily clean it. Some people advise against trying to clean it at all, others claim you can satisfactorily hand wash it, while still others advocate only dry cleaning by an expert who has the proper "know how" and equipment. Do not attempt to dry clean it yourself unless you have received complete instructions from a reliable source. After dry cleaning, do not sleep in the bag until it has been thoroughly aired out for several days, for noxious fumes often linger and can cause severe illness or even death to someone sleeping in it when it is tightly zippered.

Figure 26–7 "Happiness is Finding Out the Camper Who Put Frogs in Your Bed Caught Poison Ivy."

SELECTING A SLEEPING BAG

A sleeping bag is a highly personal item and there is no one bag which will suit everyone's tastes and needs. In selecting the particular one that is right for *you,* consider such factors as the season of the year, the altitude and probable minimum and maximum temperatures you will encounter, the prevalence of winds, the likelihood of rain or other precipitation, your own personal characteristics (some people sleep much "warmer" than others), how much and what type of clothing you will wear to bed, how extensively you will use it, how much bulk and weight you are willing to carry, and how much you are willing to spend.

Despite its cost and the difficulty of cleaning it, a good down bag may well be a wise purchase in the long run, especially if you will be camping out frequently in all kinds of weather, for when properly cared for, it will give you years of dependable service and will have a good resale value if you should decide to sell it. However, a down bag might well be a foolish luxury for someone who camps out only occasionally in the summer, when the bag might often be too warm, causing him to spend more time sleeping *on* than *in* it. A light-weight bag made of synthetic materials costs less and would probably adequately meet the needs of the occasional summer camper.

So-called three-season bags are satisfactory in all but the coldest weather. Some of them come with an extra-warm inner bag that zips inside, and this can sometimes be used separately to provide an extra bag. A serious camper who goes out in all types of weather may want to invest in two bags, a light one for summer and a heavy one for winter.

Since there are now so many bags on the market, you should delay making a final choice until you have looked at several different types. Study the catalogs of outfitters (see Appendix E), visit stores, and talk to experienced campers. If possible, borrow several bags from friends or rent them from outfitters so that you can test them in actual use. It is usually best to avoid buying so-called "bargains" made by relatively unknown manufacturers; stick to reputable manufacturers who are willing to stand behind their products. When you find a bag you think you may like, take off your shoes and crawl into it, zip it up, and see how it feels. Are your feet comfortable in it? If you want it for cold weather, is there a hood which will give good protection for your head and neck? Bags come in several lengths with corresponding variations in width. Buy the smallest one you feel comfortable in; it will save you money, bulk, and weight and will even be warmer. The price quoted for a down bag usually includes the cost of a waterproof stuff bag for it.

Note the quality of workmanship throughout the bag; this is usually one of the best measures of its overall quality. Turn the bag inside out to check the inside too. Is the stitching even, and are there from 8 to 10 stitches per inch (neither more nor less)? Is there adequate backstitching or tacking (made by stitching back and forth over the same spot several times) at all points of stress and at the ends of the rows of stitching, and are there double rows of stitching at such points of stress as seams, zippers, and the place where the hood is attached? Is good thread used and is it of Dacron or cotton with a nylon core for strength?

Read all the labels on the bag, for the government requires that the manufacturer disclose such information as (1) the amount and type of filling used (be wary of reprocessed materials which may be some manufacturer's castoffs or the leftovers from some other product), (2) the type of outer covering, and (3) the cut and size of the bag (these dimensions are usually given in terms of the uncut material with no allowance for hems and seams).

Some bags feature a pocket for inserting an air mattress, but these are not usually satisfactory since it is difficult to inflate the mattress inside the bag and, when it is inflated, there isn't much space left inside for the sleeper.

It is often difficult to buy suitable bags for children, since many manufacturers do not make them and others use inferior materials (this is particularly true of down bags). Fortunately, there is now a greater selection of bags made from synthetic materials and these are generally inexpensive and serve quite well for summer camping.

GROUND SHEET OR TARP

The ground is always more or less cold and damp, and since neither a blanket roll nor a sleeping bag is or should be completely waterproof, you will need a good waterproof tent floor, a sleeping pad, or a good tarp or ground sheet to protect your bedroll from dampness, dirt, and abrasion. Since any material you use for this purpose will eventually develop tiny tears and even larger holes from contact with the rough ground, many people use only an inexpensive, lightweight sheet of plastic (polyethylene), considering it expendable and easily replaceable. Although coated nylon costs more, it will last several times as long as polyethylene. Carry a roll of plastic or ripstop tape with you to mend holes as they appear.

PREPARING A BED SITE

Hikers often sleep with only a bed roll or sleeping bag and ground sheet for a mattress. To the uninitiated, this may sound like pure torture, but it is surprisingly easy for a vigorous person, particularly when young, to become accustomed to it after a possibly uncomfortable first night or two. This type of bedding cuts down on a backpacker's load, but even Pollyanna would have to admit that softness is not one of its virtues and that it may well have been the source of the expression "making mountains out of mole hills."

For maximum comfort, choose smooth ground and go over every inch of it on your hands and knees, removing each twig, pebble, or tough weed before putting down your bedding. Try to select a level spot, but if that is impossible, select one with as little slope as possible and place your head at the higher end. If you are on sand or bare dirt, hollow out depressions for your hips and shoulders, repeatedly trying them out until they fit. You would, of course, not do this where it would damage vegetation.

Figure 26-8 "I Just Gotta Get Up and Rest A While."

MATTRESSES

As we have noted, the weight of your body will compress the bottom of your sleeping bag, particularly if it has a down filler, until very little thickness or loft remains, thus reducing softness and insulation. Although campers of the past cut branches or gathered leaves, grass, or hay to supply a comfortable "mattress," such practices cannot be sanctioned today because of the need to conserve our natural resources. Therefore, if a modern backpacker finds sleeping on the ground too uncomfortable, he must carry his own mattress. When he wants the ultimate in lightness and compactness, he settles for a "shorty" pad which is just long enough to support him from his shoulders to his hips or mid-thighs. If he wants a pillow for his head or support for his legs, he can choose between using an inflatable air pillow, forming an earth pillow if he is on sand or bare dirt, or stuffing soft clothing into his stuff bag or other bag.

TYPES OF MATTRESSES

Three types of outdoor mattresses are in current use: (1) air mattresses, (2) open cell foam pads, and (3) closed cell foam pads.

Air Mattresses. Air mattresses, although favorites for many years, are now seldom used by backpackers for several reasons. Although they provide softness when properly used, they take some time to get used to and have other more serious drawbacks. They make for cold sleeping since they confine quantities of air in relatively large air spaces; this air moves about with every movement of the sleeper, even his breathing, and as we have seen, moving air carries away body heat. This characteristic, of course, might be welcome in hot weather. Since it is usually not practical to carry along a pump, you must inflate them by mouth and this can become a dreaded and onerous task at the end of a hard day on the trail. Perhaps their worst feature is that they will eventually develop leaks, all too often in the middle of the night when they really let you down with a bump.

Their main advantage is that they can be deflated and compressed into a very small package for transporting. To carry one, roll it up and place it vertically in your pack; don't fold it because repeated folding in the same place will cause the material to deteriorate, resulting in leaks.

Mattresses of rubberized materials are heavy and cold to sleep on, and the cheap, plastic variety are not worth buying for they wear out very quickly and are totally undependable, even developing pin-prick holes while not in use. Vinyl is more satisfactory and, with care, will last an appreciable length of time, and nylon is probably best of all.

Figure 26-9 "Happiness Is To Get Home to My Own Little Bed."

Always test your air mattress before starting out on a trip, for it is much more convenient to repair it at home then when out in the wilds. Inspect the valve to see that it is working properly and inflate the mattress and leave it overnight to check for slow leaks. If it does leak, inflate it again and draw it slowly past your ear as you listen for the sound of escaping air, or immerse it in water and watch for air bubbles.

The secret of sleeping comfortably on an air mattress is to underinflate it so that you sleep *in* not *on* it and won't bounce around like a cork on the ocean. Inflate the mattress fully, then lie down on your side on it so you can easily reach the valve. Now slowly let out air until your hip just barely touches the ground.

To save time when deflating the mattress in the morning, open the valve when you first get up and let it deflate while you eat breakfast and pack.

To store a mattress, do not fold it but inflate it slightly and stand it on end in a cool place.

Open Cell Foam Pads. An open cell foam pad, as the name suggests, has cells which open into each other like the cells of a sponge. This allows the air to circulate freely, and as we noted, moving air carries away body heat making them cold to sleep on. Like a sponge, they also absorb dampness, so it is necessary to encase them in a waterproof covering which adds to their weight and cost. The pad is soft to sleep on but insulates poorly and is so heavy and bulky that backpackers seldom choose it.

Closed Cell Foam Pads. A closed cell pad is much warmer to sleep on since the cells are completely separate and so confine the air in small spaces. Since it does not absorb moisture, it needs no covering, although you may want to use a ground sheet or a washable cover to protect it from soil and abrasion. The closed cell pad is quite washable, smooths out ground bumps nicely, and provides good insulation. It is sold under various trade names, such as Ensolite, Thermobar, and Voltek, and comes in sheets from 1/4 to 1/2 inch thick (the 3/8-inch size is probably the most popular). A pad can be purchased ready to use or can be cut from a sheet of the material. This type of pad is less bulky and less expensive than the open cell pad and can be rolled up into a compact package to attach to your pack. It is fast becoming a favorite with "go-light" campers.

ADDITIONAL READINGS

(For an explanation of abbreviations and abbreviated forms, see page 25.)

Bridge: *America's Backpacking Book,* ch. 12.
Cardweff: *America's Camping Book,* ch. 5.
Colwell: *Introduction to Backpacking,* pp. 108–122.
Fletcher: *The Complete Walker,* pp. 165–196.
Langer: *The Joy of Camping,* pp. 29–43.
Learn and Tallman: *Backpacker's Digest,* ch. 3.
Manning: *Backpacking One Step at a Time,* ch. 11.
Merrill: *The Hiker's and Backpacker's Handbook,* pp. 85–95.
Rethmel: *Backpacking,* pp. 2-1 to 2-5.
Riviere: *Backcountry Camping,* ch. 4.
Scout Handbook, pp. 234–235.
Sunset Camping Handbook, pp. 21–26.
Wood: *Pleasure Packing,* ch. 4.

MAGAZINE ARTICLES

Backpacker:
"Backpacker's Equipment." *Backpacker-2,* Summer, 1973, pp. 45–51, 64–76.
Kutik, William: "You and Your Gear—Cleaning Your Bag." *Backpacker-2,* Summer, 1973, p. 12.
Packer, Nelson: "How to Buy a Duck Down Sleeping Bag." *Backpacker-8,* Winter, 1974, p. 59.
"The Pick of the Polyester Bags." *Backpacker-6,* Summer, 1974, pp. 73–85.

Boys' Life:
Cost, Rick: "Sleeping Comfort at Camp." July, 1971, p. 66.

Camping Journal:
Heyl, Frank: "Bag a Good Night's Sleep." Jan., 1971, p. 22.

Consumer Reports 1974 Buying Guide:
"Warm Weather Sleeping Bags." p. 342.
"Down-Filled Sleeping Bags." p. 343.

Wilderness Camping:
Wood, Robert S.: "Outdoor Insulation; Down vs. Dacron Vs. Foam." Part I, Jan./Feb., 1973, p. 8; Part II, Mar./Apr., 1973.

Chapter 27

Camp Stoves and Wood Fires

Figure 27-1 Stop!! Don't You Know It Will Take Nature Many, Many Years to Replace That Tree?

Then after a day filled with pleasure and work,
As you trudge back to camp with your trout,
The smell of bacon that's cooking up there,
Is the sweetest of odors, no doubt.

—E. K. Berry, Cooking in Camp.

THE CASE OF THE DISAPPEARING WOOD FIRE

Whereas the sight of a backpacker using a camp stove was a rare thing only 20 to 25 years ago, it is now quite commonplace. There are several reasons for this, and one of the main ones is that a stove is simply more convenient, for you can unpack, assemble and put it into operation in a matter of minutes; you don't have to scamper about searching for suitable dry wood, then arrange it carefully in the type of fire you want, and wait for it to burn down to the good bed of coals so essential for successful cooking. Stoves produce an even heat of any intensity desired while leaving your pots and pans shiny bright, for there is no smoke or soot to coat them. When handled properly, a stove will not explode and offers little chance of starting a destructive forest fire. When through with it, you can simply turn it off; you don't have to wait for it to burn down and then carefully extinguish each ember and partially burned stick. A stove is so quick and easy to use that you need not hesitate to stop to heat your lunch or an afternoon snack as you might with a wood fire.

An increasing number of states now prohibit the building of wood fires, especially along the more popular trails. This is partly because of the greatly increased number of backpackers who literally crowd the trails, leaving behind an assortment of ugly, pock-marked fire sites as each group apparently feels impelled to build its fire in a brand new spot. All available wood has long since been burned, and some neophytes have even chopped down green saplings, little realizing that green wood will not burn satisfactorily anyway. Some areas that still permit controlled wood fires have compromised by establishing certain fire sites and requiring that all fires be built in them, using only the wood provided beside the site.

Another important reason for the prohibition against wood fires is the numerous disastrous forest fires that have been started by careless or ignorant campers, which annually burn over thousands of acres of woodlands, destroying valuable timber and undergrowth and destroying the homes of countless wild creatures, sending them fleeing with fear-crazed eyes in a vain attempt to escape the flames which advance so rapidly that they can outdistance even a man on horseback. Forest fires are, of course, more likely during long, dry spells, so that restrictions are particularly likely then.

A third reason has been our awakened interest in and understanding of ecology, which teaches us that burning wood disrupts nature's balance and permanently destroys a natural resource instead of leaving it to decay and return its nutrients to the soil as nature intended.

SOME ALTERNATE SOURCES OF HEAT

Several substitute sources of heat have enjoyed various degrees of favor.

CANNED HEAT

Jellied fuel such as that found in Sterno canned heat and heat tabs is relatively safe for use by even young campers but, unfortunately, gives out so little heat that it is scarcely useful for anything beyond heating a bowl of soup or stew or cooking such a simple thing as an egg. To use jellied fuel, place the can of fuel between two rocks to support the pan or use the portable folding wind screen and kettle support that is available.

CHARCOAL

Cooking with charcoal is a backyard activity familiar to almost all chil-

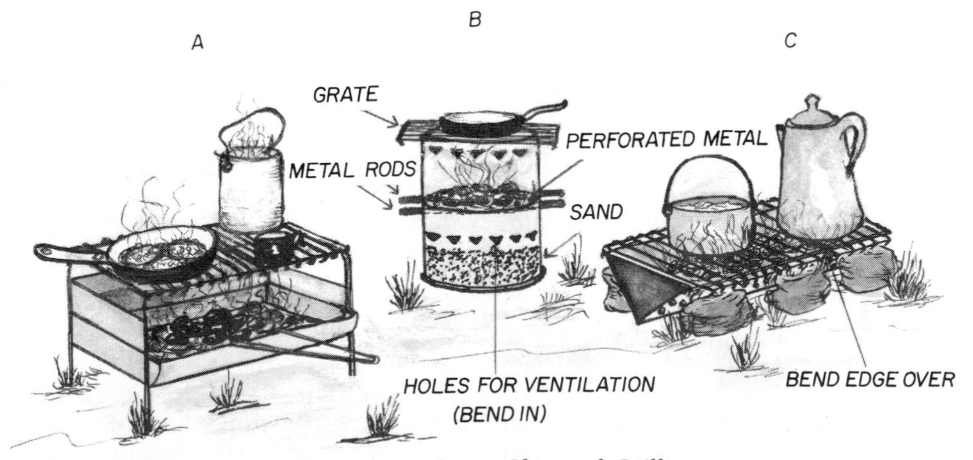

Figure 27-2 Some Charcoal Grills.

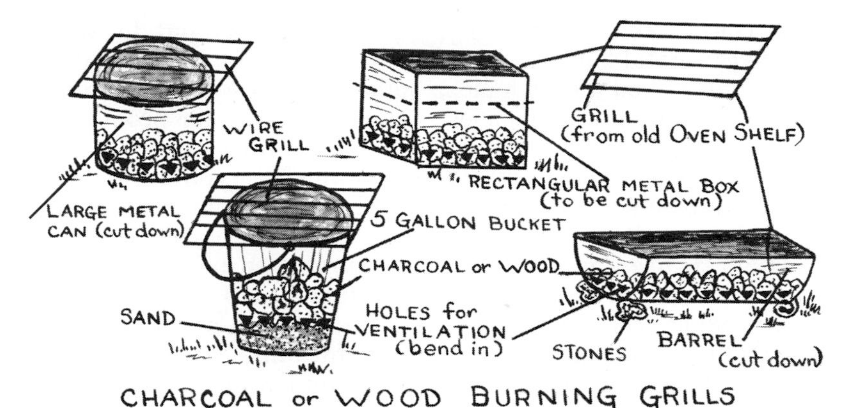

Figure 27–3 Some Other Grills to Make and Use With Wood or Charcoal.

dren and is a fairly safe and satisfactory method for them to use. Charcoal briquettes are relatively light and easy to carry and you can extinguish them when through and save them for future use. It is best to carry some sort of charcoal starter to get them started, and you will need some type of grill to contain the fire and support cooking utensils. Several types are available commercially that fold up to fit in a carrying case. The one shown in Figure 27–2*A* features a pull-out fire pan to contain the charcoal. Grills can also be handmade; the one shown in Figure 27–2*B* is made of a 5-gallon tin can in which ventilator holes are punched in the sides with a juice can opener. A metal grate on top supports the pans, and the charcoal is supported on a metal disc placed across two metal rods inserted in holes in the sides of the can. Figure 27–2*C* features a fire pan formed by cutting diagonally across two opposite corners of a large rectangular can and placing a metal grate on top to support cooking utensils. You will find instructions for working with metal in Chapter 16.

Figure 27–3 shows additional homemade grills suitable for use with either wood or charcoal. One of the most serious drawbacks of most homemade grills is that they cannot be folded up, so that they are somewhat cumbersome to take on a trip. You can usually find materials for making the grill, as well as necessary metal rods and pieces of wire screening, in trash heaps, or you can buy a piece of gravel screening to use as a pan support.

GASOLINE AND KEROSENE

Both gasoline and kerosene stoves once enjoyed great popularity, but nearly all backpackers now prefer small butane or propane stoves. Kerosene is less desirable than gasoline since it burns less efficiently, is both smelly and sooty, and necessitates carrying some more volatile fuel such as gasoline to get it going.

Gasoline stoves use white, unleaded appliance gas, which is relatively inexpensive and available at most outfitters, often under some trade name such as Coleman fuel. Although many ordinary gasoline stations carry white gasoline, it is often too dirty to burn satisfactorily and will eventually damage your stove. Ordinary automobile gasoline is quite unsuitable, for even though unleaded, it contains additives that destroy its usefulness. Although it takes a little time to get the hang of lighting and using gasoline stoves, they are efficient and maintain a steady heat as long as any fuel remains in the tank. Gasoline's very volatility, however, makes careful handling mandatory, since any spilled on the hands, clothing, or surroundings or even escaping vapors can go off like a torch when exposed to open flame or even a hot surface such as a stove or lantern.

Never use a gasoline or kerosene stove in a small, enclosed area such as a tent or cabin. Like all fuel-burning stoves, they produce carbon monoxide, which, if inhaled, can cause serious illness or even death from asphyxiation or carbon monoxide poisoning. They also give off vapors from unburned and partially burned fuels that are highly flammable and can easily build up to dangerous proportions. These, together with the carbon monoxide, gradually displace the oxygen, resulting in a vicious circle wherein the stove burns less and less efficiently and gives off more and more carbon monoxide and vapors from improperly burned fuel, thus intensifying the danger of fire and explosion. Using a stove in cramped quarters also increases the danger of upsetting it or having something flammable come in contact with it.

Carry your extra fuel in a conspicuously marked, leakproof round or flat container (Fig. 27–4), preferably of aluminum and with a tightly fitting rubber gasket and screw-on lid. You will also need to carry a small funnel with a fine mesh filter to sift out dirt when the fuel is poured. Fill the stove only 3/4 full to allow room for the gasoline to expand, as is necessary for proper burning.

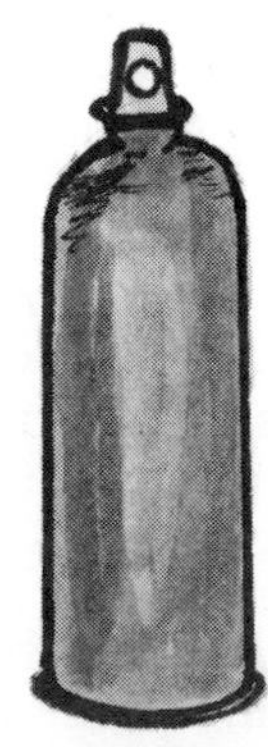

Figure 27–4 Container for Carrying Gasoline or Kerosene.

Never fill a stove when it is hot, for escaping fumes or any liquid spilled on the hot surface may burst into flame. To avoid the danger of a flashback or explosion when lighting the stove, strike the match and apply it to the burner *before* turning on the gas. If your first attempt fails, turn off the gas immediately and wait a short time to let the vapors dissipate before trying again.

Since both stoves and fuel containers give off unpleasant odors, someone not carrying food should place them in the outside pockets of his pack. Gasoline weighs about 1.5 pounds per quart and two persons on a 7-day trip will need about 2 quarts.

One of the greatest advantages of a gasoline or kerosene stove is the ease with which you can determine the amount of fuel left in the stove and add any needed before starting to cook. As we will see, that is not possible with propane or butane stoves, and in using them you may run out in the middle of cooking and have to wait until the stove is cold before adding a new cylinder of fuel to finish cooking.

PROPANE AND BUTANE

Although relative newcomers to the field, propane and butane stoves are now much preferred by most backpackers. Propane and butane are gases compressed under low pressure (LP) and contained in a thin metal cylinder or cartridge that attaches directly to the stove. This eliminates the danger and messiness of having to pour a flammable liquid. They are clean-burning and soot-free and as easy to light and regulate as your kitchen stove. They require no priming or preheating, and a new cylinder of fuel is easy to attach. Although both fuels burn well in warm weather, only propane is recommended for use in cold weather. When used with caution, there is little danger of starting a forest fire or causing an explosion; however, you should never crush or puncture a used cartridge since it may still contain enough fuel to cause an explosion. Instead, place the used cartridge in your pack to carry out and dispose of properly; too many ignorant or lazy campers have cast away their old cartridges, leaving behind a cluttered landscape, which has brought disfavor to the whole field of camping.

Since the cartridges for different stoves are not usually interchangeable, you may have to search around to find the particular type you need. This is not usually too much of a problem, however, since good outfitters usually stock a fairly wide selection of the more popular types.

A variety of sizes and types of stoves are now on the market, and some popular backpacker models are so small and compact that an entire outfit consisting of a burner, a couple of pots, a frying pan, and a windscreen all nest into a package that weighs only 2 to 3 pounds and is small and compact enough to fit into the pocket of an ordinary rucksack. Such small stoves, however, have only one burner, so you will need to either carry more than one stove or cook your meal in courses. Larger 2- or 3-burner stoves are available for larger groups or those willing to carry the extra weight.

Propane and butane stoves have several disadvantages. These fuels are less efficient than gasoline or kerosene and cooking therefore takes more time. They are also slightly more expensive, although the difference is negligible. They weigh more per unit of heat, largely because of the weight of the nonrefillable cartridge. Another disadvantage is that both pressure and heat decrease during the last 10 minutes of burning of a cartridge. As previously mentioned, there is also no way to accurately determine the amount of fuel remaining in a partly used cartridge so that you may run out in the middle of cooking and have to wait until the stove gets cold before adding a new cartridge.

Use a windscreen to concentrate the heat under the cooking vessel, and turn off the fuel supply before you extinguish the stove. As with all fuel-burning stoves, avoid using a stove in a small, poorly ventilated area such as a tent or cabin.

SOME POPULAR BACKPACKER STOVES

Figure 27-5*A* shows a French Bluet stove, which burns butane and, together with windscreen and cartridge, weighs only about 1 pound, 13 ounces. The cartridge will burn from 2 to 3 hours at maximum flame.

An 8R Optimus, or 8R Primus, Stove (these are identical except for the name) is shown in Figure 27-5*B*. It burns white gasoline and folds up neatly into a metal box that furnishes a firm, steady base with a low center of gravity. It has a self pressure system, and a half pint of gasoline burns about an hour. The stove weighs about 24 ounces without fuel.

A little grasshopper stove (Fig. 27-5*C*) is available in models that burn either propane or butane. The fuel cylinder forms the third leg of its wide tripod base, which gives it good stability. The legs fold flat for carrying and the burner comes with pan supports that can be adjusted to accommodate different-sized pans. The stove weighs about 12 ounces and the cartridge of fuel weighs about 30 ounces and will burn about 6 hours.

A Svea 123 stove (Fig. 27-5*D*), which burns white gasoline, has an internal windscreen that also serves to support the small pot that is included with the stove. The whole outfit is small enough to fit into an ordinary rucksack pocket and weighs about 25 ounces

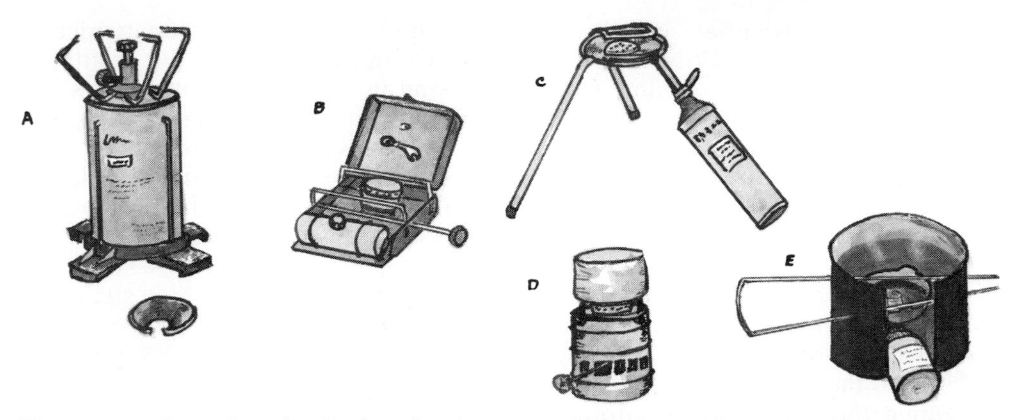

Figure 27-5 Some Popular Backpacker Stoves. *A,* Bluet (butane). *B,* Optimus 8R or Primus 8R (white gasoline). *C,* Grasshopper (propane or butane). *D,* Svea (white gasoline). *E,* Gerry Mini Stove (butane).

with fuel. A nested set of additional cooking pans is also available.

A Gerry Mini Stove, which burns butane and has a windscreen around the burner, is shown in Figure 27-5*E*. The stove itself weighs 18 ounces, and the fuel cartridge weighs 9½ ounces and burns from 2 to 3 hours.

FOREST CONSERVATION

One of the penalties of an ecological education is that one lives alone in a world of wounds. Much of the damage inflicted on land is quite invisible to the layman.

—ALDO LEOPOLD

OUR CHANGING ATTITUDES

If our first settlers could return today, they would no doubt be utterly astounded at our concern for conserving our remaining forests and woodlands. To them, the supply must have seemed inexhaustible and the forests almost an enemy, for the trees had to be cut down and disposed of to make room for homes and growing crops. The dense growth harbored both wild animals that preyed upon their meager supplies of livestock and unfriendly Indians, made so by our outrages committed against them. "Chop and burn" was a way of life to them. On the other hand, the woodlands served them well by furnishing raw materials for their furniture, homes and barns, posts and rails for their fences, and lumber for their stockades to protect them from their enemies and wild predators. The wilderness also provided fruit and herbs as well as fish and wild game to add variety to their otherwise monotonous diets.

Soon these hard-working, resourceful people discovered that there was an eager market for wood products in England and other foreign countries that would supply the ready cash needed to buy the manufactured products young America was not yet equipped to produce. Consequently, lumbering became a major industry, and lumber camps were established, from which many of our towns and cities developed.

But what was the effect of all this on the forests? The practice of the money-hungry logging companies was "clean cutting," which meant cutting everything in their paths. Young saplings and shrubbery were sacrificed, leaving behind a desolate wasteland of stumps and debris that it would take nature from 50 to 100 years to replace. In those days, few citizens were farseeing enough to grasp the significance of what was happening, although William Penn as early as 1653 made an unsuccessful plea to "save one acre of forests for every one that is cut."

RECENT PROGRESS

Fortunately, we are now undergoing a belated awakening to the need to conserve at least part of what was once our great natural heritage. One important step has been the development of the science of *forest management,* which seeks means to use forest land in ways most beneficial to both present and future generations. These include, among other things, research into the control of insects, diseases, and destructive grazing, as well as finding the best ways to replace the trees that are lost through logging or natural processes. We have also made some progress in preventing and controlling forest fires, which were once so devastating.

Tree farming is now a science that considers that trees, like any other crop, need to be planned for, nurtured, and harvested with great care. Highly trained specialists go through commercial forests, marking mature trees that have attained their maximum growth for cutting. At the same time, they plant enough seedlings to maintain a steady crop. Three-fourths of our remaining woodlands are owned by commercial growers, and together with our federal- and state-owned parks and forests, these provide most of the habitat for our depleted numbers of birds and other wildlife.

HOW FORESTS HELP US

Trees and woodlands serve us in many ways. Of special interest to us as campers is the fact that they provide the environment for organized camping, where youth can live simply, surrounded by plants and animals in their natural habitats. These same benefits are also available to the rapidly increasing number of adults and family groups who are discovering the joys of taking to the woods for such pastimes as backpacking, hiking, swimming, boating, family or group camping, and hunting and fishing.

New uses are constantly being found for lumber, so that nearly all of a felled tree, including even the bark and sawdust, is now used to produce such things as construction lumber, furniture, pulp and paper, fuel, charcoal, plastics, drugs, and pressed wood. Trees also supply maple syrup, resins, fruit, nuts, turpentine, chemicals, and even trees to make our Christmas merry. Standing timber protects our watersheds and minimizes erosion by means of their intermingled root systems and underlying carpet of grass, shrubs, debris, and underbrush that absorb moisture and gradually return it to the leaves, where it evaporates to eventually return to earth as rain. Without such vegetation on our slopes, rains and melting winter snows would cascade unimpeded down the hillsides to augment the already swollen streams and produce devastating floods; in fact, this frequently occurs in areas where the growth has been cleared away.

WOOD FIRES

Each color or tint that a tree has known
  In the heart of a wood-fire glow.
Look into the flames and you will see
  Blue dusk and the dawn's pale rose,
The golden light of the noonday sun,
  The purple of darkening night.
The crimson glow of the sunset,
  The sheen of the soft moonlight.
Fire brings forth from the heart of a tree
Beauty stored there in memory.

MARY S. EDGAR *

*From *Wood-Fire and Candle-Light.* Permission by The Macmillan Company, Ltd., of Canada.

Among the fondest memories of older campers is that of sitting in peaceful camaraderie with good friends around a blazing camp fire. Nothing else is so cheerful, has such an enchanting aroma, is so attractive to watch, imparts such a delicious taste to food, dries out wet clothing so well, or warms you so pleasantly when it is chilly. In addition, it helps destroy your rubbish and signals searchers if you are lost.

Although, as we have stated, wood fires can no longer be widely encouraged for general camp use, there are probably some situations in which they are still permissible. This is particularly true in camps that have extensive woodlands, especially those that practice scientific methods of forest management, promoting the health of all trees and systematically replacing those that are used or die of old age. In fact, this may well provide valuable conservation lessons as youngsters observe what is being done and learn to be quite selective in choosing what wood to use and how to use it. For this reason and for the benefit of those who feel that every camper should attain some proficiency in building wood fires for use in an emergency such as when his camp stove has become inoperative or he is lost and needs to signal for help, we are including a discussion of some of the principles of building wood fires.

CHOOSING A FIRE SITE

When choosing a fire site, you must be sure, above all, to choose one that will offer little chance for your fire to spread. No matter how pleasant and romantic a fire in a deeply wooded area sounds, it is always dangerous, for there are usually low-hanging dry branches to catch on fire, and even green ones may dry out enough to burn if your fire is hot. In camp, it is usually better to choose a few spots and confine all fires to them to avoid destroying any more of the natural environment than necessary.

If you must build a fire in a grassy area, use a shovel to skin off sizable divots of sod and pile them neatly so that you can replace them just as they were after your fire is out and the ground has cooled off.

The floor of the forest is usually covered with a litter of dead leaves, broken branches, and other debris called *duff,* with some underlying organic matter such as leaf mold and decomposing branches, which is called *humus.* These are combustible, and a fire may smolder in them and break out in an open blaze several hours after you have left the vicinity and forgotten all about it. Therefore, you will need to clear away all this material down to hard ground for an area of at least 6 to 10 feet in diameter. Be especially careful with the soil known as "peat" or "muck," for it is itself combustible and may burn underground for several days before breaking out. Place a ring of rocks around your firesite if they are available (see Figure 27–9).

It is best to lay a foundation of sand, gravel, or flat stones first. Avoid shale and limestone, for they may crack and fly like shrapnel when heated. Rocks near water or in a creek bed are often so waterlogged that they create enough steam to burst when heated. If you dry them out *gradually* by *gentle* heat, they may eventually prove satisfactory.

Never build a fire against a tree, for if dead, it might catch on fire; if green, you will injure or even kill it.

CONTROLLING YOUR FIRE

Keep an orderly campsite with everything in its place and dispose of all debris promptly to minimize the danger of having your fire spread.

Before lighting the fire, be prepared to handle it quickly if it should start to spread and to put it out when through with it. Certain tools are useful for this purpose. A shovel or spade comes in handy for clearing off combustible debris before building your fire and for smothering it with dirt if it starts to spread. You can also use it to move coals into the exact position needed for baking or other cooking and to push blazing firebrands over to one side where they will not burn or smoke your food. Lastly, you can use it to bury your garbage and extinguish your fire.

Place a container of water nearby to use for dousing the fire in an emergency; if not so needed, you can use it to extinguish your fire when through with it.

If you will be working with grease near the fire, never put water on it if it starts to burn for it will only spread it and make it worse. Instead, keep a quantity of baking soda, salt, or sand handy to smother it. Avoid using flour or cornmeal for they themselves will burn.

Never leave a campfire unattended for even a few minutes—that is all it needs to spread and get completely out of control.

If a Fire Starts to Spread

If a fire starts to run wild, immediate action is imperative, for a situation that you alone could easily control at its start can get completely out of hand in moments. Send or go for help unless you are *absolutely certain* you can handle it yourself.

To extinguish it, you must cut off the supply of oxygen or combustible material. To smother it (deprive it of oxygen), douse it with water, beat it with a broom, a green evergreen switch with top branches still on, a wet burlap bag or other heavy material saturated with water, or cover it with sand, dirt, or gravel. Beat *toward* the wind so that you will not simply fan the fire and spread sparks ahead of you. To deprive it of fuel, go up far enough ahead on the windward side to allow time to dig a trench 12 to 18 inches wide and deep enough to reach mineral soil; throw all flammable material *away* from the path of the fire so that it will simply burn itself out for lack of anything to burn. Watch over the area long enough to make sure that it does not blaze up again.

FUEL FOR YOUR CAMPFIRE

The disappointment and discomfort of campers when no one in the group can produce more than a smudge fire is enough to disenchant them with camping forever. Your expertise at building the right fire in the right place at the right time tells a great deal about how good a camper you are.

The kindling's dwindling
  The log won't catch,
The only blaze
  Is the new-struck match.
The flames are low,
  The smoke is high.
The wood is green
  And so am I.

—Author Unknown

Tinder, Kindling, and Firewood. Three components are necessary for successful firebuilding: (1) good *tinder* that will catch immediately when you apply the match and burn long enough to ignite (2) the *kindling,* which, in turn, sets fire to (3) the *firewood,* which burns with enough force to provide the heat, light, or atmosphere you want. You must select, prepare, and arrange each of these exactly right to get a "just right" fire. An expert fire builder does not carelessly pick up any old wood, toss it into a hit-or-miss pile, and apply a match. He works quickly and deftly, selecting and arranging each bit of fuel for a definite purpose. A balky fire that burns sluggishly or coughs spasmodically and finally dies results from choosing the wrong kind of wood or from arranging it incorrectly.

TINDER. Many things will serve satisfactorily as tinder, that highly inflammable material that ignites at the touch of a match. Curls of white birchbark are excellent, since they burn well, even when wet or rotten. Look for them on a dead or fallen tree or where quantities of them are hanging loose or have peeled off a live tree and fallen to the ground. Pieces of fat pine, dry evergreen cones, last year's dry weed stalks, dried goldenrod, grape, and honeysuckle vines, Queen Anne's lace, old birds' or squirrels' nests, milkweed silk, sagebrush, dried cactus, corn stalks, and dry corncobs are also excellent.

Three fuzz clumps or fuzz sticks, pyramided together as the base of a fire (Fig. 27–6), make good timber. Thin, curly shavings or a handful of twigs, each hardly bigger than a match, split and broken in the middle, also serve adequately.

Such things as waxed bread paper, waxed milk cartons, and crumpled up newspapers are fine if you happen to have them, but don't bring them just to build fires for there are too many other things available almost anywhere you go.

Don't depend on dry grass and leaves, for although they blaze brightly, they burn out too quickly to set fire to anything else.

Never use gasoline or aerosols not specifically intended for starting fires.

KINDLING. You will need kindling that will catch readily from the tinder and burn strongly enough to ignite the firewood. Split it for best results and keep it small in size, ranging from the size of a matchstick to about the length of your little finger or longer. Fat pine, cedar, or paper birch are best, but all the birches are satisfactory and you can also use evergreen, basswood, tulip, sumac, white pine and nearly all other kinds of pine, spruce, balsam, or box elder, as well as the frayed bark of cedar or hemlock.

FIREWOOD. Firewood is divided roughly into hard woods and soft woods, each with its own special uses for camping. Kinds of wood vary in different sections of the country, so that you must study your own particular region to determine what it provides. It isn't enough to be able to glibly recite the names of trees in full leaf, for campers use dead, dry wood with no leaves; you must identify firewood by its bark and the character of the wood itself.

Soft Woods. The lumbering industry regards as soft woods only the *evergreens* or *conifers,* while the broad-leaved trees (*deciduous,* or those that shed their leaves annually) are considered hard woods. Campers, however, consider as soft woods any that are actually softer and weigh less for their size. This includes the evergreens as well as some broad-leaved trees.

To distinguish between soft woods

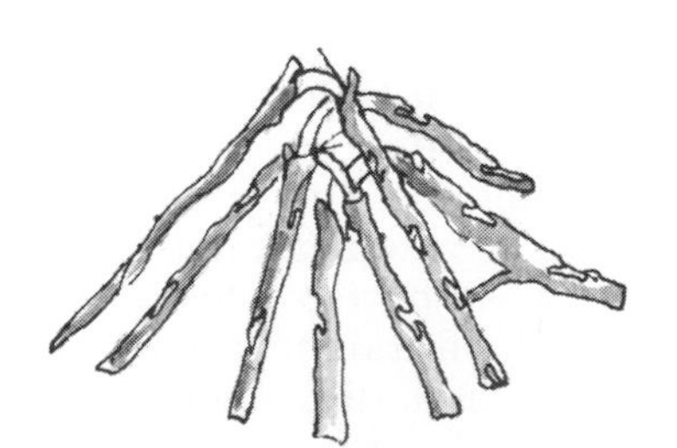

Figure 27–6 Fuzz Clumps, Broken Sticks, and Fuzz Sticks Pyramided as Tinder.

and hard woods, pick them up and weigh them in your hand; since hard woods are more compact, they weigh more. Soft woods burn quickly and briskly, making them good for kindling, providing quick flames for rapid boiling or baking, and blazing brightly for a campfire gathering. They are inclined to be somewhat smokey and sooty, however.

Good soft woods include alder, quaking aspen (poplar), balsam, basswood (linden), the birches, chestnut, cottonwood, soft or silver maple, pine (jack or Labrador and white or loblolly), pitch pine (fine for kindling, but even when burning brightly, emits a resin that taints foods and coats utensils), and spruce.

Hard Woods. Hard woods are preferable for extended cooking and providing a long-lasting fire. They kindle slowly, so soft wood must be mixed with them to get them started, but once ablaze, they last a long time and provide a good bed of glowing coals that remains hot indefinitely. Hickory, oak, and maple are usually considered best; however, apple, white ash, beech, dogwood, hornbeam (ironwood), locust, mulberry, yellow pine, and tamarack (lodgepole pine) are also good.

Figure 27–7 Fresh Fish Taste Great.

Spitfire Woods. These are woods that in general, burn well enough, but tend to spit, make alarming noises, and, worst of all, throw sparks that may start forest fires or burn holes in tents or blankets. Soft woods in this category are the conifers (pine tree type), basswood (linden), box elder, chestnut, sassafras, spruce, tamarack, tulip (yellow poplar), and willow (which is also undesirable because it imparts an acrid taste to food cooked over it).

Slow-Burning Green Woods. These are woods that, when green, will scarcely burn at all and so are worthless for either cooking or warmth. However, this very quality makes them valuable as fire dogs, backlogs, and fire banks. The following belong in this class: black ash, balsam, basswood (linden), box elder, buckeye, butternut (white walnut), chestnut, cypress, hemlock, red (scarlet) maple, red and water oak, persimmon, pine (black or white and pitch), poplar (aspen), sassafras, sourwood, sycamore (plane tree or buttonwood), tamarack, tulip (yellow poplar), and tupelo (sour gum).

Making a Selection. You must use discrimination when selecting firewood. Green wood, because of its moisture content, seldom burns well. On the other hand, wood that is extremely old has lost much of its valuable heat-producing qualities. A little intelligent experimentation will help you select wisely.

The forest floor tends to hold moisture, so that even in comparatively dry weather, branches lying on it may be somewhat damp and questionable as firewood. As each tree in a crowded forest grows, it constantly struggles with its neighbors to reach up and absorb as much sunlight as possible. As the tree grows, its bottom limbs get so little sunlight that they often die. Their position under the tree and the free circulation of air about them keeps them quite dry except during a severe storm. Their value as fuel seems to have been recognized even in feudal times. Then, all of the land belonged to the lord of the manor and the peasants were not allowed to cut trees or use any wood except what they could find on the ground or reach in the trees with their pruning hooks and shepherd's crooks (an ingenious way for the lord to keep his woodlands clean and neat). It is easy to imagine what devious methods they invented to get more than was rightfully theirs—thus the expression "by hook or by crook." Branches extending upward from downwood, driftwood, dry weathered roots, and knots also make excellent, long-lasting fuel.

Break wood to test it for dryness. Small, dry sticks snap and break cleanly, whereas wet or green ones bend and finally break with jagged edges. Large, dry sticks feel firm and heavy in the hand and will usually snap if you hit them sharply against the edge of a rock, and if you tap two of them together, they emit a clear, sharp sound instead of the dull, muffled sound of wet or green sticks. Sticks that crumble or break up too easily when you give them a sharp blow are rotten and would only smolder and smoke if put on a fire. Wood picked up from the ground is called *squaw wood* and, if perfectly dry, should not be ignored. The Indians probably used little else, for they had no implements comparable to our sharp hatchet for chopping and splitting.

Modern campers differ as to how much to use a hatchet for preparing firewood. It is only common sense and not at all unwoodsman-like to break sticks by hand or under your foot if you can do it easily. You can also avoid chopping by laying long pieces of wood across the fire to burn apart. On the other hand, skill in using a hatchet is a big asset, particularly for splitting wood, which always burns better. Walt Whitman said, "We are warmed twice by wood, once when we cut it and again when we burn it." You should ordinarily split pieces of wood over 2 inches thick before placing them on the fire.

Your Stockpile of Wood. If you are going to stay at a campsite for any length of time, arrange your wood in piles, ranging in size from large sticks for extensive cooking and council fires down to kindling and tinder (Fig. 27-8). Place the wood conveniently near but not in the way of activity around the fire site. Throw a tarpaulin or poncho over your woodpile to keep it dry and place a small emergency supply of wood under your sleeping tent in case of an unexpected rain.

Figure 27-8 Arranging Your Woodpile.

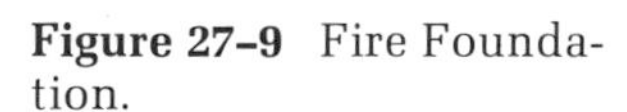

Figure 27-9 Fire Foundation.

BUILDING THE FIRE

Laying the Fire. Collect a big handful of tinder, about twice as much kindling, and quite a supply of firewood before you start, for no self-respecting camper should have to scamper about getting more fuel to keep his fire going after he has once started it. Place these materials within easy reach.

Make a fire foundation by crossing three small sticks (Fig. 27-9) with an end of each resting on one of the others to provide good air circulation. Pile the tinder loosely within this framework, leaving a little tunnel at the bottom on the *windward side* (side from which the wind is blowing). Now pile on a quantity of kindling in a loose pyramid. This completes what is known as a *basic fire lay* and forms the basis of any kind of fire you want to build (see photo).

Now add some larger pieces of wood, preferably split, in pyramid fashion. Burning consists of *combustion*, or the uniting of fuel with oxygen,

(Courtesy of Camp Kooch-I-Ching, International Falls, Minnesota.)

and when you apply a match through the tunnel to the bottom of the tinder, this loose structure permits the flame to travel upward and soon sets the whole thing ablaze. Most fire failures result from piling the fuel on too compactly or in such a way as to let it fall down as it burns so that it smothers itself, resulting in a dead fire or at best one that is smokey and balky. Remember that fire burns upward and only materials directly in its path will ignite. Keep cautiously adding still larger pieces of wood until your fire is as big as you need.

Starting the Fire. Use only *kitchen* or *torch matches* to start your fire. Safety or book matches are practically worthless for camp use.

CARRYING MATCHES. Matches are so essential to comfortable camping that when preparing for a trip you should pack them separately, placing the bulk in a waterproof container in a well-protected spot in your pack. Carry a small emergency supply, also waterproofed, in a safe spot on your person.

Figure 27–10 shows several varieties of containers for the smaller emergency supply. A metal box (*A*), such as a typewriter ribbon or bouillon cube box, although not waterproof in itself, can be sealed shut or used for carrying matches that have already been waterproofed. A common and inexpensive metal type case (*B*), available at most supply houses and equipment stores, is watertight and its screw-on top is attached so that you can't lose it. Another type of waterproof case (*C*) is made of hard black rubber of composition material and has a compass embedded in its screw-on top and a whistle on the other end. The latter two types of cases are especially good if you are camping around water, for they will float.

WATERPROOFING MATCHES. You can waterproof bunches of matches by crimping some aluminum foil around them or wrapping them in Saran-type kitchen wrap, sealing it tightly with twist-ems.

You can also waterproof the matches themselves. The best way is to buy some paraffin at a grocery store and place some of it in an old No. 10 tin can which you immerse in a pan of water. Place the water over the fire and heat it until the paraffin melts. Do not cover the paraffin or place it directly over the fire for it is quite flammable and can ignite into a ball of fire in a matter of seconds. Use tongs or pliers to remove the can of hot paraffin from the water. Tie your matches in bundles of six to eight, leaving a piece of string attached to *each* bundle with which to manipulate it. Dip each bundle of matches into the melted paraffin to coat them. When you are ready to use a match, pick it out of its paraffin bed and scrape off any excess paraffin; what little remains will make the match burn better.

Only counselors or older, very responsible campers should handle par-

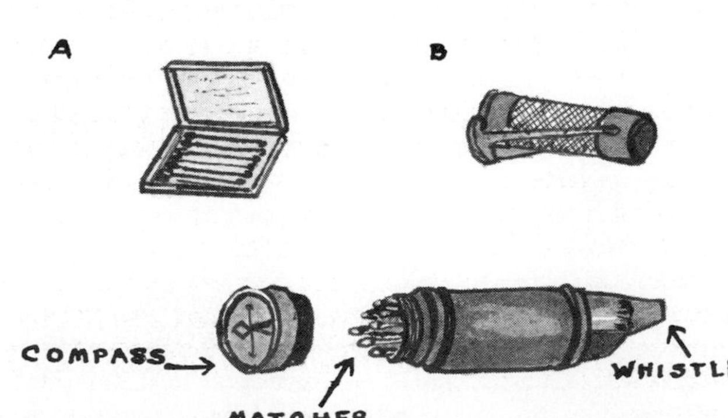

Figure 27–10 Some Match Cases.

affin because of the fire danger and the fact that hot paraffin causes nasty burns. Never pour paraffin down a sink, for it will clog it as it hardens.

You can also waterproof matches by dipping them in a thin solution of shellac, varnish, or fingernail polish.

LIGHTING THE FIRE. Pride yourself on laying your fire so well that you will need only one match to start it. Only a greenhorn chooses his material and arranges it so poorly that he must strike enough matches to make his surroundings look like a game of "pick-up-sticks."

Use a small rock or other abrasive material to strike your match on, kneel on the windward side in front of the little tunnel, take out one match, and close the container to protect the rest. Grasp the match well down its shaft to avoid breaking it, strike it, and hold it downward so the flame burns up the shaft. Cup your hands around it to shield it from the wind and, as soon as it is burning well, cautiously insert it through the tunnel to the *bottom* of the tinder.

If your fire lay is good, it will blaze up immediately and you need only stand by to add more fuel as it is needed. Place it on loosely to avoid smothering the fire. If your fire doesn't catch after two or three matches, the fault obviously lies in your fire lay and you'll save time in the long run by tearing it down and starting all over again. Don't toss away a match until you're sure it is dead out; then drop it in the fire or break it in two and stick the head in the ground.

General Hints About Fires. One of the commonest errors in building fires is to build one much bigger than you need. The Indian expressed his disdain for this practice by saying, "White man big fool; make big fire, can't go near; Indian make little fire and sit happy."

You need a fire only as big as your hat to cook a simple meal. Big fires take more work, are hot, waste fuel, burn the food or cook it too rapidly, and create greater fire hazards. They are called *bonfires* to distinguish them from proper campfires. If many people are to eat, separate them into groups and let each group cook separately or have a separate fire for each item on the menu.

Let your fire burn down to coals before you start to cook. This cooks your food slowly and clear through instead of leaving it burned and with charcoal on the outside while the inside remains raw. Coals are also more comfortable to cook over and do not leave your kettle with a black, sooty mask. To get good coals, light a good hardwood fire well in advance and keep it going until you have a thick bed of glowing embers.

To burn large, heavy sticks, raise them on a pair of green stick *fire dogs* (large sticks) to improve the draft. This is especially important on a damp, muggy day.

Smoke follows a vacuum. To keep from having smoke in your face, create a vacuum on the other side by building your fire in front of a cliff, placing your canoe on its side, or suspending a poncho or blanket on a framework of sticks.

A forked green stick *fire poker,* 3 to 4 feet long, serves well to rearrange fuel and embers to better advantage. You can use a shovel instead but must be careful not to let hot coals remain on it, for prolonged heat will ruin its temper.

The *inspirator* (Fig. 27-11), attributed to Steward Edward White, is an indispensable device for encouraging stubborn fires. Use a piece of garden hose $1\frac{1}{2}$ to 2 feet long and place a slightly flattened piece of metal on one end. Place the metal end at strategic

Figure 27-11 Using an Inspirator.

points at the *bottom* of the fire and blow gently to supply the extra oxygen needed to set it ablaze.

KINDS OF FIRES

Wigwam or Tepee Fire (Fig. 27–12). An 18-inch wigwam or tepee fire burns quickly, with enough heat to boil water

Figure 27–12 Wigwam or Tepee Fire.

or cook a quick, one-pot meal or provide light and cheer for a small group meeting. Its rapid flame renders it a good foundation for getting more long-lasting fires going.

Hunter-Trapper Fire (Fig. 27–13). This is one of the most thoroughly satisfactory cooking fires. Lay rocks in the form of an open **V** with the wide end toward the wind and about 15 to 16 inches wide, tapering to the small end, which is just wide enough to support your smallest kettle. Build a wigwam fire inside and keep it going until you have a good bed of coals to distribute along under your kettles. Keep a brisk fire going at one end to produce coals to replenish those under your kettles. This fire is cooler to cook by and conserves fuel, since the rocks reflect all the heat up onto your kettles.

Figure 27–14 Log Cabin or Crisscross Fire.

Log Cabin or Crisscross Fire (Fig. 27–14). This is a good cooking fire, especially when you need a good bed of coals for continued heat. It also makes a good council ring fire. Use sticks an inch or less in diameter if you want it to burn briskly. Build the structure loosely and light a small tepee fire on top to set the whole thing going quickly.

Reflector Fires (Fig. 27–15). Reflector fires give steady heat for baking

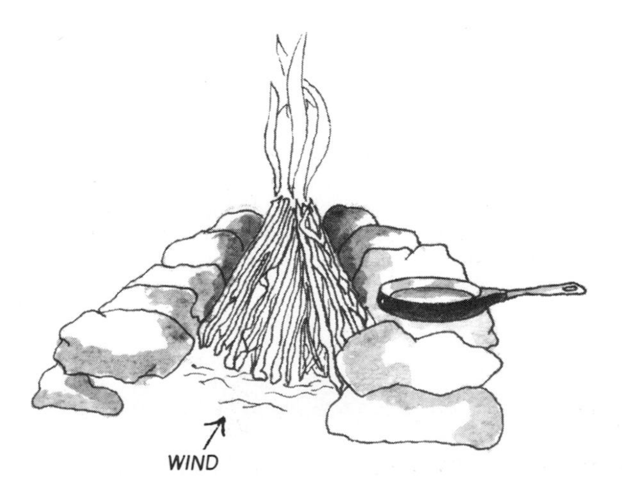

Figure 27–13 Stone Hunter-Trapper Fire.

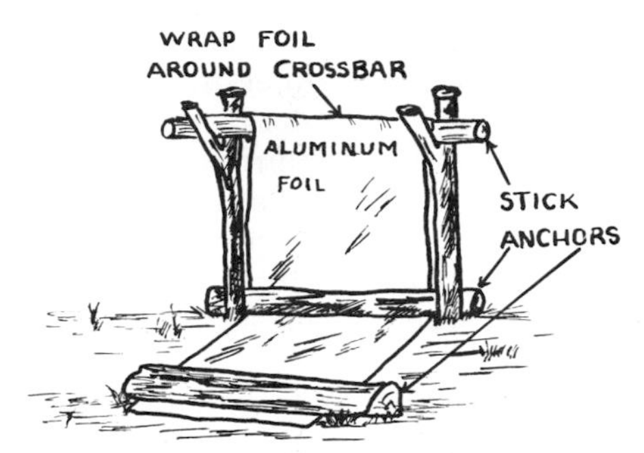

Figure 27–15 Aluminum Foil Reflector.

in a reflector oven or for throwing heat into an open tent. Place the reflector on the leeward side of the fire so that it will draw the smoke and flames and reflect back only the heat.

You can make a *fire bank* by piling up stones or stacking logs against uprights driven into the ground at a 75 degree angle. Pile dirt in front of it to keep it from catching on fire. Figure 27–15 shows a piece of aluminum foil converted into a reflector. Wrap the foil several times around a stick laid between the notches in two upright forked sticks. Then bring the foil down and anchor it at the bottom by a stick placed behind the forked sticks. Now bring the aluminum forward and anchor it with some rocks or a heavy stick. These would be most suitable at an outpost camp or permanent cook site where you can use the sticks over and over.

Altar Fires (Fig. 27–16). Altar fires are labor-saving devices for more or less permanent campsites since you do not have to stoop either to tend the fire or to stir your food. They also minimize the danger of having the fire spread through the duff. Cement rocks together or notch logs and fit them together to form a hollow base and fill it with some nonflammable material such as flattened tin cans, sand, or rocks. Build it a convenient height for those using it—1½ to 2 feet high for children, 2½ to 3 feet high for adults. If you extend one side of the base up a foot or two, it will make an excellent reflector fire.

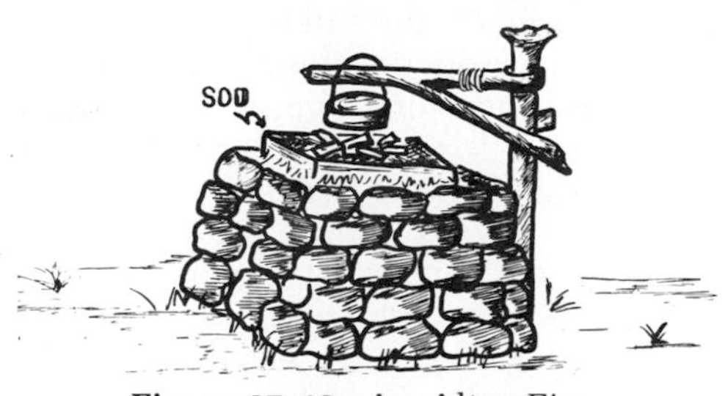

Figure 27–16 An Altar Fire.

Council Fires. When a group meets for a summer campfire program, they want a maximum of light and cheer with a minimum of heat. Adapt the size of your fire to the size of your group and avoid using varieties of wood that crackle and pop, for they are dangerous and distract attention from the program. Use a plentiful supply of tinder and kindling as a base and intersperse larger split kindling among your logs so that the fire will get underway quickly. A mixture of soft and hard woods usually gives best results. It is a hazardous practice to use kerosene or gasoline to produce a spectacular blaze, for such fires can easily get out of hand. Since the average campfire program seldom lasts more than an hour, you should be able to lay a fire that will last that long without having to replenish it, but you should have fuel available in case you need it.

LOG CABIN FIRE (Fig. 27–14). This cooking fire is also a favorite for campfire programs. Start the base with two logs about 3 feet long and 5 to 6 inches thick, placed about 2½ feet apart. Then build up five or six layers of successively smaller and shorter sticks, laid parallel, leaving small spaces between. Build a foundation fire on top that will burn brightly and soon drop enough hot embers down to set the whole thing ablaze.

WIGWAM FIRE (Fig. 27–12). As previously mentioned, a small wigwam fire is excellent for a small group. Although a tall bonfire towering high in the air is spectacular, it is not appropriate for

Figure 27–17 "No, No, Oscar! Not a Smudge Fire. You're Not Lost; You're Just Confused!"

camp use, for it is extremely hazardous since no matter how well you wire or otherwise fasten it together, there is always a danger that the long poles will work loose or burn in two and fall perilously close to those around it or set fire to the surroundings. It is also usually too hot for comfort in summer.

Smudge Fires (Fig. 27–17). Directions for making a smudge fire to send messages to others or to signal others that you are lost or need help were given on p. 395.

EXTINGUISHING YOUR CAMPFIRE

Water is the best thing to use for extinguishing a campfire. Scatter all the embers that remain and douse them thoroughly with water, sprinkling it on with the back of your hand to make it go as far as possible, yet making sure that every bit of living fire is thoroughly drenched. Carefully pull aside all blazing pieces for a special dousing, saturating them or immersing them in a nearby stream or lake. Stir the fire bed repeatedly and keep sprinkling it with water. Place your hand at various spots on it to search for any remaining heat. Make sure it's *dead out;* it's not safe to leave it if there is even a trace of heat, flame, smoke or steam.

If water is unavailable, smother the fire with sand, gravel or dirt, but choose the soil carefully, for some types contain enough vegetable matter to smolder for days before breaking out into a full-fledged flame. If you have to move hot ashes, wet them down thoroughly and deposit them at a fireproof spot.

WET WEATHER FIRES

The novice at fire making has enough trouble producing a bright, steady flame in clear, dry weather, but that is nothing compared to his difficulties when the heavens have been pouring buckets of rain for hours and everything is squashy under foot. Then comes the real test, for now a fire is more necessary than at any other time. It is quite important psychologically as well as physically to send everyone to bed with warm, dry clothing, hot food in their stomachs, and memories of fun and fellowship around a cheerful blaze. Bedding down on a dismal night without these comforts is enough to quell anyone's ardor for camping.

If you are a wise counselor, you will be prepared for just such an emergency. Midst the deluge, you can calmly produce your waterproof matches and some good tinder you have saved for just this occasion and capably set to work. Whenever you are in camp, always keep a supply of dry kindling and firewood under a tent or tarpaulin. If caught without it, search for it under overhanging rocks or fallen trees or on the dead bottom limbs of standing trees. Even wet wood is usually damp only on the top layers and you can get dry wood by stripping off the bark or shaving off a few layers. Splitting large sticks will also reveal an inner core of dry wood to use as kindling or to make fuzz clumps or fuzz sticks.

Trench Candles. *Trench candles* (Fig. 27-18), carried in a plastic bag or waterproof tin box, are excellent for starting a fire anytime, but especially on a rainy day. To make them, lay a strip of cloth, twine, or thick cord in the center of six to ten sheets of newspaper and roll and twist them into a tight cylinder. Tie pieces of string snugly about the roll at intervals of 2 to 4 inches, leaving an end of the string on each section long enough to handle it by. Sever the roll midway between the strings and pull out the center cloth or cord of each segment far enough to serve as a wick. Dip each piece several times in melted paraffin or old candle wax, letting it harden a few minutes in between so that the paper becomes thoroughly saturated with the wax.

Trench candles are almost impervious to rain and wind and will burn long enough to start a fire under almost any conditions. By themselves, they will provide enough heat to cook on a hobo stove or give a fairly adequate light when burned flat in a dish or other container.

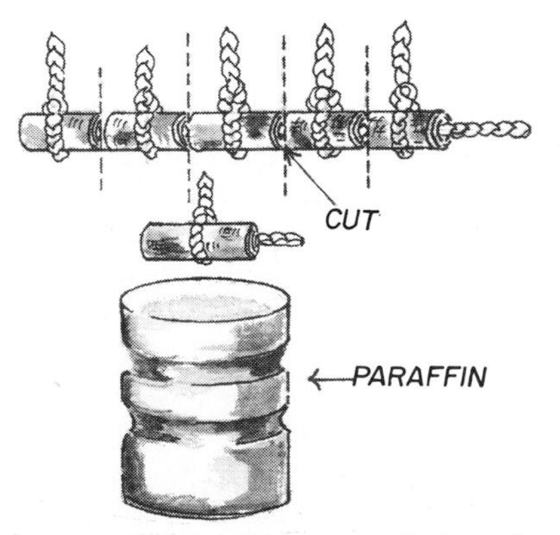

Figure 27-18 Making Trench Candles.

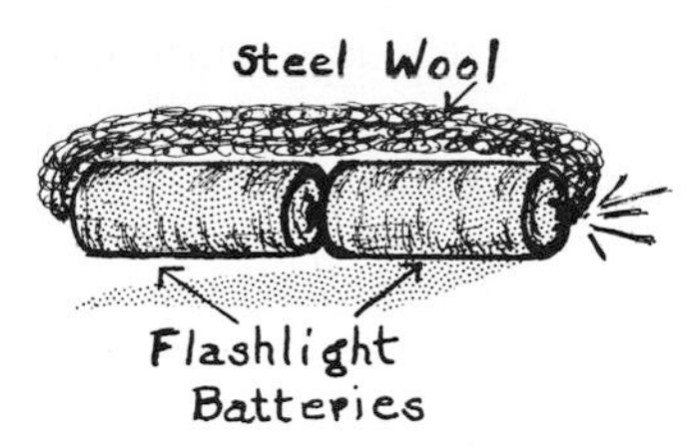

Figure 27-19 Using Flashlight Batteries and Steel Wool to Start a Fire.

A plain candle stub or, even better, a plumber's candle will serve the same purpose, although not nearly so well.

Flashlight Batteries and Steel Wool. Number 00 (very fine) steel wool will burn. Take a length of it and place the two ends in contact with flashlight batteries as shown in Figure 27-19. Hold it over your tinder and drop it in when it begins to glow. Now blow on it until it becomes red hot and bursts into flame; then push it under your prepared fire lay. Use fresh batteries and carry them in a plastic bag.

Peas. Barbara Ellen Joy and Jeanne Bassett* describe a method for making "peas," which are good to start wet weather fires. Mix ashes from a soft wood fire with kerosene and roll them into small balls about the size of large peas. Let them dry out and carry them in a tin box. A match will set them burning brightly enough to start any stubborn fire.

Laying a Wet Weather Fire. A fire built on sopping-wet ground can produce enough steam to smother itself. To avoid this, scoop away the wet top ground and build a little platform of aluminum foil, stones, or sticks as a base.

A wigwam fire works best on wet ground. Lay it with even more than usual care, using fuzz sticks, peas, or trench candles and good tinder and kindling at first, adding other fuel gradually as your fire gains momentum.

---

*Barbara Ellen Joy and Jeanne Bassett: "Wet Weather Fires." *Camping Magazine,* April, 1939.

Damp fuel dries out with surprising rapidity when leaned gingerly up against already flaming sticks and you can place an additional supply close to the fire to gradually dry out.

An inspirator is especially helpful for wet weather fires.

If rain is falling, suspend a piece of tarpaulin or an extra poncho on a framework of sticks at least 5 feet above the fire to shield it until you have it going well. If it is windy, anchor the corners with guy ropes. Since this is rather hard on good material, some camps set aside a few special pieces for this purpose. If the wind is especially strong, erect a windbreak of branches or a tarpaulin on the windward side.

ADDITIONAL READINGS

(For an explanation of abbreviations and abbreviated forms used, see page 25.)

Camp Stoves

Angier: *Wilderness Gear You Can Make Yourself,* pp. 65–66. (Instructions for grills)

Bridge: *America's Backpacking Book,* pp. 86–89, 206–209.

Fletcher: *The Complete Walker,* pp. 105–114.

Langer: *The Joy of Camping,* pp. 56–64.

Manning: *Backpacking One Step at a Time,* pp. 224–237.

Riviere: *Backcountry Camping,* pp. 132–135.

Riviere: *Family Camper's Cookbook,* chs. III, IV.

Sunset Camping Handbook, pp. 29–31.

Whelen and Angier: *On Your Own in the Wilderness,* ch. 10.

Wood: *Pleasure Packing,* pp. 55–62.

MAGAZINE ARTICLES

Camping Journal:

Bigwood, Steve: "How to Prevent Fuelish Accidents," Aug./Sept., 1975, p. 32.

"Buyer's Guide." Mar., 1973.

Consumer Reports:

"Camp Stoves." June, 1969, p. 338.

Fire Without Matches

Angier: *How to Stay Alive in the Woods,* pp. 109–116.

Angier: *Survival with Style,* pp. 45–52.

Angier: *Wilderness Gear You Can Make Yourself,* pp. 21–26.

Bale: *What On Earth,* pp. 31–36.

Boy Scout Handbook, pp. 179–181.

Dalrymple: *Survival in the Outdoors,* pp. 207–223.

Fieldbook for Boys and Men, pp. 310–312.

Hamper: *Wilderness Survival,* pp. 19–21.

Merrill: *The Survival Handbook,* pp. 81–86.

Olsen: *Outdoor Survival Skills,* ch. 3.

Shivers: *Camping,* pp. 240–241.

Shockley and Fox: *Survival in the Wilds,* ch. 6.

Wood: *Pleasure Packing,* ch. 5 to p. 64.

Wood Fires

Angier: *Home in Your Pack,* ch. 9.

Angier: *How to Stay Alive in the Woods,* chs. 10, 11.

Angier: *Skills for Taming the Wilds,* ch. 5.

Angier: *Survival with Style,* ch. 3.

Bridge: *America's Backpacking Book,* pp. 83–86.

Cardwell: *America's Camping Book,* chs. 16–18.

Dalrymple: *Survival in the Outdoors,* pp. 195–207.

Fieldbook for Boys and Men, ch. 8.

Fire Building. Girl Scouts, $10. (Flip charts)

Firemanship (No. 3317). Boy Scouts, 1968, 64 pp., 45¢, paper.

Garrison: *Outdoor Education,* ch. IV.

Gould: *The Complete Book of Camping,* pp. 32–44.

Langer: *The Joy of Camping,* pp. 67–72.

Learn and Tallman: *Backpacker's Digest,* ch. 10.

Manning: *Backpacking One Step at a Time,* pp. 29–33, 223–224.

Merrill: *All About Camping,* ch. 13.

Merrill: *The Survival Handbook,* ch. 6.

Miracle and Decker: *Complete Book of Camping,* ch. 22.

Ormond: *Complete Book of Outdoor Lore,* ch. 7.

Riviere: *Backcountry Camping,* ch. 6 to p. 132.

Riviere: *The Camper's Bible,* ch. 5.

Riviere: *Family Camper's Cookbook,* ch. II.

Shivers: *Camping,* pp. 238–247.

Whelen and Angier: *On Your Own in the Wilderness,* ch. 11.

MAGAZINE ARTICLES

Camping Journal:

Duffey, Dave: "How to Choose Campfire Wood." Jan., 1968, p. 32.

Camping Magazine:

Clark, E. W.: "Organization Guide for Camp Fire Safety." Mar., 1962, p. 20.

Chapter 28

Foods and Outdoor Cooking

Figure 28-1 "Will This Never End?"

OUTDOOR COOKERY*

Half the fun of campin' out
And trampin' here and there
Is buildin' up your appetite
'Til you're hungry as a bear.

Then sittin' down at mess time
With swell victuals all about—
Boy! that's livin' what is livin'
And you get it campin' out!

—VAN DER SMISSEN AND GOERING:
A Leader's Guide to Nature-Oriented Activities,
p. 97.

We may live without friends,
We may live without books,
But civilized man
Cannot live without cooks.†

—NESSMUK

PLANNING AND PACKING FOR TRIPS

PLANNING MENUS

No matter how much other fun there is in camp, nothing can quite take the place of good, nourishing meals, tastily prepared and attractively served. With the variety of mixes and dehydrated foods now on the market, there is no excuse, even on long trips, for serving dull, monotonous meals. All that is required is a little imagination, a pinch of good common sense, some forethought and planning, and a good outdoor recipe book. Then even the inexperienced can turn out a tasty meal.

Young beginners should start out by planning simple *nosebag* or *poke* lunches, such as sandwiches, fruit, and a cold drink to be packed at the main camp and taken out and eaten, the paper bags being burned at the campsite. The next step might be cooking a one-pot meal for a supper cookout,

*By permission from the State University of Iowa Press.

†Nessmuk (George W. Sears): *Woodcraft.* Dover Publications, Inc., 1963.

then an aluminum-foil menu with meat and vegetables all cooked together in a package, followed by cooking in hot coals, and so on through the whole category of wonderful cooking methods available in primitive surroundings. It is usually best to add only one new item at a time so that the whole meal won't be ruined if the new technique doesn't turn out as anticipated. Such shake-down ventures give experience in gauging appetites and preparing food before longer trips are taken.

Some of the more elaborate dishes and methods of cooking may prove quite challenging when you are near camp and have ample time and when carrying out extra utensils won't be a burden, but on trips you will want to stick to simple, substantial meals that can be prepared in jig time and require only a minimum of utensils to be carried and washed out after each meal. This explains why stews and other one-pot meals are so popular.

Above all, shun the inevitable and indigestible picnic menu of wieners, buns, potato chips, pickles, and marshmallows, which apparently constitutes the average American's idea of the only possible outdoor menu. It is important from a psychological as well as a health standpoint to have meals that are just as nutritious, well-cooked, and attractively served as those indoors. The fact that vigorous exercise and breathing large quantities of fresh air produce ravenous appetites isn't an adequate excuse for serving half-raw, unappetizing conglomerations.

Let campers share in planning and cooking their own meals, learning the principles of good nutrition and imaginative food selection and preparation as they do so. Toward this end, many camps make it possible for campers and counselors to work closely with the dietitian or a well-trained trip counselor. If you wish, you can include a consideration of costs, giving them a budget and letting them figure costs per meal, per day and per week. They will soon realize that those in average financial circumstances can't afford steak for every meal but can have good, tasty food all the time, with enough money left over for an occasional splurge.

There are now many excellent outdoor recipe books, so that anyone who can read and follow directions can plan and prepare a variety of delicious, nutritious meals. After some experience in outdoor cooking, you may even want to adapt regular recipes for out-of-doors use.

PLANNING MEALS

On the trail, breakfast is usually simple but must be substantial enough to stick to the ribs throughout a morning of activity; the usual home menu of toast, cereal, orange juice, and coffee just won't fill the bill. Lunch is also hearty and likewise simple, often consisting of sandwiches and other cold foods, possibly supplemented by hot soup or a hot drink if the weather is rainy or chilly. A cold lunch enables you to get back on the trail quickly without having to consume time in building and putting out a fire or unpacking your stove. Supper can be more leisurely, with a hot, filling stew or other one-pot dish along with a hot bread, perhaps some side dishes, and dessert.

To satisfy the appetites of growing youngsters, sharpened by vigorous exercise, most trippers carry some sort of snack food to munch along the trail or at brief rest stops. These may consist of a combination of such items as dried fruits, hard candy, non-melting chocolate or candy bars, unsalted peanuts or other nuts, and sugar-coated cereal. (Such snacks are commonly called *birdseed* or *glop*.) Each camper carries his own supply in a plastic bag, secured at the top with a twist-'em or pipe cleaner.

Including enough roughage in the diet to prevent constipation is often a problem, but it can be remedied by including plenty of dried fruit (prunes, figs, dates, etc.); put them to soak the night before if you want them soft for breakfast.

Plan each meal in detail, following recipes exactly and putting down the exact amount of each ingredient needed. In selecting recipes consider such things as: (1) ease of preparation, (2) time required for cooking, (3) number and type of utensils needed (these add bulk and weight to the pack), (4) amount of fuel required, (5) amount and type of weight to be disposed of or carried back with you, (6) age, and personal preferences of those going on the trip, and (7) religious and cultural characteristics of the group. If possible, try out each recipe before planning to use it on a trip.

Most camps furnish blank trip forms to be filled out before the trip. These ask for such information as the names of those going, the date and time of departure, destination, date and time of return, number of days and meals planned for, the actual menus planned for each meal, the exact quantities of each foodstuff needed, and a summary of the total number of utensils needed for the trip. After your plans have been approved, it is well to copy the menu for each meal on a 3 by 5 inch card, stating the exact quantities of foodstuffs required, cooking utensils needed, type of fire required, and complete directions for preparing everything; give the card to the head cook well ahead of the meal so that he or she can study it and make plans for preparing it. After your plan has been approved, representative campers, with one or more counselors, serve as *mar-*

(Courtesy of the Boy Scouts of America, New Brunswick, N. J.)

keters, working with the dietician or trips counselor to assemble and pack the supplies requisitioned.

When a group is large, it is usually best to divide it into small groups of six to eight, each cooking and perhaps even planning its own meals, for coping with large numbers sometimes proves quite overwhelming to inexperienced youngsters.

NEW LIGHTWEIGHT FOODS

Serious backpackers today seldom take ordinary foods on a trip of any duration, for in addition to the danger of eating certain foods that have been kept for even a few hours without refrigeration, they are simply too bulky and heavy for comfortable carrying. From 70 to 90 per cent of such foods are just plain water, which weighs a pound for each pint (2 cups). Modern methods of food preparation seek to remove much of this water, leaving foods that are dry, light, and compact and that, when properly packed, will keep a year or more without refrigeration. They can usually be reconstituted in from 10 to 30 minutes by adding water and cooking quickly, and they produce a finished product that closely resembles the original food in taste, eye appeal, and nutritional value.

Figure 28–2 Flippity-Flap (or Flop?)

Various methods are used to make these lightweight foods, such as puff drying and vacuum drying, which produce foods that are commonly called dehydrated foods, and actual freeze drying, which involves rapidly reducing the temperature to 40° to 50° below zero and then placing them in a near vacuum where the water comes off as vapor. Freeze drying is superior for many foods since it removes as much as 97 per cent of the water content, but it is the most expensive method because of the large investment in plant and equipment that is required. After being freeze dried, a pound of meat weighs only 2 ounces, 10 pounds of potatoes only 1.7 pounds, and a pound of peaches that will serve four only 3 ounces. A whole cooked meal can be freeze dried and then reconstituted merely by adding boiling water. Many foods carelessly referred to as freeze dried are actually dehydrated by one of the methods previously mentioned, and although not as much of the water is removed, they are cheaper and often quite satisfactory.

The increasing popularity of camping has created a brisk demand for these foods, and a number of specialized firms have been established to produce them. Their constant experimentation and efforts to produce something better have resulted in the availability of well over 200 imaginative products, including all kinds of fruits, puddings, stews, breads, eggs and egg products, applesauce, milk shakes, fruit juices, hamburger, casseroles, beefsteak, chicken, pork chops, pizza, chow mein, and even ice cream. You will find the names of several such firms in Appendix E and you may want to write to them to learn more about their products and prices.

In addition to individual foodstuffs, whole meals are available in 1-man, 2-man, 4-man, and 8-man packets. However, some users find the portions in some brands too skimpy to satisfy appetites, so you may want to do a little experimenting before starting out on a long trip. An active teenager or adult will burn up 3,000 to 4,000 calories a day, and growing children may surprise you with what they can tuck away. Daily rations per person usually weigh from 1¾ to 2 pounds.

Each item in a prepackaged meal usually comes packed in its own individual light-weight plastic (polyethylene) waterproof bag, and those for the whole meal are then assembled in a larger bag, clearly marked with the name of the meal and the contents. Some items come in a bag in which you can soak, cook, or even eat them. You can then burn the bag, leaving no garbage to carry back or dishes to wash.

As mentioned, individually packaged items are also available so you can make up your own menus. Foods can also be bought in bulk, which allows individuals or camps expecting to take several trips during the summer to save money by measuring out and repackaging what is needed for meals.

Although buying these special light-weight foods and prepackaged meals from suppliers does cost a little more, the difference is not as great as it might seem and the fact that there is absolutely no waste and the convenience afforded may well make it seem like a very good investment.

Figure 28-3 "Scat!"

Some people involved in camping object to using such foods exclusively, feeling that campers thereby miss out on valuable experience in planning nutritious, well-balanced meals and in learning to budget. Preplanned meals also fail to allow for individual tastes and for giving experience in using various outdoor cooking methods.

Lightweight Foods Available at Your Grocery

An increasing variety of dehydrated and freeze dried foods, often called "dried," "instant," or "minute" foods, can be found on the shelves of your local supermarket. They are usually cheaper than those purchased from specialized suppliers. If you are planning substantial purchases, ask the manager to help you find what he has available. You will also find suitable foods at Oriental and health food stores. Here are some possibilities:

Bread, biscuit, muffin, cornbread, and pancake mixes
Cake, cookie, brownie, and gingerbread mixes
Oatmeal, grits, cornmeal, farina, Granola, Grapenuts
Dried peas, lentils, and beans of all types
Instant rice
Skillet dinners
Dried soups
Dried fruits (apricots, raisins, apples, prunes, dates, figs, fruit cocktail)
Macaroni, spaghetti, noodles, pizza
Hard cheese
Pream and other non-dairy products
Instant pudding, Jello (cool in a stream)
Dried milk (a pound makes a gallon of milk)—this is usually skim milk, but dried whole milk is available
Instant potatoes

- Powdered fruit juices
- Parsley, onion, and carrot flakes
- Instant cocoa, coffee and tea, malted milk tablets, Ovaltine
- Popcorn (excellent for campfire nibbling)
- Peanuts and other nuts, hard candy, and non-melting chocolate
- Dried beef, codfish flakes and cakes
- Pemmican (dried meat pounded to a pulp and then mashed with fat and sometimes raisins and sugar and formed into cakes or bars)
- Beef jerky (thin, brown strips that you can suck on)
- Wilson bacon bar
- Hard cookies, such as ginger snaps
- Bouillon cubes, dried mushrooms, and gravy mixes (excellent for adding flavor to soups and casseroles)
- Pie and cobbler mixes
- Herbs and spices—choose a few favorites, such as ground cummin, oregano, thyme, herb mixtures, cinnamon, cloves, bay leaves, dried dill, rosemary, and sage

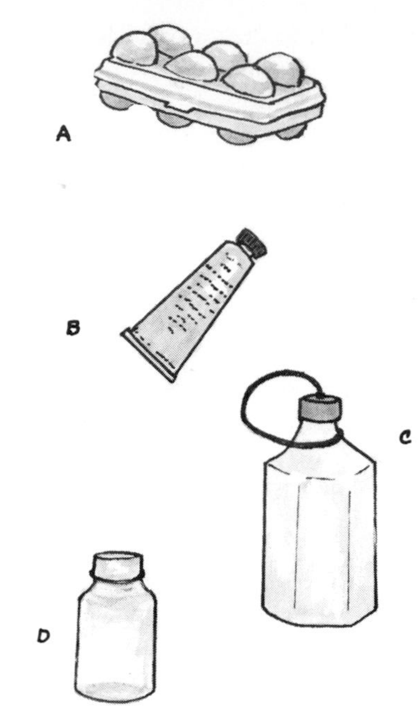

Figure 28–4 Some Containers for Packing Food.

PACKING FOOD

Any kind of trip, particularly one on foot, offers a challenge to plan menus using foods that require no refrigeration and are not too bulky and cumbersome. Many items purchased at the grocery store come in packages too fragile to stand the wear and tear of a trip or have sharp corners that may gouge into other things in your pack. They also do not contain the exact amounts you will need, so that you would be carrying excess bulk and weight; why carry ten pounds of flour when you need only six or a whole jug of molasses when you need only a cupful? Measure out and package exactly what you need for each meal, being careful to detach any essential directions for preparations.

Pack semiliquids such as oleo, syrup, peanut butter, jams, jellies, honey, catsup, and mustard in refillable wide-mouthed squeeze tubes such as that shown in Figure 28–4*B* or in plastic (poly) bottles like those in Figure 28–4*C* and *D*; these can be purchased from suppliers. Light-weight aluminum cans such as baking powder cans can also be used. Other packing possibilities are Tupperware, old plastic prescription bottles, and plastic containers intended for home freezing.

Place dry materials in strong plastic bags available from suppliers or in those intended for home freezing, squeezing out excess air and fastening them at the top by pressing with a warm iron or using plastic twist-'ems or half of a pipe stem cleaner, crimping back the ends with pliers so they won't puncture other things. Double bag (one inside the other) fine-particle foods such as flour and sugar. Be sure the bags are strong enough to hold up under trail use, and label them with a felt tip pen before you fill them. Include the name of the contents, the amount, and the meal they are to be used in. If there are printed directions for preparation, place them inside so that you can read them through the clear plastic. These bags are particularly valuable since you can often use them over again or dispose of them by burning. When planning to cook such things as flapjacks, biscuits, soups, and cakes, mix all the dry ingredients at home and pack them in a labelled plastic bag; this cuts down on the number of bags necessary and saves having to measure out and mix ingredients on the trail.

Glass bottles are heavy and breakable, so remove the contents and place them in wide-mouthed plastic bottles or light aluminum cans with screw-on or press-in tops, saved from commercial products or purchased from outfitters.

Hard cheese (not processed) in chunk form will keep quite well without refrigeration if properly packed. Package it in meal-size quantities, wrapping each portion in two or three layers of cheesecloth, pressed lightly against the cheese. Dip each package quickly into melted paraffin so that it acquires a good coating, then place the packages in a rigid metal container to prevent other objects from breaking the paraffin shield. Although a little mold may form around the edges of the cheese, it is merely a harmless form of penicillin, which you can scrape off if you find it objectionable.

Fresh eggs will not keep well for long without refrigeration; it is better to depend on the several dried egg products available from outfitters. If you prefer to take fresh eggs for use early in the trip, wrap them in paper to make them fit snugly in a plastic container such as that shown in Figure 28–4*A*.

Spices and other flavorings do wonders in perking up prosaic foods, so include a few well-chosen favorites. Large quantities of salt will be needed to replace that lost through perspiration. Since salt draws moisture, it will eventually rust out tin containers, so carry it in a plastic bottle or bag or in one of the poly shakers for both salt and pepper that are available from suppliers. Fasten doubtful corks and lids with adhesive tape.

For a one-meal cookout, you can simply carry your food in your cooking kettle or in a No. 10 tin can hobo stove (see Figure 29–7). For longer trips, assemble all the bags for a single meal into a larger bag, carefully labelled as to the meal for which it is intended. Place all your bags for a day (breakfast, lunch, and supper) into a larger bag, labelled with the day for which it is intended, and place these bags in your food duffel bag, arranged in the order in which they will be used, with that to be used first on top. Although it may be advisable occasionally to substitute one meal for another, as when rainy or cool weather makes a warm meal seem more desirable than the cold meal that was planned, do it rarely lest you end up with all the less attractive meals for the end of the trip. Confine portions allowed to what was planned; your extra snack foods should take care of any lack. Keep a running diary of comments and observations on each meal regarding such things as amounts, preparation, palatability, and so forth. Use this to help you plan better for each succeeding trip.

When going on an extended trip, investigate the possibilities of lightening your load and adding fresh supplies by purchasing from groceries and roadside stands along the way. You may also be able to arrange a rendezvous with the camp truck at some point en route to get fresh clothes and food or arrange with some supplier to make a drop shipment to you at some post office along the way. You may also be able to add variety to your diet by picking fruit or catching fish along the way, but don't count too much on it or you may end up hungry.

OUTDOOR COOKING

Since camps often have cookout sites near their cabins or the main camp

(Courtesy of Missouri Valley College, Marshall, Mo.)

or take short trips involving only one or two meals, we have included some recipes and cooking methods that are especially suitable for use with wood fires in such situations. For additional recipes and cooking methods, consult the references at the end of the chapter.

SOME GENERAL NOTES ABOUT COOKING

For general cooking over wood fires, ordinary kettles with wire handles that can be hung over lug poles or on pot hooks (see Figure 29–13) are recommended.

When cooking over a wood fire, coat the outside surfaces of your kettles with a thick paste of detergent and water or rub a moistened bar of laundry soap over them. When you wash the kettle, the soap washes off easily, taking the smoke and soot with it. Not all campers are agreed on this, however; some feel that kettles heat better and more evenly if you leave the coating of smoke and soot on them, and in that case, you will need to carry each kettle in it's own carrying bag so that the soot won't rub off on other things in your pack.

When preparing fresh vegetables, do not leave them standing in water longer than necessary, for it removes some of their precious vitamins. Add them to rapidly boiling salted water and cook quickly, using as little water as possible. Avoid overcooking, keeping them on just long enough to tenderize them without destroying their crispness. Add them to water below the boiling point only if you want to extract their flavor, as in making soups or stews.

You can skin tomatoes quickly by scalding them with boiling water or holding them over the flames until their skins crack. However, it is more healthful to wash the skin well and eat it too.

Use a glass bottle or tin can when you need a rolling pin.

Grease the vessel in which you melt chocolate or measure molasses to keep it from adhering to the sides.

Test eggs for freshness by dropping them into water. If they sink quickly, they are fresh; if they sink slowly, proceed with caution, for they are doubtful; if they float, don't use them at all, for they are ancient.

Put a container of water over the fire when you first light it and you'll have hot water all ready for your main cooking by the time the fire burns down to coals.

When a recipe calls for sour milk, you can produce it immediately by adding two tablespoons of lemon juice or a few drops of vinegar for each cup of sweet milk.

You can improvise double boilers for cooking rice and other cereals by supporting the food vessel on three or four small stones inside a larger vessel partly filled with water.

Line your frying pan with aluminum foil before cooking meat or other hard to remove food and you'll have no pans that are difficult to scrub.

A little vinegar and water boiled inside the utensils in which fish has been cooked removes the fishy odor.

When cooking meat, use low or moderate heat. This requires more time, but the meat will not shrink so much and will be much more palatable and tender. When you want to draw the juices and flavor out of meat, as in making soup or stew, start it in cold water and cook it with low heat. To seal the juices and flavor in, drop it into boiling water or sear it on all sides over a hot fire, then cook it over low or moderate heat. Do not season meat until it is nearly done, for seasonings draw out juices. Neither overcook nor undercook fresh meat, but cook pork especially thoroughly because of the danger of trichinosis.

Dried milk will taste better if you mix it and let it stand for some time before drinking it.

To test breads and cakes for doneness, stick a straw or sliver of wood into them; if it comes out clean, they are done; if doughy or sticky, they need to bake longer.

Be sure to follow recipes and directions carefully.

Long, slow cooking usually im-

(Courtesy of Paul Parker, Girl Scouts U.S.A.)

proves the flavor of food. When using a wood fire, start the fire early and let it burn down to a glowing bed of coals. You can regulate the heat by changing the distance of the food from the fire or by drawing more coals under the pot, keeping a brisk fire going over at one side to produce more coals if they are needed.

Remember to allow more time for cooking at high altitudes.

In general, keep a cover on your cook pot to conserve heat and help preserve moisture.

When preparing to cook, it is a good idea to spread a plastic sheet on the ground and place all your foodstuffs and cooking utensils on it. This will keep them readily visible and prevent misplacing some essential item.

Frying is frequently overused in camp cookery and, when incorrectly done, results in an unappetizing and indigestible dish. The chief problem comes from letting fried foods absorb too much fat as they cook. To avoid this, have the food as dry as possible and heat the grease to just under the smoking stage before you put the food in. The hot grease sears the food, sealing the juices in and the grease out. Drain fried foods on a paper napkin or paper towel to remove excess grease. When frying in a skillet over an open fire, avoid high flames lest they set fire to the grease in the pan.

Pan broiling is a healthful and highly recommended form of frying that uses low heat. You start with very little grease in the pan and pour off the excess as it forms, leaving barely enough in the pan to keep the food from sticking. Turn the meat several times.

Broiling is cooking by direct exposure to the heat from glowing coals. Build a fire of hard wood well in advance of cooking time and keep it going until it burns down to a good bed of coals. Place the meat over the flame to sear it quickly on both sides, then place it over the coals; watch it carefully. Beware of letting fat drip into the flame, for it may catch on fire and burn the meat. Avoid using resinous or strong-tasting woods lest they impart a disagreeable flavor to the food.

Wilderness cookery is done without utensils and includes cooking in ashes or coals, in an imu or beanhole, or on a stick or spit. It is fun to plan a whole meal using only wilderness cookery, and it is surprising what a variety of tantalizing foods you can serve.

COMMON MEASURES

3 teaspoons (tsp.) = 1 tablespoon (T)
16 T = 1 cup (C)
1 C = 1/2 pint (pt.)
2 pts. = 1 quart (qt.)
4 qts. = 1 gallon (gal.)

No. 1/2 can = 1 cup
No. 1 can = 1 1/2 cups
No. 2 can = 2 1/2 cups
No. 2 1/2 can = 3 1/2 cups
No. 3 can = 4 cups
No. 5 can = 5 cups
No. 10 can = 1 gal. (12 cups)

2 T butter = 1 oz.
2 C butter or lard = 1 lb.
4 T flour = 1 oz.
4 C flour = 1 lb.
2 C granulated sugar = 1 lb.
3-3 1/2 C brown sugar = 1 lb.
3-3 1/2 C powdered sugar =1 lb.
4 C cocoa = 1 lb.
3 1/2-4 C cornmeal = 1 lb.
2 C rice = 1 lb.
2-2 1/2 C dry navy beans = 1 lb.

OUTDOOR RECIPES

ONE-POT MEALS

These are stews or mixtures that, as the name suggests, are cooked in one kettle and furnish a whole meal in themselves. They are usually built upon a base of macaroni, spaghetti, dumplings, rice, potatoes, or noodles with various dehydrated vegetables, broth cubes, and your favorite seasonings. They may be served hot on rice, toast, or crackers.

Slumgullion (Serves 5)

6 to 10 slices of bacon
2 onions, diced

(Courtesy of Miami Valley Council, B.S.A., Dayton, Ohio)

1 No. 2 can tomatoes
$\frac{1}{4}$ to $\frac{1}{2}$ lb. cheese, diced
2 C meat, already cooked
$\frac{1}{2}$ tsp. salt

Cut the bacon into small pieces and fry the onion with it; drain off part of the fat, and add the tomatoes, meat, and salt. Cook for about 20 minutes; then add the cheese and continue cooking until it is melted.

Irish Stew (Serves 5)

5 onions, sliced
1 lb. meat cut in 1 inch cubes
5 potatoes
Other vegetables such as carrots, as desired
Salt and pepper

Melt a little fat in a kettle and fry the onions and meat until brown. Cover them with cold water and bring to a boil. Cook slowly for $1\frac{1}{2}$ hours, add the potatoes, and continue to cook slowly until they are tender. Season to taste.

Ring Tum Diddy (Serves 5)

6 slices bacon, diced
2 onions, sliced
$\frac{1}{4}$ lb. cheese, diced
1 No. 2 can tomatoes
1 No. 2 can corn
Salt and pepper

Fry the bacon and onions until brown, and pour off part of the fat. Add them to the tomatoes and corn and bring to a boil. Add the cheese and cook slowly until it is melted. Season to taste.

Komac Stew (Serves 8)

1 small can tomatoes or 4 fresh tomatoes (diced)
1 green pepper
2 onions, diced
3 eggs
4 T butter
Salt and pepper

Melt the butter and fry the onions until brown. Wash and dice the pepper and add to the tomatoes and onions and cook slowly for $\frac{1}{2}$ hour, stirring frequently. Season to taste and add the eggs one at a time, stirring meanwhile. Avoid cooking over a fire that is too hot, for it will make the mixture curdle and look unappetizing, although this won't impair the taste or quality.

STICK COOKERY

For stick cookery, use a metal skewer or peel and sharpen a green stick about 2 feet long. Resinous woods and willow impart an unpleasant taste. If in doubt about the suitability of the wood, peel the end and bite it. Cook over coals, not flames. You can support the stick above the fire by laying it across a rock or forked stick and weighting the handle end down with a rock or other heavy object.

1. Bread Twister or Doughboy. Use a regular biscuit mix, adding just enough water to make it sticky. Roll out flat about $\frac{1}{4}$ to $\frac{1}{2}$ inch thick and cut into long strips about 2 inches wide. Remove the bark from the end of a stick about twice the size of your thumb, heat the end, flour it, and wind a strip of dough spirally around it, leaving a slight gap between the spirals. Bake for 10 to 15 minutes over coals, turning it so that all sides bake evenly. It will come off the stick in the form of a cylinder closed at one end. When filled with jam, jelly or cheese, it is known as *a cave woman cream puff.*

Figure 28–5 Bread Twister or Doughboy.

2. Pig-in-a-Blanket. Cook a wiener or long sausage on a stick, then cover it with biscuit dough and bake.

3. Bacon Twister. Cook a piece of bacon thoroughly, cover it with dough and bake like a pig in a blanket. You can use sausage instead of the bacon.

Pioneer Drumsticks (Serves 5)

$1\frac{1}{4}$ lbs. beef, chopped fine
$\frac{3}{4}$ C cornflakes, crumbled fine
1 egg
Onion (if desired)
Salt and pepper

Thoroughly mix the ingredients and wrap a thin portion tightly around the peeled end of the stick and squeeze firmly into place. Toast it slowly over coals, turning frequently, and serve in a roll. Some prefer to put the cornflakes on after the meat has been placed on the stick, so that they form a sort of crust over the outside.

5. Angel on Horseback. For each serving, thread one slice of bacon on the sharpened end of a stick, and partially cook. Then wrap the bacon tightly around a 1-inch square of cheese, and hold over the fire until the bacon is done and the cheese melted. Serve with lettuce in a bun.

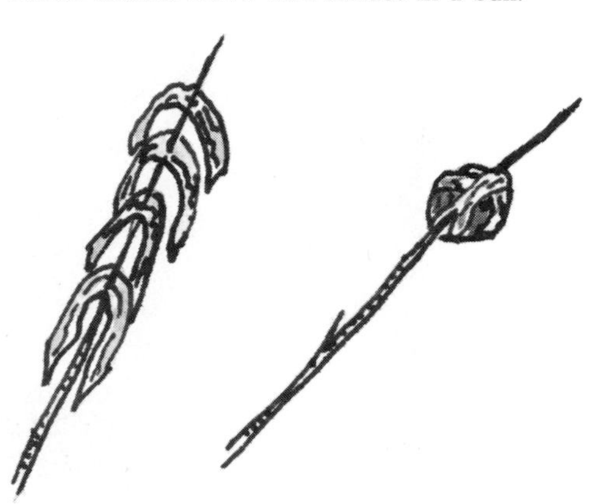

Figure 28–6 Angel on Horseback.

6. Shish Kebabs. Lace a slice of bacon in and out among alternate 1-inch squares of steak, chops, slices of onion, oysters, small tomatoes, green peppers, and so forth, as desired, impaled on a stick. Place the pieces close together if you want the meat rare, farther apart if well done. The bacon will serve to baste them. Broil over gradual heat from coals. Shish kebab got its name from two Turkish words, "shish" meaning skewer, and "kebab" meaning "broiled meat."

Figure 28–7 A Shish Kebab.

7. Cooking on a Forked Stick. A forked stick or a wire fork (Fig. 16–5C) may be used for cooking steaks, oysters, wieners, sausages, bacon, toast, green corn, apples, parsnips, marshmallows, or chops or for toasting sandwiches. When cooking meats, toast, and similar foods, run the tines into the food lengthwise or lace them through the food several times to hold it securely so it can be turned to cook evenly on all sides.

8. Date Dreams. Make these by alternating pitted dates with halved marshmallows on a stick and toasting slowly over the fire.

COOKING IN ASHES OR COALS

The secret of cooking in ashes or coals is to build a hardwood fire early and let it burn to coals. To keep a new supply of hot coals coming, keep a fire going at one side and draw coals over as you need them. Parsnips, fish (wrapped in clay), oysters (in the shell), and squash may be cooked in this way.

1. Potatoes. Scrub well Irish potatoes, sweet potatoes, or yams of medium size and without blemishes, and place them on hot coals in a single layer so that they do not touch each other; cover with coals to a depth of about 1 inch, replenishing them frequently. They are done when a sharp stick will penetrate them easily (45 to 60 minutes, depending on their size). Jab a small hole in each end to let the steam escape. Some like to coat potatoes with skins on with a thick layer of wet mud or clay before roasting; both skins and mud come off cleanly when they are done. Cook fish in the same way.

2. Onions. Cook them as you cook potatoes.

3. Eggs. Prick a small hole through the egg shell (but not the membrane) on the large end of the egg and another through membrane and all at the small end (these holes are to let the steam escape and to keep the egg from bursting). Balance the egg carefully on its large end close to the fire where it will get moderate heat; avoid too much heat lest the egg explode. The eggs should be ready to eat in five to twelve minutes, depending on whether you want them hard or soft. Some prefer to wrap the egg in wet leaves, wet mud or clay before baking.

4. Little Pig Potatoes. Slice the end off a potato and hollow out enough of the center to insert a small, thin sausage (cheese, bacon or raw egg may be used instead). Replace the end of the potato and fasten it with slivers of wood and bake it as previously described.

5. Roasting Ears. Turn back the husks from young, tender roasting ears and remove the silks. Sprinkle lightly with salt, replace the husks, soak the whole thing in water a few moments, and bake in the same way as potatoes.

6. Roasted Apples. Core the apple and fill the cavity with raisins, brown sugar, nuts, and the like. Bake them as you bake a potato.

7. Ash Bread. Build a hard wood fire, preferably on top of a large rock, at least a half hour before baking. Rake the embers aside and place the loaf of bread, well floured and rolled out to a thickness of ½ to ¾ inches, on the hot surface. Cover it with ashes and a layer of coals, replenishing them as they cool. It is ready to eat when a sliver of wood inserted in it comes out without dough adhering to it. Unlikely as it seems, the loaf will emerge quite clean and any adhering ashes can be quickly brushed away.

You may use any bread dough, but baking powder biscuit dough is preferred because of the short baking time necessary. If desired, raisins, nuts, berries or other fruit may be mixed with the dough.

8. Popcorn. Few things are more delightful than sitting around a blazing campfire eating popcorn. To pop properly, the kernels must be stored so they won't lose their moisture, so keep them in a moisture-proof, air-tight container, and open it only when you are ready to pop the corn. Place about ¼ cup of cooking oil in the bottom of a fairly heavy skillet or pan with a tight fitting lid and heat it over your camp stove or campfire. It is hot enough when a trial grain spins in the hot oil. Cover the bottom of the utensil with a layer of kernels, put the lid on, and start to shake it gently over the heat; continue shaking until most of the kernels have popped. Pour into a large container and mix in salt and melted oleo.

BAKING POTATOES IN A NO. 10 TIN CAN

Scrub the potatoes well and wrap each in a layer of waxed paper, then in damp newspaper. Pack them in enough wet dirt or sand in a No. 10 tin can to keep them from touching each other or the sides of the can. Place the can among hot coals and leave about 45 minutes, adding additional glowing coals as needed. Keep the dirt in the can moist by adding more water if necessary.

BAKING IN A REFLECTOR OVEN

Reflector ovens are very useful cooking utensils and should be a part of every outdoor cooking kit, although you may hesitate to carry their two or three pounds of weight on a trip. Purchase them from outfitters or make

Figure 28-8 Reflector Oven Made From Aluminum Foil.

them from tin cans as described on page 285. Commercial varieties are hinged so that they fold up and fit into a carrying case. You can also fashion an oven on the spot, using heavy duty aluminum foil (Fig. 28-8). Make a framework of lashed sticks and fasten a piece of foil across them for a shelf. Then take another 24-inch piece of foil, place the center of it behind the stick at the back and wrap it around other sticks to form the top and bottom of the oven. It will be still more efficient if you place other pieces of foil at the ends. Prop up the oven so the shelf is level and about 8 to 12 inches away from the fire and on the windward side, so that the ashes and flames will be blown away from the contents; it works even better if you place a reflector wall of rock or wood on the leeward side of the fire (Fig. 28-9). Use flames, not coals, and keep them brisk and about as high and wide as the oven shelf. When the shelf is hot enough to sizzle when you sprinkle water on it, place the food directly on it or use a baking pan. The sloping top and bottom reflect the heat onto the food from both above and below, insuring thorough cooking and even browning, but the metal must be kept bright and shiny to do its job well. If the surface of the shelf becomes tarnished, line it with aluminum foil to restore its brightness. Handles on the oven permit you to adjust it to a position just far enough from the fire to get the right amount of heat.

1. **General Baking.** Rolls, biscuits, pies, gingerbread, cornbread, cakes, cookies, meat, and small cut up birds such as chickens can be baked to a turn in a reflector oven.
2. **Sweet Potato Soufflé.** This can be baked in hollowed-out oranges (be sure to remove all the bitter lining) or in scooped-out apples.
3. **Eggs Baked in Orange Shells.** Prepare the orange as above and break an egg into it; season, and set in the reflector oven to bake.
4. **Potatoes.** Scrub Irish potatoes, sweet potatoes or yams. Grease their jackets with oleo or bacon fat to keep them tender. Bake them in a reflector oven for 45 minutes turning them and testing to see when they are done.
5. **Some Mores.** Make a sandwich of a marshmallow and a piece of a chocolate candy bar between two graham crackers. Press gently together and place in a reflector oven to bake.
6. **Banana Boats.** Peel back a narrow strip of peeling from the inside curve of a banana, scoop out part of the banana and fill with marshmallow, chocolate, nuts, or raisins. Replace the strip of peeling and bake in a reflector oven.

Figure 28-9 Baking in a Reflector Oven.

Figure 28–10 Baking in a Skillet.

BAKING IN A SKILLET

Support the skillet at a 45 degree angle against rocks on the windward side of the fire and over coals (Fig. 28–10).

1. Bannock. This is a traditional woodsman's bread, made by baking biscuit dough in a floured skillet. Shape the dough about one inch thick and of a form just big enough to fit the skillet. Flour it on both sides. Turn the loaf over when done on one side; both sides will be ready in about 15 minutes. Coals shoveled out and put behind the pan hasten the baking of the underside.

2. Pancakes (Flapjacks). Grease skillet lightly and brace as described. Use only moderate heat from a small fire or from coals and heat the skillet to just under the smoking point. Drop the batter from a spoon and turn the flapjacks as soon as bubbles appear on top. Avoid too much heat for it is easy to burn them. Add blueberries or other fruit for variety. You can make your own syrup by mixing a cup of white or brown sugar with ½ cup of water, then bringing it to a boil as you stir it. Add a small amount of vanilla for a different flavor.

COOKING IN A DUTCH OVEN

The heavy, black, cast iron Dutch oven of our pioneers is still an outstanding favorite, for you can bake, broil, fry, roast, or stew in it—in fact, do anything you could in your oven at home. Unlike the reflector oven, which reflects heat, it absorbs heat slowly and steadily and stays hot for a long time. Unlike indoor Dutch ovens, an outdoor oven has three stubby legs that leave enough room to rake coals under it to heat it from below, and its flat, tight-fitting lid with a turned-up edge lets you put coals on top to heat from above. It has a strong wire handle to manipulate it with. Ovens come in diameters of 10, 12, and 14 inches. Some lighter-weight ovens are now made of heavy aluminum, which lightens them by about 2 pounds, but they are not nearly as satisfactory as those of cast iron. You may not want to carry an oven on a long trip but you will enjoy using it near camp.

"Season" a new cast iron oven before using it to keep it from rusting or having food stick to it. Scrub the inside with soap and water and dry it thoroughly. Then coat the inside with a layer of unsalted fat and place it in your home oven for 2 hours at 450°, swabbing the sides occasionally with the melted fat. Let it cool slowly and wipe off the excess fat. Each time after you use it, wash it out with hot, soapy water, letting it stand a little while if there are particles of food sticking to it. Never use steel wool or metal scouring pads on it, for they will destroy the effects of the "seasoning" you did and may allow it to rust. Dry it thoroughly and apply a light coating of grease if you will not be using it again soon.

Its tight-fitting lid and heavy construction retain the heat and steam so that it cooks the food thoroughly without letting moisture and any of the suc-

Figure 28–11 An Outdoor Dutch Oven

Figure 28-12 An Improvised Dutch Oven

culent flavors escape. Be careful not to let the hot coals under the oven actually touch it or it may burn the food.

The most common error made in cooking with a Dutch oven is to use too much heat. Experience is the best teacher here. Check on progress by using a forked stick or wire hook to carefully remove the lid occasionally to see what is happening; then add or take away coals as needed.

You can improvise a Dutch oven by inverting a *heavy* skillet so it fits tightly over a *heavy* kettle. Support this legless oven on green sticks or rocks to provide a little space for coals underneath.

1. Pot Roast. Put bits of fat meat or other fat in the bottom of the kettle. Sear all sides of the roast over an open fire and put it in the kettle, adding such vegetables as onions, parsnips, carrots, turnips, Irish or sweet potatoes about a half hour before it is ready to serve. This provides a delicious meal in itself, and you can use the stock left in the bottom to make gravy if desired. A five-pound piece of meat requires about three hours to cook. This is a good way to cook tough meat, for it combines frying, baking, and steaming, and the long exposure to even, moderate temperature tenderizes almost any cut. If the meat is quite lean, rub it with fat or lay a few strips of bacon across it to baste it as it cooks.

2. Baking. A Dutch oven is excellent for baking corn bread, biscuits, rolls, pies, cookies, potatoes in their skins, chicken; in fact, almost anything to be baked will come out cooked to a turn.

THE IMU OR PIT BARBECUE

This is another splendid method to cook by steam with moderate even heat. It is really a variety of fireless cookery, and the excellent results obtained justify the long cooking time required. About three hours are necessary to cook a chicken, about a half-day for a ten-pound roast, and as much as fifteen or sixteen hours for anything as big as a whole sheep.

To begin the *imu,* dig a hole about two to three times as large as the food to be cooked and line the sides and bottom with nonpopping rocks; build a good hard wood fire in it and keep it going for an hour or two until the rocks are sizzling hot and there is a good bed of coals. Get all the food ready and place it in the pit as rapidly as possible so that no more heat than necessary escapes. Remove part of the coals and hot rocks, place the food in the pit, and pack the hot rocks and coals back in around and over it. Then shovel on about 6 inches of dirt to make a steamproof covering (if you see smoke or steam escaping, shovel more dirt over the leak). You can now forget the food until you dig it up, ready to eat, three to

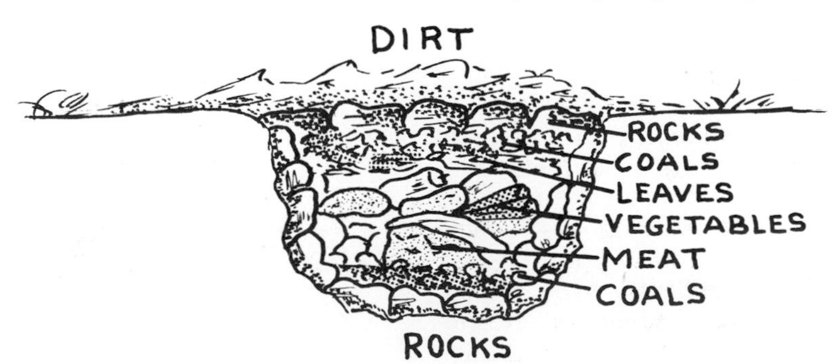

Figure 28-13 An Imu or Pit Barbecue.

twenty hours later. You can cook green corn, parsnips, carrots, onions, ham, clams, potatoes with meat, and many other foods in this way.

A preheated Dutch oven makes the best container for the food, but if none is available you may wrap the meat and vegetables in damp butcher paper, damp paper towels, damp grass or seaweed, or damp nontasting leaves, such as lettuce, cabbage, sassafras, or sycamore. Bitter resinous leaves and burlap bags may be used if kept several layers away from the food.

Bean Hole Beans

$\frac{3}{4}$ lb. (2 C) dried navy beans
$\frac{1}{2}$ lb. salt pork or bacon, diced
$1\frac{1}{2}$ tsp. salt
$\frac{1}{8}$ C sugar
$\frac{1}{8}$ C molasses
2 onions, chopped fine

These are excellent when cooked in a Dutch oven inside an imu, or a bean hole made like an imu. Wash the beans and soak them overnight until their skins start to crack. Then mix all the ingredients and place them in a bean hole and let cook for six to eight hours. This cooking time can be shortened several hours by first cooking the beans in water over an open fire until they are soft, then pouring off the water and mixing in the ingredients before placing them in the imu.

COOKING ON A STONE GRIDDLE

Prop a large, flat, nonpopping rock on stones, leaving plenty of room underneath for draft. Build a fire both on and under the well-scrubbed stone, and when it is sizzling hot, clean off the top, grease it well with a swab, and fry such foods as bacon and eggs or flapjacks on it.

Figure 28-14 Cooking on a Stone Griddle

BARBECUING

There are several ways to barbecue meat; you can place it directly over coals (never flames) or a short distance away at the side of the fire. Barbecuing is a satisfactory method for cooking anything from a small chicken to large cuts of meat or even whole animals.

1. Barbecuing on a Spit over the Fire. Dig a pit, build a good hard wood fire in it, and let it burn down to coals. Place the meat on the spit and fasten it firmly in place so that it will turn as the stick does and so cook evenly on all sides. The coals will cool off and must be replaced frequently, so keep a separate fire at one side of the pit to provide a constantly fresh supply.

When barbecuing a chicken, select a young, tender bird, commonly known as a springer or broiler. One weighing two pounds serves two people and you can cook several side by side on the same spit. Clean the chicken well and insert the spit firmly from tail to neck. Protect the wings and legs from burning by pinning them close to the body with wooden slivers. Rotate the spit slowly over the coals, and baste the bird every ten minutes with melted butter, bacon fat, or other shortening applied with a swab made by tying a cloth to the end of a stick.

Make the handle of the spit long enough to let you stay well back from the fire and place nails at varying heights on the uprights for adjusting the spit to the proper height above the heat. You can use a peeled green stick for a spit, but a metal rod with a non-heating handle does a better job, since it conveys the heat into the meat and cooks it from the inside as well as the outside. Cook roasts of beef or pork,

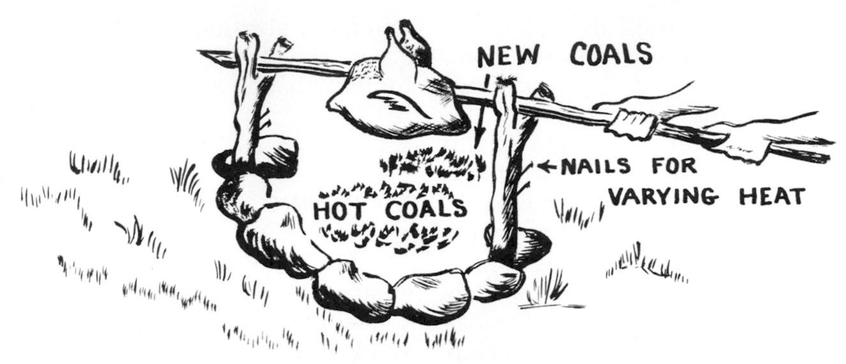

Figure 28–15 Barbecuing on a Spit.

ducks, turkeys, and small game in this way.

2. Barbecuing on a Wire Grill. Fit a wire grill or piece of gravel screen on a framework of rocks, two logs, or metal poles over a pit. Build a fire of charcoal or hard wood and let it burn down to coals; place the food to be cooked (wieners, chickens, spareribs, chops, steaks, and the like) on the grill over at one side of the pit. Two persons using garden forks or similar tools can fasten them in the food-laden grill to draw it into position over the coals. Use a long-handled spatula, further lengthened by tying a long stick to the end of it, to turn the meat. Do not prick the meat with a fork, for holes allow juices to escape. Baste the meat occasionally with a cloth swab to keep it from drying out.

3. Barbecuing at the Side of the Fire. For this style of cookery, suspend the meat by a cord or wire from a lug pole 5 to 6 feet above the ground and on the leeward side of the fire. Insert a flat piece of wood or flattened No. 10 tin can about halfway down the string. Even on a seemingly still day, the tin can will catch enough breeze to keep the meat turning automatically so that it cooks evenly. Prepare the chicken as described for cooking over the fire, and reverse the lug pole and meat periodically to cook both sides. Set a pan under the meat to catch the drippings, and

Figure 28–16 Barbecuing on a Wire Grill

Figure 28–17 Barbecuing at the Side of the Fire

baste it every ten or fifteen minutes. A reflector wall on the leeward side speeds up the process.

ALUMINUM FOIL COOKING

Aluminum foil is a versatile material, for you can waterproof matches or food with it, line cooking utensils to avoid hard scrubbing, make a reflector oven (see Fig. 28–8) and dishes from it; you can fashion cooking utensils from it and then eat right out of the utensils. Since foil will not burn, place it in the fire to burn off the food after use, then crumple it into a ball and take it home with you. If you want to save the foil, you can wash it off and use it again.

How to Cook Pressure-Cooker Style. Heavy duty foil is best for outdoor cooking, since it is about twice as thick as the ordinary variety. To prepare a meal in it, tear off a piece large enough to surround the food, allowing 2 to 3 inches of excess on the three

Figure 28–18 An Aluminum Foil Package.

open sides. Lay the food on one half of the piece, bring the other half over, and fold the two edges up into at least ½ inch folds and crimp them to make an airtight envelope; the all-important thing is to make it absolutely airtight so that no steam can escape, carrying with it the juices and wonderful flavor. If you have ordinary rather than heavy-duty foil, use two layers, wrapping them around in opposite directions and crimping each separately.

Cook in a good bed of coals from a hard wood fire, made well ahead of time. Round out a depression in the coals big enough for the food, place the package in it, and pull the coals back over and around it. Turn the food over halfway through the cooking process. When it is done, rake it out carefully, let it sit a minute to cool, and then make a slit down the center or open the ends and eat right from the foil.

When cooking vegetables, wash them just before you wrap them in the foil; the moisture will provide the necessary steam to cook them. When cooking meat that has little fat, put in a slight amount of oleo, cooking fat or oil, or a few strips of bacon. Add very little, if any, water, and salt and pepper to taste.

What to Cook. To cook a hamburger meal, place a patty in the foil along with strips of potato, green pepper, onions, carrots, and tomato. Flavor with a pinch of salt and cook 15 minutes.

Lamb or pork chops, steaks, fish, and chicken can be cooked in this way, surrounding them with such vegetables as sliced carrots, turnips, potatoes, onions, or green beans. Wet a roasting ear thoroughly, leaving it in its husks, wrap a hot dog in biscuit dough, core an apple and fill the hole with brown or white sugar, cinnamon, and raisins, and cook similarly. You can wrap the ingredients for several meals before you start out, labeling them so that you can select the right one and toss it into the coals when ready to eat. If you want to take extra foil with you, tear off a strip and roll it around a small stick; folding it might cause holes at the creases.

Cooking Time. Cooking time will depend on such factors as the size of the package and the heat of the coals; if necessary, peep into the package to see if it is done but be sure to seal it up airtight again before replacing it in the coals. When cooking several things together, you must, of course, allow enough time for the slowest one to cook. The following are suggested cooking times:

Meats

Chicken (cut up)	20–30 minutes
Fish (whole)	15–20 minutes
Fish (fillets)	10–15 minutes
Shish kebab	14 minutes
Beef cubes (1 inch)	20–30 minutes
Frankfurters	10–15 minutes
Pigs-in-blanket	15–17 minutes
Lamb chops	20–30 minutes
Pork chops	30–40 minutes

Vegetables

Corn (silks and husks removed)	6–10 minutes
Potatoes (Irish)	60–70 minutes
Potatoes (sweet)	45–50 minutes
Carrots (sticks)	15–20 minutes
Squash (acorn)	30 minutes

Miscellaneous

Apple (whole)	20–30 minutes
Banana (whole)	8–10 minutes
Biscuits (wrap loosely in foil to allow for rising)	6–10 minutes
Stew (1 inch meat chunks, potato cubes, onions, carrots, salt, etc.)	20 minutes

IMPROVISED COOKING UTENSILS

Fashion stew pans and frying pans from a double layer of heavy-duty foil, fastening the top securely around a loop formed by lashing the tips of a forked stick together and shaping the middle portion of the foil into whatever sort of vessel you want. Let the butt end of the forked stick extend backward for a handle. Fry in it or make soup, cocoa, or anything else you want in it. You can also make a framework from a coat hanger, twisting the top into a long handle with a loop at the end to form the basis for the body of the utensil.

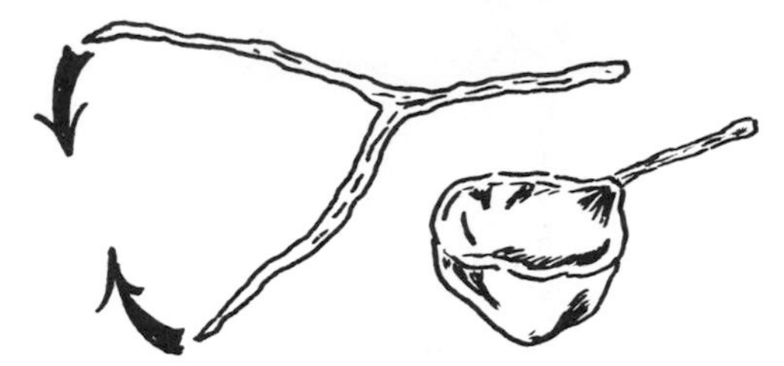

Figure 28–19 An Aluminum Foil Stew Pan.

ADDITIONAL READINGS

(For an explanation of abbreviations and abbreviated forms, see page 25.)

General

Angier: *Home in Your Pack*, chs. 10, 11, 12.

Angier: *Living off the Country.*

Angier: *Skills for Taming the Wilds*, chs. 14, 15, 16.

Angier: *Wilderness Cookery.*

Basic Fish Cookery (#1.49:39:2/2). Supt. of Documents, 26 pp., 25¢, paper.

Bates, Joseph D., Jr.: *The Outdoor Cook's Bible.* Doubleday, 1963, 212 pp., $2, paper.

Beard, James: *The James Beard Cookbook.* Dutton, $4.95.

Better Homes and Gardens Barbecue Book. Bantam, 1972, $1.25.

Better Homes and Gardens Family Camping Book, chs. XI, XII, XIII, XIV.

Betty Crocker's New Outdoor Cookbook. Golden, $2.95.

Boy Scout Handbook, pp. 247–251, 261–273.

Bridge: *America's Backpacking Book*, ch. 6 to p. 83 and pp. 89–111.

Brower: *Going Light with Backpack or Burro*, ch. 5.

Bunnelle, Hasse, with Shirley Sarvis: *Cooking for Camp and Trail.* Sierra, 1972, 198 pp., $3.95.

Bunnelle, Hasse, with Winnie Thomas: *Food For Knapsackers.* Sierra, rev., 1970, 144 pp., $1.95.

Cardwell: *America's Camping Book*, pp. 171–172, chs. 19, 20.

Carhart, A. H.: *The Outdoorsman's Cookbook.* Macmillan, rev., 1962, 95¢, paper.

Casola, Matteo: *Successful Mass Cookery and Volume Feeding.* Ahrens, 1969, 308 pp., $10.75.

Cooking (No. 3257). Boy Scouts, 1967, 96 pp., 45¢, paper.

Cooking Out-of-Doors (no. 19-9842). Girl Scouts, $3, spiral.
Dutch Oven Cooking. AAA Tent and Awning Co., 24 West 5th South, Salt Lake City, Utah 84101, $1, paper.
Fieldbook for Boys and Men, pp. 122–123, ch. 9.
Fletcher: *The Complete Walker,* pp. 66–137.
Friedlander, Barbara: *Earth, Water, Fire, Air.* Collier, 1972, 192 pp., $3.95, paper.
Germain: *When You Go Canoe Camping,* ch. V.
Groene, Janet: *Cooking on the Go: A Camping and Galley Cookbook.* Grosset & Dunlap, 1971, 140 pp., $5.95.
Holm, Don: *The Old-Fashioned Dutch Oven Cookbook.* Caxton, 1970, 106 pp., $3.95, paper.
Johnson: *Anyone Can Camp in Comfort,* chs. 5, 6, 7.
Langer: *The Joy of Camping,* pp. 79–99, 287–291.
Learn and Tallman: *Backpacker's Digest,* ch. 9.
Macfarlan: *The Boy's Book of Hiking,* ch. 5.
MacKay: *Creative Counseling for Christian Camps,* pp. 48–54.
Manning: *Backpacking One Step at a Time,* pp. 235–246, ch. 14.
Merrill: *All About Camping,* chs. 14, 15, 16.
Merrill: *The Hiker's and Backpacker's Handbook,* ch. 6.
Miracle and Decker: *Complete Book of Camping,* chs. 12, 13, 24, 25.
Oetting, Rae, and Mabel Otis Robinson: *Camping and Outdoor Cooking.* Denison, 1958, 260 pp., $5.95.
Ormond: *Outdoorsman's Handbook,* Part 4.
Rethmel: *Backpacking,* chs. 4–6.
Riviere: *Backcountry Camping,* ch. 7.
Riviere: *The Camper's Bible,* ch. 7.
Riviere: *Family Camper's Cookbook.*
Shivers: *Camping,* pp. 228–238, Appendix A.
Stephens, Mae Webb, and George S. Wells: *Coping With Camp Cooking.* Stackpole, 1968, 96 pp., $2.95.
Sunset Barbecue Cook Book. Lane, 1965, 159 pp., $1.95, paper.
Sunset Camping Handbook, pp. 40–57, 65–67.
Sunset Ideas for Building Barbecues. Lane, 1971, 71 pp., $1.95, paper.
Tarr, Yvonne Young: *The Complete Outdoor Cookbook.* Quadrangle, 1973, 308 pp., $8.95.
van der Smissen and Goering: *A Leader's Guide to Nature-Oriented Activities,* pp. 101–125.
Walrath, Arthur J.: *Camp Cookery for Small Groups.* Walraths, P. O. Box 245, Blacksburg, Va. 24060, 1967, 84 pp., $1.75, paper.
Whelen and Angier: *On Your Own In the Wilderness,* chs. 27, 28, 29 and pp. 315–320.
Winnett: *Backpacking For Fun,* ch. 4.
Wood: *Pleasure Packing,* pp. 64–71 and ch. 6.

MAGAZINE ARTICLES

Backpacker:
"The Best of the Freeze-Dried Dinners." *Backpacker-7,* Fall, 1974, p. 63.
"How to Round Out Your Freeze-Dried Dinner Menu." *Backpacker-10,* Summer, 1975, p. 64.
Packer, Nelson: "How to Pick a Freeze-Dried Dinner." *Backpacker-7,* Fall, 1974, p. 65. (See also pp. 67–80.)
Saijo, Albert: "Go Light Backpacking." *Backpacker-3,* Fall, 1973, p. 86.
Van Lear, Denise: "You and Your Gear—Supermarket Substitutes." *Backpacker-6,* Summer, 1964, p. 26.

Camping Journal:
"Build Your Own Backpack Oven." Apr., 1972, p. 97.
Stebbins, J. Ray: "Food for Backpackers." Aug., 1972, p. 30.
Steindler, Gerry: "Cooking With Foil." July, 1970, p. 24.
Steindler, Gerry: "5 Minute Meals." Apr., 1973, p. 54.
Steindler, Gerry: "Trail Chow: How to Pick It, Pack It, Cook It." Mar., 1970, p. 38.
Steindler, Gerry: "Wagon Tongue." July, 1970, p. 14. (Convenience foods)

Camping Magazine:
Burkart, Audrey C.: "Dear Mom, the Food Is Great." Mar., 1974, p. 9.
"Lighten Canoe Trip Loads With Modern Food Products." May, 1965.
MacRae, Rod: Part I—"Outdoor Cooking Can Be Fun and Nourishing," Apr., 1961, p. 15; Part II—"Good Equipment Leads to Good Outdoor Cooking." May, 1961, p. 24.
Proud, Dorothy M.: "Planning Nutritious Camp Meals." Feb., 1966.
Treadwell, Dawn D.: "Planning Meals for Young Campers." May, 1972, p. 18.

Wild Foods

Angier, Bradford: *Feasting Free on Wild Edibles.* Stackpole, 1972, 320 pp., $7.95; $4.95, paper.
Angier, Bradford: *Gourmet Cooking For Free.* Stackpole, 1970, 192 pp., $4.95.
Angier: *How to Stay Alive in the Woods.*
Angier: *Living Off the Country.*
Angier: *Skills for Taming the Wilds,* chs. 17, 18, 19, 23.
Angier: *Survival With Style,* chs. 9–11.
Angier, Bradford: *We Like It Wild.* Macmillan, 1973, $1.50, paper.
Angier: *Wilderness Cookery,* chs. 3–6, 10.
Barnett, Harriet and James: *Game and Fish Cookbook.* Grossman, 1968, 162 pp., $7.95.
Berglund, Berndt, and Clare E. Bolsby: *The Edible Wild.* Scribner's, $2.45.

Coon, Nelson: *Using Wayside Plants,* 4th ed. Hearthside, 1969, 254 pp., $5.95.
Dalrymple: *Survival in the Outdoors,* ch. 8.
Edible and Poisonous Plants of the Eastern States and *Edible and Poisonous Plants of the Western States.* Plant Deck, 2134 S.W. Wembley Park Road, Lake Oswego, Oregon 97304. Two decks of 52 cards each, with a picture of the plant on one side of the card and its description on the other, $4.95, each.
Fernald, Merritt L., Alfred Kinsey, and Reed Rollins: *Edible Wild Plants of Eastern North America.* Harper & Row, rev., 1958, $10.95.
Fieldbook for Boys and Men, pp. 322–331.
Gibbons, Euell: *Stalking the Blue-Eyed Scallop.* McKay, 1964, 332 pp., $7.95; $2.95, paper.
Gibbons, Euell: *Stalking the Good Life.* McKay, 1971, 247 pp., $5.95.
Gibbons, Euell: *Stalking the Healthful Herbs.* McKay, 1970, $8.95; $2.95, paper.
Gibbons, Euell: *Stalking the Wild Asparagus.* McKay, 1962, 303 pp., $2.95, paper.
Hall, Alan: *The Wild Food Trail Guide.* Holt, Rinehart, 1973, 195 pp., $3.45, paper.
Hamper: *Wilderness Survival,* pp. 22–59.
Kirk, Donald: *Wild Edible Plants of the Western United States.* Naturegraph, 1970, 307 pp., $5.95; $3.95, paper.
Langer: *The Joy of Camping,* pp. 287–291.
Medsger, Oliver P.: *Edible Wild Plants.* Macmillan, rev., 1972, 323 pp., $2.95, paper.
Merrill: *The Survival Handbook,* chs. 7, 8.
Olsen: *Outdoor Survival Skills,* chs. 4–6, pp. 146–178.
Shockley and Fox: *Survival in the Wilds,* chs. 5, 8–10, 13.
Sweet, Muriel: *Common Edible and Useful Plants of the West.* Naturegraph, 1962, 64 pp., $3.50; $1.50, paper.
Wilderness Pocket 'n Pack Library, Vols. 1 and 2.

Chapter 29

Outdoor Food Storage and Cooking Devices

Figure 29–1 That's Shiftlessness.

None is so poor that he need sit on a pumpkin; that is shiftlessness.

—HENRY THOREAU

KEEPING FOOD COOL AND SAFE

"Oh, this is the life," you say, as you sink back with a few of your pals on the first night away from permanent camp. Just a handful of friends, a delicious supper under your belt, dishes all washed up and put away, and nothing to do but gather around the campfire and enjoy yourself until its time to turn in for the night. You've escaped from civilization for a few days and there's no danger of outsiders crashing in.

You may be right insofar as human intrusion is concerned, but do you realize that hundreds of forest eyes are, or soon will be, focused upon your camp? Friendly eyes, to be sure, but they belong to curious creatures that will want to investigate this strange assortment that has established itself in the midst of their forest home. These creatures are hungry, too, and will nibble on anything and everything they can find after you have gone to bed.

Unless you are camping in true wilderness country, you are extremely unlikely to be visited by such animals as the wolves, foxes, and bears that constantly plagued the early settlers of this country, but such animals as chipmunks, squirrels, roving dogs, pack rats, and field mice are likely to be your neighbors. In some regions, porcupines are numerous and may prove troublesome, for their sharp teeth can be very destructive. Anything with a salty taste has an irresistible attraction for them, and perspiration-soaked paddles, axes, shoes, belts, bridles, and saddles must be kept well beyond their reach. Any food with an odor is particularly likely to draw uninvited guests.

PROTECTION FROM INSECTS

You must anticipate the ever-present flies, ants, and other tiny crawling and flying creatures that love to sample your food and literally get in your hair. To protect food from ants and other crawling insects, you can erect a water barrier by placing the

Figure 29-2 An Insect-Proof Hook for Suspending Food.

food on a table with each leg resting in a small container of water or you can make a hanger by poking a piece of stiff wire, such as a straightened-out coat hanger, through the bottom of a shallow tin can and soldering it to make it watertight (Fig. 29-2). Fill the can with water, then bend the ends of the wire over to make two hooks; hang the food on one and suspend the other over a limb or on your camp rope tied between two trees. Also effective is a sprinkling of common moth flakes or moth balls around the legs of a table or on the path ants would have to take to reach the food.

To keep out flying insects, place the food in jars or cans with tight-fitting suction or screw-on lids or plastic covers; wrap it in cloth, mosquito netting, cheesecloth, or waxed paper; or place it in plastic bags, sealed at the top with a warm iron.

PROTECTION FROM ANIMALS

The type of marauders you expect will, of course, determine the kind of cache or protection you must provide. Even tin cans are not safe, for some animals, including dogs, can pierce them with their teeth and suck out the contents. The usual method of caching food is to suspend it on a tree limb about 10 to 20 feet above the ground, far enough away from the tree trunk and overhanging branches that neither jumping nor climbing animals can get to it. Fasten one end of a $\frac{1}{8}$-inch nylon rope to the food package, then tie a small rock or other small heavy object to the other end and throw it over a tree limb to use as a pulley to raise the food to a safe height (Fig. 29-3).

Cupboard Cache. Make this convenient cupboard from an oblong box, such as an old orange crate, and insert appropriate shelves in it. Fit it with an insect-proof covering of cheesecloth or plastic and a protective front of canvas, oilcloth, or cheesecloth with tabs to tie into eyes or loops to slip over hooks placed around the bottom and sides of the crate. To attach a rope for suspending the box, anchor the rope to large screw eyes fastened in the top of the box or tie overhand or figure-of-eight knots in holes in the box. This cupboard is awkward to take on a hiking trip, but it is excellent for a wagon or canoe trip. It is also a practical refinement to leave at an outpost camp.

Figure 29-3 A Cupboard Cache.

You can construct a similar cupboard that can be folded or rolled up from canvas, leaving wide hems at the top for inserting a stick or metal support upon arrival at the campsite.

KEEPING FOOD COOL

One of the main problems when trip camping is keeping such perishable foods as butter and milk cool. When stored in an airtight container, milk will keep for 24 hours or a little longer and butter will remain sweet and relatively firm for 2 weeks or more. In general, however, when going out for more than a day, it is better to take nonperishable foods or some of the multitude of dehydrated foods now available than to take chances with perishable foods, for even the most efficient refrigeration devices are too bulky to take for the kind of camping we are talking about. For short stays, you can use various methods to keep your food cool, depending upon what materials are available at your campsite.

Cooling With Ice. Though it isn't practicable when backpacking, it is entirely feasible to take ice for cooling when you are transporting your supplies by automobile or truck. A fifty-pound cake of ice will last four days when properly cared for and a hundred-pound cake will last twice as long.

As soon as possible after you arrive at the campsite, dig a hole big enough for the ice and the food you want to pack with it. Line the bottom and sides with small rocks or gravel and a layer of grass or leaves. Insulate the ice by wrapping it tightly with several layers of newspaper and an outside covering of burlap. Thoroughly moisten the insulation and place the package in an old cardboard box or tin can with holes punched in it to allow the ice water to drain off. Pack the food in close to the ice and lower the container into the pit; then shovel wet sand or gravel in all around and cover the whole thing with wet burlap or dampened newspapers.

Figure 29-4 Who Needs an Electric Fan?

Plan your cooking program so that you will need to open your "refrigerator" as seldom as possible and the ice will last surprisingly well.

Cooling With Water

When water from a stream or lake is available, you can devise several varieties of satisfactory coolers. If the water may be disturbed by strong waves, swift currents, or boats, weight the food down with rocks or anchor it to trees or rocks on the shore so that it can't be overturned or washed away. Place the food in waterproof containers to keep impure water from contaminating it.

A Spring Box. A large box, can, or barrel can be sunk at the water's edge to hold food. Insert a shelf large enough to hold all the food that is not in watertight containers and leave the underpart unshelved to accommodate tall watertight containers. Make large holes near the bottom of the container to promote a free flow of water through it (Fig. 29-5).

By feeling about in the water of a lake, you can often locate one or more spots that seem appreciably cooler than

Figure 29-5 A Spring Box.

the rest; these are places where underground streams feed into the lake. Place your spring box in one of these spots, preferably in the shade. Weight it down with heavy rocks and cover it with newspapers or a heavy piece of burlap. This covering should either be kept constantly wet or its ends should be left dangling in the water to absorb moisture to cool the contents by evaporation.

Immersing Directly in Water. You can place your food in a large watertight container, such as a five-gallon milk can, a cupboard cache, a bucket, or a pan, and submerge it in a cool spot in the lake or stream, using rocks to weight it down if necessary. Place it in the shade and cover it with newspapers, kept constantly wet, or with a piece of burlap or cheesecloth long enough to extend down into the water for cooling by evaporation as described for the spring box.

Cooling by Evaporation

Cooling by evaporation is effective, particularly on a hot day when there is a fairly good breeze. Putting salt in the water will hasten the evaporation, making the system more efficient.

An Oriole Cache. This is one of the best methods for storing food, because it cools it and at the same time protects it from animals and insects (Fig. 29-6).

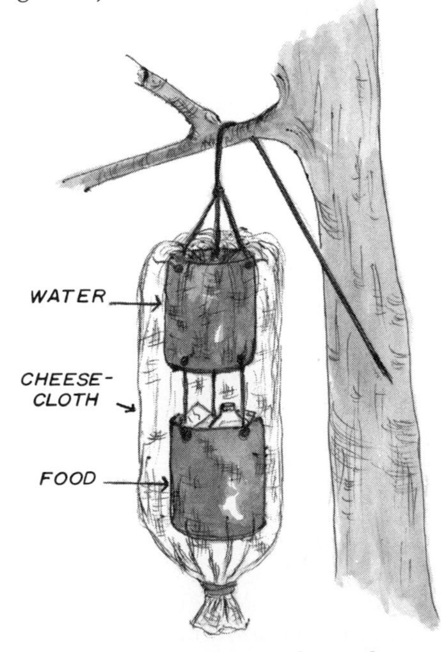

Figure 29-6 An Oriole Cache.

Make three or four holes near the tops of two buckets or number 10 tin cans, spacing the holes evenly so that the cans will hang straight. Join the cans with rope, as shown in Figure 29-6, leaving enough space between them to insert food into the lower one.

Take a piece of cheesecloth large enough to cover both cans and use small rocks to anchor the center of it in the upper can, which is kept about two-thirds full of water. Bring the cheesecloth down under the cans and fasten it tightly to form an insect-proof cover.

The cheesecloth absorbs water from the top can and the resulting evaporation keeps the food cool. Hang the cache in the shade in a fairly strong breeze. Swing the rope over a limb and raise the cache to a level where it will be safe from insects and animals.

Additional Cooling Methods

If you dig a shallow pit in the bank close to a lake or stream, it will usually fill up quickly with underground water that is even cooler than that in the lake or stream. Place food in suitable receptacles in the pit and cover the top with wet burlap or newspapers as described previously.

Dig a hole in a shady place under a tree and line it with rocks, gravel, or leaves. Place the food in it and cover the top and sides with dampened leaves, newspapers, or burlap, and redampen them frequently.

Keep your drinking water cool by suspending it in the breeze in a desert bag; the water seeps out slowly through the canvas and cools the contents by evaporation.

COOKING DEVICES

A good camper is able to adapt himself happily to using whatever resources for camp life he finds plentiful in his particular region. If you want to practice good ecology or are in an area where cutting green saplings for kettle supports is prohibited, you can usually find nonpopping rocks which will do beautifully. A dump or salvage yard in the vicinity may provide flat or odd-shaped bits of metal, old stove parts, and similar items which you can convert into cooking devices and other gadgets for use around the campsite. Ingenuity and skill will aid you in improvising cooking devices, and your satisfaction will be greatly enhanced by knowing that you built your creation "from the ground up."

CAMPFIRE PARAPHERNALIA

It is essential to take time to prepare properly for work; a camper disabled through carelessness is about as welcome around camp as a rainstorm. Canvas or other work gloves and a large bandanna are useful for handling hot objects around the fire and for keeping the hands clean for cooking. When cooking over a wood fire, a green forked-stick fire poker and a shovel are indispensable for moving hot rocks, burning embers, and glowing coals into more advantageous positions for cooking.

Tin Can or Hobo Stove. A *hobo stove* (Fig. 29-7) is made from a number 10 tin can and provides a fine little device for making toast, bacon and eggs, or other quickly cooked foods. Cut a three-inch hole at the bottom to contain the fire and use a can opener to punch several triangular holes around the top to provide ventilation and a smoke outlet. A small amount of fuel is all that is necessary; in fact, you must be careful to avoid burning the food. In the interest of ecology, it is best to use canned heat (Sterno), a warming candle, a buddy burner, or a trench candle to provide the heat, but, if necessary, you can use a few small

Figure 29–7 A Hobo Stove.

twigs. Light the fire and place the hobo stove over it, making sure that is is level so the food won't spill.

Paraffin Stove or Buddy Burner. A little *paraffin stove* or *buddy burner* (Fig. 29-8) is excellent for quick cooking, for it will burn for several minutes, throwing out enough heat to cook simple foods. You can also place it under a charcoal or stubborn wood fire to get it started.

Make the stove by placing about two-thirds of a medium or small-sized cake of paraffin or some old candle stubs in a tuna can or a can cut down to about that height and immerse the can in boiling water, using the method described for waterproofing matches in Chapter 27. Use extreme care in handling the paraffin, for it is flammable and can cause very severe burns if it gets on your skin. Wind a piece of cardboard or corrugated paper into a loose spiral, and insert it into the wax when it begins to harden, leaving enough of the edge extending above the wax to act as a wick. You can use the paraffin stove in your cooking fireplace for quick, simple cooking, and it will also serve as an emergency light. Placing it under a charcoal or stubborn wood fire will help to get it started quickly. When you are through with it, smother the flame by placing a lid over the can and save it to use another time.

Figure 29–8 A Paraffin Stove or Buddy Burner.

Pan Tree. To make a handy *pan tree* (Fig. 29-9), find a dead but solid branch or small tree and trim the small branches to make pegs for hanging things. Sharpen the end of the shaft and drive it into the ground near your campfire or work table. Another way to keep your pans and other paraphernalia handy and off the ground is to tie your camp rope between two

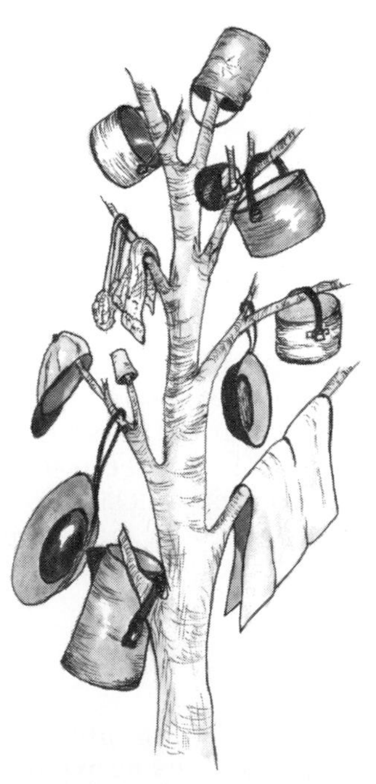

Figure 29–9 A Pan Tree.

trees and hang your utensils on the rope with wire pot hooks.

SUPPORTS FOR THE KETTLE

Ingenious campers find many ways to support kettles over the fire. Some sort of griddle or grate is almost a necessity for successful cooking, because it keeps things from tipping or upsetting, usually can be adjusted to bring the heat nearer to or farther from the kettles, and increases the efficiency of the fire by reflecting the heat up onto the kettles.

Stone Griddles. You can place three rocks in a triangle to support a one-pot meal (Fig. 29-10*A*) or you can line up several rocks in rows, spacing them just widely enough to support your kettles and making them several rocks high if you wish (Fig. 29-10*B*). A popular variation is the *keyhole fireplace* shown in Figure 29-10C. The fire is kept going in the broad end of the keyhole to furnish fresh coals to put under the kettles supported at the narrow end. Be sure to use only nonpoppable rocks; porous ones from in or near a stream are particularly likely to explode and fly in dangerous pieces, because they often contain enough water to build up an enormous amount of steam when heated. Choose the least porous rocks you can find.

Wire or Metal Grates. Figure 29-11*A* shows a lightweight grill suitable for a backpacker, which can be supported across the fire on rocks, green logs, cinder blocks, or bricks. It weighs only about 4 ounces and usually comes with a carrying case.

Figure 29-11*B* shows a folding grate with legs which can be extended and placed in the ground so no other support is necessary. The type shown here has closely spaced bars at one end for grilling directly over the fire. Models are available that weigh as little as 14 ounces.

Creative campers may want to im-

Figure 29-10 Stone Griddles.

Figure 29-11 A Backpacker's Grill and a Folding Grate.

provise, and it is usually possible to find metal bars or old pieces of flat metal in scrap heaps that will serve nicely. Other possibilities are a piece of gravel screen or even chicken wire, the shelf from an old oven, or an unpainted shelf from an old refrigerator.

Pot Hooks. The pot hooks shown on the standard crane (Fig. 29-13) are made of metal and so are ecologically sound because they take the place of the time-honored wooden pot hooks that were once a standard item at every campsite. The pot hook on the left in Figure 29-13 is made of strong wire or a coat hanger bent over to form two hooks, one to place over the lug pole and the other to hold the pot. The pot hook on the right is made by inserting two hooks in the links at each end of a chain; it is easy to adjust the length by varying the position of the top hook in the chain.

An assortment of pot hooks of various lengths is desirable so that the pot can be hung at just the right height above the fire. They are also useful for many other purposes, such as hanging pots, kitchen utensils, clothing, and other camp paraphernalia on your camp rope or even on low-hanging branches of a live tree.

The Standard Crane. Few things are more valuable around a campsite than the good old *crotched stick;* there are a thousand-and-one uses for it, including providing the supports for a standard crane. When seeking one, there is no use wasting time in trying to find the variety shown in Figure 29-12*A*; it is quite rare and would be unsatisfactory anyway for it is likely to split when you pound on the crotch to drive it into the ground. The type shown in Figure 29-12*B* is easily found, serves quite well, and minimizes the danger of splitting the crotch since you pound on the main part to drive it in. For ease in driving, sharpen the end into a four-sided point.

The *standard crane* (Fig. 29-13) has long been used to suspend several kettles over the fire simultaneously. Modern campers should not ordinarily use it, however, because it requires too much precious wood. It consists of a *lug pole* of metal or wood supported on two forked sticks about 3 to 4 feet above the fire. Pot hooks of various lengths can be hung on the lug pole for varying the distance of the kettles from the fire. After the meal is over, the lug

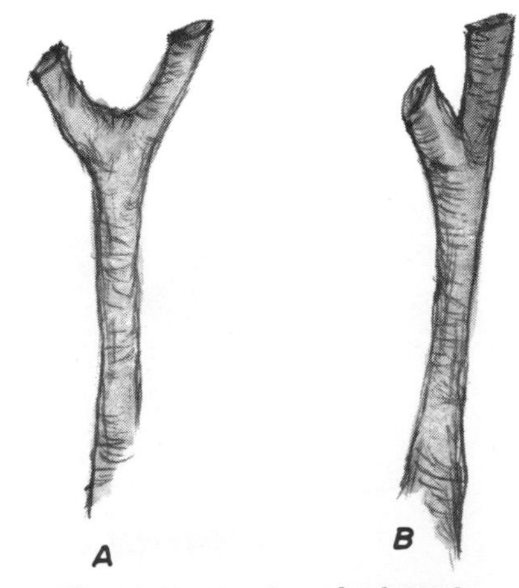

Figure 29-12 Crotched Sticks.

Figure 29–13 A Standard Crane With Pot Hooks.

pole can be removed and the fire built up for the evening program.

CLAY OVENS

The various types of clay ovens are interesting to construct and, if properly made, give excellent results when roasting meats and vegetables or baking pies, cakes, or cookies. If the ovens are to be durable and satisfactory, they must be made of clay that is cohesive and that will bake hard.

Satisfactory clay is available in most regions, and published geological surveys or persons in the neighborhood who are interested in geology may provide help in locating it. You may be able to find it in cellars, road cuttings, and other places of excavation and along the banks of streams. To test the clay for cohesiveness and workability, allow it to dry out for a little while, then knead it thoroughly and curl it around your finger. If you can curl and uncurl it without breaking or cracking it, it will probably be satisfactory.

Dig enough clay to make your oven, taking care not to mix any dirt with it. Allow it to dry for a while and then work and knead it until it is quite pliable. If it does not seem to stick together well, weave in a little hay or grass to give it added body.

To make a clay oven over a large round or rectangular metal can (Fig. 29-14), cut a hole in the top for a chimney and build up a platform of clay or rocks for it to rest on. Place a layer of rocks over the sides, ends, and back of

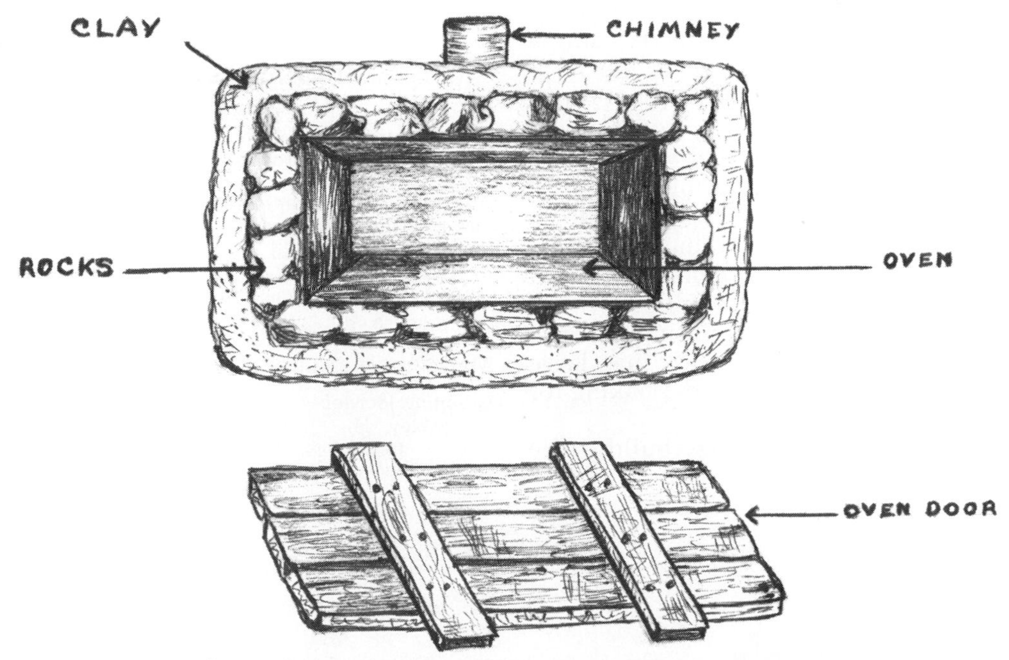

Figure 29–14 Clay Oven Made Over a Metal Can Base.

Figure 29–15 Other Varieties of Clay Ovens.

the can and cover them with clay to a depth of about a foot, making sure to leave the chimney hole uncovered. Bake the clay in the sun for a couple of days, and then build a slow-burning fire of partly green wood inside it and keep it going for two or three hours to bake it hard and firm. The fire must not be too hot or it will cause cracks to appear.

There are other forms over which you can build a clay oven (Fig. 29–15). One form consists of small sticks bound into a round bundle of the desired size and shape; another is made from a wooden packing box, and a third from a half-keg. Make the form for the chimney by inserting a tin can with both ends removed or a small wooden box or bundle of sticks of the appropriate size. Cover the form with clay and bake as previously described, letting the fire inside burn out the wooden form as it hardens the clay. If cracks appear, fill them with new clay and let it harden the next time you use the oven. Make the oven just large enough to accommodate the baking for your group.

When ready to bake, build a fire in the oven and keep it going until it is as hot as desired. If the wood does not burn well, place rocks or green stick fire dogs under the fuel to improve the ventilation. When the proper temperature has been reached, rake out the fire, place the food inside, and close the oven up tightly by placing a flat stone over the chimney and fitting some sort of door tightly into place. You can use a flat stone or a piece of metal for the door, or you can make one by joining a few pieces of wood together (Fig. 29–14).

ADDITIONAL READINGS

(For an explanation of abbreviations and abbreviated forms, see page 25.)

Angier: *Skills for Taming the Wilds,* ch. 14.
Jaeger: *Wildwood Wisdom.*
Mason: *Junior Book of Woodcraft.*
Rutstrum: *The New Way of the Wilderness.*
Whelen and Angier: *On Your Own in the Wilderness,* ch. 10.

MAGAZINE ARTICLES

Camping Journal:
Sibley, Hi: "Jury Rigs for Cooking." Jan., 1968, p. 44.

Chapter 30

Duffel for Camping and Trips

Figure 30–1 What's She Doing in an "Organized Camp"?

Look out, when you start for the day,
That your kit is packed to your mind;
There is no use going away,
With half of it left behind.

—Rudyard Kipling*

Follow the trail to the open air
Alone with the hills and sky;
A pack on your back, but never a care,
Letting the days slip by!

—Agathe Deming†

"ROUGHING IT SMOOTHLY"

A newcomer to camp usually brings with him all sorts of unnecessary *duffel* or *gear* (camp jargon for your possessions), most of which lies unused, collecting dust and occupying valuable space. The secret of happy camp living is to have everything you need for health, safety, and happiness without being surrounded by a collection of unnecessary claptrap. Remember that the keynote of camp living is simplicity. Your camp living quarters will probably be clean, comfortable, and quite adequate for your needs but without extra embellishments or an unlimited amount of storage space. The ultimate goal, both in camp and on the trail, is perhaps best expressed by the title of Elon Jessup's book, *Roughing It Smoothly*. However, unless you are engaging in the type of camping known as "survival camping," it is just as bad to go to the opposite extreme by trying to live too primitively.

DUFFEL FOR TRIPS

When planning for a trip, choosing what to take and how to pack it is truly

*From "A Boy Scout's Patrol Song," 1909. *In Rudyard Kipling's Verse,* Definitive Edition, 1940, Doubleday & Co., Inc. Reprinted with permission from the publishers.

†Reproduced by permission of Miss Deming.

an art in itself, especially if you plan to carry everything on your back, for even after traveling only a few miles over a trail that is rough or steep, perhaps in disagreeable weather, each inch of bulk seems like a foot and each ounce a pound. Transportation by canoe, pack saddle, or covered wagon allows a bit more latitude, but compactness and lightness are important even then, since space is still at a premium and every unnecessary thing you have will need to be picked up and handled many times as you search for needed items.

SOURCES OF EQUIPMENT

Camps and counselors should not promote long expeditions into the woods unless a minimum of equipment of the right sort is available for doing it comfortably and safely. However, elaborate outlays suitable for going on an African safari aren't at all necessary, for campers can initially get along with little more than the things they or the camp already have, adding to them as their experience dictates and their finances permit. Camps sometimes rent or lend pieces of personal equipment to campers and customarily furnish such group equipment as tents, tools, and group cooking and eating outfits. Campers can also make many items, perhaps as a special project before the trip begins. You can find instructions for making such things as ponchos, ground cloths, tents, packsacks, and sleeping bags in the references listed at the end of the chapter or you can make them from kits available from outfitters. You can also make or assemble your own cooking utensils, mess kits, and other items.

Army-navy surplus stores are good sources of inexpensive gear, and quantity discounts are often available from suppliers.

DITTY BAGS

A camper's pack is a series of bags within bags, with similar things, such as toilet articles or underwear, collected in small *ditty bags;* this allows you to put your hand on just what you want without having to turn everything topsy-turvy. Articles packed singly or in disorderly fashion have a way of dropping to the bottom of your pack or being left behind at some stopping place.

The number of ditty bags you will need depends upon the length of your

Figure 30–2 Some Ditty Bags.

trip and your personal preferences. A minimum is one for toilet articles, one for clothing, one for eating utensils, and one for miscellaneous items. You may want to add others for such things as tools and repair materials, shoes, and food.

Many campers like ditty bags made of strong plastic (outfitters sell these) since they are waterproof, tough, and readily reveal what is in them. You can collect your own assortment by saving such things as home freezer bags and bags in which food and other items are sold. For extra security when packing fine substances such as flour, place one bag inside another. Fold over the tops and fasten them with rubber bands or "twist-'ems." Bear in mind that some plastics are highly inflammable and must be kept away from an open flame.

Outfitters also offer zippered pouches and cloth ditty bags that close with drawstrings, which are usually waterproofed and made from strong, lightweight materials. However, it is easy to make your own. The very best material to use is probably parachute nylon, which is light and compact, so strong you can hardly tear it, so tightly woven that it sheds rain, and will neither shrink nor rot. Other possibilities are balloon silk, Egyptian cloth, denim, and unbleached muslin, which you can waterproof if you wish. To determine the size you need for an individual bag, assemble all the items that are to go in it and fashion a paper pattern big enough to surround them, leaving enough extra width for double-stitched seams and enough room at the top for a hem wide enough to admit a pair of shoestrings to serve as a drawstring.

A broad ditty bag with a round bottom, such as the case for toiletries shown in Figure 30-2, will stand open and upright while you use it, although it is not as simple to construct as one made by simply sewing two rectangular pieces of cloth together. Use distinguishing colors and draw a representative picture on each bag or list the contents on the side with enamel for permanence, Mystik Tape, or a wax crayon for a temporary job. Label long, narrow bags on top so that you can slip them into your bag upright and remove them without disturbing the rest of the contents. You can pack various pieces of equipment in an ordinary cloth shoe bag, (Fig. 30-3), which you can roll up to put in your pack, and you can quickly set up some woodland "dresser drawers" by tying the bag to a tree or the foot of your bed.

Figure 30-3 A Handy Shoe Bag Hold-all.

CLOTHING

Clothing and outfitting stores display attractive camping outfits of almost every type and description, but the wise novice goes slowly and chooses carefully before making a large investment. Although everyone wants to look well dressed and attractive, comfort, suitability, and durability are far more important considerations. Since, as a beginner, you will gradually build up experience and stamina by

Figure 30–4 Fledglings Must Stay Close to the Nest.

starting with trips that are short in both distance and duration, you can usually find enough suitable garments in your present wardrobe. Add new ones as you become assured that you really like camping and intend to continue with it.

Your choices will be influenced by such factors as the season and weather expected, the length of the trip, the terrain, and your own personal preferences. Remember that your body has a built-in thermostat and its own heating and cooling devices, and choose your clothing with a view to helping them perform efficiently. During warm summer months, you will need garments that "breathe," or permit a flow of air that cools you by contact and by evaporating perspiration; loosely woven clothing does this best, and light-colored clothing does not absorb the heat of the sun's rays as dark colors do. Figured or checked patterns show less soil than plain colors. Besides keeping you warm or cool, clothing also protects you from insects, brush and other rough objects, poison ivy and oak, burrs, nettles, cool breezes, rain, and even hail and snow.

Clothing should fit snugly and comfortably, yet be cut full enough to permit freedom of movement when hiking, climbing, canoeing, or working around camp. It should be plain and serviceable, snag-resistant, and washable. Camp is not the place for fragile or dressy things. For the most part, men and women will find the same type of clothing suitable.

A camper dresses in layers. As previously discussed, several layers of clothing are warmer for cool weather because of the air trapped between them. They also allow you to adapt readily to changing conditions by simply adding or subtracting layers. On a cool summer morning, for instance, you may start out wearing fishnet underwear, shorts, trousers, a shirt or two, and even a light sweater and a lightweight windbreaker. As it warms up, you keep removing garments until by noon you are wearing only your underwear, shorts, and a lightweight shirt. In reverse order, you add garments to meet the cool of the evening.

Underwear. Although almost any well-fitting, comfortable cotton underwear will do for summer wear, the experienced backpacker prefers *fishnet underwear,* which consists of a network of large diamond-shaped holes. The mesh feels quite comfortable as it soaks up perspiration and allows it to evaporate. You will need at least one extra set of underwear so that you can wash out the soiled set at night to always have a pair in reserve for an emergency.

Pants. Pants should be of sturdy, closely woven material that will resist snagging and picking up trailside impedimenta such as burrs and nettles. Although wool is preferable for cold weather, cotton or part cotton is better for summer. Blue jeans, once a camping favorite except during cold or rainy weather, are still a good choice if you can find a pair of the old-fashioned roomy kind; unfortunately, most of today's jeans are cut in the form-fitting Western style that fits too tightly for comfort and does not permit free movement. You will find several types of work pants at your local stores which will do nicely, and a large selection of suitable pants are available from outfitters. Stout whipcord, denim,

(Courtesy of Girl Scouts, U.S.A.)

khaki, drill, and corduroy are some of the more satisfactory materials.

Cuffless pants are preferable since cuffs collect dirt and catch on snags, causing tears and possibly accidents. If the pants you want to wear have cuffs, cut them off and rehem the bottoms of the legs.

Although you may find it handy to store a few things in your pants pockets when hiking without a pack or working around camp, leave them practically empty when you are using a pack, for bulging pockets prove oppressively heavy and hamper you as you walk. It is also difficult to extract things from them; items are much more convenient when placed in the outside pockets of your pack. Pants pockets should be fastened shut with a zipper, button, or snap so you don't lose things from them. They should be of sturdy construction and should hang from the waist of the pants rather than from holes cut in the fabric.

Wearing a belt or having buckles, belt loops, or ridges on your pants will prove quite irritating when worn under the tightly cinched hipbelt of your pack. Suspenders are likewise undesirable when worn with a pack, for they are likely to get tangled up with your pack straps or catch on brush along the trail.

Long pants are recommended for general hiking through the woods to protect you from scratches, poison ivy or oak, insect bites, chiggers, and too much sun. If you wish, you can slit them up the sides and roll them up for coolness when such protection is not needed. While walking through sand or an infestation of insects, tape your pant legs snugly about your ankles.

Some prefer shorts for walking on city sidewalks, along country roads, or on open woodland trails. They should be of rugged construction and comfortably cut. You can make "cut-offs" by cutting off the legs of a suitable pair of trousers.

Riding breeches or jodhpurs make very poor camp attire since they bind about the knees and hamper free stooping and bending.

Shirts. Cotton shirts or those of part cotton are desirable for summer wear, although they may become uncomfortably soggy and chilly when wet. For this reason, many prefer a lightweight shirt or a combination of wool and cotton.

Long sleeves discourage mosquitoes and other biting insects and protect against sunburn, scratches, and poison ivy and oak. A long shirt tail keeps your shirt inside your trousers, or you can wear it outside for better ventilation when it is hot. One or two breast pockets with button down flaps are a convenience.

Take at least one extra shirt to wear for extra warmth and to allow you to wash one out at night.

Sweaters. Sweaters make pretty poor outer attire since they collect every burr in sight, snag on bushes, stretch out of shape and become soggy and heavy when wet. However, they are excellent for warmth when worn under an extra shirt or windbreaker.

Windbreakers. Your summer outfit should include a lightweight windbreaker jacket. One with a hood is called a *parka*. It should be of closely woven, water repellent (not waterproof) material so that it "breathes" to keep your perspiration from being trapped inside where it will condense, making you cold, clammy, and almost as wet as if you had no protection at all. Long-fiber cotton, tough nylon, or a combination of the two are the most satisfactory materials. The garment should be long enough to pretty well cover your hips and should be roomy enough to permit free arm movement even when worn over several layers of clothing. Most jackets have elasticized wrists, and there should be several large pockets. Windbreakers come in two styles: one a slipover jacket, the other opening down the front. Although slipover is simpler and lighter, it cannot be worn open to adjust to temperature changes.

Headgear. You will need a hat with a fairly wide brim to protect you from sun and glare and to keep the water from running down your neck when it rains. It should fasten under your chin with a strap or ties so it can't blow away. There should be holes in the crown, and these should be placed high enough to permit ventilation; add some triangular ventilation holes of your own if there aren't enough. A roller-crusher type hat of soft material, which you can roll up and store in your pack is good. Some prefer to wear a hat of terry cloth which you can keep wet to cool your head. Berets, although worn by some, obviously do not meet all of these requirements. Other campers like a duckbill visored tennis, hunting, or baseball cap. For cooling your head, you can knot your bandanna into the semblance of a hat and wear it damp; you can also use it to keep perspiration from running down into your eyes.

Sleepwear. Never sleep in the clothes you have worn all day, for the perspiration in them will lie about you

Figure 30–5 Packin' Up.

like a wet blanket. Change into fresh clothing, such as pajamas, a T-shirt and shorts, or a sweat suit. If you are chilly, add an extra shirt or sweater and wear two pairs of socks to keep your feet warm.

Boots and Socks. The choice of boots and socks and the care of the feet are discussed on pages 407 to 412.

Rainwear. *Getting wet* will probably not cause a cold or any ill effects whatsoever, but *staying* wet likely will, so stop immediately, change into dry clothing, and get thoroughly warm in front of a blazing fire. Better yet, don't get wet! A wise camper always goes prepared for rain. He carefully packs his own waterproofing, uses waterproof packs and bedrolls, or carries extra tarpaulins or ponchos to cover any duffel not so protected.

Keep rainwear near the top of your pack where you can find it in a hurry when you need it. There is little agreement as to the best rain protection but none disputes the inadequacy of the gossamer, oiled-silk cape with hood.

Raincoats that are too long are a pure nuisance, for they flap about at every step, tripping you when you climb hills, and constantly flying open to expose the lower part of your body to the elements. They are usually hot and binding and cause profuse sweating.

As we have previously noted, snug-fitting, waterproof garments trap perspiration and make you almost as wet as if you had no rain protection at all. Therefore, have rainwear that fits loosely to admit some ventilation, and make sure that wrists, collars, and fronts can be opened during breaks in the weather. To make garments absolutely rainproof, they must be coated with rubber, which makes them heavy, or made of some light material with a rainproof coating, such as urethane-coated nylon. Garments of thin plastic vinyl are adequate for occasional wear but will quickly disintegrate under rugged use.

PONCHO. The most popular garment for general rainwear around camp is probably a poncho. This is a waterproof sheet with a center hole and hood for the head (Fig. 30-6*A*). The type shown has a long flap in the back that can be draped over your pack to protect it or snapped up when not needed

Figure 30-6 A Poncho (*A*) and a Rain Suit (*B*).

for this purpose. This loose construction provides ample ventilation. The hood can be held close about your face with a drawstring. A poncho is especially useful in a canoe, where you can drape the loose flap over your duffel on the bottom of the canoe. The garment proves rather unsatisfactory, however, when trying to walk in a strong wind, which sets it flapping, or when trying to walk through heavy brush or weeds. A poncho is particularly valuable because of its versatility—there is usually a covering for the head hole which allows you to convert it into a flat waterproof sheet to cover gear, use it as a ground cloth under your sleeping bag, or construct an improvised shelter with it (see pp. 455–456). Two ponchos can be snapped together to form a larger sheet.

RAIN SUITS. For complete protection, you will want a rain suit (Fig. 30-6*B*), which consists of a hip length jacket with a hood and full cut trousers that slip on or off easily over your shoes and are roomy enough to wear over several other garments. The suit should be well-constructed and of a strong, lightweight, and durable material.

RAIN CHAPS. Rain chaps slip onto each leg individually and tie at the waist. Since they have no front, back, or crotch, they weigh very little. They protect your legs well and should be worn with a fairly long rain jacket to protect the rest of the body.

CAGOULE. A *cagoule* is a knee-length pullover parka, usually made of coated nylon. It is roomy, provides good protection in any but extreme weather conditions, and allows free body movement. Some are provided with snaps to shorten them when their full length is not needed.

RAIN HAT. As noted, many items of rainwear come with built-in or detachable head protectors. If you need a separate hat, you can either carry a rainproof cover for your regular hat or get one of the various sou'westers or light waterproof hats with medium brim and strings to tie under your chin.

FOOTWEAR. Although your boots may be made water resistant, it is practically impossible to waterproof them. Light rubbers are available to slip on over them if you expect to do extensive hiking under wet conditions. Rubber boots are heavy and clumsy and tiring to walk in and are recommended only for actually wading through water.

Gloves. A pair of lightweight leather gloves or washable canvas work gloves are a very important part of your equipment. They are indispensable for handling hot cooking utensils and for protecting your hands from blisters, abrasions, and splinters when doing heavy work, building fires, or clearing brush. They also keep your hands clean and can be slipped off when actually working with food. They should fit snugly, for if too large, they are awkward and tend to slip, making them dangerous to use.

Bandanna. A large-sized bandanna is another piece of equipment that adapts itself to many purposes. You can use it to handle hot pans, to tie up a homemade mess kit, to hold specimens gathered along the trail, to double as a triangular bandage or tourniquet, to shield your neck and face from sunburn and insects, to wear around your forehead to keep perspiration out of your eyes, to dampen and make into a turban to wear wet around your head to cool you in hot weather, or to place folded under your tump line or the straps on your pack to keep them from cutting into you. Carry it in your hip pocket or an outside pocket of your pack or wear it around your neck, cowboy fashion, ready for instant use.

Swimming Suit and Cap. You will need these for refreshing dips.

TOILET ARTICLES

Carry a few well-chosen toilet articles in a ditty bag approximately 9 by

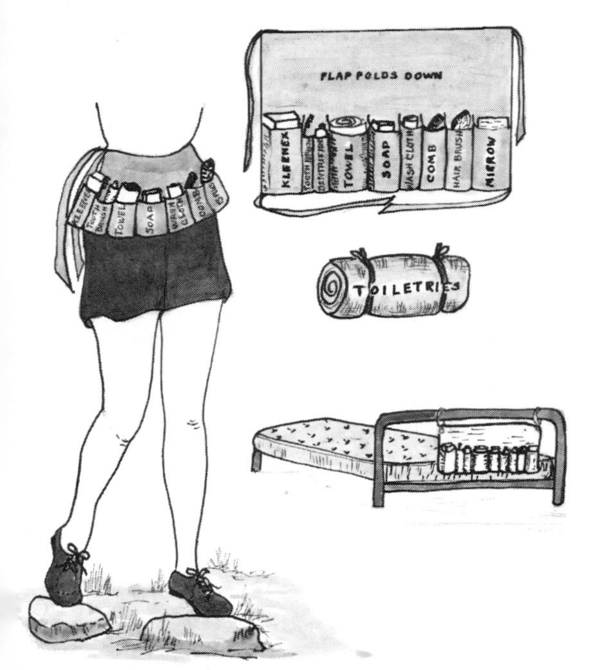

Figure 30–7 A Kit for Toilet Articles.

19 inches or in a specially constructed case. The case shown in Figure 30–7 is particularly handy, for you can wear it around your waist while using it, tie it at the foot of your bed, or roll it up and place it in your pack en route. Fashion it from strong material such as unbleached muslin, denim, or toweling. Spread out all the articles you want to include in logical sequence and make a paper pattern to fit, allowing enough space for hems and turning up 6 or 7 inches of the material for pockets; be sure to allow enough fullness to accommodate the thickness of the objects.

For a trip, you need take only small quantities of toilet supplies (a small piece of soap instead of the whole bar, a small quantity of tooth powder instead of the whole can, and the like). Pack them in unbreakable containers. Such planning is the secret of successful *go-light* trips. You may sometimes have to pack such articles as your toothbrush, toilet soap, washcloths and towels wet, so it is best to fit them with individual oiled-silk or plastic ditty bags. You need take no great supply of washcloths and towels, for you can wash them out and hang them up to dry overnight. A small metal mirror is superior to the breakable type.

By carefully saving and washing out the plastic bottles and bags that home products commonly come in, you can soon accumulate almost all the containers and bags you need.

MISCELLANEOUS EQUIPMENT

Include a few tools in your trip outfit. If several campers are going, you need not burden each member of the party with duplicates. Two axes or bow saws will serve a whole party, for few will be using them at the same time; however, one would be inadequate owing to the danger of loss or breakage.

TOOLS AND REPAIR KIT

Such tools as a screwdriver and pliers with wire cutter are useful. A compact tool haft is available that consists of a hollow handle filled with various attachments for converting the tool into a hammer, a screwdriver, an awl, and so on. Carry a trowel or small shovel, preferably with detachable handle, for digging sanitary facilities and manipulating and putting out fires.

Axe, Knife, Sheath Knife, and Bow Saw. If you will be building wood fires, you will need to take an axe, knife, and perhaps a bow saw and

Figure 30–8 A Handy Trowel or Shovel.

sheath knife, as discussed in Chapter 24.

Always keep your axe in its sheath, and wear it on your belt around camp; pack it in your bag where you can find it quickly en route.

Carry your knife in your pocket, attached to your belt or belt loop, or in a "catch-all" ditty bag in one of the pockets of your packsack.

One or two sheath knives for the group are convenient to use as cooking knives or as strong knives for heavy work. Include at least one file and one sharpening stone for group use.

Other Items. Some lengths of fish line or strong nylon cord, twine, glue, thin copper or picture wire, shoe thread, a bit of wax, canoe and tent repair kits, and a small assortment of nails and tacks will also prove helpful. You will find many uses for ½ to 2-inch strips of old inner tube (tying packages, fastening them to your pack frame, etc.). Keep these things together in a repair ditty bag.

ADHESIVE TAPE

Adhesive tape serves many functions in addition to its first aid use in applying bandages and supporting sprains. It will stick to almost anything that is dry, especially if pressed on with a little heat, as from a heated spoon or frying pan. You can use it to temporarily mend a leaky tent or canoe, a rip in clothing, or a leak in a bucket or kettle. It will also secure a cork in a bottle, fasten the lid on a box or tin can, and even make hinges for a lid.

CAMERA

Only a high-quality camera and equipment will give superior results in nature photography, for you must take shots where and when you find them, often in the shade or in other difficult situations. Keep your camera where you can snatch it up and use it in the brief period nature poses. Be sure to take extra film and have a small plastic cover or ditty bag for covering your camera in case of a sudden rain.

PURSE AND MONEY

You may need a small amount of money for telephone calls, supplies along the way, or other emergency uses. Pin it fast in your pocket, keep it in a secure place in your packsack, or wear it in a money bag around your waist.

WATCH

At least two people in the group should have watches. Luminous dials are an advantage at night.

GLASSES

On long trips, campers wearing glasses should take along an extra pair in a strong case.

MAPS

Even though you may not actually need a map to find your way, a topographical map of the region will prove interesting and will help you to choose the most intriguing path. Prepare it for hard use on the road as described on page 391.

COMPASS

You will need a compass for following or making a trail map. Slip it into your shirt pocket and secure it with a strong cord or thong.

(Courtesy of Crystal Lake Camps, Hughesville, Pennsylvania.)

STATIONERY

Never take ordinary ink, for it is likely to leak and ruin valuable duffel and anything written with it runs and becomes indecipherable when it gets damp. Prestamp your postal cards or envelopes and write with a hard pencil or ball point pen.

NOTEBOOK AND PENCIL

Always keep a small (about $3\frac{3}{4}$ inches by $6\frac{3}{4}$ inches) loose-leaf notebook and a pencil in your jacket or shirt pocket or in an outside pocket of your pack. A hard pencil is best, for it will not smear as the pages of the book rub together. An excellent habit to form is to jot down and file anything you run across that might be of later help in camping and counseling. Games, stories, songs, bits of nature lore, and so on are veritable gold mines during counseling days and may be stored in a file box or large-capacity notebook cover for ready reference. Select a few choice items to take on a trip for "program" and include a few blank pages for making notes along the way.

PROTECTION FROM THE SUN

You will need a broad-brimmed hat or visored cap, long sleeves and full-length trousers, a bandanna for your neck, a *good* pair of sunglasses, and some suntan oil if you are to be much in the open, particularly on water. Observe all the precautions listed on page 102 when trying to achieve a tan, but carry sunburn ointment, too, in case someone is foolish enough to overexpose himself. Avoid cheap sunglasses, for their faulty lenses often cause eye strain. Wear sunglasses to protect your eyes from bright sunlight, dust and wind, but don't make a habit of wearing them indoors, in shade, on cloudy days, or just any old time. If you wear regular glasses, you will probably find the flip type sunglasses most convenient.

(Courtesy of Harold M. Lambert.)

PROTECTION FROM INSECTS

Take a good insect repellent to apply to your face, neck, and hands, a head net, and insect protection for your tent. Many good sprays are now available that will aid greatly in keeping your campsite free from irritating insects, though scientists are still debating and experimenting in regard to the safety of pestcides, for some are excessively harmful to friendly wildlife under certain conditions. In addition, there is evidence that aerosol sprays containing fluorocarbons are damaging to the environment. Before purchasing or using them, get expert advice and be sure to follow directions carefully.

SLEEPING EQUIPMENT

This consists of a poncho or ground cloth to place under a sleeping bag or a bed roll made of blankets and safety pins, tied with a rope (see pages 461–462). You can use a ditty bag filled with soft materials, such as socks and extra underwear, for a pillow.

SIT-UPONS

These inventions of the Girl Scouts are useful around main camp when sitting on damp ground and also make good pillows. Make them by placing a few layers of newspaper between two pieces of oilcloth about a foot square and binding the edges together with a blanket stitch. You may paint your name on your sit-upon. Roll it up and tie it with a string for carrying.

TENTS

Tents or extra tarpaulins and ponchos are necessary in case of rain.

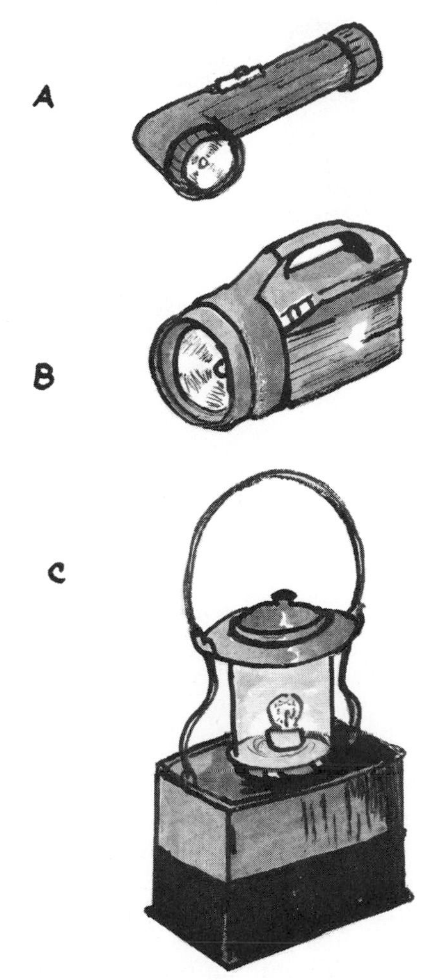

Figure 30-9 Two Types of Flashlights and a Camp Lantern.

FLASHLIGHTS AND LANTERNS

Each person should have a good flashlight with extra bulbs and batteries. Figure 30-9*A* and *B* shows two types of individual flashlights, while Fig. 30-9*C* shows a camp lantern that is suitable for group use. When not using your flashlight, reverse the top battery so that the two negative poles meet; this will prolong the life of the batteries.

You will probably use a flashlight less than you think, for when on a trip you will usually make maximum use of daylight hours by stopping early to make camp, eat supper, and clean up before dark so that you will be ready to be up and on your way early.

CANDLES

Short, fat plumbers' or miners' candles are best, for they burn strongly enough to start even a wet-weather fire and also give off quite a bit of light. Some prefer to use a candle in a lantern (Fig. 30-10) that has a shatterproof plastic chimney to shield the flame and a chain at the top to hang it by. The lantern folds down compactly for carrying. Candles are not recommended as a means of light for campers because of the danger of starting a fire.

BINOCULARS

Good quality, lightweight binoculars are valuable for studying bird and animal life, locating a landmark from a

Figure 30-10 A Candle Lantern.

high vantage point, mapping out the most desirable trail, enjoying distant scenery, and giving or receiving messages from a distance. The *power* of binoculars is usually printed on them as 6×, 8×, 10×, and so on, which indicates the amount by which they magnify. For instance, 8× binoculars make an object a ½ mile away seem as if it were only 1/16 mile away because they magnify it to 8 times normal size.

You might naturally assume that it is best to get the highest power binoculars available, but this depends largely upon the purpose for which you intend to use them. Bear in mind that binoculars magnify what you don't want to see as well as what you do. Thus, they intensify haze, smoke, the trembling of your hands as you hold them, the movements of a boat, or even a gnat that happens to cross your line of vision. Also, the higher the power, the narrower the field of vision—in other words, you see more and more of less and less. Another drawback is that the weight of the binoculars increases with the power, so that powerful ones are too bulky and heavy for go-light backpacking. For ordinary camp purposes, you will usually find it desirable to get a clear view of a fairly wide field, and so your choice will be a 6× or 7× pair.

When you want to have your binoculars instantly available, as for studying animal or bird life, wear them on a short lanyard around your neck, with the lenses covered by protective rubber caps that you can slip off in a jiffy. To keep them from excessive swaying and dragging down on your neck, you can add a pocket to your shirt made to fit them from denim or other heavy material. Ordinarily, keep your binoculars in their case, stashed away in an outside pocket of your pack.

WATER SUPPLY

You will need to carry a supply of water with you, the amount depending upon your ability to replenish your supply from known safe sources along the way. When you are not absolutely certain of the water's purity, you will need to take equipment to purify it by one of the methods discussed in Chapter 31. Several types of containers are available for carrying your supply.

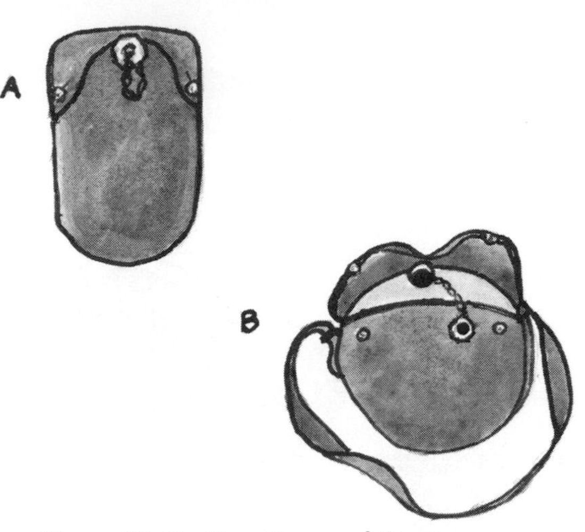

Figure 30–11 Two Types of Canteens.

Figure 30–11*A* shows a favorite wide-mouthed, flat type of canteen, usually made of plastic, for carrying an individual supply. It is shaped to slip conveniently into an outside pocket of your pack. The canteen shown in Figure 30–11*B* is usually made of aluminum, which is lightweight and rustproof and will not taint the contents. It has an adjustable strap for carrying it over one shoulder. Several types of collapsible water bags and desert bags are available for carrying larger quantities of liquid for a group, which are usually available in ½ to 3 gallon capacities. Individual canteens ordinarily come in 1- and 2-quart sizes.

If your camp has established routes that are frequently used for trips, it will pay you to take samples of all water sources along the way and have them tested for purity, as carrying large quantities of water becomes burdensome since it weighs 8 pounds per gallon. Having to purify it can also be a time-consuming nuisance.

PEDOMETER

This interesting instrument records the distance you cover on foot. For more details, see pages 387 and 418.

MENDING KIT

Pack mending equipment in a tin box or ditty bag and include such items as needles (laced through a small piece of cardboard), both straight and safety pins, a few yards of thread wound on a piece of cardboard, small pointed scissors, buttons, patches of cloth and leather, assorted rubber bands, adhesive tape, and strong waxed linen thread.

FISHING GEAR

Fresh fish make a welcome addition to your camp menu.

TOILET PAPER

BOOKS AND PAMPHLETS

Sources for songs, games, nature identification, poetry, or stories are welcome.

Figure 30–12 Carry Thread like This.

MATCHES

A small supply of matches is always a good thing to take for emergency use on a trip, and if you plan to build wood fires, you will need a large supply. Your matches should be waterproofed, carried in a waterproof container, or wrapped in aluminum foil.

EQUIPMENT FOR BUILDING WOOD FIRES IN WET WEATHER

Trench candles, "peas," plumbers' candles, and bits of dry tinder help a great deal. An inspirator, coiled up in one of your cooking kettles is worth its weight in gold for starting fires in wet weather. All these are discussed in Chapter 27.

EXTRA PADDLES

In case you are travelling by canoe, take one or more extra paddles in case any are lost or broken.

WHISTLES

Several whistles on lanyards should be available so that any person or group going even a short distance away from the main group can carry one. It is easier than you think to become confused or lost when going even a short distance as to gather fire wood, and it can turn out to be a very serious thing. A whistle blast carries much farther than the voice and, of course, the universal signal for help is three blasts on the whistle.

COOKING AND EATING OUTFITS

Nested cooking kits are available to serve 1, 2, 4, 8, or 12 persons. These cooking utensils usually have no han-

Figure 30–13 A Mess Kit with Detachable Handle.

dles, but instead are manipulated by a detachable handle that fits any of them. This lightens the weight of the outfit and allows the vessels to fit more compactly together (see Fig. 30–13). This arrangement has an added advantage in that the handle stays comfortably cool to the touch, since it is never left over the fire.

Although aluminum utensils are lightest in weight, those of lightweight steel are better since they weigh only a little more, are less likely to become dented or misshapen, and spread the heat more uniformly under the food so that there is less tendency for it to stick or burn. Porcelain or enamel utensils chip too easily to be practical for continued use on the trail.

The frying pan in some kits comes with a folding handle that sometimes has a slot in it for inserting a stick to lengthen the handle so that the user can stay farther away from the hot fire. As mentioned in Chapter 27, some camp stoves come with their own set of nested cooking utensils.

You can assemble your own mess kit by purchasing odds and ends at a variety or hardware store, using the trial and error method to find ones that nest together. Cut off the handles and buy a pot gripper to handle them by or use a pair of needle-nosed pliers (these will also be useful for other purposes around camp). Carry this mess kit in a homemade bag with a drawstring, a bandanna, or make a ditty bag to fit it. Fold-down rings instead of knobs on lids and shallow spouts and bail ears on pots also make for compact nesting. Pot covers should fit tightly to keep the juices in and dirt and ashes out. Low, wide utensils are less liable to be upset than tall ones and the contents also cook faster. Knives, forks, and spoons can be placed inside the kettles or carried inside a bag made on the order of the toilet kit shown in Figure 30–7. You can use the largest pot on the outside of your kit for a water bucket and thus keep it clean for contact with the kit cover. When cooking over a wood fire, some advocate not washing the outsides of your cooking kettles, claiming that the accumulation of carbon on them improves their heat-retaining properties. If you follow this practice, you may want to put layers of newspapers between them.

A reflector oven that folds flat is greatly enjoyed on a trip, perhaps even to the extent that you will be willing to carry the extra weight. Most people consider a Dutch oven entirely too cumbersome to take when backpacking.

Nonbreakable plastic is considered by many to be superior for cups, plates, and other dishes, and sectioned plates are available. Others prefer pie tins or aluminum plates, and even aluminum containers such as TV dinners come in will last a week or two on the trail.

Aluminum cups burn your lips when filled with hot liquid. Enameled cups are better, especially the type with a handle that is open at the bottom so that you can hang it on your belt or pack. Best of all is probably the Sierra Club cup (Figure 30–14) which, although made of stainless steel, weighs

Figure 30–14 A Sierra Club Cup.

only 3 ounces. It is constructed so that it keeps the contents warm while staying cool at the brim so that it will not burn your lips. You can hang it on your belt or pack by means of the handle. The cup is also wide enough to be suitable for use as a dish when eating such things as soups and stews.

Each person will need a fork and spoon, but he can use his pocket knife instead of carrying a table knife.

Careful menu planning will eliminate utensil problems. You can combine ingredients into many tasty one-pot dishes and can cook many things in ashes or in aluminum foil, as described in Chapter 28.

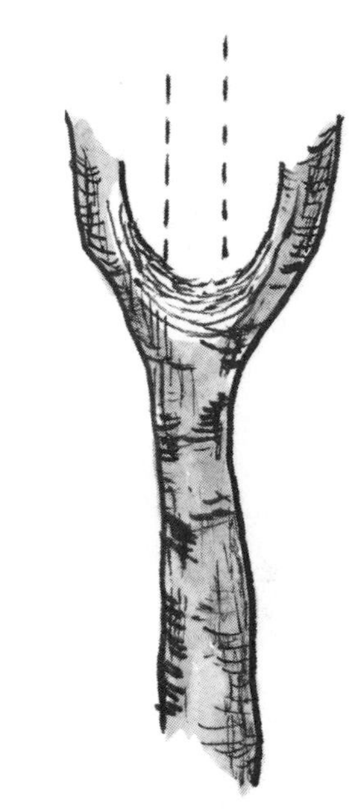

Figure 30-16 An Emergency Crutch.

FIRST AID KIT

By observing safety precautions you can cut down on the number of injuries and accidents. However, no expedition, even a very brief one, should leave camp without the necessary supplies for emergencies. Campers should not take individual first aid supplies and try to treat themselves but should go to the trained person or persons designated to take care of first aid. Although you can buy first aid kits designed for camper use, many camps prefer to assemble their own with the aid of the camp doctor or nurse.

A lightweight, aluminum fishing tackle box with compartments or a special kit with pockets makes a good container. You will need only small quantities of many supplies, which you can place in small plastic vials available at the drug store or in ones you bring from home. If you take glass bottles, wrap them in corrugated cardboard, sponge rubber, or several layers of paper towels or toilet tissue. Some medications are available in ampules just large enough for a single treatment. Here are some suggestions for supplies, but the final decision should be made by your local health personnel.

Figure 30-15 A First Aid Kit.

Instruction book
Triangular bandage (a clean bandanna will do)
Absorbent cotton
Adhesive tape
Ace bandages
Adhesive bandages
Gauze squares—roller gauze
Aromatic spirits of ammonia—for bites, stings, and fainting
Boric acid solution—for minor eye irritations
Aspirin
Baking soda—for bites, stings, indigestion, or sunburn
Oil of cloves—for toothache
Disinfectant
Sunburn ointment
Treatment for burns
Tweezers—sharp pointed

Treatment for poinson ivy or oak
Snake bite kit
Small scissors
Safety pins
Insect repellent
Moleskin—for preventing blisters

You can make an emergency crutch from a branch, as illustrated in Figure 30-16. The top, which rests under the armpit, should be smoothed with sandpaper or sand held in a piece of cloth or leather and padded with sponge rubber, gauze, or some folds of soft cloth bound on with adhesive tape. A stretcher, improvised from a coat or blankets and sticks, is described on page 343.

CHECK LISTS FOR PACKING EQUIPMENT

Select from the following list to make out your own check list. Then check and recheck your list until you have eliminated everything not really essential. After you return from your trip, revise your list on the basis of your experience and keep it handy for use the next time.

PERSONAL EQUIPMENT

Essential

Wearing Apparel
Extra trousers and shirts
Shorts
Sunglasses
Moccasins or extra shoes
Socks (several pairs)
Wide brimmed hat or duckbill visor cap
Pajamas
Rainwear
Leather or heavy canvas gloves
Bandanna
Extra underclothes
Windbreaker, wool shirt, sweatshirt, or sweater
Hiking stick

Toilet Articles
Biodegradable soap in plastic box
Towels and washcloths
Pocket mirror (metal preferred)
Toothbrush and paste
Comb
Suntan lotion
Insect repellent
Sanitary napkins or tampons

For Food
Canteen
Mess kit, including cup, fork, and spoon

Tools, Etc.
Pocket Knife
Waterproofed matches or matches in waterproof matchbox
Flashlight, extra bulb and batteries
Packsack

Optional

Wearing Apparel
Insect head-net or mosquito netting
Leather belt for hatchet, knife, etc.
Light rubbers
Swim suit and cap

Toilet Articles
Shaving kit (men)
Tissues
Lotions for hair or skin
ChapStick

Tools, Etc.
Hatchets or saws
Tump line
Fishing equipment and license
Whistle
Pedometer

Camp rope
Maps
Pocket notebook
Hard pencil or ball point pen
Bedroll with ground cloth

Mending kit
Sheath Knife
Compass
Money
Binoculars
Camera and film (in waterproof bag)
Nature books, poetry books, games
Air mattress or foam pad and repair kit
Stationery (already stamped)
Musical instrument
Songbooks
Extra eyeglasses in case
Tent
Watch
Hammock (can be rolled up to size of a fist

GROUP EQUIPMENT

Essential

For Food
Menus and recipes
Water purification equipment
Aluminum foil
Cooking forks, spatula, spoons
Cooking utensils
Water pail (plastic or canvas folding)
Paraffined cloth or plastic food bags
Salt and pepper in shakers (fit piece of waxed paper inside tops)
Food (carefully checked against check list)

Tools
Axes or saws
Repair kit for mending tents, air mattresses, etc.
Nails, twine, etc.
Adhesive tape
Tarpaulins, ponchos or pup tents for sheltering equipment, dining porch, etc.
Spade or shovel
File and shaprening stone
Can opener
Electric lantern
String, wire

Fires and Sanitation
Extra supply of waterproofed matches
Toilet paper
Insect repellent
Wash pan or canvas wash basin
Dishcloths, towels
Yellow soap or detergent
Metal or plastic sponge for cleaning pans
Steel wool

Miscellaneous
Check list of equipment
Mending kit (buttons, thread, shoelaces, etc.)
First aid kit and instruction book
Tents or tarps and accessories
Snake bite kit

Optional

For Food
Hobo stoves, reflector oven, Dutch oven
Paper towels
Grates
Paper napkins

Tools
Extra paddles
No. 10 tin can buckets, etc.
Candles
25 or 50 feet of strong cord
Camp Lantern

Fires and Sanitation
Inspirator, "peas," trench candles, etc.

Miscellaneous
Maps of area
Old newspapers
Extra shoelaces (twine will do)

BACK PACKING

Traveling on foot with your bedding, food, and clothing on your back offers the ultimate in freedom, for only when you leave the beaten path and learn to walk unobtrusively through the forest do you experience the wonderful world of wildlife.

Stow all your equipment in some form of a packsack, even though you're only going out for a sightseeing tour or a simple lunch. In that way, you'll be able to take extras that you might want, such as your knife, binoculars, containers for gathering interesting specimens, and camera; you won't lose precious gear as you lay it down to examine something you find along the way, and you'll have your hands free for pushing aside underbrush, for examining, or for helping you climb. Only a rank beginner trails along with objects dangling and flapping from his waist and bulging out of his pockets, making him look like a veritable porcupine.

Even a light pack may bother you at first, but day-by-day use will strengthen your muscles until you will scarcely notice it and would indeed feel ill-equipped without it.

Packs of almost any size and description are available so that you should be able to find one exactly suited to your needs, no matter what you are doing.

BELT, WAIST, OR FANNY PACK

The pack known as a *belt, waist,* or *fanny pack* is the smallest of all. It consists simply of a small container attached to a nylon or web belt which is worn around the waist. It will hold from 3 to 5 pounds of supplies, including your lunch, a camera and film, and a water bottle, and is useful mainly to free your hands when you are going on short expeditions. It is made of the same materials as larger packs and usually opens by means of a zipper on top which is covered by a protective rain flap. Some packs also have one or two zippered pockets on the side. The belt is worn with enough slack so that you can turn it around to extract the contents without having to remove the belt. Some backpackers wear one of these packs in addition to their regular pack to provide a handy place for special equipment such as a first aid or survival kit.

DAY PACKS

There are several types of day packs, varying in size from those just large enough to carry what you would want for a daytime expedition to those suitable for a weekend trip. A day pack is essentially a bag supported by two straps worn over the shoulders. Since almost all the weight of the bag is borne by the shoulders and back, it is uncomfortable if it weighs more than 15 to 20 pounds and should be supported on a pack frame, as will be discussed later. If you will be staying overnight, your bedroll or sleeping bag is customarily attached in the shape of an inverted U across the top and sides of the bag.

Knapsack. A knapsack is a small bag suitable for younger campers or for daylight jaunts and cook outs.

Haversack. A haversack is usually somewhat larger than a knapsack and is suitable for adolescents on light trips for it will hold the things necessary for an overnight stay. You may even be able to find room for your sleeping bag in it if you have one of the extremely lightweight models that fold up into a package scarcely larger than a long loaf of bread. There are usually two or more outside pockets for storing odds and ends or things you want to keep readily available.

Rucksack. A rucksack is a favorite for carrying a heavier load. It has

Figure 30–17 Some Day Packs.

the usual shoulder straps and often a waist strap which holds it close to your body so that it will not bounce and sway excessively as you walk along. The name is of German origin and literally means "back sack." Rucksacks come in many sizes, some being large enough to carry ample supplies for a weekend or longer stay. The shoulder straps can usually be adjusted for size by means of buckles. A rucksack is usually a narrow bag that hugs the back well, making it an excellent bag for those climbing over rocks, scrambling through brush, or traveling in other close quarters. Two shapes are common: (1) straight-sided or rectangular and (2) teardrop-shaped which is narrow at the top and broad toward the bottom so that it permits free arm action.

A rucksack usually has two compartments: a large upper compartment that opens by means of a zipper and has a protective rain flap on top, and a lower one that has a zippered side opening. There are usually two zippered outside pockets. The shoulder straps, usually of nylon, webbing, or leather, are wide and padded where they cross the shoulders and narrow where they attach to the pack. The bottom of the bag is reinforced with leather, plastic or a double layer of pack material to protect it from excessive wear.

A disadvantage of the rucksack in hot weather is its very tendency to hug the back—there is no space for air circulation, making it hot and uncomfortable. For this reason, and because the weight will be distributed more comfortably, it is recommended that you support it on a pack frame. This type of pack finds great favor with skiiers, cross country hikers, and bicyclists.

Adirondack Pack Basket. The Adirondack pack basket is a part of our

Figure 30–18 Carrying a Rucksack.

Figure 30-19 Adirondack Pack Basket.

heritage from the Indians of the Northeast, and some campers still prefer it. One advantage is that its construction of oak or ash splints protects the contents, and it is rigid enough to keep canned goods and other hard objects from gouging into your back. It is shaped to fit the back and has straps for carrying it. Though not waterproof itself, it usually comes with a waterproof cover. You can arrange your bedding in the shape of an inverted U across the top. The Adirondack pack basket is available in several sizes. Among its disadvantages are that is is awkward to fit into a canoe or automobile, it may catch on brush and trees as you pass through the woods, and it takes up the same amount of space whether full or empty.

LARGER PACKS

Since larger packs are designed to carry heavy loads, they are usually sold as a unit with a matching pack frame. A favorite material is tough, closely woven nylon, which bears up well under the rough usage the pack receives. Although most packs are nearly waterproof, they often have a tendency to develop leaks, especially at the seams and along the zippers, so that it is advisable to cover it with a waterproof rain cover or poncho when out in a rain.

The pack usually has two main compartments. The upper one is about twice as large as the lower and closed by means of a large flap. The lower compartment opens by means of a full width zipper, which may or may not have a protective rain flap. There seems to be a growing tendency to add more and more outside pockets, and a modern pack may have as many as five or more, with two on each side and one or two across the back. They ordinarily have protective flaps to keep out dirt and moisture. These pockets increase carrying space and provide a place to carry things needed en route so that you won't have to open the whole pack and paw through everything in an effort to find what you want. Strong nylon coil zippers are best since they combine strength and flexibility, are easier to repair, and have less tendency to jam. Packs often have a see-through map pocket on the outside of the top

Figure 30-20 Pack Bag Supported on a Pack Frame.

flap. This allows you to fold the map to the appropriate area and consult it without having to remove it from the pocket, saving both time and wear and tear on the map. The pockets and compartments allow you to be quite selective when packing and distributing the weight of your gear.

Most packs have collapsible *spreader bars* at the top which serve to hold the top of the upper compartment open to simplify packing and unpacking.

When a good pack is properly loaded and mounted on a suitable frame, the average healthy male who is accustomed to it can walk comfortably and nearly upright while carrying a load of 35 pounds or more.

A *Duluth Packsack* is one of a variety of big sacks or bags capable of holding a very large supply of food and clothing. It is sometimes used by husky men, especially for hauling goods for only a short distance, as at a canoe portage, but is too heavy for inexperienced or adolescent campers to handle.

Selecting a Pack. Your pack should, of course, be selected to meet your own particular needs. There are many models from which to choose, and new ones are constantly appearing on the market. In general, select the smallest pack that will carry your needs. If you will be taking trips of various lengths, especially in different seasons, you may even want to invest in several packs since more duffel is needed for cold weather.

The first thing to look for in a pack is good workmanship. Stitches should be close together and there should be reinforcements at all points of strain. Seams should be well sewed and reinforced where necessary so that they can't pull or ravel out. All zippers should be strong, operate smoothly, and be protected by rain flaps. The hardware on the pack should be well constructed and should serve to attach

(Courtesy of Cheley Colorado Camps, Estes Park, Colorado.)

the pack firmly to the frame so that it will not shift about, which is irritating and causes undue wear on the pack. Pick out a few packs that appeal to you, pack them with an approximation of the gear you will take and walk around with them to see how comfortably they ride.

PACK FRAMES

As we have mentioned, heavy packs should be supported on a pack frame. If you try to carry a pack by the shoulder straps alone, the straps will cut into your shoulders, and since the weight is borne almost entirely by the shoulders, you will have to proceed in a fatiguing, bent-over position in order to balance the pack. A pack frame shifts as much as 75 percent of the weight to the powerful muscles of your hips, pelvis, and legs, where it rides easily as you step forward in a nearly erect positon. Other benefits of a pack frame are that it prevents the pack from bulging out of shape, keeps its contents from gouging into your back, provides air space to cool your back and allow perspiration to evaporate, and distributes the weight so that the shoulder straps do not cut into your shoulders.

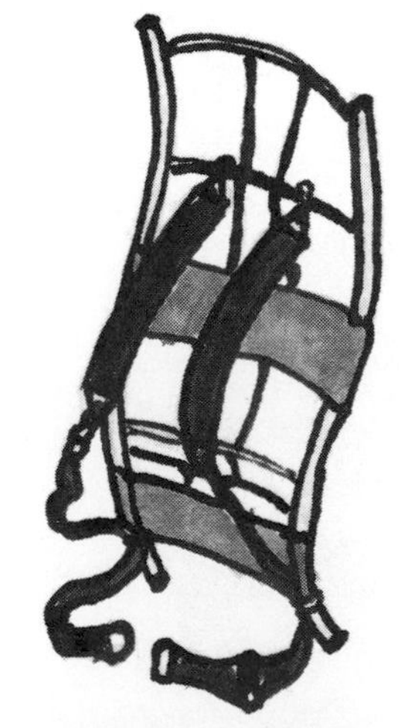

Figure 30–21 A Pack Frame.

A pack frame (Fig. 30–21) consists of a metal framework, shoulder straps, upper and lower *back bands,* and a hip belt. The best frames are made of aluminum tubing, which, when properly welded, is both strong and lightweight. Although magnesium is lighter, it is more expensive and often not durable. Steel frames, although quite strong, are entirely too heavy to be practical. The frame is shaped roughly like a shallow S, which follows the contours of the body when properly fitted and slants forward slightly over the shoulders at the top.

The padded shoulder straps do not lift the pack but rather stabilize it and hold the top of it close to your body. The upper and lower back bands are positioned about even with your shoulders and waist and are taut enough to keep the middle part of the pack from coming into contact with your body. These bands are usually made of strong webbing, nylon, or several layers of other strong material and can be adjusted up or down to coincide with your own physique.

Buy a hip belt if your pack doesn't have one. Be sure that it is at least 2 inches wide, for it will cut you in two if it is too narrow. The belt is worn cinched tight so that it can perform its important function of holding the bottom of the pack close to your body and transferring most of the weight to your strong hip region. Hip belts that reach clear around you like a pants belt are superior to the partial belts that reach only to the outside edges of the frame.

The pack bag is ordinarily supported on the top two thirds of the pack frame, leaving room below for lashing on your sleeping bag or bed roll, covered by a waterproof stuff sack, ground cloth, or poncho. If you take a foam rubber pad, lash it on either above or below your pack bag. Many hikers attach their raingear to the top of the frame where they can get at it in a hurry in case of a sudden storm. Most packs have rings or other means of attaching extra items, such as snow skis, an ice axe, a fishing rod, or a Sierra Club cup. Various devices are used to attach the pack bag to the frame. The best are probably *clevis pins,* which extend from holes in the frame to grommets in the bag. These devices should allow for adjusting to the width and length of the bag and their wide variations largely explain why it is wise to buy a bag and frame as a unit or at least ones that are made by the same manufacturer.

The most important consideration in buying a pack frame is to get one that fits you; otherwise it will hit you at all the wrong places, and if too small, it will bind at the shoulders, and if too large, it will teeter and wobble about above your head in a most distressing manner.

Pack frames usually come in four sizes: small, medium, large, and extra large, but these classifications are actually of little value since a proper fit really depends mostly upon the actual size and shape of your own torso. Although pack bands, shoulder straps, and hip belt are all adjustable, they cannot satisfactorily compensate for a frame that is not basically of the right proportions for you. Therefore, if you are inexperienced, you will need to seek expert advice before making a choice. As always, it is ideal if you can borrow or rent and try out several packs and frames before making a final purchase. In each case, try adjusting the bag and frame in various ways to find the most comfortable combination.

A pack frame is also useful for lashing on and carrying irregular objects such as firewood or even a bedroll wrapped in a poncho or ground sheet.

IMPROVISED PACKSACKS

(Note that none of these are waterproof, so that you will need to waterproof the contents or cover them with a poncho or piece of plastic.)

Shoulder Stick Pack. The most picturesque and romantic way to carry your possesions is to tie them in a big bandanna, hang it on the end of a stick, tramp-style, and jauntily stride along with it perched over your shoulder. Unfortunately, your jaunty feeling lasts only a short time, for this is, in reality, a most uncomfortable way to carry your gear.

Blanket Roll. You may roll your gear in a blanket, secure it with three-inch horse blanket pins and a short rope, and wear it in a U around your shoulder. This works well enough for a short trip, but the roll will make you hot and sweaty and catch on every tree and branch along the way, making it ill-adapted for any but short trips. Use your poncho or ground cloth as the outside layer to render it waterproof.

Figure 30-22 A Blanket Roll Pack.

Figure 30–23 A Slack Pack.

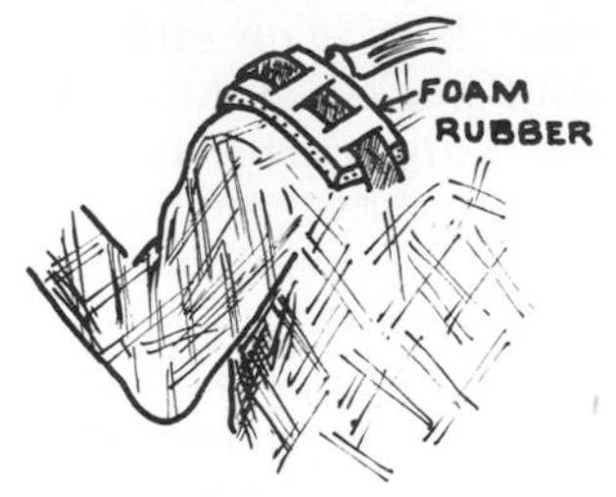

Figure 30–25 An Improvised Shoulder Pad.

Blue Jeans or Slack Pack. Jaeger* describes a novel way to make a packsack out of blue jeans or slacks. Tie your duffel into a secure parcel and slip it into the body of your slacks; secure it by running a rope through the belt loops and up around the crotch. Convert the legs of the slacks into pack straps, bringing them up across your shoulders and under your arms; fasten them about 2 inches apart at the center (not the edges) of the pack so it hugs your shoulders snugly and centers the weight well down on your back.

Burlap Bag Pack. You can convert a burlap bag or other large bag, four pebbles, and a strong rope about 2½ to 3 feet long into a pack. Place a pebble in one corner of the sack and tightly fasten the rope, slightly off center, around the corner with a clove or timber hitch. Place another pebble in the other lower corner and again fasten the long end of the rope around it. You should now have left two ends of the rope that are about equal in length. Bring them up and fasten them to the upper two corners with pebbles in them, leaving enough slack to slip your arms through the rope for carrying straps for the sack. Pad the ropes with old socks or other improvised padding where they cross your shoulders, as shown in Figure 30–25. Pin the top of the bag shut with large safety pins.

*Jaeger, Ellsworth: *Wildwood Wisdom,* New York, Macmillan, Inc., 1945, p. 54.

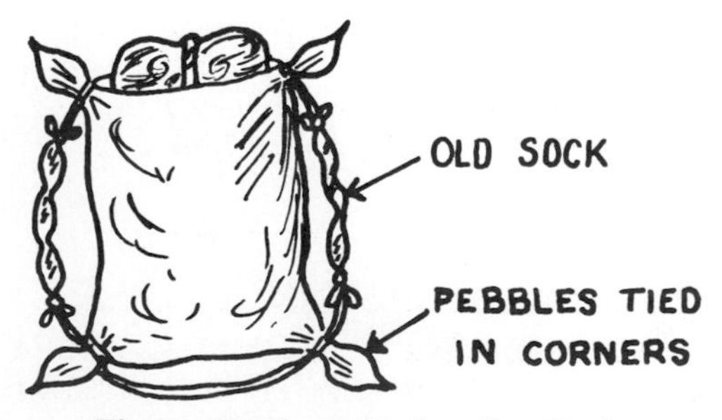

Figure 30–24 A Burlap Bag Pack.

IMPROVISED SHOULDER PADS

Narrow shoulder straps or those made of flimsy material that wrinkles will cut into you and soon become uncomfortable. You can buy pads to slip over the straps or make your own. Use a strip of leather, webbing, or other heavy material 2 to 2½ inches wide for the framework, padding it with foam rubber or thick felt. Fasten the padding to the straps or slit it so you can slip the straps through it.

TUMP LINE

Shoulder straps alone are used to support most packs, but some experienced foot travelers who make a practice of carrying heavy packs day after day use a *tump line* in conjunction with them (Fig. 30–26). This consists of a narrow strip of leather or webbing, 16 to 20 feet long that widens to 2½ to 3 inches at the center, where it rests at about your hairline just above your forehead. Its most important use is for safety in climbing steep mountains or crossing swift streams where the footing is precarious; when you support your pack only by the tump line, a mere flick of your head will release it if you start to fall. It also serves to rest you, for when used with shoulder straps, it distributes the weight between your head, neck, and shoulders and when used alone, it shifts all of the weight from your shoulders.

Figure 30–26 Using a Tump Line

Figure 30–27 A Duffel Bag.

Although of use to hardened backpackers, a tump line is probably impractical for campers in an organized camp and other inexperienced individuals, since to use it successfully, extremely strong neck and shoulder muscles are required, which develop only after months or even years of use.

DUNNAGE BAGS

There are various types of large bags and boxes for transporting large quantities of equipment to and from camp. The *duffel bag* is one of the most widely used. It is made of waterproof material and is designed for shipping equipment by automobile, wagon, train, pack horse, or canoe, but not for carrying on the back except for short distances. The most convenient model has a zipper running across the top so that you can easily obtain anything in it

Figure 30–28 Stuff Bags

without having to remove a lot of other things first. Some prefer wooden or metal lockers with partitioned shelves that can also be used as storage boxes or tables in camp. *Stuff bags* come in various sizes and close with a drawstring at the top (Fig. 30-28).

THE GOOD OLD PONCHO

The poncho, a waterproof cloth available in a variety of sizes, is a perfect example of a piece of equipment that pays its way by serving many purposes. It has a hole near the center large enough to slip your head through so that you can wear it as a large waterproof cape (Fig. 30-6), and many come with a hood already attached. There are overlapping flaps to cover the hole and make it waterproof for use as a flat piece. There are snaps along the edges so that you can fasten it around blankets arranged as a bedroll and use it both as a waterproof cover and ground cloth. The metal *grommets* along the sides are for inserting ropes to convert it into a shelter or lean-to (Fig. 25-9), and it is also useful to shield a fire when you must build one in the rain or in a strong draft. Some varieties have snaps along the sides so that two of them can be snapped together to form a large piece for a tent, a fly over a light tent, or as a dining porch in rainy weather. They come in a variety of materials: vinyl plastic weighing only 12 ounces, treated nylon weighing 19 ounces, and so on; the featherweight ones can be folded almost to the size of a bandanna.

GROUND CLOTH

A ground cloth is similar to a poncho, but it does not have a center hole for wearing it as a rain cape. It is even simpler to construct and takes about four yards of material. Be sure that it is larger than your bedroll.

In making either a ground cloth or a poncho, allow for wide seams that won't pull out, and use double or triple stitching throughout. Snaps and grommets (not less than ½ inch in size) may be purchased and inserted. Many water repellent or waterproof materials are available for making either a poncho or a ground cloth. Among them are coated nylon, Egyptian cotton, duck, neoprene, and vinyl plastic (the lightest of all). Oil cloth, an old shower curtain, or even a plastic tablecloth will serve temporarily.

ADDITIONAL READINGS

(For an explanation of abbreviations and abbreviated forms, see page 25.)

General References

Backpacking Equipment. Backpacker Magazine, Room 1000, Dept. A, West 44th St., New York, New York: 10036. 160 pp., 1975, $5.45.
Bridge: *America's Backpacking Book,* chs. 2, 7, 9, 13, 22.
Cardwell: *America's Camping Book,* chs. 9–11, 51.
Colwell: *Introduction to Backpacking,* chs. 4, 5, 9.
Fieldbook for Boys and Men, pp. 33–37, 272–273.
Fletcher: *The Complete Walker,* pp. 13–43, 197–220, 221–269, 325–327.
Langer: *The Joy of Camping,* pp. 44–55.
Learn and Tallman: *Backpacker's Digest,* chs. 6, 8.
Lightweight Equipment for Hiking, Camping and Mountaineering. Potomac, 1972, $1, paper.
Macfarlan: *The Boy's Book of Hiking,* chs. 6, 9.
Manning: *Backpacking One Step at a Time,* chs. 7, 9, 15.
Merrill: *The Hiker's and Backpacker's Handbook,* ch. 5.
Rethmel: *Backpacking,* pp. 2-5 to 3-8, chs. 2, 3.
Riviere: *Backcountry Camping,* ch. 5.
Boy Scout Handbook, pp. 218–221.
Sunset Camping Handbook, pp. 26–29, 31–37.
Winnett: *Backpacking for Fun,* chs. 2, 3, 5, 11, and Appendix II.
Wood: *Pleasure Packing,* ch. 3.

MAGAZINE ARTICLES

Backpacker:
Hastings, Honey C.: "Make & Fix It." *Back-*

packer-6, Summer, 1974, p. 30. (Repairing Equipment)
Mensinger, Bruce: "You and Your Gear—Camera Care." *Backpacker-5,* Spring, 1974, p. 18.
Pomeranz, Maurice H.: "Backpacking Becomes Big Business." *Backpacker-5,* Spring, 1974, p. 33.
Saijo, Albert: "Go-Light Backpacking." *Backpacker-3,* Fall, 1973, p. 86.

Camping Journal:
Annual Buyer's Guide Issue.
"Cameras." Sept., 1972, p. 30.
Elliott, Bob: "Timber Country Camp-Out." Oct., 1971, p. 28.
Hamft, Martin: "Backpacking—What to Pack and How to Pack It." June, 1974, p. 24.
Heiner, Lou: "Binoculars." Aug., 1972, p. 24.
Heyl, Frank: "How to Choose and Use Rainwear for Camp." Oct., 1971, p. 22.
Laredo, Lorraine: "Basic Camping." Sept., 1972, p. 10. (Disposable equipment)
Laycock, George: "What to Take (Backpacker Check List)." Apr., 1973, p. 73.
Ormond, Clyde: "On the Trail." Mar., 1970, p. 25. (Keeping tools sharp)
Ormond, Clyde: "On the Trail." May, 1970, p. 6. (Combination tools)
Ormond, Clyde: "On the Trail." Nov., 1971, p. 5. (Gloves)
Ormond, Clyde: "On the Trail." Feb., 1972, p. 8. (Binoculars)

Wilderness Camping:
Coggeshall, Almy D.: "The Old Woodchuck's Winter Closet." Dec./Jan., 1977, p. 260.
Ruhl, Jim: "The Other Side of the Coin." Sept./Oct., 1973, p. 45.
Strong, Steve: "Gadgets of Back Packing—Essential Materials or Trivial Frills." Jan./Feb., 1974, p. 28.

Making and Repairing Your Own Equipment

Angier: *Wilderness Gear You Can Make Yourself.*
Bridge: *America's Backpacking Book,* pp. 118–128, 167–172.
Burch, Monte: *Outdoorsman's Fix-It Book.* Harper & Row, 1972, 274 pp., $6.95.
Cardwell: *America's Camping Book,* Part III (pp. 115–169).
Cunningham, Gerry, and Margaret Hansson: *Lightweight Camping Equipment and How To Make It.* Gerry, 3rd ed., 1964, 130 pp., $2.50.
Fieldbook for Boys and Men, pp. 540–549.
Hiking and Camping Equipment. Boy Scouts, 35 ¢ paper.
Learn and Tallman: *Backpacker's Digest,* ch. 5.
Litepac Camping Equipment. Boy Scouts, 35¢, paper.
Ormond: *Outdoorsman's Handbook.*
Spielman, Patrick E.: *Make Your Own Sports Gear.* Bruce, 1970, 154 pp., $7.95.

MAGAZINE ARTICLES

Backpacker:
Hastings, Honey C.: "Make & Fix It." *Backpacker-1,* Spring, 1973, p. 14 (Miscellaneous)
Hastings, Honey C.: "Make & Fix It." *Backpacker-2,* Summer, 1973, p. 14. (Belt pouch)
Hastings, Honey C.: "Make & Fix It." *Backpacker-3,* Fall, 1973, p. 18. (Tents)
Hastings, Honey C.: "Make & Fix It." *Backpacker-4,* Winter, 1973, p. 18. (Mittens, boots)
Hastings, Honey C.: "Make & Fix It." *Backpacker-5,* Spring, 1975, p. 22. (Ponchos)

Camping Journal:
Bolton, Dick: "Make Your Own Pack Frame." Aug., 1971, p. 20.
Collier, Ed J., Jr.: "Backpacker's Delight." Nov., 1973, p. 54. (Lightweight simple-to-construct cot just right for backpackers)
Engerbretson, Dave: "Kits for Campers." Mar., 1974, p. 68.
Richards, Chuck: "Sew Your Own Sleeping Bag." Mar., 1972, p. 40.
"You Built Backpacker Tent," Jan., 1972, p. 26.

Packs

Bridge: *America's Backpacking Book,* ch. 10.
Cardwell: *America's Camping Book,* ch. 7.
Colwell: *Introduction to Backpacking,* ch. 3.
Fieldbook for Boys and Men, pp. 42–47.
Fletcher: *The Complete Walker,* pp. 53–66.
Langer: *The Joy of Camping,* pp. 110–124.
Learn and Tallman: *Backpacker's Digest,* chs. 4, 5, pp. 266–284.
Manning: *Backpacking One Step at a Time,* ch. 10.
Merrill: *The Hiker's and Backpacker's Handbook,* ch. 4.
Rethmel: *Backpacking,* pp. 2-11 to 2-13.
Riviere: *Backcountry Camping,* ch. 1.
Wood: *Pleasure Packing,* ch. 1.

MAGAZINE ARTICLES

Backpacker:
"The Best of the Weekend Packs." *Backpacker-5,* Spring, 1974, pp. 49–61.
Packer, Nelson: "How to Pick a Pack." *Backpacker-1,* Spring, 1973, p. 57.
"The Pick of the Packs." *Backpacker-1,* Spring, 1973, p. 48.

"The Pick of the Polyester Bags." *Backpacker-6,* Summer, 1974, pp. 73–85.
Shepard, Bill: "The Wrap-Around Controversy—One Man's Opinion." *Backpacker-1,* Spring, 1973, p. 61.

Camping Journal:
Bauer, Erwin: "Camping Journal's 1970 Guide to Backpacks." Oct., 1970, p. 30.
"Packs and Frames." Feb., 1973.

Consumer Reports:
"Backpacks." Aug., 1974, p. 572.
"Day Packs." Aug., 1975, p. 472.

Wilderness Camping:
"Tempest in a Backpack." Mar./Apr., 1973, pp. 38–43.
Wood, Robert S.: "Pleasure Packing." Mar./Apr., 1974, p. 21. (The birdcage pack and a new awareness)

Chapter 31

Trip Camping

I cannot indulge in such sports as water skiing, mountain climbing, and water polo because of my poor back—it has a big yellow streak running up it.

—RALPH REPPERT in the Baltimore *Sunday Sun.*

When there's a yellow sun on the hill
And a wind is light as a feather
And the clouds frisk gaily, as young clouds will,
Oh, then it is gypsy weather!
That's the weather to travel in,
With the sun and wind against your skin,
No matter how glad to rest you've been,
You must go when it's gypsy weather.

—MARY CAROLYN DAVIES, *Gypsy Weather.*

Figure 31-1 "Where Do You Think We Ought to Put This?"

TRIPS AND TRIP CAMPING

THE PROBLEM OF THE OLDER CAMPER

Monotony is repugnant to all of us, and this is particularly true of children. Those of high school age, in particular, crave excitement, new experiences, and a chance to test their growing maturity. All of us are aware of the increasing involvement of this age group in police baiting, robbery, mugging, car stealing, drug and alcohol abuse, abortion, venereal disease, and even suicide. The logical conclusion must be that one of the reasons for this lies in the failure of society to provide means for satisfying their desire for thrills, excitement, and high adventure in legitimate and socially approved ways.

Many camps have recently reported that their campers are becoming proportionately younger and younger as older campers lose interest and fail to return. Obviously, this carries a loud and clear message insofar as camp programming is concerned. To keep these youngsters eager to return, we must provide innovation, variety, and progression in our programs so that they are not doing the same old things but find a challenge to their developing abilities.

Can and will we as a camping profession have enough imagination and willingness to change to meet the challenge? More and more camps are succeeding in this effort, and one means has been through a good trips program that progresses from simple cookouts and overnights to longer trips that make full use of growing skills and knowledge.

However, although it may seem almost unbelievable, some camps are still dragging their feet in following the modern trend toward rustic programming, as they continue to offer programs similar to those one might expect to find in glorified children's resorts. In the most flagrant cases, their activities consist largely of the same things the child has been or would be doing at home or in school, such as basketball, football, and other team sports, city-type arts and crafts, and elaborate dramatic events. Campcraft and woodcraft skills, if included at all, are practiced as neat little exercises to pass tests, quite divorced from any practical use for living in the out-of-doors.

Their routine includes eating three meals a day in a soon-familiar dining room, with a kitchen staff to prepare the meals and paid employees to serve them, clear the tables, clean the dining room, and wash the dishes in an electric dishwasher. Any "trips" taken consist of excursions to a nearby spot to eat more food prepared and served by someone else. Excitement? Challenge? What is there about such procedures to answer a child's needs and make him want to come back again?

It is our honest conviction that a good camp will take full advantage of its unique setting and the unparalleled opportunities it offers. Although nearly every camp finds such daily routines as those just mentioned necessary for smooth running, there should also be numerous opportunities for youngsters to do the unusual, the previously unknown, the heretofore untried.

Perhaps the very fact that today's youth has so much given to him without having done a thing to earn it and so many things done for him without his having to raise a finger explains the extreme exultation he feels at being given a chance to carry the ball and plan and do things for himself, as in rustic camping situations. Standing on one's own two feet and pulling one's weight are a part of our American tradition whose roots go back to our very beginnings. We in camping should be among the first to take a stand against the growing tendency to reach out and ask, even demand, that the government and other agencies do for us things we might better do for ourselves. Trip camping is a step in this direction.

VALUES OF TRIP CAMPING

As anyone who has dealt extensively with youngsters knows, they never tire of hearing of the exploits of our pioneers in their struggle to conquer the wilderness and wrest a living from the soil by their strength and the use of crude tools and methods. Almost invariably, history pictures them as rugged individualists, brave, hard-working, ingenious, and persistent. In those times, a man established his position with his fellow men by those characteristics most needed for the circumstances—resourcefulness, physical prowess, bravery, and a willingness to work hard, and it mattered little if he had wealth and social background. These true values have persisted in our thinking through the years and we must recognize them to evaluate our present ideals and our great American heritage.

These same values are evident in a modern camp that promotes rugged living. The boy who was sought after by his peers at home because of his ample spending money and material possessions but who can't build a fire or keep up on the trail is soon scorned by his trail mates. He is judged solely on his own merits—mama and papa can't run interference for him now. Following a trail and making camp in comparatively virgin country is hard work and the boy or girl with the stamina and know-how to do it successfully can be rightfully proud of his achievements.

Helping to plan and carry out a trip successfully results in a lot of growing up. A camper must learn to anticipate and plan ahead as he makes check lists and uses them for packing. He must work and cooperate closely with others, accepting responsibility and carrying his own duffel as well as his share of group supplies. The vigorous activity and ample quantities of good nutritious food, which he has helped to prepare, serve to promote exuberant good health and physical fitness.

(Courtesy of the U. S. Forest Service.)

What better way to instill a love of nature than to live intimately with it 24 hours a day? How better to instill a sense of the urgency for practicing good conservation than to live it day by day? Attitudes and practices acquired will probably last through a lifetime of family camping, picnicking, or hunting and fishing.

A trip camper puts into practice what he has learned about finding his way with map and compass, using tools, outdoor cooking, tent pitching, striking, lashing, packing, and carrying equipment to make himself safe and comfortable in his "home away from home."

When well-trained youngsters become an integral part of the planning of an exciting trip, they enjoy it to the utmost. Their pleasure comes from three sources: (1) anticipating and planning for it, (2) actually doing it, (3) talking about it and remembering it all the rest of their lives. Deep and lasting friendships form as a small trail group goes off into a little world of its own. Sharing inner thoughts, laughing together over amusing incidents, working and struggling together toward a common goal all develop a true knowledge of the meaning of "one for all and all for one." As in any intimate association, of course, occasional frictions and misunderstandings will arise. Some camper will surely at some time display selfishness, thoughtlessness, or a tendency to rationalize and blame others for his failures and mishaps. However, he will most certainly be subjected to what is generally considered to be the most effective of reforming influences—the disapproval and lack of acceptance by his peers.

While each person in the group learns to be self-reliant and independent, he must also learn to fit in as part of the group, which eventually develops the spirit of "we-ness" and cooperation so essential for living happily in today's society.

You, as a counselor, will never

Figure 32-2 Lucky You!

have a better opportunity to get intimately acquainted with your campers and exert your subtle influence on them in various ways, as you see them in all sorts of circumstances and listen to their unrestrained chatter as well as more serious discussions.

WHY CAMPS HESITATE

There are many reasons why some camps still make only a token effort to sponsor a real program of trip camping. One important one is the fact that some camp directors, boards of directors or absentee owners, responsible for programming, are unversed in trip camping. Like produces like, and those who have done their own camping where no such program existed will be understandably reluctant to promote it. This may be all to the good, however, for it is better to have no trips at all than to send campers out without competent people to plan and lead them. Those who are undecided may well be swayed by parents, who are often unenthusiastic or even averse to having their precious offspring subjected to imaginary dangers way out in the "great unknown." Some campers themselves may be fearful, for even the youngest has probably heard some of the tales that circulate periodically about wild animals attacking humans and snakes crawling in bed with unwary sleepers. It matters little that the tales may be completely unauthenticated or that, even if there is a basis of fact in them, they have been exaggerated out of all proportion to what actually happened. However, you should have a healthy respect for all forms of wildlife. Don't tease wild animals or try to get too close or pet them, for you are unfamiliar to them and they might strike back, just as even you would do if frightened.

Uninitiated counselors likewise hesitate, for many of them have had little if any training and experience along these lines. Some college counselor training courses either cannot or do not find the time for proper training in outdoor skills and actual camping experiences, and the pre-camp training course is usually all too short to permit thoroughness.

Camps are wise indeed not to sponsor such activities unless they have enough experienced personnel and the necessary equipment to do it safely. Fortunately, the lack of qualified leaders is being somewhat overcome as the American Camping Association proceeds with its efforts to improve and expand counselor training. Schools and other organizations are also becoming more realistic about what is needed. As campers participate in these better programs, they eventually mature to occupy positions of leadership as administrators and counselors.

Expense may be another handicapping factor, for trip safety and comfort require at least a minimum of special equipment and supplies. Camps must usually invest enough to supply such group necessities as tents, and group cooking equipment, and they, or the campers, must provide what personal gear is needed. However, elaborate outlays are unnecessary and good care and handling will lengthen the life of what you have. Where finances are limited, campers can make many things for themselves, using the methods de-

(Courtesy of Barbara Ellen Joy and Marjorie Comp.)

scribed in this book as well as those included in some of the additional readings listed at the end of this chapter and Chapter 30. Creating their own equipment will be quite appealing to them in this age of having everything provided gratis to an extent unheard of by any previous generation. Problems of "what to do next" fade into thin air when campers are happily engaged in making gear for that trip which is just a few days or weeks away. Remember, nothing is so highly treasured as something you have made yourself.

TRIP PROGRESSION

Perhaps you doubt the wisdom of such an enthusiastic promotion of trips for everyone. Let us hasten to explain that a trip can include a wide variety of experiences. For a quite young, inexperienced camper, it may mean only a very simple lunch or supper cookout. Next may come an overnight, perhaps only a few feet from the cabin door, but it will involve making a bedroll, packing up a few belongings, getting the provisions for a simple meal or two and sleeping under the open sky or out in a tent. Nevertheless, the neophyte will be gaining experience as he helps to plan what supplies and equipment will be needed and uses a check list to see that nothing is left behind. Perhaps the group will enjoy pretending that they are part of a covered wagon train bound for Californ-i-a, which is so far from their cabin that they will just have to get along without anything they were careless enough to forget. See that this first overnight is really fun, with a good program and a special treat, such as marshmallows to toast or popcorn to pop. If they are really leery about the surrounding darkness, you may want to consider placing a lighted lantern where all can see its reassuring blaze.

A successful first experience whets

Figure 31-3 Hope He Comes Too.

a camper's appetite to return to main camp and start mastering the necessary skills for going on a still longer trip.

A good trip program will provide for progressively longer and more exciting trips with each succeeding summer, so that a returning camper always has something new and more challenging to look forward to. Note that extended trips are not recommended for those who are under the age of twelve or thirteen and who have not built up to them through a program of easy jaunts.

HOW AND WHERE TO GO

Some camps are fortunate enough to have several possibilities for trip camping right within their own confines. Picking out a suitable route and destination and perhaps establishing there an *outpost* or *primitive camp* with a permanent Adirondack shack (Fig. 25-17) to provide shelter overnight can well become a camper project ("program," if you please) that will keep them happily engaged for days or even weeks. It is best to have several alternate destinations which vary in distance and difficulty, and different groups may forage about, vying with each other in trying to find and develop the one "perfect" spot with the most natural advantages. Each group can then clear the necessary area, erect camp "fixings" for comfortable living, pick out a colorful name, erect a sign, and lay a trail for others to follow to attend their camp christening and dedication. (Be careful to do as little damage to the environment as possible.) This will soon produce a variety of little outpost camps for trip destinations. Make it a tradition to have all future users leave the campsite better than they found it and add some little convenience as a thank-you for using it. It is good practice to change the location of an outpost camp frequently so that the site can return to its wild state.

When a camp has only limited acreage available or when older campers have pretty much explored their own grounds, you may find it advisable to look elsewhere for new places to go. There may be some farmer with suitable facilities who will agree to let you use them, perhaps upon payment of a modest fee. Most people enjoy having well-behaved youngsters around and will cooperate 100 per cent if you can assure them that you and your campers understand the meaning of good outdoor manners and will take every precaution to maintain the property as they found it.

It may be possible to travel by canoe, sailboat, rowboat, or even raft to a distant shore where sites are available for cookouts or overnight stops. Bicycles are an often neglected means of covering distances in a surprisingly short time; stay off dangerous main highways and seek the always more interesting back roads. Campers, supplies, and bicycles may be transported to suitable take-off points in order to visit more distant areas and can be picked up again at the same spot after the trip.

Figure 31-4 Pannier Style Bicycle Pack.

Nearly every camp will find public areas with camping facilities somewhere nearby, where arrangements can be made to take a group. Some enterprising camps, such as Camp Wakeela,* have converted an old, unused farm wagon into a covered wagon, with an old tent to cover the wagon bed. A neighboring farmer supplied the "horse power" to pull the wagon, loaded with duffel, while the twelve- and thirteen-year-old campers took turns riding and walking, pioneer style. Other camps convey heavy equipment to outlying districts by pack animal, jeep, camp truck, or station wagon. Horseback trips are always popular.

Good possibilities lie also in national, state, county, and local parks, forests, and wildlife refuges, where arrangements can often be made to camp and explore well-marked trails. It is best to avoid the more popular areas, especially during their peak seasons, for they offer little chance for privacy. Most of them have restrictions about cutting timber and burning wood, thus making it mandatory to cook over charcoal or on some form of camp stove. These are minor handicaps and give campers actual experience in situations they will meet as adult citizens. Trail maps, guide books, and professional personnel are usually available to help.

It may be possible to affiliate with the AYH (American Youth Hostels) and make use of their maps, trails and hostels if any of them are located near you (see pp. 13-14). The Appalachian Trail is a 2050-mile footpath leading from Mount Katahdin in Maine to Mount Oglethorpe in Georgia that winds through the beautiful scenery of the Green and White Mountains, the Berkshires, Alleghenies, Catskills, Blue Ridge and Smokies. The Pacific Coast Trail of about 2150 miles leads from Canada to Mexico through the Cascades and Sierra Nevada and Sierra Madre Mountains. Though both these trails contain rugged sections suitable only for seasoned trippers, other parts can be reached by automobile or public transportation and are quite suitable for young, inexperienced groups under good leadership. Both offer some campsites and permanent shelters at convenient stopping places. The reader can gain further information by writing to the addresses listed in Appendix C at the back of this book.

HOW RUGGED SHALL THE TRIP BE?

Always bear in mind that no trip is good camp practice or fun when it degenerates into an endurance contest or a race against time. Ten miles a day may be enough for average hikers, or even five if the going is rough, while seasoned "trippers" might well go at least twice as far. Those going by canoe may cover 12 to 20 miles or more a day

* Segal, Harvey C.: "Westward Ho." *Recreation,* March, 1957, p. 82.

and cyclists may count on 20 to 50 miles. Allow plenty of opportunity for seeing, exploring, and just plain having fun, for it's not "how far" but "how much" that counts when evaluating a trip. On long excursions, it is wise to take it easy the first day while the group warms up. Later, allow for at least one "lazy" day out of five, with campers remaining at the same site to sleep late and do their laundry and mending, explore the country, play games, fish, sing, enjoy cheerful banter, or "just set" as the mood dictates. Trippers should return alert and rested, not mentally and physically fagged out so that they have to spend an extra day or two recuperating.

Before taking a group over a proposed route, at least two counselors and perhaps some especially able campers should survey it. They may make a trail map, indicating good places to stop overnight, sources of water and firewood (if needed), scenic views and other points of interest, and so on. Plan to return by a different route if it seems feasible.

At the end of frequently used routes or at overnight stops along the way you may want to establish outpost or primitive camps. Equip them with rustic cooking devices, sleeping quarters, and other things to save time, make trippers more comfortable during their stay, and minimize the damage to the environment that would occur if each incoming group made its own.

WHO SHOULD GO ON TRIPS?

The best number for a trip group is six to ten campers with at least one counselor for each five campers, depending on their ages. No group, no matter how small, should ever start out without at least two leaders, for in case of an emergency, there must be one adult to stay with the group while the other goes to use the telephone or secure help. At least one of the counselors must be a trained and experienced trip camper, having learned by practice as well as through training courses and extensive reading. At least one should have had training in first aid and preferably hold a current American Red Cross certificate.

Campers should be of approximately the same age, strength, and ex-

(Courtesy of Cheley Colorado Camps, Estes Park, Colorado.)

perience, lest the young and inexperienced wear themselves out or be unjustly called "lazy" or "tenderfoot" while trying to keep up with the others. Campers on extended trips should be at least twelve years old.

Every person going on a trip should have a physical check-up and "O.K." from the camp nurse or physician just before starting. Knowing that such a requirement exists may stimulate those wanting to go to get plenty of rest and sleep and put themselves in tip-top physical condition beforehand.

It is wise to set up a progressive set of skills in campcraft and woodcraft that campers must master before going. The list can be brief and easy for first trips, with additional skills added for succeeding, more difficult trips. A chart on which a camper can check off the tests as he passes them acts as an incentive and shows him exactly how much he has to do before he can qualify. Campcraft and woodcraft instruction and practice can be set up as regular parts of the program just as canoeing, arts and crafts, or swimming are. Set up an exhibit at the main camp showing examples of such techniques as fire building, lashing, knot tying, and building outdoor fireplaces as models for those trying to perfect their own skills and pass tests. Use bulletin boards and keep a supply of helpful books and pamphlets handy.

A set of tests might cover such areas as the following:

A demonstrated knowledge of good manners in the out-of-doors
Use and care of knife, hatchet, and saw
Selection and use of appropriate forms of fuel
Conservation and proper extinguishing of campfires, if used
Outdoor cookery
Using or making a bedroll and having experience in sleeping out-of-doors
Knowledge of trip equipment and proper packing of duffel
Pitching and striking a tent
Camp sanitation and proper disposal of garbage

Figure 31-5 A Good Neighbor.

Knowledge of weather and weather prediction
Lashing and tying various useful knots
First aid and safety
Experience in one-meal, all-day, and overnight trips
Paddling, horseback or bicycle riding, if the trip involves such methods of transportation

Such requirements impart real zest to learning and perfecting camping skills. In addition, they help insure that participants will be safe, happy, and comfortable on the trip.

THE TRIPS COUNSELOR

Many camps appoint one person, at least on a part-time basis, known by some such title as "Trips Counselor," to take charge of the entire trips program, with one or more assistants to help as needed. Such persons can set up a program of "enabling skills," variously known as *campcraft, pioneering,* or *woodcraft.*

The trips counselor should be a mature, seasoned person who is thoroughly versed in his field through wide experience as well as reading and instruction in it. He should be level-headed, resourceful, completely dependable, and, most of all, enthusiastic about the possibilities of his program. He must be an expert with map and compass as well as general campcraft skills and be able to construct campsite refinements and makeshift devices in various ways. He must be a good organizer and have tact and forcefulness, for he must coordinate the whole program and, at some time or other, work with counselors, campers, and almost everyone else in camp. He must be able to arouse enthusiasm and possess a sense of fairness, so that everyone gets an equal chance to use camp equipment, trails, and camping-out spots.

One of his main responsibilities is to see that there is adequate equipment of the right type on hand and that it is kept in good repair and replenished when necessary. He must arrange for storing equipment efficiently and safely in the equipment room or rooms. He must keep careful lists as he checks group equipment out and in. Though each group is responsible for returning its gear dry, clean, and in good condition for storage, the trips counselor must check to see that this is done. He must know how to care for leather goods, tents, and other gear to keep them always in A-1 condition. He will be expected to keep a complete and up-to-date running inventory of equipment, turning in a final list at the end of the season and suggesting repairs and acquisitions that need to be made before the next year. It will also be his job to see that things are stored properly for the winter. He must be aware of the necessity for seeing that equipment is not lost and lasts as long as possible, for it occupies an important place in the camp budget, and he must impart this attitude to others. Anything lost or ruined through misuse must be replaced, thus leaving that much less to buy additional equipment or develop other phases of the program. He goes along on trips himself or at least sees that those responsible are well-prepared for their duties.

PLANNING THE TRIP

POINTS TO CONSIDER

Much of the pleasure of a trip consists in planning and anticipating it. Decisions must be made as to where to go, how to get there, what to take, and how long to stay, and they will depend upon such factors as:

1. The ages and experience of those going.
2. The probable temperature and weather conditions.
3. The means of transportation—canoe, hiking, horseback, bicycle, pack animal, covered wagon, etc.
4. The possibilities for restocking at farmhouses or stores along the way.
5. The ruggedness of the terrain—hills, density of underbrush, etc.
6. Means of cooking and facilities for camping along the way. Will some areas require the use of charcoal or camp stoves for cooking?
7. Availability of safe water for drinking, cooking, and washing. Will you need to purify it? Remember that thirsty campers and dehydrated food require large quantities.
8. The amount of time you want to devote to cooking and the type and variety of cooking utensils you have available and want to burden yourself with.
9. The number and length of stopovers desired to take side excursions or do special things, such as swim, visit an old mill, and so on.
10. Do some areas require you to have permits to camp, build fires, or fish?
11. Is the trail clearly marked or will you need good maps and compasses? No one should venture along an unmarked or poorly marked trail unless at least one person in the group is thoroughly versed in using map and compass.
12. Are there places convenient to the trail from which you can

(Courtesy of Girl Scouts, U.S.A.)

reach a telephone, a physician, or forest ranger in case an emergency arises? The person in charge should have complete information about this.

PLANNING WITH A GROUP

Start planning well ahead of time and elicit help from campers at every step of the way. Let it be *their* trip, not *yours,* to give them all the joy of helping to make decisions, solving problems, and striving to make it a success. Only indifference, or even resentment, results from dragging them on trips someone else has planned and made arrangements for. How much responsibility they can take will, of course, depend somewhat upon their ages and experience, but you may be pleasantly surprised by the worthwhile suggestions campers make and the amount of work their willing hands accomplish when they are given the opportunity. A counselor who makes a workhorse of himself and tries to do everything, carrying all the responsibility, is showing poor leadership and, instead of serving children, is actually cheating them out of much of the joy and growth which is rightfully theirs. Someone has wisely said that "work is only work when you would rather be doing something else," and youngsters enjoy toiling like little demons on a project they have really set their hearts on.

Ask them for their preferences and make use of the power of suggestion by saying, "Let's," "Wouldn't it be fun?" or "How shall we?" Don't make the mistake however, of letting them make all decisions or carry too much responsibility. After all, you are ultimately responsible and supposedly have been chosen for your position because of your greater experience and maturity. The ability to *guide* followers into making wise decisions is the mark of a good leader, but when it becomes a question of violating principles of good judgment, safety, or good camp practices, you must have the courage to come out with a big, loud "NO" and then stick to it. You will have less to regret in the future and they'll respect you much more in the long run. To avoid the unpleasantness of direct denials or confrontations, try to swing them to wise decisions so tactfully that they do not realize that the decisions were not wholly their own.

FILLING THE INNER MAN

Menus must be compiled and amounts and food lists turned in far enough ahead to allow time for measuring out or assembling stock items and ordering any necessary extras. The dietitian or person in charge of food will usually help with this and his knowledge and experience will be of inestimable value. Each camp usually sets up its own procedures for doing this, and you, as a counselor, should learn what they are and follow them to the letter.

Consider what cooking utensils various items will require. With how many utensils do you want to burden yourselves? You can cut down on the number by planning to cook one-pot or aluminum foil meals.

Figure 31-6 "Hold Everything! Here's Food!"

You will also want to consider how much time you want to take out for cooking. Some foods require elaborate preparations and long cooking times, while others are quite simple and can be finished up in jig time.

GROUP EQUIPMENT

Determine what group equipment you will need, such as tents, cooking outfits, and the like. Make out duplicate lists, carrying one to check against along the way and leaving the other back at camp with the trips counselor or other person in charge to check against when you return. Assemble everything and weigh it to determine how much of it each camper will need to carry in order to have his proportionate share.

Distribute equipment equitably, taking into consideration the strength and stamina of the hikers, and don't hesitate to make changes on the road if they seem advisable. For instance, if one camper is carrying an unusually heavy piece of group equipment, someone else with less might take over some of his personal gear to compensate.

As with personal equipment, place related items together in ditty bags—

one for fire building, one for small tools, one or more for cooking utensils and equipment, and so on. Have distinctive colors for each bag or label it conspicuously so that you can locate what you want quickly. Attach a tag securely, listing its exact contents to check against each time you pack up to move on.

Select a counselor or responsible camper to make and carry a master list of the exact location of each item; for instance, Joe has the reflector oven, Harry has Friday's lunch and Danny has the extra poncho for protecting the cooking equipment. Some person should also take responsibility for the food, making a similar master list, together with menus, cooking directions, and the names of persons in charge of cooking each meal.

PERSONAL EQUIPMENT

Using the lists and information given in Chapter 30, help each camper to make out his own check list of personal equipment, completing it at least a week ahead of time. The inexperienced will probably think such concern entirely unnecessary, for the average person is inclined to say, "That's a bunch of tommyrot. I can throw everything I need together in fifteen minutes"—and "throw" is probably just what he would do. However, his first sad experience with the results of his haphazardness will undoubtedly put him in a more receptive mood. Certain items are mandatory for everyone but a few choices can depend on individual preferences.

A common error in packing is to assume that the weather will stay just as it is at the moment. However, mornings and evenings will undoubtedly be chilly, and unless you have a rabbit's foot in one shoe and a four-leaf clover over your ear, you will encounter at least one cool, rainy spell. Plan for it and be prepared.

Mark each article, including clothing, with the owner's name. You can use India ink, a marking pen, or a name tape, or you can type or print your name on a piece of iron-on tape (put a bit of waxed paper beneath it) and then iron it on the article. Use a wood-burning set to burn names into wooden articles such as the handles of hatchets or shovels.

A day or two ahead of time, let each camper assemble all his duffel, checking it against his master list, and try it for fit by packing it into his pack. Then place everything, including his pack frame and his share of the group equipment, on the scales and weigh it to the ounce. Take a half day or overnight hike with it to see how it rides. Does it weigh too much? Then take everything out and see how many items are actually nonessential. The mark of an experienced backpacker is the small amount of bulk and weight he carries; one way he does this is by taking advantage of every saving offered by modern freeze dried food and lightweight equipment.

An average man in good condition can carry a pack of 30 to 35 pounds, juniors and women 20 to 25 pounds, and younger children proportionately less. Around 30 pounds is suggested for trips by canoe, bicycle, or horseback. The lighter the pack the better, however, just as long as you have what you need.

Hints on Packing. Use a definite system for packing your gear into your pack, striving to see that: (1) everything fits well without rattling or breaking; (2) you can find what you need quickly and with a minimum of effort; and (3) your pack rides well on your shoulders and is comfortable to carry. In general, a pack rides better if you place heavier things in the upper compartment of your pack and as close to your back as possible, with light, bulky things toward the bottom. This distribution lets you walk easily, as you can stand almost upright instead of having to lean forward.

Place things needed first (the next meal, a snack, and so forth) and those used frequently or in a hurry (map, compass, binoculars, rain wear, canteen, camera and film, insect spray, first aid kit, and pocket knife) into the convenient side pockets of your pack or at the very top of it. Place soft things such as extra clothing on the side next your body and pad breakables and sharp edges that might gouge you or damage other things in your pack. Try to fit everything in compactly to minimize friction and jarring. Avoid carrying quantities of things in your pockets or attached to your belt, for they will weigh you down and eventually become most uncomfortable. Use only pockets that are deep and strong, and if they have no fasteners of their own, pin them shut or attach each object by a strong cord or chain long enough to permit using it without detaching it. Objects dropped along the trail have an uncanny knack for losing themselves in the brush and duff where you can't find them, even if you take the time to go back to look for them.

Garments such as slacks and shirts can be more easily located and will come out less wrinkled if you fold them neatly, then roll them fairly tight and place them on end in a ditty bag or in your pack.

Experiment until you have worked out a system of packing that seems most logical, with a place for everything and everything in its place so that you could almost locate an item in the dark.

HOISTING A PACK

The easiest way to get into your pack is to have a companion hold it while you wriggle into it. If you must do it by yourself, elevate the pack on a stump or tree trunk and place your arms in the straps or sit down in front of the pack, slip your arms through the straps, turn over on your hands and knees and then stand up. If your pack is fairly light, you can swing it up onto your raised thigh, put one arm through a strap, raise the bag a bit higher and slip your other arm into the other strap. When removing a pack, reverse one of these processes; be careful never to just drop the pack to the ground.

(Courtesy of Y.M.C.A. Camp Widjiwagan, Ely, Minnesota.)

WAYS TO LIGHTEN THE LOAD

Some camps minimize the problem of transportation on long trips by sending such heavy materials as food, clean clothing, and bedding ahead by auto, truck, or pack horse. You may also be able to replenish food supplies at stores along the way or by shipping supplies ahead by parcel post. Fresh clothing can be supplied in this way and the soiled returned to camp.

Cut down on both weight and expense by finding ways to make one piece of equipment serve several purposes and by making do at the campsite.

OTHER THINGS TO PLAN FOR

Make out a kapers chart or schedule of trip duties as described on page 93, rotating responsibilities so that no one will feel that he has been unfairly burdened. Place different combinations of campers to work together at various times to prevent the development of cliques or personal animosities. Outline duties clearly so that no one fails to do what he was supposed to because he misunderstood; this also makes it easier to prevent shirking. Tempers can flare very quickly over this.

Pool all money and divide it among two or three responsible persons. Usually no money will be needed except for emergencies, for good trip country usually lies away from towns. If campers do have occasion to go into town, set a low limit on how much each can spend for sweets and other appetite spoilers. A well-planned menu includes all the sweets that are good for them, and those who are more affluent should not be encouraged to show off before the others.

Ask for volunteers to keep a trip diary or log. If they have the ability to see the funny side of things and put it into words, so much the better. Include exact times of arrival and departure and record just what you did at each stop and along the way. Official artists and photographers may also be selected. The diary will make good reading around the campfire at night, and by adding pictures, poems, souvenirs and perhaps a marked trail map, it can be made into a booklet, adorned by the trippers themselves or in the arts and crafts department and presented to each person as soon after the trip as possible. The pages can be mounted in a spiral notebook with special covers pasted on.

Figure 31-7 That Was a Good One.

Work out a complete itinerary of just where you expect to be at any given time and leave a copy at the camp office so that they can locate you if it becomes necessary.

Give some thought to things to do for recreation at odd moments on the trip and take suggestions for games, songs, stunts, and poems to use as they fit in. A spelling bee, nature quiz, or round-robin story may be just the thing for a rest stop along the trail or just before crawling into your "downy soft" beds. Such activities help people forget how tired they are and how heavy their packs are. Likewise, a serious discussion or devotional program may be just the thing to improve everyone's morale.

Although a lengthy lecture is not necessary, you should impress upon the group the importance of sticking together at all times so that no one gets lost. Counselors should have whistles with perhaps a few extra for campers who must temporarily leave the group for water or firewood. Agree upon an exact procedure for both the group and the camper if someone should become separated.

ON THE ROAD

CHOOSING A CAMPSITE

It is well to begin looking for a good campsite at least an hour or two

(Courtesy of H. Armstrong Roberts.)

before sundown. You will be tired and thankful to have supper over, the dishes washed, and everything made shipshape for the night well before dark, since camp lighting is usually something less than brilliant.

When you wish to camp on other than camp property, it is not only illegal but discourteous to do so without the owner's permission. If you explain the nature of your group and what you are doing and assure the owner that you will be careful with your fire and leave a neat campsite, he will usually willingly give his permission. Remind your group that they represent *camp* and that the camp's continued good name depends on their observance of all the rules of consideration for others and out-of-door courtesy and good conservation practices. If others are sleeping nearby, be careful not to keep them awake or make yourselves obnoxious in any way.

In choosing a campsite, there are a number of points to consider. It will probably be impossible to find one combining all of them, but you can at least look for one embodying as many as possible.

Privacy, a certain amount of isolation, and a beautiful view are much to be desired. Good drinking water and water for cooking and bathing are, of course, a big advantage, but you should take no chances, always sterilizing water in some way if there is any doubt.

If you plan to use wood for a fire, an open spot just at the edge of a woods is most desirable since firewood will be handy. The Indians, always wise in matters of camping, usually pitched their tepees on open fields or plains where they would not be endangered by falling trees and branches during a storm. Though trees may give some shelter during a deluge, they will continue to drip on your tent for hours after the rain is over. Stay clear of a lone or unusually tall tree for it is particularly likely to attract lightning.

Select an elevated gentle slope with fairly porous soil to insure good drainage in case of a storm. Avoid a place covered with a growth of lush grass, for it indicates that the ground is water-soaked and too damp for good sleeping or sitting. Sand is also undesirable for it gets into everything you eat and wear. Nearby bushes and high grass shut off the breeze and tend to harbor bothersome insects. The ground should be smooth enough for good sleeping.

Dry stream beds, ravines and the banks of streams are risky, for a sudden storm may catch your camp in the midst of a flash flood and an island may be completely inundated during a storm. Look for high water marks before deciding to camp on such spots.

Rock piles may harbor snakes and ant hills; old, rotten trees infested with ants bring hordes of uninvited bedfellows that will also get into your food and make you miserable.

Mosquitoes also make mighty uncomfortable camp mates. They are so small that they rarely fly far against the breeze, so that a spot on the leeward side of a lake or stream some distance away from the water is usually comparatively safe. A spot not too near water or high grass and exposed to a good breeze is usually relatively free from them, but it may prove to be a somewhat dangerous place to build a fire there. A fairly dense growth of trees between camp and their breeding places also serves as pretty good protection.

MAKING CAMP

After you have chosen your campsite, survey it carefully to decide just how to lay it out, locating the cooking area, latrine, tents, garbage disposal area, and so on. Place personal duffel in one area and group equipment in another, arranged with labels clearly in evidence so that anyone can easily find what he wants. Each person then starts to complete his preassigned tasks as quickly as possible.

(Courtesy of Drury College, Springfield, Missouri.)

In setting up camp, remember to:
1. Put perishable supplies to cool.
2. Pitch tents fairly close for companionship and, preferably, facing north or northeast if a storm seems likely. (Most violent summer storms come from the southwest—hence the sailor's name, "Sou'wester," for his hat.) If fair weather seems likely, you may want to face tents southeast to catch the morning sun or vice versa if you want to sleep late.
3. Make beds, clearing away all pebbles, sticks, and clumps of grass. Have each person place his individual duffel inside his tent. Get anything needed out of the packs. If you are going to unpack or rearrange large quantities of your duffel, it is best to place it on a blanket or poncho to prevent losing or misplacing small articles.
4. Dig a latrine and grease pit.
5. If you need firewood, get it and arrange your fireplace. Otherwise, set up your stove and cooking paraphernalia.
6. Get water for drinking and cooking; purify it if necessary.
7. Take care of general camping equipment, such as boats, canoes, lanterns, and so forth.

(Courtesy of Robert E. Smallman, Girl Scouts, U.S.A.)

DIVIDING TRIP DUTIES

It is ordinarily best to divide trippers into committees for each meal, with duties assigned somewhat as follows:

Cooks. Consult the menu and figure out methods and approximate cooking times, type of fire and fireplace needed, and so forth.

If you are going to use wood, tell the fire builders the kind of fire and fireplace you want and where and when to build them.

At the proper time, get the food out and measure out the proportions, putting the rest away so that it will not be contaminated by insects and dirt.

If cooking with wood, *soap the entire outsides* of the kettles before cooking the food. Take pride in seeing that everything is palatable and well-seasoned.

Get out eating utensils and set the table or arrange to serve the food cafeteria-style.

Act as hosts or hostesses and serve the plates. As soon as everyone has finished eating, put left-over food away and replace unused portions.

Fire Builders. Prepare to furnish the heat necessary for cooking in the proper manner. For a wood fire, you will need an axe, a knife or a saw, gloves, and matches. Have handy a fire poker, shovel, and other equipment to use in case the fire should start to spread.

Consult the cooks and prepare the type of fire and fireplace needed. Build it early enough to let it burn down to coals by the time the cooks are ready.

Gather enough wood to last through the meal, chopping or breaking it up into appropriate sizes and arranging a neat woodpile convenient to the fire but not in the way or where sparks might be blown into it.

Keep the fire going, with at least one person constantly standing by to replenish fuel, rearrange coals and so forth, at the direction of the cooks. Keep up the fire long enough to heat dishwater.

Completely extinguish the fire as soon as everyone is through with it and leave the fireplace neat and with enough fuel to start the next meal if it is to be eaten there.

If breakfast is next or there are signs of rain, gather some tinder, kindling, and firewood and put them under a tent or extra tarpaulin.

Clean up and Sanitation. Dig and line a grease pit.

Arrange a refrigerating or cooling system for perishable foods.

Put dishwater on to heat as soon as the cooks are through with the fire and there are large containers available for it. Heat enough for sterilizing, too.

Wash all dishes and sterilize them. Keep your dishwater clean by wiping dishes out first with dry leaves, napkins, or paper towels before immersing them in the dishwater. Fill one pan with hot soapy water, another with hot water for rinsing and sterilizing. Sand or wood ashes make good substitutes for scouring powder.

Dishes and silverware can be sterilized by placing them in a net bag or one made from a double thickness of cheesecloth and immersing them in boiling water for two minutes; then hang bag and all up to drain and dry.

Wash out dishcloths and towels and hang them out to dry. Scald them after the evening meal.

Bury and cover all garbage or prepare it to take with you.

Burn out and flatten tin cans to take with you.

Be sure there is enough properly sterilized water on hand for drinking and for taking pan baths if desired.

MAKING A LATRINE

Make some sort of latrine whenever you are staying away from camp.

(Courtesy of Girl Scouts, U.S.A.)

An easy one is the *straddle trench*, dug 2 to 3 feet deep, downhill from camp and at a distance of at least 100 feet. Pile the dirt along the sides where a quantity of it can be kicked back into the trench or shoveled in with a homemade tin can shovel or other shovel after each use. Make a tin can shovel by compressing the ends of a forked stick and flattening a tin can over them or by splitting a stick, inserting a flattened tin can in the slit, nailing it fast, and lashing the stick to keep if from splitting further (Fig. 31–8). If you use the trench for several days, purify it periodically by covering it with a layer of chloride of lime, creosote, or ashes or by burning a fire over it.

Figure 31–8 Tin Can Shovel.

Keep toilet paper nearby on a forked stick and covered with a No. 10 tin can or a 1-pound coffee can with a detachable lid (Fig.16–5*E*) as a shelter from wind and weather. Cut a slot down one side to pull the paper through. Make holes in both ends of it and place it on a stick supported across two forked sticks driven into the ground.

The latrine should be close enough to the campsite to be convenient and easy and safe to get to at night, yet it must not be near the source of drinking water and must be far enough away to provide privacy. If no natural screen of bushes or underbrush is available construct one with a poncho or tarp suspended on trees or bushes. Arrange facilities nearby for handwashing.

MAKING DRINKING WATER SAFE

The only way to be absolutely sure a natural water supply is safe for drinking and cooking or washing dishes is to have it tested by qualified personnel. If this has not been done, you must sterilize it, no matter how clear and sparkling it looks, for it may carry serious diseases such as typhoid fever. It is best to bring water from camp in clean canteens or thermos jugs or fill them from *safe* sources along the way. When that is impossible, use one of the following methods to purify it:

1. Boil it for 10 to 20 minutes (time it from when it actually starts to boil). This causes the water to taste flat because the air has been removed, but you can restore the oxygen and the good flavor by stirring it vigorously with a spoon or pouring it back and forth several times from one container to another.
2. Use one to two drops of iodine or Halazone tablets according to the directions printed on the container. A few drops of lemon juice will improve the taste.
3. Use one part of chlorine to 100 parts of water. Let stand 30 minutes.
4. Use one to two drops of Clorox per gallon and aerate as in method 1.

When water is available at an outpost or frequently used campsite, it is worthwhile to send a sample to the state board of health for testing so that you won't have to bother to sterilize it. Directions for doing this can be secured from your state or county board of health or the camp director.

During very hot weather, you may want to add a little salt to your drinking water to prevent heat cramps and possible prostration. Consult the camp doctor or nurse about this.

FOOD

Make an earnest attempt to serve all meals on time and maintain high standards for cooking, serving, and eating them. The practice of subsisting on a diet of fried foods or on partially raw, overcooked, or poorly seasoned food is unnecessary. Never let campers make a practice of hanging around munching on bits of this or that while they're waiting for the main course to be ready. If it is long overdue or they're really quite hungry, give *everyone* something to allay hunger pangs. Every meal should be a ceremony beginning with a silent, spoken or sung grace and with everyone sitting down to eat together in pleasant surroundings. An invariable rule should be that no one eats without clean hands and face and neatly arranged hair just as when dining at home or back at the main camp. Singing well-loved songs or playing an interesting game makes time pass faster for those waiting for a meal and workers may be able to join in too.

GARBAGE DISPOSAL

Keep your campsite neat and clean and dispose of all garbage immediately in an appropriate way, for slops and rubbish dumped about a campsite look unsightly, draw flies and other pests, and may give off offensive odors.

Making a Grease Pit. To make a grease pit for disposing of liquid wastes, dig a hole on the downslope from camp and line it with small stones or gravel. Pour your dishwater and other liquid slops, waste fats, and the like into it and burn it out each time with a quick-burning fire. Mark it prominently so that no one will stumble into it by mistake.

Disposing of Solid Wastes. Solid wastes should be dried out on a frame of screening, as shown in Figure 31–10, until they become dry enough to burn in a brisk fire. Do not bury them, for some prowling animal will be sure to dig them up. Such wastes as aluminum foil, and banana, orange, and

Figure 31-9 You Brought It—Pack It Out!

apple peelings will not burn and should be carried in a litter bag back to camp with you unless you are on an extended trip, in which case they should be burned dry and then buried at some distance from camp. Remove both ends from tin cans and place them in the fire to burn out the inside contents and soften the solder so that you can mash them flat under your foot. Carry them back home with you (after all, they won't be nearly as heavy as they were when you brought them out full of food). Do not bury them, for it will take many years for them to disintegrate. Never just toss them out, for they catch water in which mosquitoes can breed and are an eyesore on the landscape. In addition, animals can get claws, hoofs, or heads caught in them.

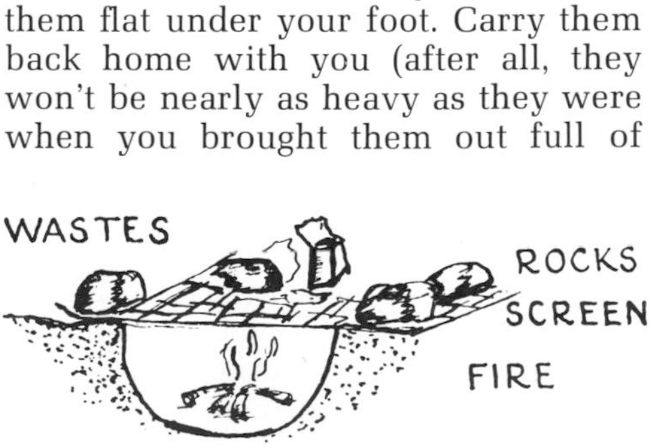

Twist paper to be burned tightly and burn it a little at a time, holding it down with a green stick poker so that the gases produced will not cause it to fly into the air and become a potential source of a forest fire. Tear cardboard boxes into bits and feed them to the fire a little at a time.

WASTES
ROCKS
SCREEN
FIRE

Figure 31-10 Drying Kiln for Solid Wastes.

BEDDING DOWN FOR THE NIGHT

Cache all food safely against roving dogs and other animals (see Chapter 29 for techniques). Turn pots and kettles upside down and stow everything

Figure 31–11 "Don't Do This to Me."

neatly away for the night. See that your fire is completely out and safe from spreading.

Many animals like to chew on candles, soap, and the like; securely hide them or suspend them from tree limbs so that they are inaccessible. Porcupines, in particular, crave salt and consequently may chew and completely ruin articles which have been perspiration-soaked such as axe, paddle or oar handles, saddles, shoes, belts, bridles, and so forth. These, too, should be suspended from ropes or taken inside your tent with you.

If you are sleeping outside, turn your shoes upside down as a protection against rain or heavy dew and place them close beside your bed roll where you can locate them quickly if you need them in the night. If you wear glasses, place them in their case inside your shoes or in your pack to avoid losing or breaking them.

Keep your flashlight nearby where you can locate it instantly in the dark.

If mosquitoes or other insects prove bothersome, spray your tent and surroundings with a good insect repellent before retiring.

IN CASE OF RAIN

Trippers should be experts at reading weather signs, for it's much better to foresee the rain and get everything ready before it comes than to have to scamper about in a deluge. If you decide to pitch your tent for the night, you should make a few variations from your usual procedures; many of these have already been discussed. If you must continue to work in the rain, a poncho gives better protection than a raincoat, for it is ample enough to cover a share of what you're carrying in addition to yourself.

If you have tents with front flies, you can make a connecting porch between two of them by pitching them facing each other and just far enough apart for the flies to slightly overlap. Slant them downward toward the tent so the water will run off down over the roof. This provides a "breezeway" (Fig. 31–12) in which you can actually do a little *light* cooking if you keep your fire quite small and put it out if your tent flies dry out.

If you expect to be rained in for an evening or several daylight hours, it is more sociable to pitch your tents in a semicircle so that you can sit in your tent doorways and have the cheeriness of a campfire in the midle. You can cook under a tarp.

Stake down guy wires deeper than usual. A well-chosen tent, when properly pitched, will stay put through anything less than a hurricane. Remember to place your tents with backs to the wind and rain. Loosen hemp guy ropes enough to prevent their shrinking and pulling out, leaving you with a wet tent around your neck.

Place all your duffel under tents, tarps, or ponchos, and do not unroll your bed roll until you are ready to get into it, so it won't collect dampness.

Figure 31–12 Tents with Breezeway.

HEALTH AND CLEANLINESS ON TRIPS

Keep yourself and your clothing clean. Stay in camp a half or a whole day occasionally on a long trip to wash out your clothing or stop at a nearby town to use the laundromat.

All the rules of health and sanitation are doubly important on a trip, where the illness or incapacity of a single person is most inconvenient. A stimulating and refreshing bath or sponge-off every day is a "must." Wash well before each meal and use strong soap immediately after possible exposure to poison ivy.

Never sleep in the clothes you have worn all day, for they contain body moisture that will chill you as it evaporates. A change to clean pajamas is restful and stimulating and permits you to wash out your soiled clothing and hang it up to dry overnight (Fig. 31–13). It is particularly important to wash out your socks and underwear each night.

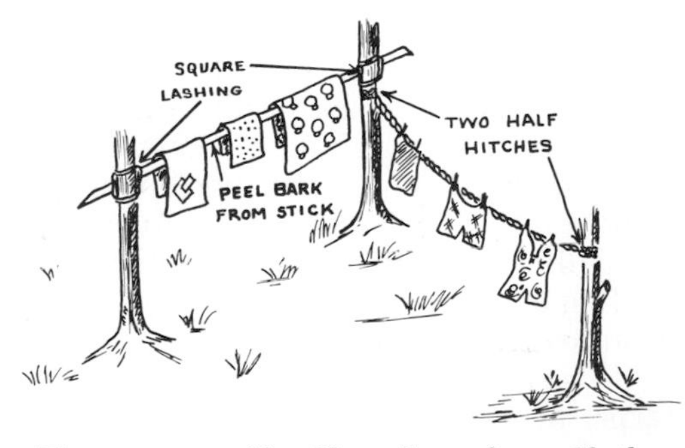

Figure 31–13 Use Your Rope for a Clothes Line.

Take care of minor ailments, which clearly fall within the realm of first aid; they may turn into major ones if neglected. The counselor best trained in first aid should administer all treatments except in emergencies when he is not available; he should keep an exact record of everything he does. He must carefully avoid doing the wrong thing and should never try to play doctor or nurse.

We have already pointed out that no trip should be taken without at least two counselors; if a camper should be seriously injured or show signs of serious illness, one counselor should take him to the nearest physician or back to camp while the other stays with the rest of the group.

If a camper shows symptoms of appendicitis (nausea and vomiting, abdominal pains that may be general at first but eventually become localized, inability to straighten the leg comfortably while lying down or to stand up straight) *do not apply heat or give a laxative under any circumstances.*

You can make a good emergency hot-water bottle by wrapping a heated stone or a canteen or plastic bottle filled with hot water in a towel or flannel shirt. If you need a stretcher, button up two coats, insert two saplings or long tent poles and lash in spreaders to keep them apart. A blanket and safety pins can be used in the same way (see page 343). Improvise a crutch as shown in Figure 30-16.

Digestive disturbances can be very "upsetting," so observe the principles of moderation and good nutrition. Many such cases can be traced to rancid food particles and germs left on dishes not thoroughly washed and sterilized.

Strenuous days on the trail necessitate a maximum of rest and sleep. This means an early bedtime, for the sun is an early riser and is likely to shine rudely right into your eyes to disturb you, in addition to the birds and other wildlife that will be noisily searching for an early breakfast.

Be on guard against cuts, scratches, blisters, sunburn, and exposure to poison ivy; carrying a pack on already sore shoulders can be pure torture. Summer colds are also miserable, so change wet clothing immediately and be especially careful to keep your head, shoulders, and feet dry.

BREAKING CAMP

Pack your food with the makings for lunch, usually an easily prepared meal, on top where they will be readily available.

Burn out your latrine and grease and garbage pits and cover them with dirt. (Don't dump grease over an open fire; the blaze might cause severe burns or start a forest fire.)

Restore any sod removed, fill in holes, and place the ground in condition to prevent erosion.

Leave your campsite even neater than it was when you came. Try to restore it so that no one will even know you were there and so that it is in condition to return to its natural state as soon as possible.

Take a last look around your campsite to see that you are not leaving anything behind.

Your fire should be completely dead.

> Let no man say,
> And say it to your shame,
> That all was beauty here
> Until *you* came.
>
> —AUTHOR UNKNOWN

BACK AT THE MAIN CAMP

Each camper and counselor should have a physical check-up by the physician or nurse within 24 hours after arriving back in camp. All should return in the pink of condition, and cases of sunburn, indigestion, overfatigue, and the like are unforgivable; they indicate poor planning or management of the trip.

Having a weeding-out party: unpack all gear, both personal and group, and carefully sort it into three piles: (1) items used many times, (2) those used occasionally, and (3) those never used. See how many items from piles (2) and (3) you can strike off your equipment list for the next trip.

Repair, air out, and store all personal equipment and check in unused food to the proper person.

Check all group equipment against the inventory you left at camp and make necessary repairs. Air and clean everything thoroughly and return it to its proper place.

"Trippers" should take it easy for a day or two after returning from a hard journey, taking time for laundry and getting personal effects in order. You may want to complete copies of your trip log, write up your adventures for the camp newspaper, or dramatize episodes for yourselves or your fellow campers at a subsequent campfire program.

Within a short time after returning, call a group meeting to evaluate the trip, noting both the good and bad points of your preliminary planning and preparations, the suitability of the food, morale of the group, and so on. Carefully make a note of all suggestions that will help you to improve future trips. You may want to relay some of your ideas to the director and trips counselor for the benefit of other trippers.

CANOE TRIPS

Canoe trips are favorites, especially with senior campers, for travel is relatively easy; also proportionately greater loads of equipment and food can be taken than by any other mode of travel except wagon, automobile, or truck. A person must be a triple-threat man, however, to undertake long canoe trips safely, for he must be a good camper, an excellent swimmer, and a skilled canoeist. He should also have toughened himself by short trips. Camps nearly always have rigid standards or tests that a camper must pass before he can qualify; they usually include passing the American Red Cross Intermediate swimming test or its equivalent as well as tests of camping and canoeing skills.

You can cover 3 or 4 miles an hour on a lake and even more when traveling with the current of a river. However, on long voyages, plan to lay over one out of every three or four days for rest and relief from the constant paddling.

EQUIPMENT

A 16-foot cruising model canoe seems to be the general favorite for

(Courtesy of Y.M.C.A. Camp Widjiwagan, Ely, Minnesota.)

camp trips, and you can choose from among canvas-covered, fiber glass, plywood, aluminum, or any of the new materials entering the market. Each type has its adherents but aluminum seems to be gaining in favor, for it is strong and durable, yet light in weight, an especially important consideration when portaging must be done. Aluminum canoes need very little upkeep and, with care, should last for years. They usually dent instead of puncturing when encountering obstacles with moderate force and have built-in air chambers that make them float and even right themselves when overturned.

Carefully choose your trip canoe for strength, stability in the water, and lightness if you will need to portage. For lake travel, choose a canoe with a slightly rounded bottom and a width that continues well out to the ends. A flat-bottomed, shoe-type curved keel, giving higher and slim ends, is better. Though long, tapered ends give more speed, a flat-bottomed boat gives more stability in the water. Put your canoe in first class repair and equip it with a painter and proper thwarts. When paddling, most people like to remove the seats and kneel on the bottom of the canoe with knees well apart and buttocks resting against a thwart; others prefer to leave the seats in so they can change position in calm water. Kneeling is the safest position since it keeps the center of gravity low; it also helps you to travel more rapidly and keeps the canoe steadier and well under control. You will need a light, waterproof kneeling pad that will float so that it can serve as a life preserver in an emergency; it will also serve as a pillow for sleeping or a seat for sitting on damp ground around the campfire. Buy one or make it from two layers of sponge rubber inserted inside an inner tube.

The sternman's paddle should reach up to his chin when he stands it on the ground; the bowman's is about three inches shorter. Maple paddles are best for trips, since they are springier and less likely to break. Label your paddle with a piece of adhesive tape on which you have printed your name in India ink so that you can always use the same paddle and get accustomed to it. Carry an extra paddle on the floor of each canoe in case one is lost or broken, and take a repair kit suitable for mending your type of canoe.

You will need dark glasses and a map of the route, and you should have light moccasins or low rubber sneakers for paddling, though some prefer to slip off their shoes and paddle in their socks.

Each person should wear a life jacket at all times when in a canoe.

Take a piece of mosquito netting to weight down around you if you want to sleep in your canoe.

ON THE WATER

On a trip, a canoe usually holds two people and their duffel, though a large craft can carry three. The sternman should be experienced and a master of the "J" stroke, for he is responsible for steering. The bowman, paddling on the opposite side, sets the rhythm of the stroke and keeps a sharp lookout for half-hidden rocks or snags. He must be able to use the "draw" stroke to pull the canoe away from suddenly-revealed obstacles in the path. Keep the personnel in each craft about two or three canoe lengths apart for companionship and for help if one gets into trouble.

Some prefer to pack their duffel in boxes made especially to fit into a canoe, but you can also use regular packs or duffel bags. Assemble all the gear for the canoe and pack it while it is entirely afloat, keeping it in shallow water and wading along the side.

It is very important to *trim your*

Figure 31–14 A Loaded Canoe.

load, keeping the weight balanced crosswise and toward the center of the canoe so that the bow and stern are kept as light as possible (Fig. 31–14). Place heavy things on the bottom and leave three to four inches of *freeboard,* or clear space, below the gunwales. Pack your duffel under the thwarts, if possible, and tie it so it can't slip about and throw the canoe off balance and so you won't lose it if you should capsize. Distribute the weight so that with passengers and duffel aboard the bow rides about an inch or two higher than the stern; take the canoe, loaded with both duffel and crew, out a little distance from shore and test it before you start on the trip. Pack things you might want in a hurry on top.

When you are ready to take off, the bowman steadies the bow between his legs while the sternman walks down the *exact center* of the canoe with his weight low and both hands on the gunwales. As he reaches the stern, his weight raises the bow so that the bowman can push off as he enters to send the canoe out into the clear and set it in motion.

Beware of sunburn; it is easy to unwittingly get a case bad enough to incapacitate you, for you will probably be too far from shore to have any shade at all and won't begin to feel the hot sun rays until it's too late. Keep your body, face, and neck well covered and use a good suntan lotion.

Keep your eye out for a good shady place to stop about noon and take a couple of hours off for lunch and rest. Confine most of your paddling to the cool of early morning and evening. When putting in to shore, ease in slowly, for rocks or snags can do serious damage. Before disembarking, make sure your canoe is well supported throughout its length either by the beach or water; fasten it by its painter to a tree or stake so you won't lose it by having it wash away. Never leave your canoe moored in the water for a long time, especially if there is a strong wind or waves, for lashing about on pebbles or rocks can damage or even make holes in it or carry it away. Carry, don't drag it, well back from shore and turn it upside down.

Choose an experienced and prudent canoeist for the lead canoe and the second most experienced to serve as "tail" man. Work out a system of hand signals to convey messages and see that everyone understands that they are to be obeyed instantly and implicitly.

SAFETY

A canoe is, for its size, one of the safest means of water travel since it won't capsize if used properly, and even if it should, you are in no danger *if* you'll hang on, for even when filled with water a canoe will support three or four people. The main thing is to swim to it, catch hold and stay with it, for it is just as foolish to abandon it and try to swim to shore as it would be to throw away a life preserver. Hang on with one hand and paddle to shore with the other; in fact, if there's a wind or current, it will probably carry you there without any effort at all on your part. If you've fastened your duffel to the canoe, it will be coming right along with you. This is all fine and dandy but it is still better not to capsize in the first place; here are some hints to help prevent it.

Never paddle in unknown water after dark unless some emergency makes it necessary.

Change seats only in shallow water and keep your weight as low as possible and exactly in the center of the canoe, grasping a gunwale with each hand as you proceed. Move slowly and deliberately. Save your horseplay for land—a canoe is no place for it!

On large bodies of water, stay close to shore. Learn to anticipate changes in the weather. (In some circumstances you might even want to carry a small portable radio for getting weather reports.) Get *off* the water if a storm is approaching. It is particularly danger-

(Courtesy of Camp Kooch-I-Ching, International Falls, Minnesota.)

ous to remain on it during squalls or lightning as well as in high winds. If necessary to continue paddling during a light sprinkle, raise your duffel a little off the floor, if possible, and cover it with an extra tarp or ground cloth. If you should ever be so unfortunate as to be caught in rough water, sit on the floor to keep your weight low and paddle vigorously to keep your canoe at an angle to the waves instead of letting it get crosswise where there is much danger of shipping water and swamping. If you should lose a paddle, kneel and paddle with your hand. In a real emergency, use two poles crosswise to lash two canoes together broadside and exactly parallel.

Never wear heavy or tight clothing or weight yourself down with knives, axes, heavy shoes, or rubber boots, lest you suddenly be thrown into the water and have to swim for it. Avoid overloading your canoe.

If it comes to a question of whether to portage or paddle through white water, remember the old Indian saying, "No Indian ever drowned on a portage." Portaging gives you a chance to stretch your legs and insures your safety. It is also better to portage than to try to canoe through rock-strewn water where it is easy to do irreparable damage to your canoe. For a two-man portage, invert your canoe and place one person at the bow to support it above his shoulder and choose the path, while his companion supports it over his head and follows. For a short portage, you can carry a canoe upright with one person grasping it underneath at each end. Counselors and senior campers will probably prefer the one-man carry.

Thus the Birch Canoe was builded
In the valley by the river,
In the bosom of the forest;
And the forest's life was in it,

(Courtesy of Camp Manito-Wish, Y.M.C.A., Milkwaukee, Wisconsin.)

All its mystery and its magic,
All the lightness of the birch tree,
All the toughness of the cedar,
All the larch's supple sinews;
And it floated on the river
Like a yellow leaf in Autumn
Like a yellow water lily.

—LONGFELLOW, *The Song of Hiawatha.*

WILDERNESS TRIPS AND SURVIVAL METHODS

*Changing Times** reports that about 35 camps specialize in canoe and wilderness trips of various lengths and degrees of difficulty, usually lasting from 10 days to 2 months. Among the most challenging are those associated with the 26-day wilderness survival courses promoted by Outward Bound,† a nonprofit organization that sponsors five schools located in Colorado, Oregon, Minnesota, North Carolina, and Maine. Each school holds about three sessions a summer and the first three have programs for both boys and girls. Those attending receive intensive training in survival methods under expert instruction and participate in grueling expeditions of their own planning. A culminating event is a three-day trip alone into the wilds to live almost entirely off what nature provides.

Several camps and other organizations are promoting survival experiences or living off the land with only a meager amount of equipment. Food consists of such things as fish, small animals, insects, wild fruit, and wild vegetation. Just what the survival kit carried should consist of varies somewhat with the season, the region of the country, and the personal opinions of the sponsoring person or organization. Most lists include such things as bandages, iodine or iodine swabs, burn ointment, a snakebite kit, flashlight, matches or other means of starting a fire, a small candle, compass, pocketknife and small sharpening stone, safety pins, 15 feet of copper wire for making snares and for other purposes, a plastic bag and halazone tablets for purifying water, a 20 foot nylon fishline for fishing and other purposes, fish hooks and sinkers, a poncho, and a blanket. Get expert information before you try it. You will find the sources listed in the Additional Readings helpful.

Fig. 31–15 Misery Is the End of Camp.

**Changing Times,* This Year a Different Summer for the Kids, March, 1969, p. 31.

†Outward Bound, Inc., Andover, Mass. 01810.

ADDITIONAL READINGS

(For an explanation of abbreviations and abbreviated forms used, see page 25.)

Bicycling

Asa, Warren: *North American Bicycle Atlas.* Am. Youth Hostels, Inc., 20 West 17th Street, New York, New York 10011, 1969, 127 pp., $2.50.
Bridge, Raymond: *Freewheeling: The Bicycle*

Camping Book. Order from Galloway, 192 pp., $5.95.
Browder, Sue: *The American Biking Atlas and Touring Guide.* Workman, 1974, 318 pp., $5.95.
Cardwell: *America's Camping Book,* ch. 43 to p. 459.
Coles, Clarence W., and Harold T. Glenn: *Glenn's Complete Bicycle Repair Manual.* Crown, 1973, 339 pp., $5.95, paper.
Cuthbertson, Tom: *Anybody's Bike Book: An Original Manual of Bicycle Repairs.* Ten Speed Press, 2510 Bancroft Way, Berkeley, California 94704, 1971, 176 pp., $6.95; $3, paper.
Cuthbertson, Tom: *Bike Tripping.* Ten Speed Press, 2510 Bancroft Way, Berkeley, California 94704, 1972, $6.95; $3, paper.
Cycling (No. 3330). Boy Scouts, 1971, 48 pp., 45¢, paper.
Frankel, Lillian and Godfrey: *The Bicycle Book.* Cornerstone, $1.50.
Henkel, Stephen C.: *Bikes: A How-To-Do-It Guide to Selection, Care, Repair, Maintenance, Decoration, Safety, and Fun on Your Bicycle.* Bantam, 1972, 189 pp., $1.25, paper.
Macfarlan, Alan A.: *Boy's Book of Biking.* Stackpole, 1968, 160 pp., $4.50.
MacGonagle, S.: *Bicycle.* Barnes, $4.95.
McIntyre, Bibs: *The Bike Book: Everything You Need to Know About Owning and Riding a Bike.* Harper & Row, 1972, $6.95.
Savage, John H.: *The Gold Medal Bicycle Handbook.* Fawcett, 274 pp., 95¢, paper.
Shaw, R.: *Teach Yourself Cycling.* Dover, $2.50.
Sherman, Steve: *Bike Hiking.* Backpacker Books, 1974, 160 pp., $1.45.
Sloane, Eugene A.: *The New Complete Book of Bicycling.* Simon & Schuster, 1974, 531 pp., $9.95.
Thiffault, Mark: *Bicycle Digest.* Digest Books, 288 pp., $5.95.
Tobey, Peter W.: *Two Wheel Travel: Bicycle Camping and Touring.* Dell, $3.
Wagenvoord, James: *Bikes and Riders.* Van Nostrand, 1972, 157 pp., $7.95.

MAGAZINE ARTICLES

Boy's Life:
"Bicycle Safety Check." Aug., 1972, p. 47.
Marshall, Joe: "Bike Hiking." Mar., 1972, p. 64.
Spencer, Billie: "Bike Safety." Mar., 1972, p. 58.
"Your Personal Bike Rack." Oct., 1972, p. 51.

Camping Journal:
Camping Journal, Mar., 1974. (Several articles)
Franey, Joseph: "Cross-Country Bicycle Tour: Washington State to Washington, D. C." June, 1972, p. 50.
Millar, Randall: "Cycle Care and Maintenance." July, 1974, p. 30.
Thomas, Bill: "Cycling the Backroads of America." July, 1974, p. 29.

Camping Magazine:
Stein, Bernard: "Bikecology." Mar., 1974, p. 16.

Consumer Reports:
"Three-Speed Bicycles." *1974 Buying Guide Issue,* p. 368.

Wilderness Camping:
Hayes, Chuck: "Bicycling Camping—The Only Way to Fly." Mar./Apr., 1974, p. 39.
Moran, Margot: "Island Hopping by Bicycle." Mar./Apr., 1974, p. 34.
Spadaro, Tony: "Gear Right for Touring." Mar./Apr., 1974, p. 43.
Sumner, Lloyd: "Two-Wheel Freedom." May/June, 1973, p. 31.
Walters, Bill: "1400 Mile Summer—A Northeastern Cycling Tour." Mar./Apr., 1974, p. 28.

Boat and Canoe Camping

(See also related material and the bibliography in Chapter 18.)

Angier: *Skills for Taming the Wilds,* ch. 11.
Bearse, Ray: *The Canoe Camper's Handbook.* 1974, Winchester, $7.95.
Berger: *Program Activities for Camps,* pp. 93–97.
Better Homes & Gardens Family Camping Book, ch. 21.
Cheney, Theodore A.: *Camping by Backpack and Canoe.* Funk & Wagnalls, 1971, 210 pp., $7.95.
Fieldbook for Boys and Men, pp. 274–277.
Germain: *When You Go Canoe Camping.*
Handel, Carle W.: *Canoe Camping.* Ronald, 1953, 192 pp., $4.
Malo, John W.: *Malo's Complete Guide to Canoeing and Canoe Camping.* Collier, 1969, 278 pp., $1.95, paper.
Malo, John W.: *Wilderness Canoeing.* Macmillan, 1971, 176 pp., $6.95.
Merrill: *All About Camping,* ch. 5.
Ormond: *Complete Book of Outdoor Lore,* ch. 3.
Riviere: *Backcountry Camping,* ch. 2 to p. 37.
Riviere: *The Camper's Bible,* ch. 14.
Riviere, Bill: *Pole, Paddle and Portage.* Van Nostrand, 1969, 260 pp., $6.95.
Shivers: *Camping,* pp. 288–294.

MAGAZINE ARTICLES

Camping Journal:
McKeown, William: "Boat Camping." Apr., 1970, p. 23.
Morrow, Les: "Canoe Portage Rig." Apr., 1973, p. 56.
Richards, Blaine; "How to Pack a Canoe." Mar., 1967, p. 42.

Wilderness Camping:
Burrell, Bob: "Canoe Back Packing." July/Aug., 1973, p. 20.
Corbeille, Roger L.: "The Canoe Cargo Box." May/June, 1974, p. 28.
LeBrant, Howie, and Harry N. Roberts: *On Canoe Design.* Aug./Sept., 1976, p. 16.
Wilderness Camping's Canoe Buyer's Guide. Aug./Sept., 1976, p. 50.

Camping with Children

Bridge: *America's Backpacking Book,* ch. 23.
Langer: *The Joy of Camping,* pp. 125–132.
Manning: *Backpacking One Step at a Time,* ch. 18.
Silverman, Goldie: *Backpacking with Babies and Small Children.* Backpacker Books, 175 pp., $4.50.
Stout, James and Ann: Backpacking With Small Children. Funk & Wagnalls, 1976, $6.95.
Wood: *Pleasure Packing,* ch. 12.

MAGAZINE ARTICLES

Backpacker:
Clark, Michael J.: "You're Taking . . . Who? . . . Where?" *Backpacker-3,* Fall, 1973, p. 29.

Camping with Horse and Burro

Brower: *Going Light—With Backpack or Burro.*
Cardwell: *America's Camping Book,* ch. 47.
Merrill: *All About Camping,* chs. 11, 21. 22.
Merrill: *The Hiker's and Backpacker's Handbook,* ch. 9.
Ormond: *Outdoorsman's Handbook,* Part 7.
Shivers: *Camping,* pp. 294–295.

Desert Camping

Bridge: *America's Backpacking Book,* ch. 19.
Merrill: *All About Camping,* ch. 7.
Merrill: *The Hiker's and Backpacker's Handbook,* ch. 10.
Merrill: *The Survival Handbook,* ch. 14.

Mountaineering

Bridge: *America's Backpacking Book,* ch. 18.
Cardwell: *America's Camping Book,* ch. 27.
Casewit, Curtis: *The Hiking-Climbing Handbook.* Hawthorn, 1969, 182 pp., $2.50, paper.
Ferber, Peggy (Ed.): *Mountaineering: The Freedom of the Hills.* The Mountaineers, Seattle, Washington, 3rd ed., 1974, 478 pp., $9.95.
Graves, Richard: *Bushcraft.* Skimeister Sport Shop, Box 168B, North Woodstock, New Hampshire 03262, $3.95.
Greenbank, Anthony: *The Book of Survival.* Order from Backpacker Books, 250 pp., 95¢, paper.
Kelley, Dennis: *Mountain Search for the Lost Person.* Order from the author, P.O. Box 153, Montrose, California 91020, $3.95, paper.
Mendenhall, Ruth and John: *Introduction to Rock and Mountain Climbing.* Stackpole, 1969, 192 pp., $5.95.
Merrill: *All About Camping,* ch. 10.
Merrill: *The Survival Handbook,* ch. 11.
Paulicke, Wilhelm, and Helmut Dumler: *Hazards in Mountaineering.* Oxford U., $8.95.
Wilderness Pocket 'n Pack Library.

Survival, First Aid, etc.

(See also the section "Wild Foods" in the bibliography in Chapter 30.)

Angier: *How to Stay Alive in the Woods.*
Angier, Bradford: *Living off the Country.* Stackpole, 1956, 241 pp., $5.
Angier: *Skills for Taming the Wilds.*
Angier: *Survival with Style.*
Angier: *Wilderness Cookery.*
Bale, Robert O.: *Outdoor Living.* Burgess, 1961, 199 pp., $3.95, spiral.
Berglund, Berndt: *Wilderness Survival,* Scribner, 1974, 175 pp., $2.95, paper.
Bridge: *America's Backpacking Book,* chs. 15, 16.
Cardwell: *America's Camping Book,* chs. 32, 34.
Dalrymple: *Survival in the Outdoors.*
Fear, Gene: *Surviving the Unexpected Wilderness Emergency.* Survival Education Association, 9035 Golden Given Road, Tacoma, Washington 98445, 1972, 196 pp., $3.95.
Fieldbook for Boys and Men, ch. 16 and pp. 550–551.
Greenbank, Anthony: *The Book of Survival.* Signet, 265 pp., 95¢, paper.
Hamper: *Wilderness Survival.*
Johnson, James R.: *Anyone Can Live off the Land.* McKay, 1961, 121 pp., $3.11.
Learn and Tallman: *Backpacker's Digest,* ch. 16.
MacInnes, Hamish: *International Mountain Rescue Handbook.* Scribner's, 1972, 218 pp., $10.
Medicine for Mountaineering. Order from Backpacker Books, 350 pp., $7.50.
Merrill: *All About Camping,* chs. 23–25.
Merrill: *The Hiker's and Backpacker's Handbook,* ch. 11.
Merrill: *The Survival Handbook.*
Mountaineering First Aid. Backpacker Books, 96 pp., $1.95, paper.
Olsen, Larry: *Outdoor Survival Skills,* BYU, 1973, $4.95; $2.95, paper.
Outdoor Living—Problems, Solutions, Guidelines. Mountain Rescue Council, P.O. Box 696, Tacoma, Washington 98401, 103 pp., $2.50.
Outdoor Survival: A Game About Wilderness Skills. Stackpole, $10. (A game for 2, 3 or 4 players testing the player's knowledge about what to do when lost away from civilization)
Rethmel: *Backpacking,* ch. 7 and Appendix H.
Shivers: *Camping,* pp. 261–267.
Shockley and Fox: *Survival in the Wilds.*

MAGAZINE ARTICLES

Camping Journal:
Haddon, E. P.: "Make Your Own Pocket Survival Kit." Nov., 1970, p. 20.
Johnson, E. C.: "Camp Chef." Apr. and May, 1974.
"Survival Seminar—C. A. P. Style." Apr., 1970, p. 36.

Trip Camping

Abel, Michael: *Backpacking Made Easy.* Naturegraph, 1972, $5.50; $2.50, paper.
Angier: *Home in Your Pack,* chs. 1, 8.
Angier: *Skills for Taming the Wilds,* chs. 6, 10, 13.
Bridge: *America's Backpacking Book,* chs. 3, 5, 21.
Cardwell: *America's Camping Book,* chs. 22, 42.
Colwell: *Introduction to Backpacking,* chs. 6, 10.
Dalrymple: *Survival in the Outdoors,* ch. 6.
Fieldbook for Boys and Men, ch. 5.
Fletcher: *The Complete Walker,* pp. 270–295.
Guide to Group Backpacking. Backpacker Books, 45 pp., $3.50, mimeographed.
Johnson, James Ralph: *Advanced Camping Techniques.* McKay, 1967, 149 pp., $3.75.
Langer: *The Joy of Camping,* pp. 133–143.
Learn and Tallman: *Backpacker's Digest,* ch. 19.
Macfarlan, Allan A.: *The Boy's Book of Hiking,* ch. 10.
Manning: *Backpacking One Step at a Time,* chs. 2, 3, 18.
Merrill: *All About Camping,* ch. 9.
Merrill: *The Hiker's and Backpacker's Handbook,* ch. 3.
Miracle and Decker: *Complete Book of Camping,* chs. 1, 17–21.
Ormond: *Complete Book of Outdoor Lore,* chs. 8–11.
Ormond: *Outdoorsman's Handbook,* Parts 3, 5, 8.
Primitive Camp Sanitation. Girl Scouts, $10. (Caches, latrines, garbage disposal, and dishwashing) (Flip charts)
Rethmel: *Backpacking,* chs. 7–10.
Riviere: *Backcountry Camping,* ch. 9.
Van Lear, Denise (Ed.): *The Best About Backpacking.* Sierra Club, 1974, 384 pp., $6.95, paper.
Whelen and Angier: *On Your Own in the Wilderness.*
Winnett: *Backpacking for Fun,* chs. 7, 10.
Wood: *Pleasure Packing,* chs. 8, 10, 14.

MAGAZINE ARTICLES

Camping Journal:
Gibbs, Jerry: "How to Pack a Pack." Oct., 1972, p. 36.
Huypia, Jorma: "Backpacking—Backwoods Basics." June, 1974, p. 22.
Lockwood, Daniel: "A Low Budget Plan for Building a Unique Program for Pioneering." Feb., 1973, p. 12.
Schmidt, Ernest F.: "Today's Campers Should Learn How to be 'Lazy' on Trips. June, 1971, p. 16.

Camping Magazine:
Jambro, Thomas A.: "Visual Aids Spark Tripping Calendar." Feb., 1969, p. 21.

Wilderness Camping:
Reiche, Carl A.: "A Proposal—50 Hikers' Huts for America." Jan./Feb., 1974, p. 14.

Where to Go

(See also the section "Where To Go" in the bibliography in Chapter 1.)

Bridge: *America's Backpacking Book,* ch. 25.
Cardwell: *America's Camping Book,* ch. 21.
Colwell: *Introduction to Backpacking,* ch. 11.
Colwell, Robert: *Introduction to Foot Trails in America.* Stackpole, 1972, 224 pp., $5.95.
Colwell, Robert: *Introduction to Water Trails in America.* Stackpole, 1973, 221 pp., $5.95; $2.95, paper.
Johnson, J. R.: *Everglades Adventure.* McKay, $4.95.
Learn and Tallman: *Backpacker's Digest,* ch. 20.
Makens, James C.: *Maken's Guide to U.S. Canoe Trails.* La Voyageur Publishing Co., 1319 Wentwood Dr., Irving, Texas 75061, 1971, 86 pp., $4.95, paper.
Merrill: *All About Camping,* chs. 2, 3, 12.
Merrill: *The Hiker's and Backpacker's Handbook,* chs. 2, 12, 13, Appendix.
National Scenic and Recreation Trails. Produced by Dept. of Interior, Bureau of Outdoor Recreation and U. S. Forest Service, Supt. of Documents, 1970, 30¢.
Nickels, Nick: *Plan Now, Paddle Later.* Order from the author, P.O. Box 479, Lakefield, Ontario, Canada, $5.50, paper.
Rethmel: *Backpacking,* pp. A-9 to A-12.
Riviere: *Backcountry Camping,* ch. 15.
Sutton, A. and M.: *Appalachian Trail: Wilderness on the Doorstep.* Lippincott, 1967, $9.95.

MAGAZINE ARTICLES

Camping Journal:
"Best Trails Known and Unknown." June, 1974, p. 26.

Wilderness Camping:
Hixson, Robert: "20,000 Miles of Walking—the National Trails System." Sept./Oct., 1973, p. 14.

Winter Camping

Angier: *Survival with Style,* pp. 30–42, chs. 6, 7.
Bennett, Margaret: *Crosscountry Skiing for the Fun of It.* Order from Backpacker Books, 206 pp., $5.95.
Bridge: *America's Backpacking Book,* ch. 20.

Bridge, Raymond: *The Complete Snow Camper's Guide*. Scribner's, 1973, 39 pp., $4.95, paper.
Caldwell, John: *The New Crosscountry Ski Book*. Order from Backpacker Books, 144 pp., $3.95, paper.
Fieldbook for Boys and Men, ch. 15.
Langer: *The Joy of Camping,* pp. 192–226, 261–270.
Manning: *Backpacking One Step at a Time,* ch. 19.
Merrill: *All About Camping,* ch. 8 and pp. 367–372.
Merrill: *The Survival Handbook,* ch. 12.
Osgood, William E., and Leslie J. Hurley: *Ski Touring: An Introductory Guide*. Charles E. Tuttle Co., Inc., Rutland, Vermont 15701, 1969, 148 pp., $5.
Osgood, William E., and Leslie J. Hurley: *The Snowshoe Book*. Order from Backpacker Books, 127 pp., $3.95, paper.
Rethmel: *Backpacking,* Appendix I.
Riviere: *Backcountry Camping,* ch. 11.
Rossit, Edward A.: *Snow Camping and Mountaineering*. Funk & Wagnalls, 1970, 276 pp., $10.
Rutstrum, Calvin: *Paradise Below Zero*. Macmillan, 1968, 244 pp., $2.45, paper.
Tapely, Lance: *Ski-Touring in New England*. Stone Wall Press, Lexington, Massachusetts 02173, 1973, $6.50; $3.50, paper.
Winter Activities (No. 26-092). Boy Scouts, 25¢.
Wood: *Pleasure Packing,* ch. 11.

MAGAZINE ARTICLES

Backpacker:
"How to Build a Campfire in Deep Snow." *Backpacker-8,* Winter, 1974, p. 33.
Curtis, Sam: "How to Track Wildlife on Skis." *Backpacker-8,* Winter, 1974, p. 40.
Frisch, Bob: "Silence and Magic." *Backpacker-4,* Winter, 1973, p. 30. (Snowshoeing)
Henley, Thomas: "How to Build An Igloo." *Backpacker-8,* Winter, 1974, p. 54.
Nourse, Alan E., M. D.: "Cold Weather Killers: Hypothermia & Frostbite." *Backpacker-4,* Winter, 1973, p. 36.
Perry, Phillip M.: "Putting the Brakes on the Snowmobile Menace." *Backpacker-8,* Winter, 1974, p. 50.
"Snowshoeing and Skis." *Backpacker-4,* Winter, 1973, pp. 30–35.
Waterman, Laura and Guy: "How to Keep Warm in Winter Without a Campfire." *Backpacker-8,* Winter, 1974, p. 32.

Boys' Life:
Pryce, Dick: "Sit Tight and Survive." Jan., 1972, p. 57.

Camping Journal:
Bridge, Raymond, "Go-Shoes for Snow." Dec., 1971, p. 30.
Grant, Ken: "Make Yourself Freeze-Proof." Dec., 1972, p. 23.
Roberts, Harry: "How to Choose a Ski." Feb., 1974, p. 90.
Seeghers, Carroll II: "Winter Camping." Feb., 1974, p. 23.
Stebbins, J. Ray: "Backpack Into Snow Country." Dec., 1971, p. 22.

Wilderness Camping:
Bentley, Bill: "The Universal Ski Binding." Nov./Dec., 1973, p. 11.
Dayton, Gene: "Night Touring." Nov./Dec., 1973, p. 41. (Ski touring)
Foster, John R.: "Snowshoeing the Rugged Belts." Nov./Dec., 1973, p. 41.
Hatcher, C. L.: "Cold Weather Canoeing." Sept./Oct., 1973, p. 24.
Martin, Emilie: "A Killer For All Seasons—Hypothermia." Jan./Feb., 1973, p. 38.
Neuwirth, Joseph G., Jr.: "Principles of Cold Weather Adaptability." Nov./Dec., 1973, p. 26.
"Ski-Touring Potpourri." Jan./Feb., 1974, p. 42.
Wood, Robert S.: "Pleasure Packing—The Great Breathability Myth." Part I, Sept./Oct., 1973, p. 10; Part II, Nov./Dec., 1973, p. 18.

Appendix A

Selected General Bibliography

Note: This listing of books includes only those that have been cited in the bibliographies in two or more chapters. Other excellent sources can be found in the bibliography in each chapter. For an explanation of abbreviations and abbreviated forms used, see page 25.

Angier, Bradford: *Home in Your Pack.* Collier, rev., 1972, 202 pp., $1.50, paper.

Angier, Bradford: *How to Stay Alive in the Woods.* Macmillan, 1966, 286 pp., 95¢, paper.

Angier, Bradford: *Living Off the Country.* Stackpole, 1965, 241 pp., $5.

Angier, Bradford: *Skills for Taming the Wilds.* Stackpole, 1967, 288 pp., $6.95.

Angier, Bradford: *Survival with Style.* Stackpole, 1972, 256 pp., $6.95.

Angier, Bradford: *Wilderness Cookery.* Stackpole, rev., 1970, 256 pp., $1.95, paper.

Angier, Bradford: *Wilderness Gear You Can Make Yourself.* Macmillan, 1973, 115 pp., $2.95, paper.

Bale, R. O.: *What On Earth.* ACA, 1969, 160 pp., $3.95, paper.

Basic Outboard Boating Textbook. ARC, 1964, 98 pp., 75¢, paper.

Berger, H. Jean: *Program Activities for Camps.* Burgess, 2nd ed., 1969, 179 pp., $5, paper.

Better Homes and Gardens Family Camping Book. Meredith, 1961, 160 pp., $2.95.

Bloom, Dr. Joel: *Camper Guidance—In the Routines of Daily Living.* ACA, 1965, 16 pp., 60¢, paper.

Bloom, Dr. Joel W., et al.: *Camper Guidance—A Basic Handbook for Counselors.* ACA, 1961, 24 pp., 85¢, paper.

Bridge, Raymond: *America's Backpacking Book.* Scribner's, 1973, 417 pp., $12.50.

Brower, David R. (Ed.): *Going Light—With Backpack or Burro.* Sierra, 1972, 152 pp., $3.50.

Brown, Vinson: *The Amateur Naturalist's Handbook.* Little, Brown, 1948, 475 pp., $6.50.

Camp Job Descriptions. ACA, 20 pp., 50¢, paper.

Campcraft Instructor's Manual (Including Tripcraft). ACA, 1973, 96 pp., $2, paper.

Camping (No. 3256). Boy Scouts, 1966, 96 pp., 45¢, paper.

Camping Is Education. ACA, 1960, 24 pp., 75¢, paper.

Cardwell, Paul, Jr.: *America's Camping Book.* Scribner's, 1969, 591 pp., $10.

Chappell, Wallace: *When You Go Trail Camping.* ACA, 1969, 96 pp., 75¢, paper.

Colwell, Robert: *Introduction to Backpacking.* Stackpole, 1970, 192 pp., $5.95.

Convention Highlights. ACA, 1962, 106 pp., $5, paper.

Corbin, H. Dan: *Recreation Leadership.* Prentice-Hall, 3rd ed., 1970, 418 pp., $8.95.

Cunningham, Gerry, and Margaret Hansson: *Lightweight Camping Equipment and How To Make It.* Colo. Outdoor Sports, 1964, 131 pp., $3.25.

Dalrymple, Byron: *Survival in the Outdoors.* Dutton, 1972, 309 pp., $6.95.

Danford, Howard G., and Shirley Max: *Creative Leadership in Recreation*. Allyn and Bacon, 2nd ed., 1970, 398 pp., $8.95.

Eisenberg, Helen and Larry: *Omnibus of Fun*. Ass'n Press, 1956, 625 pp., $7.95.

Ensign, John and Ruth: *Camping Together as Christians*. Knox, 1958, 148 pp., $1.50, paper.

Fieldbook for Boys and Men (No. 3201). Boy Scouts, 1967, 576 pp., $1.95, paper.

Fletcher, Colin: *The Complete Walker*. Knopf, 1972, 353 pp., $7.95.

Gabrielson, M. Alexander, Betty Spears, and Bramwell W. Gabrielson: *Aquatics Handbook*. Prentice-Hall, 2nd ed., 1968, 224 pp., $11.30.

Garrison, Cecil: *Outdoor Education: Principles and Practice*. Thomas, 1966, 239 pp., $9.50.

Germain, Donald L.: *When You Go Canoe Camping*. ACA, 1968, 69 pp., 75¢, paper.

Gould, Heywood: *The Complete Book of Camping*. Signet, 1972, 156 pp., $1, paper.

Hammerman, Donald R., and William M. Hammerman (Eds.): *Outdoor Education: A Book of Readings*. Burgess, 2nd ed., 1973, 412 pp., $7.95, paper.

Hammerman, Donald R., and William M. Hammerman: *Teaching in the Outdoors*. Burgess, 2nd ed., 1973, 144 pp., $3.95, paper.

Hammett, Catherine T.: *Your Own Book of Campcraft*. Pocket Books, 1950, 197 pp., 35¢, paper.

Hamper, Stan: *Wilderness Survival*. Order from ACA, 1963, 97 pp., $1, paper.

Harbin, E. O.: *The Fun Encyclopedia*. Abingdon, 1940, 1008 pp., $6.95.

Harty, William T.: *Science for Camp and Counselor*. Ass'n Press, 1964, 320 pp., $9.95.

Hillcourt, William: *New Field Book of Nature Activities and Conservation*. Putnam, 1971, 420 pp., $5.95.

Jaeger, Ellsworth: *Wildwood Wisdom*. Macmillan, 1966, 228 pp., $6.95.

Johnson, James R.: *Anyone Can Camp in Comfort*. McKay, 1964, 154 pp., $3.75.

Kjellstrom, Bjorn: *Be Expert with Map and Compass*. Scribner's, rev., 1972, 136 pp., $3.50.

Kraus, Richard G.: *Recreation Leader's Handbook*. McGraw-Hill, 1955, 299 pp., $9.

Kujoth, Jean Spealman (Compiler): *The Recreation Program Guide*. Scarecrow, 1972, 437 pp., $10.

Langer, Richard: *The Joy of Camping*. Saturday Review, 1973, 320 pp., $8.95; Penguin, 1974, $2.50, paper.

Learn, C. R., and Anne S. Tallman: *Backpacker's Digest*. Digest Books, 1973, 288 pp., $5.95, paper.

Ledlie, John A., and Francis W. Holbein: *Camp Counselor's Manual*. Ass'n Press, rev., 1969, 128 pp., $1.75, paper.

Lightweight Equipment for Hiking, Camping and Mountaineering. Potomac Appalachian Trail Club Equipment Co., Washington, D.C., 13th ed., 1972, $1.

Litepac Camping Equipment. Boys' Life, 20¢. (Articles reprinted from Boys' Life)

Macfarlan, Allan A.: *The Boy's Book of Hiking*. Stackpole, 1968, 159 pp., $4.50.

MacKay, Joy: *Creative Counseling for Christian Camps*. Scripture, 1966, 129 pp., $1.95, paper.

Mand, Charles L.: *Outdoor Education*. Pratt, 1967, 192 pp., $2.95, paper.

Manning, Harvey: *Backpacking One Step at a Time*. Random, 351 pp., $7.95, paper.

Mason, Bernard S.: *The Book of Indian Crafts and Costumes*. Ronald, 1946, 118 pp., $6.50.

Mason, Bernard S.: *The Junior Book of Camping and Woodcraft*. Ronald, 1943, 120 pp., $6.

Merrill, Bill: *The Hiker's and Backpacker's Handbook*. Winchester, 1971, 320 pp., $5.95; Arco, $2.95, paper.

Merrill, Bill: *The Survival Handbook*. Winchester, 1972, 312 pp., $5.95.

Merrill, W. K.: *All About Camping*. Stackpole, 1970, 399 pp., $2.95, paper.

Miracle, Leonard, and Maurice H. Decker: *The Complete Book of Camping*. Harper & Row, 1961, 594 pp., $5.95.

Mooers, Robert L., Jr.: *Finding Your Way in the Outdoors*. Dutton, 1972, 275 pp., $5.95.

Moser, Clarence G.: *Understanding Girls*. Ass'n Press, 1957, 252 pp., $3.50.

Mountaineering: The Freedom of the Hills. The Mountaineers, Seattle, 1967, $7.95.

Mulac, Margaret E.: *Fun and Games*. Macmillan, 1963, 350 pp., 95¢, paper.

National Directory of Accredited Camps for Boys and Girls. ACA, published annually, 300 pp., $3, paper.

Olsen, Larry Dean: *Outdoor Survival Skills*. BYU Press, 1973, $4.95; $2.95, paper.

Ormond, Clyde: *Complete Book of Outdoor Lore*. Harper & Row, 1965, 498 pp., $5.95.

Ormond, Clyde: *Outdoorsman's Handbook*. Dutton, 1971, 336 pp., $5.95.

Ott, Elmer F.: *So You Want To Be a Camp Counselor*. Ass'n Press, 1946, 112 pp., $1.50.

Outdoor Safety Tips. Supt. of Documents, 15¢, paper.

Outdoor Tips. Remington, 1972, 190 pp., $2.95.

Rethmel, Robert C.: *Backpacking*. Burgess, rev., 1972, 144 pp., $6.95; $3.95, paper.

Riviere, Bill: *Backcountry Camping*. Doubleday, 1971, 320 pp., $6.95.

Riviere, Bill: *The Camper's Bible*. Doubleday, 1960, 176 pp., $1.95, paper.

Riviere, Bill: *The Family Camper's Cookbook*. Holt, Rinehart, 1965, 244 pp., $4.95; Doubleday, $1.95, paper.

Rodney, Lynn S., and Phyllis M. Ford: *Camp Administration*. Ronald, 1971, 402 pp., $8.75.

Rutstrum, Calvin: *The New Way of the Wilderness*. Macmillan, rev., 1973, 280 pp., $2.95, paper.

Scout Handbook. Boy Scouts, 8th ed., 1972, 480 pp., $1.60, paper.

Scoutmaster's Handbook. Boy Scouts, 1972, 384 pp., $2.25, paper.

Shivers, Jay S.: *Camping.* Appleton-Century, 1971, 424 pp., $8.95.

Shockley, Robert O., and Charles K. Fox: *Survival in the Wilds.* Barnes, 1970, 150 pp., $6.95.

Shuttlesworth, Dorothy E.: *Exploring Nature with Your Child.* Hawthorn, 1952, 448 pp., $5.95.

Smith, Julian W., et al.: *Outdoor Education.* Prentice-Hall, 2nd ed., 1972, 335 pp., $9.95.

Strean, Herbert S. (Ed.): *New Approaches in Child Guidance.* Scarecrow, 1970, 313 pp., $7.50.

Sunset Camping Handbook. Lane, 1970, 96 pp., $1.95, paper.

Todd, Floyd and Pauline: *Camping for Christian Youth.* Harper & Row, 1968, 198 pp., $2.50, paper.

van der Smissen, Betty, and Oswald H. Goering: *A Leader's Guide to Nature Oriented Activities.* Iowa State U., 1965, 210 pp., $3.95, spiral.

Van Krevelan, Alice: *Children in Groups: Psychology and the Summer Camp.* Brooks/Cole, 1972, 136 pp., $4.35.

Vinal, Dr. William: *Nature Recreation.* Dover, 2nd ed., 1963, 310 pp., $2.75, paper.

Webb, Kenneth B. (Ed.): *Light From a Thousand Campfires.* ACA, 1960, 384 pp., $3.95, paper.

Webb, Kenneth B.: *Summer Camps—Security in the Midst of Change.* ACA, 1968, 52 pp., $1, paper.

Wells, George and Iris: *Handbook of Wilderness Travel.* Harper & Row, 1956, 294 pp., $4.

Whelen, Townsend, and Bradford Angier: *On Your Own in the Wilderness.* Stackpole, 1958, 330 pp., $5.

Wilderness Pocket'n Pack Library. Life Support, 1969–1972, five pocket-sized books, $4.95 the set or $1 each. (*Survival in the Wilderness, Edible Plants in the Wilderness* [2 Volumes], *Poisonous Plants in the Wilderness,* and *Primitive Medical Aid in the Wilderness.*)

Winnett, Thomas: *Backpacking for Fun.* Wilderness, 1972, 131 pp., $2.95, paper.

Wood, Robert S.: *Pleasure Packing.* Condor, 1972, 211 pp., $3.95, paper.

Appendix B

Magazines

American Forests. Published monthly by The American Forestry Association, 919 17th St., N.W., Washington, D.C. 20006, $6.

Audubon. Published six times a year (Jan., Mar., May, July, Sept., Nov.) by the National Audubon Society, 950 Third Ave., New York, N.Y. 10022, $10.

Backpacker. Published quarterly (Mar., June, Sept., Dec.) by Backpacker, Inc., 28 W. 44th St., New York, N.Y. 10036, $7.50.

Boys' Life. Published monthly by the Boy Scouts of America, North Brunswick, N.J. 08902, $5.

Camping Journal. Published monthly by Davis Publications, Inc., P. O. Box 2600, Greenwich, Conn. 06830, $8.95.

Camping Magazine. Published monthly Jan.–June and bi-monthly Sept.–Dec. by the American Camping Association, Martinsville, Ind. 46161. ACA membership includes subscription; to others, $9.

Consumer Reports. Published monthly by Consumers Union of the United States, Inc., P. O. Box 1000, Orangeburg, N.Y. 10962, $8.

J.O.H.P.E.R. Journal of Health, Physical Education and Recreation. Published monthly except July and August, with November-December combined, by the American Association for Health, Physical Education and Recreation, 1201 16th St., N.W., Washington, D.C. 20036. AAHPER membership includes subscription; to others, $25.

The Living Wilderness. Published quarterly by The Wilderness Society, 729 15th St., N.W., Washington, D.C. 20005, $7.50.

National Wildlife. Published bimonthly by the National Wildlife Federation, 1412 16th St., N.W., Washington, D.C. 20036, $6.50.

Recreation. Official magazine of the National Recreation Association. Published monthly except July and August.

Wilderness Camping. Published six times a year (Jan., Mar., May, July, Sept., Nov.), 1255 Portland Place, Boulder, Colo. 80302, $4.

Appendix C

Organizations Promoting Outdoor Activities

Note: This list is necessarily selective; the names and addresses of many other organizations promoting outdoor activities can be found, listed by state, in Appendix III of Fletcher: *The Complete Walker.*

Amateur Bicycle League of America, 6411 Orchard St., Dearborn, Mich. 48120.

American Canoe Association, 4260 East Ave., Denver, Colo. 80222.

American Forestry Association, 919 17th St., N.W., Washington, D.C. 20006.

American Water Ski Association, 7th St. and Avenue G, S.W., Winterhaven, Fla. 33880.

American Whitewater Affiliation, 3115 Eton Ave., Berkeley, Calif. 94705.

American Youth Hostels, Inc., National Campus, Delaplane, Va. 22025.

Appalachian Mountain Club, 5 Joy St., Boston, Mass. 02108.

Appalachian Trail Conference, P. O. Box 236, Harpers Ferry, W.Va. 25425.

Archery Institute, 715 N. Rush St., Chicago, Ill.

Association of Private Camps, 55 W. 42nd St., New York, N.Y. 10036.

Bicycle Club of America, 9 Central Park W., New York, N.Y. 10023.

Boy Scouts of America, North Brunswick, N.J. 08902.

Boys' Clubs of America, 771 First Ave., New York, N.Y. 10017.

Camp Archery Association, 200 Coligni Ave., New Rochelle, N.Y. 10801.

Camp Fire Girls, Inc., 450 Avenue of the Americas, New York, N.Y. 10011.

Colorado Mountain Club, 1400 Josephine St., Denver, Colo. 80206.

Family Camping Federation, Bradford Woods, Martinsville, Ind. 46151.

Federation of Western Outdoor Clubs, Route 3, P. O. Box 172, Carmel, Calif. 93921.

Friends of the Earth, 529 Commercial Street, San Francisco, Calif. 94111.

Fund for the Advancement of Camping, Room 1414, 19 S. La Salle St., Chicago, Ill. 60603.

Girl Scouts of the U. S. A., 830 Third Ave., New York, N.Y. 10022.

The National Audubon Society, 950 Third Ave., New York, N.Y. 10022.

National Campers and Hikers Association, P. O. Box 182, 7172 Transit Road, Buffalo, N.Y. 14221.

National Parks and Conservation Association, 1701 18th St., N.W., Washington, D.C. 20009.

National Parks Association, 1300 New Hampshire Ave., Washington, D.C. 20036.

National Wildlife Federation, 1412 16th St., N.W., Washington, D.C. 20036.

The New England Trail Conference, 26 Bedford Terrace, Northampton, Mass. 01060.

The Sierra Club, 1050 Mills Tower, 270 Bush St., San Francisco, Calif. 94104.

South Eastern Alaska Mountaineering Association, P. O. Box 1314, Ketchikan, Alaska 99901.

United States Canoe Association, 6338 Hoover Road, Indianapolis, Ind. 46260.

United States Ski Association, The Broadmoor, Colorado Springs, Colo. 80906.

Isaak Walton League of America, 1326 Waukegan Road, Glenview, Ill. 60025.

The Wilderness Society, 1901 Pennsylvania Ave., N.W., Washington, D.C. 20006.

Appendix D

Directory of Publishers and Other Organizations

Note: Publishers and organizations are listed by the abbreviations and contractions used throughout this book.

AAHPER: American Association for Health, Physical Education and Recreation, 1201 16th St., N.W., Washington, D.C. 20036.

Abingdon: Abingdon Press, 201 Eighth Avenue, Nashville, Tenn. 37203.

ACA: American Camping Association, Bradford Woods, Martinsville, Ind. 46151.

Allyn & Bacon: Allyn & Bacon, Rockleigh, N.J. 07647.

Amer. Orienteering: American Orienteering Service, P. O. Box 547, La Porte, Ind. 46350.

Appleton-Century: Appleton-Century-Crofts, Educational Division, 440 Park Ave. S., New York, N.Y. 10016.

ARC: American National Red Cross, 17th and D Sts., Washington, D.C. 20006. (Books may usually be purchased from local chapters)

Arco: Arco Publishing Co., Inc., 219 Park Ave. S., New York, N.Y. 10003.

Ass'n Press: Association Press, 291 Broadway, New York, N.Y. 10007.

Atheneum: Atheneum Publishers, 122 E. 42nd St., New York, N.Y. 10017.

Augsburg: Augsburg Publishing House, 426 S. 5th St., Minneapolis, Minn. 55415.

Backpacker Books: Backpacker Books, Bellows Falls, Vt. 05101.

Baker: Baker Book House, 1019 Wealthy St., S.E., Grand Rapids, Mich. 49506.

Ballantine: Ballantine Books, Inc., 201 E. 50th St., New York, N.Y. 10022.

Bantam: Bantam Books, Inc., 666 Fifth Ave., New York, N.Y. 10019.

Barnes: A. S. Barnes & Co., Forsgate Dr., Cranbury, N.J. 08512.

Barnes & Noble: Barnes & Noble, Inc., 10 E. 53rd St., New York, N.Y. 10022.

Basic Books: Basic Books, Inc., 10 E. 53rd St., New York, N.Y. 10022.

Bennett: Charles A. Bennett Company, Inc., 809 West Detwiler Dr., Peoria, Ill. 61614.

Better Homes and Gardens. See *Meredith Press.*

Boy Scouts: Boy Scouts of America, National Council, North Brunswick, N.J. 08902.

Branford: Charles T. Branford Co., 28 Union Street, Newton Centre, Mass. 02159.

Brooks/Cole: Brooks/Cole Publishing Co., 540 Abrego St., Monterey, Calif. 93940.

Brown: Wm. C. Brown & Co., 2460 Kerper Blvd., Dubuque, Iowa 52001.

Bruce: Bruce Publishing Co., 2642 University Ave., St. Paul, Minn. 55114.

Burgess: Burgess Publishing Co., 7108 Ohms Lane, Minneapolis, Minn. 55435.

BYU: Brigham Young University Press, 209 University Press Building, Provo, Utah 84601.

Chilton: Chilton Book Co., Chilton Way, Radnor, Pa. 19089.

CLC Press: Covenant Life Curriculum Press. See *John Knox Press.*
Cokesbury: Cokesbury, Southwestern Regional Service Center, 1910 Main St., Dallas, Tex. 75221.
Collier: P. F. Collier, Inc., 866 Third Ave., New York, N.Y. 10022.
Condor: Condor Books, 1000 Mariposa, Berkeley, Calif. 94707.
Consumer Reports: Consumer Reports, P. O. Box 1000, Orangeburg, N.Y. 10962.
Coop. Rec. Service: Cooperative Recreation Service, Publishing Department, Radnor Rd., Delaware, Ohio 43015.
Cornell: Cornell University Press, 124 Roberts Place, Ithaca, N.Y. 14850.
Cornell Maritime: Cornell Maritime, P. O. Box 109, Cambridge, Md. 21613.
Coward-McCann: Coward-McCann & Geoghegan, Inc., 200 Madison Ave., New York, N.Y. 10016. (Carried by Putnam)
Crowell: Thomas Y. Crowell Co., 666 Fifth Ave., New York, N.Y. 10019.
Crown: Crown Publishers Inc., 419 Park Ave. S., New York, N.Y. 10016.
Davis: Davis Publications, Inc., 50 Portland St., Worcester, Mass. 01608.
Day: The John Day Co., Inc., 257 Park Ave. S., New York, N.Y. 10010.
Dell: Dell Publishing Co., Inc., 1 Dag Hammarskjold Plaza, 245 E. 47th St., New York, N.Y. 10017.
Denison: T. S. Denison and Co., Inc., 5100 W. 82nd St., Minneapolis, Minn. 55431.
Devin-Adair: The Devin Adair Co., 1 Park Ave., Old Greenwich, Conn. 06870.
Dial: The Dial Press, 1 Dag Hammarskjold Plaza, 245 E. 47th St., New York, N.Y. 10017.
Digest Books: Digest Books, 540 Frontage Rd., Northfield, Ill. 60093.
Dodd, Mead: Dodd, Mead & Co., Inc., 79 Madison Ave., New York, N.Y. 10016.
Doubleday: Doubleday and Co., Inc., 501 Franklin Ave., Garden City, N.Y. 11531.
Dover: Dover Publications, Inc., 180 Varick St., New York, N.Y. 10014.
Drake: Drake Publishers, Inc., 381 Park Ave. S., New York, N.Y. 10016.
Duke: Duke University Press, Box 6697, College Station, Durham, N.C. 27708.
Dutton: E. P. Dutton & Co., Inc., 201 Park Ave. S., New York, N.Y. 10003.
Eerdmans: William B. Eerdmans Publishing Co., 255 Jefferson Ave., S.E., Grand Rapids, Mich. 49502.
Emerson: Emerson Books, Reynolds Lane, Buchanan, N.Y. 10511.
Exposition: Exposition Press, Inc., 50 Jericho Tpk., Jericho, N.Y. 11753.
Fawcett: Fawcett Publications, Inc., Fawcett Place, Greenwich, Conn. 06830.
Fearon: Fearon Publishers, Inc., 6 Davis Dr., Belmont, Calif. 94002.
Fell: Frederick Fell, Inc., 386 Park Ave. S., New York, N.Y. 10016.
Fleet: Fleet Press Corp., 156 Fifth Ave., New York, N.Y. 10010.
Follett: Follett Publishing Co., 1010 West Washington Blvd., Chicago, Ill. 60607.
Forest Service: Forest Service, U. S. Department of Agriculture, Washington, D.C. 20250.
Fox: Sam Fox Publishing Co., 1540 Broadway, New York, N.Y. 10023.
Funk & Wagnalls: Funk & Wagnalls, 666 Fifth Ave., New York, N.Y. 10019.
Galloway: Galloway Publications, 5 Mountain Ave., North Plainfield, N.J. 07060.
Gerry: Gerry, Inc., Box 910, Boulder, Colo. 80301.
Girl Scouts: Girl Scouts of the U.S.A., 830 Third Ave., New York, N.Y. 10022.
Golden: Golden Press, Educational Division, Western Publishing Co., Inc., 850 Third Ave., New York, N.Y. 10022.
Greene: The Stephen Greene Press, Fessenden Road, Indian Flat, P. O. Box 1000, Brattleboro, Vt. 05301.
Grosset & Dunlap: Grosset & Dunlap, Inc., 51 Madison Ave., New York, N.Y. 10010.
Hallmark: Hallmark Cards, Inc., 25th and Magee Trafficway, Kansas City, Mo. 64108.
Hammond: Hammond, Inc., 515 Valley St., Maplewood, N.J. 07040.
Harcourt: Harcourt Brace Jovanovich, Inc., 757 Third Ave., New York, N.Y. 10017.
Harper & Row: Harper & Row Publishers, Inc., 10 E. 53rd St., New York, N.Y. 10022.
Harvey: Harvey House, Inc., Publishers, South Buckout, Irvington-on-Hudson, N.Y. 10533.
Hawthorn: Hawthorn Books, Inc., 260 Madison Ave., New York, N.Y. 10016.
Hoffman: Hoffman Publications, Inc., P. O. Box 7196, Fort Lauderdale, Fla. 33304.
Holt, Rinehart: Holt, Rinehart and Winston, Inc., 383 Madison Ave., New York, N.Y. 10017.
Horizon: Horizon Press, Inc., 156 Fifth Ave., New York, N.Y. 10010.
Horn: Horn Books, Inc., 585 Boylston St., Boston, Mass. 02116.
Houghton Mifflin: Houghton Mifflin Co., Educational Division, 1 Beacon St., Boston, Mass. 02108.
Int'l Textbook: International Textbook Co., Scranton, Pa. 18515.
Interstate: The Interstate Printers and Publishers, 19-27 North Jackson St., Danville, Ill. 61832.
Iowa State U.: Iowa State University Press, Press Building, Ames, Iowa 50010.
Knopf: Alfred A. Knopf, 201 E. 50th St., New York, N.Y. 10022.
Knox: John Knox Press, 801 E. Main St., Box 1176, Richmond, Va. 23209.
Lane: Lane Magazine and Book Co., Menlo Park, Calif. 94025.
La Siesta: La Siesta Press, Box 406, Glendale, Calif. 91209.

Lea & Febiger: Lea & Febiger, 600 S. Washington Sq., Philadelphia, Pa. 19106.

Libra: Libra Publishers, Inc., 391 Willets Rd., Box 165, Roslyn Heights, N.Y. 11577.

Life Support: Life Support Technology, Inc., P. O. Box 16, Manning, Ore. 97125.

Lion: Lion Books, 111 E. 39th St., New York, N.Y. 10016.

Lippincott: J. B. Lippincott Co., E. Washington Sq., Philadelphia, Pa. 19105.

Little, Brown: Little, Brown & Co., 34 Beacon St., Boston, Mass. 02106.

Longman, Green: Longman, Green and Co., Inc. See *David McKay Company, Inc.*

Luce: Robert B. Luce, Inc., 2000 North St., N.W., Washington, D.C. 20036.

McGraw-Hill: McGraw-Hill Book Co., 1221 Avenue of the Americas, New York, N.Y. 10020.

McKay: David McKay Co., Inc., 750 Third Ave., New York, N.Y. 10017.

McKnight: McKnight and McKnight Publishing Co., U. S. Route 66 at Towanda Ave., Bloomington, Ill. 61701.

Macmillan: The Macmillan Publishing Co., 866 Third Ave., New York, N.Y. 10022.

Meredith: Meredith Corporation—Better Homes & Gardens Books, 1716 Locust St., Des Moines, Iowa 50303.

Morrow: William Morrow and Co., Inc., 105 Madison Ave., New York, N.Y. 10016.

Mountain Press: Mountain Press Publishing Co., 279-287 West Front St., Missoula, Mont. 59801.

Nat'l Audubon: National Audubon Society, Audubon House, 1130 Fifth Ave., New York, N.Y. 10028.

Nat'l Ed. Ass'n: National Education Association Publications, 1201 16th Street, N.W., Washington, D.C. 10036.

Nat'l History: Natural History Press. See *Doubleday and Company, Inc.*

Nat'l Park Service: National Park Service, Department of the Interior, Washington, D.C. 20240.

Nat'l Press: National Press Books, 850 Hansen Way, Palo Alto, Calif. 94304.

Nautilus: Nautilus Books, 5 Mountain Ave., North Plainfield, N.J. 07060.

N.R.P.A.: National Recreation and Park Association, 1700 Pennsylvania Avenue, N.W., Washington, D.C. 20006.

Nat'l Safety Council: National Safety Council, 425 North Michigan Ave., Chicago, Ill. 60611.

Nat'l Wildlife Fed.: National Wildlife Federation, 1412 16th Street, N.W., Washington, D.C. 20036.

Nature Study: Nature Study Aids, Inc., 411 Dakota St., Red Wing, Minn. 55066.

Nature Study Guild: Nature Study Guild, P. O. Box 972, Berkeley, Calif. 94701.

Naturegraph: Naturegraph Publishers, 8339 Dry Creek Rd., Healdsburg, Calif. 95448.

Nelson: Thomas Nelson and Sons, 407 Seventh Ave. S., Nashville, Tenn. 37203.

New Am. Library: The New American Library, 1301 Avenue of the Americas, New York, N.Y. 10019.

Norton: W. W. Norton and Co., Inc., 55 Fifth Ave., New York, N.Y. 10003.

Oak: Oak Publications, Inc., 165 W. 46th St., New York, N.Y. 10036.

Outdoor Ed. Ass'n: The Outdoor Education Association, Inc., 606 S. Marion Ave., Carbondale, Ill. 62901.

Owen: F. A. Owen Publishing Co., Danville, N.Y. 14437.

Oxford: Oxford University Press, Inc., 200 Madison Ave., New York, N.Y. 10016.

Peek: Peek Publications, 164 E. Dana St., Mountain View, Calif. 94040.

Phoenix: Phoenix Publishing, Dept. 112, Woodstock, Vt. 05091.

Plant Deck: Plant Deck, Inc., Dept. W. C., 2134 S.W. Wombley Park Rd., Lake Oswego, Ore. 97034.

Plays: Plays, Inc., 8 Arlington St., Boston, Mass. 02116.

Pocket Books: Pocket Books, Inc., 630 Fifth Ave., New York, N.Y. 10020.

Popular Library: Popular Library, Inc., 600 Third Ave., New York, N.Y. 10011.

Praeger: Praeger Publishers, Inc., 111 Fourth Ave., New York, N.Y. 10003.

Pratt: J. Lowell Pratt, 15 East 48th St., New York, N.Y. 10017.

Prentice-Hall: Prentice-Hall, Inc., Englewood Cliffs, N.J. 07632.

Presscraft: Presscraft Papers, Benzonia, Mich. 49616.

Putnam: G. P. Putnam's Sons, 200 Madison Ave., New York, N.Y. 10016.

Quadrangle: Quadrangle/The New York Times Book Co., 10 East 53rd St., New York, N.Y. 10022.

Rand McNally: Rand McNally and Co., P. O. Box 7600, Chicago, Ill. 60608.

Random: Random House, Inc., 201 East 50th St., New York, N.Y. 10022.

Recreational: Recreational Equipment, Inc., Box 22088, Seattle, Wash. 98122.

Regnery: Henry Regnery, 114 West Illinois St., Chicago, Ill. 60601.

Remington: Remington Arms Co., Inc., Bridgeport, Conn. 06602.

Revell: Fleming H. Revell Co., Old Tappan, N.J. 07675.

Ronald: The Ronald Press, 79 Madison Ave., New York, N.Y. 10016.

Rubin: Louis D. Rubin, Box 8615, Richmond, Va. 23226.

Saturday Review: Saturday Review Press. See *E. P. Dutton and Co., Inc.*

Saunders: W. B. Saunders Co., 218 West Washington Sq., Philadelphia, Pa. 19105.

Scarecrow: Scarecrow Press, Inc., 52 Liberty St., P. O. Box 656, Metuchen, N.J. 08840.

Schocken: Schocken Books, Inc., 200 Madison Ave., New York, N.Y. 10016.

Scholastic Book Service: Scholastic Book Service, 50 West 44th St., New York, N.Y. 10036.
Science Research: Science Research Associates, Inc., 259 East Erie St., Chicago, Ill. 60611.
Scott, Foresman: Scott, Foresman and Co., 1900 East Lake Ave., Glenview, Ill. 60025.
Scribner's: Charles Scribner's Sons, 597 Fifth Ave., New York, N.Y. 10017.
Scripture: Scripture Press Publications, Inc., 1825 College Ave., Wheaton, Ill. 60187.
Sequoia: Sequoia, 300 Kalamazoo Ave., Kalamazoo, Mich. 49006.
Sierra: Sierra Club Books, 597 Fifth Ave., New York, N.Y. 10017.
Signet: See *New American Library.*
Silva: Silva, Inc., Highway 39 North, La Porte, Ind. 46350.
Silver-Burdett: Silver-Burdett Co., 250 James St., Morristown, N.J. 07960.
Simon & Schuster: Simon and Schuster, Inc., One West 39th St., New York, N.Y. 10018.
Sing Out: Sing Out, 589 Broadway, New York, N.Y. 10012. (Publishers of *Sing Out! The Folk Song Magazine*)
Stackpole: Stackpole Books, Cameron and Kelker Sts., Harrisburg, Pa. 17105.
Sterling: Sterling Publishing Co., Inc., 419 Park Ave. S., New York, N.Y. 10016.
Supt. of Documents: The Superintendent of Documents, U. S. Government Printing Office, Washington, D.C. 20402.
Syracuse: Syracuse University Press, Box 8, University Station, Syracuse, N.Y. 13210.
Thomas: Charles C Thomas, Publisher, 301 East Lawrence Ave., Springfield, Ill. 62703.
Tiresias: Tiresias Press, Inc., 116 Pinehurst Ave., New York, N.Y. 10033.
Trail-R-Club: Trail-R-Club of America, 3211 Pico Blvd., Santa Monica, Calif. 90405.
Tudor: Tudor Publishing Co., 221 Park Ave. S., New York, N.Y. 10003.
U. of Chicago: University of Chicago Press, 5801 Ellis Ave., Chicago, Ill. 60637.
U. of Mich.: University of Michigan Press, Ann Arbor, Mich. 48106.
U. of Minn.: University of Minnesota Press, 2037 University Avenue, S.E., Minneapolis, Minn. 55455.
U. of Okla.: University of Oklahoma Press, 1005 Asp Ave., Norman, Okla. 73069.
U. of Ore.: University of Oregon, Eugene, Ore. 97403.
U. of Wash.: University of Washington Press, Seattle, Wash. 98105.
U. of Wis.: University of Wisconsin Press, Box 1379, Madison, Wisc. 53701.
U. S. Coast and Geodetic Society: U. S. Coast and Geodetic Society, Washington, D.C. 20025.
U. S. Geological Survey: U. S. Geological Survey, Department of the Interior, Washington, D.C. 20242.
U. S. Naval Institute: U. S. Naval Institute, Naval Institute Press, Annapolis, Md. 21402.
Van Nostrand: Van Nostrand-Reinhold Co., 430 West 33rd St., New York, N.Y. 10001.
Vantage: Vantage Press, Inc., 516 West 34th St., New York, N.Y. 10001.
Viking: The Viking Press, Inc., 625 Madison Ave., New York, N.Y. 10022.
Wadsworth: Wadsworth Publishing Co., Inc., Belmont, Calif. 94002.
Walck: Henry Z. Walck, Inc., 3 East 54th St., New York, N.Y. 10022.
Washington Square: Washington Square Press, 630 Fifth Ave., New York, N.Y. 10020.
Watts: Franklin Watts, Inc., 845 Third Ave., New York, N.Y. 10022.
Welch: G. R. Welch Co., Ltd., 222 Evans Ave., Toronto 18, Ontario, Canada.
Western: Western Publishing Co., Inc., 1220 Mound Ave., Racine, Wisc. 53404.
Westminster: The Westminster Press, Witherspoon Bldg., Philadelphia, Pa. 19107.
Whitman: Whitman Publishing Co., 1220 Mound Ave., Racine, Wisc. 53404.
Whittlesey: Whittlesey House, 330 West 42nd St., New York, N.Y. 10036.
Wilderness: Wilderness Press, 2440 Bancroft Way, Berkeley, Calif. 94704.
Wiley: John Wiley and Sons, Inc., 605 Third Ave., New York, N.Y. 10016.
Winchester: Winchester Press, 460 Park Ave., New York, N.Y. 10022.
Workman: Workman Publishing Co., Inc., 231 E. 51st St., New York, N.Y. 10022.
World: The World Publishing Co., 110 East 59th St., New York, N.Y. 10022.
Y.M.C.A.: National Board of the Y.M.C.A., 600 Lexington Ave., New York, N.Y. 10022.
Y.W.C.A.: National Board of the Y.W.C.A., Bureau of Communications, 600 Lexington Ave., New York, N.Y. 10022.
Zondervan: Zondervan Publishing House, 1415 Lake Dr., S.E., Grand Rapids, Mich. 49506.

Appendix E

Where to Get Equipment and Supplies

Arts and Crafts

American Handicrafts, 1011 Foch St., Fort Worth, Tex. 76107.
Bersted's Hobby-Craft, Inc., 521 W. 10th Ave., Monmouth, Ill. 61462.
Boin Arts and Crafts Co., 87 Morris St., Morristown, N.J. 07960.
Customade Leather Goods, 265 Highway 55, Hamel, N. Mex. 55343.
Economy Handicrafts, 50-21 69th St., Woodside, N.Y. 11377. (Kilns)
Grey Owl Indian Craft Co., Inc., 150-02 Beaver Road, Jamaica, N.Y. 11433.
Lily Mills Co., Shelby, N.C. 28150.
Magnus Craft Materials, Inc., 109 Lafayette St., New York, N.Y. 10013.
Rit Dye, Best Foods Div., CPC International, International Plaza, Englewood Cliffs, N.J. 07632.
S and S Arts and Crafts, Colchester, Conn. 06415.
School Products Co., 312 E. 23rd St., New York, N.Y. 10010.
Signature Graphics, Box 125, Nevada, Iowa 50201.
Tandy Leather Co., 1001 Foch St., Fort Worth, Tex. 76107.

Boats, Canoes, Waterfront

Adventurer Canoe Co., P. O. Box 296, Wilton, Conn. 06897.
Alumni-Span, 122 N. Main St., Pittsford, Mich. 49271.
Aqua/matic Lifeguard Mfg. Corp., 7173 Northern Blvd., East Syracuse, N.Y. 13057.
Aqua-matic Piers, Inc., 3238 W. Pierce St., Milwaukee, Wisc. 53215.
Flaghouse, 18 W. 18th St., New York, N.Y. 10011.
Grumman Boats, Marathon, N.Y. 13803.
Hans Kepper Corp., 35 Union Square, New York, N.Y. 10003.
IPCO Inc., 541 W. 79, Minneapolis, Minn. 55420.
Lifeguard Mfg. Corp., 1224 W. Genesee, Syracuse, N.Y. 13204.
Old Town Canoe Co., 58 Middle St., Old Town, Me. 04468.
P.Z.P. Associates, Inc., 396 Sharon Drive, Cheshire, Conn. 06410.
Ouachita Marine & Industrial Corp., P. O. Box 420, Arkadelphia, Ark. 71923.
Rolf Godon Co., 15 California St., San Francisco, Calif. 94111.
Select Service and Supply Co., 180 Allen Road NE, Atlanta, Ga. 30328.
Tyne Kayaks, 14 Alpha Road, Chelmsford, Mass. 01824.
United Flotation, United McGill Corp., 2400 Fairwood Ave., Columbus, Ohio 43216.

Camping and Trip Equipment

(Most of these firms furnish catalogues that are excellent sources of information, even if you intend to shop in person locally.)

Abercrombie and Fitch, Madison Ave. at 45th St., New York, N.Y. 10017.

Alaska Sleeping Bag Co., 701 N.W. Dawson Way, Beaverton, Ore. 97005.
Alpine Designs, 6185 E. Arapahoe, Boulder, Colo. 80303.
Alpine Hut, 4725 30th Ave., N.E., Seattle, Wash. 98105.
Alpine Outfitters, 328 Link Lane, Fort Collins, Colo. 80521.
Atlantic Products Corp., 1 Johnston Ave., Trenton, N.J. 08605.
Eddie Bauer, 1737 Airport Way St., Seattle, Wash. 98124.
L. L. Bean, Inc., 902 Main St., Freeport, Me. 04032.
Bell Manufacturing Co., 25 Bell Bldg., Lewiston, Me. 04240. (Name tapes)
The Camp & Hike Shop, 4674 Knight-Arnold Rd., Memphis, Tenn. 38118.
Camp and Trail Outfitters, 21 Park Place, New York, N.Y. 10007.
Camp Supply Co., 1151 S. 7th St., St. Louis, Mo. 63104.
Camp Trails, P. O. Box 14500-9, Phoenix, Ariz. 85019.
Champion Products, 115 College Ave., Rochester, N.Y. 14603. (Camp clothing)
Class 5 Mountaineering Equipage, 2010 Seventh St., Berkeley, Calif. 94710.
Coleman Company, Inc., 250 N. Francis St., Wichita, Kan. 67201.
Colorado Outdoor Sports Corp., P. O. Box 5544, Denver, Colo. 80217.
Co-op Wilderness Supply, 1432 University Ave., Berkeley, Calif. 94702.
Eureka Tent Inc., P. O. Box 966, Binghamton, N.Y. 13902.
Gerry, 5450 North Valley Highway, Denver, Colo. 80216.
Don Gleason's Campers Supply, 21 Pearl St., Northampton, Mass. 01060.
Hi-Camp, P. O. Box 17602, Charlotte, N.C. 28211.
Highland Outfitters, 3579 University Ave. (8th St.), P. O. Box 121, Riverside, Calif. 92502.
Himalayan Industries, 807 Cannery Row, P. O. Box 950, Monterey, Calif. 93940.
Hirsch-Weis/White Stag, 5203 S.E. Johnson Creek Blvd., Portland, Ore. 97206.
Holubar Mountaineering, Ltd., Box 7, Boulder, Colo. 80302.
Kelty, 1801 Victory Blvd., Glendale, Calif. 91201.
Recreational Equipment, P. O. Box 22088, Seattle, Wash. 98122.
Redhead Brand Corp., 4100 Platinum Way, Dallas, Tex. 75237.
Select Service and Supply Co., 180 Allen Road, N.E., Atlanta, Ga. 30328.
Sierra Designs, 4th and Addison Sts., Berkeley, Calif. 94710.
Ski Hut, 1615 University Ave., Berkeley, Calif. 94703.
Skimeister Sport Shop, Main St., No. Woodstock, N.H. 03262.
The Smilie Co., 575 Howard St., San Francisco, Calif. 94105.
Sports Chalet, 951 Foothill Blvd., P. O. Box 626, LaCanada, Calif. 91011.
Velva-Sheen Mfg. Co., 3860 Virginia Ave., Cincinnati, Ohio 45227. (Camp clothing)
Walter E. Stern, 254 Nagle Ave., New York, N.Y. 10034.
Webb Mfg. Co., 4th & Cambria Sts., Philadelphia, Pa. 19133.

Do-It-Yourself Kits

Boat Builder, 229 Park Ave., New York, N.Y. 10003.
Carakit Outdoor Equipment Kits, P. O. Box 7, Boulder, Colo. 80302.
Eastern Mountain Sports, 1041 Commonwealth Ave., Boston, Mass. 02215.
Frostline, Box 2190, Boulder, Colo. 80302.
Trailcraft, Inc., P. O. Box 60601, Concordia, Kan. 66901. (Canoe kits)
Vermont Tubbs Snowshoe Kits, Wallingford, Vt. 05773.

Lightweight Foods

Bernard Food Industries, Box 487, St. James Park Station, 222 S. 24th St., San Jose, Calif. 95103. (Kamp Pack Foods)
Chuck Wagon Foods, Micro Drive, Woburn, Me. 01801.
Dri-Lite Foods, 11333 Atlantic, Lynwood, Calif. 93001.
S. Gumpert Co., 812 Jersey Ave., Jersey City, N.J. 07302.
Natural Food Backpack Dinners, P. O. Box 532, Corvallis, Ore. 97330.
Oregon Freeze Dry Foods, Inc., P. O. Box 1048, Albany, Ore. 97321. (Mountain House Foods)
Perma-Pak Camping Foods, 40 East 2430 So., Salt Lake City, Utah 84115. (Camplite Foods)
Rich-Moor Corp., P. O. Box 2728, Van Nuys, Calif. 91904.
Ad. Seidel & Son, Elk Grove Village, Ill. 60007. (Seidel's Trail Packets)
Stow-A-Way Sports Industries, Inc., 66 Cushing Hiway (Rt. 3A), Cohasset, Mass. 02025. (Stow-Lite Food)

Riflery Program and Supplies

Benjamin Air Rifle Co., 826 Marion St., St. Louis, Mo. 63104.
Daisey Division, Victor Comptometer Corp., Box 220, Rogers, Ariz. 72756.
National Rifle Association, 1600 Rhode Island Ave., N.W., Washington, D.C. 20036.
National Target Co., Inc., 4960 Wyaconda Road, Rockville, Mo. 20853.
Remington Arms Co., Inc., 939 Barnum Ave., Bridgeport, Conn. 06602.

Index